The Oxford Handbook of Emotion, Social Cognition, and Problem Solving in Adulthood

OXFORD LIBRARY OF PSYCHOLOGY

EDITOR-IN-CHIEF

Peter E. Nathan

AREA EDITORS:

Clinical Psychology
David H. Barlow

Cognitive Neuroscience
Kevin N. Ochsner and Stephen M. Kosslyn

Cognitive Psychology
Daniel Reisberg

Counseling Psychology
Elizabeth M. Altmaier and Jo-Ida C. Hansen

Developmental Psychology
Philip David Zelazo

Health Psychology
Howard S. Friedman

History of Psychology
David B. Baker

Methods and Measurement
Todd D. Little

Neuropsychology
Kenneth M. Adams

Organizational Psychology
Steve W. J. Kozlowski

Personality and Social Psychology
Kay Deaux and Mark Snyder

OXFORD LIBRARY OF PSYCHOLOGY

Editor in Chief PETER E. NATHAN

The Oxford Handbook of Emotion, Social Cognition, and Problem Solving in Adulthood

Edited by

Paul Verhaeghen and

Christopher Hertzog

OXFORD
UNIVERSITY PRESS

OXFORD
UNIVERSITY PRESS

Oxford University Press is a department of the University of Oxford.
It furthers the University's objective of excellence in research, scholarship,
and education by publishing worldwide.

Oxford   New York
Auckland   Cape Town   Dar es Salaam   Hong Kong   Karachi
Kuala Lumpur   Madrid   Melbourne   Mexico City   Nairobi
New Delhi   Shanghai   Taipei   Toronto

With offices in
Argentina   Austria   Brazil   Chile   Czech Republic   France   Greece
Guatemala   Hungary   Italy   Japan   Poland   Portugal   Singapore
South Korea   Switzerland   Thailand   Turkey   Ukraine   Vietnam

Oxford is a registered trademark of Oxford University Press
in the UK and certain other countries.

Published in the United States of America by
Oxford University Press
198 Madison Avenue, New York, NY 10016

© Oxford University Press 2014

Library of Congress Cataloging-in-Publication Data
The Oxford handbook of emotion, social cognition, and problem solving in adulthood / edited by Paul Verhaeghen
and Christopher Hertzog.—1 Edition.
pages cm.—(Oxford library of psychology)
Includes bibliographical references and index.
ISBN 978–0–19–989946–3
1. Emotions.   2. Social perception.   3. Problem solving.   I. Verhaeghen, Paul, editor.   II. Hertzog, C. K. (Christopher K.),
1952– editor.
BF511.O94 2014
153—dc23
2013048666

9 7 8 6 5 4 3 2 1
Printed in the United States of America
on acid-free paper

This book is in memory of Fredda Blanchard-Fields:
Passionate colleague, dedicated researcher, and inexhaustible font of positive energy

SHORT CONTENTS

OXFORD LIBRARY OF PSYCHOLOGY

The *Oxford Library of Psychology*, a landmark series of handbooks, is published by Oxford University Press, one of the world's oldest and most highly respected publishers, with a tradition of publishing significant books in psychology. The ambitious goal of the *Oxford Library of Psychology* is nothing less than to span a vibrant, wide-ranging field and, in so doing, to fill a clear market need.

Encompassing a comprehensive set of handbooks, organized hierarchically, the *Library* incorporates volumes at different levels, each designed to meet a distinct need. At one level are a set of handbooks designed broadly to survey the major subfields of psychology; at another are numerous handbooks that cover important current focal research and scholarly areas of psychology in depth and detail. Planned as a reflection of the dynamism of psychology, the *Library* will grow and expand as psychology itself develops, thereby highlighting significant new research that will impact on the field. Adding to its accessibility and ease of use, the *Library* will be published in print and, later on, electronically.

The *Library* surveys psychology's principal subfields with a set of handbooks that capture the current status and future prospects of those major subdisciplines. This initial set includes handbooks of social and personality psychology, clinical psychology, counseling psychology, school psychology, educational psychology, industrial and organizational psychology, cognitive psychology, cognitive neuroscience, methods and measurements, history, neuropsychology, personality assessment, developmental psychology, and more. Each handbook undertakes to review one of psychology's major subdisciplines with breadth, comprehensiveness, and exemplary scholarship. In addition to these broadly-conceived volumes, the *Library* also includes a large number of handbooks designed to explore in depth more specialized areas of scholarship and research, such as stress, health and coping, anxiety and related disorders, cognitive development, or child and adolescent assessment. In contrast to the broad coverage of the subfield handbooks, each of these latter volumes focuses on an especially productive, more highly focused line of scholarship and research. Whether at the broadest or most specific level, however, all of the *Library* handbooks offer synthetic coverage that reviews and evaluates the relevant past and present research and anticipates research in the future. Each handbook in the *Library* includes introductory and concluding chapters written by its editor to provide a roadmap to the handbook's table of contents and to offer informed anticipations of significant future developments in that field.

An undertaking of this scope calls for handbook editors and chapter authors who are established scholars in the areas about which they write. Many of the nation's and world's most productive and best-respected psychologists have agreed to edit *Library* handbooks or write authoritative chapters in their areas of expertise.

For whom has the *Oxford Library of Psychology* been written? Because of its breadth, depth, and accessibility, the *Library* serves a diverse audience, including graduate students in psychology and their faculty mentors, scholars, researchers, and practitioners in psychology and related fields. Each will find in the *Library* the information they seek on the subfield or focal area of psychology in which they work or are interested.

Befitting its commitment to accessibility, each handbook includes a comprehensive index, as well as extensive references to help guide research. And because the *Library* was designed from its inception as an online as well as a print resource, its structure and contents will be readily and rationally searchable online. Further, once the *Library* is released online, the handbooks will be regularly and thoroughly updated.

In summary, the *Oxford Library of Psychology* will grow organically to provide a thoroughly informed perspective on the field of psychology, one that reflects both psychology's dynamism and its increasing interdisciplinarity. Once published electronically, the *Library* is also destined to become a uniquely valuable interactive tool, with extended search and browsing capabilities. As you begin to consult this handbook, we sincerely hope you will share our enthusiasm for the more than 500-year tradition of Oxford University Press for excellence, innovation, and quality, as exemplified by the *Oxford Library of Psychology*.

Peter E. Nathan
Editor-in-Chief
Oxford Library of Psychology

ABOUT THE EDITORS

Paul Verhaeghen

Paul Verhaeghen, Ph.D., is a Professor of Psychology at Georgia Institute of Technology. He is interested in working memory, attention, executive control, creativity, aging, and the interfaces between them.

Christopher Hertzog

Christopher Hertzog, Ph.D., is a Professor of Psychology at Georgia Institute of Technology. He specializes in adult development and aging, with an emphasis on understanding individual differences in cognitive changes in old age and variables that can help predict and explain successful cognitive aging, including health, lifestyle, and adaptive self-regulation.

CONTRIBUTORS

Eric R. Allard
Department of Psychology
Boston College
Chestnut Hill, MA

Monika Ardelt
Department of Sociology
University of Florida
Gainesville, FL

Phoebe E. Bailey
School of Psychology
University of Western Sydney
Sydney, Australia

Sarah J. Barber
Davis School of Gerontology
University of Southern California
Los Angeles, CA

Cynthia A. Berg
Department of Psychology
University of Utah
Salt Lake City, UT

Cindy S. Bergeman
Department of Psychology
University of Notre Dame
Notre Dame, IN

Yiwei Chen
Department of Psychology
Bowling Green State University
Bowling Green, OH

Abby Heckman Coats
Westminster College
Salt Lake City, UT

Nathan S. Consedine
Department of Psychological Medicine
University of Auckland
Auckland, New Zealand

Michel Ferrari
Centre for Applied Cognitive Science
University of Toronto
Toronto, Ontario, Canada

Alexandra M. Freund
Department of Psychology
University of Zurich
Zurich, Switzerland

Anne-Laure Gilet
Laboratoire LPPL
Université de Nantes
Nantes, France

Julie D. Henry
School of Psychology
University of Queensland
St. Lucia, Australia

Christopher Hertzog
School of Psychology
Georgia Institute of Technology
Atlanta, GA

Thomas M. Hess
Department of Psychology
North Carolina State University
Raleigh, NC

Christiane Hoppmann
Department of Psychology
University of British Columbia
Vancouver, British Columbia, Canada

Michelle Horhota
Department of Psychology
Furman University
Greenville, SC

Mary Lee Hummert
Department of Communication Studies
University of Kansas
Lawrence, KS

Derek M. Isaacowitz
Department of Psychology
Northeastern University
Boston, MA

Emily J. Keener
Department of Psychology
Slippery Rock University
Slippery Rock, PA

Elizabeth A. Kensinger
Department of Psychology
Boston College
Chestnut Hill, MA

Anne C. Krendl
Department of Psychology
Boston College
Chestnut Hill, MA
Department of Psychology
Tufts University
Medford, MA

Gisela Labouvie-Vief
Department of Psychology
University of Geneva
Geneva, Switzerland

Mara Mather
Davis School of Gerontology
University of Southern California
Los Angeles, CA

Iris Mauss
Department of Psychology
University of California, Berkeley
Berkeley, CA

Nathalie Mella
Department of Psychology
University of Geneva
Geneva, Switzerland

Andrew Mienaltowski
Department of Psychology
Western Kentucky University
Bowling Green, KY

Erin Senesac Morgan
School of Psychology
Georgia Institute of Technology
Atlanta, GA

Samantha L. Neufeld
Global Institute of Sustainability
Arizona State University
Tempe, AZ

Anthony D. Ong
College of Human Ecology
Cornell University
Ithaca, NY

Louise H. Phillips
School of Psychology
University of Aberdeen
Aberdeen, Scotland

Tara L. Queen
Institute for Social Research
University of Michigan
Ann Arbor, MI

Antje Rauers
Max Planck Institute for Human
    Development
Berlin, Germany

Michaela Riediger
Max Planck Institute for Human
    Development
Berlin, Germany

Catherine Riffin
College of Human Ecology
Cornell University
Ithaca, NY

Johannes O. Ritter
Department of Psychology
University of Erfurt
Erfurt, Germany

Susanne Scheibe
Department of Psychology
University of Groningen
Groningen, Netherlands

Stacey B. Scott
Center for Healthy Aging
Pennsylvania State University
University Park, PA

Michelle N. Shiota
Department of Psychology
Arizona State University
Tempe, AZ

Michelle A. Skinner
Department of Psychology
University of Utah
Salt Lake City, UT

Gillian Slessor
School of Psychology
University of Aberdeen
Aberdeen, Scotland

Martin J. Sliwinski
Department of Human Development
    and Family Studies
Pennsylvania State University
University Park, PA

Jennifer Tehan Stanley
Brandeis University
Waltham, MA
Department of Adult Development and Aging
The University of Akron
Akron, OH

JoNell Strough
Department of Psychology
West Virginia University
Morgantown, WV

Bert N. Uchino
Department of Psychology
University of Utah
Salt Lake City, UT

Paul Verhaeghen
School of Psychology
Georgia Institute of Technology
Atlanta, GA

CONTENTS

Introduction

Christopher Hertzog *and* Paul Verhaeghen

Abstract

This handbook covers an emerging subfield in the psychology of adult development and aging: socioemotional development in adulthood as experienced in social contexts. The origins of the handbook stem from the untimely death of our colleague and friend, Fredda Blanchard-Fields, who was a leading contributor to research on the interplay of emotion and cognition in everyday problem solving. We briefly review her perspective on adult development and aging as background for understanding this emerging line of research and to frame an introduction of the chapters of this volume and their contributions.

Key Words: emotion, cognition, adult development, social cognition, everyday problem solving.

The inspiration for this book can be traced back to a recent tragedy in our lives. On August 10, 2010, our colleague, friend, and School of Psychology Chair, Fredda Blanchard-Fields, died at the age of 61 after losing her battle with metastatic melanoma. Fredda was both a remarkable person and a successful contributor to the field of lifespan developmental psychology. Inspired by the thinking of her Ph.D. mentor, Gisela Labouvie-Vief (e.g., Labouvie-Vief & Blanchard-Fields, 1982) and Paul Baltes (e.g., Baltes, 1987), she was a strong advocate of the need for embracing the complexity of psychological development, particularly in adulthood. She interested herself primarily in the interplay of cognition and emotion in social contexts, emphasizing both gains and losses across adulthood, but also the possibility of qualitative transformations in thought and action that render older adults different, but not necessarily deficient (e.g., Blanchard-Fields, 2007, 2009). From the beginning of her research career, she viewed older adults

through the lens of qualitative transformations in emotional self-regulation, experience-based knowledge about people embedded in social contexts, and effective coping and everyday problem solving (e.g., Blanchard-Fields, 1986; Blanchard-Fields & Irion, 1987; Irion & Blanchard-Fields, 1988; Labouvie-Vief & Blanchard-Fields, 1982).

She was a tireless advocate for the importance of developmental research on emotion, social cognition, and social problem solving. Her passion for these issues was reflected both in her research and in her service to the field as a journal editor and member of a National Institutes of Health (NIH) study section reviewing grants in the area of emotion and personality. Her vision of the field was one in which age differences were not reflexively construed as declines, where individual differences were a crucible for understanding successful aging (rather than nuisance variance), and in which one could and should consider how older adults' social choices and decisions reflect experience and pragmatic wisdom in the form of behaviors that, from a different lens, could be viewed as less complex, less effective, or less optimal.

Late in her career, she enthusiastically embraced the rapid evolution of theoretical and empirical work on the role of emotions in cognition and, particularly, social cognition. She was also excited about the emergence of work on intraindividual variability and change and was at the time of her death enthusiastically leading an ambitious research project seeking to link within-person variability in adults' goals and everyday problem solving with their affective reactivity and stress responses (e.g., Hilimire, Mienaltowski, Blanchard-Fields, & Corballis, in press; Scott, Sliwinski, & Blanchard-Fields, in press). Influenced by several visits with Paul Baltes, Ulman Lindenberger, and colleagues at the Max Planck Institute for Human Development in Berlin during the period between 2003 and 2008, she had also embraced a research program focusing on complex forms of emotion and cognition, including the concept of lifespan longing (*Sehnsucht*) that Paul Baltes interested himself in toward the end of his career (Kotter-Grühn, Scheibe, Blanchard-Fields, & Baltes, 2009; Scheibe, Blanchard-Fields, Wiest, & Freund, 2011). She was intrigued by the problem of emotion regulation and the idea that older adults might approach it differently, and perhaps more effectively, than younger adults (e.g., Isaacowitz & Blanchard-Fields, 2012; Scheibe & Blanchard-Fields, 2009). She was also very excited about the emerging field of social neuroscience, believing that it could provide new windows into some of her ideas about different forms of experience in old age (Blanchard-Fields, 2010). It is indeed unfortunate that she did not have the opportunity to bring these lines of work to completion or to be able to integrate fully their outcomes into her own perspective (e.g., Blanchard-Fields, 2009; Blanchard-Fields & Stange, 2009). She anticipated with positive affect experiencing an old age she construed as pregnant with professional possibilities and personal meaning. She reveled in Jenny Joseph's poem, "Warning" (Joseph, 1993), envisioning a future in which she would wear purple and embody the archetype of the wise woman, a future that she sadly never had a chance to realize.

Clearly, her thinking helped shaped the field, her exuberance and positive energy stimulated and encouraged a generation of young scientists, particularly early-career women, and her considerable influence is discernible in the content of this volume.

In reflecting upon Fredda and her personal and professional influences on us and others, her colleagues at Georgia Tech decided that a fitting way to remember and honor her was to hold a memorial scientific conference, which was held on the campus at Georgia Tech in March 2011 and supported by Georgia Tech's College of Science. We encouraged participants in this conference and additional other colleagues and contributors to this literature to contribute chapters to a handbook that reflected both Fredda's diverse interests and major new directions in the field of lifespan developmental psychology. We have been gratified by the enthusiasm shown by our contributors and their desire to both capture the field and to honor Fredda in doing so. This product, then, serves both as a retrospective on the field as it has emerged over the past two decades and as a signpost for exciting possibilities for future directions in interrelated research areas. This emerging set of foci need not be explicitly labeled with an integrative umbrella term, at least not yet. But whatever its intersection might be called, it is clear that it did not exist, as such, until Fredda and like-minded cohorts of friends and colleagues, such as Laura Carstensen, Tom Hess, and Cindy Berg (to name a few) began to forge it by conceptualizing and researching the intersections among socioemotional development, social cognition, emotion, coping, and everyday problem solving (e.g., Berg & Klaczynski, 1996; Blanchard-Fields & Abeles, 1996; Carstensen, Mikels, & Mather, 2006; Hess & Blanchard-Fields, 1999).

This book is organized into sections that capture separate but converging strands of research that are involved in the broader theme of adult emotional and cognitive development. One of the most rapidly evolving areas of lifespan developmental psychology involves emotional development and the interplay between emotion and cognition in influencing the thinking and behavior of adults as they grow older. Hence, the largest section of the book is devoted to emotion and emotional development across the lifespan. However, Blanchard-Fields's perspective drew from her work with Gisela Labouvie-Vief and was informed by psychological perspectives such as those articulated by Epstein (2010), Mischel and Shoda (1995), and Sloman (1996). She argued strongly that emotions framed, influenced, enhanced, and enriched adults' thinking and decision making in everyday problem solving. Her views were epitomized by her claim that successful everyday problem solving involved thinking "both with the head and the heart" (Blanchard-Fields & Stange, 2009; Watson & Blanchard-Fields, 1998). She viewed social wisdom and experience as being reflected in the sage advice that older adults could give others about effective problem-solving strategies in emotionally laden social situations (e.g., Coats & Blanchard-Fields, 2008) and in their embrace of social and emotional goals, such as generativity, that distinguished mature adult thinking from the instrumental, problem-focused mode of thought of younger adults (e.g., Hoppmann & Blanchard-Fields, 2010; Hoppmann, Coats, & Blanchard-Fields, 2008). Thus, contrary to the classic view of emotional reactions and analytic reasoning as opposing forces, Blanchard-Fields argued that life experience leads to a heuristic mode of thought that is both fast and frugal—in Gerd Gigerenzer's terms (e.g., Gigerenzer, Todd, & the ABC Research Group, 1999; Mata, 2007)—and imbued with emotional reactions that can actually enhance social and emotional problem-solving effectiveness (e.g., Blanchard-Fields, 2009).

Social cognition research emphasizes that rapid initial reactions to social stimuli often reflect automatic influences of stereotypes and social schemas. As such, and appropriately so, the "dark side" of social schematicity in terms of phenomena like bias and prejudice has been emphasized in the social cognition literature (see Blanchard-Fields & Horhota, 2006). Blanchard-Fields's work examined such reactions in several contexts, including causal attributions about relationships and relationship outcomes (e.g., Blanchard-Fields, 1994; Blanchard-Fields & Beatty, 2005; Blanchard-Fields & Norris, 1998; Chen & Blanchard-Fields, 1997). For instance, some of her later work on causal attributions emphasized the effects of strongly held social norms and beliefs as generators of blame and responsibility attributions when relationships experience problems (Blanchard-Fields, Hertzog, & Horhota, 2012). Her argument was that a foreclosed style of thought (e.g., Kruglanski & Webster, 1996) was motivated by and instantiated in the belief system of the individual. Older adults' more traditional beliefs about appropriate relationship behaviors influenced their blaming of actors whose behavior violated their social rules; however, she pointed out that younger adults behaved in a similar manner when their rule system was violated. Rather than viewing a foreclosed style of thought as an inevitable consequence of cognitive decline, she saw it as a manifestation of the content of social schemas that had accumulated over the life course. As such, she argued that reliance on chronically accessible beliefs, attitudes, and values created both losses and gains in terms of the quality of social reasoning. That is, she also viewed experiential modes of thinking and reactivity as carrying accumulated knowledge and experience that

could have costs (e.g., Horhota, Mienaltowski, & Blanchard-Fields, 2012) but, when relied upon, could also be a source of effective everyday problem solving (Blanchard-Fields, 2009; Blanchard-Fields, Mienaltowski, & Seay, 2007). This duality is fully consistent with lifespan developmental theory (e.g., Baltes, 1997; Baltes, Staudinger, & Lindenberger, 1999). These themes are reflected in the chapters contained in the Everyday Problem Solving and Social Cognition sections of the Handbook.

Of course, any Handbook of a broad and emerging field of psychological inquiry cannot and should not merely reflect the perspective of one or a few individuals, and the chapters contained in this book cover a broad range of perspectives (theoretical, experimental, correlational, physiological, and neuroscience-based) that befits the diversity of thought and research foci in this emerging set of domains within lifespan developmental psychology. Our aim in this Handbook was to provide an overview of the field as roughly fitting into four substantive themes: (a) emotion in adulthood, (b) its antecedents and consequents, (c) everyday problem solving, and (d) social cognition and goals.

Part 1 tackles how older adults perceive, process, and display *emotion*. Phillips, Slessor, Bailey, and Henry (Chapter 1) discuss how older adults decode social and emotional cues. This chapter deals with age differences in how adults label emotional signals, mimic emotion, and process limbic smiles. Kensinger, Allard, and Krendl (Chapter 2) provide a neuroscience perspective on the effects of age on memory for socioemotional material (including the often-observed age-related shift toward better memory for positive stimuli) and on processing of the Self. Hummert (Chapter 3) investigates how age-related changes in facial morphology change the perception of emotions displayed by older adults and elucidate how these changes might elicit negative age stereotypes. Riediger and Rauers (Chapter 4) review the growing literature on ambulatory affective assessment in older adults, with an emphasis on work on the prevalence of and affective reactivity to unpleasant experiences in daily life.

Part 2 explores the *antecedent and consequents of age-related differences in emotion*. Labouvie-Vief, Gilet, and Mella (Chapter 5) discuss emotions in the context of Labouvie-Vief's cognitive-developmental theory about mechanisms for maintaining emotion regulation—dynamic integration theory (DIT). DIT sees emotion regulation as an active response to challenges, one in which age-related deficits in regulatory mechanisms can effectively be buffered by increases in specific automated procedural and declarative knowledge. Stanley and Isaacowitz (Chapter 6) describe perceiver context (e.g., motivation), stimulus context, and emotional context as moderators of age differences in both emotion regulation and emotion recognition. They argue for an explicit consideration and integration of context into basic conceptual frameworks (such as neuropsychological theories, or theories about motivation) to move the field toward stronger predictive power. Riffin, Ong, and Bergeman (Chapter 7) examine the health significance of positive emotions across the lifespan, linking age-related positivity effects to positive health behaviors, psychological coping, and well-being, as well as to physiological outcomes. Sliwinski and Scott (Chapter 8) review the longitudinal evidence on one boundary condition for emotional well-being: the occurrence and impact of daily stress. They note gains in emotional well-being through middle age, with a slow down and eventual reversal during the late 60s. Consedine and Mauss (Chapter 9) offer a skill-based conceptualization of emotion regulation across the lifespan through the lens of developmental functionalism, with an emphasis on age-related differences in regulatory tasks and capacities and in the specific tactics used to accomplish regulatory ends. Finally, Senesac Morgan and Scheibe (Chapter 10) describe the role of increased emotion regulation efficiency in reconciling cognitive decline and increased well-being over the adult lifespan.

Part 3 deals with *everyday problem solving*. Skinner, Berg, and Uchino (Chapter 11) investigate contextual variations in emotion regulation during everyday problem solving. They paint a complex picture in which contextual conditions can either tax or support skill use in older adults. Strough and Keener (Chapter 12) discuss links between goals and strategies for solving interpersonal everyday problems across the whole lifespan and outline a contextual and motivational model for this type of problem solving. Heckman Coats, Hoppmann, and Scott (Chapter 13) bridge the clinical and cognitive literature by offering an integrated perspective on goals, strategies, and well-being based on the coping and everyday problem-solving literature. Shiota and Neufeld (Chapter 14) review the evidence on age-related autonomic physiological changes in responding to emotions and examine how these changes impact the emotional experience.

Part 4 focuses on *social cognition and goals*. Hess and Queen (Chapter 15) investigate how aging influences judgment and decision processes, with an emphasis placed on the complex interactions among declining resources, increasing experience, and the resultant adaptive and compensatory processes. Ritter and Freund (Chapter 16) trace personal values across adulthood. They argue that values serve as a cognitive compass and are especially relevant with regard to life planning in adolescence and life review in late adulthood. Horhota, Mienaltowski, and Chen (Chapter 17) review age-related differences in causal attributions in social situations. They point out that both limited resources and increased social knowledge (including schematic beliefs) make older adults more prone to making dispositional attributions. Barber and Mather (Chapter 18) review the growing literature on stereotype threat and its influence on cognitive performance in older adults, examining the role of regulatory focus and regulatory fit, and delineating contexts in which the effect is especially likely to operate. Finally, Ardelt and Ferrari (Chapter 19) investigate the relationship between emotions and wisdom, concluding that wisdom necessitates the integration of emotion and cognition to develop toward self-awareness, self-transcendence, and wholeness, thus leading wise people to promote a good life for themselves and their communities.

As stated earlier, our goal as editors was to bring together a wide selection of topics and perspectives. We think we have succeeded. At the same time, when reading the chapters as they came in, we were very happy to discover that, amid the variety of voices, a strong set of themes emerged; these themes clearly resonate with the main themes and emphases in Blanchard-Fields's work, as discussed earlier. We mention four.

First, there is clear convergence that the deficit model of aging, that is, the view that aging is best (or even uniquely) characterized as a story of irreparable losses, is patently wrong. To be sure, losses do occur. Several instances of age-related loss are mentioned throughout this Handbook, including: (1) older adults have difficulty decoding information from smiles; (2) there is an age-related decrease in facial expressivity; (3) cognitive control declines over the adult lifespan, with implications for analytic reasoning in everyday life; (4) older adults show decreased ability to cope with heightened arousal; (5) older age is associated with increased blood pressure reactivity, coupled with decreases in emotional heart rate reactivity; and (6) aging is associated with elevated sympathetic neurotransmitter activity. However, such losses occur in the context of stability (not only in relatively isolated areas such as the automatic mimicry of emotions but also in wider ranging aspects of life such as affective well-being) and, more importantly, of notable gains. Several instances of gains in function are identified in this Handbook, including: (1) older adults show increased attention toward and memory for positive emotions, (2) older adults demonstrate lowered reactivity to daily stressors, older adults are more efficient at proactive down-regulation of unpleasant emotions, (3) they demonstrate increased experience with life in general and specific problem-solving context in particular, (4) they show increased crystallization of cognitive-emotional representations, (5) they are better at effectively avoiding stressful situations and selecting situations that optimize positive emotions or minimize negative emotions, (6) they are more likely to use positive reappraisal, (7) they make better use of social resources, and (8) they show increased emotion regulation efficiency. This pattern is obviously good news. It becomes very good news indeed if one considers that the areas of life where gains are observed might be exactly those that older adults themselves consider of vital importance for quality of life and everyday functioning.

A second theme concerns the dynamic nature of socioemotional development and a radical individualization of this development, with the living ecology of the individual at its heart. That is, well-being is viewed as being achieved through the balanced dynamic interplay between an individual's gains and losses in service of the individual's values and goals. Most, if not all, of the chapters in this Handbook exude this flavor, but it is a very explicit part of the theoretical conceptualization in Chapters 5, 6, 9, 11, 12, 13, 15, and 17.

A third theme is the emphasis on a cross-level examination of the determinants of emotional and socioemotional behavior—from biology and neuroscience to cognitive and social psychology. A good example is reactivity to stress: increases in sympathetic neurotransmitter activity combined with growing arterial stiffness can lead to greater increases in diastolic blood pressure during daily hassles (Chapter 14), which might explain why older adults are less likely to tolerate high levels of arousal (e.g., Chapter 11), which in turn might lead them to be more selective in the environments they seek out (e.g., Chapter 10), which then might ultimately lead to increased well-being (e.g., Chapter 7). Baltes (1997) would consider such patterns as possible reflections of the orchestration of selection, optimization, and compensation to achieve goals in everyday life. Others would view the balance between losses and gains in different terms, but there is a growing appreciation in the literature that processes of adaptation occur at multiple levels within and between persons and their environmental contexts. We note that many of the chapters in this Handbook explicitly point at the necessity of integrating biological/neuroscientific data with those of psychological studies for a full understanding of socioemotional development in adulthood.

Finally, and perhaps more controversially, many (but not all) of the chapters in this Handbook display a growing awareness that it might be fruitful to consider the different theories or frameworks in the field (traditionally often viewed as competing) as complementary ways of explaining the relevant phenomena, rather than as rival explanations. These theories fall broadly into two categories: accounts that center on time perspective and motivation (most notably Carstensen's socioemotional selectivity theory; e.g., Carstensen et al., 2006) and accounts that stress the balances between goals and age-related hindrances and affordances set by the body and the mind (e.g., dynamic integration theory, Labouvie-Vief, 2003; the strength and vulnerability integration [SAVI] model, Charles, 2010).

In a way, harmonizing these two broad families of accounts might be an example of what Ardelt and Ferrari (Chapter 19) consider to be true wisdom: the integration of a social and a cognitive perspective on life, with ultimate understanding (and compassion) as its final goal. We welcome this development, which we see very much as in line with Fredda's contributions to the field. We miss her, and we are glad that so many of her colleagues were willing to memorialize her in this volume and help continue the spirit of her work and her personality so beautifully into the future.

References

Baltes, P. B. (1987). Theoretical propositions of lifespan developmental psychology: On the dynamics between growth and decline. *Developmental Psychology, 23*, 611–626.

Baltes, P. B. (1997). On the incomplete architecture of human ontogeny: Selection, optimization, and compensation as a foundation for developmental theory. *American Psychologist, 52*, 366–380.

Baltes, P. B., Staudinger, U. M., & Lindenberger, U. (1999). Lifespan psychology: Theory and application to intellectual functioning. *Annual Review of Psychology, 50*, 471–507.

Berg, C. A., & Klaczynski, P. (1996). Practical intelligence and problem solving: Searching for perspectives. In F. Blanchard-Fields & T. M. Hess (Eds.), *Perspectives on cognition in adulthood and aging* (pp. 323–357). New York: McGraw-Hill.

Blanchard-Fields, F. (1986). Attributional processes in adult development. *Educational Gerontology, 12*, 291–300.

Blanchard-Fields, F. (1994). Age differences in causal attributions from an adult developmental perspective. *Journal of Gerontology: Psychological Sciences, 49*, P43–P51.

Blanchard-Fields, F. (2007). Everyday problem solving and emotion: An adult developmental perspective. *Current Directions in Psychological Science, 16*, 26–31.

Blanchard-Fields, F. (2009). Flexible and adaptive socio-emotional problem solving in adult development. *Restorative Neurology and Neuroscience, 27*, 539–550.

Blanchard-Fields, F. (2010). Neuroscience and aging. In J. C. Cavanaugh, C. K. Cavanaugh, J. Berry, & R. West (Eds.), *Aging in America, Volume 1: Psychological aspects* (pp. 1–25). Santa Barbara, CA: Praeger/ABL-CLIO.

Blanchard-Fields, F., & Abeles, R. (1996). Social cognition and aging. In J. Birren & K. W. Schaie (Eds.), *Handbook of the psychology of aging* (4th ed.,). San Diego: Academic Press.

Blanchard-Fields, F., & Beatty, C. (2005). Age differences in blame attributions: The role of relationship outcome ambiguity and personal identification. *Journals of Gerontology: Psychological Science, 60*, P19–P26.

Blanchard-Fields, F., Hertzog, C., & Horhota, M. (2012). Violate my beliefs? Then you're to blame! Belief content as an explanation of causal attribution biases. *Psychology and Aging, 27*, 324–337.

Blanchard-Fields, F., & Horhota, M. (2006). How can the study of aging inform research on social cognition? *Social Cognition, 24*, 207–217.

Blanchard-Fields, F., & Irion, J. (1988). Coping strategies from the perspective of two developmental markers: Age and social reasoning. *Journal of Genetic Psychology, 149*, 141–152.

Blanchard-Fields, F., Mienaltowski, A., & Seay, R. (2007). Age differences in everyday problem-solving effectiveness: Older adults select more effective strategies for interpersonal problems. *Journals of Gerontology: Psychological Science. 62*, P61–P64.

Blanchard-Fields, F., & Norris, L. (1994). Causal attributions from adolescence through adulthood: Age differences, ego level, and generalized response style. *Aging and Cognition, 1*, 67–86.

Blanchard-Fields, F., & Stange, A. (2009). Challenges for the current status of adult developmental theory: A new century of progress. In M. C. Smith, & T. Reio (Eds.), *Handbook of research on adult development and learning* (pp. 3–33). Mahwah, NJ: Lawrence Erlbaum Associates.

Carstensen, L. L., Mikels, J. A., & Mather, M. (2006). Aging and the intersection of cognition, motivation, and emotion. In J. E. Birren & K. W. Schaie (Eds.), *Handbook of the psychology of aging* (6th ed., pp. 343–362). New York: Academic Press.

Charles, S. T. (2010). Strength and vulnerability integration: A model of emotional well-being across adulthood. *Psychological Bulletin, 136*, 1068–1091.

Chen, Y., & Blanchard-Fields, F. (1997). Age differences in stages of attributional processing. *Psychology and Aging, 12*, 694–703.

Coats, A. H., & Blanchard-Fields, F. (2008). Emotion regulation in interpersonal problems: The role of cognitive-emotional complexity, emotion regulation goals, and expressivity. *Psychology and Aging, 23*, 39–51.

Epstein, S. (2010). Demystifying intuition: What it is, what it does, and how it does it. *Psychological Inquiry, 21*, 295–312.

Gigerenzer, G., Todd, P., and the ABC Research Group (1999). Simple heuristics that make us smart. New York: Academic Press.

Hess, T. M., & Blanchard-Fields, F. (Eds.). (1999). *Social cognition and aging*. San Diego: Academic Press.

Hilimire, M., Mienaltowski, A., Blanchard-Fields, F., & Corballis, P. (in press). Age-related differences in event-related potentials for early visual processing of emotional faces. *Social, Cognitive, and Affective Neuroscience*.

Hoppmann, C. A., & Blanchard-Fields, F. (2010). Goals and everyday problem solving: Manipulating goal preferences in young and older adults. *Developmental Psychology, 46*(6), 1433–1443.

Hoppmann, C., Coats, A. H., Blanchard-Fields, F. (2008). Examining the link between age-related goals and problem-solving strategy use. *Aging, Neuropsychology, and Cognition, 15*, 401–423.

Horhota, M., Mienaltowski, A., & Blanchard-Fields, F. (2012). If only I had taken my usual route: Age-related differences in counter-factual thinking. *Aging, Neuropsychology, and Cognition*.

Irion, J., & Blanchard-Fields, F. (1987). A cross-sectional analysis of adaptive coping in adulthood. *Journal of Gerontology, 42*, 502–504.

Isaacowitz, D. M., & Blanchard-Fields, F. (2012). Linking process and outcome in the study of emotion and aging. *Perspectives on Psychological Science, 7*, 3–17.

Joseph, J. (1993). *Selected poems*. London, England: Bloodaxe Books, Ltd.

Kotter-Grühn, D., Scheibe, S., Blanchard-Fields, F., & Baltes, P. B. (2009). Developmental emergence and functionality of Sehnsucht (life longings): The sample case of involuntary childlessness in middle-aged women. *Psychology and Aging, 24*, 634–644.

Kruglanski, A. W., & Webster, D. M. (1996). Motivated closing of the mind: "Seizing" and "freezing". *Psychological Review, 103*, 263–283.

Labouvie-Vief, G. (2003). Dynamic integration: Affect, cognition, and the self in adulthood. *Current Directions in Psychological Science, 12*, 201–206.

Labouvie-Vief, G., & Blanchard-Fields, F. (1982). Cognitive aging and psychological growth. *Ageing and Society, 2*, 183–209.

Mata, R. (2007). Understanding the aging decision maker. *Human Development, 50*, 359–366.

Mischel, W., & Shoda, Y. (1995). A cognitive–affective system theory of personality: Reconceptualizing situations, dispositions, dynamics, and invariance in personality structure. *Psychological Review, 102*, 246–268.

Scheibe, S., & Blanchard-Fields, F. (2009). Effects of regulating emotion on cognitive performance: What is costly for young adults is not so costly for older adults. *Psychology and Aging, 24*, 217–223.

Scheibe, S., Blanchard-Fields, F., Wiest, M., & Freund, A. M. (2011). Is longing only for Germans? A cross-cultural comparison of Sehnsucht in Germany and the United States. *Developmental Psychology, 47*, 603–618.

Scott, S. B., Sliwinski, M. J., & Blanchard-Fields, F. (in press). Age differences in emotional responses to daily stress: The role of timing, severity, and global perceived stress. *Psychology and Aging*.

Sloman, S. A. (1996). The empirical case for two systems of reasoning. *Psychological Bulletin, 119*, 3–22.

Watson, T., & Blanchard-Fields, F. (1998). Thinking with your head and your heart: Age differences in everyday problem-solving strategy preferences. *Aging, Neuropsychology, and Cognition, 5*, 225–240.

PART 1

Emotion During Adulthood

Older Adults' Perception of Social and Emotional Cues

Louise H. Phillips, Gillian Slessor, Phoebe E. Bailey, *and* Julie D. Henry

Abstract

Adult aging influences the decoding of social and emotional cues. Older adults perform worse than younger adults in labeling some types of emotional expression from faces, bodies, and voices. Age-related declines also occur in following social cues from eye gaze. Other aspects of social perception show age-related stability, including automatic mimicry responses to emotional stimuli. There are also age-related improvements or positivity biases in some social perception tasks such as decoding information about smiles. Evidence to date indicates that age-related deficits in social perception are not caused by general cognitive or perceptual decline. Other plausible explanations for age effects on social perception include structural changes in the aging brain, or age-related alterations in motivational goals. To date, there is not enough direct evidence to evaluate these possibilities. It is important to learn more about how the social and emotion perception changes in old age influence everyday interpersonal interactions and well-being.

Key Words: aging, emotion, social perception, emotion perception, joint attention

Perceiving the Social World

Cognitive aging research has for many years been wedded to information processing models of human functioning, which emphasize computer metaphors of the mind. This has meant a focus on "cold" cognitive tasks, such as speed of processing, memory paradigms, and intelligence tests. Fredda Blanchard-Fields was one of the first researchers in the field of cognitive aging to recognize that it is important to also consider social and emotional influences on cognition when trying to understand lifespan development (e.g., Blanchard-Fields, Jahnke, & Camp, 1995; Blanchard-Fields & Norris, 1994; Blanchard-Fields, Stein, & Watson, 2004). After all, humans are animals, not computers, and much of our everyday behavior is determined by social and emotional goals.

There is growing evidence that aging interacts with emotion to influence cognition in interesting ways. The predominant model of cognitive changes with age for many years emphasized loss of speed and decreased novel processing capacity, with some preservation of acquired skills and knowledge. How social and emotional information is processed also changes with age. An important skill in everyday communication is the ability to decode and react appropriately to the social signals sent out by other people, including cues to emotional states. Adult aging influences these social perception skills, but not in a uniform manner. Although older adults are worse at perceiving some social cues, this age difference disappears or is reversed for others. There may be a role for neural, perceptual, and cognitive decline in some of these age-related changes (Mill, Allik, Realo, & Valk, 2009; Ruffman, Henry, Livingstone, & Phillips, 2008).

Age-related cognitive decline such as reduced information processing speed or working memory capacity might be important, given that these cognitive resources are essential to social perception tasks (e.g., Phillips, Channon, Tunstall, Hedenstrom, & Lyons, 2008; Bull, Phillips, & Conway, 2008). Age differences in social perception may also be related to changing neural systems with age (e.g., Calder et al., 2003; Ruffman et al., 2008; Suzuki, Hoshino, Shigemasu, & Kawamura, 2007; Williams et al., 2006).Widespread networks of neural systems are involved in social perception tasks, with key areas including prefrontal regions (e.g., medial prefrontal cortex, anterior cingulate) and medial-temporal regions (e.g., superior temporal sulcus, amygdala). Because many of these regions are also prone to age-related volume loss (e.g., Raz et al., 1997) and show age-related changes in functional activity during emotion perception tasks (e.g., Gunning-Dixon et al., 2003), there are plausible links to be made between the neural and social perceptual changes seen in old age.

Although cognitive and neuropsychological approaches emphasize the losses with age that might impair social perception, motivational theories indicate that there may be some gains or qualitative changes. Charles and Carstensen (2010) review a substantial body of evidence indicating that, as people get older, they tend to prioritize close social relationships, focus more on achieving emotional well-being, and attend more to positive emotional information while ignoring negative information. These changing motivational goals in old age have implications for attention to and processing of social cues from the environment. Of particular importance in considering emotional changes in old age is the presence of a positivity bias: that is, a tendency to notice, attend to, and remember more positive compared to negative information. The role of life experience in social skills also indicates that older adults might show gains in some aspects of social perception.

In this chapter, we review the pattern of age effects on perceiving emotional and other social cues. Much of the literature focuses on facial expressions of emotion, but we will also cover some auditory, bodily, and multimodal social cues. The focus of this chapter is on more basic social perception processes (decoding emotional and social cues), rather than on more complex processes of social cognition, such as emotional problem solving or Theory of Mind tasks, such as belief reasoning. Links to cognitive, neural, and motivational change will be discussed. We also discuss here the limited existing evidence for possible links between social

perception and broader aspects of well-being and social behavior in old age.

The Pattern of Age Differences in Decoding Emotional Cues
Perceiving the Six Basic Facial Expressions

The most widely used measure of social perception assesses the ability to identify facial expressions of emotions from photographs. This task has been used in many studies to investigate cultural differences in emotion understanding, the neuroanatomical loci of emotional processing, and social skill deficits accompanying brain injury or psychiatric disorder. The most commonly used measure of this construct requires participants to choose which of six verbal labels best describes a facial expression (e.g., Ekman & Friesen, 1976; Young, Perrett, Calder, Sprengelmeyer, & Ekman, 2002). Six emotions are portrayed: disgust, anger, fear, surprise, sadness, and happiness. This task involves both relatively automatic processes, such as physiological reactions to the valence of emotional information, as well as higher level cognitive processes, such as evaluating the meaning of a verbal label or weighing multiple labels to decide which one best matches a face.

Most studies to date have focused on whether aging differentially affects the recognition of these six "basic" emotions. A meta-analytic review indicated that age differences vary across the six basic emotions (Ruffman et al., 2008, see Figure 2.1). There were strong and clear age-related declines in the ability to label anger, fear, and sadness; much smaller (but reliable) age impairments in identifying happiness and surprise; and a trend toward age-related improvement in identifying disgust. These age-related changes were examined in the context of three theoretical perspectives—positivity effects, general cognitive and perceptual decline, and more specific neuropsychological change in the social brain. It was argued that the pattern of age-related change in emotion perception was most consistent with a neuropsychological model stemming from changes in frontal and temporal volume, and/or changes in neurotransmitters (for more detail, see the section "Age Differences in Perceiving the Social World: Possible Mechanisms").

It has also been proposed that age-related differences in the motivational allocation of visual attention may be relevant to understanding age differences in facial affect recognition. A number of eye-tracking studies of emotion perception indicate that there are age-related changes in the allocation of attention to different parts of the face, with

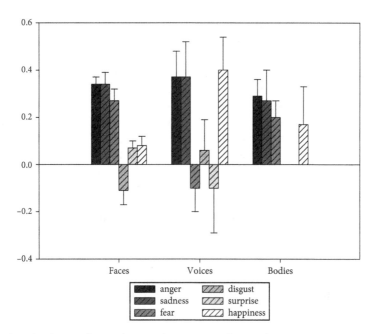

Figure 2.1. Meta-analytic data from Ruffman et al. (2008) showing mean effect sizes for age group (young vs. old) on emotion perception tasks for different emotions and modalities of presentation. Positive values indicate that older adults performed worse than young adults, whereas negative values indicate that old performed better than young. Error bars indicate standard error of effect size.

older adults tending to focus more on the mouth region and less on the eyes (Murphy & Issacowitz, 2010; Sullivan, Ruffman, & Hutton, 2007; Wong, Cronin-Golomb, & Neargarder, 2005). Given that eyes are important in identifying those emotions that older people struggle most to identify (anger, sadness, fear), this suggests a possible link between attentional biases away from the eyes and emotion recognition abilities in old age (Isaacowitz & Stanley, 2011). However, in a recent test of this possibility, Murphy and Isaacowitz (2010) did not find a clear link between problems in emotion recognition and biases in attention toward different parts of the faces in older adults.

Recent evidence indicates that the mechanisms that underlie age-related change in emotion perception may operate from relatively early in adulthood. Although most studies of aging and facial affect recognition have compared younger and older adults (i.e., extreme group contrasts—see Ruffman et al.'s 2008 review), Mill et al. (2009) conducted a cross-sectional study of 607 participants aged 18–84 years. This allows greater understanding of lifespan changes in emotion perception (see Table 2.1 for a summary of their findings). The results indicated that the trajectories of age-related change vary for different facial emotions. The largest age difference to emerge was in the recognition of sadness, followed by anger. For both of these facial emotions, deficits initially appeared from

around 30 years of age and showed linear progression with increasing age. In contrast, the other basic emotions (happiness, surprise, disgust, and fear) showed no age effect between 18 and 60, but a marked decline in recognition over the age of 60.

Table 2.1. Summary of Mill et al.'s (2009) findings in relation to lifespan aging effects on perceiving emotions from faces and voices.

Emotion	Aging effect on perceiving emotion from faces	Aging effect on perceiving emotion from voices
Anger	Linear decline	Linear decline
Sadness	Linear decline	Linear decline
Happiness	Decline 60+	Decline 60+
Neutral	No age effect	No age effect
Disgust	Decline 60+	–
Surprise	Decline 60+	–
Contempt	Improve until 60, then decline	–

In this study, 607 participants aged 18–84 completed tasks of face and voice emotion perception. Results are presented in terms of whether they indicated linear age-related declines across the lifespan, stability until mid-life followed by a decline at age 60+, or no age effect.

Another factor that has been considered in a number of recent studies is the age of the face portraying an emotion. Given own-age biases in facial identity memory (see e.g., Perfect & Moon, 2005), it seems important to understand whether such own-age biases exist in emotion perception accuracy. The evidence indicates some complex patterns of interactions between age of participant, age of face, and experience of own- and other-age social interactions (Ebner, He, & Johnson, 2011; Ebner & Johnson, 2009, 2010; Murphy, Lehrfeld, & Isaacowitz, 2010). However, there does not seem to be clear evidence of own-age biases favoring perception of emotions from similarly aged peers.

Beyond the Basic Six: Understanding Other Emotions

The majority of studies assessing age-related differences in emotion perception have used black-and-white photographs of individuals posing the six basic emotions described above. However, these are not the only emotions experienced and expressed in real-life situations. Stanley and Blanchard-Fields (2008) looked at the effects of aging on the ability to decode more complex social emotions and found that older adults had problems decoding facial expressions of shame and guilt. There are mixed findings in relation to age differences in recognition of the complex emotion of contempt from facial expressions. MacPherson, Phillips, and Della Sala (2002) found no age differences, despite this being the most difficult emotion to identify in their task. MacPherson, Phillips, and Della Sala (2006) later reported that there were age-related difficulties in distinguishing sadness from contempt in a much simpler emotion discrimination task. Mill et al. (2009, see also Table 2.1), in their lifespan study, found that middle-aged adults were better at identifying contempt compared to both younger and older adults—but the latter age groups did not differ. This could indicate that understanding of some more complex emotions, such as contempt, develops across adulthood. Mill et al.'s large lifespan aging study also included nonemotional "neutral" faces, and these were not subject to any age-related changes in labeling accuracy, unlike all the other emotions.

Younger adults have also been found to outperform their older counterparts on tasks assessing recognition of more complex emotions such as desire, interest, or sympathy from photographs of the eye-region and videos of social interactions (Bailey & Henry, 2008; Slessor, Phillips, & Bull, 2007;

Sullivan & Ruffman, 2004). In addition to problems with decoding complex mental states in these tasks, Slessor et al. (2007) reported evidence of age differences on matched control tasks involving participants judging the age and gender of people depicted in the stimuli. Therefore, these age-related declines are not specific to decoding the mental states of others but also extend to more general difficulties in perceiving social information from visual material. Further evidence is required to understand the pattern of age-related differences in decoding more complex emotional states. For example, are differences found only for negative emotions (e.g., contempt, guilt, shame) or also for positive expressions (e.g., pride, hope, excitement)?

In addition, decoding basic emotional expressions in real-life situations does not rely on the analysis of discrete, prototypical expressions, because often more than one emotion is experienced at a time. Previous studies using emotional blends found evidence of older adults' problems in interpreting the dominant emotion displayed, particularly when this was negatively valenced (e.g., anger, fear, or sadness; Bucks, Garner, Tarrant, Bradley, & Mogg, 2008; Calder et al., 2003; Sullivan & Ruffman, 2004). However, these studies have tended to focus on the perception of the dominant emotion and have not assessed age differences in the mix or intensity of emotions perceived. One study of age differences in perceived emotional intensity from faces (Phillips & Allen, 2004) indicated that older adults rate some negative expressions as being less intense. However, this might be an appropriate or adaptive response: younger adults perceived higher levels of anger in faces intended to be neutral, and this was related to the higher levels of experienced anxiety and depression in the younger participants. It would be useful to explore further whether younger and older adults might differ in their thresholds in judging a face as emotional, and how this might differ for subtle positive and negative emotions. Understanding the effects of age in identifying complex and blended emotions may be particularly important, given age differences in the complexity of experienced emotions (e.g., Labouvie-Vief & Medler, 2002).

Decoding Genuine and Posed Smiles

As indicated, there may be relative preservation in the ability to label happy facial expressions. However, it is difficult to interpret this finding: happiness recognition is generally close to 100% accurate because a smile stands out so clearly from other facial expressions. Most previous aging studies focused only on prototypical posed expressions. Some recent studies have looked at aging and perception of positive emotion in more detail, by investigating age-related differences in distinguishing between posed and genuine types of smile (Murphy et al., 2010; Slessor, Miles, Bull, and Phillips, 2010a). Slessor et al. (2010a) found no age differences in the ability to discriminate between photographs of posed and genuine smiles. However, older adults demonstrated a greater bias toward thinking that any smiling individual was "feeling happy," suggesting a positivity bias in this task. In a second study assessing social judgments of approachability, Slessor et al. (2010a) found that older adults were also more likely than younger participants to choose to approach an individual when they were displaying a posed smile. These results indicate no age-related difficulties in distinguishing between different types of smile, but an age-related positivity bias in judging and reacting to smiles.

In contrast, Murphy et al. (2010) used dynamic videos of smiles in their task. They found evidence of an age-related improvement in distinguishing posed from genuine smiles. There was no indication of an age-related bias when judging whether smiles were posed. The different pattern of results in the two smiles studies may be caused by the use of static versus dynamic emotional stimuli. Dynamic emotional stimuli (as used by Murphy et al., 2010) are likely to be more ecologically valid, more information-rich, and easier to distinguish than the static pictures used in most other aging studies, including that of Slessor et al. (2010a). The two studies also differed in the questions asked about the smiles. Whereas Murphy et al. asked participants to decide whether each smile was posed or genuine, Slessor et al. asked them to say whether the person in the photograph was feeling happy or not. More detailed research is needed to explore younger and older adults' reactions to others' smiles and how this might influence their social behavior.

Emotional Body Movements

The majority of studies investigating age differences in emotion perception look at facial expressions. Less is known about how age impacts on the ability to decode emotions from other modalities, such as body movements. It is likely that we pick up many cues to emotional states from both body posture and the dynamics of a moving body. The most widely used method to explore perception of body movement is through the use of point-light animations: these lack cues to color, contour, and texture, and so the influence of these perceptual factors can be minimized. There are relatively few studies investigating perception of emotions from body movements in older adulthood, but the available evidence indicates that older adults are less accurate than younger adults (Insch et al., 2012; Montepare, Koff, Zaitchik, & Albert, 1999; Ruffman, Sullivan, & Dittrich, 2009) in determining emotion from body movement.

In contrast to the more established pattern seen when older adults decode emotions from the face, less is known about which emotional body movements are subject to age-related decline (see the meta-analytic data in Figure 2.1, based on only three datasets). Ruffman et al. (2009) reported that older adults had more difficulty in decoding anger and sadness from point-light displays than their younger counterparts. Another recent study (Insch et al., under review) reported age differences in decoding anger, sadness, and fear from point-light displays. These results indicate a similar pattern of age-related declines to that seen in labeling facial expressions. More information is needed on age differences in decoding different types of emotional information from body postures and movement.

Other Modalities of Emotion: Auditory Expressions

Emotions are conveyed through auditory as well as visual channels: tone of voice can be a particularly evocative indicator of affective state. Several studies have assessed how age relates to the recognition of emotion from auditory cues. These studies have either presented participants with lexical tasks (situation descriptions; Isaacowitz et al., 2007) or neutral verbal material in which the emotional content of the vocal expression is manipulated (affective prosody, e.g., Ryan, Murray, & Ruffman, 2010). Other studies have used nonverbal utterances such as exclamations (Hunter, Phillips, & MacPherson, 2010). Taken together, most evidence indicates that the pattern of age-related difficulties for processing auditory emotional cues largely parallels the deficits seen for facial affect recognition. For instance, in their meta-analytic review of this literature, Ruffman et al. (2008) showed that older adults were impaired in identifying angry and sad vocal expressions, whereas decoding of fear, surprise, and disgust did not differ across age groups (see Figure 2.1). This pattern emerged whether all stimuli were included, or when restricted to the more common affective prosody stimuli only.

More recent studies particularly highlight difficulties in decoding vocal expressions of anger and sadness. For instance, Ryan et al. (2010) manipulated affective prosody and found that older adults were significantly less accurate than younger adults at labeling sadness and anger, but did not differ in their recognition of other vocal expressions (happiness, fear, surprise, or disgust). Furthermore, in their lifespan study of 607 participants aged 18–84 years, Mill et al. (2009) found that recognition of negative vocal expressions (sadness, and to a lesser degree, anger) declined from around the age of 30, whereas happiness was only impaired in the oldest group (see Table 2.1). It was concluded that the extraction of emotion information may operate analogously for speech prosody and facial expressions. Hunter et al. (2010, experiment 1) looked at the perception of nonlinguistic emotional utterances, as well as facial emotions, in an aging sample. Results indicated that there was a high degree of overlap between the emotions subject to age effects in identifying emotional utterances (anger, sadness, fear, disgust) and identifying facial expressions (anger, sadness, fear, and surprise).

Multimodal Presentation of Emotions

Studies of age differences in emotion perception mostly present stimuli in a single modality (e.g., a voice or a face). This considerably reduces ecological validity because in real-world settings, we tend to receive multimodal information about emotions; for example, from sounds and gestures as well as faces. One study that tested how age relates to emotion recognition using a more ecologically valid measure that incorporates facial expressions, body movement, paralinguistic, and auditory cues was conducted by Henry et al. (2008). Younger and older participants (as well as a sample of people with dementia) were administered the Emotion Evaluation Test from the Awareness of Social Inference Test (TASIT; McDonald, Flanagan, Rollins, & Kinch, 2002). This measure comprises 28 video vignettes in which a professional actor portrays one of seven basic emotional states (happy, sad, fearful, disgusted, surprised, angry, neutral). Henry et al. (2008) found that although older adults were impaired in labeling the emotions from these video stimuli relative to their younger counterparts, there was no interaction with emotion type. Therefore, there was no evidence that these difficulties were specific, or disproportionate, to any particular emotion. However, this test contains only four vignettes for each emotion. Consequently, although the total

measure would have had sufficient sensitivity to detect overall group differences, power to identify interaction effects with specific emotions would have been relatively low.

In another recent study of multimodal emotion perception, Hunter et al. (2010, experiment 2) investigated whether providing both visual and auditory information about emotions might actually help older people to distinguish between different affective states, compared to only having information from one of these modalities. Older adults were less able than their younger counterparts to distinguish between emotions when information was presented in faces only, and a similar age-related deficit was found in labeling emotions from auditory information only. In contrast, in the multimodal condition, there were no age differences in emotion perception, indicating that older adults may particularly benefit from the availability of multimodal information when interpreting emotions. This might be because the increased ecological validity of multimodal emotion presentations matches everyday experiences of emotional information more closely than just seeing faces or hearing voices. Also, having multiple channels of information provides a greater level of redundancy, which might help to attenuate declines in the speed or efficiency of processing emotional information in old age.

Age Differences in Implicit Measures of Emotion Perception

Most studies investigating age differences in emotion perception depend on the same basic task: explicitly choosing which emotional label best describes a particular depiction of emotion, such as a photograph of a face. But when we decode and react to the emotional states of others in our everyday lives, we do not always produce a verbal label for the emotion, we are not limited in our choice from a narrow range of labels, and we may indeed have no awareness of the emotion-decoding process. Most of the evidence reviewed indicates that older adults are impaired in explicit verbal labeling of emotional expressions. Despite the importance of implicit processes of decoding and reacting to emotional information in everyday social situations, we still have relatively little knowledge about how age influences these processes. The cognitive aging literature indicates that automatic and implicit processes are usually less affected by age than the types of complex decision-making tasks involved in emotion labeling paradigms; therefore, we might predict smaller age effects on implicit measures. Some evidence supports this: there is age-related preservation of early processes of emotional detection in facial arrays (e.g., Mather & Knight, 2006; Ruffman, Ng, & Jenkin, 2009). Ruffman et al. (2009) found both intact implicit processing (i.e., a pop-out effect) and impaired explicit processing (i.e., labeling) of angry expressions in an older adult sample.

One way of looking at implicit behavioral responses to emotional expressions is through the use of surface facial electromyography (EMG), which detects subtle changes in the electrical activity of facial muscles of participants viewing emotional stimuli. EMG is useful for detecting subtle facial expression mimicry, which the majority of studies indicate is important in successful expression recognition (e.g., Oberman, Winkielman, & Ramachandran, 2007). Because older adults have particular difficulty in labeling facial expressions of anger (Ruffman et al., 2008), Bailey, Henry, and Nangle (2009) compared young and older adults' facial mimicry responses to angry expressions. It was shown that, in the timeframe from 500 ms after stimulus onset, increases in older adults' corrugator supercilii muscle region activity, which furrows the brow, were correlated with a *reduced* ability to label expressions as angry. Since the opposite pattern was expected, whereby increased corrugator activity should correlate with *improved* anger recognition, this finding was attributed to older adults furrowing their brows in confusion rather than anger mimicry. Most importantly, the older adults were only demonstrating this confusion in the latter stage of stimulus exposure, when conscious explicit labeling processes were being activated. It was therefore suggested that older adults' brow furrowing may have been turning from a mimicry response in the early spontaneous timeframe to an expression of confusion as more explicit processing resources became engaged. Although there was no correlation between mimicry and expression labeling in the early timeframe (within 500 ms of stimulus onset), this is consistent with more recent studies also showing no link between mimicry and explicit facial expression labeling (e.g., Bogart & Matsumoto, 2010). However, although the debate surrounding such an association continues, most researchers agree that mimicry facilitates congruent emotion and smooth interaction between social partners (Blairy, Herrera, & Hess, 1999).

The contention that older adults demonstrate an intact *rapid* mimicry response was supported by Bailey and Henry (2009). In addition to the corrugator, this study used EMG over the zygomaticus major muscle region, which lifts the corner of the lips into a smile, to show that older adults mimic both happy and angry facial expressions when those stimuli are presented subconsciously and therefore processed implicitly. Together, these studies provide evidence for a possible dissociation between preserved implicit versus impaired explicit processing of negative emotion expressions among older adults. This type of dissociation is widely recognized in the cognitive aging literature (see Phillips & Henry, 2008), but may also be apparent in the domain of aging and emotion processing. Specifically, despite difficulty explicitly labeling expressions of anger, older adults demonstrate intact implicit detection of these stimuli and respond to them appropriately.

Going Beyond Emotions: Age Differences in Decoding Other Types of Social Cue
Detecting and Following Eye Gaze

Numerous studies indicate age-related declines in the forced choice labeling of emotional expressions. However, fewer studies have investigated the effects of aging on more basic aspects of social perception, such as eye gaze processing. Given repeated demonstrations that older adults attend less to the eye region of emotional faces than do young people (e.g., Murphy & Issacowitz, 2010; Sullivan et al., 2007; Wong et al., 2005), it is of interest to understand whether there are age differences in processing other social cues from eyes. The ability to detect whether another person is attending to you or somewhere else in the environment is important in social interaction. Slessor, Phillips, and Bull (2008) assessed age-related differences in the ability to detect subtle differences in gaze direction, including direct gaze and gaze averted by 0.13, 0.25, or 0.38 degrees to the left or right. Participants were asked to determine whether the person photographed was looking directly at them or averting their gaze. There was an age-related decline in the detection of subtle gaze aversion (i.e., when gaze was averted by 0.13 and 0.25 degrees) that was not fully explained by age differences in more general visual perception. Older adults had intact ability to detect both direct gaze and gaze that was more clearly averted by 0.38 degrees to the left or right.

Another social skill that develops early in life is joint attention (D'Entremont, Hains, & Muir, 1997; Morales, Mundy, & Rojas, 1998)—following the gaze of another. Successfully engaging in joint attention with another person enables early detection of socially relevant information (Langton, Watt, & Bruce, 2000; Stone & Yoder, 2001). Therefore, age-related difficulties in gaze processing may have negative implications for social interactions in old age. Using a measure of joint attention, Slessor et al. (2008) found that younger and older adults were quicker to detect a target when gaze direction of a centrally presented face predicted a target location (congruent trial) than when gaze direction cued participants in the wrong direction (incongruent trial). However, older adults showed considerably smaller joint attention effects: in other words, they had a reduced tendency to follow gaze direction to facilitate detection of the target. These age differences in joint attention could not be explained by difficulties in *detecting* gaze patterns, because in these stimuli the gaze was very clearly averted.

Slessor et al. (submitted) further investigated these age differences in gaze following by comparing congruent and incongruent trials with no-cue trials, in which gaze remained straight ahead and thus provided no cues to target location. This allows separation of facilitation effects from congruent gaze, and inhibition effects from incongruent gaze. Unlike younger participants, older adults showed no facilitation effects from congruent gaze. This is quite a striking pattern of findings. The ability to follow gaze is critical to engaging in joint attention, and thus the finding that older adults have specific difficulties following these congruent gaze cues suggests that they avoid establishing eye contact and joint attention with others. It remains a puzzle as to whether this reflects decreased ability to focus social attention, perhaps linked to neural change in old age, or instead motivational differences, such as reluctance to engage in direct eye contact with unfamiliar people.

Like the majority of research assessing the effects of aging on social perception, these gaze-following studies only employed images of younger adults. In a study including both young and old adult faces as stimuli, Slessor, Laird, Bull, Phillips, and Filippou (2010b) found that age differences in gaze following were influenced by the age of the stimulus face. Younger adults demonstrated an own-age bias, being more likely to follow the gaze of people their own age. Previous findings of age-related differences in gaze following may reflect this advantage that younger adults seem to have when decoding gaze cues from younger adult faces. It is important to note that in the Slessor et al. (2010b) study there was no evidence for an own-age bias in older adults' gaze-following. The finding that younger participants show less evidence of following older adults' gaze cues could impact negatively on intergenerational communication, perhaps contributing to findings of poor quality and less satisfying interactions between different age groups (Giles et al., 2003; Giles, Makoni, & Dailey, 2005) and reports that younger people tend to avoid social contact with older generations (Wenger, Davies, Shahtahmasebi, & Scott, 1996).

Detecting Deception From Auditory and Visual Information

The accurate perception of social cues is critical in the detection of deception. Recent media reports suggest that older adults are at increased risk of becoming victims of fraudulent activities. For example, in the United States, more than 7.3 million people over the age of 65 have been victims of financial exploitation (Investor Protection Trust, 2010) and, according to reports from the Scottish Police, in Edinburgh 86% of incidents of fraudulent selling were reported by those over the age of 60 (Smith, 2010). Rates of financial exploitation are expected to rise due to increases in the size of the older adult population, coupled with increasing financial assets (Kemp & Mosqueda, 2005).

The first study to investigate age differences in detection of deceit found that older women were better than younger women at identifying whether someone was lying or telling the truth (Bond, Thompson, & Malloy, 2005). Bond et al. (2005) argued that greater experience in interacting with others enhanced older adults' ability to accurately interpret social behavior. However, other evidence suggests that there is an age-related decline in detecting deception. Stanley and Blanchard-Fields (2008) found that older adults were less accurate than younger participants when detecting deceit from muted video clips of crime interrogations and video clips with both visual and audio cues. This is consistent with evidence that older adults are less aware than their younger counterparts of some of the paraverbal and nonverbal cues that are reliably linked to deceit (Slessor, Phillips, Bull, Venturini, Bonny, & Rokaszewicz, 2012). For example, older participants reported being less likely to interpret behaviors such as stuttering as an indication that someone was lying. In addition, older adults were more likely to hold stereotypical but inaccurate beliefs that liars tend to tell longer stories and make more hand gestures.

Ruffman, Murray, Halberstadt, and Vater (2012) also found that older adults were less successful than young at discriminating truth and lies from video recordings. This age difference was mainly driven by older adults having a greater bias to label liars as being truthful. It was also shown that both young and older adults find it easier to determine when an older adult is lying relative to a young adult, suggesting age-related decline in the skills needed to successfully deceive others. However, there was no evidence for an own-age bias in the detection of deception.

Both Stanley and Blanchard-Fields (2008) and Ruffman et al. (2012) found that age-related deficiencies in detecting deception from visual information are mediated by difficulty in recognizing facial expressions of emotion. The broader literature suggests that deception detection partly relies on the ability to detect emotions that are briefly leaked, or more specifically, the detection of microexpressions (Ekman, 2007). For example, deceivers will often briefly reveal their fear of being caught out in a lie. However, Stanley and Blanchard-Fields (2008) and Ruffman et al. (2012) showed that difficulty recognizing expressions at durations of 50 ms, 250 ms, 1.5 s, and even unlimited durations all contribute to older adults' poor performance in the domain of deception detection. Thus, it appears that older adults may be impaired in deception detection due to poor ability to accurately label facial expressions.

Smiles can also be cues to deceit in some circumstances, since they can reflect an attempt to mask an intention or emotion and thus deceive the perceiver (Ekman & O'Sullivan, 1991). It is therefore of note that, compared to their younger counterparts, older adults might have a greater tendency to approach an individual displaying a posed smile (Slessor et al., 2010a). These findings indicate that older adults may be more susceptible to deception due to the misinterpretation of disingenuous smiles.

Given recent concerns about older adults' vulnerability to fraud and financial exploitation (Smith, 2010), more understanding is needed of the mechanisms underlying age-related increases in susceptibility to fraud and deceit. One potential mechanism may be related to the automatic tendency to imitate behaviors of an interaction partner (i.e., mimicry). Indeed, Stel, van Dijk, and Olivier (2009) showed that inhibiting mimicry of a liar's false facial expression (i.e., a posed smile) improves an observer's ability to detect deceit. As outlined above, older adults demonstrate both subconscious (Bailey & Henry, 2009) and conscious (Bailey et al., 2009) mimicry of angry and smiling facial expressions commensurate with that of young adults. However, previous studies only assessed older adults' rapid facial mimicry responses (within 1 s of stimulus exposure),

and evidence of age-related behavioral disinhibition (Butler & Zacks, 2006) suggests that older adults may experience extended mimicry responses relative to their younger counterparts. Thus, future research should assess whether older adults' mimicry of posed smiling is disinhibited, and whether this is associated with difficulty in detecting deceit.

Combining Emotional and Eye Gaze Cues

In everyday interpersonal situations, social cues are not decoded in isolation but require integration of a number of different dimensions to accurately interpret information. For example, someone behaving angrily might invoke a different response if they were looking directly at you, as opposed to when their attention was focused on someone else. Previous findings suggest that gaze direction influences the perception of emotion expressions, with direct gaze enhancing the perception of anger and joy, whereas averted gaze enhances the perception of fear (Adams & Kleck, 2003, 2005). To investigate adult age-related differences in the integration and interpretation of emotion and gaze cues, Slessor, Phillips, and Bull (2010c, study 1) asked younger and older participants to decide whether faces with direct or averted gaze looked more emotional. Pairs of faces that differed only in gaze direction were used: in some trials, both faces were angry; in other trials, both faces were happy. Younger and older adults perceived happy faces to be more emotionally intense when coupled with direct (vs. averted) gaze, thus supporting previous findings. However, older participants did not differentiate angry faces with direct and averted gaze, unlike younger adults. These findings suggest that older adults may be less adept at integrating different social cues when making explicit emotion perception judgments, at least for negative emotions.

However, in real-life situations, people are not required to make explicit and conscious judgments about the intensity of emotional expressions. Therefore, Slessor et al. (2010c) conducted a second study more relevant to everyday social functioning and found that older adults also showed less integration of gaze and emotion cues than younger adults when making social judgments of approachability (e.g., to ask a favor). In this study, younger participants integrated gaze and emotion cues in a socially adaptive way, being less likely to approach an angry person looking toward them as opposed to an angry person who was looking elsewhere. However, older adults rated themselves as more likely to approach an angry person looking at them as opposed to looking away, despite the fact that the former might be more likely to be angry with the participant themself. These results may indicate that older adults have problems identifying which individuals in the social environment are most likely to respond positively to their own social efforts.

Implications of Age Changes in Social Perception for Interpersonal Functioning

Social functioning in late adulthood shows a pattern of gains and losses. On the one hand, life experiences and the wisdom that accompanies them can lead to more harmonious social relationships (Blanchard-Fields, 2007; Charles & Carstensen, 2010). Indeed, socioemotional models of aging propose that social functioning in late adulthood does not follow the same course of decline as cognitive and biological aging, in part as a consequence of increased prioritization of emotion-related goals (Antonucci, 2001; Charles & Carstensen, 2007). Competing with these facilitative effects, however, are other changes in late adulthood that are likely to have a detrimental impact on social functioning. Cognitive losses associated with normal adult aging might affect older adults' social functioning by limiting their ability to negotiate complex social relationships. For example, cognitive deficits in aging have been linked to socially insensitive behaviors, such as increased difficulty in taking another's perspective (Bailey & Henry, 2008), off-target and verbose speech (Pushkar et al., 2000), prejudicial and other socially inappropriate comments (von Hippel & Dunlop, 2005; Henry, von Hippel, & Baynes, 2009), and less socially appropriate conversational style (Bull et al., under review). In one of these studies, Henry et al. (2009) found that older adults were rated by their peers as engaging in more socially inappropriate behavior than were younger adults, such as excessive verbosity, gratuitous argumentation, and public inquiry about private matters, and that these age-related changes were mediated by changes in executive functioning.

Recent evidence indicates that problems in emotion perception in old age may also relate to socially important behaviors. Ruffman, Murray, Halberstadt, and Taumopeau (2010) report that, among a group of older adults, those who have most problems with emotion perception tend to also show more off-topic verbosity. This result may indicate that difficulties with emotion perception influence the ability to read interpersonal cues that indicate when to stop talking. In a subsequent study, Halberstadt, Ruffman, Murray, Taumoepeau,

and Ryan (2011) found that older adults had difficulty differentiating between behaviors that were socially appropriate or inappropriate, and that these difficulties were mediated by age-related deficits in emotion perception. Bull et al. (under review) present evidence that, in a group of older adults, those who had poorest social perception used gestures and eye contact less effectively when involved in a social interaction with a stranger. Taken together, these studies indicate that it is important to look more closely at how problems with emotion perception in old age relate to other behavioral measures of interpersonal communication skills.

Relatively few studies simultaneously measure problems in social perception in old age and aspects of interpersonal functioning. In one recent study, Phillips, Scott, Henry, Mowat, and Bell (2010) reported on correlations between the ability to perceive facial expressions of emotion and self-reported quality of life in three groups of older adults: healthy controls, people with depression, and people with Alzheimer disease. In the healthy older adults, there was a significant and positive association, so that those with poorer emotion perception also reported poorer quality of life. Regression analyses indicated that this relationship could not be explained by levels of cognitive functioning. This evidence indicates that older adults who struggle to perceive emotions also experience poorer quality of life. Clearly, we need to understand more about the links between age-related changes in social perception and everyday interpersonal functioning.

Age Differences in Perceiving the Social World: Possible Mechanisms

The weight of evidence thus far presented indicates that older adults have difficulties with many aspects of social perception, such as interpreting emotional cues. However, there are also some areas of preserved performance and some qualitative changes in social perception. Next, we will consider the three primary explanations that have been put forward to explain the pattern of age effects on social perception (Isaacowitz & Stanley, 2011; Mill et al., 2009; Ruffman et al., 2008): cognitive and perceptual changes with age, neural change with age, and motivational factors.

Cognitive and Perceptual Explanations for Age Differences in Social Perception

An obvious explanation for the age-related problems in many social perception tasks is that they reflect more general difficulties in cognitive processing in old age. A number of studies have tested this directly by using statistical techniques to investigate overlapping variance in age effects on emotion perception tasks (e.g., Keightley, Winocur, Burianova, Hongwanishkul, and Grady, 2006; Orgeta & Phillips, 2008; Sullivan & Ruffman, 2004). These indicate that key variables such as fluid intelligence, visual perception, and processing speed cannot explain the pattern of age effects. For example, Orgeta and Phillips (2008) report that covarying scores on a face *identity* perception task did not reduce age effects on *emotion* perception. In contrast, covarying processing speed (as assessed by the Digit Symbol test) reduced the size of the age effect, although it remained significant. This suggests some commonalities between age differences in cognitive speed and emotion perception that should be explored in more detail. One key cognitive variable that may be particularly important in age differences in emotion perception is executive function (Krendl & Ambady, 2010; Phillips et al., 2010). Executive control processes are involved in emotion labeling (Phillips et al., 2008) and are impaired in old age (Phillips & Henry, 2008), so it is a plausible hypothesis that problems with control processes, such as inhibition or updating, could explain some of the age effects reported, and this has not been explored in detail in the literature.

Another way of exploring the relationship between general cognitive decline and emotion perception is to examine the relative difficulty of labeling individual emotions. Age differences tend to increase as a task becomes more difficult (e.g., Verhaeghen & Cerella, 2002). If age differences in emotion perception reflect more general decline in basic information processing parameters, aging effects should be greatest on those emotions that are most difficult to identify. Ruffman et al. (2008) investigated this issue and concluded that the pattern of age effects did not match the difficulty levels of the emotions. For instance, although sadness was the easiest of the negative emotions for younger people to identify, it proved among the most difficult for older adults.

An important issue in a literature that largely investigates processing of faces is the complex visual perceptual processes involved in making decisions about these information-dense visual stimuli. However, age differences in emotion perception remain significant after covarying for indices of visual perceptual ability, such as contrast sensitivity (MacPherson et al., 2006). Also, the findings of age-related impairments in labeling emotions from verbal utterances suggests that a specific visual perceptual mechanism is unlikely to underlie the

changes. It would be useful to explore in more detail the perceptual mechanisms likely to be important in making affective judgments about faces, voices, or bodies, and the extent to which they are influenced by age (e.g., Pilz, Bennett, & Sekuler, 2010).

Relatively few studies have used experimental manipulations in which age differences are investigated in both emotion perception tasks and matched perception tasks that do not include emotional judgments. This may partly reflect the difficulty in designing suitable nonemotion tasks of similar perceptual and cognitive complexity as classic emotion labeling tasks. Sullivan and Ruffman (2004) matched emotional and nonemotional tasks and found evidence of specificity of age-related deficits in making intensity judgments about auditory and facial expressions of emotion. Mitchell, Kingston, and Barbosa Boucas (2011) compared age-related difficulties in emotional prosody tasks (judging whether a tone of voice was happy or sad) and nonemotional linguistic prosody tasks (judging whether the tone indicated a statement or a question). These indicated that age differences were present but smaller in the linguistic compared to the emotional prosody judgment, thus suggesting some specificity in the age differences in emotion perception.

Some evidence indicates specificity of age-related differences in other aspects of social perception. Older adults' difficulties in detecting subtle differences in gaze direction and establishing joint attention with others cannot be explained by declines in aspects of visual perception, such as contrast sensitivity (Slessor et al., 2008). In addition, different patterns of age effects have been found when comparing shifts of attention to social (eye gaze) and nonsocial (arrow) stimuli, suggesting that general impairments in attentional processes cannot account for age-related differences in joint attention (Slessor et al., submitted). However, there are fundamental differences between eyes and arrows that could explain the differential pattern of age effects found in these tasks. To further understand the mechanisms underlying age-related differences in social perception, the development of additional control tasks is necessary. Nevertheless, the evidence to date indicates that age differences in social perception are unlikely to be caused primarily by more general declines in cognitive or perceptual processes.

Neural Changes With Age and Links to Social Perception

Some recent reviews have concluded that the most plausible explanation for declining emotion perception in old age is of changing neural function (e.g., Ruffman et al., 2008). Similar arguments have been made for the role of changes in the "social brain" in age declines in other aspects of social perception, such as gaze following (Slessor et al., 2008). Emotion perception relies on multiple cognitive processes that are subserved by a large array of neural structures (Britton, Taylor, Sudheimer, & Liberzon, 2006). But there are also clearly dissociable neural substrates implicated in the recognition of specific emotions, and this could be important in understanding the pattern of age differences. For instance, the orbitofrontal cortex has been particularly linked to decoding expressions of anger (Blair, Morris, Frith, Perrett, & Dolan, 1999; Fine & Blair, 2000; Iidaka et al., 2000), the right temporal network to sadness (Blair et al., 1999; Rosen et al., 2006), the amygdala to fear (Adolphs, Tranel, Damasio, & Damasio., 1995), and the basal ganglia and insula to disgust (Calder, Keane, Manes, Antoun, & Young, 2000). Ruffman et al. (2008) therefore proposed that age-related difficulties in identifying anger might relate to structural changes in the orbitofrontal region, sadness to changes in the anterior cingulate cortex and temporal areas such as the amygdala, and fear to changes in the amygdala. In contrast, the relative sparing of some structures within the basal ganglia have been argued to underlie the absence of deficits recognizing disgust (Calder et al., 2003; Williams et al., 2006).

There is some evidence for links between physical changes in the aging brain and higher level aspects of social cognition (Charlton, Barrick, Markus, & Morris, 2009). Charlton et al. (2009) report that the ability to make social inferences declined with age and was associated with brain white matter integrity but not whole-brain volume. This indicates that changing white matter connectivity in the brain could be particularly important in high-level social cognition tasks. However, we still do not have sufficient direct evidence to evaluate whether age differences in emotion perception and other aspects of basic social perception are linked to changes in specific neural structures and their linkages (Somerville, Fani, & McClure-Tone, 2011). It is an important issue for future research to identify whether changes with age in the size and connectivity of key emotional and social brain regions are related to performance on social perception tasks.

There is compelling evidence that older adults have different patterns of functional brain activation when viewing facial expressions of emotion compared to younger adults. In particular, older adults show decreased amygdala activation and increased frontal lobe activation when looking at emotional faces (e.g., Gunning-Dixon et al., 2003; for reviews, see St. Jacques, Bessette-Symons, & Cabeza, 2009; Somerville et al., 2011). It would be interesting to know how these changing neural reactions to emotional information relate to structural and connectivity changes in the aging brain. It is also possible that age differences in neural patterns in response to emotional stimuli may relate to more motivational changes with age, which act to direct attention away from negative information in the environment (St. Jacques et al., 2009; Williams et al., 2006). In other words, it is not only potential structural changes in the aging brain that might influence functional brain response to emotional stimuli: top-down motivational factors might be important, too.

Motivational Factors, Positivity Biases, and Life Experience

Changes with age in the motivation to prioritize particular social and emotional goals might be an important influence on social behavior in old age (Charles & Carstensen, 2010). There is evidence that older adults have a "positivity bias"; that is, they attend to and remember more positive compared to negative information (e.g., Mather & Carstensen, 2003). It has been suggested that positivity biases in old age may relate to the pattern of emotion perception problems found for different emotions—difficulties in identifying primarily the negative emotions of sadness, anger, and fear, with relative preservation in identifying happy expressions (e.g., Somerville et al., 2011; Williams et al., 2006). However, it is unclear why this would result in age-related stability or even *improvement* in identifying disgust (Calder et al., 2003, Ruffman et al., 2008; Suzuki et al., 2007). One possible reason for relatively good identification of disgust may relate to biases in the choice of emotional labels. Insch et al. (under review) reported that older adults were more biased to choose disgust erroneously when identifying other emotions. When that bias to choose disgust was controlled for, an overall age-related *deficit* in identifying disgusted faces was found. This indicates that the apparent preservation in identifying disgust in old age may be an artifact of an overall bias to choose the label "disgust." Returning to the possible role of positivity biases in emotion perception, there is no direct evidence that these operate to influence performance on emotion labeling tasks: Insch et al. found no age differences in the tendency to choose happiness as a label for emotional expressions.

Positivity biases therefore seem unlikely to explain the age differences in labeling emotional expressions. But, as noted, choosing a label to describe the portrayal of an emotion does not reflect the way in which we use social cue information in everyday interactions. More exploration is needed of how motivational factors, and positivity biases in particular, might influence more ecological and implicit emotional and social tasks. For example, there is some evidence that older adults may show positivity biases when making some types of emotional judgment, such as deciding whether a smile reflects a genuine experience of happiness (Slessor et al., 2010a). Also, older adults show some positivity biases when making intensity judgments about facial expressions of emotion (Kellough & Knight, 2011). There are some suggestions that the emotional state of the perceiver could be important in influencing age differences in emotion perception: self-ratings of negative affect have been found to explain age differences in ratings of emotion intensity (Phillips & Allen, 2004) and accuracy of emotion labeling (Suzuki et al., 2007).

Another motivational bias of potential social importance that has been highlighted in a few studies of social perception in old age is differences in attending to the eye region of the face. As described earlier, a number of eye-tracking studies indicate that older people tend to spend proportionally more time looking at mouths and less time looking at eyes compared to younger counterparts (e.g., Murphy & Issacowitz, 2010). Also, older adults do not seem to follow the eye gaze of others as readily as younger people do (Slessor et al., 2008), and do not integrate eye gaze information with emotional cues adaptively (Slessor et al., 2010c). Why do older people seem to be avoiding using information from the eyes? Does this extend to more realistic everyday social interactions? Better understanding of this potential bias is needed.

Older adults have had extensive life experience analyzing emotional cues in interpersonal communication, and therefore it might be predicted that some aspects of social cue decoding would be preserved or improve with age (Dougherty, Abe, & Izard, 1996; Magai, 2001). The bulk of evidence we have presented here does not support that prediction: there are many examples of age-related decline in social perception tasks. An important factor to bear in mind when considering the role of life experience is that the vast majority of tasks used to measure social perception are very artificial and do not represent the way that we decode and utilize cues to socioemotional states in everyday life (Isaacowitz & Stanley, 2011). Where more implicit measures have been used to record older adults' sensitivity to emotional cues, some results indicate that older adults retain, for example, mimicry responses to facial expressions (Bailey et al., 2009; Bailey & Henry, 2009). To really understand how the losses and gains with old age influence social skills in everyday life, tasks that possess greater ecological validity than traditional emotion perception labeling tasks are needed.

Conclusion

In the last decade, research into the psychology of aging has moved away from considering cognitive, neural, emotional, and social change as completely separate domains of functioning, thanks to the influence of a few pioneering researchers such as Fredda Blanchard-Fields. To get a complete picture of age differences in social perception, it is necessary to use experimental techniques derived from cognitive and perceptual psychology, while incorporating key theories from social psychology with knowledge of the emotional systems of the brain. Evidence to date indicates that adult aging is associated with poorer emotion perception and declines in the ability to decode a range of different social cues. For example, older adults are less accurate in labeling emotions such as sadness, anger, and fear from facial and auditory expressions. Older adults who have problems with emotion perception also tend to show impaired social behavior and poorer quality of life. However, there are some examples of preserved functioning in old age, such as mimicry of facial expressions. The pattern of age effects on social perception indicates that they are unlikely to be caused entirely by general cognitive and perceptual change in old age. The possible role of motivational factors and structural and functional brain changes in explaining the aging pattern remain underexplored. We still do not have a good understanding of why aging causes reliable losses in some aspects of social perception but not others, and that remains a key issue for future research.

Future Directions for Research Into Adult Age Differences in Social Perception

Two key issues must be addressed by future research to better understand age differences in social perception. The first is the *nature* of age differences in decoding and reacting to emotional and other social cues in richer and more naturalistic tasks and settings. The second is better integration of motivational, neural, and behavioral data to understand the proximal *causes* of the pattern of age differences in social perception. Here, some key questions are raised that should help to address these two main issues.

Are age declines in social perception influenced by the use of more lifelike stimuli? Most emotion perception studies still use variants of the classic Ekman and Friesen (1976) black-and-white photographs of facial expressions of emotion, and with good justification: these are the best standardized and validated stimuli available. However, they also have obvious limitations: the emotions are posed, static, represent only six emotions, and the photographs are all of people who are either young or approaching middle age (Phillips & Slessor, 2011). Some advances have been made in developing stimuli sets that involve the full age range (e.g., Ebner & Johnson, 2009), and these will be useful for future studies. However, information is still lacking about the effects of aging in identifying emotions that are genuine rather than posed or acted. There may be some difficult ethical issues associated with acquiring stimuli that record people displaying genuine emotions, but this is an important goal for future research. Also, the vast majority of aging studies looking at facial expressions use static photographs. It is important that more studies follow the lead of Murphy and Issacowitz (2010) and use dynamic stimuli. In everyday life, facial cues to emotion are often subtle and fleeting, and this can best be captured through looking at dynamic information.

Are age declines attenuated when more realistic settings or familiar people are involved? To explore the possible role of life experience in age differences in social perception, it is important to acquire data on how aging influences social behavior in more realistic settings. Older adults pay less attention to others' eyes when viewing static facial expressions of emotion (e.g., Wong et al., 2005). It would be useful to look at age differences in visual attention when viewing more complex social scenes, as has previously been done in autism and schizophrenia (Riby & Hancock, 2008a, b; Sasson et al., 2007). Also, patterns of eye gaze could be video recorded during real social interactions, providing more direct information about any age differences in eye contact and joint attention in everyday settings.

One problem with all of the research to date on age differences in social perception is that the participant is always making judgments about a stranger. Given that (a) we behave very differently with strangers and those known to us, (b) we may become much more expert in judging the emotional and social signals of our friends, workmates, and family over time, and (c) older adults invest more in close others compared to younger people (who may be more open to new encounters), it seems important to explore how older adults' social perception is influenced by familiarity. Future studies could use familiar famous people as stimuli for social perception tasks or compare social perception and behavior of older adults when interacting with strangers as opposed to friends.

What do more implicit measures of behavior tell us about age differences in social perception? It would be useful to extend previous research that uses approach/avoidance judgments as a measure of sensitivity to social cues (e.g., Slessor et al., 2010c), rather than relying on explicit verbal labeling as the main measure of emotion perception. As reviewed earlier, the use of behavioral techniques such as EMG, eye-tracking, or video recording participants' social behaviors and emotional expressions should be more widely used to widen our understanding of how social perception changes with age.

What is the role of motivation in age differences in social perception? To date, most studies of aging and emotion perception have not directly investigated the role of motivational issues such as changing social goals favoring close others, or positivity biases in evaluating emotions (for a recent exception, see Kellough & Knight, 2011). It would be useful in future studies that include social perception measures to consider including assessments of social goals and positivity biases. Also, future research should include manipulations that act to alter motivation, such as changing future time perspective or weighting particular social goals, to explore their effect on emotional and social judgments.

Which changes in the brain are important for social perception in old age? It has frequently been proposed that age-related changes in social decoding are likely due to structural decline in emotion-social circuits in the brain, but there is little empirical evidence on this issue. There are relatively well-agreed upon brain networks that are involved in social perception more generally (e.g., medial prefrontal cortex, superior temporal sulcus, temporal pole) and emotion perception specifically (e.g., orbitofrontal cortex, amygdala, insula). It should be possible to test whether age declines in the size of these structures or connectivity between them relate to performance on social perception tasks.

In answering each of these questions, we can achieve a clearer picture of age differences in social perception and the social and neuropsychological factors underpinning both costs and advantages of aging in this domain. This knowledge will be particularly important for those older adults for whom social perception difficulties might influence everyday interactions and quality of life.

References

Adams, R. B., & Kleck, R. E. (2003). Perceived gaze direction and the processing of facial displays of emotion. *Psychological Science, 14*, 644–647.

Adams, R. B., & Kleck, R. E. (2005). Effects of direct and averted gaze on the perception of facially communicated emotion. *Emotion, 5*, 3–11.

Adolphs, R., Tranel, D., Damasio, H., & Damasio, A. (1995). Fear and the human amygdala. *Journal of Neuroscience, 15*, 5879–5891.

Antonucci, T. C. (2001). Social relations: An examination of social networks, social support, and sense of control. In J. E. Birren & K. W. Schaie (Eds.), *Handbook of the psychology of aging*, 5th ed. (pp. 427–453). San Diego, CA: Academic Press.

Bailey, P. E., & Henry, J. D. (2008). Growing less empathic with age: Disinhibition of the self-perspective. *Journal of Gerontology: Psychological Sciences, 63B*, 219–226.

Bailey, P. E., & Henry, J. D. (2009). Subconscious facial expression mimicry is preserved in older adulthood. *Psychology and Aging, 24*, 995–1000.

Bailey, P. E., Henry, J. D., & Nangle, M. R. (2009). Electromyographic evidence for age-related differences in the mimicry of anger. *Psychology and Aging, 24*, 224–229.

Blair, R. J. R., Morris, J. S., Frith, C. D., Perrett, D. I., & Dolan, R. J. (1999). Dissociable neural responses to facial expressions of sadness and anger. *Brain, 122*, 883–893.

Blairy, S., Herrera, P., & Hess, U. (1999). Mimicry and the judgment of emotional facial expressions. *Journal of Nonverbal Behavior, 23*, 5–41.

Blanchard-Fields, F. (2007). Everyday problem-solving and emotion: An adult developmental perspective. *Current Directions in Psychological Science, 16*, 26–31.

Blanchard-Fields, F., Jahnke, H. C., & Camp, C. (1995). Age differences in problem-solving style: The role of emotional salience. *Psychology and Aging, 10*, 173–180.

Blanchard-Fields, F., & Norris, L. (1994). Causal attributions from adolescence through adulthood: Age differences, ego level and generalized response style. *Aging and Cognition, 1*, 67–86.

Blanchard-Fields, F., Stein, R., & Watson, T. L. (2004). Age differences in emotion-regulation strategies in handling everyday problems. *Journals of Gerontology: Psychological Sciences, 59*, 261–269.

Bogart, K. R., & Matsumoto, D. (2010). Facial mimicry is not necessary to recognize emotion: Facial expression recognition by people with Moebius syndrome. *Social Neuroscience, 5*, 241–251.

Bond, G. D., Thompson, L. A., & Malloy. (2005). Vulnerability of older adults to deception in prison and non-prison contexts. *Psychology and Aging, 20*, 1–11.

Britton, J. C., Taylor, S. F., Sudheimer, K. D., & Liberzon, I. (2006). Facial expressions and complex IAPS pictures: Common and differential networks. *Neuroimage, 31*, 906–919.

Bucks, R. S., Garner, M., Tarrant, L., Bradley, B. P., & Mogg, K. (2008). Interpretation of emotionally ambiguous faces in older adults. *Journal of Gerontology: Psychological Sciences, 63B*, 337–343.

Bull, R. B., Phillips, L. H., Allen, R., Burr, K., Hoare, S., & Slama, D. (under review). Belief reasoning and emotion recognition as predictors of interpersonal interactions in healthy aging.

Bull, R. B., Phillips, L. H., & Conway, C. A. (2008). The role of control functions in mentalizing: Dual task studies of Theory of Mind and executive function. *Cognition, 107*, 663–672.

Butler, K. M., & Zacks, R. T. (2006). Age deficits in the control of prepotent responses: Evidence for an inhibitory decline. *Psychology and Aging, 21*, 638–643.

Calder, A. J., Keane, J., Manes, F., Antoun, N., & Young, A. W. (2000). Impaired recognition and experience of disgust following brain injury. *Nature Neuroscience, 3*, 1077–1078.

Calder, A. J., Keane, J., Manly, T., Sprengelmeyer, R., Scott, S., Nimmo-Smith, I., & Young, A. W. (2003). Facial expression recognition across the adult life span. *Neuropsychologia, 41*, 195–202.

Charles, S. T., & Carstensen, L. L. (2007). Emotion regulation and aging. In J. J. Gross (Ed.), *Handbook of emotion regulation* (pp. 307–327). New York: Guilford Press.

Charles, S. T., & Carstensen, L. L. (2010). Social and emotional aging. *Annual Review of Psychology, 61*, 383–409.

Charlton, R. A., Barrick, T. R., Markus, H. S., & Morris, R. G. (2009). Theory of Mind associations with other cognitive functions and brain imaging in normal aging. *Psychology and Aging, 24*, 338–348.

D'Entremont, B., Hains, S. M. J., & Muir, D. W. (1997). A demonstration of gaze following in 3–6 month olds. *Infant Behavior and Development, 20*, 569–572.

Dougherty, L. M., Abe, J. A., & Izard, C. E. (1996). Differential emotions theory and emotional development in adulthood and later life. In C. Magai & S. H. McFadden (Eds.), *Handbook of emotion, adult development, and aging* (pp. 27–41). San Diego, CA: Academic Press.

Ebner, N. C., He, Y. I., & Johnson, M. K. (2011). Age and emotion affect how we look at a face: Visual scan patterns differ for own-age versus other-age emotional faces. *Cognition and Emotion, 25*, 983–997.

Ebner, N. C., & Johnson, M. K. (2009). Young and older emotional faces: Are there age-group differences in expression identification and memory? *Emotion, 9*, 329–339.

Ebner, N. C., & Johnson, M. K. (2010). Age-group differences in interference from young and older emotional faces. *Cognition and Emotion, 24*, 1095–1116.

Ekman, P. (2007). *Emotions revealed: Recognizing faces and feelings to improve communication and emotional life.* New York: Henry Holt & Co.

Ekman, P., & Friesen, W. V. (1976). *Pictures of facial affect.* Palo Alto, CA: Consulting Psychologists Press.

Ekman, P., & O'Sullivan, M. (1991). Who can catch a liar? *American Psychologist, 46*, 913–920.

Fine, C., & Blair, R. J. R. (2000). Mini review: The cognitive and emotional effects of amygdala damage. *Neurocase, 6*, 435–450.

Giles, H., Makoni, S., & Dailey, R. M. (2005). Intergenerational communication beliefs across the lifespan: Comparative data from Ghana and South Africa. *Journal of Cross Cultural Gerontology, 20*, 191–211.

Giles, H., Noels, K. A., Williams, A., Ota, H., Lim, T., Ng, S. H., Ryan, E. B., & Somera, L. (2003). Intergenerational communication across cultures: Young people's perceptions of conversations with family elders, non-family elders and same-age peers. *Journal of Cross Cultural Gerontology, 18*, 1–32.

Gunning-Dixon, F. M., Gur, R. C., Perkins, A. C., Schroeder, L., Turner, T., Turetsky, B. I., et al. (2003). Age-related differences in brain activation during emotional face processing. *Neurobiology of Aging, 24*, 285–295.

Halberstadt, J., Ruffman, T., Murray, J., Taumoepeau, M., & Ryan, M. (2011). Emotion perception explains age-related differences in the perception of social gaffes. *Psychology and Aging, 26*, 133–136.

Henry, J. D., Ruffman, T., McDonald, S., Peek O'Leary, M-A., Phillips, L. H., Brodaty, H., & Rendell, P. G. (2008). Recognition of disgust is selectively preserved in Alzheimer's disease. *Neuropsychologia, 46*, 203–208.

Henry, J. D., von Hippel, W., & Baynes, K. (2009). Social inappropriateness, executive control, and aging. *Psychology and Aging, 24*, 239–244.

Hunter, E. M., Phillips, L. H., & MacPherson, S. E. (2010). Age benefits in emotion processing from integrating multimodal sensory cues. *Psychology and Aging, 25*, 779–787.

Iidaka, T., Omori, M., Murata, T., Kosaka, H., Yonekura, Y., Tomohisa, O., & Sadato, N. (2001). Neural interaction of the amygdala with the prefrontal and temporal cortices in the processing of facial expressions as revealed by fMRI. *Journal of Cognitive Neuroscience, 13*, 1035–1047.

Insch, P., Bull, R., Phillips, L. H., Allen, R., & Slessor, G. (2012). Adult aging, processing style and the perception of biological motion. *Experimental Aging Research, 38*, 169–185.

Insch, P. M., Slessor, G., Phillips, L. H., & Bull, R. (under review). Older adults' emotion labeling errors differ for faces and bodies.

Investor Protection Trust. (2010, June 15). *Elder investment fraud and financial exploitation.* Retrieved from www.investorprotection.org/downloads/pdf/learn/research/EIFFE_Survey_Report.pdf

Isaacowitz, D. M., Loeckenhoff, C., Lane, R., Wright, R., Sechrest, L., Riedel, R., et al. (2007). Age differences in recognition of emotion in lexical stimuli and facial expressions. *Psychology and Aging, 22*, 147–259.

Isaacowitz, D. M., & Stanley, J. T. (2011). Bringing an ecological perspective to the study of aging and recognition of emotional facial expressions: Past, current and future methods. *Journal of Nonverbal Behavior, 35*, 261–278.

Keightley, M. L., Winocur, G., Burianova, H., Hongwanishkul, D., & Grady, C. L. (2006). Age effects on social cognition: Faces tell a different story. *Psychology and Aging, 21*, 558–572.

Kellough, J. L., & Knight, B. G. (2011). Positivity effects in older adults' perception of facial emotion: The role of future time perspective. *The Journals of Gerontology. Series B, Psychological Sciences and Social Sciences, 67*, 150–158.

Kemp, B. J., & Mosqueda, L. A. (2005). Elder financial abuse: An evaluation framework and supporting evidence. *American Geriatrics Society, 53*, 1123–1127.

Krendl, A. C., & Ambady, N. (2010). Older adults' decoding of emotions: Role of dynamic versus static cues and age-related cognitive decline. *Psychology and Aging, 25*, 788–793.

Labouvie-Vief, G., & Medler, M. (2002). Affect optimization and affect complexity: Modes and styles of regulation in adulthood. *Psychology and Aging, 17*, 571–588.

Langton, S. R. H., Watt, R. J., & Bruce, V. (2000). Do the eyes have it? Cues to the direction of social attention. *Trends in Cognitive Sciences, 4*, 50–59.

MacPherson, S., Phillips, L. H., & Della Sala, S. (2002). Age, executive function and social decision-making: A dorsolateral prefrontal theory of cognitive aging. *Psychology and Aging, 17*, 598–609.

MacPherson, S. E., Phillips, L. H., & Della Sala, S. (2006). Age related decline in the ability to perceive sad facial expressions. *Aging: Clinical and Experimental Research, 18*, 418–424.

Magai, C. (2001). Emotions over the life span. In J. E. Birren & K. W. Schaie (Eds.), *Handbook of the psychology of aging* (pp. 165–183). San Diego, CA: Academic Press.

Mather, M., & Carstensen, L. L. (2003). Aging and attentional biases for emotional faces. *Psychological Science, 14*, 409–415.

Mather, M., & Knight, M. (2006). Angry faces get noticed quickly: Threat detection is not impaired among older adults. *Journal of Gerontology: Psychological Sciences, 61*, 54–57.

McDonald, S., Flanagan, S., Rollins, J., & Kinch, J. (2002). TASIT: A new clinical tool for assessing social perception after traumatic brain injury. *Journal of Head Trauma Rehabilitation, 18*, 219–238.

Mill, A., Allik, J., Realo, A., & Valk, R. (2009). Age-related differences in emotion recognition ability: A cross-sectional study. *Emotion, 9*, 619–630.

Mitchell, R. L.C., Kingston, R. A., & Barbosa Boucas, S. L. (2011). The specificity of age-related decline in interpretation of emotion cues from prosody. *Psychology and Aging, 26*, 406–414.

Montepare, J., Koff, E., Zaitchik, D., & Albert, M. (1999). The use of body movements and gestures as cues to emotions in younger and older adults. *Journal of Nonverbal Behavior, 23*, 133–152.

Morales, M., Mundy, P., & Rojas, J. (1998). Following the direction of gaze and language development in 6-month-olds. *Infant Behavior and Development, 21*, 373–377.

Murphy, N. A., & Isaacowitz, D. M. (2010). Age effects and gaze patterns in recognizing emotional expressions: An in-depth look at gaze measures and covariates. *Cognition and Emotion, 24*, 436–452.

Murphy, N. A., Lehrfeld, J. M., & Isaacowitz, D. M. (2010). Recognition of posed and spontaneous dynamic smiles in young and older adults. *Psychology and Aging, 25*, 811–821.

Oberman, L. M., Winkielman, P., & Ramachandran, V. S. (2007). Face to face: Blocking facial mimicry can selectively impair recognition of emotional expressions. *Social Neuroscience, 2*, 167–178.

Orgeta, V., & Phillips, L. H. (2008). Effects of age and emotional intensity on the recognition of facial emotion. *Experimental Aging Research, 34*, 63–79.

Perfect, T. J., & Moon, H. C. (2005). The own-age effect in face recognition. (pp. 317–337). In J. Duncan, L. H. Phillips, & P. McLeod (Eds.), *Measuring the mind: Speed, control and age.* Oxford: Oxford University Press.

Phillips, L. H., & Allen, R. (2004). Adult aging and the perceived intensity of emotions in faces and stories. *Aging: Clinical and Experimental Research, 16*, 190–199.

Phillips, L. H., Channon, S., Tunstall, M., Hedenstrom, A., & Lyons, K. (2008). The role of working memory in decoding emotions. *Emotion, 8*, 184–191.

Phillips, L. H., & Henry, J. D. (2008). Adult aging and executive function. (pp. 57–80). In V. Anderson, P. Anderson, & R.

Jacobs (Eds.), *Executive function and the frontal lobes: A life span perspective*. Hove: Psychology Press.

Phillips, L. H., Scott, C., Henry, J. D., Mowat, D., & Bell, J. S. (2010). Emotion perception in Alzheimer's disease and mood disorder in old age. *Psychology and Aging, 25*, 38–47.

Phillips, L. H., & Slessor, G. (2011). Moving beyond basic emotions in aging research. *Journal of Nonverbal Behavior, 35*, 279–286.

Pilz, K. S., Bennett, P. J., & Sekuler, A. B. (2010). Effects of aging on biological motion discrimination. *Vision Research, 50*, 211–219.

Pushkar, D., Basevitz, P., Arbuckle, T., Nohara-LeClair, M., Lapidus, S., & Peled, M. (2000). Social behavior and off-target verbosity in elderly people. *Psychology and Aging, 15*, 361–374.

Raz, N., Gunning, F. M., Head, D., Dupuis, J. H., McQuain, J., Briggs, S. D., et al. (1997). Selective aging of the human cerebral cortex observed in vivo: Differential vulnerability of the prefrontal gray matter. *Cerebral Cortex, 7*, 268–282.

Riby D. M., & Hancock, P. J. B. (2008a). Do faces capture the attention of individuals with Williams Syndrome or autism? Evidence from tracking eye movements. *Journal of Autism and Developmental Disorders, 39*, 1–11.

Riby D. M., & Hancock, P. J. B. (2008b). Viewing it differently: Social scene perception in Williams syndrome and autism. *Neuropsychologia, 46*, 2855–2860.

Rosen, H. J., Wilson, M. R., Schauer, G. F., Allison, S., Gorno-Tempini, M., Pace-Savitsky, C., et al. (2006). Neuroanatomical correlates of impaired recognition of emotion in dementia. *Neuropsychologia, 44*, 365–373.

Ruffman, T., Henry, J. D., Livingstone, V., & Phillips, L. H. (2008). A meta-analytic review of emotion recognition and aging: Implications for neuropsychological models of aging. *Neuroscience & Biobehavioral Reviews, 32*, 863–881.

Ruffman, T., Murray, J., Halberstadt, J., & Taumoepeau, M. (2010). Verbosity and emotion recognition in older adults. *Psychology and Aging, 25*, 492–297.

Ruffman, T., Murray, J., Halberstadt, J., & Vater, T. (2012). Age-related differences in deception detection. *Psychology & Aging, 27*, 543–549.

Ruffman, T., Ng, M., & Jenkin, T. (2009). Older adults respond quickly to angry faces despite recognition difficulty. *Journal of Gerontology: Psychological Sciences, 64B*, 696–703.

Ruffman, T., Sullivan, S., & Dittrich, W. (2009). Older adults' recognition of bodily and auditory expressions of emotion. *Psychology and Aging, 24*, 614–622.

Ryan, M., Murray, J., & Ruffman T. (2010a). Aging and the perception of emotion: Processing vocal expressions alone and with faces. *Experimental Aging Research, 36*, 1–22.

Sasson, N., Tsuchiya, N., Hurley, R., Couture, S. M., Penn, D. L., Adolphs, R., & Piven, J. (2007). Orienting to social stimuli differentiates social cognitive impairment in autism and schizophrenia. *Neuropsycholgia, 45*, 2580–2588.

Slessor, G., Laird, G., Bull, R., Phillips, L. H., & Filippou, D. (2010b). Age-related differences in gaze following: Does the age of the face matter?. *Journal of Gerontology: Psychological Sciences, 65*, 536–541.

Slessor, G., Miles, L., Bull, R., & Phillips, L. H. (2010). Age-related changes in detecting happiness: Discriminating between enjoyment and non-enjoyment smiles. *Psychology and Aging, 25B*, 246–250.

Slessor, G., Phillips, L. H., & Bull, R. (2007). Exploring the specificity of age-related differences in theory of mind tasks. *Psychology & Aging, 22*, 639–643.

Slessor, G., Phillips, L. H., & Bull, R. (2008). Age-related declines in basic social perception: Evidence from tasks assessing eye-gaze processing. *Psychology and Aging, 23*, 812–822.

Slessor, G., Phillips, L. H., & Bull, R. (2010c). Age-related changes in the integration of gaze direction and facial expressions of emotion. *Emotion, 10*, 555–562.

Slessor, G., Phillips, L. H., Bull, R., Venturini, C., Bonny, E., & Rokaszewicz, A. (2012). Investigating the "deceiver stereotype": Do older adults associate averted gaze with deception?. *Journal of Gerontology: Psychological Sciences, 67*, 178–183.

Slessor, G., Venturini, C., Bonny, E., Insch, P., Rokaszewicz, A., & Finnerty, A. N. (submitted). Older adults do not follow the gaze of others: Evidence from social and non-social stimuli.

Smith, K. (2010, May 17). "Smiling" face of fraud that targets OAPs. *The Scotsman*. Retrieved from http://thescotsman. scotsman.com/scotland/39Smiling39-face-of-fraud-that.6298166.jp.

Somerville, L. H., Fani, N., & McClure-Tone, E. B. (2011). Behavioral and neural representations of emotional facial expressions across the lifespan. *Developmental Neuropsychology, 36*, 408–428.

Stanley, J. T., & Blanchard-Fields, F. (2008). Challenges older adults face in detecting deceit: The role of emotion recognition. *Psychology & Aging, 23*, 24–32.

Stel, M., Van Dijk, E., & Olivier, E. (2009). You want to know the truth? Then don't mimic!. *Psychological Science, 20*, 693–699.

St. Jacques, P., Bessette-Symons, B., & Cabeza, R. (2009). Functional neuroimaging studies of aging and emotion: Fronto-amygdalar differences during emotion perception and episodic memory. *Journal of the International Neuropsychological Society, 15*, 819–825.

Stone, W. L., & Yoder, P. J. (2001). Predicting spoken language in children with autistic spectrum disorders. *Autism, 5*, 341–361.

Sullivan, S., & Ruffman, T. (2004). Emotion recognition deficits in the elderly. *International Journal of Neuroscience, 114*, 403–432.

Sullivan, S., Ruffman, T., & Hutton, S. B. (2007). Age differences in emotion recognition skills and the visual scanning of emotion faces. *Journal of Gerontology: Psychological Sciences, 62B*, 53–60.

Suzuki, A., Hoshino, T., Shigemasu, K., & Kawamura, M. (2007). Decline or improvement? Age-related differences in facial expression recognition. *Biological Psychology, 74*, 75–84.

Verhaeghen, P., & Cerella, J. (2002). Aging, executive control, and attention: A review of meta-analyses. *Neuroscience and Biobehavioral Reviews, 26*, 849–857.

von Hippel, W., & Dunlop, S. M. (2005). Aging, inhibition, and social inappropriateness. *Psychology and Aging, 20*, 519–523.

Wenger, G. C., Davies, R., Shahtahmasebi, S., & Scott, A. (1996). Social isolation and loneliness in old age: Review and model refinement. *Ageing and Society, 16*, 333–338.

Williams, L. M., Brown, K. J., Palmer, D., Liddell, B. J., Kemp, A. H., Olivieri, G., et al. (2006). The mellow years?: Neural basis of improving emotional stability over age. *The Journal of Neuroscience, 26*, 6422–6430.

Wong, B., Cronin-Golomb, A., & Neargarder, S. (2005). Patterns of visual scanning as predictors of emotion identification in normal aging. *Neuropsychology, 19*, 739–749.

Young, A., Perrett, D., Calder, A., Sprengelmeyer, R., & Ekman, P. (2002). *Facial Expressions of Emotion—Stimuli and Tests (FEEST)* (software manual v2.1 ed.). Bury St Edmunds, England: Thames Valley Test Company.

The Effects of Age on Memory for Socioemotional Material: An Affective Neuroscience Perspective

Elizabeth A. Kensinger, Eric R. Allard, *and* Anne C. Krendl

Abstract

Many of the benefits conveyed to memory by socioemotional processing are preserved even as adults age. Like young adults, older adults are more likely to remember emotional information than neutral information and to benefit from self-referential processing of information. There is, however, one age-related change in emotional memory that has garnered widespread discussion in the psychological literature: the "positivity effect," or the tendency for older adults to remember proportionally more positive information than do young adults. This essay discusses how an affective neuroscience perspective is revealing what aspects of socioemotional processing change with aging, shedding light on why aging preserves the memory benefits conveyed by socioemotional processing while at the same time influencing the valence of information that is most likely to be remembered.

Key Words: memory, socioemotional processing, aging, emotional memory, positivity effect, affective neuroscience

As we age, we experience many cognitive declines (reviewed by Park, 2000). Our speed of processing slows (Salthouse, 1996), we have more difficulty ignoring irrelevant information in our environment (Hasher & Zacks, 1988; Zacks & Hasher, 1997), and we have a harder time remembering details of events and the context in which they occurred (Chalfonte & Johnson, 1996; Hashtroudi, Johnson, & Chrosniak, 1989; Mitchell et al., 2000; Naveh-Benjamin, 2000; Schacter, Osowiecki, Kaszniak, Kihlstrom, & Valdiserri, 1994). Yet some of the cognitive deficits that older adults experience are mitigated when the information being processed has affective meaning. Like young adults, older adults are faster to detect emotional information in their environment (Hahn, Carlson, Singer, & Gronlund, 2006; Leclerc & Kensinger, 2008a; Mather & Knight, 2006), and older adults are more likely to remember affectively or self-relevant

information than other types of details (reviewed by Mather, 2006; Kensinger, 2008).

In this essay, we first present evidence for an age-related preservation in the enhancement of memory by emotion, reviewing studies that have revealed a behavioral enhancement of memory by emotion and describing the neural processes that may allow the enhancement to occur across the adult lifespan. We then describe an important age-related change that can occur in the retention of emotional information: older adults sometimes can remember proportionally more positive information than can young adults, referred to as the "positivity effect" in memory (Mather & Carstensen, 2005). We outline some of the proposals that have been put forth to explain this effect, describing how age-related changes in emotion-processing strategies or in neuroanatomical connections could contribute to it. The final section of this essay focuses on the preserved self-referential processing benefits that are conveyed to memory across the adult lifespan. Throughout this essay, we present an affective neuroscience perspective on age-related changes in memory, describing evidence revealed through behavioral and neural assessments. The goal is to combine evidence from analyses of brain structure, brain function, and behavioral outcomes to provide a more stable base from which to examine the information-processing changes that lead to effects of age on socioemotional memory (see Kosslyn & Intriligator, 1992; Cosmides & Tooby, 2000, for discussion of the role of cognitive neuroscience).

Emotional Memory Enhancement Is Preserved in Aging

Experiences that evoke an emotional reaction are often remembered better than are those that do not. This effect has been referred to as the *emotional enhancement of memory* (e.g., Talmi, Anderson, Riggs, Caplan, & Moscovitch, 2008), and it has been shown to occur for a variety of stimuli, including words, pictures, and film shows (reviewed by Cahill and McGaugh 1998; Dolan 2002; LaBar and Cabeza 2006). The enhancement of memory by emotion appears to occur regardless of an individual's age. Young, middle-aged, and older adults can benefit from the emotional relevance of information to boost the amount of information retained (Charles, Mather, & Carstensen, 2003; Denburg, Buchanan, Tranel, & Adolphs, 2003; Kensinger, Brierley, Medford, Growdon, & Corkin, 2002) and to reduce the likelihood of memory distortion[1] (Kensinger & Corkin, 2004a; Kensinger et al., 2007a; Kensinger et al., 2007c). This memory enhancement occurs not only in laboratory settings, but also for autobiographical experiences. Older adults, like young adults, are more likely to remember emotional events—such as the deaths of Princess Diana and Mother Teresa (Davidson & Glisky, 2002), the explosion of the Columbia shuttle (Kensinger, Krendl, & Corkin, 2006), or the September 11, 2001 terrorist attacks (Kvavilashvili, Mirani, Schlangman, Erskine, & Kornbrot, 2010)—than they are to remember more mundane events that took place around the same time.

Importantly, the presence of emotion not only benefits older adults' memories, it can sometimes erase the detrimental effects of age on memory. Older adults typically have difficulty remembering past events vividly (Craik & Byrd, 1982; Howard, Kahana, & Wingfield, 2006; Prull, Dawes, Martin, Rosenberg, & Light, 2006), and

they struggle to remember the context in which events took place (Bayer et al., 2011; McIntyre & Craik, 1987; Naveh-Benjamin, 2000). Yet if those events or contexts have emotional relevance, older adults often perform as well as young adults. For instance, although older adults often have difficulty remembering details such as who told them a piece of information or whether food should be served hot or cold, they perform as well as young adults if asked to remember whether a "good" or "bad" person revealed information (Rahhal, May, & Hasher, 2002) or whether food is "safe" or "unsafe" to eat (May, Rahhal, Berry, & Leighton, 2005). Older adults also find it easier to remember the affective meaning of a passage than the nonaffective details (Adams, Labouvie-Vief, Hobart, & Dorosz, 1990; Carstensen & Turk-Charles, 1994; Yoder & Elias, 1987), and they remember internal details—what they thought or felt about an experience—better than external event features (Comblain, D'Argembeau, Van der Linden, & Aldenhoff, 2004; Hashtroudi et al., 1990; Schaefer & Philippot, 2005).

Age-related preservation of memory has been noted within the "flashbulb memory" literature. Older adults often are as likely as young adults to meet the criteria for a "flashbulb memory" (Brown & Kulik, 1977), retaining an extremely vivid representation of the personal details surrounding the experience (Tekcan & Peynircioglu, 2002), and, in many instances, they are as likely to remember the details as are young adults. For instance, older adults remember the details surrounding the deaths of Princess Diana and Mother Teresa as well as young adults (Davidson & Glisky, 2002), and there are no age differences in the phenomenology or consistency of memory for highly emotional events such as the September 11, 2001 terrorist attacks (Kvavilashvili et al., 2010; Davidson, Cook, & Glisky, 2006). By contrast, older adults show significant deficits recalling details of neutral events—public or private in nature—that occurred around the same time as the emotional experiences (Davidson & Glisky, 2002; Kensinger et al., 2006; see Table 3.1 for a summary of the studies comparing young and older adults' memories for emotional public events).

Why Do Older Adults Show Enhanced Memory for Emotional Material Despite Other Cognitive Declines?

Older adults' preservation of memory for emotional experiences often has been interpreted within the framework of the *socioemotional selectivity theory*

Table 3.1. Studies comparing young and older adults' memories for emotional public events

Authors	Age Groups Assessed	Emotional Event Assessed	Control Event Assessed	Key Finding with Regard to Aging
Berntsen & Rubin, 2006	Study 2: adults born after 1945 (mean age 40.1)	Study 2: self-nominated stressful events	None	For participants who were older than 7 at the time, no relation was found between their age and the vividness of the stressful memories.
Cohen et al., 1994	Young adults (mean age 22.4) Older adults (mean age 71.6)	Margaret Thatcher's resignation on November 22, 1990	None	More young adults (90%) met the criteria for flashbulb memories than older adults (42%).
Conway et al., 2009	Adults ranging in age from 18 to 60+.	Terrorist Attacks of September 11, 2001	None	Age did not affect the likelihood of showing evidence for a consistent flashbulb memory across either a 1- or 2-year time period.
Davidson & Glisky, 2002	Young adults (mean age 19.87) Older adults (mean age between 72 and 74 depending on condition)	Deaths of Mother Teresa and Princess Diana (both around Labor Day weekend, 1997)	Most interesting event experienced during Labor Day weekend in 1997.	Young and older adults showed similar memory performance initially and over a 6-month period. Older adults' memory performance did not correspond with their performance on tasks assessing frontal-lobe or medial temporal-lobe function.
Davidson, Cook, and Glisky, 2006	Young adults (mean age 22) Older adults (mean age 74)	Terrorist Attacks of September 11, 2001	Most interesting event from the few days before September 11, 2001.	Older adults performed as well as young adults when remembering the terrorist attacks, but were less likely to retain details of the control event.
Holland and Kensinger, in prep	Young adults (mean age 26.1) Middle-aged adults (mean age 44.8) Older adults (mean age 75.0)	2008 Presidential Election	Self-selected event	Regardless of age, participants who felt negative about the outcome of the election remembered the election details more consistently than did those who felt positive about the outcome.
Kensinger, Krendl, and Corkin, 2006	Young adults (mean age 24.8) Older adults (mean age 72.6)	Space Shuttle *Columbia* disaster, 2003	2003 Super Bowl	After a 7-month delay, both age groups remembered more about the shuttle disaster than they did about the Super Bowl. The age discrepancy in memory was less pronounced for details of the shuttle explosion than of the Super Bowl event.
Kvavilashvili et al., 2010	Young adults (mean age 33.4) Older adults (mean age 71.3)	Terrorist Attacks of September 11, 2001	Staged event: receiving news that the participant was not a winner in a raffle conducted by the experimenter.	No significant age effects for either phenomenological characteristics or test-retest consistency for the emotional memory; age effects on both dimensions for the nonemotional memory.

Table 3.1. (Continued)

Authors	Age Groups Assessed	Emotional Event Assessed	Control Event Assessed	Key Finding with Regard to Aging
Otani et al., 2005	Adults living nearby the accident site stratified into: Young adults (mean age 21.3) Middle-aged adults (mean age 40) Older adults (mean age 57.8)	Japanese nuclear accident, 1999	None	Only a small percentage of participants formed flashbulb memories. No age-related decline in flashbulb memories was found.
Tekcan & Peynircioglu, 2002	Young adults (mean age 20.29) Older adults (mean age 71.53)	Death of Turkey's 8th president (1993) and death of Turkey's 1st president (1939). Tested in 1996.	Inclusion of Hatay into Turkey, 1939 (only for older adult participants)	For the 1993 death, 72% of older adults and 90% of young adults had flashbulb memories. For the 1938 death, 70% of the older adults had flashbulb memories.
Wolters & Goudsmit, 2005	Young adults (mean age 24.8) Older adults (mean age 70.5)	Terrorist Attacks of September 11, 2001	None	Similar memory performance in young and older adults.
Wright et al., 1998	Large sample of participants aged 16 to 75+	Memory for Margaret Thatcher's resignation and for the Hillsborough disaster	None	Older adults did not report less clear memories than young adults. In fact, for some events young adults reported *lower* clarity than older adults.
Yarmey & Bull, 1978	Americans and Canadians, stratified age samples ranging from 18-65+ yrs	Assassination of J. F. K., 12 years prior to study	None	23- to 27-year-olds were more likely than younger (aged 18-22) or older (28+) adults to remember what they were doing when they learned of the assassination, but these adults had poor memory for their actions prior to or preceding receipt of the news.

(Carstensen, Fung, & Charles, 2003; Carstensen, Isaacowitz, & Charles, 1999). This theory states that social and emotional goals take on increasing importance when individuals view time as limited, as happens with advancing age. According to this theory, older adults remember socioemotional information well because that information is given privileged attention and because that information is elaborated (discussed by Mather & Carstensen, 2005).

Although some behavioral studies have provided evidence consistent with this framework (Hashtroudi, Johnson, Vnek, & Ferguson, 1994; Mather & Knight, 2005), it is difficult, within a behavioral paradigm, to isolate the memory effects due to the initial allocation of attention or elaborative resources from other effects related to the subsequent rehearsal or retrieval of an experience because the ability to retrieve a memory (i.e., the behavioral manifestation of the memory) will always reflect a combination of those factors. Neuroimaging methods provide a means to examine the processes that initially give rise to a memory by measuring the neural engagement during an experience. This activity can then be related to subsequent memory: the regions that show greater engagement for experiences that are later remembered than for experiences that are later forgotten are those that are presumed to underlie successful *encoding*. By encoding, we refer to the set of processes that enable an experience to be converted into a format that can allow its storage into memory. An often-used metaphor is that of the computer keyboard, which enables us to transform our thoughts into a format that can be recorded and saved.

A plethora of studies conducted in young adults have revealed that, at least for moderate-to-high arousal stimuli, the memory enhancement for emotional material is caused by interactions between the amygdala and the hippocampus during the initial experience of an event (Hamann, 2001; LaBar & Cabeza, 2006; see Figure 3.1 for approximate locations of amygdala and hippocampus). This reciprocal relation—between a region important for the processing of salient information (the amygdala) and a region important for the successful encoding and storage of information in memory (the hippocampus)—increases the likelihood that the event is encoded and stored in memory (e.g., Kensinger & Corkin, 2004b; Richardson, Strange, & Dolan, 2004).

Older adults typically show weaker activity in the hippocampus than do young adults, both during the initial encoding of an experience (e.g., Dennis et al. 2008; Gutchess et al., 2005) and also during its later retrieval (e.g., Tsukiura et al., 2011). The hippocampus also is subject to structural atrophy with aging (Malykhin, Bouchard, Camicioli, & Coupland, 2008; Rajah, Kromas, Han, & Pruessner, 2010; Raz et al., 2005), particularly among those older adults with hypertension (Raz et al., 2005; Shing et al., 2011). These age-related changes in the hippocampus are believed to account for the reductions in the vividness and detail with which older adults remember past experiences (e.g., Dennis et al., 2008) and

with their increased susceptibility to memory distortions (e.g., Giovanello, Kensinger, Wong, & Schacter, 2010). The hippocampus is known to bind together the different details of an event into a coherent episode (see Jones & McHugh [2011] and Ranganath [2010] for recent reviews) and to use pattern-separation processes to ensure that representations of distinct events are represented in distinguishable fashions (see Yassa & Stark [2011] for recent review). Older adults' memory deficits therefore are exactly what would be expected to emerge with faulty hippocampal function: details are not recorded well, and pattern-separation processes do not effectively distinguish memory representations, thereby increasing the likelihood of memory distortions and retrieval failures.

In contrast to age-related declines in hippocampal structure and function, the amygdala tends to be relatively preserved with aging. Although some studies report significant age-related volumetric decline in the amygdala (e.g., Malykhin et al., 2008), the volumetric decline often is on par with the decline in whole-brain volume (e.g., Coffey et al., 1992; Good et al., 2001; Raz et al., 1997; Tisserand, Visser, van Boxtel, & Jolles, 2000), and the amygdala shows only modest structural connectivity reductions with advancing age (Chow & Cummings, 2000; Salat, Kaye, & Janowsky, 2001). It is important to note that, presently, relatively little is known about the relation between amygdala structure in older age and emotional memory. Although many studies have noted a link between amygdala *function* and emotional memory, links

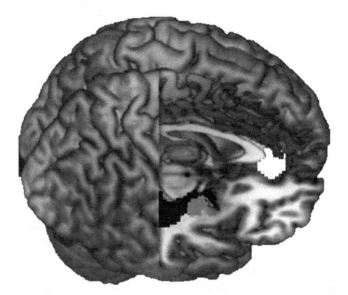

Figure 3.1. Approximate locations of the medial prefrontal cortex (mPFC, white), amygdala (gray) and hippocampus (black).

to amygdala *structure* have been less thoroughly examined. It is known that when the amygdala is significantly atrophied, the benefit in memory for emotional material no longer exists (e.g., Hamann, Cahill, & Squire, 1997), but it is not clear whether individual variability in amygdala structure has a significant effect on emotional memory performance among older adults. One study (Gerritsen et al., 2011) has provided intriguing evidence for such a relation in young adults, but the results have not yet been extended to an older adult population.

The function of the amygdala also seems to be relatively preserved with aging. Older adults engage the amygdala during the encoding of emotional experiences, and the activity in this region corresponds with the likelihood that they will later remember the emotional events (Fischer, Nyberg, & Bäckman, 2010; Kensinger & Schacter, 2008). This relative preservation of amygdala function may explain why many aspects of emotion processing seem to be preserved with aging: older adults remain able to detect emotionally arousing stimuli (e.g., Leclerc & Kensinger, 2008a), and they often show normal skin conductance responses to emotional information (e.g., Fontani, Lodi, Felici, Corradeschi, & Lupo, 2004). The intact amygdala may also explain why older adults are able to form vivid memories for affective details of experiences and for arousing events, despite their declines in hippocampal function: when the amygdala modulates hippocampal function, it may enable the hippocampus to reach a threshold of activation needed for successful encoding of event details and for effective pattern separation. This could explain why older adults do best when remembering information that initially co-activates the amygdala and the hippocampus and why some of the age-related deficits in memory for detail (e.g., Kensinger et al., 2006) or in the propensity for false memories (e.g., Kensinger & Corkin, 2004a) can be eliminated when information has affective significance.

Although the amygdala's modulation of hippocampal function may explain some of the age-related preservation in emotional memory, as noted earlier in this section, older adults also seem to elaborate on the affective meaning of information more than do young adults. It is well known that information is remembered best when it is processed in a way that encourages deep, meaning-based encoding (see Lockhart, 2002, and Craik, 2002, for relatively recent reviews on the levels of processing framework). Thus, it makes sense that if older adults elaborate on affective information, they would remember it particularly well. Evidence to support this hypothesis has come from studies that manipulate the way in which young and older adults are asked to focus on experiences. If older adults are encouraged to focus on the facts, they no longer show a bias to remember affective contexts (Hashtroudi et al., 1994), and asking young adults to attend to the affective relevance of information will often lead them to remember the affective qualities better (Hashtroudi et al., 1994).

The elaboration of material is typically a process associated with controlled processes implemented within the prefrontal cortex (PFC; Garoff-Eaton, Kensinger, & Schacter, 2007; Kirchhoff, Shapiro, & Buckner, 2005). Thus, it would be expected that if older adults elaborated more on emotional information than did young adults, they should show a greater engagement of prefrontal processes during the processing of the emotional information. Indeed, older adults sometimes show a shift toward engagement of prefrontal regions during the encoding of emotional information (e.g., Fischer et al., 2010; Kensinger & Schacter, 2008; reviewed by St. Jacques, Bessette-Symons, & Cabeza, 2009). As compared to young adults, older adults often overengage both lateral (Gunning-Dixon et al., 2003; Tessitore et al., 2005) and medial (Leclerc & Kensinger, 2008b; 2011; Tessitore et al., 2005; Williams et al., 2006) portions of the PFC when processing emotional material. This prefrontal engagement has been linked to more effective subsequent memory for emotional information (Kensinger & Schacter, 2008).

Why Might Older Adults Show a Shift Toward Prefrontal Processing, and What Are the Implications of This Shift?

It is unclear what this shift toward prefrontal processing reflects (also discussed by Kensinger & Leclerc, 2009, and Nashiro, Sakaki, & Mather, 2011). Interactions between the PFC and the amygdala have often been discussed in the context of emotion regulation (e.g., Ochsner & Gross, 2005; Quirk & Beer, 2006), and so some have speculated that older adults' shift toward prefrontal engagement reflects their tendency to regulate their reactions to emotional information (e.g., Mather & Knight, 2005; Williams et al., 2006). However, prefrontal regions are not only engaged in regulatory efforts; these regions are more generally involved in the contextual or personal interpretation of emotion-evoking information and in the elaboration of self-relevant material (Amodio & Frith, 2006;

D'Argembeau, Jedidi, Balteau, Bahri, Phillips, & Salmon, 2011; Qin & Northoff, 2011; Salzman & Fusi, 2010). Moreover, if older adults were engaging prefrontal processes to minimize negative affect, then it would be expected that such engagement would occur most often for negative information; yet, as we will discuss, at least in some instances, older adults show a greater shift toward prefrontal processing when information is of positive valence (reviewed by Kensinger & Leclerc, 2009). Thus, the shift toward prefrontal processing of emotional information could reflect older adults' increased tendency to think about affective information in a personal context or to elaborate on the meaning and relevance of emotional information, a point we will return to later in this essay.

One reason why it seems prudent to consider other explanations for older adults' prefrontal shift, aside from a regulatory one, is that older adults show a shift toward prefrontal processing in many other domains. Older adults' shift toward a more frontally driven processing of emotional information may be part of a general phenomenon, referred to as the *posterior-to-anterior shift with aging* (PASA; Davis, Dennis, Daselaar, Fleck, & Cabeza, 2008). This shift has been revealed across a number of cognitive domains, including attention and perception (Cabeza et al. 2004; Grady et al., 1994; Madden et al. 2002), working memory (Grossman et al. 2002; Rypma and D'Esposito 2000), and episodic memory for nonemotional material (Anderson et al. 2000; Dennis et al. 2007; Grady, Bernstein, Beig, & Siegenthaler, 2002; Madden et al. 1999). One plausible explanation of this posterior-to-anterior shift is that older adults approach many tasks—ranging from memorizing words to evaluating affective stimuli—in a more top-down and controlled fashion than do young adults, perhaps in an effort to compensate for declines in the bottom-up, sensory-driven processing of information (see also Grady, McIntosh, & Craik, 2003). Thus, older adults' tendency to process emotional material using prefrontal processes may not reflect a shift toward regulatory processes that is specific to the domain of emotion processing but rather a shift to top-down and controlled processing that occurs across a number of cognitive domains (see also Mather, 2006, for discussion of the role of cognitive control in older adults' emotional memory performance).

Regardless of the reason for older adults' shift toward prefrontal engagement, because prefrontal processes are essential to the encoding of episodic information (Wagner et al., 1998), it would be predicted that older adults' disproportionate engagement of these processes could serve as a mechanism to enhance their encoding of affective information. It is well known that information that is elaborated on is remembered well (Craik & Lockhart, 1972), regardless of whether that elaboration is serving to reappraise a situation (Dillon, Ritchie, Johnson, & LaBar, 2007; Steinberger, Payne, & Kensinger, 2011), to connect information to personal traits or goals (Grilli & Glisky, 2011; Gutchess, Kensinger, Yoon, & Schacter, 2007; Kesebir & Oishi, 2010), or to extract a deeper meaning from the information (Becker et al., 2010; Staeresina, Gray, & Davachi, 2009 Taevs, Dahmani, Zatorre, & Bohbot, 2010). Thus, older adults' successful encoding of emotional information is likely to be explained both by the interactions between the amygdala and the hippocampus, which may be able to mask some of the age-related deficits in hippocampal function, and by the engagement of elaborative processes implemented by the PFC, which may increase the likelihood that information is encoded in a deep and durable fashion.

An important caveat to these findings is that the shift toward prefrontal processing may not occur equally for all stimulus types and for all individuals. There are debates as to whether age-related enhancements in prefrontal engagement occur equally for positive and negative stimuli, with some research suggesting that older adults' prefrontal engagement habituates more quickly for negative stimuli than for positive (Roalf, Pruis, Stevens, & Janowsky, 2011). Research from our laboratory has shown age-related valence reversals in the types of stimuli that lead to the strongest activity within the medial PFC (mPFC). Across a range of paradigms, older adults have shown greater activity for positive than negative stimuli, whereas young adults have shown the reverse effect (see Figure 3.2). We also have shown that older adults' connectivity between the amygdala and the PFC can be particularly strong for information of a positive valence (Addis, Leclerc, Muscatell, & Kensinger, 2010; Waldinger, Kensington, & Schultz, 2011). However, age-related shifts toward prefrontal-based processing can occur for negative information as well (Gunning-Dixon et al., 2003; Tessitore et al., 2005), and, for some individuals and stimulus types, the shift is not disproportionate for positive information. For instance, when participants are asked to process facial expressions, prefrontal engagement is greater for negative expressions than for positive ones (Williams et al., 2006). When participants are asked to process high-arousal

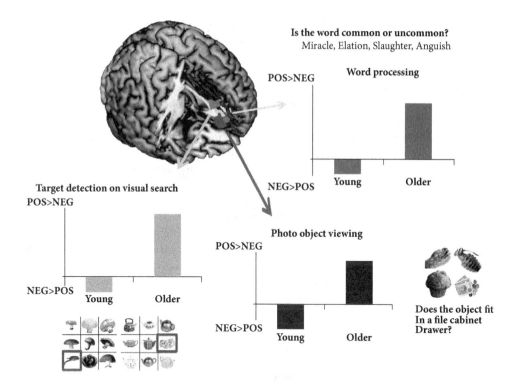

Figure 3.2. Although the medial prefrontal cortex often shows valence-dependent activity in young and older adults, the direction of its engagement is affected by age. In older adults, medial prefrontal and anterior cingulate regions are disproportionate for positive compared to negative stimuli, whereas in young adults, the engagement is stronger for negative compared to positive stimuli. This figure presents data from three different studies: Leclerc and Kensinger (2010) examined the effect of age on visual search performance; Leclerc and Kensinger (2008) revealed the effect of age on the processing of photo objects; and Leclerc and Kensinger (2011) uncovered a similar interaction between age and valence when participants processed verbal stimuli.

colored photographs (from the IAPS set; Lang, Bradley, & Cuthbert, 2005), only the subset of participants who rate themselves higher in life satisfaction (as assessed via the Satisfaction with Life Scale; Diener, Emmons, Larsen, & Griffin, 1985) show stronger connectivity between the amygdala and the PFC when the photographs are positive rather than negative (Waldinger et al., 2011). We will expand our consideration of the effects of valence on the memories of young and older adults in the next section.

Age-Related Changes in Emotional Memory: Evidence for a "Positivity Effect"

Research on the preservation of emotional memory enhancement in old age has revealed specific patterns of age-related change as a function of valence. Widespread attention has been given to findings of an age-related "positivity effect" in memory, whereby older adults remember a higher proportion of positive information or a decreased proportion of negative information as compared to younger adults; thus, the pattern of emotional memory performance is explained by an interaction

between age and emotional valence (see Carstensen & Mikels, 2005; Mikels, Larkin, Reuter-Lorenz, & Carstensen, 2005). Positivity effects in emotional memory have been observed in a variety of tasks and using diverse stimulus sets. For instance, studies have observed a positivity effect in long-term episodic memory tasks using facial expressions (Mather & Carstensen, 2003) and real-world pictures (Charles et al., 2003; Fernandes, Ross, Wiegand, & Schryer, 2008; Langeslag & van Strien, 2009), and older adults' working memory performance has been shown to benefit from processing positive relative to negative information (Mikels et al., 2005). Additionally, age-related positivity effects have been observed in assessments of autobiographical memory (Kennedy, Mather, & Carstensen, 2004; Schlagman, Schulz, & Kvavilashvili, 2006; but see Fernandes et al., 2008).

Theories Proposed to Explain the "Positivity Effect"

Several theories have been offered to account for these effects. One popular proposal in the literature asserts that age-related positivity effects may be motivationally based. As mentioned earlier, socio-emotional selectivity theory (SST; Carstensen et al., 1999) argues that with an awareness of limits on time left in life, older adults are motivated to pursue goals that are more present-oriented, such as feeling good in the here and now. Thus, older adults may focus more attention and resources toward processing and remembering positive rather than negative events as a means of producing or maintaining a positive affective state. With research suggesting that older adults may benefit from superior emotion regulation abilities as compared to their younger counterparts (Blanchard-Fields, 2007), positivity effects in emotional information processing may be one method by which emotion regulation is enhanced in old age.

Although emotion regulation explanations for the age-related positivity effect have attracted much research attention, alternative explanations have been proposed. For instance, Cacioppo and colleagues' *aging brain model* (ABM; Cacioppo, Berntson, Bechara, Tranel, & Hawkley, 2011) suggests that the positive affective shift in old age may have a biological basis. They argue that structural degradation to the amygdala leads to a decreased sensitivity to negative emotional inputs, while activation in response to positive information is spared. Furthermore, the decreased activation of the amygdala in response to negative information decreases felt emotional arousal to such information, which in turn influences a decrease in memory for arousing (namely, negative) stimuli.

Additional models have used declines in other domains to explain age-related changes in emotional memory. Labouvie-Vief and colleagues (2007) argue that age-related decline in cognitive functioning may best explain older adults preference for positive and/or avoidance of negative emotional information. They propose a framework that consists of dual modes of processing emotional information: affect optimization and affect complexity. Affect optimization refers to the tendency to process information in a way that helps to increase positive and decrease negative affect. Affect complexity refers to the ability to coordinate the experience of dual positive and negative states, enabling a focus on objectivity, personal growth, and emotional and conceptual complexity. The interaction of these two processing modes provides the basis for Labouvie-Vief's (2003) *dynamic integration theory* (DIT). This theory suggests that affect optimization and affect complexity are coordinated, so that decreases in affective complexity can result in compensatory increases in

affect optimization or in the momentary positive affect achieved, whereas increases in affective complexity can lead to a decreased tendency to optimize affect in the moment.

Rates of affect complexity tend to decline linearly after about age 60 (Labouvie-Vief & Medler, 2002); furthermore, measures of affect complexity tend to be highly correlated with measures of cognitive functioning and executive control, suggesting that the maintenance of affective complexity requires these cognitive processes. In contrast to the pattern of change in affect complexity, rates of affect optimization tend to increase linearly with advanced age. Therefore, given age-related declines in cognitive resources, older adults may be compensating for declines in affective complexity by using affect optimization strategies[2] (Labouvie-Vief, 2005).

How Well Do the Theories Fit the Data?

The biological and cognitive explanations outlined by the ABM and DIT, although initially providing plausible alternatives for changes in age-related emotional processing, have become less tenable recently. As mentioned earlier, there is evidence for increased structural degradation of the amygdala in some studies (e.g., Malykhin et al., 2008); however, other studies do not find such decline in structure and function of the amygdala (see Grieve, Clark, Williams, Peduto, & Gordon, 2005). Furthermore, whereas some studies find age-related increases in amygdala activation in response to positive relative to negative stimuli (Mather et al., 2004), others have observed that negative valence, when combined with stimulus novelty, can produce comparable activation patterns in the amygdala within both young and older adult samples (Wright, Wedig, Williams, Rauch, & Albert, 2006). More generally, explanations focused on the effects of global age-related neurobiological or cognitive decline cannot easily be reconciled with evidence suggesting that age-related positivity effects in memory can be manipulated experimentally. For instance, when older adults are provided encoding instructions to focus on information-gathering goals on episodic tasks (Löckenhoff & Carstensen, 2007) or to focus on accuracy when recalling autobiographical events (Kennedy et al., 2004), positivity effects are eliminated.

Motivational explanations for age-related positivity are bolstered by evidence suggesting the necessary role of cognitive control processing for positivity effects to emerge. Mather and Knight (2005) observed that age-related positivity effects in emotional memory were contingent on sufficient cognitive control resources being available. This finding is in contrast to the prediction of DIT, that better cognitive control and executive functioning lead to the experience of negative rather than positive affect (Labouvie-Vief & Medler, 2002), a prediction guided by research suggesting that processing negative affect may be more cognitively demanding than processing positive affect (Pratto & John, 1991, as reported in Labouvie-Vief et al., 2007). In contrast to this prediction, Mather and Knight found that only older adults who scored high on a composite measure of cognitive control ability demonstrated a memory benefit for positive relative to negative pictures as compared to younger adults (Study 2). Furthermore, when younger and older adults encoded emotional images in either conditions of full or divided attention, age-related positivity was revealed in the full attention condition but was reversed in the divided attention condition (Study 3). These results are consistent with the proposal that older adults are motivated to optimize positive affect, but that sufficient cognitive control resources may be necessary to achieve that optimization (Carstensen, Mikels, & Mather, 2006), perhaps because older adults are using cognitively demanding processes to regulate their emotions (Ochsner & Gross, 2005). Thus, when cognitive control resources are available, older adults' positive emotional processing preferences can proceed unencumbered. However, if cognitive control resources are constrained, such as when attention is divided, age-related positivity is eliminated and a more stimulus-driven (rather than a top-down) focus on the negative may result (Kryla-Lighthall & Mather, 2009).

Evidence to support a regulation account has come not only from the behavioral data but also from the neural data we outlined in the earlier section, revealing a shift toward prefrontal processing of emotional information in older age. However, although prefrontal engagement is consistent with the exertion of regulatory processes, it also would be consistent with the engagement of any other form of top-down processing of emotional information. Thus, although shifts in prefrontal processing of emotional information may be indicative of older adults' attempts at emotion regulation (Williams et al., 2006), another likely explanation might be an age-related shift toward more general processing of stimuli in a self-relevant fashion (see Kensinger & Leclerc, 2009). The following section extends our discussion beyond the preservation of emotional information in memory to an examination of the benefit of self-relevant processing in memory across adulthood and old age.

The Processing of Self-Relevant Information in Young and Older Adults

Thus far, we have discussed older adults' memory enhancement for emotional information. However, emerging research suggests that there is another domain in which older adults may also demonstrate a memory enhancement effect: remembering self-relevant information. It has been widely observed that young adults remember information better when it is encoded relevant to self than when it is encoded in other manners (Bower & Gilligan, 1979; Klein & Kihlstrom, 1986; Klein & Loftus, 1988; Maki & McCaul, 1985; Markus, 1977; Rogers, Kuiper, & Kirker, 1977). For instance, in one of the first studies on the self-referential memory effect, Rogers and colleagues (1977) found that asking people to make personal judgments on trait adjectives (e.g., "Are you mean?") produced significantly improved memory for the words than if the participants were asked to make semantic judgments (e.g., "Define the word mean").

Despite the relative consistency with which the self-referential memory enhancement effect has been observed, it has been widely debated why it occurs. Specifically, is self-relevant information supported by discrete cognitive systems (e.g., Rogers et al., 1977), or do individuals encode self-relevant information more elaborately because they have greater knowledge about the self (Greenwald & Banaji, 1989; Klein & Kihlstrom, 1986), thereby leading to superior memory performance? On a behavioral level, either explanation would lead to the same outcome (improved memory for self-relevant information). Thus, researchers have tried to answer this question through patient and neuroimaging research to isolate the mechanisms involved.

Understanding the mechanisms that give rise to the self-referential memory enhancement effect is particularly important when considering whether this enhancement effect would also benefit older adults' memories. Simply put, if self-referential processing relies on cognitive systems (which are not impaired by healthy aging) distinct from those engaged in general memory encoding and retrieval (which have been shown to be impaired in healthy aging; Chalfonte & Johnson, 1996; Hashtroudi et al., 1989; Mitchell et al., 2000; Naveh-Benjamin, 2000; Schacter et al., 1994), then memory for self-relevant information may be relatively preserved over the lifespan. In this section, we first review the extant behavioral and neuroimaging research examining the self-referential memory enhancement effect with young adults and patients and then explore parallels and disparities that have been noted in emerging behavioral and neuroimaging research on older adults' memory enhancement for self-relevant information.

Do Individuals With Severe Memory Impairments Have Improved Memory for Self-Relevant Information?

One way to investigate the mechanisms underlying the self-referential memory enhancement effect is by studying individuals with profound memory impairment. If individuals have superior memory for self-relevant information because it is encoded more deeply, then one would expect individuals with profound memory impairments not to show a preserved memory for self-relevant information. However, if the memory enhancement emerges because self-relevant information is processed by cognitive systems that are distinct from those engaged in general memory processing, then individuals with profound memory loss may still show relatively preserved self-relevant knowledge (provided they did not suffer damage to the neural regions that support self-relevant knowledge).

To investigate this question, researchers observed patients who suffered from severe amnesia (resulting from brain injury or Alzheimer's disease). Of particular interest was whether these individuals retained the ability to accurately determine whether specific traits accurately described themselves (Tulving, 1993; Klein, Loftus, & Kihlstrom, 1996; Klein, Chan, & Loftus, 1999; Klein, Rozendal, & Cosmides, 2002). For instance, Tulving (1993) reported that a patient who had suffered complete loss of episodic memory following a motorcycle accident (K. C.) could still accurately identify his personality traits. K. C. was asked to rate how self-descriptive a series of adjectives were on two separate occasions. His mother was also asked to rate how well the same adjectives described K. C. Tulving found remarkable agreement between K. C.'s two sessions, as well as the ratings provided by his mother, suggesting that despite his severe amnesia, K. C. retained a relatively preserved sense of his self-relevant traits. Similarly, Klein and colleagues (1996) found that patient W. J., who suffered from temporary retrograde amnesia following a head injury, was still able to make accurate trait judgments about herself. W. J. was asked to indicate the self-relevance of a series of adjectives both during the time she was amnesic and after her memory had returned. The authors found that her reported self-knowledge during the onset of her amnesia was remarkably consistent with her self-knowledge when her memory had returned.

Interestingly, patients with Alzheimer's disease who suffer from severe loss of episodic memory and even have difficulty recognizing their own family have also shown evidence of self-knowledge. Patient K. R., for instance, suffered from profound Alzheimer's and was unable to remember mundane details (such as the name of simple objects such as batteries or pencils), yet she was still able to identify self-relevant personality traits accurately (Klein, Cosmides, & Costabile, 2003).

Thus, even patients who experienced head injuries that impaired their episodic memory or who had severe dementia resulting in severe memory deficits still retained accurate self-knowledge. However, although individuals with severe memory deficits retain a sense of self, this does not clarify whether these patients retain a normal *memory benefit* for information pertaining to self. This is a difficult issue to address in patients with amnesia or dementia because overall memory performance is often at floor, making it difficult to reliably compare different memory conditions. Here, we may benefit from exploring whether the self-referential memory enhancement effect extends to older adults who do not have dementia or severe memory deficits. Extensive research suggests that although this group of older adults do show overall memory declines relative to young adults, they still perform well above chance on memory tasks, thereby allowing for a meaningful assessment of the self-referential memory enhancement effect (Chalfonte & Johnson, 1996; Hashtroudi, Johnson, & Chrosniak, 1990; Mitchell et al., 2000; Naveh-Benjamin, 2000; Schacter et al., 1994). Thus, if the self-referential memory enhancement effect does indeed rely on neural mechanisms that are not impaired by normal aging, then healthy older adults should show a comparable memory boost for self-relevant information as compared to young adults. In the next section, we discuss emerging findings on the effects of aging on the self-relevant memory enhancement effect.

The Self-Reference Memory Enhancement Effect and Aging

Emerging research suggests that the self-relevant memory effect is relatively preserved in aging (e.g., Derwinger, Stigsdotter Neely, MacDonald,

& Backman, 2005; Gutchess, Kensinger, Yoon, & Schacter, 2007a; Mueller, Wonderlich, & Dugan, 1986), despite the fact that healthy older adults experience overall declines in memory (Chalfonte & Johnson, 1996; Hashtroudi, Johnson, & Chrosniak, 1990; Mitchell et al., 2000; Naveh-Benjamin, 2000; Schacter et al., 1994). In an examination of overall memory recall, Mueller, Wonderlich, and Dugan (1986) found that older adults showed a memory benefit on a surprise recall test for adjectives they had identified as being self-descriptive as compared to words that they identified as being descriptive of young adults. Interestingly, Derwinger and colleagues (2005) found that the self-referential memory strategies could benefit older adults' memory recall even for seemingly mundane items. Specifically, they found that older adults were able to better remember a string of four digits when using strategies that relied on personally relevant self-generated strategies (i.e., important birthdates) relative to other mnemonic strategies.

Gutchess and colleagues (2007a) extended this line of research by examining whether self-referential processing improved older adults' memory recognition in a unique manner. In their study, Gutchess and colleagues asked participants to make one of three judgments on a list of positive and negative adjectives: self (i.e., Does this word describe me well?), other (i.e., Does this word describe Albert Einstein or a close friend well?), or case (i.e., Is this word displayed in uppercase?). After a short delay, participants were given a surprise recognition test. Two important findings emerged. First, older adults showed the expected self-reference memory enhancement effect (better memory for words that were encoded with respect to self as compared to other or case), although their memory performance overall was still lower than it was for young adults. Second, the valence of the words they encoded did not affect memory performance. That is, young and older adults' memory performance was unaffected by whether they had encoded a positive or negative word—it was only affected by the encoding instructions that had been paired with the word.

In subsequent research, Gutchess and colleagues had the rather intriguing finding that self-referential memory enhancement effect may also boost older adults' memory for the source of the information they encoded (Hamami, Serbun, & Gutchess, 2011; Rosa & Gutchess, 2011). Memory for source is often disproportionately impaired with age compared to memory for items (Johnson, Hashtroudi, & Lindsay, 1993; Old & Naveh-Benjamin, 2008;

Spencer & Raz, 1995; but see Siedlecki, Salthouse, & Berish, 2005). This specific type of memory impairment may be particularly pernicious for older adults because accurately remembering the source of information is a crucial skill in every day life. For instance, if an older adult recalls being told that he should invest his retirement money in a new fund, it is equally important that he be able to recall whether his financial advisor or a neighbor gave him that advice because one source may be more credible than the other.

To determine whether self-referential encoding would boost source memory performance, Hamami and colleagues (2011) asked participants to encode words by making one of three judgments on them: self (e.g., Does this word describe you?), common (e.g., Do you encounter this word in everyday life?), or case (e.g., Is this word in upper- or lowercase). During a surprise recognition test, participants were asked to indicate whether they had made a self, common, or case decision about each word, or whether it was a new word they had not studied. The authors found that both young and older adults were more accurate in correctly identifying the decision made about the words they had encoded relative to self as compared to words that had been encoded in other manners. Thus, self-referencing enhanced memory for details of the encoded item.

In an attempt to isolate the source memory benefits to self-referential processing, Rosa and Gutchess (2011) examined whether older adults would also experience a memory boost when the source of the information they encoded was a spouse or close friend. In the study, a group of three participants took turns placing items either into a suitcase or into a picnic basket. Within each group, two of the participants knew one another (e.g., were spouses, roommates, or close friends), whereas the remaining participant in the group was unknown. Following a brief delay, all participants were given a surprise memory task in which they were asked to indicate which of the three members of the group had placed each of the items in either the suitcase or picnic basket. The authors demonstrated that source memory for self-performed actions was better than source memory for actions performed both by close or unknown others. The authors suggested that source memory for self-performed actions might be better because performing an action oneself allows for deeper encoding of the event.

Although older adults exhibited improved memory for information encoded relative to self as compared to others across all these studies, it is important to note that the benefits from self-referencing do not eliminate or reduce age differences in memory (Glisky & Marquine, 2009; Gutchess et al., 2007a; Mueller et al., 1986). Indeed, older adults' overall memory for information encoded as it pertains to the self is still impaired as compared to young adults. However, their memory for items encoded relevant to self is enhanced as compared to their memory for items encoded relevant to others or about which they made semantic judgments. Thus, like the emotional memory enhancement effect, the self-referential enhancement effect and aging demonstrates that encoding information relative to the self improves older adults' memory overall, but age-related memory deficits still remain.

Together, these findings suggest that self-referential processing may occur in neural regions that are distinct from those engaged in general episodic memory (e.g., the hippocampus). But what might those neural regions be? Emerging research in social and affective neuroscience has begun to identify the neural mechanisms that give rise to the self-referential memory enhancement effect. We discuss those findings in the next section.

Neural Mechanisms Engaged in Self-Referential Memory

Emerging neuroimaging research extends the behavioral research just discussed by demonstrating that encoding self-relevant information is supported by the mPFC (for review and meta-analysis, see Northoff, Heinzel, de Greck, Bermpohl, Dobrowolny, & Panksepp, 2006), not the hippocampus or amygdala, which support the encoding of general episodic or emotional information (as discussed earlier). In addition to processing self-relevant information, the mPFC has been implicated in numerous social tasks such as making judgments about others (Mason, Banfield, and Macrae, 2004; Mitchell, Heatherton, and Macrae, 2002) and inferring the mental states of others (Fletcher et al., 1995; Gallagher et al., 2000; Gallagher & Frith, 2003; Stuss, Gallup, and Alexander, 2001). Interestingly, the mPFC is otherwise deactivated during most cognitive tasks (Raichle et al., 2001). It is thus thought that the mPFC is engaged when the brain is "inactive," suggesting perhaps that the "default state" of the brain is introspection (a topic we will not discuss in detail here, but see Mason et al., 2007, and Raichle et al., 2001, for more information). For the purposes of the current section, we will focus on the mPFC's role in processing self-relevant information.

Indeed, numerous neuroimaging studies have identified the mPFC as playing a central role in the self-referential memory enhancement effect. For instance, Gusnard and colleagues (2001) instructed participants to evaluate positive and negative pictures either in an internally cued manner (e.g., Do you find this image to be pleasant or unpleasant?) or in an externally cued manner (e.g., Is this image indoors or outdoors?). The authors postulated that the internally cued judgments required self-referential knowledge (since knowing whether one finds an item to be pleasant or unpleasant requires self-knowledge), whereas the externally cued judgments did not. Interestingly, the authors observed heightened mPFC activity that was associated with self-referential (internally cued) judgments, but not with non–self-referential (externally cued) judgments.

Direct examinations of the neural correlates engaged in self-reflective thought have also implicated the mPFC as playing a central role in self-relevant processing. For instance, Kelley and colleagues (2002) asked participants to judge 270 trait adjectives in one of three ways: self ("Does the trait describe you?"); other ("Does the trait describe George Bush?"); and case ("Is the trait presented in uppercase letters?") while undergoing functional magnetic resonance imaging (fMRI). They found that a direct comparison of the neural activation in "self" trials as compared to "other" trials revealed heightened activation in the mPFC. Similarly, Johnson et al. (2002) asked participants to respond to a series of questions that demanded access to either personal knowledge (e.g., "I have a quick temper") or general semantic knowledge (e.g., "Ten seconds is more than a minute"). Their results revealed that self-reflective thought was accompanied by activity in anterior regions of mPFC. Finally, Cabeza et al. (2004) presented participants with photographs that either they had taken around campus or that someone else had taken. The participants showed heightened mPFC activity for photographs they themselves had taken.

Although these studies demonstrate that the mPFC plays a central role in processing self-relevant information, what role does it play, if any, in remembering self-relevant information? Macrae, Moran, Heatherton, Banfield, and Kelley (2004) investigated this question by asking participants to evaluate how self-descriptive a series of adjectives were while undergoing fMRI. Following the encoding task, participants were given a surprise recognition task. The authors found that greater mPFC activity during the encoding of self-relevant words predicted subsequent memory for these words, suggesting that the heightened activation of mPFC during self-referential processing subserves the self-referential memory enhancement effect.

One question that has arisen from this research is whether the mPFC is uniquely responsive to self-relevant information, or, instead, is engaged when individuals encode any personally relevant information, such as information about close personal others. An important theoretical reason for examining this question is that closeness is often considered to be an extension of self into other, such that one's cognitive processes about a close other develop in a way so as to include that person as part of the self (Aron & Aron, 1996; Aron, Aron, Tudor, & Nelson, 1991; Aron & Fraley, 1999). To examine this question, Heatherton and colleagues (2006) asked participants to evaluate adjectives as they pertained to self or their best friend. Although differences in recognition memory performance for self and intimate other judgments were modest, neural response differences in the mPFC were robust, with self showing much greater activity in mPFC than for best friend judgments. These results indicate an mPFC response that is self-specific; that is, in the brain, judgments pertaining to the self were distinct from those made for close others. Interestingly, Ochsner and colleagues (2005) found that evaluating trait words as an individual imagines how other people view him or her showed robust activation in the mPFC, likely because these judgments require self-knowledge to perform. These findings clearly demonstrated that the mPFC plays a central role in self-relevant processing.

Aging and the Neural Mechanisms Underlying Self-Referential Memory Enhancement

The fact that the self-referential memory enhancement effect is supported by neural activity in the mPFC may elucidate why older adults have relatively preserved memories for information processed in a self-relevant manner. The mPFC is relatively preserved with aging (Salat et al., 2004), although its functionality may change (Williams et al., 2006). For instance, Williams and colleagues (2006) found that aging led to a shift in greater recruitment of the mPFC when older adults evaluated negative stimuli (e.g., angry faces). The authors argued that this shift reflected older adults' enhanced control over their emotional responses as compared to young adults. If the structure, but not necessarily functionality, of

the mPFC is relatively preserved with aging, what are the patterns of neural activity that emerge when older adults process self-relevant information? We will explore that question in this final section.

Gutchess and colleagues (2007b) asked young and older adults to evaluate trait adjectives as being relevant to self or other (Albert Einstein) or to make case judgments on the words while undergoing fMRI. They found that young and older adults had heightened activation in the same neural networks (mPFC and mid-cingulate) when they made self-relevant as compared to other and case judgments. However, the authors also found that the activity in the mPFC differed between the two age groups in response to the valence of the words being encoded. Specifically, older adults showed greater mPFC activity in response to positive as compared to negative words, whereas young adults had greater activation in this region for negative as compared to positive words. This finding is particularly noteworthy given that no behavioral differences were observed in memory performance for positive versus negative trait words in a behavioral study (Gutchess et al., 2007a). Thus, the use of neuroimaging to examine self-referential memory revealed a valence effect that was not apparent from a behavioral paradigm alone. Further, the valence effect that emerged in this study (older adults better remembered positive as compared to negative items) is consistent with previous work showing that older adults have a memory bias toward positive information (e.g., Carstensen et al., 1999).

In a subsequent study, Gutchess and colleagues (2010) identified neural regions that predicted successful encoding of self-relevant information in young and older adults. They found that, as compared to young adults, older adults had heightened activity in the left superior mPFC, left anterior cingulate cortex, right posterior cingulate cortex, and left inferior PFC that predicted greater subsequent memory for words encoded in a self referential manner. However, those same regions (with the exception of left inferior PFC) were more active for young adults than older adults when individuals encoded words related to others that were subsequently remembered. The authors concluded that the results suggested that older adults might encode information about the self in a more normative manner (i.e., thinking about traits they possess that are shared with many people), whereas young adults focus on encoding the unique aspects of their personality and distinguishing the self from others. Alternatively, it is also possible that young adults may process traits by referring everything (including others) to self. In other words, they may evaluate how others compare to self on specific traits. On the other hand, older adults may make a stricter distinction between self and other, and not include other in their self-concept when making evaluations.

Although neuroimaging research on the neural correlates engaged by older adults during self-referential processing is only just beginning to emerge, several key findings have become clear. First, the mPFC plays a prominent role in the self-referential memory enhancement effect for both young and older adults. However, there appear to be some minute but important differences in how the mPFC supports memory performance for self-relevant information between the two groups. One difference is the role that valence may play in the mPFC's level of activity. Another difference appears to be the manner in which older adults operationalize self-relevant information as compared to young adults. Although more research is needed to further parse apart these distinctions, it is clear that memory for self-referential information is enhanced for everyone, regardless of age.

Conclusion: The Benefits of an Affective Neuroscience Perspective

As we hope has been clear from the research outlined in this article, aging results in preservation of memory enhancement for socioemotional material. Yet the processes contributing to that enhancement are not always the same in younger and older adults. Some age-related divergence is observable in behavior, as with the positivity effect in memory, but additional age-related divergence becomes apparent only when examining the underlying neural processes engaged, as with the effects of age on engagement of the mPFC during encoding of emotional or self-referential material. There have been a number of proposals to explain the patterns of preservation and alteration that arise with aging, yet, in many cases, there is not sufficient empirical evidence to validate (or disprove) these theories. In this concluding section, we briefly review how neuroimaging methods may provide critical data to elucidate the effects of aging on the mechanisms that support the retention of socioemotional information.

Positivity Effect

Neuroimaging methods can be particularly useful for reconciling divergent theoretical explanations for the age-related positivity effect. The main distinction regarding the three theories discussed in this article (SST, ABM, DIT) relates to a "bottom-up, salience view" versus a "top-down, regulatory view" in the processing positive information. Theories in support of the bottom-up view (ABM and DIT) suggest that preferential processing of positive information occurs in response to biological or cognitive changes that diminish processing of the negative. These changes can come from decreases in amygdala activation and felt arousal to negative information (ABM) or from cognitive declines that elevate the processing of positive affect due to an inability to integrate complex affective experiences (DIT). Conversely, SST provides a top-down regulatory explanation suggesting that these effects are not the result of age-related decline but are motivational in nature.

Older adults' shift toward prefrontal processing of emotional information may be most consistent with a regulatory explanation of the effect, and the regulatory account also fits nicely with the data revealing a role for cognitive control in the positivity effect (Mather & Knight, 2005). However, although it is plausible that older adults' reliance on prefrontally mediated, cognitively demanding processes reflects their emotion regulation efforts, this shift might be related to a number of other top-down influences. For instance, many of the same mPFC regions engaged by older adults during the processing of emotional information are also engaged in studies of self-referential memory enhancements in old age. Future research is needed to distinguish whether top-down differences in emotional memory are regulatory in nature, self-referential, or result from something else. The PFC plays a complex role in higher-level cognition, including memory, and thus its contribution to the positivity effect may be multifaceted.

Self-Referential Processing

Neuroimaging research on the self-referential memory enhancement effect suggests that a unique neural network is engaged in processing self-relevant information as compared to other forms of distinctive information, with the mPFC being a central structure within that network. However, it remains an open question what the precise role of the mPFC may be in processing self-relevant information. One possibility is that the mPFC focuses attention inward for self-reflection when resources are available. Indeed, emerging research on the so-called "default network"—regions of the brain that are tonically active when the brain is "at rest" (i.e., not performing a specified task) but that seemingly "deactivate" when individuals perform a myriad of cognitive tasks (e.g., Raichle et al., 2001)—suggests that the brain may default toward integration of self-relevant information and engagement in self-relevant thought (e.g., Mason et al., 2007). Alternatively, the mPFC may be engaged in binding together any experience (physical, cognitive, or sensory) that has implications for self. Neuroimaging and aging research will play an important role in dissociating these processes. In particular, aging research may elucidate the role of the mPFC in the self-referential memory enhancement effect because although healthy older adults experience overall memory declines, they demonstrate relatively preserved memory for self. This functional dissociation in memory may be particularly relevant for isolating the role of the mPFC in global evaluations and memory of self. Future research will shed light on these questions and the role of the mPFC in self-referential processing.

Linking Together the Affective and the Self-Relevant

Research examining the effects of aging on retention of affective material has largely proceeded in isolation from research examining the effects of aging on retention of self-referent information. Yet affective experiences are often self-relevant, and making information self-relevant can increase its affective import. It remains to be tested whether older adults' preserved memory enhancement and recruitment of the mPFC within both domains is reflective of a common underlying mechanism that extends across both of these areas, but we suggest that an integration of these literatures will be an important step forward in understanding the effects of age on the retention of socioemotional information.

Acknowledgments

Preparation of this manuscript was supported by grants from the National Institute on Aging, the National Institute of Mental Health, and the Searle Scholars Program. We thank Donna Addis, Lisa Feldman Barrett, Kelly Bennion, Kelly Giovanello, Angela Gutchess, Todd Heatherton, Alisha Holland, Christina Leclerc, John Morris, Brendan Murray, Katherine Mickley Steinmetz, Robert Waldinger, and Jill Waring for thoughtful discussion related to the issues presented in this essay. We additionally thank John Morris for assistance with preparing this essay.

Notes

1. The valence of an event (whether it is positive or negative) may influence the amount of detail and the accuracy of information retained in memory. Across the lifespan, negative emotion may reduce false memory (Kensinger & Corkin, 2004; Kensinger et al., 2007) whereas positive emotion may enhance it (Piguet et al., 2008), and event details may be better remembered for negative events than for positive ones (Holland & Kensinger, 2012; Kensinger, Garoff-Eaton, & Schacter, 2007)

2. Note that this is a potential point of divergence from a regulatory account of the positivity effect, which argues that it is only those older adults who have *good* cognitive control who will have the resources necessary to regulate their reactions to emotional information and thus will show a positivity effect.

References

Adams, C., Labouvie-Vief. G., Hobart, C. J., & Dorosz, M. (1990). Adult age group differences in story recall style. *Journal of Gerontology, 45,* 17–27.

Addis, D. R., Leclerc, C. M., Muscatell, K., & Kensinger, E. A. (2010). There are age-related changes in neural connectivity during the successful encoding of positive, but not negative, information. *Cortex, 46,* 425–433.

Amodio, D. M., & Frith, C. D. (2006). Meeting of minds: The medial frontal cortex and social cognition. *Nature Reviews Neuroscience, 7,* 268–277.

Anderson, N. D., Lidaka, T., Cabeza, R., Kapur, S., McIntosh, A. R., & Craik, F. I. (2000). The effects of divided attention on encoding- and retrieval-related brain activity: A PET study of younger and older adults. *Journal of Cognitive Neuroscience, 12,* 775–792.

Aron, A., & Aron, E. N. (1996). *Self and self-expansion in relationships* Hillsdale, NJ: Lawrence Erlbaum Associates, Inc.

Aron, A., Aron, E. N., Tudor, M., & Nelson, G. J. (1991). Close relationships as including other in the self. *Journal of Personality and Social Psychology, 60*(2), 241–253.

Aron, A., & Fraley, B. (1999). Relationship closeness as including other in the self: Cognitive underpinnings and measures *Social Cognition. Special Issue: Social Cognition and Relationships, 17*(2), 140–160.

Bayer, Z. C., Hernandez, R. J., Morris, A. M., Salomonczyk, D., Pirogovsky, E., & Gilbert, P. E. (2011). Age-related source memory deficits persist despite superior item memory. *Experimental Aging Research, 37,* 473–480.

Becker, D. V., Anderson, U. S., Neuberg, S. L., Maner, J. K., Shapiro, J. R., Ackerman, J. M., Schaller, M., & Kenrick, D. T. (2010). More memory bang for the attentional buck: Self-protection goals enhance encoding efficiency for potentially threatening males. *Social Psychological & Personality Science, 1,* 182–189.

Berntsen, D., & Rubin, D. C. (2006). Flashbulb memories and posttraumatic stress reactions across the life span: Age-related effects of the German occupation of Denmark during World War II. *Psychology and Aging, 21,* 127–139.

Blanchard-Fields, F. (2007). Everyday problem solving and emotion: An adult developmental perspective. *Current Directions in Psychological Science, 16,* 26–31.

Bower, G. H., & Gilligan, S. G. (1979). Remembering information related to one's self. *Journal of Research in Personality, 13,* 420–432.

Brown, R., & Kulik, J. (1977). Flashbulb memories. *Cognition, 5,* 73–99.

Cabeza, R., Prince, S. E., Daselaar, S. M., Greenberg, D. L., Budde, M., Dolcos, F., et al. (2004). Brain activity during episodic retrieval of autobiographical and laboratory events: An fMRI study using a novel photo paradigm. *Journal of Cognitive Neuroscience, 16*, 1583–1594.

Cahill, L., & McGaugh, J. L. (1998). Mechanisms of emotional arousal and lasting declarative memory. *Trends in Neuroscience, 21*, 294–299.

Cacioppo, J. T., Berntson, G. G., Bechara, A., Tranel, D., & Hawkley, L. C. (2011). Could an aging brain contribute to subjective well-being? The value added by a social neuroscience perspective. In A. Todorov, S. T. Fiske, & D. Prentice (Eds.), *Social neuroscience: Toward understanding the underpinnings of the social mind* (pp. 249–262). New York: Oxford University Press.

Carstensen, L. L., Fung, H., & Charles, S. (2003). Socioemotional selectivity theory and the regulation of emotion in the second half of life. *Motivation and Emotion, 27*, 103–123.

Carstensen, L. L., Isaacowitz, D., & Charles, S. T. (1999). Taking time seriously: A theory of Socioemotional selectivity. *American Psychologist, 54*, 165–181.

Carstensen, L. L., & Mikels, J. A. (2005). At the intersection of emotion and cognition: Aging and the positivity effect. *Current Directions in Psychological Science, 14*, 117–121.

Carstensen, L. L., Mikels, J. A., & Mather, M. (2006). Aging and the intersection of cognition, motivation and emotion. In J. Birren & K. W. Schaie (Eds.), *Handbook of the psychology of aging*. San Diego: Academic Press, Sixth Edition.

Carstensen, L. L., & Turk-Charles, S. (1994). The salience of emotion across the adult life course. *Psychology and Aging, 9*, 259–264.

Chalfonte, B. L., & Johnson, M. K. (1996). Feature memory and binding in young and older adults. *Memory and Cognition, 24*, 403–416.

Charles, S., Mather, M., & Carstensen, L. L. (2003). Aging and emotional memory: The forgettable nature of negative images for older adults. *Journal of Experimental Psychology: General, 132*, 310–324.

Chow, T. W., & Cummings, J. L. (2000). The amygdala and Alzheimer's disease. In J. P. Aggleton (Ed.). *The amygdala: A functional analysis*. (pp. 656–680). Oxford: Oxford University Press.

Coffey, C. E., Wilkenson, W. E., Parashos, I. A., Soady, S. A., Sullivan, R. J., Patterson, L. J. et al. (1992). Quantitative cerebral anatomy of the aging human brain: A cross-sectional study using magnetic resonance imaging. *Neurology, 42*, 527–536.

Cohen, G., Conway, M. A., & Maylor, E. A. (1994). Flashbulb memories in older adults. *Psychology and Aging, 9*, 454–463.

Comblain, C., D'Argembeau, A., Van der Linden, M., & Aldenhoff, L. (2004). The effect of ageing on the recollection of emotional and neutral pictures. *Memory, 12*, 673–684.

Conway, A. R. A., Skitka, L. J., Hemmerich, J. A., & Kershaw, T. C. (2009). Flashbulb memory for 11 September 2001. *Applied Cognitive Psychology, 23*, 605–623.

Cosmides, L., & Tooby, J. (2000). The cognitive neuroscience of social reasoning. In M. S. Gazzaniga (Ed.), *The new cognitive neurosciences* (2nd ed., chapter 87, pp. 1259–1270). Cambridge, MA: MIT Press.

Craik, F. I. (2002). Levels of processing: Past, present, and future? *Memory, 10*, 305–318.

Craik, F. I. M., & Byrd, M. (1982). Aging and cognitive deficits: The role of attentional resources. In F. I. M. Craik & S. Trehub (Eds.), *Aging and cognitive processes* (pp. 191–211). New York: Plenum Press.

Craik, F. I. M., & Lockhart, R. (1972). Levels of processing: A framework for memory research. *Journal of Verbal Learning & Verbal Behavior, 11*, 671–684.

D'Argembeau, A., Jedidi, H., Balteau, E., Bahri, M., Phillips, C., & Salmon, E. (2011). Valuing one's self: Medial prefrontal involvement in epistemic and emotive investments in self-views. *Cerebral Cortex*. Advance online publication. doi: 10.1093/cercor/bhr144

Davidson, P. S., Cook, S. P., & Glisky, E. L. (2006). Flashbulb memories for September 11th can be preserved in older adults. *Neuropsychological Development and Cognition, 13*, 196–206.

Davidson, P. S. R., & Glisky, E. L. (2002). Is flashbulb memory a special instance of source memory? Evidence from older adults. *Memory, 10*, 99–111.

Davis, S. W., Dennis, N. A., Daselaar, S. M., Fleck, M. S., & Cabeza, R. (2008). Que PASA? The posterior-anterior shift in aging. *Cerebral Cortex, 18*, 1201–1209.

Denburg, N. L., Buchanan, T. W., Tranel, D., & Adolphs, R. (2003). Evidence for preserved emotional memory in normal older persons. *Emotion, 3*, 239–253.

Derwinger, A. A., Stigsdotter Neely, A. A., MacDonald, S. S., & Backman, L. L. (2005). Forgetting numbers in old age: Strategy and learning speed matter. *Gerontology, 51*(4), 277–284.

Dennis, N. A., Daselaar, S., & Cabeza, R. (2007). Effects of aging on transient and sustained successful memory encoding activity. *Neurobiology of Aging, 28*, 1749–1758.

Dennis, N. A., Hayes, S. M., Prince, S. E., Madden, D. J., Huettel, S. A., & Cabeza, R. (2008). Effects of aging on the neural correlates of successful item and source memory encoding. *Journal of Experimental Psychology: Learning, Memory, and Cognition, 34*, 791–808.

Diener, E., Emmons, R. A., Larsen, R. J., & Griffin, S. (1985). The Satisfaction with Life Scale. *Journal of Personality Assessment, 49*, 71–75.

Dillon, D. G., Ritchey, M., Johnson, B. D., & LaBar, K. S. (2007). Dissociable effects of conscious emotion regulation strategies on explicit and implicit memory. *Emotion, 7*, 354–365.

Dolan, R. J. (2002). Emotion, cognition, and behavior. *Science, 298*, 1191–1194.

Fernandes, M., Ross, M., Wiegand, M., & Schryer, E. (2008). Are memories of older adults positively biased? *Psychology and Aging, 23*, 297–306.

Fischer, H., Nyberg, L., & Bäckman, L. (2010). Age-related differences in brain regions supporting successful encoding of emotional faces. *Cortex, 46*, 490–497.

Fletcher, P. C., Happe, F., Frith, U., Baker, S. C., Dolan, R. J., Frackowiak, R. S., et al. (1995). Other minds in the brain: A functional imaging study of "theory of mind" in story comprehension. *Cognition, 57*, 109–128.

Fontani, G., Lodi, L., Felici, A., Corradeschi, F., & Lupo, C. (2004). Attentional, emotional and hormonal data in subjects of different ages. *European Journal of Applied Physiology, 92*, 452–461.

Gallagher, H. L., & Frith, C. D. (2003). Functional imaging of "theory of mind." *Trends in Cognitive Sciences, 7*, 77–83.

Gallagher, H. L., Happe, F., Brunswick, N., Fletcher, P. C., Frith, U., & Frith, C. D. (2000). Reading the mind in cartoons and stories: An fMRI study of "theory of mind" in verbal and nonverbal tasks. *Neuropsychologia, 38*, 11–21.

Garoff-Eaton, R. J., Kensinger, E. A., & Schacter, D. L. (2007). The neural correlates of conceptual and perceptual false recognition. *Learning & Memory, 14*, 684–692.

Gerritsen, L., Riipkema, M., van Oostrom, I., Buitelaar, J., Franke, B., Fernandez, G., & Tendolkar, I. (2011). Amygdala to hippocampal volume ratio is associated with negative memory bias in healthy subjects. *Psychological Medicine, 11*, 1–9.

Giovanello, K. S., Kensinger, E. A., Wong, A. T., & Schacter, D. L. (2010). Age-related neural changes during memory conjunction errors. *Journal of Cognitive Neuroscience, 22*, 1348–1361.

Glisky, E. L., & Marquine, M. J. (2009). Semantic and self-referential processing of positive and negative trait adjectives in older adults. *Memory, 17*, 144–157.

Good, C. D., Johnsrude, I. S., Ashburner, J., Henson, R. N. A., Friston, K. J., & Frackowiak, R. S. J. (2001). A voxel-based morphometric study of ageing in 465 normal adult human brains. *NeuroImage, 14*, 21–36.

Grady, C. L., Bernstein, L. J., Beig, S., & Siegenthaler, A. L. (2002). The effects of encoding task on age-related differences in the functional neuroanatomy of face memory. *Psychology of Aging, 17*, 7–23.

Grady, C. L., Maisog, J. M., Horwitz, B., Ungerleider, L. G., Mentis, M. J., Salerno, J. A., et al. (1994). Age-related changes in cortical blood flow activation during visual processing of faces and location. *Journal of Neuroscience, 14*, 1450–1462.

Grady, C. L., McIntosh, A. R., & Craik, F. I. (2003). Age-related differences in the functional connectivity of the hippocampus during memory encoding. *Hippocampus, 13*, 572–586.

Greenwald, A. G., & Banaji, M. R. (1989). The self as a memory system: Powerful, but ordinary *Journal of Personality and Social Psychology, 57*(1), 41–54.

Grieve, S. M., Clark, C. R., Williams, L. M., Peduto, A. J., & Gordon, E. (2005). Preservation of limbic and paralimbic structures in aging. *Human Brain Mapping, 25*, 391–401.

Grilli, M. D., & Glisky, E. L. (2011). The self-imagination effect: Benefits of a self-referential encoding strategy on cued recall in memory-impaired individuals with neurological damage. *Journal of the International Neuropsychological Society, 17*, 929–933.

Grossman, M., Cooke, A., DeVita, C., Alsop, D., Detre, J., Chen, W., & Gee, J. (2002). Age-related changes in working memory during sentence comprehension: An fMRI study. *Neuroimage, 15*, 302–317.

Gunning-Dixon, F. M., Gur, R. C., Perkins, A. C., Schroder, L., Turner, T., Turetsky, B. I. et al. (2003). Age-related differences in brain activation during emotional face processing. *Neurobiology of Aging, 24*, 285–295.

Gusnard, D. A., Akbudak, E., Shulman, G. L., & Raichle, M. E. (2001). Medial prefrontal cortex and self-referential mental activity: Relation to a default mode of brain function. *Proceedings of the National Academy of Sciences of the USA, 98*(7), 4259–4264.

Gutchess, A. H., Kensinger, E. A., & Schacter, D. L. (2007b). Aging, Self-referencing and Medial Prefrontal Cortex. *Social Neuroscience, 2*(2), 117–133.

Gutchess, A. H., Kensinger, E. A., & Schacter, D. L. (2010). Functional neuroimaging of self-referential encoding with age. *Neuropsychologia, 48*, 211–219.

Gutchess, A. H., Kensinger, E. A., Yoon, C., & Schacter, D. L. (2007a). Aging and the self- reference effect in memory. *Memory, 15*(8), 822–837.

Gutchess, A. H., Welsh, R. C., Hedden, T., Bangert, A., Minear, M., Liu, L. L., & Park, D. C. (2005). Aging and the neural correlates of successful picture encoding: Frontal activations

compensate for decreased medial-temporal activity. *Journal of Cognitive Neuroscience, 17*, 84–96.

Hahn, S., Carlson, C., Singer, S, & Gronlund, S. D. (2006). Aging and visual search: Automatic and controlled attentional bias to threat faces. *Acta Psychologica, 123*, 312–336.

Hamami, A., Serbun, S. J., & Gutchess, A. H. (2011). Self-referencing enhances memory specificity with age. *Psychology and Aging*, 26, 636–46.

Hamann, S. (2001). Cognitive and neural mechanisms of emotional memory. *Trends in Cognitive Sciences, 5*, 394–400.

Hamann, S. B., L. Cahill, & L. R. Squire. 1997. Emotional perception and memory in amnesia. *Neuropsychology, 11*, 104–113.

Hasher, L., & Zacks, R. T. (1988). Working memory, comprehension, and aging: A review and a new view. In G. H. Bower (Ed.), *The psychology of learning and motivation: Advances in research and theory* (vol. 22., pp. 193–225). San Diego, CA: Academic Press, Inc.

Hashtroudi, S., Johnson, M. K., & Chrosniak, L. D. (1990). Aging and qualitative characteristics of memories for perceived and imagined complex events. *Psychology and Aging, 5*, 119–126.

Hashtroudi, S., Johnson, M. K., Vnek, N., & Ferguson, S. A. (1994). Aging and the effects of affective and factual focus on source monitoring and recall. *Psychology and Aging, 9*, 160–170.

Heatherton, T. F., Wyland, C. L., Macrae, C. N., Demos, K. E., Denny, B. T., & Kelley, W. M. (2006). Medial prefrontal activity differentiates self from close others. *Social Cognitive and Affective Neuroscience, 1*, 18–25.

Holland, A. C., & Kensinger, E. A. (2012). Younger, middle-aged, and older adults' memories for the 2008 presidential election. *Journal of Applied Research on Memory and Cognition, 1*, 163–170.

Howard, M. W., Kahana, M. J., & Wingfield, A. (2006). Aging and contextual binding: Modeling recency and lag recency effects with the temporal context model. *Psychonomic Bulletin & Review, 13*, 439–445.

Johnson, M. K., Hashtroudi, S., & Lindsay, D. S. (1993). Source monitoring. *Psychological Bulletin, 114*, 3–28.

Johnson, S. C., Baxter, L. C., Wilder, L. S., Pipe, J. G., Heiserman, J. E., & Prigatano, G. P. (2002). Neural correlates of self-reflection. *Brain, 125*(Pt 8), 1808–1814.

Jones, M. W., McHugh, T. J. (2011). Updating hippocampal representations: CA2 joins the circuit. *Trends in Neurosciences.* Advance online publication. doi:10.1016/j.tins.2011.07.007

Kelley, W. M., Macrae, C. N., Wyland, C., Caglar, S., Inati, S., & Heatherton, T. F. (2002). Finding the self? An event-related fMRI Study. *Journal of Cognitive Neuroscience, 14*, 785–794.

Kennedy, Q., Mather, M., & Carstensen, L. (2004). The role of motivation in the age-related positivity in autobiographical memory. *Psychological Science, 15*, 208–214.

Kensinger, E. A., & Corkin, S. (2004a). The effects of emotional content and aging on false memories. *Cognitive, Affective, and Behavioral Neuroscience, 4*, 1–9.

Kensinger, E. A., & Corkin, S. (2004b). Two routes to emotional memory: Distinct neural processes for valence and arousal. *Proceedings of the National Academy of Sciences, USA, 101*, 3310–3315.

Kensinger, E. A., Brierley, B., Medford, N., Growdon, J. H., & Corkin, S. (2002). Effects of normal aging and Alzheimer's disease on emotional memory. *Emotion, 2*, 118–134.

Kensinger, E. A., Garoff-Eaton, R. J., & Schacter, D. L. (2007c). Effects of emotion on memory specificity in young and older adults. *Journals of Gerontology Series B: Psychological Sciences and Social Sciences, 62*, 208–215.

Kensinger, E. A., Gutchess, A. H., & Schacter, D. L. (2007b). Effects of aging and encoding instructions on emotion-induced memory trade-offs. *Psychology and Aging, 22*, 781–795.

Kensinger, E. A., Krendl, A. C., & Corkin, S. (2006). Memories of an emotional and a nonemotional event: Effects of aging and delay interval. *Experimental Aging Research, 32*, 23–45.

Kensinger, E. A., & Leclerc, C. M. (2009). Age-related changes in the neural mechanisms supporting emotion processing and emotional memory. *European Journal of Cognitive Psychology, 21*, 192–215.

Kensinger, E. A., O'Brien, J., Swanberg, K., Garoff-Eaton, R. J., & Schacter, D. L. (2007c). The effects of emotional content on reality-monitoring performance in young and older adults. *Psychology and Aging, 22*, 752–764.

Kensinger, E. A., & Schacter, D. L. (2008). Neural processes supporting young and older adults' emotional memories. *Journal of Cognitive Neuroscience, 20*, 1161–1173.

Kesebir, S., & Oishi, S. (2010). A spontaneous self-reference effect in memory: Why some birthdays are harder to remember than other. *Psychological Science, 21*, 1525–1531.

Kirchhoff, B. A., Schapiro, M. L., & Buckner, R. L. (2005). Orthographic distinctiveness and semantic elaboration provide separate contributions to memory. *Journal of Cognitive Neuroscience, 17*, 1851–1854.

Klein, S. B., Chan, R. L., & Loftus, J. (1999). Independence of episodic and semantic self- knowledge: The case from autism. *Social Cognition, 17*, 413–436

Klein, S. B., Cosmides, L., & Costabile, K. A. (2003). Preserved knowledge of self in a case of Alzheimer's dementia. *Social Cognition, 21*(2), 157–165.

Klein, S. B., & Kihlstrom, J. F. (1986). Elaboration, organization, and the self-reference effect in memory. *Journal of Experimental Psychology: General, 115*, 26–38.

Klein, S. B., & Loftus, J. (1988). The nature of self-referent encoding: The contributions of elaborative and organizational processes. *Journal of Personality and Social Psychology, 55*, 5–11.

Klein, S. B., Loftus, J., & Kihlstrom, J. F. (1996). Self-knowledge of an amnesic patient: Toward a neuropsychology of personality and social psychology. *Journal of Experimental Psychology: General, 125*(3), 250–260.

Klein, S. B., Rozendal, K., & Cosmides, L. (2002). A social–cognitive neuroscience analysis of the self. *Social Cognition, 20*, 105–135.

Kosslyn, S. M., & Intriligator, J. M. (1992). Is cognitive neuropsychology possible? The perils of sitting on a one-legged stool. *Journal of Cognitive Neuroscience, 4*, 96–106.

Kryla-Lighthall, N., & Mather, M. (2009). The role of cognitive control in older adults' emotional well-being. In V. Berngston, D. Gans, N. Putney, & M. Silverstein (Eds.), *Handbook of theories of aging* (2nd ed., pp. 323–344). New York: Springer.

Kvavilashvili, L., Mirani, J., Schlagman, S., Erskine, J. A., & Kornbrot, D. E. (2010). Effects of age on phenomenology and consistency of flashbulb memories of September 11 and a staged control event. *Psychology and Aging, 25*, 391–404.

LaBar, K. S., & Cabeza, R. (2006). Cognitive neuroscience of emotional memory. *Nature Neuroscience Reviews, 7*, 54–56.

Labouvie-Vief, G. (2003). Dynamic integration: Affect, cognition, and the self in adulthood. *Current Directions in Psychological Science, 12*, 201–206.

Labouvie-Vief, G. (2005). Self-with-other representations and the organization of the self. *Journal of Research in Personality, 39*, 185–205.

Labouvie-Vief, G., Diehl, M., Jain, E., & Zhang, F. (2007). Six-year change in affect optimization affect complexity across the adult life span: A further examination. *Psychology and Aging, 22*, 738–751.

Labouvie-Vief, G., & Medler, S. M. (2002). Affect optimization and affect complexity: Modes and styles of regulation in adulthood. *Psychology and Aging, 17*, 571–587.

Lang, P. J., Bradley, M. M., & Cuthbert, B. N. (2005). *International affective picture system (IAPS): Technical manual and affective ratings*. Gainesville, FL: Center for Research in Psychophysiology.

Langeslag, S. J. E., & van Strien, J. W. (2009). Aging and emotional memory: The co-occurrence of neurophysiological and behavioral positivity effects. *Emotion, 9*, 369–377.

Leclerc, C. M., & Kensinger, E. A. (2008a). Effects of age on detection of emotional information. *Psychology and Aging, 23*, 209–215.

Leclerc, C. M., & Kensinger, E. A. (2008b). Age-related differences in medial prefrontal activation in response to emotional images. *Cognitive, Affective, & Behavioral Neuroscience, 8*, 153–164.

Leclerc, C. M., & Kensinger, E. A. (2010). Age-related valence-based reversal in recruitment of medial prefrontal cortex on a visual search task. *Social Neuroscience, 5*, 560–576.

Leclerc, C. M., & Kensinger, E. A. (2011). Neural processing of emotional pictures and words: A comparison of young and older adults. *Developmental Neuropsychology, 36*, 519–538.

Löckenhoff, C. E., & Carstensen, L. L. (2007). Aging, emotion, and health-related decision strategies: Motivational manipulations can reduce age differences. *Psychology and Aging, 22*, 134–146.

Lockhart, R. S. (2002). Levels of processing, transfer-appropriate processing, and the concept of robust encoding. *Memory, 10*, 397–403.

Macrae, C. N., Moran, J. M., Heatherton, T. F., Banfield, J. F., & Kelley, W. M. (2004). Medial prefrontal activity predicts memory for self. *Cerebral Cortex, 14*(6), 647–654.

Madden, D. J., Langley, L. K., Denny, L. L., Turkington, T. G., Provenzale, J. M., Hawk, T. C., & Coleman, R. E. (2002). Adult age differences in visual word identification: Functional neuroanatomy by positron emission tomography. *Brain and Cognition, 49*, 297–321.

Madden, D. J., Turkington, T. G., Provenzale, J. M., Denny, L. L., Hawk, T. C., Gottlob, L. R., & Coleman, R. E. (1999). Adult age differences in the functional neuroanatomy of verbal recognition memory. *Human Brain Mapping, 7*, 115–135.

Maki, R. H., & McCaul, K. D. (1985). The effects of self-reference versus other reference on the recall of traits and nouns. *Bulletin of the Psychonomic Society, 23*, 169–172.

Malykhin, N. V., Bouchard, T. P., Camicioli, R., & Coupland, N. J. (2008). Aging hippocampus and amygdala. *Neuroreport, 19*, 543–547.

Markus, H. (1977). Self-schemata and processing information about the self. *Journal of Personality and Social Psychology, 35*, 63–78.

Mason, M. F., Banfield, J. F., & Macrae, C. N. (2004). Thinking about actions: The neural substrates of person knowledge. *Cerebral Cortex, 14*, 209–214.

Mason, M. F., Norton, M. I., Van Horn, J. D., Wegner, D. M., Grafton, S. T., & Macrae, C. N. (2007). Wandering minds: The default network and stimulus independent thought. *Science, 315(5810)*, 393–395.

Mather, M. (2006). Why memories may become more positive with age. In B. Uttl, N. Ohta, & A. L. Siegenthaler (Eds.), *Memory and emotion: Interdisciplinary perspectives* (pp. 135–159). Malden, MA: Blackwell Publishing.

Mather, M., & Carstensen, L. L. (2003). Aging and attentional biases for emotional faces. *Psychological Science, 14*, 409–415.

Mather, M., & Carstensen, L. L. (2005). Aging and motivated cognition: The positivity effect in attention and memory. *Trends in Cognitive Science, 9*, 496–502.

Mather, M., & Knight, M. (2005). Goal-directed memory: The role of cognitive control in older adults' emotional memory. *Psychology and Aging, 20*, 554–570.

Mather, M., & Knight, M. R. (2006). Angry faces get noticed quickly: Threat detection is not impaired among older adults. *Journals of Gerontology Series B: Psychological Sciences and Social Sciences, 61*, 54–57.

May, C. P., Rahhal, T., Berry, E. M., & Leighton, E. A. (2005). Aging, source memory, and emotion. *Psychology of Aging, 20*, 571–578.

McIntyre, J. S., & Craik, F. I. (1987). Age differences in memory for item and source information. *Canadian Journal of Psychology, 41*, 175–192.

Mikels, J. A., Larkin, G. R., Reuter-Lorenz, P. A., & Carstensen, L. L. (2005). Divergent trajectories in the aging mind: Changes in working memory for affective versus visual information with age. *Psychology and Aging, 20*, 542–553.

Mitchell, K.J., Johnson, M.K., Raye, C.L., Mather, M., & D'Esposito, M. (2000). Aging and reflective processes of working memory: binding and test load deficits. *Psychology and Aging, 15*, 527–541.

Mitchell, J. P., Heatherton, T. F., & Macrae, C. N. (2002). Distinct neural systems subserve person and object knowledge. *Proceedings of the National Academy of Sciences, USA, 99*, 15238–15243.

Mueller, J. H., Wonderlich, S., & Dugan, K. (1986). Self-referent processing of age-specific material. *Psychology and Aging, 1*(4), 293–299.

Nashiro, K., Sakaki, M., & Mather, M. (2011). Age differences in brain activity during emotion processing: Reflections of age-related decline or increased emotion regulation? *Gerontology*. Advance online publication. doi: 10.1159/00032846

Naveh-Benjamin, M. (2000). Adult age differences in memory performance: Tests of an associative deficit hypothesis. *Journal of Experimental Psychology: Learning, Memory, and Cognition, 26*, 1170–1187.

Northoff, G., Heinzel, A., de Greck, M., Bermpohl, F., Dobrowolny, H., & Panksepp, J. (2006). Self-referential processing in our brain—A meta-analysis of imaging studies on the self. *NeuroImage, 31*, 440–457.

Ochsner, K. N., Beer, J. S., Robertson, E. R., Cooper, J. C., Gabrieli, J. D., Kihslstrom, J. F., et al. (2005). The neural correlates of direct and reflected self-knowledge. *Neuroimage, 28*(4), 797–814.

Ochsner, K. N., & Gross, J. J. (2005). The cognitive control of emotion. *Trends in Cognitive Science, 9*, 292–249.

Old, S. R., & Naveh-Benjamin, M. (2008). Differential effects of age on item and associative measures of memory: A meta-analysis. *Psychology and Aging, 23*, 104–118.

Otani, H., Kusumi, T., Kato, K., Matsuda, K., Kern, R. P., Widner, R., Jr., & Ohta, N. (2005). Remembering a nuclear accident in Japan: Did it trigger flashbulb memories? *Memory, 13*, 6–20.

Park, D. C. (2000). The basic mechanism, accounting for age-related decline in cognitive function. In D. C. Park & N. Schwarz (Eds.), *Cognitive aging: A primer* (pp. 3–21). Philadelphia: Psychology Press.

Piguet, O., Connally, E., Krendl, A. C., Huot, J. R., & Corkin, S. (2008). False memory in aging: Effects of emotional valence on word recognition accuracy. *Psychology of Aging, 23*, 307–314.

Prull, M. W., Dawes, L. L., Martin, A. M., 3rd, Rosenberg, H. F., & Light, L. L. (2006). Recollection and familiarity in recognition memory: Adult age differences and neuropsychological test correlates. *Psychology and Aging, 21*, 107–118.

Qin, P., & Northoff, G. (2011). How is our self related to midline regions and the default-mode network? *Neuroimage, 57*, 1221–1233.

Quirk, G. J., & Beer, J. S. (2006). Prefrontal involvement in the regulation of emotion: Convergence of rat and human studies. *Current Opinion in Neurobiology, 16*, 723–727.

Rahhal, T., May, C. P., & Hasher, L. (2002). Truth and character: Sources that older adults can remember. *Psychological Science, 13*, 101–105.

Raichle, M. E., MacLeod, A. M., Snyder, A. Z., Powers, W. J., Gusnard, D. A., & Shulman, G. L. (2001). A default mode of brain function. *Proceedings of the National Academy of Sciences, USA, 98*, 676–682.

Rajah, M. N., Kromas, M., Han, J. E., & Pruessner, J. C. (2010). Group differences in anterior hippocampal volume and in the retrieval of spatial and temporal context memory in healthy young versus old adults. *Neuropsychologia, 48*, 4020–4030.

Ranganath, C. (2010). A unified framework for the functional organization of the medial temporal lobes and the phenomenology of episodic memory. *Hippocampus, 20*, 1263–1290.

Raz, N., Gunning, F. M., Head, D., Dupuis, J. H., McQuain, J., Briggs et al. (1997). Selective aging of the human cerebral cortex observed in vivo: Differential vulnerability of the prefrontal gray matter. *Cerebral Cortex, 7*, 268–282.

Raz, N., Lindenberger, U., Rodrigue, K. M., Kennedy, K. M., Head, D., Williamson, A. et al. (2005). Regional brain changes in aging healthy adults: General trends, individual differences and modifiers. *Cerebral Cortex, 15*, 1676–1689.

Richardson, M. P., Strange, B., & Dolan, R. J. (2004). Encoding of emotional memories depends on the amygdala and hippocampus and their interactions. *Nature Neuroscience, 7*, 278–285.

Roalf, D. R., Pruis, T. A., Stevens, A. A., & Janowsky, J. S. (2011). More is less: Emotion induced prefrontal cortex activity habituates in aging. *Neurobiology of Aging, 32*, 1634–1650.

Rogers, T. B., Kuiper, N. A., & Kirker, W. S. (1977). Self-reference and the encoding of personal information. *Journal of Personality and Social Psychology, 35*, 677–688.

Rosa, N. M., & Gutchess, A. H. (2011). Source memory for action in young and older adults: Self vs. close or unknown others. *Psychology and Aging, 26*, 625–30.

Rypma, B., & D'Esposito, M. (2000). Isolating the neural mechanisms of age-related changes in human working memory. *Nature Neuroscience, 3*, 509–515.

Salat, D. H., Buckner, R. L., Snyder, A. Z., Greve, D. N., Desikan, R. S. R., Busa, E., et al., 2004). Thinning of the cerebral cortex in aging. *Cerebral Cortex, 14*, 721–730.

Salat, D. H., Kaye, J. A., & Janowsky, J. S. (2001). Selective preservation and degeneration within the prefrontal cortex in aging and Alzheimer's Disease. *Archives of Neurology, 58,* 1403–1408.

Salthouse, T. A. (1996). The processing-speed theory of adult age differences in cognition. *Psychological Review, 103,* 403–428.

Salzman, C. D., & Fusi, S. (2010). Emotion, cognition, and mental state representation in amygdala and prefrontal cortex. *Annual Review of Neuroscience, 33,* 173–202.

Schacter, D. L., Osowiecki, D., Kaszniak, A. W., Kihlstrom, J. F., & Valdiserri, M. (1994). Source memory: Expending the boundaries of age-related deficits. *Psychology and Aging, 9,* 81–89.

Schaefer, A., & Philippot, P. (2005). Selective effects of emotion on the phenomenal characteristics of autobiographical memories. *Memory, 13,* 148–160.

Schlagman, S., Schulz, J., & Kvavilashvili, L. (2006). A content analysis of involuntary autobiographical memories: Examining the positivity effect in old age. *Memory, 17,* 161–175.

Shing, Y. L., Rodrigue, K. M., Kennedy, K. M., Fandakova, Y., Bodammer, N., Werkle-Bergner, M., et al. (2011). Hippocampal subfield volumes: Age, vascular risk, and correlation with associative memory. *Frontiers in Aging Neuroscience, 3,* 1–8.

Siedlecki, K. L., Salthouse, T. A., & Berish, D. E. (2005). Is there anything special about the aging of source memory? *Psychology and Aging, 20,* 19–32.

Spencer, W. D., & Raz, N. (1995). Differential effects of aging on memory for content and context: A meta-analysis. *Psychology and Aging, 10,* 527–539.

Staresina B.P., Gray J.C., & Davachi L. (2009). Event Congruency Enhances Episodic Memory Encoding through Semantic Elaboration and Relational Binding *Cerebral Cortex, 19,* 1198–120.

Steinberger, A., Payne, J. D., & Kensinger, E. A. (2011). The effect of cognitive reappraisal on the emotional memory trade-off. *Cognition & Emotion.* Advance online publication. doi:10.1080/02699931.2010.53837

St. Jacques, P. L., Bessette-Symons, B., & Cabeza, R. (2009). Functional neuroimaging studies of aging and emotion: Fronto-amygdalar difference during emotional perception and episodic memory. *Journal of the International Neuropsychological Society, 15,* 819–825.

Stuss, D. T., Gallup, G. G., & Alexander, M. P. (2001). The frontal lobes are necessary for 'theory of mind.' *Brain, 124,* 279–286.

Symons, C. S., & Johnson, B. T. (1997). The self-reference effect in memory: A meta-analysis. *Psychological Bulletin, 121,* 371–394.

Taevs, M., Dahmani, L., Zatorre, R. J., & Bohbot, V. D. (2010). Semantic elaboration in auditory and visual spatial memory. *Frontiers in Psychology.* doi: 10.3389/fpsyg.2010.00228

Talmi, D., Anderson, A. K., Riggs, L., Caplan, J. B., & Moscovitch, M. (2008). Immediate memory consequences of the effect of emotion on attention to pictures. *Learning & Memory, 15,* 172–182.

Tekcan, A. I., & Peynircioglu, Z. F. (2002). Effects of age on flashbulb memories. *Psychology and Aging, 17,* 416–422.

Tisserand, D. J., Visser, P. J., van Boxtel, M. P. J., & Jolles, J. (2000). The relation between global and limbic brain volumes on MRI and cognitive performance in healthy individuals across the age range. *Neurobiology of Aging, 21,* 569–576.

Tessitore, A., Hariri, A. R., Fera, F., Smith, W. G., Das, S., Weinberger, D. R., & Mattay, V. S. (2005). Functional changes in the activity of brain regions underlying emotion processing in the elderly. *Psychiatry Research, 139,* 9–18.

Tsukiura, T., Sekiguchi, A., Yomogida, Y., Nakagawa, S., Shigemune, Y., Kambara, T. et al. (2011). Effects of aging on hippocampal and anterior temporal activations during successful retrieval of memory for face-name associations. *Journal of Cognitive Neuroscience, 23,* 200–213.

Tulving, E. (1993). *Self-knowledge of an amnesic individual is represented abstractly.* Hillsdale, NJ: Erlbaum.

Wagner, A. D., Schacter, D. L., Rotte, M., Koutstaal, W., Maril, A., Dale, A. M., et al. (1998). Building memories: Remembering and forgetting of verbal experiences as predicted by brain activity. *Science, 281,* 1188–1191.

Waldinger, R. J., Kensinger, E. A., & Schultz, M. S. (2011). Neural activity, neural connectivity, and the processing of emotionally valenced information in older adults: Links with life satisfaction. *Cognitive, Affective, & Behavioral Neuroscience, 11,* 426–236.

Williams, L. M., Brown, K. J., Palmer, D., Liddell, B. J., Kemp, A. H., Olivieri, G., et al. (2006). The mellow years? Neural basis of improving emotional stability over age. *Journal of Neuroscience, 26,* 6422–6430.

Wolters, G., & Goudsmit, J. J. (2005). Flashbulb an event memory of September 11, 2001: Consistency, confidence, and age effects. *Psychological Reports, 96,* 605–619.

Wright, C. I., Wedig, M. M., Williams, D., Rauch, S. L., & Albert, M. S. (2006). Novel fearful faces activate the amygdala in healthy young and elderly adults. *Neurobiology of Aging, 27,* 361–374.

Wright, D. B., Gaskell, G. D., & O'Muircheartaigh, C. A. (1998). Flashbulb memory assumptions: Using national surveys to explore cognitive phenomena. *British Journal of Psychology, 89,* 103–121.

Yarmey, A. D., & Bull, M. P. (1978). Where were you when President Kennedy was assassinated? *Bulletin of the Psychonomic Society, 11,* 133–135.

Yassa, M. A., & Stark, C. E. (2011). Pattern separation in the hippocampus. *Trends in Neuroscience, 34,* 515–525.

Yoder, C. Y., & Elias, J. W. (1987). Age, affect, and memory for pictorial story sequences. *British Journal of Psychology, 78,* 545–549.

Zacks, R, & Hasher, L. (1997). Cognitive gerontology and attentional inhibition: A reply to Burke and McDowd. *Journals of Gerontology: Series B: Psychological Sciences and Social Sciences, 52,* 274–283.

Age Changes in Facial Morphology, Emotional Communication, and Age Stereotyping

Mary Lee Hummert

Abstract

Age-related changes in facial morphology may affect how others assess the emotions of older individuals. Specifically, these changes in facial structure may resemble facial expressions of negative emotions such as sadness or anger, which, in turn, can elicit trait judgments consistent with negative age stereotypes. The chapter explores the evidence for these relationships and considers their implications for intergenerational interactions, theory development, and future research.

Key Words: facial morphology, babyfaceness, facial structure, aging face, emotion communication, intergenerational interaction, age stereotypes, communication predicament of aging, age stereotypes in interaction, ecological theory, perceived age, physiognomic cues to age

Individuals rely not only on words, but also on nonverbal cues to interpret others' emotional states and to communicate their own. Often, when words and nonverbal cues send conflicting messages, people give greater credence to the nonverbal message, perhaps because they judge nonverbal communication as more spontaneous and difficult to control than verbal communication (DePaulo, 1992). Thus, the ability to interpret and communicate emotions appropriately through nonverbal modes is a key to achieving satisfactory interpersonal interactions. Facial expressions serve as the primary nonverbal mode of emotional communication (Ekman, 1993; Ekman & Friesen, 1971) and are one of the main influences on person perception (Milord, 1978). Yet, as discussed in this volume, cognitive, perceptual, and motivational changes with aging may affect older individuals' accuracy in recognizing emotions in facial expressions (see Phillips et al. Chapter 2; Stanley & Isaacowitz, Chapter 7).

This chapter takes the discussion in a different direction, considering the ways in which age-related changes in facial morphology may affect how others assess the emotions of older individuals. Specifically, these changes in facial structure may suggest to perceivers that older adults are experiencing negative emotions such as sadness or anger, emotions consistent with negative age stereotypes. In turn, these stereotypes can contribute to problematic intergenerational interactions between older individuals and family members or caregivers that reinforce and perpetuate both negative emotions and stereotypes. The chapter highlights these relationships among facial morphology, emotional expression, facial aging, and age stereotyping.

The chapter begins with an overview of research and theory on the association of facial morphology with emotions and traits in the person perception process. It then considers how facial aging maps onto facial expression of negative emotions, with attention to their association with age stereotypes and their influence on age stereotyping of older individuals. The third section examines the implications of these relationships for intergenerational interactions. Last, the chapter outlines theoretical issues and directions for future research on these topics.

Facial Expression and Structure as Cues in Person Perception

The ways in which facial expressions and structure influence the person perception process have long been of interest to psychologists. One line of research has considered the effects of facial expressions of specific emotions on perceivers' judgments of targets' personality traits (Hess, Blairy, & Kleck, 2000; Keating et al., 1981; Montepare & Dobish, 2003; Secord, 1958). Results have demonstrated that people tend to assume that transitory facial expressions of emotions such as happiness, fear, and anger are indicative of corresponding, stable personality traits. For example, Montepare and Dobish (2003) found that participants evaluated targets with angry expressions as high on dominance but low on affiliation traits. However, participants who evaluated the same targets displaying different emotional expressions came to different conclusions about their personality traits: when displaying happy expressions, targets were judged as high in both dominance and affiliation; and when they looked sad, they were rated as low in dominance.

Another prominent line of research has examined perceivers' associations between the structure of facial features and personality traits, with emphasis on the impact of facial maturity on perceptions of individuals (Berry & McArthur, 1985, 1986). This line of research revealed that adults whose facial features were more consistent with those of a baby's face (i.e., large, round eyes; wide, small nose; small ears; large forehead with low vertical placement of features on the face; rounded cranium, etc.) were associated with greater warmth, kindness, and honesty than were adults with more mature facial features (Berry & McArthur, 1985, 1986; Zebrowitz, Fellous, Mignault, & Andreoletti, 2003; Zebrowitz & Montepare, 1992). At the same time, those with babyfaced features were viewed as less dominant and strong than were those with more mature features (Zebrowitz, 1996). These results have been consistent across a variety of stimuli, including line drawings of craniofacial profiles, schematics of faces, computer-generated faces, and photographs of individuals, even when controlling for facial attractiveness (Berry & McArthur, 1986; Zebrowitz, 1996; Zebrowitz et al., 2003).

Intersection of Facial Maturity and Emotional Expression

Recently, these two lines of research have come together as scholars investigated the interaction of facial structure and emotional expression on trait assessment (Adams, Nelson, Soto, Hess, & Kleck, 2012; Marsh, Adams, & Kleck, 2005; Sacco & Hugenberg, 2009; Said, Sebe, & Todorov, 2009; Zebrowitz, Kikuchi, & Fellous, 2007, 2010). Marsh, Adams, and Kleck (2005) showed, for example, that facial expressions of fear and anger were rated as expected on dominance (low for fear, high for anger), physical characteristics of babyfaced and mature faces (more babyfaced for fear, more mature for anger), and traits associated with babyfaceness such as dependence and weakness (high for fear, low for anger). Sacco and Hugenberg (2009) demonstrated that digital manipulation of facial features to reflect variations in facial maturity affected identification of emotional expressions. Manipulations that increased babyfaced characteristics (e.g., enlarging eyes, rounding the face) enhanced identification of fearful expressions, whereas manipulations to increase facial maturity (reducing eye size, narrowing the face) enhanced identification of angry expressions.

Of special relevance to perceptions of older faces, similar results have emerged in judgments of emotionally neutral faces (Adams et al., 2012; Said et al., 2009; Zebrowitz et al., 2010). Notably, two of these studies (Said et al., 2009; Zebrowitz et al., 2010) included objective measures of emotional expression through the use of computer networks trained to identify structural components of facial expressions of emotions. Both found that the objective measures of emotional expression in the neutral faces were related to participants' trait judgments.

Theoretical Perspectives

Two theoretical explanations have been advanced to account for the relationships among facial structure, emotional expressions, and trait judgments. The first is ecological, suggesting that humans' association of the physical characteristics of a baby's face with greater affiliation and less dominance is adaptive because it facilitates the approach behaviors necessary to preserve the species through care for infants (McArthur & Baron, 1983; Zebrowitz, 1996, 2006). A corollary is that the documented preference for attractive over unattractive faces has an evolutionary basis by functioning to preserve the quality of the gene pool (Zebrowitz et al., 2010). Similarly, according to ecological theory, the association of the emotional expression of anger with greater dominance is adaptive because it serves a protective function (Marsh, Ambady, & Kleck, 2005). Further evidence comes from the correspondence between babyfaced characteristics and emotional expressions associated with affiliation on the one hand and, on the other, greater facial maturity and emotional expressions associated with dominance (Marsh, Adams, et al., 2005; Sacco & Hugenberg, 2009; Zebrowitz et al., 2003, 2007, 2010).

The second theoretical explanation is that these judgments reflect social stereotypes. For instance, Hess, Adams, Grammer, and Kleck (2009) asked participants to judge the gender of androgynous computer-generated faces expressing anger, fear, or happiness. Results showed that participants associated anger with masculinity and fear and happiness with femininity, consistent with gender stereotypes.

Yet it is difficult to establish which theoretical perspective has more explanatory power because the results that Hess, Adams, Grammer, and Kleck (2009) attribute to gender stereotypes could also be attributed to structural differences in the adult male and female face (Hess, Adams, & Kleck, 2009). In comparison to adult female faces, adult male faces have features that indicate greater facial maturity and are associated with dominance; female faces, in contrast, have more characteristics of a babyface and are associated with affiliation (Brown & Perrett, 1993; Zebrowitz & Collins, 1997).

Recent research suggests that these theoretical perspectives describe processes that operate jointly to influence the person perception process. Hess, Thibault, Adams, and Kleck (2010) were able to remove the effects of gender-related facial structure on judgments of emotions and traits using computer-generated images of a fictional community of aliens. However, they were only able to do so by disassociating gender-related social roles with physical signals to gender. Considering racial stereotypes, Zebrowitz et al. (2010) examined the role of facial structure in judgments of white, black, and Korean targets photographed with neutral emotional expressions. This research revealed that structural resemblance to emotions in the neutral faces served to mediate and suppress "stereotypes of social categories that differ in their resemblance to emotion expressions" (p. 187). For instance, although the white participants judged black targets as more dangerous and less likeable than white targets, the greater structural resemblance of black faces to happy expressions and their lesser resemblance to angry expressions partially suppressed these trait assessments. Together, the results of these two studies imply that, in everyday interaction, facial structure and social stereotypes are jointly implicated in social judgments. This conclusion provides a theoretical foundation for understanding the roles of facial aging, emotional expression, and age stereotypes in judgments of older adults (Hummert, 1999, 2011; Montepare & Zebrowitz, 2002).

The Aging Face, Facial Expression of Emotions, and Age Stereotyping

The aging process involves physical changes to the face just as it does to other parts of the body, with the most noticeable changes occurring to the skin. As aging progresses, the deep cutaneous layers of the skin lose collagen and ligaments of the facial musculature become more lax (Chauhan, Warner, & Adamson, 2012; Henry, Pierard-Franchimont, Cauwenbergh, & Pierard, 1997). The structure of the skull also changes, with bone thinning and contraction leading to enlargement of the eye socket and shortening of the jaw (Farkas et al., 2004; Shaw et al., 2011). These changes underlie the thin lips, wrinkles (e.g., crow's feet, frown lines, laugh lines, etc.), and sagging skin around the eyes, mouth, jowls, and neck of the aging face, as well as contribute to hollows around eyes and in cheeks. The top layer of the skin also thins with age and becomes more fragile. Combined with exposure to sun and other environmental factors over the lifetime, this contributes to a blotchy complexion marked by heavily pigmented areas or age spots (Goyarts, Muizzuddin, Maes, & Giacomoni, 2007). Unlike collagen and bone, cartilage continues to grow throughout the lifespan so that the nose and ears may increase in size with age (Sforza, Grandi, De Menezes, Tartaglia, & Ferrario, 2010). Although hair on the head may thin with age and lose pigment (become gray), hair on the face may increase and coarsen, especially in the eyebrows, nose, and ears (Gross, 2007).

Such age-related changes have an impact on judgments of babyfaceness and attractiveness. Zebrowitz, Olson, and Hoffman (1993) asked young adult participants to evaluate photographs of the same individuals taken during childhood, puberty, adolescence, their thirties, and their fifties. Results showed that the individuals were judged as both less babyfaced and less attractive over time. Using a cross-sectional design and including photographs of individuals older than 64, Ebner (2008) also found that photographs of the older adults were judged as less attractive than those of adults aged 18–32.

Facial aging—particularly as it affects the skin, eye area, and neck—also appears to be a primary factor influencing age judgments of older men and women (Aznar-Casanova, Torro-Alves, & Fukusima, 2010; Chauhan et al., 2012; Gross, 2007; Hummert, 1994; Hummert, Garstka, & Shaner,

1997; Hummert, Gartska, Zhang, & Slegers, 2013). For example, Chauhan et al. (2012) found that age estimates of women who had undergone cosmetic surgery decreased by an average of 7.2 years from the presurgery estimates, with the greatest decrease found for women who had surgery on both the upper and lower eye areas in addition to a face and neck lift. Other research on perceived age suggests that the surgical reduction in the number and depth of wrinkles contributed to the lower postsurgery age estimates (Aznar-Casanova et al., 2010).

Age changes in facial morphology are influenced not only by genetic factors, but also by environmental factors and other individual differences (Rexbye et al., 2006). As a result, perceived age often differs from a person's chronological age. Hummert et al. (1997) asked young, middle-aged, and older participants to sort photographs of older men and women aged 60–95 into five age groups: Younger than 60, 60–69, 70–79, 80–89, and 90 and older. The resulting groupings included several individuals whose perceived age, as judged by participants in all age groups, was younger or older than their chronological age, at times by a decade or more.

Voelkle, Ebner, Lindenberger, and Riedinger (2012) provide further evidence that age-related changes to the face contribute to the disparity between perceived age and chronological age, but their results also show that perceiver age plays a role in such judgments. They collected perceived age judgments of the 171 men and women in the *FACES Lifespan Database of Facial Expressions* (Ebner, Riediger, & Lindenberger, 2010). The photos included individuals who were young (19–31 years), middle-aged (39–55 years), and older (69–80 years), and age judgments were provided by participants from the same three age groups. Results indicated that the accuracy of the perceived age judgments (defined as the absolute difference between the perceived and chronological age) decreased as the age of the face in the photo increased, but that the strength of this effect differed across the three participant age groups. Young participants, in particular, were significantly more accurate in judging the age of their peers than of the middle-aged and older individuals in the photos.

Voelkle et al. (2012) also analyzed the bias in the perceived age judgments by considering the direction of their difference from the individual's chronological age. In general, participants overestimated the age of the younger faces and underestimated the age of the older faces. However, young and older participants were less biased in judging the age of their peers than in judging the age of the faces of those at the opposite end of the lifespan (i.e., young faces for older participants and older faces for young participants). Together, these results are consistent with the well-documented own-age bias in face recognition (Rhodes & Anastasi, 2012), suggesting that developmental and in-group/out-group processes are factors in the relationship between age-related changes to facial morphology and social perceptions.

Morphology of the Aging Face and Emotional Expression

Just as age-related changes in facial morphology affect perceived age judgments of older individuals, they can also affect interpretations of the emotion in their facial expressions. Some changes can result in facial features that resemble negative emotional expressions (Ekman, Friesen, & Tomkins, 1971; Hess, Adams, Simard, Stevenson, & Kleck, 2012; Hummert et al., 2013; Malatesta, Fiore, & Messina, 1987). The loss of collagen and elasticity that leads to drooping eyelids, a furrowed and lower brow, sagging jaw line, deep wrinkles from the nose to the chin, and thin lips could mean that the older face in repose mimics the down-turned mouth and hooded eyes associated with the facial expression of anger (Ekman & Friesen, 1978). Several of these elements are associated with facial expressions of other negative emotions such as sadness or distrust (Ekman & Friesen, 1978). In contrast, these age-related changes to the face show less relationship to a happy expression, since it requires an upward curve of the mouth and raising of the musculature in the cheeks. Ebner (2008), for example, found that young and older raters were twice as likely to assign a sad mood over a neutral mood to older faces as to younger ones, whereas they were one and a half times as likely to assign a happy mood over a neutral mood to young faces as to older ones.

Other research indicates that the aging of the face may make it more difficult to assess the emotion in facial expressions of older individuals than of younger individuals, even in judgments of the emotion in young and old faces with computer-generated, identical emotional expressions (Hess et al., 2012). In two studies using the *FACES* database (Ebner et al., 2010; Riediger, Voelkle, Ebner, & Lindenberger, 2011), young, middle-aged, and older participants judged the emotional expressions of young, middle-aged, and older individuals photographed in six poses: neutral, angry, disgusted, fearful, happy, and sad. Ebner et al. asked participants to choose the one emotion that best characterized the facial expressions of the individuals in the photos. With the exception of happiness and fear, participants were less able to identify correctly the emotions in facial expressions of the older adults than of the other two age groups.

Riediger et al. (2011) allowed participants to select and rate the intensity of all the emotions they saw in each individual's facial expression. They found that participants saw more than one emotion in the majority of the facial expressions of targets from all three age groups, but the number of emotions identified increased with the age of the person in the photograph. These results support the conclusion advanced by Hess et al. (2012) that the wrinkles in older faces reduce the clarity of the emotion in older individuals' facial expressions.

As with perceived age judgments, however, interpretation of the emotion in the facial expressions of the older targets varied with participant age (Riediger et al., 2011). Older and middle-aged participants saw fewer additional emotions in the neutral, happy, sad, and angry facial expressions of older targets than did the young participants. They also saw less sadness and anger in facial expressions of those emotions by older individuals than did the young participants. These results are consistent with the own-age bias in facial perception noted earlier and suggest an in-group/out-group effect, in that the older participants were better able to discriminate among the emotions in the facial expressions of their peers. At the same time, the results implicate developmental processes in two ways: (1) middle-aged participants were also better able than young participants to discriminate among the emotional expressions of the older targets, albeit not as well as the older participants; and (2) older participants saw less intensity in the facial expressions of negative emotions of their peers (i.e., viewed those expressions as more positive) than did the young participants, reflecting the age-related increase in preference for positive emotions predicted by socioemotional selectivity theory (Carstensen, 1992; Carstensen & Mikels, 2005).

INDIVIDUAL DIFFERENCES IN FACIAL AGING AND EMOTIONAL EXPRESSION

The extent to which some changes to the aging face reflect cumulative effects of preferred emotional expressions over time is a subject of debate. Malatesta et al. (1987) asked fourteen older women and men to complete a personality scale indicating which of ten fundamental emotions the person experienced most often. These individuals were also photographed displaying four emotions (anger, happiness, fear, sadness) and a neutral expression. Subsequently young adult coders selected which of ten emotions was displayed in each photo. Analysis of the misattributions of the coders revealed that several (anger, guilt, sadness, and fear) were significantly correlated with the emotions identified by the older individuals in the personality test as ones they most frequently experience. Of particular interest were the correlations that occurred for misattributions to the neutral facial expressions. At the same time, Malatesta et al. acknowledged that this study cannot rule out the possibility that the results reflect general age-related changes in facial structure rather than traces of long-term facial expressions.

Recent research on the influence of environmental factors in facial aging illustrates the complexity of the issues. Rexbye et al. (2006) asked nurses to examine photographs of elderly participants in the Danish Twins Registry and to judge the age of each individual twin. Because this study used twins as the targets, genetic influences on the perceived age differences were controlled. The research team then used demographic, personal habit, and psychological measures from the study's longitudinal database as predictors of the age judgments. Results indicated that smoking, sun exposure (measured by occupation), and low body mass index were significant predictors of older perceived age for men, whereas lower social class and low body mass index were significant predictors for women. The authors discussed these in terms of their impact on the development of wrinkles, which Aznar-Casanova et al. (2010) confirmed have an influence on perceived age judgments. Although depressive symptoms approached significance as a predictor of older perceived age for women, these results provide evidence that there are many factors besides preferred emotional expressions that can affect the extent and nature of facial aging.

Perceived Age and Emotion as Influences in the Stereotyping Process

The correspondence between facial features signaling advanced age and facial expression of negative emotions may account for associations between perceived age of targets and positive or negative age stereotyping of those targets (Hummert, 1994; Hummert et al., 1997; Montepare & Zebrowitz, 2002). As shown in Table 4.1, age stereotypes are multidimensional and vary in valence consistent with the traits associated with subtypes (Brewer,

Table 4.1. Age stereotype subcategories

Valence	Stereotype Label	Trait Set
Positive	*Golden Ager*	Lively, adventurous, alert, active, sociable
		Witty, independent, well-informed, skilled
		Productive, successful, capable, volunteer
		Well-traveled, future-oriented, fun-loving, happy
		Curious, healthy, sexual, self-accepting, health-conscious, courageous, interesting
	Perfect Grandparent	Kind, loving, family-oriented, generous
		Grateful, supportive, understanding, wise
		Trustworthy, intelligent, knowledgeable
	John Wayne Conservative	Patriotic, religious, nostalgic, reminiscent
		Retired, conservative, emotional, mellow
		Determined, proud
Negative	*Despondent*	Depressed, sad, hopeless, afraid, neglected, lonely
	Shrew/Curmudgeon	Complaining, ill-tempered, bitter, prejudiced,
		Demanding, inflexible, selfish, jealous, stubborn, nosy
	Severely Impaired	Slow-thinking, incompetent, feeble, incoherent, inarticulate, senile

From Hummert et al., 1994. Stereotype traits from three positive and three negative subcategories shared by young, middle-aged, and older adult participants in Hummert et al. (1994) and used in Hummert et al. (1997).

Dull, & Lui, 1981; Hummert, Garstka, Shaner, & Strahm, 1994; Schmidt & Boland, 1986; see review in Hummert, 2011). Hummert et al. (1997) asked young, middle-aged, and older participants to pair eighteen photographs of older men and women with one of the six sets of traits (without stereotype labels) presented in Table 4.1 or with a "miscellaneous" category. Half of the participants received photographs of smiling individuals and half photographs of the same individuals with a neutral facial expression. Six photos (three men and three women) in each set were judged as young-old (60s), six as middle-old (70s), and six as old-old (80 and older) in an initial study. Results supported the hypothesis that photographs of individuals with older facial features and neutral facial expressions would be paired more often with negative age stereotypes than would individuals with younger facial features and smiling expressions. These general patterns were similar across participant age groups, with one exception: older participants selected more negative stereotypes for the photos of old-old

individuals than did the young and middle-aged participants.

Examination of the traits defining these subtypes in Table 4.1 reveals that, with the exception of the Severely Impaired subtype, all include traits that directly or indirectly map onto emotions. Hummert and colleagues conducted two studies to further explore the relationships among facial cues to age, perceptions of negative emotions, and age stereotyping (Hummert et al., 2013). In the first study, two groups of young adult participants rated the eighteen neutral expression photographs from Hummert et al. (1997) on their expression of twelve emotions (e.g., anger, happiness, fear, interest, sadness, etc.) or on facial features associated with physiognomic age (see Table 4.2). A third group selected which of the six sets of stereotype traits in Table 4.1 best fit the individual in each photo. Regression analyses indicated that older physiognomic features significantly predicted higher ratings of negative emotions and selection of negative stereotypes for the photographs. Furthermore, the emotion ratings

Table 4.2. Physiognomic cues to age scale

Skin		
	Color	**Pale**–Rosy
	Texture	**Wrinkled**–Smooth
	Tone	Firm–**Loose**
	Complexion	Clear–**Spotty/blotchy**
Features		
	Cheeks	Full–**Sunken**
	Eyelids	**Droopy**–Firm
	Jawline	**Sagging**–Firm
	Neck	**Loose skin**–Firm skin

From Hummert et al., 2013. Seven-point semantic differential scale. Confirmatory factor analysis of fourteen items identified the eight items in the table as a unidimensional measure of physiognomic age. Anchors in bold indicate older physiognomic age. Items were recoded so that higher values on the composite measure indicated older physiognomic age.

partially mediated the effect of physiognomic age on stereotype selection, reducing its effect significantly but not eliminating it.

To examine whether older participants would judge the age cues and emotions similarly to young participants, the second study included both young and older participants, each of whom engaged in all three judgment tasks of the eighteen photographs, with task order counterbalanced within age group. These data were analyzed using multilevel modeling procedures with photographs as a repeated factor nested within rater. Again, emotion ratings partially mediated but did not eliminate the predictive effects of older physiognomic features on selection of negative age stereotypes. Tests of the equivalence of the hypothesized model for judgments of young and older participants confirmed their similarity, suggesting that unconscious associations between facial markers of age and negative emotions may be a factor in negative age stereotyping for older as well as younger individuals.

The Role of Facial Aging, Emotional Expressions, and Age Stereotypes in Intergenerational Interaction

The relationships identified between physiognomic cues to age, facial expressions of negative emotion, and activation of negative age stereotypes have implications for intergenerational interactions. Ecological theory regarding the relationship of facial morphology and facial expression to person perception argues that these relationships have an adaptive communicative function for humans. Although the relationship between facial maturity and angry expressions to perception of dominance is well-documented, Marsh, Ambady, et al. (2005) demonstrated that these factors can have behavioral effects as well: participants' muscular responses indicated that viewing angry faces triggered avoidance reactions whereas viewing fearful expressions triggered approach reactions. Although such responses may be reflexive, they suggest that higher order behavioral effects on perceiver responses to facial morphology and emotional expression in interaction also occur. Research and theory on intergenerational communication support this conclusion.

The *communication predicament of aging* (CPA) model (Ryan, Giles, Bartolucci, & Henwood, 1986) introduced the hypothesis that age cues could affect the process of intergenerational communication (Giles & Gasiorek, 2011; Hummert, Garstka, Ryan, & Bonnesen, 2004). The CPA is grounded in *communication accommodation theory* (Giles, Coupland, & Coupland, 1991), which posits that, in most cases, people want to be effective communicators and to adapt appropriately to the communication needs of their partners. The CPA model outlines how that positive goal can create a negative feedback cycle in interactions between younger and older people, beginning when the physical cues to age activate the younger person's negative age stereotypes and associated beliefs about age-related declines in cognitive or perceptual skills that affect communication. By adapting or overaccommodating his or her communication to those presumed declines, perhaps by speaking more loudly or using simpler words or sentence structure than normal, the younger person may adopt a speech style that has been variously termed patronizing talk, elderspeak, or, in its extreme form, secondary babytalk (Caporael, 1981; Hummert, 1999; Hummert et al., 2004; Kemper & Harden, 1999). The danger in such well-meaning overaccommodations to negative age stereotypes, according to the CPA model, is that they can contribute to declines in the psychological and physical health of older people (Baltes & Wahl, 1996; Edwards & Noller, 1998; O'Connor & Rigby, 1996; Williams, Herman, Gajewski, & Wilson, 2009). For younger people, such interactions lead to avoidance of intergenerational interaction and reinforcement of negative age stereotypes (Giles & Gasiorek, 2011).

Facial Cues to Age and the CPA Model

The negative feedback cycle outlined in the CPA model can be initiated by a variety of contextual and physical cues to age, including the age-related changes to the face (e.g., appearing to be in one's 80s or older) that are associated with negative emotions and age stereotypes. A study by Hummert, Shaner, Garstka, and Henry (1998) examined the role of facial morphology and emotional expression in initiating the CPA feedback cycle or an alternative, positive cycle outlined in the *age stereotypes in interaction* (ASI) model (Giles & Gasiorek, 2011; Hummert, 1999; Hummert et al., 2004). The ASI model proposes that a positive feedback cycle can be facilitated when the age cues (e.g., appearing to be in one's 60s) activate positive rather than negative age stereotypes. The resulting messages would constitute an affirming style of mutual respect characterized by the paralinguistic and linguistic features of standard adult-to-adult communication. In addition, the ASI model introduced a developmental perspective by considering the role of communicator age in initiating the negative feedback cycle of the CPA model or the alternative, positive feedback cycle. Drawing on research demonstrating that the tendency to associate characteristics of negative age stereotypes with declining communication skills decreases from young to middle-aged to older individuals, the ASI model predicts that the positive feedback cycle is most likely to occur when older persons interact with their age peers and least likely to occur when young persons communicate with older persons (Hummert, 1999; Hummert et al., 2004).

To test these predictions, young, middle-aged, and older participants viewed photographs of older men or women who had been associated with either the Despondent or Golden Ager stereotypes (see Table 4.1) in an earlier study (Hummert et al., 1997). The photographs were presented on a television monitor alone and then with the relevant stereotype traits. First, participants rated their beliefs about how they would speak to the targets on nine Likert scales (e.g., fast, hesitant, loud, understandable, wavering, etc.). Then they rated how they believed the target's voice would sound on the same dimensions as an indirect way to assess their perceptions of the target's age. Subsequently, participants engaged in a role-playing task in which they provided advice to the target, and these advice messages were audiotaped for analysis.

Results supported the predictions of the ASI model. The advice messages conformed to the characteristics of patronizing talk or elderspeak significantly more often when directed to targets whose photograph and traits were associated with the Despondent stereotype than with the Golden Ager stereotype. Conversely, advice messages to Golden Ager targets fit the characteristics of the affirming, adult-to-adult style more often than did messages to Despondent targets, as predicted. Thus, although the targets with features consistent with a negative age stereotype elicited from participants the overaccommodations predicted by the CPA model, the targets with features corresponding to a positive age stereotype elicited instead the adult-to-adult style predicted by the ASI model.

Furthermore, these effects varied with participant age: Young and middle-aged participants produced a higher proportion of messages with the characteristics of elderspeak to the Despondent than to the Golden Ager and a higher proportion of such messages in general than did older participants. Older participants, in contrast, delivered a higher proportion of affirming messages to both targets (65 percent of messages to the Despondent target and 75 percent to the Golden Ager target) than did young and middle-aged participants. An additional difference emerged in the characteristics of elderspeak messages from young and middle-aged participants. In comparison to elderspeak messages from young participants, those from middle-aged participants were more likely to be nurturing as opposed to directive and controlling, suggesting an age-related increase in communication competence and a move toward an affirming style.

Contributions of Perceived Age Versus Facial Expression in Interaction

Two facts about the photographs used for the targets in Hummert et al. (1998) are relevant to the topic of this chapter. First, the photographs used to represent the Despondent stereotype were of men and women with a neutral facial expression rather than a sad expression, whereas the photographs used to represent the Golden Ager stereotype were of men and women who were smiling. Second, the men and women in the Despondent photographs were judged as older (in their 80s) than the men and women in the Golden Ager photographs (60s) in the earlier research (Hummert et al., 1997). Perceived age of the targets was measured indirectly in Hummert et al. (1998) by asking participants to rate each target's voice on several qualities associated with the aging voice. Analysis confirmed that participants perceived similar age differences in the photographs as did participants who directly evaluated their age in the earlier study: they indicated that the voice of the Despondent target would sound older (less loud and fast, but more wavering and thin) than that of the Golden Ager. Thus, both perceived age and facial expression were presumably factors evaluated by these participants, but the photographs selected do not enable identification of whether one factor played a stronger role than the other.

Although perceived age and facial expression were confounded in the photographs of the older targets used in Hummert et al. (1998), other research suggests that a positive facial expression can function in two ways to reduce the activation of negative age stereotypes. First, it may lower perceived age: Ebner et al. (2010) and Voelkle et al. (2012) found that young, middle-aged, and older participants provided younger age estimates for older targets with a happy facial expression in comparison to facial expressions of other emotions. Second, it may reduce the association between perceived age and negative age stereotypes: Hummert et al. (1997) reported that young, middle-aged, and older participants were less likely to select negative stereotypes for individuals perceived to be 80 and older when those individuals were smiling than when they had a neutral facial expression, although they still associated the oldest individuals with significantly more negative age stereotypes than individuals perceived to be in their 60s.

Conclusion

The research evidence that links age-related changes to facial structure, facial expressions of negative emotions, perceived age, and age stereotyping is strong. The behavioral implications of these relationships find support in theory and research on intergenerational interaction. Together, these lines of research create challenges for social psychologists concerned with theory development, as well as with the promotion of positive emotional experiences for older individuals and their communication partners in day-to-day interactions.

Implications for Theory

As noted earlier, recent research on the relationship of facial maturity (as assessed by babyfaceness) and emotional expression to trait judgments suggests that ecological influences and social stereotypes operate jointly in the person perception process. However, the age of the individual who is the focus of judgment may affect the nature of the

ecological influences and their relationship to social stereotypes (Zebrowitz et al., 1993, 2003), and the age of the perceiver may affect the nature of the resulting social judgments (Hummert et al., 1997, 1998; Riediger et al., 2011; Voelkle et al., 2012).

Zebrowitz et al. (2003) used neural networks to collect objective measures of babyfaceness and facial anomaly of younger and older adult faces. Facial anomaly refers to structure that differs from the average symmetric face and constitutes a conceptualization of the *good gene* aspect of ecological theory. The objective measures indicated that older faces were structurally more babyfaced and anomalous than young faces.

Additional analyses assessed the ability of the objective measures to account for trait judgments of the older and younger adult faces by human judges. The judges' evaluations were consistent with age stereotypes of older adults as less attractive, sociable, warm, healthy, and strong, but more shrewd (perhaps analogous to wise) than young adults. Babyfaceness was a significant mediator only of the judges' evaluation of older faces as less strong than young faces, whereas anomaly mediated the judges' evaluation of older faces as less sociable and warm than young faces and partially mediated their judgment of the older faces as less attractive than the young faces. However, neither objective measure mediated judgments of older adults as less healthy, but shrewder than young adults. Thus, although both ecological influences and social stereotypes were evident in the judgments about young and old targets, facial anomaly or deviation from the average structure was a more potent ecological factor than babyfaceness.

Although Zebrowitz et al. (2003) controlled for effects of smiling in the mediation analyses, the fact that the objective measure of anomaly mediated judgments of sociability and warmth suggests some correspondence between anomalous structures and facial expressions of negative emotions. Research comparing objective measures of anomaly and negative emotional expression, as well as their ability to account for stereotypical evaluations of older and younger individuals, could clarify the nature of the ecological influences in the age stereotyping process.

An additional implication for theory, supported by evidence from the use of objective measures of facial structure, is that ecological influences may affect judgments of older faces implicitly, that is, outside conscious awareness (Greenwald & Banaji, 1995). Research on implicit age attitudes using the Implicit Association Test (IAT; Greenwald,

McGhee, & Schwartz, 1998) is consistent with that view: the IAT involved responses to *faces* of younger and older individuals, not to verbal age descriptors (Hummert, Garstka, O'Brien, Greenwald, & Mellott, 2002). Results confirmed implicit attitudes favoring young over older individuals that were similar in magnitude for young, middle-aged, and older participants.

Although theory regarding the effects of facial aging and emotional expression has tended to emphasize the age of the target individual, research studies have demonstrated that the age of the perceiver can also affect social judgments (Hummert et al., 1997, 1998; Riediger et al., 2011; Voelkle et al., 2012). In general, results suggest that perceivers' judgments reflect in-group/out-group and developmental processes, in addition to ecological influences. For instance, the observed own-age bias, whereby young and older individuals are better able to identify the emotion in facial expressions of their age peers than of those in the other age group, is consistent with in-group/out-group processes (Rhodes & Anastasi, 2012; Riediger et al., 2011). That is, greater familiarity and interaction with those in one's own age group than in other age groups results in greater discrimination about the characteristics of in-group members in comparison to out-group members, exemplifying the complexity-extremity effect identified by Linville (1982).

Yet in-group/out-group processes cannot account entirely for age group differences, such as an ability to identify emotional expressions of older adults that increases from young to middle-aged to older participants or an age-related increase in the tendency to see greater positive components of negative emotional expressions (Riediger et al., 2011). Similarly, in-group/out-group processes cannot explain why the incidence and form of elderspeak to older targets differs for young, middle-aged, and older individuals (Hummert et al., 1998). Instead, these results suggest that developmental processes serve to moderate in-group/out-group processes as individuals integrate lifespan experiences into age-related person perception schemas so that those schemas become richer and more complex, although not necessarily more positive, across the adult age range (Heckhausen, Dixon, & Baltes, 1989; Hummert et al., 1994; Hummert, 1999). When emotion is the focus of judgment, a developmental increase in a preference for positive emotional experiences and relationships also contributes to observed differences in the judgments of young, middle-aged, and older individuals (Carstensen, 1992; Carstensen &

Mikels, 2005). Both in-group/out-group and developmental processes remain to be integrated into ecological theory about the relationship between age-related changes to facial morphology, emotional expressions, and social judgments.

Directions for Future Research

Three areas of investigation will expand scientific knowledge of the mechanisms underlying the relationship of facial aging and emotional expressions to age stereotyping and increase understanding of their effects on intergenerational interactions. First, the research using neural networks to gather objective measures of facial structure suggests that the human brain might use similar algorithms to identify meaningful facial structures. For example, Zebrowitz, Luevano, Bronstad, and Aharon (2009) found that functional magnetic resonance imaging (fMRI) of participants revealed that the same neural substrates were activated when viewing babies and babyfaced adult men. Other researchers have used fMRI to identify neural markers of processing facial expressions of emotion (Adolphs, 2002; Adolphs, Damasio, Tranel, & Damasio, 1996; Sprengelmeyer, Rausch, Eysel, & Przuntek, 1996). The fMRI technology could be applied to investigate (1) the patterns of neural activation in processing old and young faces and (2) the correspondence between the patterns of neural activation for old faces and for facial expressions of negative emotions. Such studies would also have implications for our understanding of implicit processes in person perception and age stereotyping.

Second, research on facial structure, facial expression, and trait judgments has primarily used photographs of faces or other static representations of faces as the stimuli. Such stimuli have enabled investigators to build and test theory about facial processing in person perception, but they lack the richness of nonverbal cues available to perceivers in natural settings. Facial expressions are not static, but dynamic; and they do not occur in isolation, but are accompanied by other nonverbal cues such as vocal quality and paralanguage, gestures, and movement. Like facial morphology and expressions, such cues affect age judgments, trait assessments, and age stereotype associations (Harnsberger, Shrivastav, Brown, Rothman, & Hollien, 2008; Hummert, Mazloff, & Henry, 1999; Montepare & Zebrowitz, 1993; Montepare & Zebrowitz-McArthur, 1988; Mulac & Giles, 1996; Ryan & Capadano, 1978). Vocal qualities, in particular, not only carry information about age, but also convey emotion that could reinforce or modulate that expressed in the face (Whiteside, 1999).

The studies reviewed here have provided a strong foundation for moving toward research designs with greater ecological validity. These could be as simple as using videos that focus solely on the face and head rather than photographs or as complex as having participants engage in interactions with a confederate (Hemmesch, Tickle-Degnen, & Zebrowitz, 2009; Sparko & Zebrowitz, 2011; Tickle-Degnen, Zebrowitz, & Ma, 2011). Such studies are essential for exploring further the effects of nonverbal cues to age and emotion on age stereotyping and behavioral choices in intergenerational interactions, as well as for identifying and testing effective strategies that older individuals can use to promote positive emotional experiences and mitigate negative age stereotyping (Ryan, Kennaley, Pratt, & Schumovich, 2000; Hummert et al., 2004).

Third, although researchers acknowledge the limitations of their conclusions when participants and targets are primarily white individuals of European descent (Ebner et al., 2010; Zebrowitz et al., 2003), only a few studies have considered race/ethnicity in investigating the relationship of facial morphology and facial expression to trait judgments (Tickle-Degnen et al., 2011; Zebrowitz et al., 2010). Furthermore, only one of those studies has included older individuals as targets of judgment (Tickle-Degnen et al., 2011). Although the evidence is strong that facial expressions of the basic emotions are interpreted similarly across cultures (Ekman, 1994), research has not established that the intersection of age-related changes in facial morphology and emotional expressions is also interpreted similarly across cultures. Future research should address this gap in the literature, systematically investigating the role of culture, race/ethnicity, and age by increasing the diversity of the targets of evaluation as well as of the study participants.

Closing Comment

The adage "beauty is only skin deep" serves to remind us that the face presented to the world is not always an accurate assessment of an individual's characteristics. However, the face, and the emotion it expresses, is a primary nonverbal cue in first impressions (Ekman, 1993; Ekman & Friesen, 1971; Milord, 1978). Overgeneralizations about the characteristics of any individual based solely on facial features are likely to be inaccurate. The research reviewed here supports the conclusion that such inaccuracies in perceptions of older individuals are influenced by age-related changes in facial morphology that resemble negative emotional expressions and elicit overgeneralizations to negative age stereotypes. The age-related changes to the face vary across individuals, reflecting diversity in genetic, demographic, and environmental influences. For all, however, these changes are ultimately irreversible, a fact acknowledged even by plastic surgeons (Chauhan et al., 2012). Further research into the psychological mechanisms leading to these overgeneralizations, attention to the ecological validity of study designs, and increases in the diversity of targets and participants will enhance understanding of the role of nonverbal cues to age and emotion in age stereotyping. Such understanding is essential to inform strategies for reducing the potential negative effects of age stereotyping on intergenerational interactions and increasing the emotional satisfaction and psychological well-being of older adults and their communication partners.

References

Adams, R. B., Nelson, A. J., Soto, J. A., Hess, U., & Kleck, R. E. (2012). Emotion in the neutral face: A mechanism for impression formation? *Cognition and Emotion, 26*(3), 431–441.

Adolphs, R. (2002). Neural systems for recognizing emotions. *Current Opinions in Neurobiology, 12*, 169–177.

Adolphs R., Damasio, H., Tranel, D., & Damasio, A. R. (1996). Cortical systems for the recognition of emotions in facial expressions. *Journal of Neuroscience, 16*, 7678–7687.

Aznar-Casanova, J., Torro-Alves, N., & Fukusima, S. (2010). How much older do you get when a wrinkle appears on your face? Modifying age estimates by number of wrinkles. *Aging, Neuropsychology, and Cognition, 17*, 406–421.

Baltes, M. M., & Wahl, H. W. (1996). Patterns of communication in old age: The dependence-support and independence-ignore script. *Health Communication, 8*, 217–231.

Berry, D. S., & McArthur, L. Z. (1985). Some components and consequences of a babyface. *Journal of Personality and Social Psychology, 48*(2), 312–323.

Berry, D. S., & McArthur, L. Z. (1986). Perceiving character in faces: The impact of age-related craniofacial changes on social perception. *Psychological Bulletin, 100*(1), 3–18.

Brewer, M., Dull, V., & Lui, L. (1981). Perceptions of the elderly: Stereotypes as prototypes. *Journal of Personality and Social Psychology, 41*, 656–670.

Brown, E., & Perrett, D. I. (1993). What gives a face its gender? *Perception, 22*, 829–840.

Caporael, L. R. (1981). The paralanguage of caregiving: Baby talk to the institutionalized aged. *Journal of Personality and Social Psychology, 40*, 876–884.

Carstensen, L. L. (1992). Social and emotional patterns in adulthood: Support for socioemotional selectivity theory. *Psychology and Aging, 7*, 331–338.

Carstensen, L. L., & Mikels, J. A. (2005). At the intersection of emotion and cognition: Aging and the positivity effect. *Current Directions in Psychological Science, 14*, 117–121.

Chauhan, N., Warner, J. P., & Adamson, Peter A. (2012). Perceived age change after aesthetic facial surgical procedures: Quantifying outcomes of aging face surgery. *Archives of Facial Plastic Surgery, 14,* 258–262.

DePaulo, B. M. (1992). Nonverbal behavior and self-presentation. *Psychological Bulletin, 111,* 203–243.

Ebner, N. C. (2008). Age of face matters: Age-group differences in ratings of young and old faces. *Behavior Research Methods, 40,* 130–136.

Ebner, N. C., Riediger, M., & Lindenberger, U. (2010). FACES—A database of facial expressions in young, middle-aged, and older women and men: Development and validation. *Behavior Research Methods, 42,* 351–362.

Edwards, H., & Noller, P. (1998). Factors influencing caregiver-carereceiver communication and its impact on the well-being of older carereceivers. *Health Communication, 10,* 317–341.

Ekman, P. (1993). Facial expression and emotion. *American Psychologist, 48*(4), 384–392.

Ekman, P. (1994). Strong evidence for universals in facial expressions: A reply to Russell's mistaken critique. *Psychological Bulletin, 115,* 268–287.

Ekman, P., & Friesen, W. V. (1971). Constants across cultures in the face and emotion. *Journal of Personality and Social Psychology, 17,* 124–129.

Ekman, P., & Friesen, W. V. (1978). *The facial action coding system: A technique for the measurement of facial movement.* Palo Alto, CA: Consulting Psychologists Press.

Ekman, P., Friesen, W. V., & Tomkins, S. S. (1971). Facial affect scoring technique: A first validity study. *Semiotica, 3,* 37–58.

Giles, H., Coupland, N., & Coupland, J. (1991). Accommodation theory: Communication, context, and consequence. In H. Giles, J. Coupland, & N. Coupland (Eds.), *Contexts of accommodation: Developments in applied linguistics* (pp. 1–68). Cambridge: Cambridge University Press.

Giles, H., & Gasiorek, J. (2011). Intergenerational communication practices. In K. W. Schaie & S. L. Willis (Eds.), *Handbook of the psychology of aging* (7th ed., pp. 233–248). London: Academic Press.

Farkas, L. G., Eiben, O. G., Sivkov, S., Tompson, B., Katic, M. J., & Forrest, C. R. (2004. Anthropometric measurements of the facial framework in adulthood: Age-related changes in eight age categories in 600 healthy white North Americans of European ancestry from 16 to 90 years of age. *Journal of Craniofacial Surgery, 15,* 288–298.

Goyarts, E., Muizzuddin, N., Maes, D., & Giacomoni, P. (2007). Morphological changes associated with aging: Age spots and the microinflammatory model of skin aging. *Annals of the New York Academy of Sciences, 1119,* 32–39.

Greenwald, A. G., & Banaji, M. R. (1995). Implicit social cognition: Attitudes, self-esteem, and stereotypes. *Psychological Review, 102,* 4–27.

Greenwald, A. G., McGhee, D. E., & Schwartz, J. L. K. (1998). Measuring individual differences in implicit cognition: The implicit association test. *Journal of Personality and Social Psychology, 74,* 1464–1480.

Gross, T. F. (2007). Developmental changes in the perception of adult facial age. *The Journal of Genetic Psychology: Research and Theory on Human Development, 168,* 443–464.

Harnsberger, J. D., Shrivastav, R., Brown, W. S., Rothman, H., & Hollien, H. (2008). Speaking rate and fundamental frequency as speech cues to perceived age. *Journal of Voice, 22,* 58–69.

Heckhausen, J., Dixon, R. A., & Baltes, P. B. (1989). Gains and losses in development throughout adulthood as perceived by different adult age groups. *Developmental Psychology, 25,* 109–121.

Hemmesch, A. R., Tickle-Degnen, L., & Zebrowitz, L. A. (2009). The influence of facial masking and sex on older adults' impressions of individuals with Parkinson's disease. *Psychology and Aging, 24,* 542–549.

Henry, F., Pierard-Franchimont, C., Cauwenbergh, G., & Pierard, G. E. (1997). Age-related changes in facial skin contours and rheology. *Journal of the American Geriatrics Society, 45,* 220–222.

Hess, U., Adams, R. B., Grammer, K., & Kleck, R. E. (2009). Face gender and emotion expression: Are angry women more like men? *Journal of Vision, 9* (12):19, 1–8.

Hess, U., Adams, R. B., & Kleck, R. E. (2009). The categorical perception of emotions and traits. *Social Cognition, 27,* 320–326.

Hess, U., Adams, R. B., Simard, A., Stevenson, M. T., & Kleck, R. E. (2012). Smiling and sad wrinkles: Age-related changes in the face and the perception of emotions and intentions. *Journal of Experimental Social Psychology, 48,* 1377–1380.

Hess, U., Blairy, S., & Kleck, R. E. (2000). The influence of facial emotion displays, gender, and ethnicity on judgments of dominance and affiliation. *Journal of Nonverbal Behavior, 24,* 265–283.

Hess, U., Thibault, P., Adams, R. B., & Kleck, R. E. (2010). The influence of gender, social roles, and facial appearance on perceived emotionality. *European Journal of Social Psychology, 40,* 1310–1317.

Hummert, M. L. (1994). Physiognomic cues and the activation of stereotypes of the elderly in interaction. *International Journal of Aging and Human Development, 39,* 5–20.

Hummert, M. L. (1999). Age stereotyping: Social cognitive and developmental issues. In T. M. Hess & F. Blanchard-Fields (Eds.), *Social cognition and aging* (pp. 175–196). New York: Academic Press.

Hummert, M. L. (2011). Age stereotypes and aging. In K. W. Schaie & S. L. Willis (Eds.), *Handbook of the psychology of aging* (7th ed., pp. 249–262). London: Academic Press.

Hummert, M. L., Gartska, T. A., O'Brien, L. T., Greenwald, A. G., & Mellot, D. S. (2002). Using the implicit association test to measure age differences in implicit social perceptions, *Psychology and Aging, 17,* 482–495.

Hummert, M. L., Garstka, T. A., Ryan, E. B., & Bonnesen, J. L. (2004). The role of age stereotypes in interpersonal communication. In J. F. Nussbaum & J. Coupland (Eds.), *The handbook of communication and aging* (2nd ed., pp. 91–114). Mahwah, NJ: Erlbaum.

Hummert, M. L., Garstka, T. A., & Shaner, J. L. (1997). Stereotyping of older adults: The role of target facial cues and perceiver characteristics. *Psychology and Aging, 12,* 107–114.

Hummert, M. L., Garstka, T. A., Shaner, J. L., & Strahm, S. (1994). Stereotypes of the elderly held by young, middle-aged and elderly adults. *Journal of Gerontology: Psychological Sciences, 49,* P240–P249.

Hummert, M. L., Garstka, T. A., Zhang, Y. B., & Slegers, D. (2013). The role of facial cues to age and emotion in age stereotyping. Manuscript in preparation.

Hummert, M. L., Mazloff, D. C., & Henry, C. (1999). Vocal characteristics of older adults and stereotyping. *Journal of Nonverbal Behavior, 23,* 111–132.

Hummert, M. L., Shaner, J. L., Garstka, T. A., & Henry, C. (1998). Communication with older adults: The influence of age stereotypes, context, and communicator age. *Human Communication Research, 25,* 125–152.

Keating, C. F., Mazur, A., Segall, M. H., Cysneiros, P. G., Divale, W. T., Kilbride, J. E., et al. (1981). Culture and the perception of social dominance from facial expression. *Journal of Personality and Social Psychology, 40,* 615–626.

Kemper, S., & Harden, T. (1999). Experimentally disentangling what's beneficial about elderspeak from what's not. *Psychology and Aging, 14,* 656–670.

Linville, P. W. (1982). The complexity-extremity effect and age-based stereotyping. *Journal of Personality and Social Psychology, 42,* 193–211.

Malatesta, C. Z., Fiore, M. J., & Messina, J. J. (1987). Affect, personality, and facial expressive characteristics of older people. *Psychology and Aging, 2,* 64–69.

Marsh, A. A., Adams, R. B., & Kleck, R. E. (2005). Why do fear and anger look the way they do? Form and social function in facial expressions. *Personality and Social Psychology Bulletin, 31,* 73–86.

Marsh, A. A., Ambady, N., & Kleck, R. E. (2005). The effects of fear and anger facial expressions on approach—and avoidance-related behaviors. *Emotion, 5*(1), 119–124.

McArthur, L. Z., & Baron, R. M. (1983). Toward an ecological theory of social perception. *Psychological Review, 90,* 215–238.

Milord, J. T. (1978). Aesthetic aspects of faces: A (somewhat) phenomenological analysis using multidimensional scaling methods. *Journal of Personality and Social Psychology, 36,* 205–216.

Montepare, J. M., & Dobish, H. (2003). The contribution of emotion perceptions and their overgeneralizations to trait impressions. *Journal of Nonverbal Behavior, 27*(4), 237–254.

Montepare, J. M., & Zebrowitz, L. A. (1993). A cross-cultural comparison of impressions created by age-related variations in gait. *Journal of Nonverbal Behavior, 17,* 55–68.

Montepare, J. M., & Zebrowitz, L. A. (2002). A social-developmental view of ageism. In T. D. Nelson (Ed.), *Ageism: Stereotyping and prejudice against older persons.* Cambridge, MA: MIT Press.

Montepare, J. M., & Zebrowitz-McArthur, L. A. (1988). Impressions of people created by age-related qualities of their gaits. *Journal of Personality and Social Psychology, 55,* 547–556.

Mulac, A., & Giles, H. (1996). "You're only as old as you sound": Perceived vocal age and social meanings. *Health Communication, 8,* 199–215.

O'Connor, B. P., & Rigby, H. (1996). Perceptions of baby talk, frequency of receiving baby talk, and self-esteem among community and nursing home residents. *Psychology and Aging, 11,* 147–154.

Rexbye, H., Petersen, I., Johansen, M., Klitkou, L., Jeune, B., & Christensen, K. (2006). Influence of environmental factors on facial ageing. *Age and Ageing, 35,* 110–115.

Rhodes, M. G., & Anastasi, J. S. (2012). The Own-Age Bias in Face Recognition: A Meta-Analytic and Theoretical Review. *Psychological Bulletin, 138,* 146–174.

Riediger, M., Voelkle, M. C., Ebner, N. C., & Lindenberger, U. (2011). Beyond "happy, angry, or sad?": Age-of-poser and age-of-rater effects on multi-dimensional emotion perception. *Cognition and Emotion, 25,* 968–982.

Ryan, E. B., & Capadano, H. L. (1978). Age perceptions and evaluative reactions toward adult speakers. *Journal of Gerontology, 33,* 98–102.

Ryan, E. B., Giles, H., Bartolucci, G., & Henwood, K. (1986). Psycholinguistic and social psychological components of communication by and with the elderly. *Language and Communication, 6,* 1–24.

Ryan, E. B., Kennaley, D. E., Pratt, M. W., & Shumovich, M. A. (2000). Evaluations by staff, residents, and community seniors of patronizing speech in the nursing home: Impact of passive, assertive or humorous responses. *Psychology and Aging, 15,* 272–285.

Sacco, D. F., & Hugenberg, K. (2009). The look of fear and anger: Facial maturity modulates recognition of fearful and angry expressions. *Emotion, 9,* 39–49.

Said, C. P., Sebe, N., & Todorov, A. (2009). Structural resemblance to emotional expressions predicts evaluation of emotionally neutral faces. *Emotion, 9,* 260–264.

Schmidt, D. F., & Boland, S. M. (1986). The structure of impressions of older adults: Evidence for multiple stereotypes. *Psychology and Aging, 1,* 255–260.

Secord, P. F. (1958). Facial features and interpersonal processes in interpersonal perception. In R. Tagiuri & L. Petrullo (Eds.), *Person perception and interpersonal behavior* (pp. 300–315). Stanford, CA: Stanford University Press.

Sforza, C., Grandi, G., De Menezes, M., Tartaglia, G. M., Ferrario, V. F. (2010). Age—and sex-related changes in the normal human external nose. *Forensic Science International. 204,* 205.e1–205.e9.

Shaw, R., Katzel, E., Koltz, P., Yaremchuk, M., Girotto, J., Kahn, D., & Langstein, H. (2011). Aging of the facial skeleton: Aesthetic implications and rejuvenation strategies. *Plastic and Reconstructive Surgery, 127,* 374–383.

Sparko, A. L., & Zebrowitz, L. A. (2011). Moderating effects of facial expression and movement on the babyface stereotype. *Journal of Nonverbal Behavior, 35,* 243–257.

Sprengelmeyer, R., Rausch, M., Eysel, U. T., & Przuntek, H. (1996). Neural structures associated with recognition of facial expressions of basic emotions. *Proceedings of the Royal Society of London. Series B: Biological Sciences, 265,* 1927–1931.

Tickle-Degnen, L., Zebrowitz, L. A., Ma, H. -I. (2011). Culture, gender, and health care stigma: Practitioners' response to facial masking experienced by people with Parkinson's disease. *Social Science & Medicine, 73,* 95–102.

Voelkle, M. C., Ebner, N. C., Lindenberger, U., & Riediger, M. (2012). Let me guess how old you are: Effects of age, gender, and facial expression on perceptions of age. *Psychology and Aging, 27,* 265–277.

Whiteside, S. P. (1999). Note on voice and perturbation measures in simulated vocal emotions. *Perceptual and Motor Skills, 88,* 1219–1222.

Williams, K. N., Herman, R., Gajewski, B., & Wilson, K. (2009). Elderspeak communication: Impact on dementia care. *American Journal of Alzheimer's Disease and Other Dementias, 24,* 11–20.

Zebrowitz, L. A. (1996). Physical appearance as a basis of stereotyping. In N. MacRae, M. Hewstone, & C. Stangor (Eds.), *Foundations of stereotypes and stereotyping* (pp. 79–120). New York: Guilford Press.

Zebrowitz, L. A. (2006). Finally, faces find favor. *Social Cognition, 24,* 657–701.

Zebrowitz, L. A., & Collins, M. A. (1997). Accurate social perception at zero acquaintance: The affordances of a Gibsonian approach. *Personality and Social Psychology Review, 1,* 204–223.

Zebrowitz, L. A., Fellous, J., Mignault, A., & Andreoletti, C. (2003). Trait impressions as overgeneralized responses to adaptively significant facial qualities: Evidence from connectionist modeling. *Personality and Social Psychology Review, 7,* 194–215.

Zebrowitz, L. A., Kikuchi, M., & Fellous, J. (2007). Are effects of emotion expression on trait impressions mediated by babyfaceness? Evidence from connectionist modeling. *Personality and Social Psychology Bulletin, 33,* 648–662.

Zebrowitz, L. A., Kikuchi, M., & Fellous, J. (2010). Facial resemblance to emotions: Group differences, impression effects, and race stereotypes. *Journal of Personality and Social Psychology, 98,* 175–189.

Zebrowitz, L. A., Luevano, V. X., Bronstad, P. M., & Aharon, I. (2009). Neural activation to babyfaced men matches activation to babies. *Social Neuroscience, 4,* 1–10.

Zebrowitz, L. A., & Montepare, J. M. (1992). Impressions of babyfaced individuals across the life span. *Developmental Psychology, 28,* 1143–1152.

Zebrowitz, L. A., Olson, K., & Hoffman, K. (1993). Stability of babyfaceness and attractiveness across the life span. *Journal of Personality and Social Psychology, 64,* 453–466.

Do Everyday Affective Experiences Differ Throughout Adulthood?: A Review of Ambulatory-Assessment Evidence

Michaela Riediger *and* Antje Rauers

Abstract

Do adults from different age groups vary in the intensity or the variability of their everyday affective experiences? Are there age-related differences in the likelihood of encountering, and in the intensity of affectively reacting to, affect-eliciting events in daily life? Do individuals from different age groups differ in the complexity of their everyday affective lives? We review evidence on these questions currently available from ambulatory assessment studies. Ambulatory assessment refers to a group of research techniques-such as diary or experience sampling methods-that repeatedly capture everyday experiences as they naturally occur in people's daily lives. We summarize the strengths and challenges of ambulatory assessment methods, discuss the available evidence from ambulatory assessment studies on age differences in everyday affective experiences and stability, and summarize research on possible factors that may contribute to these effects. Here, we address findings on age differences in the likelihood of encountering distressing experiences, on age differences in people's affective reactions to such events, and on age differences in people's affect regulation orientations. We also review ambulatory assessment evidence on age differences in the complexity of everyday affective experiences.

Key Words: affective development, age differences, ambulatory assessment, diary method, experience sampling, affective well-being, affective experiences, affective reactivity, affective complexity, affect regulation

There are probably few notions in contemporary lifespan psychology that have caused as much astonishment and disbelief as the claim that affective well-being remains stable, or even improves, well into old age (e.g., Lawton, Kleban, & Dean, 1993; Levenson, Carstensen, & Gottman, 1994), and only declines shortly before death (Gerstorf et al., 2010). The question arises how this is possible in view of the multitude of developmental losses that aging individuals face (Baltes, 1987), such as declines in fluid-cognitive or physical functioning, and the increased risk of being confronted with one's own illnesses or those of loved ones.

Historically, age-comparative research on affective well-being started out using global or retrospective measures of participants' conceptions of their "average" affective well-being "in general" or in a certain period of time (e.g., "during the past year"). Responding to these measures requires deliberate aggregations of one's remembered (and typically variable) affective life. Both remembering and aggregating are subject to multiple influences, such as biases and errors in the recall of affective experiences, or recollection and aggregation heuristics (e.g., Miron-Shatz, Stone, & Kahneman, 2009; Robinson & Clore, 2002). The nature of these influences, however, may vary with people's age (Hoppmann & Riediger, 2009). There is, for example, evidence that older as compared to younger adults may show a more pronounced preference for positive over negative information when remembering valenced material, which may lead older people to reconstruct their past more positively than younger people (e.g., Ready, Weinberger, & Jones, 2007).

Global and retrospective measures of affective well-being are thus suited to investigate whether people from different age groups recall their affective lives differently. They cannot, however, inform about age differences in actual affective experiences in everyday life. Investigating the latter requires capturing affective experiences at the moment of, or close to, their spontaneous emergence in people's natural life contexts. Since the beginning of the 21st century, there has been an upsurge in the use of so-called ambulatory assessment methods to achieve this aim. This research has addressed a variety of questions: Do individuals from different age groups vary in the intensity or variability of their everyday affective experiences? Are there age-related differences in the likelihood of encountering, and in the intensity of affectively reacting to, affect-eliciting events in daily life? Do younger and older adults differ in the complexity of their everyday affective lives? The purpose of this chapter is to review the currently available evidence from ambulatory assessment studies on these questions. Our primary focus is on age differences from younger to older adulthood. Where available, we also include age-comparative studies spanning the age range from adolescence to old age.

We start with a discussion of the strengths and challenges of ambulatory assessment methods. Following that, we summarize evidence from ambulatory assessment studies on age differences in everyday affective experiences and stability. We then review attempts to identify factors that contribute to these effects, such as age differences in the likelihood of encountering distressing experiences, or age differences in people's affective reactions to such events. We also summarize evidence on age differences in people's affect-regulation orientations. Finally, we review research on age differences in the structure of affective experiences in daily life. We conclude the chapter with a summary and an outlook on possible future research directions.

Ambulatory Assessment as a Tool for Studying Age Differences in Everyday Affective Experiences: Strengths and Challenges

Ambulatory assessment encompasses a class of research techniques that aim at capturing experiences—such as events, behaviors, feelings, thoughts, or physiological processes—as they naturally occur in the study participants' everyday lives (e.g., Hoppmann & Riediger, 2009). Many labels have been used to refer to these techniques, such as experience sampling, real-time data capture, time-situated method, ecological momentary assessment, or diary method. The distinctive characteristic that sets ambulatory assessment techniques apart from other research approaches (such as single-time global evaluations or longer-term retrospective reconstructions of past experiences) is the repeated sampling of experiences at the very moment of, or in close temporal proximity to, their spontaneous occurrence in the individual's natural environment.

Ambulatory assessment studies of age differences in affective functioning have most typically used either *diary* or *experience-sampling* techniques, which differ regarding the timeframes of the assessments. Diary techniques obtain repeated self-reports of affective experiences that occurred during short preceding time intervals, whereas experience sampling refers to the acquisition of repeated self-reports of momentary affective experiences. In diary studies, assessments are mostly obtained at fixed points in time, such as before going to bed at night, and refer to the participants' experiences since the last diary entry. In experience-sampling studies, participants are often provided with electronic assessment devices, such as handheld computers or mobile phones. Participants carry these devices with them while they pursue their normal daily routines. The devices signal participants at varying intervals when to respond to the study instrument, which refers to their momentary situation. To date, only a few developmental investigations of affective phenomena have used complementary assessment strategies in addition to repeated momentary self-reports of affective experiences, such as ambulatory monitoring of physiological processes or of physical activities (e.g., Wrzus, Müller, Wagner, Lindenberger, & Riediger, 2012).

Two important methodological advantages in the ambulatory assessment of affective experiences are brought about by the (relative) immediacy of the measurement and the fact that it takes place in the participants' natural environments. There is ample empirical evidence that global or long-term retrospective reports do not actually reflect affective experiences because respondents have to rely on their memory or use belief-based inference strategies, which results in partial recall and other response biases (Robinson & Clore, 2002). The more immediate the assessment, the less relevant are these concerns. Experience sampling is superior to diary methods in this respect, because diary measures also involve retrospection, albeit across short time intervals, which is not the case for experience sampling. Diary approaches are nevertheless a valuable approach in ambulatory assessment and are therefore included in this chapter, because they have other advantages. For example, diary approaches can describe participants' daily lives more comprehensively than experience sampling, and are more likely to capture rare phenomena. Both diary and experience sampling approaches collect information within the natural context of the participants' day-to-day lives, which enhances the ecological validity of the assessment, offering unique opportunities to understand how everyday affective experiences spontaneously unfold (Schwarz, 2007).[1]

The prevailing emphasis in early studies on age differences in affective experiences has been on differences *between* individuals. Other important characteristics of affective experiences—such as their inherently fluctuating nature reflected in short-term within-person variations, or their covariation with social, cognitive, or other processes—had initially received comparatively less attention. A compelling conceptual benefit of momentary assessment is that measurement occasions are repeated with short time intervals between them. This makes short-term processes and fluctuations accessible to scientific investigation. Another conceptual benefit is that ambulatory assessment can provide insight into the role of everyday contexts for affective experiences and their covariation with other processes.

Despite these methodological and conceptual benefits, there are also challenges to the use of ambulatory assessment strategies when studying age differences in affective experiences. For example, the burden for the participants (e.g., the necessary time commitment or confidence in being able to handle the assessment device) is comparatively large. This can create difficulties in terms of both representativeness and attrition of the sample (Scollon, Kim-Prieto, & Diener, 2003). That is, the demanding nature of the assessment strategy could lead certain types of individuals to be over- or underrepresented in the sample from the beginning, or to be more likely to drop out during the study interval. This concern can even be aggravated in developmental studies, in which selectivity effects may vary across the investigated age groups. For example, selectivity effects caused by the necessity to handle handheld computers or mobile phones as assessment devices may be larger among older participants than among their younger counterparts,

who are typically more accustomed to using mobile technologies.

Furthermore, repeatedly measuring affective experiences might cause *reactivity* effects (Scollon et al., 2003). That is, it is possible that the phenomenon under study may change as a result of measurement or reporting. Although reactivity is a general challenge in social and behavioral research, it can be even more relevant in ambulatory assessment research because the repeated assessments may lead people to pay unusual attention to their affective experiences. Another limitation, which applies to field research in general, is the difficulty of investigating causal relations between phenomena, a challenge that we will return to in more detail later. Also, the possibilities to statistically control for potentially interfering variables are limited in ambulatory assessment, because it cannot capture a given moment in its full complexity and with a plethora of influencing factors.

In short, ambulatory assessment carries methodological and conceptual advantages for the study of age differences in everyday affective processes. Nonetheless, it also presents a number of challenges that need to be considered, as we will discuss in the concluding section of this chapter. When adequately applied, however, ambulatory assessment represents a valuable approach with which to tackle questions regarding age differences in everyday affective processes. In the following sections, we review the respective, currently available empirical evidence. We begin by summarizing evidence on age differences in everyday affective experiences and on the factors that might contribute to these differences.

Age Differences in Everyday Affective Well-Being and Stability

Affective well-being refers to individuals' typical hedonic tone during a given period of time, and *affective stability* refers to the extent of within-person variability of affective experiences. It has been questioned whether global or long-term retrospective measures are suited to adequately reflect age differences in these constructs. This skepticism derived, among other things, from the argument that affective experiences cannot be stored over extended periods of time and therefore have to be reconstructed in response to such measures (Robinson & Clore, 2002). Such reconstructions might be more positively toned among older as compared to younger individuals because of age-related increases in the tendency to recall positive over negative information (e.g., Ready et al., 2007). This concern is less applicable to ambulatory assessment studies that repeatedly measure affective experiences in participants' natural life contexts at the moment of, or close to, their emergence. Here, indicators of affective well-being are obtained by averaging people's reports of their momentary affective experiences, and indicators of affective stability are captured by determining indicators of the within-person variability of momentary affective experiences throughout the study interval. In the following, we review the currently available experience sampling evidence on age differences in everyday affective well-being and variability. Table 5.1 provides a simplified summary of the main findings reviewed here.

Overall, the evidence from these studies converges in showing that older adults, on average, report relatively more positively toned and more stable affective experiences in their daily lives than do younger individuals (e.g., Carstensen, Pasupathi, Mayr, & Nesselroade, 2000; Carstensen et al., 2011; Charles et al., 2010; Kööts, Realo, & Allik, 2011; Riediger & Freund, 2008; Riediger, Schmiedek, Wagner, & Lindenberger, 2009; Steptoe, Leigh, & Kumari, 2011). This convergence is all the more compelling as these studies differed in various ways, such as in the age range investigated, in the ambulatory assessment approach taken (diaries vs. experience sampling), in the specific facets of affective experiences considered, and in the kind of well-being indicators derived. Despite notable differences in findings that we allude to in later sections, one overarching pattern of findings is

Table 5.1. Overview of central findings of the reviewed studies on age differences in everyday affective well-being and stability

Central findings	References
1) Average affective experiences in everyday life	
a) Aggregate indicators: Affect balance	
• Linear age-related increase in affect balance throughout adulthood	Riediger & Freund (2008); Riediger et al. (2009)
• Nonlinear age-related increase in affect balance throughout adulthood (effect leveling off in older age)	Carstensen et al. (2000; 2011)
b) Subfacet indicators: Positive (PA) and negative affect (NA)	
• Age-related increase in intensity of PA, and decrease in intensity of NA throughout adulthood	Kööts et al. (2011)
• Age-related increase in intensity of PA, and age invariance in intensity of NA throughout adulthood	Riediger et al. (2009)
• Age-related decrease in intensity of NA, and age invariance in intensity of PA from middle to older adulthood	Charles et al. (2009)
• Age-related decrease in the intensity of NA; age differences in intensity of PA moderated by time of assessment: more intense PA among older adults at wakeup, but less intense PA by 7 p.m.	Steptoe et al. (2011)
• Age-related decrease in the frequency of NA, age invariance in the frequency and intensity of NA and in the intensity of PA throughout adulthood	Carstensen et al. (2000)
• Age-related increase in the intensity of NA throughout adulthood	Sliwinski et al. (2009, study 1)
2) Variability of affective experiences in everyday life	
• Age-related decrease in within-person variability of affective experiences throughout adulthood	Brose et al. (2012); Carstensen et al. (2000; 2011); Röcke et al. (2009); Steptoe et al. (2011)

Note. Most reviewed studies were cross-sectional. Studies varied regarding how everyday affective experiences were measured, aggregated, and analyzed. See information in text for details.

consistent: in the overwhelming majority of these studies, one or more of the investigated well-being indicators reflected more positively toned everyday affective well-being in older than in younger participants. We are only aware of one diary study (Sliwinski, Almeida, Stawski, & Smyth, 2009, study 1) that observed the reverse pattern of results.

The finding of positive age differences is particularly unequivocal for aggregate measures of mean levels of affective well-being. An often used aggregate is *affect balance*, the average difference between momentary positive and momentary negative affect. The higher the scores of this index, the more pronounced is the predominance of positive over negative feelings in individuals' everyday lives. Age-related increases in affect balance were observed both in cross-sectional (e.g., Riediger & Freund, 2008; Riediger et al., 2009), and in a 10-year longitudinal experience-sampling study (Carstensen et al., 2011). Somewhat less consistent across these studies are findings regarding the *form* of the observed age differences. Carstensen and colleagues (2000, 2011) reported an age-related increase in aggregate indicators of everyday affective well-being from younger to middle-aged adulthood, followed by a leveling-off of this age effect into old age. There were, however, no indications of such nonlinear age effects in two other experience-sampling studies of age-heterogeneous samples (Riediger & Freund, 2008, study 2; Riediger et al., 2009), which suggested a relatively continuous adult trajectory of the age effects on affect balance.

In addition to studying age differences in average emotional experiences, research has also addressed age differences in the variability of participants' affective lives. These studies typically operationalize affect variability as the within-person standard deviation of repeated reports of the intensity of participants' momentary (positive and/or negative) affect. There is converging evidence from various experience-sampling studies that older as compared to younger adults' everyday affective experiences are more stable (i.e., fluctuate less) over time (e.g., Carstensen et al., 2000, 2011; Steptoe et al., 2011), which is consistent with evidence from measurement burst studies assessed in laboratory contexts (Brose, Scheibe, & Schmiedek, 2012; Röcke, Li, & Smith, 2009). The longitudinal experience-sampling study by Carstensen and colleagues (2011) further demonstrates that the age-related increase in affective stability is not only evident in cross-sectional comparisons of younger, middle-aged, and older adults, but also evident in longitudinal analyses of

within-person change in affect variability over the course of 10 years.

Although the evidence for better average affective well-being and less affect variability in older adults' daily lives is fairly consistent across studies, the pattern is less coherent regarding age differences in *subfacets* of everyday affective experiences, such as the average intensity or frequency of positive and negative affect. In a recent study by Kööts and colleagues (2011), for example, age effects were evident in both positive and negative affect. On seven daily experience samples throughout a 14-day study period, 55 younger (19–23 years) and 55 older participants (61–88 years) reported how well each of several positive and negative affect states represented their momentary feelings. Older as compared to younger participants reported, on average, more intense positive affect (operationalized as feelings of happiness and surprise) and less intense negative affect (operationalized as feelings of anger, contempt, disappointment, disgust, fear, irritation, and sadness), as well as less fatigue (operationalized as feelings of sleepiness and tiredness).

Other studies suggest that the overarching age effect in affect balance may not generalize to the same extent across different facets of affective experiences (Carstensen et al., 2000; Riediger et al., 2009), but there is inconsistency between these studies regarding the specific results. Riediger and colleagues (2009), who obtained an average of 54 momentary reports of several positive and negative affect facets from 378 participants ranging in age from 14 to 86 years, reported that the age-related increase in affect balance observed in this study was driven more by an age-related increase in positive affect (operationalized as average intensities of feeling joyful, content, and interested) than by an age-related decrease in negative affect (operationalized as average intensity of feeling angry, nervous, and downhearted). A different pattern emerged in the study by Carstensen and colleagues (2000). These authors obtained five daily experience samples of 19 positive and negative affect facets throughout 1 week from 184 individuals aged 18–94 years (i.e., reports of how happy, joyful, content, excited, proud, amused, angry, sad, fearful, disgusted, guilty, etc. participants momentarily felt). From these reports, the authors derived indicators of how often, on average, positive and negative affect facets were felt, at least to some extent, regardless of their intensity (affect frequency), and indicators of how intensely, on average, these positive and negative affect facets were experienced when they were present (affect intensity). The authors neither found age-related differences regarding the average frequency and intensity of positive affect, nor did they find age-related differences regarding the average intensity of negative affect. There was, however, a significant age-related decline in the frequency of experiencing negative affect.

More evidence for age differences in everyday affective experiences well into old age comes from two studies investigating the age range from late middle to old adulthood. Charles and colleagues (2010), for example, assessed everyday affective well-being in 101 older women aged 63–93 years in eight consecutive evening telephone interviews. They found that even in this older sample, the older participants were, the less negative affect they reported on average. This was particularly evident in fewer reports of feeling sad or disappointed. There was no significant age effect regarding an aggregate measure of everyday positive affect in this study, but explorations of age differences in discrete affect facets revealed that the older participants were, the less likely they reported feeling excited, enthusiastic, and inspired.

Steptoe and colleagues (2011) reported rather similar results from a large-scale study in which four assessments of momentary affective states were obtained throughout a day from 4,258 participants aged 52–79 years. Again, the older participants were, the less negative affect they reported. The age effect for an aggregate measure of positive affect depended on the timing of the assessment. Positive affect was comparatively higher among the older than the younger participants in this sample on waking, but lower by 7 p.m.

Sliwinski and colleagues (2009, study 1) report the only findings that we are aware of that diverge from the general pattern of age-related stability or increase in ambulatory assessments of everyday affective well-being. Their measure, however, was different from those used in other ambulatory assessment studies. Two waves of eight nightly telephone interviews were conducted about 10 years apart in a sample of 671 adults aged 24–75 years. Participants reported for how long during the past 24 hours they had felt (a) restless or fidgety, (b) so sad that nothing could cheer them up, (c) that everything was an effort, and (d) hopeless. There were no cross-sectional age differences in an aggregate measure of negative affect across these items, but results indicated an increase in this measure of negative affect throughout 10 years, which was more pronounced the older the participants were.

The reported inconsistencies regarding the form and pattern of age differences in various aspects of everyday affective well-being may well derive from the fact that there has been little correspondence between studies in terms of how everyday affective experiences were measured, aggregated, and analyzed. Perhaps most importantly, the various researchers have each used their idiosyncratic set of affect items (adjectives), with little or no overlap across studies. It may be possible, for example, that age effects in everyday affective experiences vary across different discrete affect states (e.g., anger vs. sadness, Blanchard-Fields & Coats, 2008). Such differential age effects would be obscured by the currently prevailing approach of analyzing aggregate indicators of affective well-being. Systematically complementing analyses of age differences in *aggregate* measures with analyses of age differences in *discrete* affective states will be necessary to explore this possibility in the future. Furthermore, the studies reviewed differed in terms of whether they used diary or experience-sampling techniques as ambulatory assessment approaches. Earlier, we alluded to the fact that both techniques differ in terms of the immediacy and the comprehensiveness of the assessment, which also may have led to differences in the results. Furthermore, the fact that the studies partly investigated samples from different nationalities may have contributed to differences in findings. Systematic cross-cultural comparisons are necessary to explore this possibility. Enhancing the comparability of assessments across studies will hence be essential to investigate the replicability of findings across different samples, cultures, and research laboratories.

In sum, there is converging evidence across studies that higher age is predictive of better overall affective well-being in everyday life, as indicated by aggregate measures of affect balance. There also is converging evidence that older age is characterized by a lower variability of everyday affective experiences. The evidence is less consistent when it comes to the form of age-related differences, although the majority of the available evidence suggests sustained associations between age and everyday affective well-being into older adulthood. The evidence on age differences in specific facets of everyday affective experiences is even less consistent. This may be a consequence of the lack of methodological overlap across studies, for example, in terms of the affect items assessed. Enhancing the comparability of assessment protocols across studies is an important task for future research. Although most of the currently available studies are cross-sectional, longitudinal experience-sampling findings indicate that the well-replicated age effects in aggregate measures of everyday affective well-being and affective stability are not entirely due to cohort differences between investigated age groups, but also reflect within-person change over time. This raises the question of why older age is associated with more stable and better reports of overall affective well-being in everyday life.

Potential Contributors to Age Trajectories in Everyday Affective Well-Being

Attempts to make sense of adult trajectories of affective well-being initially focused on older adults' ability to adapt to major aging-related losses. Research in this tradition has emphasized, for example, the adaptive value of older adults' comparing themselves to individuals who are worse off, selectively focusing their available resources, or becoming increasingly flexible in modifying or disengaging from unrealizable goals (e.g., Brandtstädter & Greve, 1994; Brandtstädter & Renner, 1990; Freund & Baltes, 2000; Heckhausen & Schulz, 1995).

With the enhanced use of ambulatory assessment methods, other explanatory themes were brought into the discussion that focused on the potential role of age-related differences in mundane day-to-day experiences and contexts. Positions within this line of reasoning theorized, for example, that age differences in everyday affective experiences might partly be due to older adults' daily lives being more predictable (e.g., Röcke et al., 2009) and less susceptible to distressing experiences (e.g., Charles et al., 2010; Riediger & Freund, 2008). It has also been speculated that age differences in everyday affective well-being may derive from older adults' being better at regulating their affective experiences vis-à-vis everyday problems than are younger individuals (e.g., Carstensen et al., 2000). Even though this is a prominent claim, direct empirical investigations using ambulatory assessment are still lacking. Indirect routes to investigating this idea have been taken by studies that examined age differences in people's affective reactivity to everyday distressing experiences. Here, we summarize the currently available empirical evidence from ambulatory assessment studies regarding these themes. First, however, we emphasize a crucial feature of the currently available investigations of this kind: they provide insights into factors that are *associated* with age-related differences in everyday affective experiences, but do not (yet) allow conclusions regarding the *causality* in these relationships.

A Word of Caution: Association ≠ Causal Relation

Even though many of the studies we review next were motivated by a conceptual interest in potential reasons for age-related differences in everyday affective experiences, reliable causal inferences cannot yet be drawn based on the currently available ambulatory assessment evidence. According to a classic analysis of causal relationships, this would require demonstrating that three fundamental conditions are met: (a) the cause precedes the effect, (b) the cause is statistically associated with the effect, and (c) there is no other plausible alternative explanation for the effect other than the cause (Mill, 1848; see also Rutter, 2007).

We emphasize this here because causal interpretations of cross-sectional mediation analyses based on linear regressions are used in some of the studies we review here. The validity of causal conclusions inferred from such analyses, however, has been questioned based on conceptual and methodological considerations (e.g., Lindenberger & Pötter, 1998; Lindenberger, von Oertzen, Ghisletta, & Hertzog, 2011; Maxwell & Cole, 2007). A detailed elaboration of the issue of testing causality is beyond the scope of this chapter. Accessible discussions of this issue that target the research interests of developmental psychologists have been provided, for example, by Foster (2010) and Rutter (2007). For the purposes of the present chapter, it is sufficient that readers are aware that the studies we review here provide valuable information on whether potential context and other factors are *associated* with age differences in everyday affective experiences. Unraveling the issue of causality in these associations remains an important task for future studies. Recent proposals of diagnostic and methodological tools suitable for application in (longitudinal) ambulatory assessment studies (e.g., Foster, 2010; Rutter, 2007) will be instrumental in pursuing this aim. With that note of caution in mind, we now turn to the argument that age-related differences in daily-life contexts, such as the exposure to daily hassles or to motivational conflicts, may be among the factors that are associated with age differences in everyday affective well-being.

Age Differences in the Exposure to Daily Hassles and Everyday Motivational Conflicts

Daily hassles are minor stressors that include, for example, challenges and disruptions of routines, everyday concerns at work, arguments, or annoyances. They often elicit an affective response in the individual encountering them, such as a momentary decline in positive and/or a momentary increase in negative affect (Almeida, 2005; Stawski, Sliwinski, Almeida, & Smyth, 2008). Frequent encounters of everyday stressors might thus result in lower average affective well-being.

Indeed, there is evidence from various studies that older adults report fewer hassles in their daily lives than younger individuals do. For example, in the National Study of Daily Experiences (NSDE), a representative U.S. national sample of 1,483 adults ranging in age from 24 to 74 years completed eight consecutive nightly semistructured telephone interviews on stressful experiences they had encountered during the preceding 24 hours. Younger (25–39 years) and middle-aged (40–59 years) adults reported more frequent everyday stressors and perceived their experienced stressors as more severe than did older adults (60–74 years, Almeida & Horn, 2004). Other analyses with data from the NSDE study focused specifically on stressors in the interpersonal domain and also showed that older as compared to younger and middle-aged adults experienced fewer interpersonal tensions (Birditt, Fingerman, & Almeida, 2005) and encountered fewer arguments, as well as fewer situations in which arguments could have occurred but were avoided (Charles, Piazza, Luong, & Almeida, 2009). The finding of an age-related decrease in the exposure to daily stressors was recently replicated with more fine-grained measurement schedules and more immediate assessments of stressful everyday situations using a mobile phone–based experience sampling technology (Wrzus et al., 2012, study 1). This study's results also correspond to results from semistructured interviews covering a timespan of 24 hours that were obtained in laboratory settings (Sliwinski, Smyth, Hofer, & Stawski, 2006; Stawski et al., 2008).

Charles and colleagues (2010) investigated whether age differences in stressor exposure were associated with age differences in daily negative affect using data from eight consecutive evening telephone interviews in a sample of 101 older women. Again, older age was associated with fewer daily stressors and a lower subjective severity of daily stressors. Furthermore, older age was also associated with lower everyday negative affect. Interestingly, significant proportions of the age-related variance in everyday negative affect were associated with stressor frequency and perceived stressor severity. Frequency of stressor occurrence accounted for 43%, and

subjective perceptions of stressor severity for 19% of the variance shared between daily negative affect and age, respectively (for a methodological discussion of such indices, see Lindenberger et al., 2011).

Riediger and Freund (2008) reported a series of studies on everyday motivational conflicts that provide further evidence that daily contexts of affective experiences are associated with age-related increases in day-to-day affective well-being. Motivational conflicts in everyday life frequently result from the co-occurrence of behavioral tendencies that cannot be followed simultaneously, so that one tendency has to be given priority at the cost of the other for the time being. An example is having to decide whether to go to a concert one has been looking forward to or stay at home to care for one's spouse who has become sick. Depending on the behavioral option chosen, such motivational dilemmas can lead to the sense that one *wants* to do something else (e.g., because that would be more pleasurable) or that one *should* do something else instead (e.g., because that would be more responsible). Such experiences of motivational conflict can often be unpleasant and accompanied by momentary declines in participants' affective well-being. Results from two studies using comprehensive activity diaries and experience sampling in age-heterogeneous adult samples showed that, with age, the frequency of motivational conflict decreased. Again, there was an age-related increase in everyday affective well-being reported by the participants in these studies. Furthermore, and consistently across both studies, this age-related decrease in motivational conflicts was associated with the age-related increase in affective well-being.

Taken together, findings on age differences in the exposure to daily hassles and motivational conflicts emphasize the role that *everyday* experiences may play in terms of positive adult trajectories in everyday affective well-being and thus complement the often prevailing focus on resilience despite major aging-related losses. Although conclusions regarding causality are not yet possible with the correlational data provided by the available studies (as explained earlier), the overall pattern of findings gives rise to the speculation that age-related decreases in the prevalence of everyday stressors and motivational-conflict experiences may be among the factors that contribute to an age-related improvement in day-to-day affective well-being. Empirical testing of the causal relations potentially involved here, however, remains an open task for future studies.

Another unresolved issue accruing from this research pertains to the reasons for the lower prevalence of everyday stressors and day-to-day motivational conflicts among older adults. There is some preliminary indication that it might not just be the reduced stressor and conflict "proneness" of older adults' life circumstances that is relevant here. Riediger and Freund (2008), for example, found that age differences in the pattern of involvement in everyday activities (e.g., older adults' having more spare time for leisure activities, and younger adults' being more involved in work or study-related activities) were not associated with age differences in the prevalence of everyday motivational conflict experiences. There also was no empirical support for the assumptions that older adults' being increasingly selective in the activities they engage in, and less confronted with sociocultural constraints and expectations in the choice of their activities, might lead to a lower conflict prevalence. Riediger and Freund speculated that regulatory processes on the part of the individuals might be involved. They assumed that it might not necessarily be the case that older adults encounter fewer motivational conflicts in their daily lives than do younger adults, but that they come to terms with (i.e., regulate their perceptions of) motivational-conflict situations more efficiently. Age differences in regulatory strategies have been proposed to contribute to the lower prevalence of other everyday stressors in older adulthood as well. For example, it has been suggested that not only a lower stressor susceptibility of older adults' life circumstances, but also older adults' stronger tendencies to actively or passively avoid distressing situations, or to appraise unavoidable situations as less severe, might play a role (Stawski et al., 2008).

The idea that aging individuals might proactively downregulate occurrences of unpleasant experiences in their daily lives is related to the more general tenet that adults of different age groups might differ in how they regulate or control their affective experiences (Blanchard-Fields, 2007). Due to the difficulty of observing affect-regulation efforts and their effectiveness, direct empirical evidence (other than participants' self-reports) regarding age differences in affective self-regulation is still missing. Several indirect lines of investigation have been pursued, however. Next, we review evidence from ambulatory assessment studies for two of these indirect approaches, addressing age differences in people's affect-regulation orientations and their affective reactivity to unpleasant but unavoidable everyday experiences (which have been regarded as indirect indicators of the direction and the effectiveness of people's affect-regulation efforts, respectively).

Age Differences in Affect-Regulation Orientations

To date, little attention has been paid to the fact that affect-regulatory behaviors are preceded and fundamentally shaped by motivational processes. This is presumably the case because most investigators have assumed that affect regulation is generally pro-hedonic, that is, directed at optimizing the individual's well-being (e.g., R. J. Larsen, 2000). Only recently has awareness increased that, occasionally, there can be situations in which people want to maintain or enhance negative affect, or dampen positive affect. Such a contra-hedonic orientation can occur, for example, when negative affect is beneficial or positive affect detrimental for attaining individuals' goals or for maintaining consistent views of themselves (e.g., Parrott, 1993; Tamir, Chiu, & Gross, 2007; Tamir, Mitchell, & Gross, 2008; Wood, Heimpel, Manwell, & Whittington, 2009). Anger, for example, can help one to stand up to somebody else in an argument, whereas joy can distract one's concentration from a difficult cognitive task. People may also sometimes seek apparently negative affective experiences because, for them, these experiences are also accompanied or followed by positive experiences (Andrade & Cohen, 2007).

Riediger and colleagues (2009, 2011) proposed that considering the proactive aspects of affective experience might contribute to the understanding of age-related differences in everyday affective experiences. They investigated this idea in an experience-sampling study with 378 participants ranging in age from adolescence to old adulthood. Participants reported, on average 54 times in 3 weeks, how they momentarily felt and whether they currently wanted to dampen, enhance, or maintain each of six positive and negative affect facets (i.e., feeling angry, downcast, anxious, interested, joyful, and content). Participants further completed two trials of a numerical memory-updating task, assessing momentary working memory capacity on each measurement occasion.

As expected, contra-hedonic orientations did not occur frequently in the daily lives of most participants. Across the entire sample, contra-hedonic orientations were reported, on average, in 15% of the measurement occasions, and were thus considerably less prevalent than pro-hedonic orientations, which were reported, on average, in 92% of the measurement occasions. (Occurrences of contra- and pro-hedonic orientations were not mutually exclusive and therefore do not add up to 100%.) There were, however, pronounced age differences in participants' reports on wanting to influence their feelings. Interestingly, these differences largely corresponded to the well-replicated finding of an age-related increase in day-to-day affective well-being. Specifically, contra-hedonic orientations to enhance or maintain negative affect, or to dampen positive affect, were most prevalent among adolescents, as compared to all other age groups. Pro-hedonic orientation, in contrast, was most prevalent in later adulthood, and this effect was driven by the motivations to maintain (but not to enhance) positive and to dampen negative affect. These age differences in pro- and contra-hedonic orientation could not be attributed to age-related differences in daily-life affective experiences, activities, or social partners. Based on these findings, the authors speculated that part of the negative emotionality that is characteristic of adolescence, and part of the positive emotionality that is characteristic of older adulthood, might be intentionally sought and maintained by the individual.

Irrespective of participants' age, findings regarding associations between pro- and contra-hedonic orientations and within-person fluctuations in working memory capacity indicated that contra-hedonic orientation is more cognitively demanding than pro-hedonic orientation (Riediger et al., 2011). Pro-hedonic orientation was only weakly associated with within-person fluctuations in working memory performance. The more momentary contra-hedonic orientation participants reported, however, the lower their momentary working memory performance, and this was independent of the participants' momentary affective experiences. Interestingly, the effects of contra-hedonic orientation on working memory performance could not be attributed to lack of effort or to differences in other individual or situational characteristics. Despite the pronounced age-related differences in the prevalence of different affect-regulation orientations, their cognitive requirements thus appear to be independent of the individual's age.

Overall, this research suggests that taking into account motivational aspects of how people want to influence their feelings can contribute to the understanding of age-related differences in affective functioning from adolescence to old age. It leaves open, however, whether age differences in affect-regulation orientation also translate into differences in behavioral efforts toward these ends. A related question is whether potential age differences in regulation efforts might also be evident in people's effectiveness in regulating affective states in desired directions. Although direct evidence regarding this idea is currently still lacking, several researchers have contended that such age differences in regulation effectiveness should be evident in how people react affectively to negative experiences they encounter in their daily lives. In the following section, we summarize the available evidence regarding this idea and discuss a recent proposal of how to reconcile apparent inconsistencies therein.

Age Differences in Affective Reactivity to Unpleasant Experiences in Daily Life

Over the past years, several studies have used diary and experience sampling methodologies to investigate potential age-related differences in people's affective reactivity to negative events they encounter in their daily lives. Although these experiences can vary in severity, the primary focus of this research has been on relatively minor everyday hassles. Although affective responses to such hassles can be evident in changes in people's feelings, behaviors, or physiological states, it has typically been studied in terms of people's psychological responses, most often operationalized as (temporary) increases in negative affect. Hardly any studies are available that addressed age differences in physiological reactions to unpleasant everyday events (but see Uchino, Berg, Smith, Pearce, & Skinner, 2006; Wrzus et al., 2012), and we are not aware of evidence from ambulatory assessment studies regarding age-related differences in behavioral responses to daily hassles.

Much of this research has implicitly or explicitly built on the assumption that interindividual differences in affective reactions to everyday stressors of comparable severity derive from differences in the ability to regulate or control one's affective response. The current lifespan literature offers seemingly opposing theoretical positions with regard to the question of whether adults from different age groups differ in this respect. On the one hand, positions deriving from socioemotional selectivity theory (e.g., Carstensen, Isaacowitz, & Charles, 1999) contend that affective responding to unpleasant events should decrease with age because older adults, due to their increasingly limited perspective of lifetime remaining, should become increasingly motivated to control their affective responses in order to maintain their well-being when confronted with unpleasant events. On the other hand, positions deriving, for example, from dynamic integration theory (e.g., Labouvie-Vief, 2009) maintain that affective responding should increase with age. These positions build on the idea that regulating affective responses is largely cognitively controlled and therefore requires an investment of cognitive capacity. As cognitive capacity declines with age, the ability to effectively regulate emotions in the face of hassles should therefore be reduced, which should result in more pronounced responding to unpleasant events.

These seemingly opposing theoretical positions are also reflected by a still inconclusive pattern of empirical evidence from ambulatory assessment studies. Some studies suggest that older adults are less psychologically responsive to everyday hassles than are younger individuals (e.g., Birditt et al., 2005; Carstensen et al., 2000; Uchino et al., 2006). But there is also evidence to the contrary, indicating more pronounced affective responding to daily hassles with higher age (e.g., Mroczek & Almeida, 2004).

A closer look at these studies reveals that different types of everyday hassles were investigated, which suggests that age-related differences in affective responding may be associated with characteristics of the everyday stressor eliciting the response. This speculation is further nourished by observations that even analyses of the same dataset, namely the NSDE, yielded opposing patterns of findings depending on which hassle events the analyses were focused on and on how affective reactivity was operationalized (e.g., Birditt et al., 2005; Charles et al., 2009; Mroczek & Almeida, 2004). As we mentioned earlier, eight consecutive nightly semistructured telephone interviews on stressful experiences during the preceding 24 hours were obtained in this study from a large-scale representative U.S. national sample of participants ranging in age from younger to older adulthood. When measures that reflected the complexity of stressful experiences encountered during a given day were aggregated (i.e., when the number of stressors were weighted by their reported severity), results indicated an age-related increase in negative affect reactivity to daily stress. That is, the association between the severity-weighted stressor count during a given day and negative affect reported for that day was more pronounced the older participants were (e.g., Mroczek & Almeida, 2004; Sliwinski et al., 2009, study 1). Other authors focused their analyses of the same dataset on more circumscribed types of stressors in the interpersonal domain and found no age-related differences in affective reactivity or even less affective reactivity to these events among older than younger participants (Birditt et al., 2005; Charles et al., 2009). Charles and colleagues (2009), for example, observed that in response to encountering interpersonal disagreements that could have resulted in an argument, but had been avoided, older adults' negative affect increased less than did younger and middle-aged adults'. They found no age differences in stress reactivity to arguments that did actually happen.

This divergent pattern of findings suggests that age-related differences in affective reactivity might be associated with characteristics of the particular type of hassle encountered. Wrzus and colleagues (2012) contended that the resource demands of the situation might play a central role in this respect. According to their *overpowering hypothesis,* older adults should respond more strongly to unpleasant events than younger individuals when the resource demands of the unpleasant event are high and the situational demands are likely to exceed older adults' available resources to successfully control their affective responses. When resource demands implied by the negative event are low, however, the authors predicted no age differences or even an age-related decrease in affective responding to negative experiences. This could be due to possible age-related increases in the motivation to maintain one's well-being even in the face of adversity. This line of argument is also consistent with the Strength and Vulnerability Model proposed by Charles (2010). Results from two ambulatory assessment studies supported these predictions for both affective and physiological responding to everyday hassles. The first study used experience sampling to obtain repeated reports of momentary negative affect and occurrences of unpleasant events in the everyday lives of an age-heterogeneous sample covering the age range from adolescence to old age. In the second study, a subsample of 92 participants wore an ambulatory psychophysiological monitoring system for 24 hours and additionally completed an average of seven experience-sampling reports while pursuing their daily routines. Affective responding was analyzed by comparing, within persons, negative affect and heart rate variability in situations with and without preceding unpleasant events. The number of life domains affected by a negative event was used as a proxy for the complexity of resource requirements imposed by the experience. Here, the idea was that unpleasant events that affect multiple life domains (e.g., when missing a bus not only meant waiting in the cold for the next bus, but also being late for an important appointment) are more complex to deal with than events with more circumscribed effects (e.g., when missing the bus only meant having to wait in the cold). The majority of hassles reported in these studies were circumscribed; that is, affected only one life domain. On average, 13% of the reported hassles qualified as complex; that is, affected multiple life domains. Both psychological and cardiovascular reactions to these complex unpleasant events were more pronounced the older the participants were. In contrast, when participants dealt with circumscribed unpleasant events, no age differences in psychological responding were observed, and cardiovascular responding was even less pronounced the older the participants were.

Taken together, theoretical predictions and empirical evidence regarding age differences in affective responding appear to contrast at first glance. Recent ambulatory assessment research, however, suggests that taking the specific characteristics of the negative event into account may help to clarify the prevailing inconsistency. Resource demands imposed by the event may be a particularly relevant characteristic in this respect. Based on their findings, Wrzus and colleagues (2012) speculate that, as long as the resource demands exerted by an event do not overtax the individual's capacities, affect-regulation competence may be maintained throughout adulthood, leading to comparable or even less affective reactivity to negative experiences among older adults as compared to younger individuals. For the few complex everyday hassles, however, the likelihood may increase that their resource demands overtax older adults' capacity to effectively regulate their affective response, leading to higher affective responsiveness to complex events with increased age.

To revisit the question of potential mechanisms associated with age differences in daily affective well-being, the studies just summarized suggest that healthy older adults, at least into young old age, often report better overall affective well-being in their daily lives than younger adults do. The studies also provide evidence that two age-related differences may be associated with this observation: an age-related decrease in the prevalence of both everyday stressors and motivational-conflict experiences. Although it is often claimed in the literature that an age-related improvement in affect-regulation competence may also be relevant here, direct empirical evidence from people's daily lives to support this claim is still lacking. Indirect evidence comes from investigations on age differences in affect-regulation orientations and in affective reactivity to negative daily events.

Research on the former—affect-regulation orientation—provided evidence for an age-related decrease in the prevalence of contra-hedonic and an increase of pro-hedonic orientations. Results on age differences in the latter—affective reactivity—are still mixed, with recent evidence suggesting that this may be due to variability across studies regarding the investigated events' characteristics. Resource demands imposed by the negative experience may be particularly important in this respect. Table 5.2 provides a brief summary of the main reviewed findings on potential contributors to age differences in everyday affective well-being.

So far, most studies on age differences in affective reactivity to negative everyday events have implicitly assumed that individuals are comparable in their motivation to maximize their affective well-being even in the face of adversity. The fact that people might differ in their affect-regulation motivation, and that there may be age-related differences therein (Riediger et al., 2009, 2011), has not yet been taken into consideration. Investigating potential implications of this possibility for age differences in affective reactivity thus remains an important task for future research.

The studies discussed so far differentiated everyday affective experiences primarily in terms of their valence. Such a perspective is in line with dimensional models that propose that every affective experience at a given point in time, as a whole, can unequivocally be described in terms of such characteristics as its valence and arousal (e.g., Russell & Carroll, 1999). Another perspective, to which we turn next, assumes that affective experiences may involve a blend of affective entities that can vary regarding their specific characteristics (Cacioppo & Berntson, 1994). This perspective brings another characteristic of affective experiences into play, namely, their structure or complexity (Schimmack, 2001).

Age Differences in the Complexity of Everyday Affective Experiences

Interest in age differences in affective complexity derived from theoretical propositions that affective complexity reflects desirable affective development and increases with age (Carstensen et al., 2011; Labouvie-Vief, & Studer, 2010). For example, socioemotional selectivity theory (Carstensen et al., 1999) posits that older adults, because of their limited time perspective, focus more on emotionally salient goals than younger adults do. These goals imply the appreciation of close relationships, including conflicting and ambivalent ones. Mixed

Table 5.2. Overview of central findings of the reviewed studies on potential contributors to age trajectories in everyday affective well-being

Central findings	References
1) Exposure to hassles and motivational conflicts in everyday life	
• Age-related decrease in number and perceived severity of everyday stressors (various types) throughout adulthood	Almeida & Horn (2004); Charles et al. (2010); Sliwinski et al. (2008); Wrzus et al. (2012, study 1)
• Age-related decrease in number of interpersonal stressors (tensions, arguments, avoided arguments) throughout adulthood	Birditt et al. (2005); Charles et al. (2009)
• Age-related decrease in number of everyday motivational conflicts throughout adulthood	Riediger & Freund (2008)
2) Affect-regulation orientations in everyday life	
• Age-related increase in pro-hedonic, age-related decrease in contra-hedonic orientation throughout adulthood	Riediger et al. (2009)
3) Affective reactivity to everyday hassles	
• Age-related decrease in affective responsiveness to everyday hassles throughout adulthood	Birditt et al. (2005); Carstensen et al. (2000); Charles et al. (2009, avoided arguments); Uchino et al. (2006)
• Age-related increase in affective responsiveness to everyday hassles throughout adulthood	Mroczek & Almeida, 2004; Sliwinski et al. (2009, study 1)
• Age invariance in psychological responsiveness to arguments throughout adulthood	Charles et al. (2009)
• Age differences in affective reactivity depend on resource demands (complexity) of the event:	Wrzus et al. (2012)
– Complex events: Age-related increase in psychological and cardiovascular responsiveness from adolescence to old age	
– Circumscribed events: Age invariance in psychological responsiveness, and age-related decrease in cardiovascular responsiveness	

Note. All reviewed studies were cross-sectional. Studies varied regarding how affective responsiveness to hassles was operationalized. See information in text for study details.

affective experiences as related to such close relationships may therefore become more frequent as people age (Carstensen et al., 2000).

Another theoretical framework assumes that affective experiences are heavily influenced by culturally shared representations of emotions during earlier phases in life, whereas across adulthood, idiosyncratic experiences become more and more incorporated into these schematic structures. This should result in increasing cognitive-evaluative complexity as a response to affect-eliciting events, and, in turn, to more idiosyncratic affective experiences and an increasing tolerance for experiencing seemingly contradicting feelings, such as positive and negative affect, at the same time (Labouvie-Vief, DeVoe, & Bulka, 1989; Labouvie-Vief & Medler, 2002).

Over the past decade, a body of research has evolved that uses ambulatory assessment techniques to investigate these theoretical ideas in terms of age differences in the complexity of everyday affective experiences. Here, we summarize the empirical findings from this research. First, however, we emphasize the conceptual and methodological heterogeneity of the respective investigations.

Conceptual and Methodological Heterogeneity of Research on Everyday Affective Complexity

A review of findings on age differences in everyday affective complexity needs to appreciate a two-fold heterogeneity of the respective investigations. First, there is a multitude of different, loosely related theoretical constructs that reflect the general idea of affective complexity. Affective complexity has been addressed using various related constructs, such as poignancy (defined as the experience of mixed positive and negative affect; Carstensen et al., 2000), emotion blends (defined as the experience of co-occurring distinct emotions; Zelenski & Larsen, 2000), or granularity (defined as the tendency to differentiate between distinct affective states; Feldman Barrett, Gross, Christensen, & Benvenuto, 2001). Second, the methods with which researchers have sought to capture these multiple constructs are similarly diverse.

Our review focuses on two conceptualizations that have been most commonly used in ambulatory assessment studies on age differences in everyday affective complexity. The first conceptualization focuses on *affect co-occurrence*, that is, the simultaneous co-occurrence of different affective states (e.g., feeling happy and sad at the same time). This construct is often operationalized as the within-person correlation of positive and negative affect over time (Carstensen et al., 2000; Grühn, Lumley, Diehl, & Labouvie-Vief, 2012; Ong & Bergeman, 2004; Zelenski & Larsen, 2000). Given the widespread use of this approach, it should be noted that interpreting such a covariation measure in terms of affective complexity may be problematic (Schimmack, 2001). Low correlations reflect the relative independence of experiencing positive and negative affect, which can, but need not, include the possibility of their simultaneous co-occurrence. Alternatively, such low correlations may also result from low within-person variance in either positive or negative affect, or both (Diener & Iran-Nejad, 1986; Russell & Carroll, 1999). Age differences in affective variability, particularly in negative affect (Grühn et al., 2012; Röcke et al., 2009) potentially aggravate the equivocality of this measure in age-comparative research. An alternative index for affect co-occurrence is to quantify the degree or frequency of experiencing different affective states at the same time (Schimmack, 2001). Although this approach has been initially used primarily for experimental data (e.g., Ersner-Hershfield, Mikels, Sullivan, & Carstensen, 2008; J. T. Larsen, McGraw, Mellers, & Cacioppo, 2004; Magai, Consedine, Krivoshekova, Kudadjie-Gyamfi, & McPherson, 2006), it has also been applied to experience-sampling data more recently (Riediger et al., 2009).

The second conceptualization of everyday affective complexity pertains to *affective differentiation*, that is, the tendency to differentiate between distinct facets of a given affective experience. This construct is often operationalized by the number of meaningful principal components derived from each participant's repeated responses to multiple-item affect scales over time (Carstensen et al., 2000; Hay & Diehl, 2011; Ong & Bergeman, 2004) or by p-technique factor analysis (Grühn et al., 2012; Ram, 2006).

The methodological diversity in investigations of age differences in affective complexity may limit the possibility to replicate empirical findings across studies, as demonstrated by Ready, Carvalho, and Weinberger (2008) and Grühn and colleagues (2012). Following recommendations by Schimmack (2001), these authors each compared different statistical indices for affective complexity within the same experience-sampling dataset. Their findings indicate that age differences in affective complexity depend on the level of data aggregation and on the choice of statistical indices, and that the associations between various indices are relatively small. Yet more methodological divergence between studies comes from disparities regarding the use of different sampling schedules and of different affect items. These multiple differences across studies have likely contributed to the heterogeneity of the empirical findings that we review next, separately for the two conceptualizations of affect co-occurrence and affect differentiation.

Empirical Investigations on Potential Age Differences in Everyday Affect Co-Occurrence

Carstensen and colleagues (2000) reported findings from an experience-sampling study in which intraperson correlations of positive and negative affect were negative throughout the investigated lifespan sample, but smaller with higher age. The authors interpret this finding as indicating a greater simultaneous co-occurrence of positive and negative affect, or poignancy, in old age (for a critical evaluation of this conclusion, however, see Schimmack, 2001). Carstensen and colleagues (2011) later followed up on this sample with two additional measurement bursts. In contrast to Carstensen et al. (2000), they found no age-differential associations of positive and negative affect 5 years later, but replicated their earlier finding with the measurement burst 10 years later. Moreover, longitudinal analyses across all measurement bursts showed that the within-person association between positive and negative affect became smaller as participants grew older. This is an important finding because it suggests that there is within-person change in the covariation of positive and negative affect over time.

Three other studies, however, did not replicate these age differences in intraperson correlations of positive and negative affect in their samples. These findings come from diary studies with younger, middle-aged, and older adults (Hay & Diehl, 2011; Ready et al., 2008) and from an experience-sampling study with an adult lifespan sample (Grühn et al., 2012). In addition, a daily-diary study with older adults by Ong and Bergemann (2004) also investigated within-person correlations of positive and negative affect over time and found no age differences within the age range from 60 to 85 years.

More divergent evidence is provided by two studies suggesting that the co-occurrence of positive and negative affect is even less prevalent in older than in younger adults. In a daily-diary study by Ready and colleagues (2008, study 2), negative within-person correlations of positive and negative affect were stronger in older than in younger adults. Similarly, data from an experience-sampling study with a lifespan sample (Riediger et al., 2009) showed that episodes of mixed affect, operationalized as the simultaneous co-occurrence of intense positive and negative affect that are both above the individual's respective averages, were less prevalent among older adults and more prevalent among adolescents as compared to all other age groups.

Empirical Investigations on Potential Age Differences in Everyday Affect Differentiation

Empirical evidence on age differences in everyday affect differentiation is similarly inconsistent. Analyses of the experience-sampling study reported by Carstensen and colleagues (2000) suggest more affect differentiation in old age. In this study, the factorial structure of older adults' affect reports yielded more principal components than that of younger adults', suggesting that older adults reported their everyday affect experiences in more differentiated terms than did younger individuals. However, application of another analytical approach, namely, p-technique factor analysis, with the longitudinal dataset from these participants yielded the opposite pattern of results, suggesting that older adults' reports of their everyday affective experiences were less differentiated than younger adults' (Ram, 2006). Diverging from both findings, p-technique factor analysis of another experience-sampling dataset found that the factorial structure of everyday affective experiences was age-invariant (Grühn et al., 2012).

In sum, so far, the empirical evidence concerning age differences in everyday affective complexity is inconclusive for measures of both affect co-occurrence and affect differentiation. Table 5.3

Table 5.3. Overview of central findings of the reviewed studies on age differences in the complexity of affective experiences

Central findings	References
1) Affect co-occurrence ("mixed affect")	
• Age-related decrease in the negative within-person correlation between momentary positive affect (PA) and negative affect (NA) throughout adulthood	Carstensen et al. (2000; 2011)
• Age invariance in the negative within-person correlation between momentary PA and NA throughout adulthood	Hay & Diehl (2011); Grühn et al. (2012); Ong & Bergemann (2004); Ready et al. (2008, study 1)
• Age-related increase in the negative within-person correlation between momentary PA and NA throughout adulthood	Ready et al. (2008, study 2)
• Age-related decrease in the prevalence of situations where the reported intensity of both PA and NA were at or above the individual's respective averages	Riediger et al. (2009)
2) Affect differentiation in everyday life	
• Age-related increase in affect differentiation throughout adulthood	Carstensen et al. (2000)
• Age-related decrease in affect differentiation throughout adulthood	Ram (2006)
• Age invariance in affect differentiation throughout adulthood	Grühn et al. (2012)

Note. Most reviewed studies were cross-sectional. Studies varied regarding how everyday affective experiences were measured, aggregated, and analyzed. See information in text for details.

provides a brief summary of the reviewed studies. To date, the theoretical notion that everyday affective complexity increases with age has received little support from ambulatory assessment research, with only two such studies (Carstensen et al., 2000, 2011) finding supporting evidence.

At present, the prevailing conceptual and methodological heterogeneity on the one hand, and the multifarious empirical picture on the other, prevent any clear conclusions about potential age differences in everyday affective complexity. Although this may seem unsatisfactory at first glance, it also provides the interesting opportunity for the field to rise to the challenge of resolving these existing inconsistencies. This challenge pertains to affect-complexity research in general, but ambulatory assessment can offer valuable contributions, both in terms of understanding people's everyday affective complexity across life, and in terms of refining methods of affect-complexity research.

Conclusion

Historically, researchers initially expected that affective well-being should decline with age throughout adulthood because of the many aging-related losses, such as those in the cognitive, social, or health domains. When these expectations could not be confirmed empirically with global or retrospective well-being measures, suspicions arose that methodological limitations with these measures might be responsible. Ambulatory assessment, the repeated sampling of experiences in close temporal proximity to their spontaneous emergence in people's natural living environments, was brought into play as a way to overcome these concerns. Over the past decade, a body of research has been growing that uses ambulatory assessment (e.g., diary and experience-sampling) approaches to investigate age-related differences in everyday affective experiences. This research has provided well-replicated evidence that, overall, older individuals do indeed tend to report better average affective well-being in their daily lives than younger individuals do. Although these findings are relatively pervasive across different studies, samples, and operationalizations, inconsistencies in the more detailed examinations of the findings are noteworthy, too. These pertain, for example, to the form of the observed age effects across different phases of the adult lifespan, or the presence or absence of age effects regarding specific facets of everyday affective experiences. Ambulatory assessment research has also gone beyond attempts to show whether age differences in everyday affective experiences exist. It has furthermore addressed the mechanisms that might be associated with such age differences. Here, the available evidence suggests that multiple aspects, some of which relate to individuals' everyday life contexts and behaviors, might be at work. Findings indicate, for example, that a lower prevalence of everyday stressors and motivational conflicts in older as compared to younger adults' daily lives are associated with age differences in everyday affective experiences. Another notion maintains that age differences in the ability to control affective responses in the face of adversity may also be relevant in this respect; however, this proposition has not yet received sufficient empirical support. Although there is evidence that older adults evince more pro-hedonic orientations (and adolescents, more contra-hedonic orientations) in their daily lives than do individuals from other age groups, the empirical picture regarding adult age differences in people's actual affective responding to everyday hassles is still inconclusive. Recent findings, however, suggest that the characteristics of the affect-eliciting event, and in particular their resource requirements, could be important in this context. Although affective responding to the majority of daily hassles with relative circumscribed resource requirements appears to be fairly age-invariant, more pronounced affective reactivity has been observed in response to everyday stressors with complex resource demands. This pattern of findings suggests stability of affect-regulation competence into older adulthood as long as the situational resource demands do not overtax the individuals' resource capacity, but a decline in affect-regulation effectiveness as soon as this is the case. Yet another series of analyses has moved beyond descriptions of everyday affective experiences in terms of their overarching hedonic tone or valence. This perspective has taken into account that affective experiences can be more complex, and hence investigated potential age-related differences in the structure of everyday affective experiences. To date, this research is characterized by considerable conceptual and methodological heterogeneity, which is likely responsible for the still inconclusive pattern of empirical findings. Future studies will have to resolve these inconsistencies to further advance the field.

Future Directions

More methodological homogeneity across studies is not only desirable for research on everyday affective complexity, but also for the entire field of ambulatory assessment research on affective development. Much of the complexity and partial inconsistency of the findings we have reviewed in this chapter may be due to the pronounced methodological heterogeneity across studies. Most important, little to no overlap exists between studies in terms of how everyday affective experiences were measured. Although most of the studies reviewed here proceeded from the assumption that different affect facets can be validly summarized into aggregate indices of positive and negative affect, or of overall affective well-being, there is controversy in the literature about the extent to which this is warranted as opposed to treating different affect facets as reflecting distinctive experiences. The possibility that differences in the subtleties of findings reviewed here are due to different sets of affect measures should be explored in a systematic fashion in the future.

Another important task for the future is to take on more openly the challenges brought forth by ambulatory assessment methods. To date, a unilateral emphasis on the strengths of the approach (e.g., the immediacy and ecological validity of the assessments, and the accessibility of short-term within-person fluctuations and their covariation with other processes and environmental characteristics over time) is typical. The fact that ambulatory assessment also involves methodological challenges that might be relevant for the interpretation of findings has been largely neglected. Particularly important here are issues of possible measurement reactivity as well as potential age-differential sample selectivity and attrition. Although measurement reactivity has been (at least rudimentarily) addressed in some of the studies reviewed here (e.g., by analyzing and controlling for potential time-related trends in the variables under investigation; Riediger & Freund, 2008; Riediger et al., 2011), this is not yet common practice and should be more routinely implemented in the analysis of ambulatory assessment datasets. Moreover, the possibility of including control groups who do not participate in the ambulatory assessment phase should be more frequently considered when planning study designs. Age-differential sample selectivity and attrition have received even less attention. Future studies should incorporate means to explore the representativeness of their investigated samples more rigorously.

Furthermore, to date, developmental investigations of everyday affective functioning have primarily focused on demonstrating potential age-related differences in characteristics of everyday affective experiences, and on investigating factors that might have contributed to such age-related differences. Not much attention has been paid yet to the potential consequences of interindividual differences in

affective functioning for developmental processes (but see mortality analyses in Carstensen et al., 2011). Incorporating such an "outcome-focused" perspective more extensively will provide fruitful impetus to further advancements of the understanding of adult affective development.

A matter of course for developmental researchers, one that should nevertheless not be forgotten, is the limited suitability of cross-sectional data for investigating human development. The currently prevailing (and pragmatically determined) emphasis on cross-sectional ambulatory assessment studies needs to be more systematically complemented in the future by long-term longitudinal, and preferably cross-sequential, study designs. This will provide more powerful possibilities to disentangle the influences that derive from differences between birth cohorts from those that are due to aging-related changes within persons over time. A related challenge for future studies, to which we have already alluded, pertains to methodological refinements that will allow for sounder explorations of causal relations involved in the phenomena under study, namely the antecedents and consequences of aging-related differences in everyday affective functioning.

Note

1. Studies that repeatedly sample momentary affective experiences in laboratory contexts (e.g., Brose, Schmiedek, Lövdén, & Lindenberger, 2011; Röcke et al., 2009; Sliwinski et al., 2009, study 2; Stawski et al., 2008) do not have the enhanced ecological validity that is characteristic for ambulatory assessment approaches and are therefore not included in the present review.

References

Almeida, D. M. (2005). Resilience and vulnerability to daily stressors assessed via diary methods. *Current Directions in Psychological Science, 14,* 64–68. doi: 10.1111/j.0963-7214.2005.00336.x

Almeida, D. M., & Horn, M. C. (2004). Is daily life more stressful during middle adulthood? In O. G. Brim, C. D. Ryff & R. C. Kessler (Eds.), *How healthy are we? A national study of well-being at midlife* (pp. 425–451). Chicago, IL: University of Chicago Press.

Andrade, E. B., & Cohen, J. B. (2007). On the consumption of negative feelings. *Journal of Consumer Research, 34,* 283–300. doi: 10.1086/519498

Baltes, P. B. (1987). Theoretical propositions of life-span developmental psychology: On the dynamics between growth and decline. *Developmental Psychology, 23,* 611–626. doi: 10.1037/0012-1649.23.5.611

Birditt, K. S., Fingerman, K. L., & Almeida, D. M. (2005). Age differences in exposure and reactions to interpersonal tensions: A daily diary study. *Psychology and Aging, 20,* 330–340. doi: 10.1037/0882-7974.20.2.330

Blanchard-Fields, F. (2007). Everyday problem solving and emotion: An adult developmental perspective. *Current Directions in Psychological Science, 16*, 26–31. doi: 10.1111/j.1467-872 1.2007.00469.x

Blanchard-Fields, F., & Coats, A. H. (2008). The experience of anger and sadness in everyday problems impacts age differences in emotion regulation. *Developmental Psychology, 44*, 1547–1556. doi: 10.1037/a0013915

Brandtstädter, J., & Greve, W. (1994). The aging self: Stabilizing and protective processes. *Developmental Review, 14*, 52–80. doi: 10.1006/drev.1994.1003

Brandtstädter, J., & Renner, G. (1990). Tenacious goal pursuit and flexible goal adjustment: Explication and age-related analysis of assimilative and accommodative strategies of coping. *Psychology and Aging, 5*, 58–67. doi: 10.1037/0882-7974.5.1.58

Brose, A., Scheibe, S., & Schmiedek, F. (2012). Life contexts make a difference: emotional stability in younger and older adults. *Psychology and Aging.* Advance online publication. doi: 10.1037/a0030047

Brose, A., Schmiedek, F., Lövdén, M., & Lindenberger, U. (2011). Normal aging dampens the link between intrusive thoughts and negative affect in reaction to daily stressors. *Psychology and Aging, 26*, 488–502. doi: 10.1037/a0022287

Cacioppo, J. X., & Berntson, G. G. (1994). Relationship between attitudes and evaluative space: A critical review, with emphasis on the separability of positive and negative substrates. *Psychological Bulletin, 115*, 401–423. doi: 10.103 7/0033-2909.115.3.401

Carstensen, L. L., Isaacowitz, D. M., & Charles, S. T. (1999). Taking time seriously: A theory of socioemotional selectivity. *American Psychologist, 54*, 165–181. doi: 10.1037/0003-066X.54.3.165

Carstensen, L. L., Pasupathi, M., Mayr, U., & Nesselroade, J. R. (2000). Emotional experience in everyday life across the adult life span. *Journal of Personality and Social Psychology, 79*, 644–655. doi: IO.1037//O022-3514.79.4.644

Carstensen, L. L., Turan, B., Scheibe, S., Ram, N., Ersner-Hershfield, H., Samanez-Larkin, G. R., et al. (2011). Emotional experience improves with age: Evidence based on over 10 years of experience sampling. *Psychology and Aging, 26*, 21–33. doi: 10.1037/a0021285

Charles, S. T. (2010). Strength and vulnerability integration: A model of emotional well-being across adulthood. *Psychological Bulletin, 136*, 1068–1091. doi: 10.1037/a0021232

Charles, S. T., Luong, G., Almeida, D. M., Ryff, C., Sturm, M., & Love, G. (2010). Fewer ups and downs: Daily stressors mediate age differences in negative affect. *Journal of Gerontology: Psychological Sciences, 65B*, 279–286. doi: 10.1093/geronb/gbq002

Charles, S. T., Piazza, J. R., Luong, G., & Almeida, D. M. (2009). Now you see it, now you don't: Age differences in affective reactivity to social tensions. *Psychology and Aging, 24*, 645–653. doi: 10.1037/a0016673

Diener, E., & Iran-Nejad, A. (1986). The relationship in experience between various types of affect. *Journal of Personality and Social Psychology, 50*, 1031–1038. doi: 10.1037/0022-3 514.50.5.1031

Ersner-Hershfield, H., Mikels, J. A., Sullivan, S. J., & Carstensen, L. L. (2008). Poignancy: Mixed emotional experience in the face of meaningful endings. *Journal of Personality and Social Psychology, 94*, 158–167. doi: 10.1037/0022-3514.94.1.158

Feldman Barrett, L., Gross, J., Christensen, T. C., & Benvenuto, M. (2001). Knowing what you're feeling and knowing what

to do about it: Mapping the relation between emotion differentiation and emotion regulation. *Cognition and Emotion, 15*, 713–724. doi: 10.1080/02699930143000239

Foster, E. (2010). Causal inference and developmental psychology. *Developmental Psychology, 46*, 1454–1480. doi: 10.1037/a0020204

Freund, A. M., & Baltes, P. B. (2000). The orchestration of selection, optimization and compensation: An action-theoretical conceptualization of a theory of developmental regulation. In W. J. Perrig & A. Grob (Eds.), *Control of human behavior, mental processes, and consciousness: Essays in honor of the 60th birthday of August Flammer* (pp. 35–58). Mahwah, NJ: Lawrence Erlbaum.

Gerstorf, D., Ram, N., Mayraz, G., Hidajat, M., Lindenberger, U., Wagner, G. G., & Schupp, J. (2010). Late-life decline in well-being across adulthood in Germany, the United Kingdom, and the United States: Something is seriously wrong at the end of life. *Psychology and Aging, 25*, 477–485. doi: 10.1037/a0017543

Grühn, D., Lumley, M. A., Diehl, M., & Labouvie-Vief, G. (2012). Time-based indicators of emotional complexity: Interrelations and correlates. *Emotion.* Advance online publication. doi: 10.1037/a0030363

Hay, E. L., & Diehl, M. (2011). Emotion complexity and emotion regulation across adulthood. *European Journal of Ageing, 8*, 1–12. doi: 10.1007/s10433-011-0191-7

Heckhausen, J., & Schulz, R. (1995). A life-span theory of control. *Psychological Review, 102*, 284–304.

Hoppmann, C., & Riediger, M. (2009). Ambulatory assessment in lifespan psychology: An overview of current status and new trends. *European Psychologist, 14*, 98–108. doi: 10.1027/1016-9040.14.2.98

Kööts, L., Realo, A., & Allik, J. (2011). The influence of the weather on affective experience. An experience sampling study. *Journal of Individual Differences, 32*, 74–84. doi: 10.1027/1614-0001/a000037

Labouvie-Vief, G. (2009). Dynamic integration theory: Emotion, cognition, and equilibrium in later life. In V. L. Bengtson, M. Silverstein, N. M. Putney, & D. Gans (Eds.), *Handbook of theories of aging* (2nd ed., pp. 277–293). New York: Springer.

Labouvie-Vief, G., DeVoe, M., & Bulka, D. (1989). Speaking about feelings: Conceptions of emotion across the life span. *Psychology and Aging, 4*, 425–437. doi: 10.1037//0882-7974.4.4.425

Labouvie-Vief, G., Grühn, D., & Studer, J. (2010). Dynamic integration of emotion and cognition: Equilibrium regulation in development and aging. In R. M. Lerner, M. E. Lamb, & A. M. Freund (Eds.), *The handbook of life-span development: Vol. 2. Social and emotional development* (pp. 79–115). Hoboken, NJ: Wiley.

Labouvie-Vief, G., & Medler, M. (2002). Affect optimization and affect complexity: Modes and styles of regulation in adulthood. *Psychology and Aging, 17*, 571–588. doi: 10.1037 //0882-7974.17.4.571

Larsen, J. T., McGraw, A. P., Mellers, B. A., & Cacioppo, J. T. (2004). The agony of victory and thrill of defeat: Mixed emotional reactions to disappointing wins and relieving losses. *Psychological Science, 15*, 325–330. doi: 10.1111/j.0956-79 76.2004.00677.x

Larsen, R. J. (2000). Toward a science of mood regulation. *Psychological Inquiry, 11*, 129–141.

Lawton, M. P., Kleban, M. H., & Dean, J. (1993). Affect and age: Cross-sectional comparisons of structure and prevalence. *Psychology and Aging, 8*, 165–175.

Levenson, R. W., Carstensen, L. L., & Gottman, J. M. (1994). The influence of age and gender on affect, physiology, and their interrelations: A study of long-term marriages. *Journal of Personality and Social Psychology, 67*, 56–68.

Lindenberger, U., & Pötter, U. (1998). The complex nature of unique and shared effects in hierarchical linear regression: Implications for developmental psychology. *Psychological Methods, 3*, 218–230. doi: 10.1037/1082-989X.3.2.218

Lindenberger, U., von Oertzen, T., Ghisletta, P., & Hertzog, C. (2011). Cross-sectional age variance extraction: What's change got to do with it? *Psychology and Aging, 26*, 34–47. doi: 10.1037/a0020525

Magai, C., Consedine, N. S., Krivoshekova, Y. S., Kudadjie-Gyamfi, E., & McPherson, R. (2006). Emotion experience and expression across the adult life span: Insights from a multimodal assessment study. *Psychology and Aging, 21*, 303–317. doi: 10.1037/0882-7974.21.2.303

Maxwell, S. E., & Cole, D. A. (2007). Bias in cross-sectional analyses of longitudinal mediation. *Psychological Methods, 12*, 23–44. doi: 10.1037/1082-989X.12.1.23

Mill, J. S. (1848). *A system of logic*. London: Parker.

Miron-Shatz, T., Stone, A., & Kahneman, D. (2009). Memories of yesterday's emotions: Does the valence of experience affect the memory-experience gap? *Emotion, 9*, 885–891. doi: 10.1037/a0017823

Mroczek, D. K., & Almeida, D. M. (2004). The effect of daily stress, personality, and age on daily negative affect. *Journal of Personality, 72*, 355–378. doi: 10.1111/j.0022-3506.2004.00265.x

Ong, A. D., & Bergeman, C. S. (2004). The complexity of emotions in later life. *Journal of Gerontology: Psychological Sciences, 59B*, P117–P122. doi: 10.1093/geronb/59.3.P117

Parrott, W. G. (1993). Beyond hedonism: Motives for inhibiting good moods and for maintaining bad moods. In D. M. Wegner & J. W. Pennebaker (Eds.), *Handbook of mental control* (pp. 278–305). Englewood Cliffs, NJ: Prentice Hall.

Ram, N. (2006). *Emphasizing individuality in developmental models of change*. (Doctoral dissertation, University of Virginia). Retrieved from http://en.scientificcommons.org/35283990

Ready, R. E., Carvalho, J. O., & Weinberger, M. I. (2008). Emotional complexity in younger, midlife, and older adults. *Psychology and Aging, 23*, 928–933. doi: 10.1037/a0014003

Ready, R. E., Weinberger, M. I., & Jones, K. M. (2007). How happy have you felt lately? Two diary studies of emotion recall in older and younger adults. *Cognition and Emotion, 21*, 728–757. doi: 10.1080/02699930600948269

Riediger, M., & Freund, A. M. (2008). Me against myself: Motivational conflict and emotional development in adulthood. *Psychology and Aging, 23*, 479–494. doi: 10.1037/a0013302

Riediger, M., Schmiedek, F., Wagner, G., & Lindenberger, U. (2009). Seeking pleasure and seeking pain: Differences in pro- and contra-hedonic motivation from adolescence to old age. *Psychological Science, 20*, 1529–1535. doi: 10.1111/j.1467-9280.2009.02473.x

Riediger, M., Wrzus, C., Schmiedek, F., Wagner, G. G., & Lindenberger, U. (2011). Is seeking bad mood cognitively demanding? Contra-hedonic orientation and working-memory capacity in everyday life. *Emotion, 11*, 656–665. doi: 10.1037/a0022756

Robinson, M. D., & Clore, G. L. (2002). Belief and feeling: Evidence for an accessibility model of emotional self-report. *Psychological Bulletin, 128*, 934–960. doi: 10.1037/0033-2909.128.6.934

Röcke, C., Li, S.-C., & Smith, J. (2009). Intraindividual variability in positive and negative affect over 45 days: Do older adults fluctuate less than young adults? *Psychology and Aging, 24*, 863–878. doi: 10.1037/a0016276

Russell, J. A., & Carroll, J. M. (1999). On the bipolarity of positive and negative affect. *Psychological Bulletin, 125*, 3–30. doi: 10.1037/0033-2909.125.1.3

Rutter, M. (2007). Proceeding from observed correlation to causal inference: The use of natural experiments. *Perspectives on Psychological Science, 2*, 377–395. doi: 10.1111/j.1745-6916.2007.00050.x

Schimmack, U. (2001). Pleasure, displeasure, and mixed feelings: Are semantic opposites mutually exclusive? *Cognition & Emotion, 15*, 81–97. doi: 10.1080/02699930126097

Schwarz, N. (2007). Retrospective and concurrent self-reports: The rationale for real-time data capture. In A. A. Stone, S. Shiffman, A. A. Atienza, & L. Nebeling (Eds.), *The science of real-time data capture* (pp. 11–26). New York: Oxford University Press.

Scollon, C. N., Kim-Prieto, C., & Diener, E. (2003). Experience sampling: Promises and pitfalls, strengths and weaknesses. *Journal of Happiness Studies, 4*, 5–34. doi: 10.1023/A:1023605205115

Sliwinski, M. J., Almeida, D. M., Stawski, R. S., & Smyth, J. (2009). Intraindividual change and variability in daily stress processes: Findings from two measurement-burst diary studies. *Psychology and Aging, 24*, 828–840. doi: 10.1037/a0017925

Sliwinski, M. J., Smyth, J. M., Hofer, S. M., & Stawski, R. S. (2006). Intraindividual coupling of daily stress and cognition. *Psychology and Aging, 21*, 545–557. doi: 10.1037/0882-7974.21.3.545

Stawski, R. S., Sliwinski, M. J., Almeida, D. M., & Smyth, J. M. (2008). Reported exposure and emotional reactivity to daily stressors: The roles of adult age and global perceived stress. *Psychology and Aging, 23*, 52–61. doi: 10.1037/0882-7974.23.1.52

Steptoe, A., Leigh, E. S., & Kumari, M. (2011). Positive affect and distressed affect over the day in older people. *Psychology and Aging, 26*, 956–965. doi: 10.1037/a0023303

Tamir, M., Chiu, C.-Y., & Gross, J. J. (2007). Business or pleasure? Utilitarian versus hedonic considerations in emotion regulation. *Emotion, 7*, 546–554. doi: 10.1037/1528-3542.7.3.546

Tamir, M., Mitchell, C., & Gross, J. J. (2008). Hedonic and instrumental motives in anger regulation. *Psychological Science, 19*, 324–328. doi: 10.1111/j.1467-9280.2008.02088.x

Uchino, B. N., Berg, C. A., Smith, T. W., Pearce, G., & Skinner, M. (2006). Age-related differences in ambulatory blood pressure during daily stress: Evidence for greater blood pressure reactivity with age. *Psychology and Aging, 21*, 231–239. doi: 10.1037/0882-7974.21.2.231

Wood, J. V., Heimpel, S. A., Manwell, L. A., & Whittington, E. J. (2009). This mood is familiar and I don't deserve to feel better anyway: Mechanisms underlying self-esteem differences in the motivation to repair sad moods. *Journal of Personality and Social Psychology, 96*, 363–380. doi: 10.1037/a0012881

Wrzus, C., Müller, V., Wagner, G. G., Lindenberger, U., & Riediger, M. (2012). Affective and cardiovascular responding to unpleasant events from adolescence to old age: Complexity of events matters. *Developmental Psychology*, Advance online publication. doi: 10.1037/a0028325

Zelenski, J. M., & Larsen, R. J. (2000). The distribution of basic emotions in everyday life: A state and trait perspective from experience sampling data. *Journal of Research in Personality, 34*, 178–197. doi: 10.1006/jrpe.1999.2275

PART 2

Emotion in Context: Antecedents and Consequences

The Dynamics of Cognitive-Emotional Integration: Complexity and Hedonics in Emotional Development

Gisela Labouvie-Vief, Anne-Laure Gilet, *and* Nathalie Mella

Abstract

In this chapter, we discuss Fredda Blanchard-Fields' important contribution to the understanding of emotional regulation in later life by relating it to a recent cognitive-developmental theory (Dynamic Integration Theory [DIT]) that posits joint development and aging of the cognitive-executive and emotional systems. This conception, inspired by the work of Jean Piaget, describes cognitive-emotional development during the first part of the lifespan as a process in which the capacity for sustaining emotional tension becomes raised as higher order cognitive representations become part of a common regulatory network. This process raises the functional tension threshold range over which emotional equilibrium is maintained. In contrast to earlier development, aging is characterized by a lowering of tension thresholds that brings greater vulnerability to high levels of activation in conditions that are novel and involve a great deal of effort. In contrast, well-automated knowledge and crystallized knowledge can provide a degree of buffering against these negative changes and is, at times, even related to increases in the depth and integration of experience.

Key Words: adult development, lifespan development, emotional development, emotion regulation, equilibrium

In this chapter, we would like to add to the celebration of Fredda Blanchard-Fields' life and work by addressing what we see as the central defining theme that has characterized Fredda's work and by proposing a theoretical solution to the questions she raised throughout her career. A unique feature of that career was her readiness to address a complex picture of emotional development and to reject any one-dimensional answer to that picture. Having begun her dissertation work with a study aimed at extending Labouvie-Vief's theory of the continuation of cognitive and emotional development from early life into adulthood (e.g., Labouvie-Vief, 1980, 1982), Blanchard-Fields was one of the first to explore how emotional development continued after adolescence. Part of that development, according to Labouvie-Vief, should be an increasing integration

of those cognitive and emotional systems that lack integration in early life and, especially, in adolescence. Working with tasks that presented an imaginary conflict between two parties, Blanchard-Fields examined the capacity to reason on and resolve this conflict in a way that resisted a simple right-wrong polarization. Instead, she looked for solutions that viewed each of the opposing perspectives as subjective viewpoints that, although inherently contrasting, could involve an attempt to reach consensus by means of trying to coordinate these perspectives through discussion and, ideally, an integrative problem resolution.

For this purpose, Blanchard-Fields used tasks that presented different viewpoints that were either abstract and of little emotional charge or were highly emotionally charged. The low emotional charge task was a modification of Kuhn and colleagues' "Livia task" (Kuhn, Pennington, & Leadbeater, 1983), which dealt with a hypothetical war between the fictional North and South Livias, as retold by the respective historians of each country. Tasks that were high in emotional charge dealt with a conflict between teenagers and their parents about a planned visit to the grandparents versus an outing with peers, or between a young woman and her partner about the pros and cons of an abortion.

Results of the study showed that, for adolescents, performance on the Livia task was equal to that of young adults, but that performance increased from young to middle adulthood. In contrast, for the emotionally charged visit and grandparent tasks, linear increments were found over the age groups, with adolescents scoring low increases from there on. Thus, adolescents scored significantly lower on the emotionally charged tasks than on the non-charged Livia task. Adults, but not adolescents, therefore, showed evidence of the capacity to reason in an emotionally balanced way even in emotionally demanding situations, thus supporting the conclusion that the cognitive or representational aspect of emotions and the dynamic aspects of their activation and regulation are well integrated in adults, but poorly so in adolescents.

Much of Blanchard-Fields' later research was aimed at the question, "does aging beyond middle adulthood bring a broadening and deepening of such processes of growth and integration?" The results of a series of her studies provided a disappointing picture (Blanchard-Fields, 1999): against the hoped-for continuation of increases into late life, instead results suggested a picture that tended to be much less positive and that even suggested a degree of decline in integrated complexity in older individuals. This was evident from a number of findings, such as a decrease in the capacity for reasoning in a dialectical fashion, a related move toward more polarizing processes of attribution, and an increasing difficulty in inhibiting irrelevant information. Blanchard-Fields thus concluded that regulation processes in later life are compromised as a result of declines in executive processes during this age period.

Since this earlier work, however, her work began to evoke a more complex picture, acknowledging that not only late middle adulthood but even later life could bring the ability for flexible and adaptive problem solving (Blanchard-Fields, 2009). For example, research often reports that the self-descriptions of elderly individuals are emotionally positive

(e.g., Mroczek & Kolarz, 1998), that older individuals can be more effective in emotion control (Gross, Carstensen, Pasupathi, Tsai, Gotestam Skorpen, & Hsu, 1997; Lawton, Kleban, & Dean, 1993), and that they place high priority on goals of emotion regulation (Blanchard-Fields, 2007; Carstensen, Mikels, & Mather, 2006); at times, they spend even less resources on emotion regulation than do younger adults.

Findings such as these, Blanchard-Fields suggested, appear to be in contrast to the tendency of much of the literature on aging and emotions to underscore massive declines in executive functions and fluid intelligence as a source of declines in emotion regulation. Rather, Blanchard-Fields' results suggest that cognitive losses do not automatically translate into losses in emotion regulation. Instead, she proposed, emotions need to be understood in the social context in which emotion regulation emerges, well as in the accumulation of life experiences that reinforce and automate emotion regulation skills.

In our opinion, Fredda Blanchard-Fields was working on an integration that has far-reaching consequences. A problem of the emotion regulation literature, particularly that of later life, has been a polarization between emotions as automatic processes and their control or regulation as effortful processes. However, classical writings such as those of Freud (see Pribam & Gill, 1976) and Piaget (1981), as well as several recent published studies (Craik & Bialystok, 2006; Labouvie-Vief, 2009; Labouvie-Vief, Grühn, & Studer, 2010; Lewis, 2010) suggest explicitly that not all of the burden of emotion regulation is on executive processes. Instead, even relatively complex emotion regulation can be accomplished through the means of regulation processes that have come to be automated into high-level cognitive-emotional structures (representations) whose efficiency does not necessarily rely on high effort and difficulty.

Nevertheless, we propose that development and aging bring both strengths and limits in such efficiency. To discuss these strengths and limits, we outline a theory initially stimulated by Piaget's (1981) writings on the parallel relationships between progressions in cognitive development and those in the domain of emotion. It was a core proposal of Piaget that, much as the development of automated representations restructures cognition, so it also restructures emotion, leading from precursor emotions that function in a reflex-like fashion to ones of greater complexity (higher levels of representation) that function with greater efficiency and integration, yet also with a greater degree of conscious awareness. Since the theory was closely tied to equilibrium models, it also implies increases in the complexity of representations that, in turn, bring changes in the conditions under which equilibrium is maintained. These conditions, furthermore, have direct consequences for the hedonics of emotion—that is, feelings of efficacy, comfort, and emotional well-being. In this way, equilibrium processes are directly tied to developing representations. Piaget referred to this aspect as the direct correspondence between, on one hand, the representational/structural aspect of emotions and, on the other hand, their energetics or dynamics of arousal from too low to comfortable to intolerable and damaging.

Generalizing this theory to the total lifespan, from *womb* to *tomb*, we present the resulting theory (DIT) in three sections. In the first section, we discuss the concept of equilibrium from a primarily physiological-biological perspective and elaborate its similarity to Piaget's notion of stages as moments of equilibrium or assimilation in a succession of changes. Second, we generalize this simple model of equilibrium to one that involves expansion and transformation through momentary disequilibrium and eventual widening of its range and level of functioning at biological and psychological levels. We also discuss the potential ideal and less positive outcomes of this process, as well as the conditions that foster or hinder it. In the third section, we then discuss how this model can be applied to the development of emotion regulation processes across the lifespan, placing particular emphasis on the process of aging.

Equilibrium in Development

Piaget's theory of development (e.g., Piaget, 1971) is well known for the fact that he loved biological metaphors for psychological processes. Even more, he proposed that psychological processes were ones that transformed and extended inborn biological ones (Piaget, 1971), and his thinking on notions of equilibrium is a prime example. Like biological processes, he proposed, psychological processes are dynamic. In joining with biological processes, they can, however, amplify the power and flexibility of those, because psychological processes can be less automatic and involve more cognitive control. Therefore, they make possible flexible adaptations to novel situations and can lead to developmental achievements of high levels of complexity and a dramatically widened range over which equilibrium

can be maintained. Yet, argued Piaget, such processes of change need to be well-coordinated to ensure not only that change can occur, but also that, in the midst of change, a degree of stability can be preserved. Such precarious coordination and balance assures "intelligent change, which does not transform things beyond recognition in one stroke, and which always preserves invariance in certain respects" (Piaget, 1970, p. 20).

Piaget's notion of development in stage-like progressions implies just such well-regulated change that preserves continuity. It describes relative moments of calm and stability in a process of change, moments that he referred to as equilibrium. At such moments, individuals possess a particular understanding of reality, characterized by the given level at which aspects of reality are represented. Each level provides a degree of stability to the child, because it implies a coherent picture of his or her world, which, as a consequence, appears coherent and controllable, and hence comfortable and nonthreatening. This does not mean, however, that the world is comfortable and nonthreatening in some absolute sense, but rather that the child construes it to be so through a process of assimilating it to a particular understanding or representation that she or he has developed so far. If what the child experiences matches her representation, the experience can be mastered and lead to feelings of success and pride. If, in turn, there is no such match, the result can be confusion and discomfort—and, in the extreme, even rage and terror. Hence, this notion of equilibrium implies that we fit or match how we experience the world with our understandings and expectations of it. The expectations we have of reality have implications, therefore, for our experiences of success and failure, joys and disappointments.

Biological Equilibrium

Piaget's analysis of developmental processes thus took as a core mechanism one already described by biologists, who similarly have been interested in organisms' capacity to maintain a relatively constant range of vital biological values (e.g., Brent, 1978; Carver & Scheier, 1998; Helson, 1964). Such systems were first described by Cannon (1939), whose interest was in the homeostatic mechanisms by which all living systems regulate themselves. As an example, take the system of body temperature regulation, which aims at preserving a "normal" human body temperature of 98.6oF. In actuality, body temperature changes upward and downward around this level through a constant play of positive and negative deviations from this ideal or *end state*. These deviations are, in turn, compensated for through equal movements in the opposite direction—as in the example of a driver who steers his car in an apparently "straight" direction by making small, alternating movements of deviation to the right and left from the ideal straight path. As a result, equilibrium systems represent not a fixed point of perfect stability, but rather a steady state—a dynamic play or *range* around an idealized *end state*. We will refer to this range as the *equilibrium range* throughout the chapter. Within those ranges, the organism functions optimally—that is, functioning is well integrated, and the organism experiences a sense of well-being. If, however, significant variations from this range occur in either direction, the play of deviations in one direction and counter-deviations in the other may become stormy and less stable, and deviations eventually may become so dramatic that they can no longer be compensated for. At such extremes, damage or even total breakdown of the system will result.

We display this state of affairs in Figure 6.1, which shows the relationship between the level of integrated functioning, on one hand, and the range of the equilibrium zone, on the other. The relationship is illustrated by an inverted U function, indicating that, to the degree that the system moves away from the end state and toward the margins of the equilibrium zone, system functioning is degraded. The system responds to these deviations with tension, which in turn implies that regulatory

effort commensurate with the degree of deviation is expended, with the aim of restoring the system to equilibrium. This homeostatic process works as long as deviations remain within the equilibrium range, keeping system tension within tolerable ranges. As tension moves toward the extremes of this range, however, the system exceeds tension thresholds, thus leading to a complete breakdown.

As in Freud's theory, Cannon's theory represented a tension reduction model. A homeostatic model based on tension reduction is "one which through the operation of a mechanism restores a certain end state unless and until the point of breakdown is reached" (Walker, 1956, p. 63). Such systems attempt to keep the discrepancy or tension between the end state and the actual state of the system at a minimum; they do this by responding to increases in discrepancy with an effortful response that matches the vigor of the deviation, but compensates for it by being in the opposite direction. As a result, such systems aim at keeping the discrepancy between the actual and end states at a minimum. As a consequence, they are called *discrepancy-reducing* or *negative feedback systems*.

Equilibrium as Psychological Construct

Equilibrium processes such as those described, despite being rather complex processes of dynamic regulation, function quite automatically to protect the organism. They can, however, be empowered by cognitive understandings; for example, knowing about the dangers of great discrepancies from

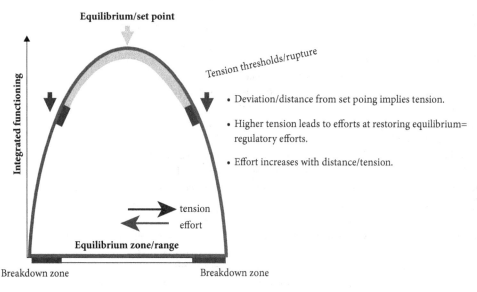

Figure 6.1. Equilibrium model of functioning.
Adapted from Labouvie-Vief (2009).

ideal temperatures, humans have developed means of creating protected environments that guard them from dangerous fluctuations. Piaget proposed that, in general, the function of cognition in development is thus to extend the range over which humans can maintain biologically evolved equilibrium mechanisms.

Piaget's use of the equilibrium construct to describe the influence of psychological processes such as cognitions closely followed already available biological models. He applied them to evolutionary processes of how the child manages to experience a sense of constancy in the midst of a dynamic back-and-forth. To do so, he (Piaget, 1980; see also Chapman, 1988) created examples that show a constant play between moments that assure a sense of stability and others that pose a challenge and threaten to undo that stability. There is, therefore, both a constant to-and-fro of tendencies that drive the system to disequilibrium, and compensatory and reparatory ones that bring the system back to equilibrium. As in the biological case of body temperature regulation, this to-and-fro often occurs outside the child's awareness, but nevertheless is evident to the adult observer in the manner in which children change their responses to changing situations.

As an example, take the example of a child who cannot conserve quantity in the familiar problem of the clay cylinder or "sausage" that is rolled out to become longer but thinner. To the mature observer, it is obvious that such actions do not change the overall volume of the clay material. Since, however, the child does not understand that increases in length are compensated for by corresponding decreases in thickness—thus preserving the total volume despite variations in both dimensions—she "focuses" (centers) on a single dimension. This focus is directed not through deliberation and cognitive understanding, but rather by purely perceptual and automatic responses: as long as the variations are very minor, the child will affirm that the volume of the sausage has not changed, but as soon as the variations become quite large, she will note the considerable change in one dimension—but to the exclusion of the other. This results in a highly unstable situation in which, at times, one dimension (e.g., length) is attended to and, at other times, the other (width). The child thus expresses constant contradictions, but neither notes nor is bothered by them—he or she lacks cognitive awareness of the contradictions. This state of affairs, according to Piaget, reflects a cognitive gap, a lack of understanding the situation.

Psychological and Biological Factors in Equilibrium Regulation

The example just cited is not particularly salient in emotions, as children show little surprise, interest, or even upset at the incoherence of their responses. As the child's cognitive understanding of the situation improves, however, as a result of gradually accumulating learning and resulting "cognitive maturation," emotions come into play as well. How the child comes to advance in his or her cognitive understanding has been described by Piaget in many studies (Piaget, 1976, 1980). Probably as a result of advances in cognitive capacity, children eventually come to notice their knowledge gaps, showing obvious astonishment at the changes of the clay cylinder display—a moment Piaget characterized as the "grasp of consciousness" (Piaget, 1976). This moment brings about notable, sometimes dramatic, changes in their behavior. Understanding that a problem exists in their understanding of the situation, they attempt to understand it, with all the tension, confusion, and conflict this implies. This is consistent with the Piaget's view that periods of disequilibrium are a sine qua non condition for advances in understanding. Such periods of development bring the acceptance of and involvement with conflict, tension, and instability (see also Harter & Monsour, 1992; Labouvie-Vief, 2008; Lewis, 2005).

As a result of such deliberate acceptance of tension, and the curiosity that comes with it, children engage in efforts to understand and resolve their contradictory perceptions. This process at first is characterized by great effort and tension, often accompanied with intense frustration at the lack of perceived coherence. Continued effortful engagement, however, brings gradual increases in more differentiated understanding of the situation. The eventual result of these efforts is integration at a higher level of complexity that integrates previous contradictions; for example, the child, now no longer confused by the changes in the perceptual appearance of the clay "sausage," may say, "Well, it is still the same because it has become longer, but also thinner!" Hence, the child evidences an integration that has both cognitive and emotional aspects. More generally, with the development of more complex representations, the child (and later adult) is able to resolve emotional tensions and conflicts, and experience positive hedonic tone instead. It is for this reason that our chapter highlights the synchrony between representational development and hedonics as its subtitle.

At first rather effortful, this process of coming to construe constancy in the face of change becomes well learned and automatic. This process of crystallization has been well researched in the domain of intellectual development (e.g., Craik & Bialystok, 2006; Horn, 1982; Horn & Cattell, 1967) and implies that even complex representations begin to take on quasi-automatic properties. As a result, events that were once difficult and even frightening eventually come to provoke a sense of pride and joy as more complex and well-integrated cognitions evolve. For example, Sroufe (1996) noted that, with development, infants are able to better support tension: for example, tasks that provoke fear at one point (e.g., as the mother loudly says "boom, boom") at a later time evoke laughter. Hence, infants become better able to modulate tension fluctuations of increasing strength.

More generally, as a result of such repeated engagements with situations that challenge equilibrium, individuals thus evolve representations that, on the one hand, are more cognitively complex and, on the other hand (i.e., on the side of emotions and their energetics), free him or her from excessive tension and award more positive emotions such as interest, joy, pride, and so forth. We propose, in fact, that this sequence and interfacing of cognitive and emotional processes forms the crux of cognitive-emotional development, as displayed in Figure 6.2.

Complexity and Tension in Development

In sum, Figure 6.2 demonstrates how, in the process of cognitive-emotional development, tension and emotion regulation become transformed. At early stages, the process of tension regulation

functions automatically, not unlike the early biological models proposed by Cannon. Simple, automatic, emotion-related processes (experiences of comfort and joy in situations close to set point, within the equilibrium zone, and below the tension thresholds; interest in situations near the set point; and annoyance, distress, or fear in situations far from equilibrium) are at the base of these regulatory processes. Whether these processes are set in motion is, in turn, related to the degree to which the child's cognitive understanding accords with the situation. If the situation is well within range of the child's understanding, these regulatory processes happen automatically and effortlessly. If, however, the situation occurs far from equilibrium (yet not so far as to be truly disorganizing), the child can engage effortful cognitive strategies (such as attention, reflection, memorizing, etc.) in an attempt to understand the situation. As a result of practice, the effort involved in these attempts is reduced to the degree at which the new strategies themselves become automated. At this point, the child has developed a new representation of the situation, one that is easily accessible and automatic and that encompasses both cognitive understanding and emotional equilibrium. At this juncture, a higher level of cognitive-emotional development is achieved, as shown in Figure 6.2.

Generally, therefore, we propose that cognitive-emotional development is synchronous with the cognitive understanding of the individual. At beginning levels and while the individual lacks understanding, experiences that deviate from the norm in terms of complexity and/or intensity are disequilibrating and associated with tension. However, once

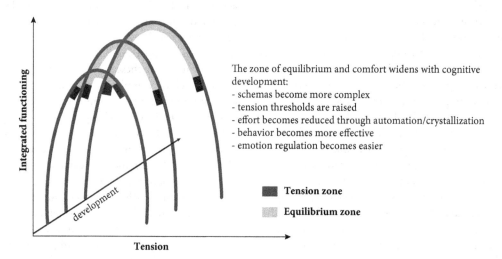

Figure 6.2. Model of dynamic integration of cognitivo-emotional schemas.
Adapted from Labouvie-Vief (2009).

these experiences have been formed into automatic cognitive-emotional representations, they are no longer disequilibrating and are, in fact, preferred. That is, individuals are better able to maintain well-integrated behavior on the cognitive side and, at the same time, experience better emotional balance on the emotional side. This process continues through a series of stages, from childhood to adulthood. Hence, development implies a parallelism between cognitive level and the kinds of situations that can be mastered emotionally. Overall, tension thresholds rise as equilibrium zones expand.

Mechanisms of the Tension and Equilibrium Expansion in Early Development

How are the expansion of equilibrium and the lowering of tension effected on a biological level? From a biological view, regulatory functions are processed along three core systems: the brainstem, and the limbic and cortical systems. At first, integration is lacking since automatic processes predominate and cortical controls are not yet established. Eventually, these systems are vertically integrated (e.g., Panksepp, 2005). This developing hierarchical system draws on brainstem-related homeostatic systems that provide the original physiological foundation for the regulation of state, attention, and emotional reactivity. With cortical growth and developing connectivity between these diverse systems, high-order self-regulatory abilities are built on these automatic forms of regulation. A first milestone is the development of attention modulation capacities, after the age of 3 months, which affords the adaptive coordination of vigilance and distress during information processing (e.g., Eckerman, Oehler, Hannan, & Molitor, 1995). The second relevant milestone is the growing connectivity between limbic and cortical systems during childhood. For example, the transition to self-regulatory behaviors during the second year of life often draws on higher control systems, reflecting the integration of the anterior cingulate gyrus that is implicated in the coordination of distress and attention. The functional connectivity to prefrontal regions marks the final steps in the development of this system by exerting inhibitory control (Diamond, 1990). The maturation of top-down frontolimbic connections then enables a better regulation of tension generated by stressful events. This emotion-regulation system—which is intimately tied to emotion processing systems—continues integrating during childhood and only achieves maturity after late adolescence (e.g., Steinberg, 2008).

Overall, the formation of connections between "automatic" centers and those that are related to effortful control processes leads to growing regulatory abilities from infancy to young adulthood. Language is a prime example of such regulation, involving as it does the emergence of representations (e.g., Hariri, Bookheimer, & Mazziotta, 2000; Lieberman, Eisenberger, Crockett, Tom, Pfeifer, & Way, 2007; Luria, 1932). For example, Luria demonstrated that the use of language acted to dampen peripheral arousal and motor excitation (Luria, 1932); more recently, research has established that the use of linguistic labels functions to downregulate activation of brain regions involved in emotional processing, such as amygdala (e.g., Hariri et al., 2000; Lieberman et al., 2007). Thus, using functional magnetic resonance imaging (fMRI), Hariri and colleagues (2000) showed that merely labeling emotional faces decreased activity in the amygdala while increasing prefrontal activation, thus indicating the inhibitory function of cortical regions on emotional processing.

In early childhood, the interconnection between cognitive and emotional processes grows in complexity and allows a better prediction of the social environment. More complex cognitivo-emotional representations will allow more precise expectations about the world, thus widening the range of the equilibrium zone as the child matures. For example, the growing ability of the child to recognize and make predictions about the mental states of self and other (Theory of Mind capacities) increasingly equips the child with a cognitive behavioral repertoire that offers increasing capacity to deal with tension and perturbation.

In early adolescence, increasing metacognitive and emotion regulation skills are sustained by the growing complexity of prefrontal and limbic connectivity. Hence, increasingly skillful emotion regulation and tension tolerance are expected with the passage from childhood to adolescence. Using event-related potentials (ERPs), Lewis and Stieben (2004) isolated the processes underlying the cognitive control of emotional outcomes. These authors tested children from 6 to 16 years in a go/no-go paradigm and showed that medial prefrontal ERP amplitudes diminish with age. At the same time, the ERP amplitudes become more sensitive to anxiety, and internalizing children showed higher amplitudes than noninternalizing children, especially when anxious. According to the authors, younger children expend more effort controlling their response in general, whereas older children recruit more effortful self-control more specifically under anxious conditions (Lewis & Stieben, 2004). Supporting developmental differences in cognitive processes dedicated to the regulation of negative emotion, this study suggests that tension reduction with increasing age is based on an automatization of processes that require effort at younger ages. Another ERP study examined changes in the form and amplitude of error-related negativity (ERN), a wave associated with cognitive control, in participants aged 7 to 20 years (Davies, Segalowitz, & Gavin, 2004). These authors found that the amplitude of the ERN increased with age, with the increase most evident at 17–20 years. According to the authors, this trend reflects a developing capacity for the cognitive control of impulsive action. In the same vein, neuroimaging research shows less prefrontal activation in adults than in children (Casey et al., 1997; Durston, Thomas, Yang, Uluğ, Zimmerman, & Casey, 2002) and adolescents (Luna et al., 2001) during tasks requiring inhibition or directed attention, suggesting that inhibition is achieved with less effort in adults, as attested to by less prefrontal engagement. All these studies suggest that increasing cognitive-emotional integration and improved emotion regulation with age is based on the development of well-automated networks between the respective functions of the brain (Casey et al., 1997; Luna et al., 2001).

Complexity and Tension in Adulthood and Later Life

The processes of automatization and increasing integration of complex representations or cognitive-emotional schemas continue well into adulthood and later mid-life, as suggested in Figure 6.2. In the literature on adult cognition, this process of formation of highly automated cognitive-emotional schemas has been referred to as an increasing "crystallization" of certain cognitive and cognitive-emotional representations (Craik & Bialystok, 2006; Horn & Cattell, 1967). These processes of crystallization reduce the burden of effortful attempts at regulation, attempts that are more dependent on fluid processes.

Nevertheless, fluid processes are well known to decrease in later life (Baltes & Lindenberger, 1997; Schaie, 1994). Eventually, these decreases can affect the smooth execution of crystallized processes, as well—the "fluidization" of crystallized capacities (Labouvie-Vief, 2009). That is, although the store of crystallized knowledge itself appears to be quite resistant to these changes, losses are particularly evident where the flexible availability and execution of knowledge are concerned. This is especially true when the situation demands that knowledge application involves stringent constraints of time, effort, and energy.

The result of these fluidization processes, we propose, is that the general process of equilibrium regulation is impaired in later life. In general, we predict that these changes have several implications. First, although not highly evident in situation of high crystallization, in less well-automated situations, aging will bring a narrowing of the equilibrium zone, along with a simultaneous lowering of tension thresholds and a lowering of the level of performance complexity (see Figure 6.3A). However, the degree to which these restrictions truly become a major problem of regulation depends, as already stated, on the degree to which tasks highlight fluid, effortful executive processes: if elderly individuals do not need to expend such effort as a result of

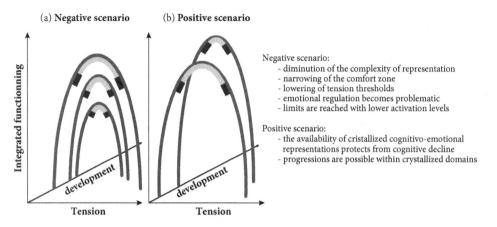

Figure 6.3. Negative (A) and positive (B) scenario linked to resources restriction. Adapted from Labouvie-Vief (2009).

crystallization, this automation will protect them from decline (in fact, there exists the possibility of *progressions* in complexity within the domain of well-crystallized representations, as we discuss later). Well-automated crystallized cognitive-emotional schemas can thus provide protection against the negative consequences of aging, although the range of situations to which this applies becomes quite restricted—depending, as it does, on the specific store of knowledge that individuals have come to be highly familiar with (see Figure 6.3B). Nevertheless, within this range, age differences can be reduced, and older adults may even show better performance than their younger counterparts.

Aging and Loss of Fluid Processes: Vulnerability of Later Life Regulation Capacities

As Figure 6.3A proposes, the consistent decline of fluid abilities with increasing age implies that, in general, elderly persons' capacity to deal with situations that are not based on well-established knowledge systems becomes increasingly restricted. Specifically, we suggest that these restrictions will be especially obvious in situations that exceed an individual's level of complexity or that require inhibition of well-automated functioning.

Older Adults Are More Vulnerable to Higher Levels of Tension

Consistent with resource limitations with advancing age, older adults should be more vulnerable to high levels of tension/arousal. In fact, older adults do not like emotionally strong stimulations, and a growing body of research indicates that highly arousing material is perceived as more negative by older adults than by younger adults. In a study examining valence and arousal ratings of emotional pictures in younger and older adults, Grühn and Scheibe (2008) found that valence and arousal were strongly correlated, and that this correlation became stronger with age. More specifically, older adults rated negative pictures as more negative and more arousing than younger adults did, whereas they judged positive pictures as more positive and less arousing. More recently, Keil and Freund (2009) investigated young, middle-aged, and older adults' perceptions of negative, neutral, and positive pictures. Their results showed that valence and arousal ratings formed a more linear relationship in older participants rather than a curvilinear relation, as was true for the younger participants. Whereas older adults showed a strong negative relation

between valence and arousal, younger adults instead perceived lower arousing pictures as neutral and highly arousing ones as either positive or negative depending on their content. The authors suggested that, with increasing age, highly arousing material is perceived as more aversive. In the same vein, Gilet, Grühn, Studer, and Labouvie-Vief (2012) examined young, middle-aged, and older adults' ratings for 835 French adjectives. Their findings indicated a strong linear association between valence and arousal ratings in younger, middle-aged, and older adults. Specifically, the most positively rated words were the lowest arousing ones; the most negatively rated words were the highest arousing ones. Consistent with past research, the size of the linear association between valence and arousal differed by age group: older adults' ratings showed a stronger linear association than did middle-aged and young adults' ratings. Taken together, the results of these studies may reflect a greater interdependence between cognitive and emotional abilities in older individuals, with a decline in fluid functioning being associated with difficulties in processing emotional material. This assumption is supported by findings showing a strong relationship between the cognitive and emotional systems, especially in the elderly (Labouvie-Vief, Chiodo, Goguen, Diehl, & Orwoll, 1995). Aging is thus thought to affect homeostatic abilities and impair tension tolerance. With advancing age, individuals should be more easily overwhelmed and should show reduced emotion regulation capacities, especially when dealing with highly arousing materials or situations.

High Arousal Levels Are More Disruptive for Cognitive Processing in Older Adults

In a study using an emotional Stroop task, Wurm and colleagues (Wurm, Labouvie-Vief, Aycock, Rebucal, & Koch, 2004) showed that older adults are more sensitive to the arousal level of stimuli than are younger adults. The authors investigated the effects of low, medium, and high arousing words on response latencies. Findings indicated no differences in response latencies between low and high arousing words for young adults. In contrast, older adults showed a significant elevation of response latencies for high arousing words compared to low and medium arousing words, reflecting inhibition difficulties with highly arousing material. Similar problems with highly arousing material have been reported by Grühn and Scheibe (2008). Here, the authors examined the ease with which pictures can be remembered according to their associated arousal level. They showed that the arousal level of stimuli was not associated with younger adults' memory scores, but was negatively associated with older adults' scores. The more arousing the pictures, the less remembered in older adults. These results are consistent with the assumption of a negative relationship between effectiveness of cognitive performance and tension levels in the elderly. Aging thus is also associated with reduced homeostatic abilities: older adults' systems are more vulnerable to high activation and more easily overwhelmed. As a consequence, high levels of activation then lead to inefficient cognitive performance or even to its disruption.

One line of recent evidence suggesting that the aging system is more easily overwhelmed emerges from research using physiological measures of effort, such as systolic blood pressure. For example, Hess and Ennis (2012) investigated age differences in effort associated with cognitive activity for young and older adults. Participants were asked to perform either a low- or a high-difficulty counting task immediately followed by a multiplication task. Findings showed that the elderly exhibited higher reactivity levels in both tasks than did their younger counterparts but also lower performances in the multiplication task. According to the authors, this association of a very high reactivity and a low performance level may reflect a breakdown of cognitive activity. As described in detail by Labouvie-Vief and collaborators (Labouvie-Vief, 2009; Labouvie-Vief et al., 2010), and consistent with the developmental view outlined earlier, this breakdown results in a lowering of tension thresholds. That is, with aging, the cognitive and emotional systems are more likely to become overwhelmed and disrupted under conditions that move the person away from ideal conditions and closer to the breakdown zone. Specifically, we describe a range of specific situations and circumstances that create challenges to regulation and an increasing likelihood of breakdown in the smooth coordination between cognitive and emotional functioning (Labouvie-Vief, 2009; Labouvie-Vief et al., 2010).

Older Adults Are More Sensitive to Stressful Situations

Evidence for the lowering of tension thresholds in later life is further supported by research on stress. Even if some studies suggest that older adults are less easily aroused than younger adults (e.g., Labouvie-Vief, Lumley, Jain, & Heinze, 2003), most of the experiments investigating age

differences in cardiac reactivity to stressful situations argue for an age-related increase of the physiological response (see Uchino, Birmingham, & Berg, 2010, for a review). For example, Jennings and colleagues (Jennings, Kamarck, Manuck, Everson, Kaplan, & Salonen, 1997) found an age-related increase in cardiovascular reactivity in men aged 46–64 years performing a mental challenge. More recently, Uchino, Holt-Lunstad, Bloor and Campo (2005) examined cardiovascular response to stress in middle-aged and older adults. They found longitudinal evidence for an age-related increase in systolic blood pressure reactivity and respiratory sinus arrhythmia. This finding was independent of other demographic (e.g., level of education) or health-related factors (e.g., self-reported health behaviors). In another study, Uchino and colleagues (Uchino, Berg, Smith, Pearce, & Skinner, 2006) highlighted a threshold effect: older adults, compared to young or middle-aged adults, show lower reactivity at lower levels of stress but stronger reactivity at higher levels of stress. In addition, in their recent meta-analysis, Uchino et al. (2010) found that systolic blood pressure reactivity was moderated by the degree of task activation. These results offer further support for the assumption that higher activation is more problematic for older adults than for their younger counterparts. Related to this, Bäckman and Molander (1986a, b) investigated young and older adults' miniature golf performance under normal-stress (training) and high-stress situations (competition). Findings showed that (a) older adults' performance was disrupted under the competitive situation whereas young adults' performance was not affected (Bäckman & Molander, 1986a), and (b) older adults were less efficient in compensating for the negative effects of nonoptimal levels of arousal (Bäckman & Molander, 1986b).

Physiological research also indicates that older adults showed a more pronounced stress-induced hormonal secretion than did younger adults during a cognitive challenge (Gotthardt, Schweiger, Fahrenberg, Lauer, Holsboer, & Heuser, 1995). More recently, Neupert, Miller, and Lachman (2006) found that older adults were more reactive (i.e., showed stronger cortisol responses) than younger adults during cognitively challenging tasks. Older adults also take more time to recover from such stress-related reaction than do younger adults (e.g., Seeman & Robbins, 1994). Thus, older adults are also more affected by high levels of stress during recovery than young adults. This deleterious physiologic effect of stressful situations has been highlighted in studies examining cortisol reactivity in rats (Sapolsky, Krey, & McEwen, 1986) and humans (Otte, Hart, Neylan, Marmar, Yaffe, & Mohr, 2005). High sustained levels of cortisol reactivity are maladaptive and impair cognitive performance (de Kloet, Oitzl, & Joels, 1999). These studies on stress provide further evidence for the greater dysregulation of the system under high levels of arousal and/or effort with advancing age.

Preexisting Individual Differences in Emotion Regulation Negatively Affect Performance of Older Adults

As mentioned earlier, tension thresholds are lowered with advancing age, leaving the system more susceptible to overactivation. This is especially true for individuals who have preexisting problems with emotion regulation, such as those related to flexible and effortful control. Overactivation problems are therefore more frequent and severe in older individuals who do not already possess well-automated crystallized schemas that function to regulate high tension levels. In contrast, young adults, even those with relatively ineffective schemas, will be less negatively affected because of their ample resources to mobilize effort and tolerate tension. As an example, Andreoletti, Veratti, and Lachman (2006) showed that older adults who were more anxious regarding their memory performances recalled fewer words than did older adults less anxious about their memory performances. Young adults, in contrast, performed well irrespective of their memory-related anxiety level. In the same vein, Deptula, Singh, and Pomara (1993) highlighted relationships between word recall and self-reported levels of anxiety, depression, and withdrawal. Whereas young adults showed slightly positive but nonsignificant correlations between these ratings and word recall, older adults showed significant negative associations between these dimensions and memory performance. Similarly, Hogan (2003) showed that higher anxiety was related to poorer divided attention performance in older but not in younger adults.

Taken together, these studies showed that older adults' memory performance was degraded by high internal negative activation, whereas young adults' memory performance was practically unaffected (but see Cavanaugh & Murphy, 1986; Whitbourne, 1976). More recently, Jain and Labouvie-Vief (2010) found an effect of regulation styles (i.e., attachment styles) on emotion processing in the elderly but not in younger adults. The authors hypothesized variation in attachment styles

to have much stronger effects on emotion processing and reactivity in the elderly than in younger adults. They expected to find signs of good response integration, such as low reactivity and positive affect, in secure individuals rather than in insecure individuals (e.g., highly anxious elders), who would show signs of overactivation. In contrast, avoidant-dismissing elders, who are known for their self-protective efforts at emotion avoidance, should show lower levels of reactivity as well as signs of breakdown of these efforts at higher levels of activation. Using an emotional Stroop paradigm, the authors found that dismissing elders showed generally decreased response times, but elevated response times for fear and anger words. In contrast, secure individuals showed increased response latencies for joy words. No attachment style differences were found in young adults. In a second study, heart rate was monitored while adult mother-daughter pairs discussed three emotion events (conflict, happy, neutral). Findings showed that, during conflict discussion, older but not younger dismissing women had the highest initial heart rates and slowest recovery. These results suggest that a dismissing style can serve a partially protective role for older individuals, but that this role breaks down if levels of activation reach a critical level.

Consistent with this proposition, several studies (for review, see Labouvie-Vief, Grühn, & Mouras, 2009; Magai, 2001; Zhang & Labouvie-Vief, 2004) have reported that the avoidant-dismissing, self-protective style of attachment just described is more prevalent in the elderly than in younger adults, thus suggesting that this style may reflect an attempt to use compensatory protection strategies against negative emotions and their consequences (Labouvie-Vief et al., 2009). Consistent with this idea, several studies reported that older adults can engage in compensatory mechanisms that break down at high levels of arousal. For example, investigating younger and older adults' working memory performances (N-back task), Mattay et al. (2006) found that at a low level of memory load (i.e., 1-back) older adults performed as well as younger adults and showed greater prefrontal cortical activity bilaterally than young adults. By contrast, at higher levels of memory load (i.e., 2- and 3-back), older adults performed worse than younger adults and, at the same time, showed relatively reduced activity in prefrontal regions. These results suggest that older adults engage in compensatory mechanisms (i.e., additional prefrontal cortical activation) to maintain their performances. But, as cognitive demand increases, a breakdown threshold is reached, compensation cannot be maintained, and a disruption in performance occurs.

In summary, increasing age and loss of fluid cognitive functioning seems to impair the capacity to cope with high tension, and high-complexity emotional information becomes affected. However, DIT also suggests that this loss can be offset by the availability of strong crystallized processes that provide a protective function. Even so, Labouvie-Vief (2009) proposes that crystallization will continue to be beneficial primarily in settings that make little demands on effortful acquisition of material, especially if that material implies high levels of activation/stress.

Aging and Crystallization: Strengths of Later-Life Regulation Capacities

We already noted that a number of studies on aging suggest that automatic functioning seems little affected in later life and may even increase in importance (Hess, 2005) or facilitate performance in some emotion regulation tasks (e.g., Blanchard-Fields, 2009). More specifically, preserved automaticity is likely to help individuals' performance in situations or tasks that do not require them to inhibit their well-automated cognitive-emotional knowledge, and in tasks that are in the range of complexity for which such crystallized knowledge already is available. Indeed, effects usually associated with aging—such as reduction of cognitive control over emotions—are not always detrimental, but actually may bring positive benefits to the extent that automated knowledge systems may provide a rich base for integrating experience. Here, we outline several domains of research demonstrating that, under specific conditions, elders show positive performances on a range of tasks—performances that hint at a certain stock of deepened knowledge and wisdom. Here, we outline a few lines of research that point to such progressive movements.

Deepened Inner Orientation

In the eyes of some theoreticians, increases in automatic functioning in later life may bring unique benefits to the aging person. Jung (1933) suggested that, with a relaxation of controlled functioning, mid to late adulthood can bring a liberation of unconscious processes and, with it, a turn away from preoccupations with the outer world. Instead, increases in understanding of those inner components of experience that form a general dimension of developmental progression may achieve its height in later life through a process of "centroversion," or focus toward the inner world (see Labouvie-Vief, 1994). One sign of this inward shift is the general way in which individuals' relationship to information becomes restructured. For the young adult, information is seen as an outer resource, given that one attempts to reproduce it in a literal way. In contrast, middle-aged and older adults turn more to the landscape of human motivations and intentions. Hence, they may become experts at the processing of information relating to subjective processes and inner dynamics. Although this symbolic processing style can result in deficits on the literal level, it may imply a richer psychological texture.

Richer Integration of Psychological Experience

Empirical evidence for a shift toward a more interpretive and subjective mode of information processing can be found in studies investigating age differences in memory for text. For example, in a study by Adams (1991), participants were asked to summarize a modified version of a Sufi teaching tale. Results showed age differences in the patterns of summarization related to the story's psychological and metaphorical meanings. Whereas adolescents produced texts that were very detailed and close to the original, middle-aged and older adults produced texts that implied qualitatively different processes. Middle-aged adults focused on the implied psychological and metaphorical meaning of the tales. Similarly, older adults were interested in the meaning of the tale, which they produced in very brief but highly integrative and abstract-thematic ways. In a similar fashion, Jepson and Labouvie-Vief (1992) reported a series of studies in which individuals were asked to summarize narratives. In one study, young, middle-aged, and older adults were asked to respond to a series of fable-like stories. Consistent with expectations, the results showed clear age-related differences in symbolic processing. With advancing age, participants were less likely to use text-based inferences but more likely to use simple or complex symbolic inferences. Young adults produced detailed, almost verbatim, reproductions of these tales, whereas older adults were primarily concerned with general meanings that were symbolic, moral, and inner-psychological. These results suggest that older individuals may continue to develop highly integrated and personally meaningful insights about life's regularities—the hallmark we think, of advanced wisdom.

Somewhat relatedly, a growing body of research suggests that age differences can diminish or even disappear if experimental tasks permit the elderly to make use of the inner orientation that draws on rich knowledge of self and psychological processes. For example, recent studies on age-related differences in everyday problem-solving tasks found that older adults can solve problems as effectively or even more effectively than younger adults do. Especially in emotionally salient and interpersonal problems, older adults are more effective than young adults (Blanchard-Fields, 2007). In fact, older people are capable of a greater flexibility and adaptability in choosing the strategy that best matches the context of the problem than are younger adults (Blanchard-Fields, Mienaltowski, & Seay, 2007).

Heightened Cognitive Performance in Situations Relevant for the Elderly

In a large body of work, Hess and colleagues suggested that the relevance of materials and tasks may largely contribute to the apparent decrement often highlighted in the literature (see Hess, 2005, for a review). Accordingly, older adults' performance appears to be more affected by the meaningfulness of the task than younger adults' performance. For example, older adults were more accurate in making trait inferences and recalled more information about a target that was similar in age (Hess, Rosenberg, & Waters, 2001). More recently, Germain and Hess (2007) conducted a series of experiments examining the impact of personal relevance on age differences in the ability to ignore distracting information. Young and older adults were asked to read short text passages either relevant to the younger or the older group. Overall, findings revealed particularly enhanced comprehension and text processing under relevant condition for the elderly. By contrast, younger adults were less sensitive to the relevance, exhibiting either similar performances or a moderate increase of relevant information processing. In the same vein, assessing younger and older adults' source memory, Rahhal, May, and Hasher (2002) showed that older adults' deficits are reduced when they have to deal with affective or value-based information, such as truth or moral character. Finally, May, Rahhal, Berry, and Leighton (2005) investigated young and older adults' ability to remember three types of contextual information about an event. The authors differentiated between contextual information that was simply contextual or meaning-based, and conceptual information that also had an emotional component. Whereas young adults outperformed older adults in the recall of contextual nonemotional information,

age differences disappeared when remembering contextual information carrying emotional significance. The data thus suggest that age differences can be eliminated when information to be remembered is relevant to older adults.

Taken together, these results suggest that the performance of elderly individuals tends to improve significantly when they can rely on their knowledge and experience. Unlike younger adults, whose performances differ only slightly from situation to situation, older adults derive particular benefit from situations that are particularly familiar and personally relevant. On one hand, these effects of personal relevance on the elderly indicate that they are well able to profit from the effects of emotional facilitation. On the other hand, they are also consistent with the suggestion of Craik and Bialystok (2006) that younger adults are very capable of generating de novo internal activation that supports efficient performance. Because older adults are lacking such facilitation effects, the burden of processing is fully placed on the effortful/conscious processing system—fluid processes. Consistent with this, Labouvie-Vief (2009) recently proposed that facilitation effects in the elderly suggest that the high level of integrated functioning found in some elderly nevertheless often goes along with a narrowing of contexts that are increasingly restricted to value-based and otherwise personally meaningful situations. In this way, the data of Hess and others are also consistent with the interpretation that the elderly become more *dependent* on the provision of such activation—for example, as a result of their accumulated experience—or else of externally provided cues.

Conclusion

In this chapter, we address the mix of positive and negative changes in emotion regulation observed with aging. We propose that this diversity of findings can be explained and systematized by a theory outlining the coevolution in individual development of cognitive structures and emotion regulation capacities in such a way that individuals develop more effective means of maintaining equilibrium. On this formulation, the growth of cognitive structures and their integration with emotional systems in early development is related to an expansion of the range over which individuals can maintain equilibrium, as well as a raising of the tension thresholds that individuals can manage. The resulting cognitive-emotional schemas or representations themselves can become highly automated or crystallized, providing individuals with the available means of regulation that, although at first dependent on the expenditure of effort, eventually come to function in a relatively effortless way.

In contrast to development from childhood to middle adulthood, later life appears to bring a cessation of this expansive developmental process as the capacity for high tension and effortful performances decreases as a result of the decline of fluid processes of cognition. As a result, aging is typically associated with a lowering of tension thresholds and a restriction of the range of equilibrium. However, these restrictions may be limiting only in cases where individuals cannot fall back on already well-developed representational systems, instead needing to expend high levels of tension, stress, and effort.

By placing cognitive-emotional processes in the context of equilibrium regulation, the proposed theory provides, we believe, a coherent framework to discuss cognitive-emotional processes from a psychological and biological perspective alike. The notion of lowered equilibrium thresholds with aging already is commonplace in the medical and biological field, such as cardiac stress tests or recommendations for physical exercise regimens. By applying a similar conception to the field of emotion regulation, the current theory provides a linkage of the cognitive functions of emotion regulation to mechanisms of arousal and activation.

References

Adams, C. (1991). Qualitative age differences in memory for text: A life-span developmental perspective. *Psychology and Aging, 6,* 323–336.

Andreoletti, C., Veratti, B. W., & Lachman, M. E. (2006). Age differences in the relationship between anxiety and recall. *Aging & Mental Health, 10,* 265–271.

Bäckman, L., & Molander, B. (1986a). Adult age differences in the ability to cope with situations of high arousal in a precision sport. *Psychology and Aging, 1,* 133–139.

Bäckman, L., & Molander, B. (1986b). Effects of adult age and level of skill on the ability to cope with high-stress conditions in a precision sport. *Psychology and Aging, 1,* 334–336.

Baltes, P. B., & Lindenberger, U. (1997). Emergence of a powerful connection between sensory and cognitive functions across the adult life span: A new window to the study of cognitive aging? *Psychology and Aging, 12,* 12–21.

Blanchard-Fields, F. (1999). Social schematicity and causal attributions. In T. M. Hess & F. Blanchard-Fields (Eds.), *Social cognition and aging* (pp. 222–236). San Diego, CA: Academic Press.

Blanchard-Fields, F. (2007). Everyday problem solving and emotion: An adult developmental perspective. *Current Directions in Psychological Science, 16,* 26–31.

Blanchard-Fields, F. (2009). Flexible and adaptive socio-emotional problem solving in adult development and aging. *Restorative Neurology and Neuroscience, 27,* 539–550.

Blanchard-Fields, F., Mienaltowski, A., & Seay, R. B. (2007). Age differences in everyday problem-solving effectiveness: Older adults select more effective strategies for interpersonal problems. *Journals of Gerontology: Series B: Psychological Sciences and Social Sciences, 62B,* P61–P64.

Brent, S. B. (1978). Motivation, steady-state, and structural development: A general model of psychological homeostasis. *Motivation and Emotion, 2,* 299–332.

Cannon, W. B. (Ed.). (1939). *The wisdom of the body* (Rev. ed.). New York: WW Norton & Co.

Carstensen, L. L., Mikels, J. A., & Mather, M. (2006). Aging and the intersection of cognition, motivation and emotion. In J. Birren & K. W. Schaie (Eds.), *Handbook of the psychology of aging,* 6th ed. (pp. 343–362). San Diego, CA: Academic Press.

Carver, C. S., & Scheier, M., F. (1998). *On the self-regulation of behavior.* New York Cambridge University Press.

Casey, B. J., Trainor, R. J., Orendi, J. L., Schubert, A. B., Nystrom, L. E., Giedd, J. N., et al. (1997). A developmental functional MRI study of prefrontal activation during performance of a go-no-go task. *Journal of Cognitive Neuroscience, 9,* 835–847.

Cavanaugh, J. C., & Murphy, N. Z. (1986). Personality and metamemory correlates of memory performance in younger and older adults. *Educational Gerontology, 12,* 385–394.

Chapman, M. (1988). *Constructive evolution: Origins and development of Piaget's thought.* New York: Cambridge University Press.

Craik, F. I. M., & Bialystok, E. (2006). Cognition through the lifespan: mechanisms of change. *Trends in Cognitive Sciences, 10,* 131–138.

Davies, P. L., Segalowitz, S. J., & Gavin, W. J. (2004). Development of response-monitoring ERPs in 7- to 25-year-olds. *Developmental Neuropsychology, 25,* 355–376.

de Kloet, E. R., Oitzl, M. S., & Joels, M. (1999). Stress and cognition: Are corticosteroids good or bad guys? *Trends in Neurosciences, 22,* 422–426.

Deptula, D., Singh, R., & Pomara, N. (1993). Aging, emotional states, and memory. *American Journal of Psychiatry, 150,* 429–434.

Diamond, A. (Ed.). (1990). *The development and neural bases of higher cognitive functions.* New York: New York Academy of Sciences.

Durston, S., Thomas, K. M., Yang, Y., Uluğ, A. M., Zimmerman, R. D., & Casey, B. J. (2002). A neural basis for the development of inhibitory control. *Developmental Science, 5,* F9–F16.

Eckerman, C. O., Oehler, J. M., Hannan, T. E., & Molitor, A. (1995). The development prior to term age of very prematurely born newborns' responsiveness in en face exchanges. *Infant Behavior and Development, 18,* 283–297.

Germain, C. M., & Hess, T. M. (2007). Motivational influences on controlled processing: Moderating distractibility in older adults. *Aging, Neuropsychology, and Cognition 14,* 462–486.

Gilet, A.-L., Grühn, D., Studer, J., & Labouvie-Vief, G. (2012). Valence, arousal, and imagery ratings for 835 French attributes by young, middle-aged, and older adults: The French Emotional Evaluation List (FEEL). European Review of *Applied Psychology-Revue Européenne de Psychologie Appliquée, 62,* 173–181.

Gotthardt, U., Schweiger, U., Fahrenberg, J., Lauer, C. J., Holsboer, F., & Heuser, I. (1995). Cortisol, ACTH, and cardiovascular response to a cognitive challenge paradigm in aging and depression *American Journal of Physiology, 268,* R865–R873.

Gross, J. J., Carstensen, L. L., Pasupathi, M., Tsai, J., Gotestam Skorpen, C., & Hsu, A. Y. C. (1997). Emotion and aging: Experience, expression, and control. *Psychology and Aging, 12,* 590–599.

Grühn, D., & Scheibe, S. (2008). Age-related differences in valence and arousal ratings of pictures from the International Affective Picture System (IAPS): Do ratings become more extreme with age? *Behavior Research Methods, 40,* 512–521.

Hariri, A. R., Bookheimer, S. Y., & Mazziotta, J. C. (2000). Modulating emotional responses: Effects of a neocortical network on the limbic system. *Neuroreport, 11,* 43–48.

Harter, S., & Monsour, A. (1992). Development analysis of conflict caused by opposing attributes in the adolescent self-portrait. *Developmental Psychology, 28,* 251–260.

Helson, H. (Ed.). (1964). *Adaptation-level theory: An experimental and systematic approach to behavior.* New York: Harper & Row.

Hess, T. M. (2005). Memory and aging in context. *Psychological Bulletin, 131,* 383–406.

Hess, T. M., & Ennis, G. E. (2012). Age differences in the effort and costs associated with cognitive activity. *The Journals of Gerontology Series B: Psychological Sciences and Social Sciences, 67,* 447–455.

Hess, T. M., Rosenberg, D. C., & Waters, S. J. (2001). Motivation and representational processes in adulthood: The effects of social accountability and information relevance. *Psychology and Aging, 16,* 629–642.

Hogan, M. J. (2003). Divided attention in older but not younger adults is impaired by anxiety. *Experimental Aging Research, 29,* 111–136.

Horn, J. L. (1982). The theory of fluid and crystallized intelligence in relation to concepts of comparative psychology and aging in adulthood. In F. I. M. Craik & S. Trehub (Eds.), *Aging and cognitive processes* (pp. 237–278). New York: Plenum Press.

Horn, J. L., & Cattell, R. B. (1967). Age differences in fluid and crystallized intelligence. *Acta Psychologica, 26,* 107–129.

Jain, E., & Labouvie-Vief, G. (2010). Compensatory effects of emotion avoidance in adult development. *Biological Psychology, 84,* 497–513.

Jennings, J. R., Kamarck, T., Manuck, S., Everson, S. A., Kaplan, G., & Salonen, J. T. (1997). Aging or disease? Cardiovascular reactivity in Finnish men over the middle years. *Psychology & Aging, 12,* 225–238.

Jepson, K. L., & Labouvie-Vief, G. (1992). Symbolic processing of youth and elders. In R. L. West & J. D. Sinnott (Eds.), *Everyday memory and aging* (pp. 124–137). New York: Springer.

Jung, C. G. (1933). *Modern man in search of a soul* (W. S. Dell, & C. F. Baynes, Trans.). London: Harcourt, Brace & World.

Keil, A., & Freund, A. M. (2009). Changes in the sensitivity to appetitive and aversive arousal across adulthood. *Psychology and Aging, 24,* 668–680.

Kuhn, D., Pennington, N., & Leadbeater, B. (1983). Adult thinking in developmental perspective: The sample case of juror reasoning. In P. Baltes & O. Brim (Eds.), *Life-span development and behavior* (vol. 5, pp. 158–197). New York: Academic Press.

Labouvie-Vief, G. (1980). Beyond formal operations: Uses and limits of pure logic in life-span development. *Human Development, 23,* 141–161.

Labouvie-Vief, G. (1982). Dynamic development and mature autonomy: A theoretical prologue. *Human Development, 25,* 161–191.

Labouvie-Vief, G. (1994). *Psyche and Eros: Mind and gender in the life course.* New York: Cambridge University Press.

Labouvie-Vief, G. (2008). Dynamic integration theory: Emotion, cognition, and equilibrium in later life. In V. Bengtson, M. Silverstein, N. Putney, & D. Gans (Eds.), *Handbook of theories of aging* (pp. 277–293). New York: Springer.

Labouvie-Vief, G. (2009). Cognition and equilibrium regulation in development and aging. *Restorative Neurology and Neuroscience, 27,* 551–565.

Labouvie-Vief, G., Chiodo, L. M., Goguen, L. A., Diehl, M., & Orwoll, L. (1995). Representations of self across the life span. *Psychology and Aging, 10,* 404–415.

Labouvie-Vief, G., Grühn, D., & Mouras, H. (2009). Dynamic emotion-cognition interactions in development: Arousal, stress, and the processing of affect. In H. B. Bosworth & C. Hertzog (Eds.), *Cognition in aging: Methodologies and applications* (pp. 181–196). Washington, DC: American Psychological Association.

Labouvie-Vief, G., Grühn, D., & Studer, J. (2010). Dynamic integration of emotion and cognition: Equilibrium regulation in development and aging. In R. M. Lerner, M. E. Lamb, & A. M. Freund (Eds.), *The handbook of life-span development: Volume 2, social and emotional development* (pp. 79–115). Hoboken, NJ: Wiley.

Labouvie-Vief, G., Lumley, M. A., Jain, E., & Heinze, H. (2003). Age and gender differences in cardiac reactivity and subjective emotion responses to emotional autobiographical memories. *Emotion, 3,* 115–126.

Lawton, M. P., Kleban, M. H., & Dean, J. (1993). Affect and age: Cross-sectional comparisons of structure and prevalence. *Psychology and Aging, 8,* 165–175.

Lewis, M. D. (2005). Bridging emotion theory and neurobiology through dynamic systems modeling. *Behavioral and Brain Sciences, 28,* 169–245.

Lewis, M. D. (2010). The emergence of consciousness and its role in human development. In R. M. Lerner & W. F. Overton (Eds.), *The handbook of life-span development: Volume 1, cognition, biology and methods* (pp. 628–670). Hoboken, NJ: Wiley.

Lewis, M. D., & Stieben, J. (2004). Emotion regulation in the brain: Conceptual issues and directions for developmental research. *Child Development, 75,* 371–376.

Lieberman, M. D., Eisenberger, N. I., Crockett, M. J., Tom, S. M., Pfeifer, J. H., & Way, B. M. (2007). Putting feelings into words: Affect labeling disrupts amygdala activity in response to affective stimuli. *Psychological Science, 18,* 421–428.

Luna, B., Thulborn, K. R., Munoz, D. P., Merriam, E. P., Garver, K. E., Minshew, N. J., et al. (2001). Maturation of widely distributed brain function subserves cognitive development. *NeuroImage, 13,* 786–793.

Luria, A. (1932). *The nature of human conflicts.* New York: Liveright.

Magai, C. (2001). Emotions over the life span. In J. E. Birren & K. W. Schaie (Eds.), *Handbook of the psychology of aging,* 5th ed. (pp. 399–426). San Diego, CA: Academic Press.

Mattay, V. S., Fera, F., Tessitore, A., Hariri, A. R., Berman, K. F., Das, S., et al. (2006). Neurophysiological correlates of age-related changes in working memory capacity. *Neuroscience Letters, 392,* 32–37.

May, C. P., Rahhal, T., Berry, E. M., & Leighton, E. A. (2005). Aging, source memory, and emotion. *Psychology and Aging, 20,* 571–578.

Mroczek, D. K., & Kolarz, C. M. (1998). The effect of age on positive and negative affect: A developmental perspective on happiness. *Journal of Personality and Social Psychology, 75,* 1333–1349.

Neupert, S. D., Miller, L. S., & Lachman, M. E. (2006). Physiological reactivity to cognitive stressors: Variations by age and socioeconomic status. *International Journal of Aging and Human Development, 62,* 221–235.

Otte, C., Hart, S., Neylan, T. C., Marmar, C. R., Yaffe, K., & Mohr, D. C. (2005). A meta-analysis of cortisol response to challenge in human aging: Importance of gender. *Psychoneuroendocrinology, 30,* 80–91.

Panksepp, J. (2005). Affective consciousness: Core emotional feelings in animals and humans. *Consciousness and Cognition, 14,* 30–80.

Piaget, J. (1970). *Structuralism* (C. Maschler, Trans.). New York: Basic Books.

Piaget, J. (1971). *Biology and knowledge* (B. Walsh, Trans.). Chicago: University of Chicago Press.

Piaget, J. (1976). *The grasp of consciousness: action and concept in the young child* (S. Wedgwood, Trans.). Cambridge: Harvard University Press.

Piaget, J. (1980). *Experiments in contradiction* (D. Coleman, Trans.). Chicago: University of Chicago Press.

Piaget, J. (1981). *Intelligence and affectivity: Their relationship during child development* (T. A. Brown & C. E. Kaegi, Trans.). Oxford: Annual Reviews.

Pribam, K. H., & Gill, M. M. (1976). *Freud's "project" reassessed.* New York: Basic Books.

Rahhal, T. A., May, C. P., & Hasher, L. (2002). Truth and character: Sources that older adults can remember. *Psychological Science, 13,* 101–105.

Sapolsky, R. M., Krey, L. C., & McEwen, B. S. (1986). The neuroendocrinology of stress and aging: the glucocorticoid cascade hypothesis. *Endocrine Reviews, 7,* 284–301.

Schaie, K. W. (1994). The course of adult intellectual development. *American Psychologist, 49,* 304–313.

Seeman, T. E., & Robbins, R. J. (1994). Aging and hypothalamic-pituitary-adrenal response to challenge in humans. *Endocrine Reviews, 15,* 233–260.

Sroufe, L. A. (1996). *Emotional development: The organization of emotional life in the early years.* New York: Cambridge University Press.

Steinberg, L. (2008). A social neuroscience perspective on adolescent risk-taking. *Developmental Review, 28,* 78–106.

Uchino, B. N., Berg, C. A., Smith, T. W., Pearce, G., & Skinner, M. (2006). Age-related differences in ambulatory blood pressure during daily stress: Evidence for greater blood pressure reactivity with age. *Psychology and Aging, 21,* 231–239.

Uchino, B. N., Birmingham, W., & Berg, C. A. (2010). Are older adults less or more physiologically reactive? A meta-analysis of age-related differences in cardiovascular reactivity to laboratory tasks. *Journal of Gerontology: Psychological Sciences, 65B,* 154–162.

Uchino, B. N., Holt-Lunstad, J., Bloor, L. E., & Campo, R. A. (2005). Aging and cardiovascular reactivity to stress: Longitudinal evidence for changes in stress reactivity. *Psychology and Aging, 20,* 134–143.

Walker, N. (1956). Freud and homeostasis. *British Journal for the Philosophy of Science, 7,* 61–72.

Whitbourne, S. K. (1976). Test anxiety in elderly and young adults. *International Journal of Aging & Human Development, 7,* 201–210.

Wurm, L. H., Labouvie-Vief, G., Aycock, J., Rebucal, K. A., & Koch, H. E. (2004). Performance in auditory and visual emotional Stroop tasks: A comparison of older and younger adults. *Psychology and Aging, 19,* 523–535.

Zhang, F., & Labouvie-Vief, G. (2004). Stability and fluctuation in adult attachment style over a 6-year period. *Attachment & Human Development, 6,* 419–437.

Putting Emotional Aging in Context: Contextual Influences on Age-Related Changes in Emotion Regulation and Recognition

Jennifer Tehan Stanley *and* Derek M. Isaacowitz

Abstract

Emotion regulation and recognition do not take place in a vacuum; instead, these emotional processes happen in specific contexts. In this chapter, we highlight context effects in the study of socioemotional aging and consider in detail three forms of context that may be relevant for age effects on both emotion regulation and emotion recognition: perceiver context, stimulus context, and emotional context. After reviewing what is known in each of these three areas for both regulation and recognition differences with age, paying particular attention to those factors that moderate the age differences, we consider the implications for theory and research of focusing on context in the study of emotional aging.

Key Words: context, emotion regulation, emotion recognition, lifespan developmental perspective

Recently, both in the general emotion perception literature and in the area of aging and emotion recognition, there has been a call to consider context in studies of emotion recognition, in order to gain a more complete picture of how emotional facial expressions are processed in daily life (Barrett, Mesquita, & Gendron, 2011; Isaacowitz & Stanley, 2011; Montepare, 2011). Barrett and colleagues (2011) reviewed the importance of considering three types of context in emotion perception: perceiver-based context (e.g., physiological arousal, cognitive abilities), cultural context (e.g., Western Caucasian vs. East Asian), and stimulus context (e.g., tone of voice, situation, body posture, surrounding facial expressions).

In this chapter, we review current findings regarding contextual effects in aging research not only in the area of emotion recognition, but in the area of emotion regulation as well. Gross (1998, p. 275) defines *emotion regulation* as "the processes by which individuals influence which emotions they have, when they have them, and how they experience and express these emotions." We include

both recognition and regulation to cast a wide net in our review of context effects in aging. We focus our review of the emotion recognition literature on the ability to identify facial expressions of emotion, because that is where most of the work has been done. Similar to the review done by Barrett and colleagues (2011), we also highlight three types of context that are critical to consider: the motivational and individual difference factors in the *context of the perceiver*, the *stimulus context*, and the *emotional context*. Throughout, we emphasize parallels between the two literatures on the types of contextual factors that influence aging effects. Please refer to Table 7.1 for a summary of context effects on age differences in emotion regulation and emotion recognition.

Perceiver Context

Both emotion regulation and emotion recognition occur within an individual who harbors specific goals, abilities, and personality characteristics. Research on how these aspects of the perceiver context influence socioemotional functioning suggests

Table 7.1. Summary of literature on contextual influences on age-related changes in emotion regulation and emotion recognition

		Emotion regulation				Emotion recognition			
		Take-home message	Example	Empirical support	Useful reviews	Take-home message	Example	Empirical support	Useful reviews
Perceiver Context	Motivation	Emotion regulation is influenced by the motivational context of the individual, including age-related shifts in goals, current task goals, and culture.	Positivity effects in information processing show that, compared to young adults, older adults prefer to attend to and remember positive vs. negative information.	Allard & Isaacowitz, under review; Charles et al., 2003; Fung et al., 2008; Isaacowitz et al., 2008; Isaacowitz et al., 2009; Isaacowitz et al., 2006a, 2006b; Kennedy et al., 2004; Mather & Carstensen, 2003; Noh et al., 2011; Thomas & Hasher, 2006; Wood & Kisley, 2006	Carstensen et al., 1999; Carstensen & Mikels, 2005; Carstensen et al., 2006; Isaacowitz, 2006; Isaacowitz & Blanchard-Fields, 2012; Murphy & Isaacowitz, 2008; Rozin & Royzman, 2001	Little current evidence that the motivational context of the individual can explain age-related differences in emotion recognition.	Some researchers suggest age differences in emotion recognition reflect age-related shifts in the motivation to process emotional information, consistent with socioemotional selectivity theory (Carstensen & Mikels, 2005).	Riediger et al., 2011; Williams et al., 2006	Ruffman et al., 2008
	Individual Differences	Executive functioning is a key individual difference variable moderating age effects in emotion regulation. Personality characteristics also moderate age differences in emotion regulation.	Older adults high (vs. low) in executive functioning are more likely to display positivity effects, or more likely to have these positivity effects result in positive mood outcomes.	Isaacowitz et al., 2008; Isaacowitz et al., 2009; Knight et al., 2007; Larcom & Isaacowitz, 2009; Lee & Knight, 2009; Mather & Knight, 2005; Noh et al., 2011; Pearman et al., 2010; Stanley & Isaacowitz, 2011	Isaacowitz & Noh, 2011; Kryla-Lighthall & Mather, 2009	Age-related decline in cognitive or perceptual abilities does not completely account for age differences in emotion recognition.	Age-related differences in emotion recognition remain when controlling for visual perception of faces and fluid intelligence.	Keighley et al., 2006; Sullivan & Ruffman, 2004b	Ruffman et al., 2008

		Emotion regulation				Emotion recognition			
		Take-home message	Example	Empirical support	Useful reviews	Take-home message	Example	Empirical support	Useful reviews
Stimulus Context	Age Relevance	When the content of the stimuli are relevant to older adults, age deficits in subjective emotional ratings and physiology are eliminated or reversed.	After viewing age-relevant clips about loss, older adults reported greater sadness than did young adults, and there were no age differences in autonomic responses.	Kunzmann & Gruhn, 2005; Kunzmann & Richter, 2009		The influence of age relevance on age differences in emotion recognition is nuanced.	When recognizing facial expressions of emotion, older faces are more difficult to interpret. Age deficits in emotion recognition are eliminated with age-relevant dynamic or multimodal material.	Ebner, 2008; Ebner & Johnson, 2009; Malatesta et al., 1987; Murphy et al., 2010; Richter et al., 2010; Richter & Kunzmann, 2011; Riediger et al., 2011	Isaacowitz & Stanley, 2011; Ruffman et al., 2008
	Stimulus & Task Form	The task type (attention, memory) and form (picture, word) of the task influences whether age differences in emotion regulation emerge.	Positivity effects are more likely to emerge in studies on recognition memory (vs. studies of attention). The arousal level of the stimulus also matters.	Grühn et al., 2005; Isaacowitz & Choi, 2011; Isaacowitz et al., 2006a, 2006b; Opitz et al., in press; Scheibe & Blanchard-Fields, 2009; Shiota & Levenson, 2009; Thomas & Hasher, 2006	Isaacowitz & Blanchard-Fields, 2012; Murphy & Isaacowitz, 2008	Different patterns of age effects emerge for emotion recognition, as a function of the modality (faces, tone of voice, words) and the degree of context provided (static vs. dynamic, single vs. multimodal presentations).	When more context is provided, such as facial expressions paired with congruent vocal tones, age differences in emotion recognition accuracy are reduced or eliminated.	Hunter et al., 2010; Isaacowitz et al., 2007; Krendl & Ambady, 2010; Murphy et al., 2010; Phillips et al., 2002; Richter et al., 2010; Slessor et al., 2010	
Emotional Context		Age differences in the regulation of anger and sadness stand out as unique compared to regulating other emotions.	Compared to young, older adults seem to avoid anger and embrace sadness.	Birditt & Fingerman, 2003; Blanchard-Fields & Coats, 2008; Charles & Carstensen, 2008; Haase et al., 2008; Kunzmann & Gruhn, 2005	Blanchard-Fields, 2007; Labouvie-Vief, 2003	Different patterns of age effects emerge for discrete emotions depending on the modality (faces, bodies, voices).	For facial expressions, age differences in emotion recognition are largest for angry, fearful, and sad faces.	Mienaltowski et al., 2011; Williams et al., 2006	Ruffman et al., 2008

that they may be especially relevant when examining age effects.

Motivation

As people go about their daily activities—in the grocery store, at the office, driving in the car—there is more information in their visual environment than they can possibly process. How do individuals choose what information to attend to and process? People are able to hone in on only the information relevant to them at the time (Simons & Chabris, 1999). Put another way, the current goals of the individual direct and guide attention (Isaacowitz, 2006). These goals are adaptive and dynamic. For example, within an individual, deciding what goals are prioritized may change depending on their developmental stage.

Socioemotional selectivity theory (SST) contends that there is a developmental uptick in the priority of social and emotional goals as individuals approach an ending, such as death (Carstensen, 1992; Carstensen, Isaacowitz, & Charles, 1999). According to SST, when future time perspective is expansive, as it is in young adulthood, individuals focus on acquiring information. But as future time perspective becomes more limited, as in old age, individuals focus on emotionally gratifying experiences, like spending time with a close social partner. For example, a number of studies found that as individuals approach an ending, they are more likely to favor spending time with familiar social partners over novel partners (Carstensen & Fredrickson, 1998; Fredrickson & Carstensen, 1990). This phenomenon persisted whether the ending was operationalized as proximity to death or some other ending, such as the sociopolitical ending created by the 1997 handover of Hong Kong to the People's Republic of China (Fung, Carstensen, & Lutz, 1999). Importantly, when imagining an expansive future, older adults' partner choices looked more like those of young adults, such that the bias toward favoring spending time with a familiar partner disappeared (Fung et al., 1999). Thus, endings bring emotional goals to the forefront, and these goals are strong top-down influences on the behaviors and choices of adults of all ages.

EMOTION REGULATION AND POSITIVITY EFFECTS

Several studies have found that older adults are more likely than young adults to preferentially attend to and remember positively valenced information relative to negatively valenced information,

a phenomenon termed *positivity effects* in information processing (Carstensen & Mikels, 2005; but see Murphy & Isaacowitz, 2008, for a meta-analysis). For example, in a dot-probe task, older adults were faster to respond to dots that appeared behind the more positive emotional face in emotional-neutral face pairs, suggesting that older adults, but not young adults, were already attending to the more positive face in each pair before the probe appeared (Mather & Carstensen, 2003). Eye tracking studies confirm positive looking preferences in older adults, such that older adults fixate more on happy faces and less on angry or sad faces (relative to neutral) in emotional-neutral face pairs, whereas young adults do not look more toward the happy faces (Isaacowitz, Wadlinger, Goren, & Wilson, 2006a,b). Young adults do not tend to exhibit this preference for positive information, but rather show the opposite tendency, to attend to and remember more negative information, relative to positive (a negativity bias; Rozin & Royzman, 2001). Although some studies show a clear age-related bias for positive material over negative or neutral material (Charles, Mather, & Carstensen, 2003; Mather & Carstensen, 2003), others may be better interpreted in terms of an age-related reduction in the negativity bias in attention (e.g., Wood & Kisley, 2006). Regardless of the mechanism, the end result is that many studies on attentional preferences show age-related increases in the ratio of positive-to-negative material.

Older adults also tend to better remember positive over negative images and faces (Charles et al., 2003; Mather & Carstensen, 2003). For example, one study that presented a slideshow of negative, neutral, and positive scenes found that age differences in recall and recognition were greatest for negative scenes and smallest for positive scenes (Charles et al., 2003). It has been suggested that these age-related positivity effects in information processing are no accident: older adults may be using their attention and memory processes to facilitate their emotion-regulatory goals (Carstensen, Mikels, & Mather, 2006; Isaacowitz et al., 2006b). The argument is that, consistent with SST, older adults have a limited future time perspective, which triggers a shift toward prioritizing emotionally gratifying goals, such as maintaining a positive mood, and this motivates older adults to attend to and remember more positive emotional information than negative information as a means to regulate their emotions.

Although this chain is certainly plausible, Isaacowitz and Blanchard-Fields point out the dearth of actual evidence for this hypothesized link between emotion regulation strategies, positivity effects, and an improvement in mood (Isaacowitz & Blanchard-Fields, 2012). Several studies have tested this link in the context of positive gaze preferences using eye tracking, and have found that older adults do activate positive looking in mood-regulatory contexts (Isaacowitz, Toner, Goren, & Wilson, 2008) and that it can lead to positive mood outcomes for *some* older adults (Isaacowitz, Toner, & Neupert, 2009; Noh, Lohani, & Isaacowitz, 2011). These complex findings suggest that there may be important moderators of age-related positivity effects in attention and memory; just the kind of situation that begs for a consideration of contextual factors (which tend to be moderating variables).

Are there motivational variables that serve as perceiver context relevant to the display of positivity effects? If older adults display positivity effects in gaze when they are in a negative mood state that needs to be regulated (Isaacowitz et al., 2008), it would suggest that motivational context is important. When older adults are instructed to focus on accuracy, positivity effects sometimes disappear where they were previously observed (Kennedy, Mather, & Carstensen, 2004; Mather & Carstensen, 2005), and a recent study suggests that motivation to regulate emotions can make positivity effects appear (Allard & Isaacowitz, n.d.). There is also evidence that the motivation to enhance emotional meaning in old age may manifest differently in different cultures. For example, one study found that older Chinese participants actually looked away from happy faces in happy-neutral face pairs, whereas young adults did not (Fung et al., 2008). The authors suggest that individuals in interdependent cultures, such as the Chinese culture, consider both negative and positive feelings as central to emotional meaning, whereas individuals in independent cultures, such as the American culture, emphasize feeling good as a goal. Clearly, the motivational context of the individual, including age (or more precisely, future time perspective), goal for the task (e.g., focus on accuracy instructions), and culture, all influence how an individual regulates their emotions.

EMOTION RECOGNITION AND MOTIVATION

Numerous studies on aging and emotion recognition have reported age-related deficits in the ability to recognize facial expressions of emotion (see Ruffman, Henry, Livingstone, & Phillips, 2008, for a meta-analytic review). The standard task used in these studies is to ask young and older adults to identify an emotional facial expression from a static photograph of an expression posed at maximum intensity and validated with the Facial Action Coding System (Ekman, Friesen, & Hager, 2002). Participants choose an emotion label from a multiple-choice list. For recognition accuracy of the basic emotions, the typical pattern of age effects is that young adults consistently outperform older adults at recognizing anger, sadness, and fear (Calder et al., 2003; Orgeta & Phillips, 2008; Sullivan & Ruffman, 2004a), with surprise and happy recognition exhibiting smaller age deficits (Ruffman et al., 2008) or age equivalence (McDowell, Harrison, & Demaree, 1994; Murphy & Isaacowitz, 2010; Orgeta & Phillips, 2008; Phillips, MacLean, & Allen, 2002). Interestingly, older adults do not seem to have trouble recognizing disgusted facial expressions; they are as good as young adults (Orgeta & Phillips, 2008; Phillips et al., 2002) or sometimes better than young adults (Calder et al., 2003; Suzuki, Hoshino, Shigemasu, & Kawamura, 2007; Wong, Cronin-Golomb, & Neargarder, 2005) at correctly identifying disgusted facial expressions. Older adults are also as accurate as young adults at identifying the emotional valence of a facial expression (i.e., positive, negative, or neutral; Keightley, Winocur, Burianova, Hongwanishkul, & Grady, 2006).

Why might older adults have a particular problem with recognizing angry, sad, and fearful facial expressions? Some researchers suggest that older adults may be motivated to avoid negative facial expressions to maximize emotional well-being (in line with SST), and this avoidance leads to older adults exhibiting worse emotion recognition for negative emotions. For example, one emotion recognition study found that older adults made fewer attributions of anger, fear, disgust, and sadness than young adults, suggesting an age-related avoidance of these negative emotion labels (Riediger, Voelkle, Ebner, & Lindenberger, 2011). Whether this avoidance of negative was related to feeling good, however, was not tested.

One study employed techniques of functional neuroimaging and event-related potentials (ERPs) to examine activation of the medial prefrontal cortex (MPFC), an area of the cortex that is activated in response to emotional stimuli (Damasio, 1998), among young and older adults viewing fearful or happy facial expressions. The study found age-related decreases in early MPFC activation while participants viewed happy facial expressions and age-related increases in later activation in the same area while participants viewed fearful facial expressions (Williams et al., 2006). The authors interpret these findings within the framework of SST, suggesting that, with age, there are decreases in the controlled processing (the later phase of activation of the MPFC) of positive emotions and increases in the controlled processing of negative emotions. In this study, they linked these age-related differences in brain activation to age-related decreases in neuroticism, suggesting that this shift in how positive and negative emotions are processed may contribute to emotional well-being in old age.

Although findings from several studies are consistent with positivity effects contributing to age differences in emotion recognition, there is also evidence that does not fit with this theory. For example, positivity effects would not explain age deficits in happiness recognition or lack of age deficits in disgust recognition (Ruffman et al., 2008). Moreover, the theory is difficult to test in an emotion recognition task because happiness is typically the only positive emotion presented along with several negative emotions. It is fairly easy to identify a happy face as happy when the only choices are happy, sad, angry, or fearful because happy is the only positively valenced emotion. Older adults perform as well as young adults at identifying the valence (positive, negative, or neutral) of an emotional facial expression (Keightley et al., 2006). Thus, many of the emotion recognition studies are constrained by ceiling effects for the positive emotion (Isaacowitz et al., 2007). Future work should test age differences in multiple positive and negative emotions within the same study to elucidate whether positivity effects are really contributing to the age differences in emotion recognition accuracy.

SUMMARY OF THE MOTIVATIONAL CONTEXT

Overall, the motivational context definitely matters when examining age differences in emotion regulation. Goals associated with future time perspective appear to play a key role in activating patterns of positivity effects in attention and memory. Furthermore, there is emerging evidence that these positivity effects sometimes actually do correspond to improvements in mood. In terms of emotion recognition, the influence of the motivational context is less clear. It does not appear that positivity effects alone can explain the patterns of age effects. Other contextual factors, such as individual differences in cognition or affect, or characteristics of the stimuli (discussed in more detail later), may play a larger role in explaining age-related differences in emotion

recognition. It may also be the case that motivational factors that have not yet been explored, such as task motivation, play a greater role in age differences in emotion recognition.

Individual Difference Characteristics

Individual difference variables may be contextual factors that moderate or mediate (or do neither to) age differences in emotion regulation and recognition. Individual differences in cognitive abilities and personality have been most often considered in these domains.

EMOTION REGULATION

In literature on age-related positivity effects in attention and memory, executive functioning has emerged as the key individual difference moderating variable of interest, primarily due to Mather's argument that older adults need adequate cognitive control abilities to display motivated positivity effects (e.g., Kryla-Lighthall & Mather, 2009). Although several studies have manipulated cognitive control through divided attention within subjects (e.g., Knight et al., 2007), other studies have investigated individual differences in executive functioning. Mather and Knight (2005, experiment 2) found that older adults who scored well on tasks measuring cognitive control were more likely to exhibit positivity effects in memory. These findings suggest that individual differences in executive functioning moderate whether positivity effects are *displayed*. We have found that individual differences in executive functioning can also moderate whether positivity effects in fixation lead to positive mood outcomes, with older adults who have better executive control being more able to resist mood decline by focusing on the less negative face in a face pair (Isaacowitz et al., 2008, 2009). It also appears that alerting ability moderates the relationship between positive looking behaviors and mood for older adults (Isaacowitz & Noh, 2011; Noh et al., 2011).

Individual differences in personality and affect also influence age differences in emotion regulation. For example, older adults who rapidly regulated out of an induced negative mood were more likely to be low in trait anxiety and depressive symptoms and have higher levels of optimism than were older adults who did not rapidly regulate their moods (Larcom & Isaacowitz, 2009). Another study found that when viewing sad pictures, levels of sad mood were better predicted by individual differences in agreeableness than in age (Pearman, Andreoletti, & Isaacowitz, 2010). Furthermore, a cluster analysis revealed four subgroups of mood change trajectories across a short time period in which older adults were overrepresented in the most positive *and* the most negative subgroups (Stanley & Isaacowitz, 2011). Individual difference characteristics differentiated group membership: the most negative group had slower processing speed, more state anxiety and neuroticism, and looked less at happy faces than did other groups. Individual differences may also influence the processing of emotion-relevant information: in a dot-probe task, low anxiety older adults avoided sad faces but high anxiety older adults did not. However, high anxiety older adults initially avoided negative words but later dwelled on them (Lee & Knight, 2009). In addition to the utility of considering personality and affective traits, these studies also highlight the importance of considering the temporal context when examining how individual differences exert influence on age differences in emotion regulation.

EMOTION RECOGNITION

In contrast with the moderating role of individual differences in age effects in emotion regulation, individual differences have been considered possible *mediators* of age differences in emotion recognition. Nevertheless, several studies have shown that age-related decline in cognitive abilities cannot completely account for age-related differences in emotion recognition (Keightley et al., 2006; Sullivan & Ruffman, 2004b). In one study, age-related deficits in recognizing fear and sadness remained even when controlling for individual differences in face processing, visual perception of faces, and fluid intelligence (Sullivan & Ruffman, 2004b). Another study was able to eliminate age differences in sadness recognition by controlling for self-reported anxiety and depression (Suzuki et al., 2007). Finally, one study found that anger recognition was related to greater emotional awareness (Keightley et al., 2006), suggesting that future work should include more social and emotional individual difference measures as possible mediators of age differences in emotion recognition.

SUMMARY OF INDIVIDUAL DIFFERENCES AS CONTEXT

In sum, individual differences in cognitive variables such as executive functioning and alerting ability are key contextual factors in determining when older adults will display positivity effects (Knight et al., 2007; Mather & Knight, 2005) and when positivity effects actually relate to mood improvement

(Isaacowitz et al., 2008; Noh et al., 2011). In addition, affective characteristics such as anxiety and depression, and personality traits such as agreeableness and neuroticism, are critical to consider when determining which older adults will regulate their moods most effectively. To date, this work has been only correlational in nature. It is very possible that differences in mood regulation cause differences in affective characteristics (e.g., depression), or that the relationship is bidirectional. Future work should focus on disentangling the direction of causation in these relationships. Whereas individual differences have most often been considered as moderators of age differences in emotion regulation, they have most frequently been investigated as possible mediators of age effects in emotion recognition. Age differences in emotion recognition have not been fully explained by cognitive, perceptual, or affective variables. A handful of studies have accounted for age differences in recognizing specific discrete emotions (e.g., anger, sad) with affective individual difference factors, suggesting that a discrete emotions perspective may be useful for understanding the causal mechanisms driving age-related differences in emotion recognition (see the section "Emotional Context").

Stimulus Context

The internal psychological state of the perceiver is one potentially relevant context, but any situation in which an individual is recognizing or regulating their response to some stimulus in his or her environment features an important external context as well. Here, we consider how the nature of the external stimuli may themselves form a key context.

Age Relevance

Individuals may be able to relate best to situations or material relevant to their current stage in life. One facet of the stimuli that has emerged as a powerful moderator of age effects in socioemotional functioning is age relevance, or whether the stimuli match what the target would typically encounter in daily life (Blanchard-Fields, Baldi, & Stein, 1999). For example, a young adult may best relate to situations in a school context, a middle-aged adult might relate to a work context, and an older adult might be most familiar with retirement. Theoretically, emotional material that is age-relevant may be more likely to trigger accessible autobiographical experiences that are similar, which could boost the impact of the emotional material. The age relevance of the stimuli also relates to motivation, because an individual may be more motivated to process emotional information that is relevant to his or her current stage in life.

EMOTION REGULATION

Much of the work on emotion regulation and aging has examined age differences in subjective responses (e.g., ratings of sadness) and physiological reactivity (e.g., heart rate, skin conductance) to emotional film clips. Several studies suggest that there is stability with age in subjective responses, but age-related decreases, or "dampening," in physiological reactivity to emotion-eliciting film clips. For example, when watching sad and amusing clips, young and older adults did not differ in online subjective responses, but older adults exhibited smaller changes in cardiovascular responding than did young adults (Tsai, Levenson, & Carstensen, 2000). However, after viewing age-relevant film clips about loss (e.g., cancer), older adults reported *greater* sadness than did young adults, and there were no age differences in autonomic responses (Kunzmann & Gruhn, 2005; Kunzmann & Richter, 2009). This suggests that when the stimuli are age-relevant for older adults, their subjective responses can be even greater in magnitude than young adults', and their physiological responses are not dampened.

EMOTION RECOGNITION

Several studies have examined whether individuals are better at recognizing the emotional facial expressions of their same-age peers, known as an *own-age bias*. Before describing the results of these studies, we first consider why the age of the face might be relevant for recognition accuracy. First, there are developmental differences in the physiognomy of young and old faces due to age-related decreases in facial collagen. Specifically, wrinkles, drooping around the eyes, and sagging jowls all contribute to age-related changes in the appearance of the face (Hooyman & Kiyak, 1996). Indeed, consistent with work on negative stereotypes about aging, older faces are rated as less attractive than young faces by both young and older adults (although older adults' ratings of old faces were more positive than young adults' ratings; Ebner, 2008). Thus, one possibility is that older adults may be more familiar with interpreting the facial expressions of old faces than are young adults (Bartlett & Fulton, 1991), which could give them an advantage when interpreting the emotions expressed in older faces. This experiential advantage may eliminate age differences in basic emotion recognition abilities with

older target faces. A second possible reason for an own-age bias may be that older adults are more motivated to recognize the emotional expression of a same-age peer because they would be more likely to interact socially with individuals their own age. If there is an own-age bias in emotion recognition, the majority of the emotion recognition and aging literature would have underestimated older adults' emotion recognition abilities because most studies use young to middle-aged adult stimuli only.

To date, there is only mixed support for this possibility (see Isaacowitz & Stanley, 2011, for a review). In one study, both young and older adults were better at identifying anger and neutral expressions in young faces than old faces (Ebner & Johnson, 2009), suggesting that older faces are more difficult for *everyone* to interpret than young faces, perhaps because of the age-related physical changes to the face just mentioned. Similarly, another study reported that young, middle-aged, and older adults found it more difficult to recognize the facial expressions of older posers than young posers, with young adults exhibiting a steeper drop-off in performance from young poser to old poser than middle-aged and older adults, for some emotions (Riediger et al., 2011). This suggests that although expressions are more difficult to identify when posed by older adults than when posed by young adults, for some emotions, older adult raters are not as negatively affected by old posers as are young adults. Nevertheless, these age-of-poser by age-of-rater effects did not change the overall main effect of young adults outperforming older adults, suggesting than an own-age bias cannot fully account for age differences in emotion recognition accuracy. Likewise, in a study with dynamic stimuli, young, middle-aged, and older women were equally poor at identifying angry, sad, and fearful emotions from older female faces (Malatesta, Izard, Culver, & Nicolich, 1987). Furthermore, older women were worse at identifying emotions expressed by their own age group than young adults were at identifying emotions expressed by young posers, providing further support that emotions expressed by older faces are more difficult to identify for all ages.

Consistent with these complex results, several studies suggest that the influence of age relevance in emotion perception and aging is quite nuanced. In one series of studies, older adults outperformed young adults at distinguishing between posed and genuine smiles when presented with both young and old dynamic target smiles, but age equivalence was found when presented with only young dynamic target smiles (Murphy, Lehrfeld, & Isaacowitz, 2010). In another study, the age of the target also influenced emotion perception in dynamic clips of participants reliving an angry, sad, or happy autobiographical experience (Richter, Dietzel, & Kunzmann, 2010). When only visual information was presented, young adults were more accurate than older adults, but when audio information was provided, describing the context of the autobiographical event, young adults' performance dropped to the level of older adults', suggesting that young adults were at a disadvantage when trying to understand the emotions of a target talking about a topic not relevant to their age group. Another study also suggests that the age relevance of the topic can influence age differences in emotion perception. When rating the emotion of a target talking about a life transition, young adults' ratings of emotions more closely matched what the target self-rated than did older adults', but these age differences were eliminated when rating the emotions of a target talking about social loss (Richter & Kunzmann, 2011). Presumably, older adults' ratings of emotional experience more closely matched the target's self-ratings in the social loss theme because this topic was more relevant to older adults.

Stimulus and Task Form

In addition to the age relevance of the target or the topic, the actual form, or mode, of the stimulus and the task involving it can influence patterns of age effects in emotion regulation and recognition. Emotional information can be conveyed via visual or auditory sensory pathways. The stimulus form can be categorized further within these two classes of stimulus presentation. For example, visual stimuli can be presented as emotional scenes, faces, or words in either static or dynamic formats. Auditory stimuli can vary in emotional tone, meaning, or both.

EMOTION REGULATION

The extent to which positivity effects emerge may be task-dependent. In a meta-analysis of studies of emotional attention and memory, there was little evidence for positivity effects in older adults overall; the only significant "positivity effects" found were that older adults exhibited less of a negativity preference than young adults in memory recognition studies (Murphy & Isaacowitz, 2008). However, several individual studies have found positivity effects in attention to emotional faces (Isaacowitz et al., 2006a,b, 2008) or scenes

(Isaacowitz & Choi, 2011), suggesting that positivity effects are quite dependent on the particular task and thus may be obscured in a meta-analysis that collapses across material type (e.g., arousal level), measure (e.g., fixations, reaction time), and task. Given evidence that certain cognitive resources and motivational priorities are necessary conditions for the emergence of positivity effects, it is not surprising that positivity effects only emerge in a subset of emotional tasks. In addition to inherent differences in the attention-capturing qualities of different materials, such as pictures tending to be more memorable than words in recognition tasks for both young and older adults (Park, Puglisi, & Sovacool, 1983), there are also likely differences between tasks in the extent to which attending to or remembering positive material could actually affect mood.

Studies on memory for emotional words have yielded further mixed results. In one study, no evidence for positivity effects was found in recall of positive, negative, or neutral words, whether presented in block format or mixed list format (Grühn, Smith, & Baltes, 2005). However, in another study, older adults showed reliable recognition only for positive words, whereas young adults were more likely to correctly recognize negative than positive words (Thomas & Hasher, 2006). One major methodological difference between these two studies is the nature of the memory task: recall or recognition. Interestingly, in another study that examined both recall and recognition, positivity effects were only apparent for nonarousing words (e.g., serenity and sorrow), but not arousing words (e.g., elation and slaughter; Kensinger, 2008). Thus, it appears that the form of the stimulus (e.g., words, pictures, arousal level) and the task (e.g., recall vs. recognition) can influence the pattern of age effects in research on positivity effects.

Task differences may also be relevant when considering different paradigms for studying potential age differences in emotion regulation. Although work on age differences in fixation have tested whether these gaze patterns could help older adults regulate their affective state (e.g., Isaacowitz et al., 2008, 2009), suggesting increased reliance with age on attentional deployment as a regulation strategy, other research has presented participants with emotionally evocative stimuli and instructed them to regulate their emotions in particular ways. This work has found older adults to be better at implementing some types of emotion regulation strategies (such as positive reappraisal) but worse at others (such as detached reappraisal and using reappraisal to decrease unpleasant emotion (e.g., Opitz, Rauch, Terry, & Urry, 2012; Shiota & Levenson, 2009), and that the cognitive costs of implementing certain strategies may vary with age (Scheibe & Blanchard-Fields, 2009). Thus, not only the form of the stimuli but the task involving the stimuli can change aspects of age differences, suggesting the need for a more nuanced consideration of not only when but how older adults regulate their emotions with different elicitors and tasks (see also Isaacowitz & Blanchard-Fields, 2012).

EMOTION RECOGNITION

The stimulus form and task also influence aging effects in emotion recognition research. A meta-analysis found age deficits in recognizing at least some of the basic emotions for faces, bodies, voices, and face–voice matching (Ruffman et al., 2008). However, the extent to which these patterns of age effects vary as a function of the stimulus type can be informative for understanding the mechanism underlying age differences in emotion recognition (e.g., Is anger consistently misidentified across modalities? Is the most difficult emotion the one with the largest age differences?).

Interestingly, age-related deficits in emotion recognition of facial expressions do not always extend to age deficits in recognizing emotions in stories (Phillips et al., 2002), although greater age deficits have been observed for recognizing the emotion felt by a target from a brief sentence (Isaacowitz et al., 2007). It appears that increasing the context in an emotion recognition task can sometimes attenuate or even eliminate age differences in recognition accuracy. For example, when facial expressions were paired with congruent vocal tones, age differences in recognition accuracy were eliminated (Hunter, Phillips, & MacPherson, 2010). Similarly, when participants had to identify the emotion expressed by a target in film clips, age-related deficits in happiness recognition were found when the sound was not available ("context poor" condition) and were eliminated when the sound was available ("context rich" condition), although age differences in anger and sadness recognition remained (Richter et al., 2010).

Age differences are also reduced, or even reversed, when dynamic rather than static stimuli are presented (again, representing an increase in contextual cues). For example, no age differences are found in distinguishing a genuine from a posed smile from static photos of young adults (Slessor, Miles, Bull, & Phillips, 2010), but older adults were better at discriminating a real smile from a fake one when dynamic stimuli of young and older adult targets were presented (Murphy et al., 2010). These results are consistent with evidence that older adults are just as good as young adults at identifying the valence (positive or negative) of facial expressions when presented in a dynamic format (Krendl & Ambady, 2010).

SUMMARY OF STIMULUS AND
TASK FORM CONTEXT

Clearly, the form and mode of the stimulus can determine the pattern of age effects in emotion regulation and emotion recognition studies. Positivity effects seem most likely to be found in studies of recognition memory. And there are differential positivity effects depending on whether pictures (faces, scenes) or words are used. Future research on whether attending to more positive pictures versus words are differentially likely to lead to positive moods could help disentangle these mixed findings. In emotion recognition research, different patterns of age deficits emerge depending on the modality (e.g., face, voice, body), but, in several studies, when additional context is added, age-related deficits are attenuated, eliminated, or even reversed. These context studies are important for understanding the locus of age-related difficulties with emotion recognition, as well as the extent to which these difficulties pose a practical problem for older adults in everyday life.

Emotional Context

A final type of context incorporates both the perceiver and the stimulus: this is the emotional context of the task itself. A discrete emotions perspective would indicate that different emotions have different stimulus contexts and elicit different types of responses in perceivers. Thus, the specific emotion involved may itself form a context that influences performance, as we consider here. Clearly, these effects incorporate aspects of both the perceiver-level context and the stimulus-level context but we wanted to highlight the discrete emotions perspective by drawing links between discrete emotion effects in the emotion regulation and the emotion recognition literature.

Emotion Regulation

Across several studies, age differences in the experience of anger and sadness show opposite trajectories. Specifically, compared with young adults, older adults seem to be avoiding anger and embracing sadness. For example, when solving interpersonal problems, older adults report experiencing less anger than young adults (Blanchard-Fields & Coats, 2008). Consistent with an age-related increase in the importance of interpersonal relationships, older adults report experiencing less anger in their daily lives (Birditt & Fingerman, 2003). Even in experimental paradigms, older adults tend to downplay anger as a response: after "accidentally" overhearing negative remarks about themselves, older adults reported less anger, but equal levels of sadness, as young adults (Charles & Carstensen, 2008). In another study, older adults reported *greater* sadness than young adults when watching loss-based film clips (Kunzmann & Gruhn, 2005). One explanation for avoiding anger is that older adults may be less able than young adults to physically tolerate the toxicity of anger (Blanchard-Fields, 2007; Labouvie-Vief, 2003). Some suggestive results come from a study linking emotional responses to neutral films with well-being: for middle-aged adults, but not young or old, greater self-reported anger was associated with greater well-being. And for older adults, but not young or middle-aged adults, greater self-reported sadness was associated with greater well-being (Haase, Seider, Shiota, & Levenson, 2011). Future work should further explore the antecedents and consequences of these experiential differences in the experience of anger and sadness among young and older adults.

Emotion Recognition

As described earlier, a clear distinction in age effects in recognition of positive versus negative emotions is not consistent with the literature. A meta-analysis of age differences in recognizing facial expressions of emotion found that older adults are the worst at identifying anger, fear, and sadness, with smaller age effects for disgust, surprise, and happy recognition (Ruffman et al., 2008). Rather than valence, one might look to arousal as a distinguishing feature of age differences in emotion recognition. Too much arousal in general may be aversive to older adults. How might this tie in with emotion recognition deficits? Perhaps older adults subconsciously process the arousal level of stimuli in their environment and thus direct attention away from fully processing stimuli that are aversive, thereby misidentifying an angry face for a disgusted one. One study found that young and older adults exhibit a different relationship between emotional valence and arousal when rating emotional pictures and verbs (Keil & Freund, 2009). Specifically,

older adults rate low-arousing stimuli as most pleasing and high-arousing stimuli as least pleasant. In another study, older adults displayed longer reaction times to high- than low-arousing stimuli, but the valence of the stimuli did not influence the reaction time of older adults (Wurm, Labouvie-Vief, Aycock, Rebucal, & Koch, 2004). Consistent with SST, older adults might avoid recognizing highly arousing negative emotions in order to regulate their own emotions.

The first question that must be considered for this hypothesis to be tenable is whether merely viewing a negative facial expression actually influences emotional experience. There is evidence that looking at positive or negative facial expressions can be related to mood and mood change (Isaacowitz et al., 2009). Furthermore, correlational evidence suggests that emotional experience and expression are related to emotion recognition. An electromyography study investigated whether there were age differences in facial mimicry (known to be important for accurate emotion recognition) when recognizing angry facial expressions. Young and older adults exhibited similar levels of corrugator (brow) activity when viewing an angry face, suggesting that both age groups "mimicked" the angry facial expressions (Bailey, Henry, & Nangle, 2009). Thus, it seems that it is at least possible that viewing an emotional facial expression could be linked to experiencing that emotion.

Earlier, we reviewed evidence that older adults appear to avoid anger but embrace sadness in the experience of emotions. Yet, in the emotion recognition research, older adults are poor at identifying both angry and sad facial expressions, but not disgust. Why might there be differences in the discrete emotion that older adults avoid in emotion regulation and emotion recognition? One possibility is that the experience versus the recognition of certain discrete facial expressions may be more or less threatening to a relationship. That is, experiencing sadness yourself may not be as great a threat to interpersonal relationship as when someone else expresses sadness. This may mean that the experience of sadness and the recognition of sadness are differentially threatening to older adults. It is important to note that we do not yet know if participants activate such relationship-preserving processes when presented with pictures of strangers in a lab setting. Future work should empirically test this possibility.

Could age deficits in emotion recognition be a reflection of older adults, at some level, intentionally avoiding "toxic" emotional expressions in order to maintain well-being? The logical question here becomes: Wouldn't older adults need to first recognize the emotion in order to avoid it? There is some evidence that suggests emotion can influence early visual processing. Older adults have been shown to be as good as young adults at detecting an angry face in an array of neutral faces (Mather & Knight, 2006). Thus, it is possible that older adults initially detect anger during preattentive or early processes, but then avoid anger as soon as it is detected. In a study with young adults, a fearful face cue enhanced contrast sensitivity compared to a neutral face cue, suggesting that the emotion of a face can influence early visual processing (Phelps, Ling, & Carrasco, 2006). Furthermore, an ERP study showed that, even in early visual processing, young and older adults differentially prioritize the processing of emotional facial expressions (Mienaltowski, Corballis, Blanchard-Fields, Parks, & Hilimire, 2011). Given this promising evidence, future work in this area might investigate the role of arousal in explaining patterns of age effects in recognizing discrete emotions.

Differential age effects for recognizing discrete emotions have also been attributed to age-related changes in the structure or function of the brain. This neuropsychological approach suggests that the areas of the brain that are responsive to specific emotions, such as the orbitofrontal cortex for anger or the insula for disgust, exhibit differential patterns of decline with age (Calder et al., 2003; Raz et al., 1997; Ruffman et al., 2008; Williams et al., 2006), and this explains the differential patterns of age effects for anger and disgust recognition. Although this argument makes logical sense, there is currently little direct evidence to support the neuropsychological explanation. Additionally, it is unclear how this approach could explain the pattern of age effects in emotion regulation.

Summary of the Emotional Context

Overall, the experience of anger and sadness clearly exhibit different age-related trajectories. The reason for these differences is still not completely understood, but it is possible that anger is avoided and sadness is embraced in order to preserve close relationships. Discrete emotion effects in emotion recognition vary by mode (face, tone of voice). The degree to which these differential emotion patterns are intentional versus side effects of other age-related changes is not clear. One hypothesis is that arousal, rather than valence, determines the

emotional expressions that older adults will recognize best, perhaps also in order to preserve their relationships. Interestingly, the most difficult emotional expression to recognize appears to be fear for both young and older adults (Rapcsak et al., 2000), but fear expressions are not the only ones missed by older adults, suggesting that age differences in emotion recognition for specific emotions may not be related to difficulty (and thus, not solely a result of cognitive decline with age). Future work should focus on whether age differences in the regulation and recognition of certain discrete emotions serve a functional role.

Conclusion

Context appears to exert an influence on both age-related differences in emotion regulation and emotion recognition, although the nature of the influence varies between the two and also depends on the type of context involved. Whereas most research on context and emotion regulation has considered potential contextual moderators, most research on context and emotion recognition has tended to treat context as a possible mediator. Our review suggests that context is probably best conceptualized as a moderator of age differences in both emotion regulation and emotion recognition. One reason for this is simply recent work questioning mediational analysis with cross-sectional age data (Lindenberger, von Oertzen, Ghisletta, & Hertzog, 2011). Even putting these data analytic problems aside, conceptually speaking, there does not seem to be any variable, context-related or otherwise, that seems able to fully account for age differences in emotion regulation or recognition. Instead, it seems that aspects of the perceiver, stimulus, and emotional context can strengthen or weaken the magnitude of age differences, thus suggesting a moderating role. One question for the future is whether there are additive effects of multiple moderating contextual variables.

Fredda Blanchard-Fields strongly believed in the importance of context in the study of socioemotional aging, but she also was concerned that potential mechanisms be specified and tested directly (i.e., Isaacowitz & Blanchard-Fields, 2012). The study of context in emotion regulation and recognition, in a sense, is all about mechanisms: what can be shown to actually vary outcomes of interest, and under what conditions? We hope that explicitly considering context and integrating context into conceptual frameworks (such as age-related positivity effects, own-age biases, and neuropsychological models) will move the field of socioemotional aging to a place of strong predictive power and conceptual specificity.

Future Directions

What are some key future directions that would help with this endeavor? In general, both the study of age differences in emotion regulation and emotion recognition would benefit more from a functional approach, in which potential mechanisms are explicitly linked to key outcomes. Although this point has already been made separately in the area of emotion regulation (Isaacowitz & Blanchard-Fields, 2012) and emotion recognition (Isaacowitz & Stanley, 2011), a consideration of context serves as a reminder that these links are not always obvious or simple. Put another way, the reliance on correlational designs (pattern *y* is consistent with process *x*) has been reasonable, but drawing out the practical and theoretical implications of such correlational results may necessitate an increased use of experimental designs that permit more direct hypothesis testing (e.g., does process *x* lead to better or worse regulation, and/or better or worse recognition, and does this vary by age?). Although not every possible moderating variable can be manipulated in the lab, constraining the processes in lab studies may permit more direct testing of how proposed mechanisms do (or do not) predict outcomes. This is particularly important in cases in which mood can be either an outcome or a predictor itself; thus, isolating the direction of causality is especially important.

Also in the service of simplicity, many studies have considered only one positive or negative emotion in their designs. Given ceiling effects with happy emotions, and differential effects of discrete negative emotions across both regulation and recognition studies, it will be important in future work to put various configurations of positive and negative emotional stimuli in competition with each other simultaneously; this will more closely approximate real-world situations and will be necessary for assessing true preferences and differences among groupings of emotions. Such designs would also be helpful for testing whether positivity effects or other supposedly regulation-related processes can actually predict outcomes such as accuracy on the emotion recognition side.

If motivation is considered to be a key context in emotion regulation and recognition, studies will need to be conducted that either assess naturalistic variation in motivation or manipulate it experimentally. Although numerous studies support SST's idea that older adults value emotional goals (Scheibe & Carstensen, 2010), it is still the case that testing these and other possible goals directly is necessary to explain key regulatory and recognition outcomes that may vary by age.

Given our assertion that moderators will be more useful to consider than mediators in this literature, the full range of potential moderators should be considered and tested. For example, task motivation may be a key moderator of how older adults perform on both regulation and recognition tasks, but has not been explored. The social context also has not been adequately considered. For example, does the familiarity of the target improve emotion recognition for older adults? Finally, future work should explore how individual difference characteristics, such as cognitive capacity, health status, and depression, contribute to socioemotional functioning. Importantly, social and emotional individual difference factors should not be overlooked as possible moderators of age effects.

Research on context in socioemotional aging should also move ahead, keeping in mind that successful emotion regulation and accurate emotion recognition are not the only important outcomes; instead, these processes move in dynamic interplay with other key behaviors and outcomes, such as those involving health. Future work should not only consider the context of the stimuli, the perceiver, and the discrete emotion, but should put the entire emotional aging enterprise in a social, ecological context as well.

References

Allard, E. S., & Isaacowitz, D. M. (n.d.). *Motivational priority and emotional processing preferences in visual fixation in younger and older adults.* Unpublished manuscript. Boston College, Boston, MA.

Bailey, P. E., Henry, J. D., & Nangle, M. R. (2009). Electromyographic evidence for age-related differences in the mimicry of anger. *Psychology and Aging, 24,* 224–229. doi: 10.1037/a0014112

Barrett, L. F., Mesquita, B., & Gendron, M. (2011). Context in emotion perception. *Current Directions in Psychological Science, 20,* 286–290. doi: 10.1177/0963721411422522

Bartlett, J. C., & Fulton, A. (1991). Familiarity and recognition of faces in old age. *Memory and Cognition, 19,* 229–238.

Birditt, K. S., & Fingerman, K. L. (2003). Age and gender differences in adults' descriptions of emotional reactions to interpersonal problems. *Journal of Gerontology, 58B,* 237–245.

Blanchard-Fields, F. (2007). Everyday problem solving and emotion: An adult developmental perspective. *Current Directions in Psychological Science, 16,* 26–31. doi: 10.1111/j.1467-872 1.2007.00469.x

Blanchard-Fields, F., Baldi, R., & Stein, R. (1999). Age relevance and context effects on attributions across the adult lifespan. *International Journal of Aging and Human Development, 23,* 665–683. doi: 10.1080/016502599383748

Blanchard-Fields, F., & Coats, A. H. (2008). The experience of anger and sadness in everyday problems impacts age differences in emotion regulation. *Developmental Psychology, 44,* 1547–1556. doi: 10.1037/a0013915

Calder, A. J., Keane, J., Manly, T., Sprengelmeyer, R., Scott, S., Nimmo-Smith, I., & Young, A. W. (2003). Facial expression recognition across the adult life span. *Neuropsychologia, 41,* 195–202. doi: 10.1016/S0028-3932(02)00149-5

Carstensen, L. L. (1992). Social and emotional patterns in adulthood: Support for socioemotional selectivity theory. *Psychology and Aging, 7,* 331–338.

Carstensen, L. L., & Fredrickson, B. L. (1998). Influence of HIV status and age on cognitive representations of others. *Health Psychology, 17,* 494–503.

Carstensen, L. L., Isaacowitz, D. M., & Charles, S. T. (1999). Taking time seriously: A theory of socioemotional selectivity. *American Psychologist, 54,* 165–181. doi: 10.1037/0003-066X.54.3.165

Carstensen, L. L., & Mikels, J. A. (2005). At the intersection of emotion and cognition: Aging and the positivity effect. *Current Directions in Psychological Science, 14,* 117–121. doi : 10.1111/j.0963-7214.2005.00348.x

Carstensen, L. L., Mikels, J. A., & Mather, M. (2006). Aging and the intersection of cognition, motivation, and emotion. In J. Birren & K. W. Schaie (Eds.), *Handbook of the Psychology of Aging,* 6th ed. (pp. 343–362). Amsterdam: Elsevier Academic Press.

Charles, S. T., & Carstensen, L. L. (2008). Unpleasant situations elicit different emotional responses in younger and older adults. *Psychology and Aging, 23,* 495–504. doi: 10.1037/a0013284

Charles, S. T., Mather, M., & Carstensen, L. L. (2003). Aging and emotional memory: The forgettable nature of negative images for older adults. *Journal of Experimental Psychology: General, 132,* 310–324. doi: 10.1037/0096-3445.132.2.310

Damasio, A. R. (1998). The somatic marker hypothesis and the possible functions of the prefrontal cortex. In A. C. Roberts, T. W. Robbins, & L. Weiskrantz (Eds.), *The prefrontal cortex: Executive and cognitive functions* (pp. 36–50). New York: Oxford University Press.

Ebner, N. C. (2008). Age of face matters: Age-group differences in ratings of young and old faces. *Behavior Research Methods, 40,* 130–136.

Ebner, N. C., & Johnson, M. K. (2009). Young and older emotional faces: Are there age group differences in expression identification and memory? *Emotion, 9,* 329–339. doi: http://dx.doi.org/10.1037/a0015179

Ekman, P., Friesen, W. V., & Hager, J. C. (2002). Facial Action Coding System: The Manual on CD ROM. Salt Lake City, UT: A Human Face.

Fredrickson, B. L., & Carstensen, L. L. (1990). Choosing social partners: How old age and anticipated endings make people more selective. *Psychology and Aging, 5,* 335–347.

Fung, H. H., Carstensen, L. L., & Lutz, A. M. (1999). Influence of time on social preferences: Implications for life-span development. *Psychology and Aging, 14,* 595–604. doi: 10.1037/0882-7974.14.4.595

Fung, H. H., Lu, A. Y., Goren, D., Isaacowitz, D. M., Wadlinger, H. A., & Wilson, H. R. (2008). Age-related positivity enhancement is not universal: Older Chinese look away from positive stimuli. *Psychology and Aging, 23,* 440–446. doi: 10.1037/0882-7974.23.2.440

Gross, J. J. (1998). The emerging field of emotion regulation: An integrative review. *Review of General Psychology, 2,* 271–299. doi: 10.1037/1089-2680.2.3.271

Grühn, D., Smith, J., & Baltes, P. B. (2005). No aging bias favoring memory for positive material: Evidence from a heterogeneity-homogeneity list paradigm using emotionally toned words. *Psychology and Aging, 20,* 579–588. doi: 10.1037/0882-7974.20.4.579

Haase, C. M., Seider, B. H., Shiota, M. N., & Levenson, R. W. (2011). Anger and sadness in response to an emotionally neutral film: Evidence for age-specific associations with well-being. *Psychology and Aging, 27,* 305–317. doi: 10.1037/a0024959

Hooyman, N., & Kiyak, H. A. (1996). *Social gerontology: A multidisciplinary perspective,* 4th ed. Boston: Allyn & Bacon.

Hunter, E. M., Phillips, L. H., & MacPherson, S. E. (2010). Effects of age on cross-modal emotion perception. *Psychology and Aging, 25,* 779–787. doi: 10.1037/a0020528

Isaacowitz, D. M. (2006). Motivated gaze: The view from the gazer. *Current Directions in Psychological Science, 15,* 68–72. doi: 10.1111/j.0963-7214.2006.00409.x

Isaacowitz, D. M., & Blanchard-Fields, F. (2012). Linking process and outcome in the study of emotion and aging. *Perspectives on Psychological Science, 7,* 3–17.

Isaacowitz, D. M., & Choi, Y. (2011). The malleability of age-related positive gaze preferences: Training to change gaze and mood. *Emotion, 11,* 90–100. doi: 10.1037/a0021551

Isaacowitz, D. M., Loeckenhoff, C., Lane, R., Wright, R., Sechrest, L., Riedel, R., & Costa, P. T. (2007). Age differences in recognition of emotion in lexical stimuli and facial expressions. *Psychology and Aging, 22,* 147–259. doi: 10.1037/0882-7974.22.1.147

Isaacowitz, D. M., & Noh, S. R. (2011). Does looking at the positive mean feeling good? Age and individual differences matter. *Social and Personality Psychology Compass, 5,* 505–517. doi: 10.1111/j.1751-9004.2011.00374.x

Isaacowitz, D. M., & Stanley, J. T. (2011). Bringing an ecological perspective to the study of aging and emotion recognition: Past, current, and future methods. *Journal of Nonverbal Behavior, 35,* 261–278. doi: 10.1007/s10919-011-0113-6

Isaacowitz, D. M., Toner, K., Goren, D., & Wilson, H. (2008). Looking while unhappy: Mood congruent gaze in younger adults, positive gaze in older adults. *Psychological Science, 19,* 848–853. doi: 10.1111/j.1467-9280.2008.02167.x

Isaacowitz, D. M., Toner, K., & Neupert, S. D. (2009). Use of gaze for real-time mood regulation: Effects of age and attentional functioning. *Psychology and Aging, 24,* 989–994. doi: 10.1037/a0017706

Isaacowitz, D. M., Wadlinger, H. A., Goren, D., & Wilson, H. R. (2006a). Is there an age-related positivity effect in visual attention? A comparison of two methodologies. *Emotion, 6,* 511–516. doi: 10.1037/1528-3542.6.3.511

Isaacowitz, D. M., Wadlinger, H. A., Goren, D., & Wilson, H. R. (2006b). Selective preference in visual fixation away from negative images in old age? An eye-tracking study. *Psychology and Aging, 21,* 40–48. doi: 10.1037/0882-7974.21.1.40

Keightley, M. L., Winocur, G., Burianova, H., Hongwanishkul, D., & Grady, C. L. (2006). Age effects on social cognition: Faces tell a different story. *Psychology and Aging, 21,* 558–572. doi: 10.1037/0882-7974.21.3.558

Keil, A., & Freund, A. M. (2009). Changes in the sensitivity to appetitive and aversive arousal across adulthood. *Psychology and Aging, 24,* 668–680. doi: 10.1037/a0016969

Kennedy, Q., Mather, M., & Carstensen, L. L. (2004). The role of motivation in the age-related positivity effect in autobiographical memory. *Psychological Science, 15*, 208–214. doi: 10.1111/j.0956-7976.2004.01503011.x

Kensinger, E. A. (2008). Age differences in memory for arousing and nonarousing emotional words. *Journals of Gerontology: Psychological Sciences, 63B*, 13–18.

Knight, M., Seymour, T. L., Gaunt, J. T., Baker, C., Nesmith, K., & Mather, M. (2007). Aging and goal-directed emotional attention: Distraction reverses emotional biases. *Emotion, 7*, 705–714. doi: 10.1037/1528-3542.7.4.705

Krendl, A. C., & Ambady, N. (2010). Older adults' decoding of emotions: Role of dynamic versus static cues and age-related cognitive decline. *Psychology and Aging, 25*, 788–793. doi: 10.1037/a0020607

Kryla-Lighthall, N., & Mather, M. (2009). The role of cognitive control in older adults' emotional well-being. In V. L. Bengston, D. Gans, N. M. Pulney, & M. Silverstein (Eds.), *Handbook of theories of aging*. New York: Springer Publishing.

Kunzmann, U., & Gruhn, D. (2005). Age differences in emotional reactivity: The sample case of sadness. *Psychology and Aging, 20*, 47–59. doi: 10.1037/0882-7974.20.1.47

Kunzmann, U., & Richter, D. (2009). Emotional reactivity across the adult life span: The cognitive pragmatics make a difference. *Psychology and Aging, 24*, 879–889.

Labouvie-Vief, G. (2003). Dynamic integration: Affect, cognition, and the self in adulthood. *Current Directions in Psychological Science, 12*, 201–206.

Larcom, M. J., & Isaacowitz, D. M. (2009). Rapid emotion regulation after mood induction: Age and individual differences. *Journal of Gerontology: Psychological Sciences, 64B*, 733–741. doi: 10.1093/geronb/gbp077

Lee, L. O., & Knight, B. G. (2009). Attentional bias for threat in older adults: Moderation of the positivity bias by trait anxiety and stimulus modality. *Psychology and Aging, 24*, 741–747. doi: 10.1037/a0016409

Lindenberger, U., von Oertzen, T., Ghisletta, P., & Hertzog, C. (2011). Cross-sectional age variance extraction: What's change got to do with it? *Psychology and Aging, 26*, 34–47. doi: 10.1037/a0020525

Malatesta, C. Z., Izard, C. E., Culver, C., & Nicolich, M. (1987). Emotion communication skills in young, middle-aged, and older women. *Psychology and Aging, 2*, 193–203.

Mather, M., & Carstensen, L. L. (2003). Aging and attentional biases for emotional faces. *Psychological Science, 14*, 409–415. doi: 10.1111/1467-9280.01455

Mather, M., & Carstensen, L. L. (2005). Aging and motivated cognition: The positivity effect in attention and memory. *Trends in Cognitive Sciences, 9*, 496–502. doi: 10.1016/j.tics.2005.08.005

Mather, M., & Knight, M. (2005). Goal-directed memory: The role of cognitive control in older adults' emotional memory. *Psychology and Aging, 20*, 554–570. doi: 10.1037/0882-7974.20.4.554

Mather, M., & Knight, M. R. (2006). Angry faces get noticed quickly: Threat detection is not impaired among older adults. *Journal of Gerontology, 61*, 54–57. doi: 10.1093/geronb/61.1.P5

McDowell, C. L., Harrison, D. W., & Demaree, H. A. (1994). Is right hemisphere decline in the perception of emotion a function of aging? *International Journal of Neuroscience, 79*, 1–11.

Mienaltowski, A., Corballis, P. M., Blanchard-Fields, F., Parks, N. A., & Hilimire, M. R. (2011). Anger management: Age differences in emotional modulation of visual processing. *Psychology and Aging, 26*, 224–231. doi: 10.1037/a0021032

Montepare, J. M. E. (2011). Aging and nonverbal behavior: The recognition of facial expressions of emotion [Special issue]. *Journal of Nonverbal Behavior, 35*.

Murphy, N. A., & Isaacowitz, D. M. (2010). Age effects and gaze patterns in recognising emotional expressions: An in-depth look at gaze measures and covariates. *Cognition & Emotion, 24*, 436–452. doi: 10.1080/02699930802664623

Murphy, N. A., & Isaacowitz, D. M. (2008). Preferences for emotional information in older and younger adults: A meta-analysis of memory and attention tasks. *Psychology and Aging, 23*, 263–286. doi: 10.1037/0882-7974.23.2.263

Murphy, N. A., Lehrfeld, J. M., & Isaacowitz, D. M. (2010). Recognition of posed and spontaneous dynamic smiles in younger and older adults. *Psychology and Aging, 25*, 811–821. doi: 10.1037/a0019888

Noh, S. R., Lohani, M., & Isaacowitz, D. M. (2011). Deliberate real-time mood regulation in adulthood: The importance of age, fixation, and attentional functioning. *Cognition & Emotion, 25*, 998–1013. doi: 10.1080/02699931.2010.541668

Opitz, P. C., Rauch, L. C., Terry, D. P., & Urry, H. L. (2012). Prefrontal mediation of age differences in cognitive reappraisal. *Neurobiology of Aging, 33*, 645–655. doi: 10.1016/j.neurobiolaging.2010.06.004

Orgeta, V., & Phillips, L. H. (2008). Effects of age and emotional intensity on the recognition of facial emotion. *Experimental Aging Research, 34*, 63–79. doi: 10.1080/03610730701762047

Park, D. C., Puglisi, J. T., & Sovacool, M. (1983). Memory for pictures, words, and spatial location in older adults: Evidence for pictorial superiority. *Journals of Gerontology, 38*, 582–588.

Pearman, A., Andreoletti, C., & Isaacowitz, D. M. (2010). Sadness prediction and response: Effects of age and agreeableness. *Aging & Mental Health, 14*, 355–363. doi: 10.1080/13607860903292586

Phelps, E. A., Ling, S., & Carrasco, M. (2006). Emotion facilitates perception and potentiates the perceptual benefits of attention. *Psychological Science, 17*, 292–299. doi: 10.1111/j.1467-9280.2006.01701.x

Phillips, L. H., MacLean, R. D. J., & Allen, R. (2002). Age and the understanding of emotions: Neuropsychological and sociocognitive perspectives. *Journal of Gerontology: Psychological Sciences, 57B*, 526–530.

Rapcsak, S. Z., Galper, S. R., Corner, J. F., Reminger, S. L., Nielsen, L., Kaszniak, A. W., et al. (2000). Fear recognition deficits after focal brain damage: A cautionary note. *Neurology, 54*, 575–581.

Raz, N., Gunning, F. M., Head, D., Dupuis, J. H., McQuain, J., Briggs, S. D., et al. (1997). Selective aging of the human cerebral cortex observed in vivo: Differential vulnerability of the prefrontal gray matter. *Cerebral Cortex, 7*, 268–282.

Richter, D., Dietzel, C., & Kunzmann, U. (2010). Age differences in emotion recognition: The task matters. *Journal of Gerontology: Psychological Sciences, 60B*, 48–55. doi: 10.1093/geronb/gbq068

Richter, D., & Kunzmann, U. (2011). Age differences in three facets of empathy: Performance-based evidence. *Psychology and Aging, 26*, 60–70. doi: 10.1037/a0021138

Riediger, M., Voelkle, M. C., Ebner, N. C., & Lindenberger, U. (2011). Beyond "Happy, Angry, or Sad?" Age-of-poser and age-of-rater effects on multi-dimensional emotion perception. *Cognition & Emotion 25*, [Special Section] 968–982. doi: 10.1080/02699931.2010.540812

Rozin, P., & Royzman, E. B. (2001). Negativity bias, negativity dominance, and contagion. *Personality and Social Psychology Review, 5*, 296–320.

Ruffman, T., Henry, J. D., Livingstone, V., & Phillips, L. H. (2008). A meta-analytic review of emotion recognition and aging: Implications for neuropsychological models of aging. *Neuroscience & Biobehavioral Reviews, 32*, 863–881. doi: 10.1016/j.neubiorev.2008.01.001

Scheibe, S., & Blanchard-Fields, F. (2009). Effects of regulating emotions on cognitive performance: What is costly for young adults is not so costly for older adults. *Psychology and Aging, 24*, 217–223. doi: 10.1037/a0013807

Scheibe, S., & Carstensen, L. L. (2010). Emotional aging: Recent findings and future trends. *Journal of Gerontology: Psychological Sciences, 65B*, P135–P144.

Shiota, M. N., & Levenson, R. W. (2009). Effects of aging on experimentally instructed detached reappraisal, positive reappraisal, and emotional behavior suppression. *Psychology and Aging, 24*, 890–900. doi: 10.1037/a0017896

Simons, D. J., & Chabris, C. F. (1999). Gorillas in our midst: Sustained inattentional blindness for dynamic events. *Perception, 28*, 1059–1074. doi: 10.1068/p2952

Slessor, G., Miles, L. K., Bull, R., & Phillips, L. H. (2010). Age-related changes in detecting happiness: Discriminating between enjoyment and nonenjoyment smiles. *Psychology and Aging, 25*, 246–250. doi: 10.1037/a0018248

Stanley, J. T., & Isaacowitz, D. M. (2011). Age-related differences in profiles of mood-change trajectories. *Developmental Psychology, 47*, 318–330. doi: 10.1037/a0021023

Sullivan, S., & Ruffman, T. (2004a). Emotion recognition deficits in the elderly. *International Journal of Neuroscience, 114*, 403–432. doi: 10.1080/00207450490270901

Sullivan, S., & Ruffman, T. (2004b). Social understanding: How does it fare with advancing years? *British Journal of Psychology, 95*, 1–18.

Suzuki, A., Hoshino, T., Shigemasu, K., & Kawamura, M. (2007). Decline or improvement?: Age-related differences in facial expression recognition. *Biological Psychology, 74*, 75–84. doi: 10.1016/j.biopsycho.2006.07.003

Thomas, R. C., & Hasher, L. (2006). The influence of emotional valence on age differences in early processing and memory. *Psychology and Aging, 21*, 821–525. doi: 10.1037/0882-7974.21.4.821

Tsai, J. L., Levenson, R. W., & Carstensen, L. L. (2000). Autonomic, subjective, and expressive responses to emotional films in older and younger Chinese Americans and European Americans. *Psychology and Aging, 15*, 684–693. doi: 10.1037/0882-7974.15.4.684

Williams, L. M., Brown, K. J., Palmer, D., Liddell, B. J., Kemp, A. H., Olivieri, G., et al. (2006). The mellow years?: Neural basis of improving emotional stability over age. *Journal of Neuroscience, 26*, 6422–6430.

Wong, B., Cronin-Golomb, A., & Neargarder, S. (2005). Patterns of visual scanning as predictors of emotion identification in normal aging. *Neuropsychology, 19*, 739–749. doi: 10.1037/0894-4105.19.6.739

Wood, S., & Kisley, M. A. (2006). The negativity bias is eliminated in older adults: Age-related reduction in event-related brain potentials associated with evaluative categorization. *Psychology and Aging, 21*, 815–820. doi: 10.1037/0882-7974.21.4.815

Wurm, L. H., Labouvie-Vief, G., Aycock, J., Rebucal, K. A., & Koch, H. E. (2004). Performance in auditory and visual emotional Stroop tasks: A comparison of older and younger adults. *Psychology and Aging, 19*, 523–535. doi: 10.1037/0882-7974.19.3.523

Positive Emotions and Health in Adulthood and Later Life

Catherine Riffin, Anthony D. Ong, *and* Cindy S. Bergeman

Abstract

Theoretical models and empirical evidence support an association between positive emotions and enhanced physical health. In this essay, we describe the current state of knowledge regarding the health significance of positive emotions in later life. We begin by exploring the contribution of lifespan theories of aging to emotion research. We then provide an overview of existing empirical evidence relevant to the role of positive emotions and adult health and well-being. We conclude with a discussion of how the integration of theoretical models and empirical findings can inform future research exploring the health effects of positive emotions across the lifespan.

Key Words: Aging, health, positive emotions, resilience

Changes in physical, cognitive, and emotional functioning pervade the aging process. In contrast with the pattern of age-related declines in physical health, emotional well-being appears to be preserved with age. Efforts to uncover this "paradox" of aging have recently begun to identify possible mechanisms that may account for age differences in emotional experience (see Charles & Carstensen, 2009; Scheibe & Carstensen, 2010; Urry & Gross, 2010, for a review). In the following sections, we review lifespan theories of emotion, with specific attention to health implications for older adults. We then discuss how age-associated gains in positive emotions may support physical well-being in later life. In doing so, we summarize recent evidence on the biobehavioral mechanisms that may account for this relationship by focusing on the approaches, empirical findings, and methodological inconsistencies that exist in present literature. Finally, we delineate future new directions in emotional aging research.

Age Differences in Emotional Well-Being

Although advanced age is marked by physical and cognitive decline, accumulating research suggests that affective well-being is maintained well into later life (e.g., Carstensen, Pasupathi, Mayr, & Nesselroade, 2000; Charles, Reynolds, & Gatz, 2001; Charles, 2010; Charles & Carstensen, 2009. In fact, increased age is associated with improved emotion regulation and emotional stability (e.g., Carstensen et al., 2000; Charles et al., 2001; Charles, 2010). Both cross-sectional (Carstensen et al., 2000; Gross et al., 1997; Mroczek & Kolarz, 1998) and longitudinal studies (Charles et al., 2001; Costa et al., 1987; Griffin, Mroczek, & Spiro, 2006) substantiate this association and further reveal that reductions in negative emotional experience are accompanied by a greater frequency in positive emotions across age cohorts. Even individuals in their eighties enjoy high levels of positive emotions; it is not until the "terminal phase" of life that older adults exhibit a precipitous decline in affective well-being (Gerstorf et al., 2010). Although some evidence calls into question whether age-related shifts in subjective well-being are moderated by functional health constraints (Kunzmann, Little, & Smith, 2000), overall, the data suggest that positive emotions remain stable throughout adulthood.

Below, we describe two theories of emotional aging that provide distinct accounts of how positive emotions are maintained into adulthood. Socioemotional selectivity theory (Carstensen, Isaacowitz, & Charles, 1999) and dynamic integration theory (Labouvie-Vief, 2003) propose different explanations for the trajectory of emotional aging across the lifespan. Although empirical evidence provides general support for each of these theories, research has yet to identify the underlying mechanisms associated with the hypotheses proposed by each framework.

Information Processing and the Positivity Effect

Socioemotional selectivity theory contends that time perception plays a key role in motivation, especially as it relates to goal selection and goal pursuit (Carstensen & Charles, 1998). When time horizons are perceived as expansive, as they often do in youth, goals focused on gaining knowledge and information are prioritized. Alternatively, as the end of life draws near and temporal horizons shrink, older adults begin to seek more emotionally satisfying experiences and avoid negative ones. Socioemotional selectivity theory points to the shift in motivation as contributing to older adults' tendency to prioritize positive over negative material. This developmental pattern, termed the "positivity effect," is proposed to have implications for age-related changes in information processing systems, such as memory and attention (Carstensen & Mikels, 2005; Kensinger, Garoff-Eaton, & Scgacter, 2007).

THE POSITIVITY EFFECT IN MEMORY

Growing evidence indicates that memory for emotional material, especially positive emotional material, is enhanced in older adults (Carstensen & Mikels, 2005). Studies of recall and recognition memory reveal that although older adults recall fewer images than younger adults, they recall more positive images as compared to negative images (Charles, Mather, & Carstensen, 2003). Furthermore, research on working memory suggests that older adults' memory performance is enhanced when they are asked to recall stimuli that are positive in valence (Mikels, Larkin, Reuter-Lorenz, & Carstensen, 2005).

Consistent with laboratory findings, studies of autobiographical memory and mutual reminiscing also point to an age-related positivity bias. For example, one study found that when asked to recount personal experiences from over a decade prior, older adults tended to remember the past in a more positive light than originally reported (Kennedy, Mather, & Carstensen, 2004). Younger adults, on the other hand, remembered the past more negatively. This experience also holds during mutual reminiscing: older adults report more positive and fewer negative emotions when engaging in retrospective retelling of the personal past (Pasupathi & Carstensen, 2003).

Although this work illustrates older adults' selective memory for positive material, other research reveals that this may not always be the case. For example, a study comparing younger (18–31 years) and older (64–75 years) adults failed to find an aging bias in memory for emotionally toned words (Gruhn, Smith, & Baltes, 2005). In general, however, an association between advanced age and positively biased memory is documented across the literature (Murphy & Isaacowitz, 2008).

THE POSITIVITY EFFECT IN ATTENTION

Studies of attention also provide evidence for the positivity effect. With advanced age, older adults selectively attend more to emotional information and exhibit a bias toward positive rather than negative stimuli. Dot-probe and eye-tracking studies of visual attention support this age-related positivity bias. For example, in a study of younger (18–24 years) and older (61–85 years) adults, Isaacowitz and colleagues (2006a) found that older individuals display a gaze pattern toward happy and away from sad faces, whereas younger adults showed no preference for happy faces, but looked away from sad faces. This same study demonstrated that older adults responded more quickly when dot probes replaced positive stimuli with negative stimuli. These results corroborate with findings from other visual attention studies showing that older adults tend to look away from emotionally negative faces (Isaacowitz, Wadlinger, Goren, & Wilson, 2006b; Mather & Carstensen, 2003).

Consistent with socioemotional selectivity theory, recent evidence suggests that positive attentional preferences may assist older adults in regulating their emotional experiences (Isaacowitz, Toner, Goren, & Wilson, 2008; Isaacowitz, Toner, & Neupert, 2009). In other words, focusing attention on positive stimuli helps to optimize affect as well as manage negative emotional experiences. Importantly, individual differences may influence attentional deployment. For instance, the ability to avoid negative stimuli may hinge on cognitive control. Whereas individuals without the necessary resources may be unable to successfully engage in regulatory strategies (Knight et al., 2007), those with good executive functioning are able to resist mood declines by displaying gaze preferences toward positive and away from negative faces when in a bad mood (Issacowitz et al., 2009).

NEURAL EVIDENCE OF THE POSITIVITY EFFECT

Additional support for the positivity effect comes from functional magnetic resonance imaging (fMRI) studies exploring neural responses to emotional stimuli. Emerging research in this area reveals age-related changes in subcortical and cortical activation (Samanez-Larkin & Carstensen, 2011). For example, older adults (70–90 years) show greater amygdala activation in response to positive images than do younger adults (18–29 years) and relatively less activation when viewing negative images (Mather et al., 2004). Such changes in brain activation patterns may reflect underlying age-related shifts in emotion regulation and processing (Scheibe & Carstensen, 2010), which in turn serve to promote emotional well-being in later life.

Cognitive Control

In contrast with socioemotional selectivity theory, which emphasizes goal selection as a key component in emotional preservation, dynamic integration theory (Labouvie-Vief, 2003) posits that developmental declines in cognitive resources may account for age differences in emotion regulation and well-being. Specifically, this theory proposes that affect regulation depends on two core elements: *optimization*, an unconscious, automatic process of enhancing affect, and *differentiation*, a complex, conscious process of incorporating one's own feelings and knowledge with the thoughts and feelings of others. Together, differentiation and optimization are hypothesized to promote optimal emotion regulation (see Labouvie-Vief et al., "The Dynamics of Cognitive-Emotional Integration: Complexity and Hedonics in Emotional Development" for details).

According to dynamic integration theory, diminishing executive functioning in older adults elicits a gradual shift from a more complex mode of emotion regulation (i.e., differentiation) to one favoring simplicity. In support of this prediction, a cross-sectional study comparing younger (15–29 years), middle-aged

(30–59 years), and older adults (60–86 years) found that older individuals tended to exhibit high levels of optimization (i.e., high positive affect) and low complexity (e.g., high denial and repression), whereas younger individuals showed high levels of affect complexity (Labouvie-Vief & Medler, 2002). Consistent with these cross-sectional results, a 6-year longitudinal study (Labouvie-Vief, Diehl, Jain, & Zhang, 2007) documented a developmental trend in increasing optimization and decreasing complexity in older adults. Taken together, these findings illustrate that age-related losses in cognitive control are associated with a compensatory response toward affect optimization.

Additionally, dynamic integration theory suggests that cognitive declines throughout the aging process result in decreases in emotion regulation capacity (Labouvie-Vief, 2003). In particular, deterioration of executive functioning may contribute to deficits in older adults' inhibitory control in emotionally charged or highly arousing circumstances. For example, a cross-sectional study by Wurm and colleagues (2004) revealed that older adults (52–92 years) had difficulty inhibiting irrelevant information as well as processing high-arousing words during emotional Stroop tasks as compared to younger adults.

Overall, the current body of research consistently documents an age-associated shift in emotional experience. Although socioemotional selectivity theory and dynamic integration theory propose divergent explanations for this developmental pattern, the empirical evidence consistently supports the association between advanced age and positive emotion, especially among high-functioning older adults.

Aging and Emotion Regulation

Integrative theories posit that increases in emotional well-being across the lifespan may be explained by older adults' enhanced ability to modulate emotional experiences. These models suggest that emotion regulation processes vary with age and further predict when and why these abilities change across the lifespan. Alongside theoretical predictions, empirical evidence supports an association between emotion regulation and positive psychological outcomes (Gross & John, 2003).

OPTIMIZING EMOTIONAL EXPERIENCE IN LATER LIFE

Extending from Baltes and Baltes' (1990) metatheory of successful aging, Urry and Gross (SOC-ER; Urry & Gross, 2010) recently put forth a framework of selection, optimization, and compensation with emotion regulation. Consistent with socioemotional selectivity theory, this model highlights motivation as a key factor in prompting the use of specific regulation strategies in the service of well-being. SOC-ER proposes that older adults compensate for changes in internal (i.e., cognition) and external (i.e., social engagement) resources through capitalizing on emotion regulatory strategies. In particular, the framework suggests five points at which emotion may be modulated in the emotion generative process: (1) selection of the situation, (2) modification of the situation, (3) deployment of attention, (4) change of cognitions, and (5) modulation of behavioral responses. Divided into antecedent- and response-focused regulatory strategies, the first four (antecedent-focused processes) are employed before emotion response tendencies are fully activated, whereas modulation of behavior (a response-focused process) appears only once an emotion is already under way (Gross & John, 2003).

Older adults tend to engage in antecedent-focused emotion regulation strategies more frequently and with greater efficiency than do younger adults, who tend to employ more response-focused strategies (John & Gross, 2004). Age differences in both types of processes (antecedent- and response-focused) have been most widely documented in studies of attention deployment, reappraisal, and suppression. Older adults use attentional deployment when confronted with negative stimuli, whereas younger adults display a looking preference in congruence with their mood (Isaacowitz et al., 2008). These gaze patterns are clearly represented in the SOC-ER framework as antecedent- versus response-focused processes and are hypothesized to contribute to age-related differences in escaping bad moods and retaining positive experiences (Isaacowitz et al., 2009).

Through mood induction procedures, studies have shown that the ability to implement *positive reappraisal* increases with age, whereas the ability to implement *detached reappraisal* (i.e., deliberate redirection of attention away from emotionally charged stimuli) declines (Shiota & Levenson, 2009). These findings reveal an age-related shift in emotion regulation and provide a framework for subsequent research aimed at exploring the influence of individual and contextual variation in emotion regulation processes across age cohorts.

PRESERVING EMOTIONAL WELL-BEING THROUGH THE STRENGTHS OF AGING

As an alternative account of emotion regulation, the model of strength and vulnerability integration (SAVI), by Charles (2010), proposes that older adults draw on specific strengths of aging (e.g., situational appraisals, selective attentional strategies, goal-oriented behaviors) to promote positive emotional well-being. In accordance with socioemotional selectivity theory, SAVI maintains that both motivation and temporal horizons each contribute to the age differences in emotion regulation. Extending the socioemotional selectivity theory framework, the SAVI model contends that, with accumulated life experience, older adults learn how to cope with and avoid negative situations.

As hypothesized by SAVI, age differences in emotion regulation have emerged in studies of situational appraisals and behavior. These findings are particularly provocative within the context of interpersonal relationships. For instance, older adults report being in a more positive and less negative mood when they interact with family members; they also tend to avoid arguments more than do younger adults (Charles & Piazza, 2007; Charles, Piazza, Luong, & Almeida, 2009). As a means of preserving interpersonal harmony and maintaining positive emotional well-being, older individuals employ passive, rather than active tactics, such as avoiding confrontation or avoiding negatively charged situations altogether (Blanchard-Fields, Chen, & Norris, 1997). Notably, these strategies are proposed to assist older adults in optimizing positive emotional experiences.

Although studies examining appraisals, memory, and behavior provide a consistent picture of age differences in emotion regulation, evidence of age differences in response to stressful situations is relatively sparse (Charles, 2010). SAVI proposes that, when confronted with unrelenting or persistent stressors, older adults may be unable to employ emotion regulation strategies. Specifically, in the face of uncontrollable stress, neurological dysfunction, and loss of social belonging (Charles, 2010), it may not be possible for older adults to disengage from or de-escalate negative experiences. Thus, a minority of individuals may experience affective distress due to prolonged physiological arousal.

FUTURE DIRECTIONS IN EMOTION REGULATION

Overall, older adults benefit from enhanced emotion regulation; however, individual and contextual variation may account for observed differences in emotional experience. Personality, for example, may differentiate individuals in their abilities to draw on positive emotions in coping processes (Charles,

2010). More specifically, those high in the trait of neuroticism may be less adept at modulating emotional experiences (Mroczek & Almeida, 2004). It has since been hypothesized that this failure to regulate emotional experience may be a result of heightened reactivity to daily stressors (Mroczek et al., 2006), as well as to increased sensitivity to physiological arousal (Eyesnck, 1963). Over time, the accumulation of these responses may leave older adults high in neuroticism less able to employ emotion regulation strategies (Charles, 2010). Thus, examining individual differences and emotion regulation in a prospective and longitudinal fashion may help illuminate changes across the lifespan. Moreover, although most people report decreasing levels of negative affect over time, individuals high in neuroticism report stable and high levels of negative affect (Charles et al., 2001) in addition to poorer emotion regulatory abilities (Mroczek & Almeida, 2004). Expanding on this work would help tease apart how positive emotion regulation strategies change across the lifespan, as well as how personality components may either facilitate or hinder these regulatory processes.

Although individual variation may account for some of the differences in well-being, research has yet to uncover whether specific regulatory strategies may serve to enhance positive emotional experience across the lifespan. However, some scholars propose that *savoring* (i.e., a deliberate and conscious awareness of pleasant emotional experiences) may be one regulatory strategy that promotes overall health and well-being for both the young and old (Bryant, 2003; Wood, Heimpel, & Michela, 2003). Whereas people who employ this mode of control experience advantages in well-being, those who engage in the converse—the *dampening* of positive emotions—may have less favorable outcomes (Tugade & Fredrickson, 2007). Notably, *savoring* has been linked with self-esteem and self-control, as well as optimism and life satisfaction (Bryant, 2003). Although correlational in nature, such findings suggest that savoring may confer an array of benefits.

In light of evidence that emotion regulation promotes affective well-being (Charles, 2010; Urry & Gross, 2010) and that positive emotions facilitate better coping and self-regulation strategies (Aspinwall, 1998), it becomes important to understand whether there is a reciprocal influence of emotional well-being and positive regulatory strategies and whether this effect varies by age. For instance, because older adults tend to experience more positive emotions as compared to younger adults (Mroczek, 2001), are they more readily able to draw on their positive emotional experiences as a means of enhancing their regulatory abilities? Recent models of attention suggest that this may be the case (Wadlinger & Isaacowitz, 2011 but have yet to explore how this may manifest differently in older and younger adults.

In sum, research points to an age-associated shift in affective well-being despite pervasive declines in cognitive processes. Although theories of emotional aging pose differing accounts of the underlying mechanisms, that positive emotions remain largely stable over the life course may have strong implications for physiological processes, especially as they contribute to overall physical health.

Pathways Linking Positive Emotions to Health

In this section, we present empirical evidence exploring four potential pathways by which positive emotions influence adult health: health behaviors, physiological systems, stressor exposure, and stress undoing (Ong, 2010). Recent reviews (Cohen & Pressman, 2006) indicate that the strongest associations between positive emotions and health are from prospective studies examining stable emotional *traits*. In addition, investigations exploring the role of naturally occurring or induced emotional *states* highlight the importance of positive emotions in delaying the onset of age-related biological decline. Taken together, the current literature provides convincing evidence of the adaptive significance of positive emotion in later life, as well as foundational support for the underlying pathways that contribute to enhanced physical health.

Health Behaviors

Growing research has identified health practices as playing a critical role in relation to risk for illness and disease (Adler & Matthews, 1994). Whereas negative habits (e.g., poor diet, physical inactivity) have health-damaging consequences, positive health practices (e.g., exercising, avoiding prolonged sun exposure) protect against the onset and development of acute and chronic conditions. Moreover, the consequences of such behaviors may have far-reaching effects, particularly as they accumulate with age; thus, maintaining positive health practices over time may be particularly crucial for older individuals.

Recent reviews document the prospective association between trait positive emotion and health-enhancing practices (Pressman & Cohen,

2005; Steptoe, Dockray, & Wardle, 2009), suggesting that positive emotions may foster engagement in positive health behaviors. One such example may be the restorative link between positive emotions and sleep. For instance, data from a study of 736 health adults (58–72 years) revealed an inverse association between trait positive emotion and sleep disturbance, even after controlling for age, sex, employment status, self-rated health, and psychological distress (Steptoe, O'Donnell, Marmot, & Wardle, 2008). Similar associations have been found in studies of narcolepsy patients and healthy controls in which positive emotions are linked with increases in sleep duration and decreases in fragmented rapid eye movement (REM) sleep (Fosse, Stickgold, & Hobson, 2002). These benefits may be particularly important for older individuals, given that poor sleep efficiency and greater sleep disturbance increase with advanced age (Bloom et al., 2009). Whereas cumulative sleep loss has negative health consequences that contribute to increased risks for adult morbidity and mortality, improved sleep quality confers a number of recuperative benefits to restore and revitalize the body (Kripke, Garfinkel, Wingard, Klauber, & Marler, 2002; Reid et al., 2006). Thus, positive emotions may indirectly promote overall health through enhancing sleep quality and rest.

Positive emotions not only promote physical recovery and rejuvenation, but also enhance psychological well-being to restore bodily function. For instance, a study of surgical patients found that individuals who had views of the natural environment (e.g., trees and animals) not only recovered more quickly but also had shorter hospital stays and fewer postoperative complications than did patients whose views lacked natural settings (Ulrich, 1984). Importantly, positive emotion was a central factor hypothesized to facilitate recovery by promoting psychological well-being. Although these studies highlight the association between trait positive emotion and salutary health outcomes (through promoting adaptive health behaviors), recent inquiries indicate that the favorable effects of psychological well-being on mortality are present after taking health behaviors into account (see Chida & Steptoe, 2008, for a review). Such evidence further indicates that there may be alternative pathways through which positive emotions influence adult health.

Physiological Systems

In addition to exploring behavioral mechanisms, research examining biological pathways has begun to illuminate the relationship between positive emotion and physiological outcomes (Ong, 2010; Steptoe, O'Donnell, Badrick, Kumari, & Marmot, 2008). Allostatic load or the "wear and tear" that results from chronic or repeated elevation of the body's stress response systems implicates deleterious physiologic changes in the body (McEwen, 1998). Over the life course, the accumulation of these alterations may confer health-damaging consequences, ultimately resulting in chronic pain and illness (Kiecolt-Glaser, McGuire, Robles, & Glaser, 2002). Although persistent physiological arousal can have detrimental effects on physical health, accruing evidence indicates that positive emotion may have direct and indirect effects on these systems and may play a role in mitigating the age-related health declines that result from physiological stress and strain (Pressman & Cohen, 2005).

Studies of diurnal cortisol, a biological marker of stress, illustrate the importance of trait positive emotion in relation to physiology. In a large-scale study of 2,873 healthy men and women (aged 57–74), Steptoe and colleagues (2007) assessed associations between inflammatory markers, cortisol levels, and positive affect. Results indicated that, for women in particular, positive affect was associated with lower levels of cortisol, even after adjusting for sociodemographic (e.g., age, gender, income, and ethnicity) and physical (e.g., body mass index, waist/hip ratio) characteristics. Other research has examined the relationship between cortisol and positive emotions within the context of life events. A recent study employing data from the Midlife in the United Sates (MIDUS) survey and the National Study of Daily Experiences (NSDE) (Ong, Fuller-Rowell, Bonanno, & Almeida, 2011) found that spousal bereavement was associated with cortisol dysregulation. Importantly, mediational analyses showed that lower levels of positive emotion following the loss accounted for the observed differences in the cortisol slopes. This finding further suggests that positive emotions may play an important role in neuroendocrine functioning. Extending existing research, a study of middle-aged men and women (45–59 years) (Steptoe, Wardle, & Marmot, 2005) examined the protective effects of positive emotions on neuroendocrine, cardiovascular, and inflammatory processes. Results revealed inverse associations between happiness and salivary cortisol, heart rate, and fibrinogen (a marker of immune competence) stress responses. Notably, the effects demonstrated by the aforementioned studies were independent of trait negative emotion, indicating that the pathway by which positive emotions promote salubrious health outcomes is distinct from that of psychological distress.

Additional evidence suggests that age-related alterations in immunocompetence may also accelerate declines in physical health. In particular, advanced age has been linked with dysregulation of normal cellular processes and decreases in natural killer cell cytotoxicity (NKCC) functionality, as well as increases in inflammatory markers, such as interleukin-6 (IL-6) and C-reactive protein (CRP). Research on older adults demonstrates the importance of positive mood on age-related decreases in immune response. Employing a sample of eighteen healthy individuals (75–91 years) who had recently received the influenza vaccine, Costanzo and colleagues (2004) found that those who reported higher levels of optimism and vigor had greater cytokine responses.

Positive emotion may also work to suppress stress-induced elevations of inflammatory markers and increase levels of certain antibodies. In a study of healthy men and women (35–55 years), Steptoe, O'Donnell, Badrick, Kumari, and Marmot (2008) found trait positive emotion was associated with reduced levels of both IL-6 and CRP in women (but not in men). This finding concurs with those from a review of eight studies that revealed associations between induced positive mood and increased levels of immunoglobulin A (sIgA), an important antibody known to protect against viral and bacterial infection (Marsland, Pressman, & Cohen, 2007).

Viral-challenge studies also substantiate the protective effect of positive emotions, particularly in relation to cold incidence and infection. For example, in a study by Cohen and colleagues (2006), healthy individuals (18–54 years) with positive emotional style (PES) exhibited lower risk of developing illness symptoms after exposure to a respiratory virus. Notably, this prospective link emerged even after controlling for sociodemographic characteristics, virus-type, and dispositional variables, including negative emotional style (NES). Similar findings were reported in a study of 327 young and middle-aged adults (18–54 years) (Doyle, Gentile, & Cohen 2006). Results revealed that, independent of NES, PES was associated not only with decreased illness expression of two rhinoviruses, but also with lower levels of IL-6.

Further, positive emotion may benefit the health of older adults by protecting against bodily deterioration and attenuating pain symptoms. A study of 124 women (35–72 years) with osteoarthritis and fibromyalgia, Zautra, Johnson, and Davis (2005) showed a prospective association between higher levels of positive affect and lower levels of pain symptoms. In addition, a large-scale study of non-institutionalized Mexican Americans (65–95 years) revealed an association between trait positive affect and a 3 percent decrease in risk of frailty. The results still held after controlling for background variables, including demographic characteristics and preexisting medical conditions (Ostir, Ottenbacher, & Markides, 2004). In general, the data suggest that positive emotion may protect against deterioration of physiological systems and contribute to salutary health outcomes as a result.

Stressor Exposure

Prolonged activation of stress-response systems confers risk for poor health outcomes. Moreover, differential exposure to stressors may contribute to heightened physiological reactions and further precipitate age-related declines in adult health and well-being (Kiecolt-Glaser & Glaser, 2001). Whereas the accumulation of stressors and negative life events accelerates physical decline, positive emotions may play a role in mitigating exposure to stressors associated with aging.

Earlier work suggests that stress may interact with age to accelerate deterioration of immune responses (Cohen & Williamson, 1991), ultimately leading to compromised health in the form of infectious disease, inflammation, and illness. Moreover, exposure to stressful events may contribute to immunosenescence among older adults, although positive emotion may dampen such effects. A prospective study of fifty-eight older adults (65–89 years) explored the relationships between participants' mood and cellular immune response before and after housing relocation (Lutgendorf et al., 2001). Overall, movers presented lower NKCC than did controls, but independent of the effects of group (mover vs. nonmover), higher levels of vigor and optimism were linked to greater NKCC at baseline and follow-up.

Positive emotion may help to reduce stressor exposure within the context of both chronic and acute conditions. More specifically, positive emotion has been linked to reduced risk for morbidity, including coronary problems. For example, in a 6-year prospective cohort study of older adults (65 years and older), Ostir and colleagues (2001) found an inverse relationship between positive affect and stroke incidence, after adjusting for sociodemographic and health characteristics. In addition, happiness has been shown to predict lower hospital readmission rates among patients with chronic disease (55 years and older), suggesting that positive emotions are protective against exposure to stressors after illness (Middleton & Byrd, 1996). Studies such as these reveal the importance of positive emotions in allaying exposure to health conditions and illness (Chida & Steptoe, 2008; Pressman & Cohen, 2005).

Collectively, these studies provide support for the association between positive emotions and reduced stressor exposure. Although increased exposure to stress may accelerate declines in physical health and exacerbate normative age-related changes in physiology, positive emotions may mitigate these effects. In sum, the findings reviewed here reveal a protective link between positive emotion and stressor exposure; however, full exploration of the underlying pathways has yet to be established by empirical research.

Stress Undoing

Positive emotions influence health not only via behavioral and physiological pathways, but also through *undoing* the adverse effects of stress. Age differences in stress reactivity and recovery have been documented in studies of cardiovascular (Uchino, Birmingham, & Berg, 2010) and immune function (Piazza, Almeida, Dmitrieva, & Klein, 2010). These studies reveal that older adults show greater physiological responses to stress-induced stimuli than do younger individuals.

Ambulatory assessments, for example, provide evidence in support of the stress undoing hypothesis, demonstrating that positive emotions may be instrumental in attenuating the effects of daily stress (e.g., Ong, Bergeman, & Bisconti, 2004; Ong, Bergeman, Bisconti, & Wallace, 2006). In particular, diary studies have explored the role of psychological well-being in reducing stress-induced elevations in blood pressure and heart rate variability. For example, one 60-day diary study of emotions and cardiovascular activity revealed an association between daily positive well-being and reduced cardiovascular reactivity to negative emotional arousal in older adults (60–87 years) (Ong & Allaire, 2005). Concurring with and adding to these findings, research examining positive mood has documented links between positive affect and lower blood pressure reactivity and suppressed cortisol levels (Brummett, Boyle, Kuhn, Siegler, & Williams, 2009). In addition, positive emotions may also facilitate stress undoing by alleviating pain symptoms and severity. For instance, in middle-aged women (42–76 years) with rheumatoid arthritis or osteoarthritis, weekly positive emotions mitigated the association between negative emotion and reports of pain (Zautra, Smith, Affleck, & Tennen, 2001). Such protocols illustrate the multiple pathways by which positive emotions may attenuate reactivity and facilitate stress recovery on a daily basis.

Not only do positive emotions attenuate stress reactivity, but they also assist with recovery from physiological arousal and pain. Such associations are most often captured in laboratory protocols. In younger adults, for example, induced positive emotion has been shown to hasten the return of heart rate and blood pressure to baseline levels (Fredrickson, Mancuso, Branigan, & Tugade, 2000), as well as to assuage induced pain. For example, when presented with a cold-pressure pain hand-immersion task, college-aged volunteers who were asked to imagine pleasant scenes showed increases in pain tolerance after treatment (Hertel & Hekmat, 1994). The link between positive emotions and reduced stress is also present within clinical samples. In an illustrative study, Rotton and Shats (1996) examined the salutary effects of induced humor in seventy-eight patients (18–65 years) admitted to the hospital for orthopedic surgery. Participants who watched humorous films not only requested smaller doses of minor medication postsurgery, but also self-administered lower doses of major analgesics.

Taken together, the previously reviewed studies illustrate plausible pathways that underlie the association between positive emotion and adult health outcomes. Through enhancing health behaviors, reducing activation of physiological processes, diminishing stressor exposure, and attenuating stress reactivity and recovery, positive emotions appear to confer an array of health benefits, especially in later life. Although the current literature provides provocative evidence for the protective effect of positive emotions on physical well-being, additional research is needed to examine this relationship in greater detail.

Emotional Experience and Health

Although the focus of this essay is on the link between positive emotions and health, alternative interpretations of this relationship certainly warrant acknowledgment. For instance, it is plausible that the experience of positive emotions may stem from a more general disposition or set of traits. Scheier, Carver, and others point to trait optimism as conferring beneficial physical and psychological outcomes. Such literature has identified pathways by which optimism may promote effective coping during stress and thus enhance overall health and well-being (Scheier & Carver, 1992). Positive thinking may also underlie self-regulation, allowing individuals to engage in health-enhancing behaviors to recover faster from acute conditions (Scheier et al., 2003) as well as to adapt to enduring and chronic illnesses (Scheier & Carver, 2001). Alternatively, personality theorists note that certain characteristics are linked with engagement in regulatory processes known to enhance health and behaviors (Booth-Kewley & Vickers, 2006). As such, positive emotions may be one piece of a more complex puzzle. The dynamic interplay among regulatory processes, emotional experience, and stress reactivity may assist individuals in overcoming illness and ultimately contribute to protective benefits for health, longevity, and quality of life.

Future Directions for Theory and Research

The data presented here, along with lifespan theories of emotion, substantiate the link between positive emotions and health; however, some gaps and inconsistencies in the literature remain. In the following section, we delineate directions for future research that illustrate the utility of applying theoretical frameworks in uncovering the role of positive emotions in maintaining health.

The Positivity Ratio and Well-Being

The link between positive emotions and health is well documented. Few studies, however, specify a particular threshold necessary for optimal human functioning (Keyes, 2002). Researchers have begun to explore this issue and propose that a ratio of positive to negative emotion at or above 2.9 to 1 may be necessary for optimal mental health in younger adults (Fredrickson & Losada, 2005). Building on these earlier findings, recent studies indicate the importance of maintaining a high positive to negative emotion ratio across variety of domains. Importantly, the balance of positive to negative emotions has been shown to increase longevity and delay mortality. In particular, empirical work suggests that positivity is predictive of survival (Carstensen et al., 2011) and lower mortality risk (Ong, Mroczek, & Riffin, 2011).

Although such evidence supports the link between positivity and flourishing, some research calls into question whether this association is, in fact, due to a "healthy aging effect." In the face advanced disease, such as breast cancer (Brown, Butow, Culjak, Coates, & Dunn, 2000) and renal disease (Devins et al., 1990), high levels of positive emotion may be detrimental to well-being. To explore this relationship further, future studies may benefit from examining the extent to which positive emotions predict survival in the context of both preventable and unpreventable causes of death. Research in this area would thus disentangle whether this association is stronger for preventable causes rather than for those that are unavoidable.

Recently, research has begun to provide a more nuanced picture of the health benefits of the positivity ratio. In particular, results from a daily diary study (Diehl, Hay, & Berg, 2011) revealed that, although the ratio predicted mental health in young adults, it did not reliably distinguish mental health status among middle-aged and older individuals. Findings such as these highlight the importance of examining this ratio not only across the lifespan, but also within a variety of contexts. Because this "critical level" of positivity may vary by age, researchers suggest that it may be important to identify age-graded positivity ratios across health domains in future studies (Diehl et al., 2011).

Positive Emotions and Physiology Across the Lifespan

Although laboratory and naturalistic studies document the salubrious effects of positive emotion across age cohorts, few explicitly compare both younger and older adults within the same investigation. Given existing empirical evidence, plausible hypotheses can be made in exploring potential age differences in the physiological manifestation of emotion. Formal tests of these predictions may further contribute to uncovering the potential pathways linking positive emotion and health.

Meta-analytic reviews suggest that physiological arousal is associated with varying levels of emotion activation (Pinquart, 2001; Pressman & Cohen, 2005). Whereas acute or high-activated emotions (e.g., enthusiasm, excitement) trigger greater physiological responses, unactivated positive emotions (e.g., calm, relaxed) tend to elicit smaller reactions. Notably, low- and high-activated emotions may have differential effects on adult health. Activated positive emotions, for instance, are associated with heightened cardiovascular and immune responses. Unactivated positive emotions, on the other hand, may benefit neuroendocrine function (Pressman & Cohen, 2005), as well as specific cognitive processes and social behavior (Isen, 2008).

Importantly, emotion activation may vary by age (Pinquart, 2001; Pressman & Cohen, 2005).

Findings from a recent study (Kessler & Staudinger, 2009) suggest that although comparable levels of high-arousal positive emotion exist across age cohorts, levels of low-arousal positive emotion increase over time. Cross-sectional investigation of age differences in activation-arousal may reveal important variations in health outcomes associated with physiological changes and, furthermore, may reveal how mild positive emotions may promote resilience across the lifespan. In addition, longitudinal work is necessary to uncover the extent to which these differences change over time. More specifically, longitudinal comparisons of cross-sectional age differences would distinguish cohort effects from developmental patterns of change, providing an integrated portrayal of age-related alterations in emotion and health.

Although study in this area appears promising, prior research on the health effects of activated and unactivated positive emotions has been hampered by methodological limitations. Experimental studies have failed to include manipulation checks of specific mood inductions. Correlational studies often neglect to control for negative emotion. In spite of these methodological shortcomings, future investigation of age-related differences in physiological manifestations of emotion would highlight a potential underlying mechanism by which emotional experience is connected to adult health (Pressman & Cohen, 2005).

Conclusion

Although growing evidence reveals age differences in emotion and emotion regulation processes, questions concerning the underlying mechanisms remain largely unanswered. Inquiries into the physiological manifestations of positive emotions are just beginning to probe this area of research, but additional work is necessary. Future exploration of age-associated changes in emotions and accompanying regulatory processes will not only reveal a nuanced picture of this phenomenon, but also aid in uncovering the importance of positive emotions in later life.

References

Adler, N., & Matthews, N. (1994). Health psychology: Why do some people get sick and some stay well? *Annual Review of Psychology, 45*, 229–259.

Aspinwall, L. G. (1998). Rethinking the role of positive affect in self-regulation. *Motivation and Emotion, 22*(1), 1–32.

Baltes, P. B., & Baltes, M. M. (1990). Psychological perspectives on successful aging: The model of selective optimization with compensation. *Successful aging: Perspectives from the behavioral sciences, 1*, 1–34.

Blanchard-Fields, F., Chen, Y., & Norris, L. (1997). Everyday problem solving across the adult life span: Influence of domain specificity and cognitive appraisal. *Psychology and Aging, 12*(4), 684–693.

Bloom, H. G., Ahmed, I., Alessi, C. A., Ancoli-Israel, S., Buysse, D. J., & Kryger, M. H. (2009). Evidence-based recommendations for the assessment and management of sleep disorders in older persons. *Journal of the American Geriatrics Society, 57*, 761–789.

Booth-Kewley, S., & Vickers, R. R. (2006). Associations between major domains of personality and health behavior. *Journal of Personality, 62*(3), 281–298.

Brown, J. E., Butow, P. N., Culjak, G., Coates, A. S., & Dunn, S. M. (2000). Psychosocial predictors of outcome: Time to relapse and survival in patients with early stage melanoma. *British Journal of Cancer, 83*, 1448–1453.

Brummett, B. H., Boyle, S. H., Kuhn, C. M., Siegler, I. C., & Williams, R. B. (2009). Positive affect is associated with cardiovascular reactivity, norepinephrine level and morning rise in salivary cortisol. *Psychophysiology, 46*, 862–869.

Bryant, F. B. (2003). Savoring beliefs inventory (SBI): A scale for measuring beliefs about savouring. *Journal of Mental Health (UK), 12*(2), 175–196.

Carstensen, L. L., & Charles, S. T. (1998). Emotion in the second half of life. *Current Directions in Psychological Science, 7*(5), 144–149.

Carstensen, L. L., Isaacowitz, D. M., & Charles, S. T. (1999). Taking time seriously: A theory of socioemotional selectivity. *American Psychologist, 54*(3), 165–181.

Carstensen, L. L., & Mikels, J. (2005). At the intersection of emotion and cognition: Aging and the positivity effect. *Current Directions in Psychological Science, 14*, 117–121.

Carstensen, L. L., Pasupathi, M., Mayr, U., & Nesselroade, J. R. (2000). Emotional experience in everyday life across the adult life span. *Journal of Personality and Social Psychology, 79*(4), 644–655.

Carstensen, L. L., Turan, B., Scheibe, S., Ram, N., Ersner-Hershfield, H., Samanez-Larkin, G. R., ... & Nesselroade, J. R. (2011). Emotional experience improves with age: Evidence based on over 10 years of experience sampling. *Psychology and aging, 26*(1), 21.

Charles, S. T. (2010). Strength and vulnerability integration: A model of emotional well-being across adulthood. *Psychological Bulletin, 136*, 1068–1091.

Charles, S. T., & Carstensen, L. L. (2009). Social and emotional aging. *Annual Review of Psychology, 61*, 383–409.

Charles, S. T., Mather, M., & Carstensen, L. L. (2003). Aging and emotional memory: The forgettable nature of negative images for older adults. *Journal of Experimental Psychology: General, 132*(2), 310–324.

Charles, S. T., & Piazza, J. R. (2007). Memories of social interactions: Age differences in emotional intensity. *Psychology and Aging, 22*, 300–309.

Charles, S. T., Piazza, J. R., Luong, G., & Almeida, D. M. (2009). Now you see it, now you don't: Age differences in affective reactivity to social tensions. *Psychology and Aging, 24*, 645–653.

Charles, S. T., Reynolds, C. A., & Gatz, M. (2001). Age-related differences and change in positive and negative affect over 23 years. *Journal of Personality and Social Psychology, 80*(1), 136–151.

Chida, Y., & Steptoe, A. (2008). Positive psychological well-being and mortality: A quantitative review of prospective observational studies. *Psychosomatic Medicine, 70*, 741–756.

Cohen, S., Alper, C. M., Doyle, W. J., & Treanor, J. J. (2006). Positive emotional style predicts resistance to illness after experimental exposure to rhinovirus or influenza A virus. *Psychosomatic Medicine, 68,* 809–815.

Cohen, S., & Pressman, S. D. (2006). Positive affect and health. *Current Directions in Psychological Science, 15*(3), 122–125.

Cohen, S., & Williamson, G. M. (1991). Stress and infectious disease in humans. *Psychological Bulletin, 109*(1), 5–24.

Costanzo, E. S., Lutgendorf, S. K., Kohut, M. L., Nisley, N., Rozeboom, K., Spooner, S., et al. (2004). Mood and cytokine response to influenza virus in older adults. *Journals of Gerontology: Series A: Biological Sciences and Medical Sciences, 59*(12), 1328–1333.

Costa, P. T., Zonderman, A. B., McCrae, R. R., Cornoni-Huntley, J., Locke, B., & Barbano, H. E. (1987). Longitudinal analyses of psychological well-being in a national sample: Stability of mean levels. *Journal of Gerontology: Psychological Sciences, 42,* 50–55.

Devins, G. M., Mann, J., Mandin, H., Paul, L. C., Hons, R. B., & Burgess, E. D. (1990). Psychosocial predictors of survival in end-stage renal disease. *Journal of Nervous and Mental Disease, 178,* 127–133.

Diehl, M., Hay, E. L., & Berg, K. M. (2011). The ratio between positive and negative affect and flourishing mental health across adulthood. *Aging and Mental Health, 15*(7), 882–893.

Doyle, W. J., Gentile, D. A., & Cohen, S. (2006). Emotional style, nasal cytokines, and illness expression after experimental rhinovirus exposure. *Brain, Behavior, and Immunity, 20,* 175–181.

Eyesnck, H. J. (1963). Biological basis of personality.

Fosse, R., Stickgold, R., & Hobson, A. (2002). Emotional experience during rapid-eye-movement sleep in narcolepsy. *Sleep, 25,* 724–732.

Fredrickson, B. L., & Losada, M. F. (2005). Positive affect and the complex dynamics of human flourishing. *American Psychologist, 60,* 678–686.

Fredrickson, B. L., Mancuso, R. A., Branigan, C., & Tugade, M. M. (2000). The undoing effect of positive emotions. *Motivation and Emotion, 24*(4), 237–258.

Gerstorf, D., Ram, N., Mayraz, G., Hidajat, M., Lingenberger, U., Wagner, G. G., et al. (2010). Late-life decline in well-being across adulthood in Germany, the UK, and the US: Something is seriously wrong at the end of life. *Psychology and Aging, 25*(2), 477–485.

Griffin, P. W., Mroczek, D. K., & Spiro, A. (2006). Variability in affective change among aging men: Longitudinal findings from the VA Normative Aging Study. *Journal of Research in Personality and Individual Differences, 40,* 942–965.

Gross, J. J., Carstensen, L. L., Pasupathi, M., Tsai, J., Goetestam Skorpen, C., & Hsu, A. Y. C. (1997). Emotion and aging: Experience, expression, and control. *Psychology and Aging, 12*(4), 590–599.

Gross, J. J., & John, O. P. (2003). Individual differences in two emotion regulation processes: Implications for affect, relationships, and well-being. *Journal of Personality and Social Psychology, 85*(2), 348–362.

Gruhn, D., Smith, J., & Baltes, P. (2005). No aging bias favoring memory for positive material: Evidence from a heterogeneity-homogeneity list paradigm using emotionally toned words. *Psychology and Aging, 20*(4), 579–588.

Hertel, J. B., & Hekmat, H. M. (1994). Coping with cold-pressor pain: Effects of mood and covert imaginal modeling. *The Psychological record, 44*(2), 207–220.

Isaacowitz, D. M., Toner, K., Goren, D., & Wilson, H. R. (2008). Looking while unhappy: Mood congruent gaze in young adults, positive gaze in older adults. *Psychological Science, 19,* 848–853.

Isaacowitz, D. M., Toner, K., & Neupert, S. D. (2009). Use of gaze for real-time mood regulation: Effects of age and attentional functioning. *Psychology & Aging, 24,* 989–994.

Isaacowitz, D. M., Wadlinger, H. A., Goren, D., & Wilson, H. R. (2006a). Is there an age-related positivity effect in visual attention? A comparison of two methodologies. *Emotion 6,* 511–516.

Isaacowitz, D. M., Wadlinger, H. A., Goren, D., & Wilson, H. R. (2006b). Selective preference in visual fixation away from negative images in old age? An eye-tracking study. *Psychology & Aging, 21,* 40–48.

Isen, A. M. (2008). Some ways in which positive affect influences decision making and problem solving. In M. Lewis, J. M. Haviland-Jones & L. F. Barrett (Eds.), *Handbook of emotions* (3rd ed., pp. 548–573). New York: Guildford Press.

John, O. P., & Gross, J. J. (2004). Healthy and unhealthy emotion regulation: Personality processes, individual differences, and life span development. *Journal of Personality, 72*(6), 1301–1333.

Kennedy, Q., Mather, M., & Carstensen, L. L. (2004). The role of motivation in the age-related positivity effect in autobiographical memory. *Psychological Science, 15*(3), 208–214.

Kensinger, E. A., Garoff-Eaton, R. J., & Scgacter, D. L. (2007). Effects of emotion on memory specificity in young and older adults. *Journal of Gerontology: Psychological Sciences, 62*(4), P208–P215.

Kessler, E. M., & Staudinger, U. M. (2009). Affective experience in adulthood and old age: The role of affective arousal and perceived affect regulation. *Psychology and aging, 24*(2), 349.

Keyes, C. L. M. (2002). The mental health continuum: From languishing to flourishing in life. *Journal of Health and Social Behavior, 43*(2), 207–222.

Kiecolt-Glaser, J. K., & Glaser, R. (2001). Stress and immunity: Age enhances the risks. *Current Directions in Psychological Science, 10*(1), 18–21.

Kiecolt-Glaser, J. K., McGuire, L., Robles, T. F., & Glaser, R. (2002). Emotions, morbidity, and mortality: New perspectives from psychoneuroimmunology. *Annual Review of Psychology, 53,* 83–107.

Knight, M., Seymour, T. L., Gaunt, J. T., Baker, C., Nesmith, K., & Mather, M. (2007). Aging and goal-directed emotional attention: Distraction reverses emotional biases. *Emotion, 7*(4), 705–714.

Kripke, D. F., Garfinkel, L., Wingard, D. L., Klauber, M. R., & Marler, M. R. (2002). Mortality associated with sleep duration and insomnia. *Archives of General Psychiatry, 59*(131–136).

Kunzmann, U., Little, T. D., & Smith, J. (2000). Is age-related stability of subjective well-being a paradox? Cross-sectional and longitudinal evidence from the Berlin Aging Study. *Psychology and Aging, 15*(3), 511–526.

Labouvie-Vief, G. (2003). Dynamic integration: Affect, cognition, and the self in adulthood. *Current Directions in Psychological Science, 12*(6), 201–206.

Labouvie-Vief, G., Diehl, M., Jain, E., & Zhang, F. (2007). Six-year change in affect optimization and affect complexity across the adult life span: A further examination. *Psychology and Aging, 22,* 738–751.

Labouvie-Vief, G., & Medler, M. (2002). Affect optimization and affect complexity: Modes and styles of regulation in adulthood. *Psychology and Aging, 17*(4), 571–587.

Lutgendorf, S. K., Reimer, T. T., Harvey, J. H., Marks, G., Hong, S-. Y., Hillis, S. L., & Lubaroff, D. M. (2001). Effects of housing relocation on immunocompetence and psychosocial functioning in older adults. *Journal of Gerontology, 56,* M97–M107.

Marsland, A. L., Pressman, S. D., & Cohen, S. (2007). Positive affect and immune function. *Psychoneuroimmunology, 2,* 761–779.

Mather, M., Canli, T., English, T., Whitfield, S., Wais, P., Ochsner, K., et al. (2004). Amygdala responses to emotionally valenced stimuli in older and younger adults. *Psychological Science, 15*(4), 259–263.

Mather, M., & Carstensen, L. L. (2003). Aging and attentional biases for emotional faces. *Psychological Science, 14*(5), 409–415.

McEwen, B. S. (1998). Stress, adaptation, and disease. Allostasis and allostatic load. *Neuroimmunomodulation, 840,* 33–44.

Middleton, R. A., & Byrd, E. K. (1996). Psychosocial factors and hospital readmission status of older persons with cardiovascular disease. *Journal of Applied Rehabilitation Counseling, 27*(4), 3–10.

Mikels, J. A., Larkin, G. R., Reuter-Lorenz, P. A., & Carstensen, L. L. (2005). Divergent trajectories in the aging mind: Changes in working memory for affective versus visual information with age. *Psychology & Aging, 20,* 542–553.

Mroczek, D. K. (2001). Age and emotion in adulthood. *Current Directions in Psychological Science, 10*(3), 87–90.

Mroczek, D. K., & Almeida, D. M. (2004). The effect of daily stress, personality, and age on daily negative affect. *Journal of Personality, 72*(2), 355–378.

Mroczek, D. K., & Kolarz, C. M. (1998). The effect of age on positive and negative affect: A developmental perspective on happiness. *Journal of Personality and Social Psychology, 75*(5), 1333–1349.

Mroczek, D. K., Spiro III, A., & Griffin, P. W. (2006). Personality and Aging.

Murphy, N. A., & Isaacowitz, D. (2008). Preferences for emotional information in older and younger adults: A meta-analysis of memory and attention tasks. *Psychology and Aging, 23*(2), 263–286.

Ong, A. D. (2010). Pathways linking positive emotion and health in later life. *Current Directions in Psychological Science, 19,* 358–362.

Ong, A. D., & Allaire, J. C. (2005). Cardiovascular intraindividual variability in later life: The influence of social connectedness and positive emotions. *Psychology and Aging, 20*(3), 476.

Ong, A. D., Bergeman, C. S., & Bisconti, T. L. (2004). The role of daily positive emotions during conjugal bereavement. *Journals of Gerontology: Psychological Sciences and Social Sciences, 59B*(4), P168–P176.

Ong, A. D., Bergeman, C. S., Bisconti, T. L., & Wallace, K. (2006). Psychological resilience, positive emotions, and successful adaptation to stress in later life. *Journal of Personality and Social Psychology, 91,* 730–749.

Ong, A. D., Fuller-Rowell, T., Bonanno, G. A., & Almeida, D. M. (2011). Spousal loss predicts alterations in diurnal cortisol activity through prospective changes in positive emotion. *Health Psychology, 30*(2), 220–227.

Ong, A. D., Mroczek, D. K., & Riffin, C. R. (2011). The health significance of positive emotions in adulthood and later life. *Social and Personality Psychology Compass, 5,* 538–551.

Ostir, G. V., Ottenbacher, K. J., & Markides, K. S. (2004). Onset of frailty in older adults and the protective role of positive affect. *Psychology and Aging, 19,* 402–408.

Ostir, V., Markides, K. S., Peek, K., & Goodwin, J. S. (2001). The association between emotional well-being and the incidence of stroke in older adults. *Psychosomatic Medicine, 63*(2), 210–215.

Pasupathi, M., & Carstensen, L. L. (2003). Age and emotional experience during mutual reminiscing. *Psychology and Aging, 18*(3), 430–442.

Piazza, J. R., Almeida, D. M., Dmitrieva, N. O., & Klein, L. C. (2010). Frontiers in the use of biomarkers of health in research on stress and aging. *Journal of Gerontology: Psychological Sciences, 65B*(5), 513–525.

Pinquart, M. (2001). Age differences in perceived positive affect, negative affect, and affect balance in middle and old age. *Journal of Happiness Studies, 2*(4), 375–405.

Pressman, S. D., & Cohen, S. (2005). Does positive affect influence health? *Psychological Bulletin, 131,* 925–971

Reid, K. J., Marinovick, Z., Finkel, S., Statsinger, J., Golden, R., Hartner, K., et al. (2006). sleep: A marker of physical and mental health in the elderly. *American Journal of geriatric Psychiatry, 14*(860–866).

Rotton, J., & Shats, M. (1996). Effects of State Humor, Expectancies, and Choice on Postsurgical Mood and Self-Medication: A Field Experiment1. *Journal of Applied Social Psychology, 26*(20), 1775–1794.

Samanez-Larkin, G. R., & Carstensen, L. L. (2011). socioemotional functioning and the aging brain. In J. Decety & J. T. Cacioppo (Eds.), *The handbook of social neuroscience.* New York: Oxford University Press.

Scheibe, S., & Carstensen, L. L. (2010). Emotional aging: Recent findings and future directions. *Journal of Gerontology: Psychological Sciences, 65,* 135–144.

Scheier, M. F., & Carver, C. S. (1992). Effects of optimism on psychological and physical well-being: Theoretical overview and empirical update. *Cognitive Therapy and Research, 16*(2), 201–228.

Scheier, M. F., & Carver, C. S. (2001). Adapting to cancer: The importance of hope and purpose. in B. L. Andersen & A. Baum (Eds.), *Psychosocial interventions for cancer* (pp. 15–36). Washington, DC: American Psychological Association.

Scheier, M. F., Matthews, K. A., Owens, J. F., Magovern, G. J., Sr., Lefebvre, R., Abbott, R., et al. (2003). Dispositional optimism and recovery from coronary artery bypass surgery: The beneficial effects on physical and psychological well-being. In A. Rothman,

J., Alexander, & P. Salovey (Eds.), *Social psychology of health* (pp. 342–361). New York: Psychology Press.

Shiota, M., & Levenson, R. W. (2009). Effects of aging on experimentally instructed detached reappraisal, positive reappraisal, and emotional behavior suppression. *Psychology and Aging, 24,* 890–900.

Steptoe, A., Dockray, S., & Wardle, J. (2009). Positive affect and psychobiological processes relevant to health. *Journal of Personality, 77,* 1747–1775.

Steptoe, A., O'Donnell, K., Badrick, E., Kumari, M., & Marmot, M. (2007). Neuroendocrine and inflammatory factors associated with positive affect in health men and women. *American Journal of Epidemiology, 187*(1), 96–102.

Steptoe, A., O'Donnell, K., Marmot, M., & Wardle, J. (2008). Positive affect, psychological well-being, and good sleep. *Journal of Psychosomatic Research, 64,* 409–415.

Steptoe, A., O'Donnell, K., Badrick, E., Kumari, M., & Marmot, M. G. (2008). Neuroendocrine and inflammatory factors associated with positive affect in healthy men and women: Whitehall II study. *American Journal of Epidemiology, 167*, 96–102.

Steptoe, A., Wardle, J., & Marmot, M. (2005). Positive affect and health-related neuroendocrine, cardiovascular, and inflammatory processes. *Proceedings of the National Academy of Sciences, 102*, 6508–6512.

Tugade, M. M., & Fredrickson, B. L. (2007). Regulation of positive emotions: Emotion regulation strategies that promote resilience. *Journal of Happiness Studies, 8*, 311–333.

Uchino, B. N., Birmingham, W., & Berg, C. (2010). Are older adults less or more physiologically reactive? A meta-analysis of age-related differences in cardiovascular reactivity to laboratory tasks. *Journal of Gerontology: Psychological Sciences, 65B*, 154–162.

Ulrich, R. S. (1984). View through a window may influence recovery from surgery. *Science, 224*, 420–421.

Urry, H. L., & Gross, J. J. (2010). Emotion regulation in older age. *Current Directions in Psychological Science, 19*, 352–357.

Wadlinger, H. A., & Isaacowitz, D. M. (2011). Fixing our focus: Training attention to regulate emotion. *Personality and Social Psychology Review, 15*(1), 75–102.

Wood, J. V., Heimpel, S. A., & Michela, J. L. (2003). Savoring versus dampening: Self-esteem differences in regulating positive affect. *Journal of Personality and Social Psychology 85*, 566–580.

Wurm, L. H., Labouvie-Vief, G., Aycock, J., Rebucal, K. A., & Koch, H. E. (2004). Performance in auditory and visual emotional Stroop tasks: A comparison of younger and older adults. *Psychology and Aging, 19*, 523–535.

Zautra, A., Smith, B., Affleck, G., & Tennen, H. (2001). Examinations of chronic pain and affect relationships: Applications of a dynamic model of affect.

Zautra, A. J., Johnson, L. M., & Davis, M. C. (2005). Positive affect as a source of resilience for women in chronic pain. *Journal of Consulting and Clinical Psychology, 73*(2), 212–220.

Boundary Conditions for Emotional Well-Being in Aging: The Importance of Daily Stress

Martin J. Sliwinski *and* Stacey B. Scott

Abstract

Understanding the limits on age-graded improvements or stability in emotional well-being may provide insights into the mechanisms that drive health-related individual differences in adulthood. Insights from daily diary and experience sampling studies highlight some boundary conditions for preserved emotional well-being and regulation in older adults, suggesting that the widely accepted "aging paradox" of increasing well-being and positive affect may not be universally correct; a late-life reduction in positive affect and an increase in negative affect may be tied to end-of-life processes. Experience sampling studies also suggest that older adults are likely to experience negative affect when confronted with everyday stressors, and it is unclear whether age is associated with increases or decreases in negative affect in this situation. Chronic exposure to stress, coupled with difficulty regulating emotional reactions to unavoidable stressors, may have long-term negative consequences for older adults' psychological well-being.

Key Words: positive affect, negative affect, stress, stress reactivity, emotional self-regulation, allostatic load

The field of adult development is concerned with describing and explaining how and why individuals change on physical, cognitive, and socioemotional dimensions of functioning as they age. The dual function of description and explanation is common to all scientific disciplines—scientific theories provide systematic and testable explanations of empirical observations. What counts as "truth" in science, however, is never final. New research holds the potential to modify or reject yesterday's observations with more accurate and current data. This possibility is especially relevant for the study of psychology and aging, which must grapple with numerous methodological and measurement challenges that can alter not only our observations of aging effects but can influence the very phenomena that we study. For example, generational differences, economic climate, advances in healthcare, and changes in nutritional practices can all influence age trends in physical, emotional, and cognitive health.

Despite these challenges to empirical description, the field of adult development and aging has enjoyed a relatively rich history of successful theories. By "successful" we mean that a theory has provided useful explanations and predictions that have advanced our understanding of aging-related phenomenon, spurring new and interesting lines of research. Cognitive aging represents one area in which there have been several well-developed theories (e.g., processing speed theory, inhibition theory, the frontal hypothesis) to explain empirical evidence that points to relatively robust and ubiquitous age-graded decrements in cognitive capacity. In contrast to the age-graded decrements in cognition, numerous experimental and observational studies suggest that aspects of emotional life, such as subjective well-being and emotion regulation, do not consistently exhibit age-graded decreasesand, in fact, may improve with advancing age (Carstensen et al., 2011). The phenomenon of maintenance or age-graded growth in emotional well-being despite the declines in physical health and objective challenges that face older adults has been termed "the paradox of well-being" (see Kunzmann, Little, & Smith, 2000).

Boundary Conditions for Emotional Well-Being

The ways that emotional well-being changes with advancing age has important implications not only for advancing developmental theory but also for elucidating pathways to healthy and unhealthy aging. Depression, anxiety, and hostility have each been identified as risk factors for cardiovascular-related death (Kiecolt-Glaser, McGuire, Robles, & Glaser, 2002). Negative emotions (e.g., depressive symptoms) predictas much or more variance in physical functioning as arthritis, gastrointestinal problems, and advanced coronary artery disease (Wells et al., 1989). Emotional well-being is comprised of both negative and positive emotional experiences, however, and an absence of positive emotions canalso be detrimental. Lower global positive affect (PA) was associated with a greater risk of stroke over 6 years among healthy older adults, whereas negative affect (NA) did not predict stroke occurrence (Ostir, Markides, Peek, & Goodwin, 2001). Self-reports of experiencing positive emotions have also been consistently linked to increased longevity among community-residing older adults (Pressman & Cohen, 2005).

Understanding the limits on age-graded improvements or stability in emotional well-being may provide insights into the mechanisms that drive health-related individual differences in adulthood. In particular, insights from daily diary and experience sampling studies, especially those examining the effects of daily stress on affect, have begun to highlight some boundary conditions for preserved emotional well-being and regulation in older adults (e.g., Mroczek & Almeida, 2004; Stawski, Sliwinski, Almeida, & Smyth, 2008; Wrzus, Müller, Wagner, Lindenberger, & Riediger, 2012). Because both the psychological resources of individuals and the resource demands of their environments can either limit or enhance opportunities and choices for coping with daily challenges, emotional responses to stressors are likely to differ across people, as well as across situations. Given aging-related changes in personal resources and environments, one should expect age-related changes in emotional responses to daily stressors. Daily stressors not only exert immediate effects on emotional functioning on the day they occur (e.g., Bolger & Schilling, 1991; Zautra, Affleck, Tennen, Reich, & Davis, 2005) but may create accumulated effects that increase vulnerability to problems, including anxiety, depression, and disease (e.g., Almeida, 2005; Cacioppo et al., 1998; Zautra, 2003). Therefore, studying the daily stress process can inform theories of aging and emotion regulation, as well as provide insights into age-related changes inrisk and resilience to mental and physical health conditions.

Chapter Overview

This chapter examines the empirical evidence regarding socioemotional aging, with an emphasis on identifying those conditions that facilitate or threaten emotional well-being in older adults. First, we examine the evidence for age trends in emotional well-being, with an emphasis placed on contrasting discrepant patterns of results across different types of cross-sectional and longitudinal analyses. In this section, we pose the question: "does (un) happiness change with advancing age?" Characterizing age trends in emotional well-being is an essential first step toward understanding how stress affects emotional functioning in people of different ages. The second section examines age trends in stress-related affect observed in studies of everyday experiences. We consider not only what the existing data show with regards to age trends in emotional responding to everyday stress but also offer recommendations for targeting elements of the daily stress process that may be more directly linked to health outcomes. The third section attempts to reconcile inconsistent findings by considering the (often unmeasured) importance of developmental shifts in the broad psychosocial context that can shape how people respond to everyday challenges. The final section then considers the implications for prevailing accounts and recent theoretical advances about emotional experiences in old age, including socioemotional aging theory.

Association BetweenAge and Emotional Well-being

The strongest form of the paradox of well-being—one that postulates improvement in emotional well-being and regulation—has been widely accepted as a scientific fact. Isaacowitz and Blanchard-Fields (2012) summarized the state of the field: "It is now almost taken for granted by researchers studying emotional processing and aging that older adults are happier because they are more effective at emotion regulation" (p.3). This statement consists of three propositions: 1) that older adults are happier than younger adults; 2) that they are more effective at emotion regulation than younger adults, and 3) that their improved emotion regulation is the reason they are happier. In their review, Isaccowitz and Blanchard-Fields (2012) critically evaluated the third proposition, namely whether there is good evidence to link age differences in specific emotion regulation processes to emotional outcomes. In the present section of this chapter we will examine the first proposition—whether there is an association between age emotional well-being—and then consider the evidence for age relations to emotion regulation in the face of daily stressors in the next section.

If it is fair to say that the phenomenon of age-graded improvements in emotional well-being has attained the status of an "empirical fact" in the field of adult development, then it is also fair to ask whether findings from different samples and methods consistently support this view. In fact, studies of age-graded trends in emotional well-being are not entirely consistent, and some researchers have characterized the relationship of age with PA and NA as complex and the empirical evidence for stability and change in emotional well-being as "mixed" (Röcke, Li, & Smith, 2009). Some studies report mostly positive age trends in emotional well-being (Charles, Reynolds, & Gatz, 2001; Mroczek & Kolarz, 1998), whereas other studies report no age-graded differences or even declines in emotional well-being (Charles et al., 2001; Griffin, Mroczek, & Spiro, 2006). Although it is sometimes tempting to minimize the importance of inconsistent results that do not fit with prevailing theoretical accounts, recent empirical and theoretical work demand more nuanced and precise explanations of emotional aging (Isaacowitz & Blanchard-Fields, 2012).

Age trends in emotional well-being. The verbal descriptions of socioemotional aging found in the literature imply age-graded decrements in levels of NA until old age, and age stability or improvements in levels of PA. It is this joint pattern of NA and PA changes that supports the claim that age-graded improvements in emotional well-being across adulthood reflect a more favorable balance between positive affect (PA) and negative affect (NA). Improvements in emotional well-being are thought to occur through most of adulthood and continue until "old" age, but exactly what "old" age

means or when it begins is not always clear. Some have claimed that NA shows decreases in adulthood until age 80 (Ready, Åkerstedt, & Mroczek, 2012) or until the very end of life (Scheibe & Carstensen, 2010). In fact, our reading of the literature is that the results are not completely consistent with respect to the shape of the age trends in different facets of emotional well-being. Nor do we believe that the evidence suggests that positive age trends in emotional well-being consistently persist until very old age. The most relevant studies are those that allow examination of longitudinal age trends rather than comparisons between extreme age groups. What follows is not a comprehensive review of the literature, but an examination of several studies that permit comparison of patterns of empirical age trends in emotional well-being. The goal of this examination is to extract some regularity in the pattern and timing of age changes in emotional well-being across a range of assessment methods, samples and designs.

A classic study by Charles, Reynolds and Gatz (2001) examined age trends in positive and negative affect over a 23-year period in individuals aged 35 to 90. Results from latent growth curve analysis showed that NA exhibited a decrease across age until about age 60, after which it leveled off. Positive affect showed very modest declines, until about age 60, after which decrements in PA accelerated. Based on the notion of well-being as reflected in the balance between NA and PA, this study has often been cited as strong evidence that emotional well-being improves into old age. In fact, in the oldest group's affect trajectories shift such that PA declined faster than NA, indicating *decreasing* emotional well-being among the oldest individuals.

Another important study examined change in NA and PA in a sample of men who participated in the VA Normative Aging Study (Griffin et al., 2006). These individuals ranged in age from 45 to 97 and were followed for up to 10 years. Similar to the study of Charles et al. (2001), Griffin and colleagues showed linear decrements in PA, but did not show an accelerated decline. As regards NA, they noted that "negative affect declined until about age 70, whereupon it then demonstrated a gradual increase" (p. 952). Because they described the age trends in NA using a quadratic function, their model implies that the decrease in NA was slowing for some time before age 70, at which the age-trend reversed direction. This implies that something began happening well before age 70 that offset whatever process (es) were driving age-graded decreases in NA (i.e., improvements in emotional well-being).

A recent and very innovative study (Carstensen et al., 2011) examined age-trends in positive emotional experiences using a measurement burst design and experience sampling. In this study, participants answered questions about their current positive and negative mood at random times throughout the day. *Positive emotional experiences* were defined as the average number of positive adjectives—average number of negative adjectives endorsed at each momentary assessment. Individuals aged 18 to 94 completed 7 days of momentary assessments at baseline, then again at 5 and 10 years follow-up bursts. The results from this study are not entirely comparable to many previous studies for two reasons. First, these assessments involved momentary reports of emotional experiences and represent measurements of *experienced* well-being, compared to global self-reports of *evaluative* well-being that have been most commonly used in longitudinal studies of emotional aging. By global emotional well-being, we mean reports of how one feels "in general" or over some relatively lengthy time interval (e.g., over the last month). By experienced well-being we mean reports of feelings experienced during discrete and recent temporal epochs (e.g., during the last day, at this moment). Global reports of evaluative well-being may be more susceptible to recollective biases, such as the positivity effect (Carstensen, Mikels, & Mather, 2006) and can reflect self-schemas (e.g., "Am I a happy person?") more than actual experiences (e.g., "Was I happy?"; Robinson & Clore, 2002). A second reason why results from this study might differ from previous studies is that separate trends for NA and PA were not reported—only the difference or affect balance was analyzed. This analytic approach makes it difficult to directly compare results across studies, although it does permit a more direct answer to the question of whether people become happier or at least experience more positive emotions as they age.

Our view of the results from the Carstensen et al. (2011) study is that they are more complex than their study title, "Emotional Experience Improves with Age," suggests. Specifically, longitudinal growth curve analysis indicated that a quadratic function described the age trend in positive emotional experiences, which peaked at age 64. This implies that the frequency of positive emotional experiences was declining, on average, after the age of 64. Furthermore, it implies that the rate at which emotional experiences improved prior to this age continuously decreased, so that persons experienced more modest improvements with advancing

age. Although we caution against directly comparing results from this study of momentary experiences with previous studies that assessed global reports, a consistent picture is emerging that there are gains in both evaluative and experienced emotional well-being until the mid-60's at which point decreases in emotional being are observed.

Another study published prior to Carstensen et al. (2011) examined longitudinal changes in emotional experiences in two independent samples, both of which were studied using a measurement burst design (Sliwinski, Almeida, Smyth, & Stawski, 2009). This study examined changes in daily NA observed in two independent and quite different samples. One sample came from the Cognition, Health and Aging Project (CHAP), and consisted of older adults (aged 65–90) who were assessed for 6 days every 6 months, for a two year period. Results showed longitudinal increases in NA that depended upon age. The estimated regression coefficients (Sliwinski et al., 2009, Table 4) imply that increases in NA began at about age 68, a value very consistent with the points of inflection in NA trends found in Charles et al. (2001), Griffin et al. (2006), and Carstensen et al. (2011). Results from the National Daily Experiences (NSDE) which is part of the Midlife in US (MIDUS) project, described in Sliwinski et al. (2009) differ from this pattern by showing longitudinal increases in daily NA across the adult lifespan that did not depend significantly on age. That is, individuals on average experienced more NA as they aged, but the rate of this increase did not accelerate with advancing age.

There could be historical and methodological reasons why the NSDE data showed a different pattern of results than previous studies. First, the follow-up NSDE assessment occurred after important historical events (i.e., the September 11th attacks, initiation of two wars) which might have historical period effects on levels of emotional well-being quite apart from developmental influences. Second, the analytic approach used in the Sliwinski et al. (2009) paper differed from the growth curve modeling used in previous studies. The Charles et al. (2001), Griffin et al. (2006) and Carstensen et al. (2011) all used an "age-convergence" approach to modeling age trends in their data. This approach relies on an age-heterogeneous or accelerated longitudinal design and pools cross-sectional age differences and intraindividual change into a common estimate of an age trend (Sliwinski, Hoffman, & Hofer, 2010). Only the Charles et al. (2001) paper checked for the presence of cohort effects (which were found), but it still pooled cross-sectional and longitudinal information within each cohort. In contrast, analysis of the NSDE data separated cross-sectional from longitudinal age trends and found them to be different— there was a positive longitudinal trend in NA compared to negative cross-sectional trend in NA. That is, individuals in the NSDE sample reported higher levels of NA as they aged, but at any given assessment, older people reported lower NA than younger people.

Similar findings that reflect cross-sectional age-graded maintenance or improvements in emotional functioning have provided the bulk of evidence on which current theories are based. Given the resources and time required to conduct longitudinal studies, reliance on cross-sectional information is to some extent inevitable. However, cohort and generational differences likely influence cross-sectional results in complex ways. For example, work by Elder and colleagues have shown that men born just before the great depression experienced more vulnerability to depression than did the generation born before them (Elder, 1991). Early childhood experiences specific to historical periods may produce long-lasting cohort differences that influence how emotions are experienced, disclosed and reported during adulthood. At this point, it is unclear how much of the foundational data underlying current theorizing about emotional well-being in old age reflect developmental processes, cohort differences or their interaction.

Is there a tipping point in socioemotional aging? There is no strong basis for believing that the results from the age convergence models, which show decreasing NA across much of the adult lifespan until the 60s, more accurately describe true development trends than the purely longitudinal analysis of intraindividual change, which showed consistent increases in experienced NA throughout the adulthood in the NSDE sample. That said, there is a relatively consistent pattern of results that suggests whatever age-graded gains in emotional well-being do exist, these gains diminish with advancing age and give way to decrements at some point in the mid to late 60s. What does this imply?

First, it does not mean that older adults are more (or less) happy than younger adults. Although people in their late 60s may, on average, begin to experience declines in emotional well-being, they still may be happier (or less unhappy) than people in their 20s (Carstensen et al., 2011), but whether this has any developmental relevance depends on ruling out cohort-based explanations of the effects.

Second, and more importantly, the shift in direction in population level trajectories of well-being during the 60's may signify that age-related vulnerabilities have begun to offset gains achieved through capitalizing on age-related strengths. The 60's may represent a critical phase in socioemotional development during which the balance of maturational gains and involutional losses can reach a tipping point. At a broad level, this reversal in socioemotional development may reflect involutional processes that manifest with increasing frequency adults in their late 60's and early 70's. "Terminal decline" is a term used to describe functional decrements associated with mortality related mechanism. Evidence of terminal decline in emotional well-being (Gerstorf, Ram, Mayraz, Hidajat, Lindenberger, Wagner, & Schupp, 2010) implies that late-life decrements in well-being may reflect "pathological" aging rather than normative development. However, end-of-life changes in socioemotional functioning has been deemed relevant for informing socioemotional aging theory when they occur in younger and middle aged adults (Carstensen & Fredrickson, 1998). We concur and hold the view that although terminal decline and normative aging effects likely reflect different mechanisms, both are relevant for theories of aging and adult development.

Understanding the processes that lead to this tipping, which may begin years or even decades earlier, represents an important challenge for identifying risk and resilience factors that determine whether an individual follows a path toward healthy or unhealthy aging. The theory of Strength and Vulnerability Integration (SAVI) proposed by Charles (2010) articulates this notion and specifies the boundary conditions under which age benefits and age deficits in emotional well-being will be observed. We discuss SAVI and other hypotheses that identify boundary conditions for socioemotional aging in the last section of this chapter. The next section addresses how the study of the daily stress process can provide unique insights into the boundary conditions for age trends in emotional well-being and their relation to health.

Aging and the Daily Stress Process

There can be many reasons why a person feels anxious, depressed, angry or frustrated. Fortunately, most people experience such negative emotions relatively infrequently, and when they do, often those emotions are precipitated by some adverse event. Therefore, in order to understand developmental shifts in emotional well-being, it is necessary to understand how those events, referred to as stressors, that elicit emotional distress (e.g., the experience colloquially referred to as "being stressed") operate in people across the adult lifespan. Although major life events such as divorce and widowhood may be the prototypical experiences that come to mind for the word stressor, a growing body of studies suggests that the negative events of day-to-day life are both stressful and important for health. Daily stressors consist of routine challenges encountered as part of day-to-day living, such as arguments with family members, commuting difficulties, work deadlines, and other occurrences that disrupt everyday life. Although less severe than major life events, people experience daily stressors much more frequently, on about 40 percent-70 percent of days (Hay & Diehl, 2010; Mroczek & Almeida, 2004; Sliwinski, Smyth, Hofer, & Stawski, 2006). Also, in comparison to life events, average monthly reports of hassles are more strongly associated with somatic illness nine months later (DeLongis, Coyne, Dakof, Folkman, & Lazarus, 1982). More compelling, daily psychological stress related to work demands are associated with greater progression of carotid artery atherosclerosis six years later (Kamarck, Shiffman, Sutton-Tyrrell, Muldoon, & Tepper, 2012).

Recent work suggests that emotions play a key role in the link between stress and health. Specifically, the extent to which an individual's NA increased when stressors were reported predicted elevated depressive symptoms two months later among a sample of college students (Parrish, Cohen, & Laurenceau, 2011) and was related to increased affective symptoms and development of depressive disorder approximately one year later (Wichers et al., 2009) in a sample of young and middle aged men. This emotional sensitivity to daily stressors also has long-term implications for both emotional well-being and physical health. In a national study of adults aged 24–74 years, NA responses to daily stressors predicted likelihood of reporting affective distress andhaving been diagnosed with an affective disorder (e.g., depressive episode, dysthymia, generalized anxiety disorder; Charles, Piazza, Mogle, Sliwinski, & Almeida, in press),as well as chronic health conditions (e.g., cardiovascular conditions, diabetes, pain-related conditions, thyroid disease, digestive conditions, cancer) 10 years later (Piazza, Charles, Sliwinski, Mogle, & Almeida, in press).

The Daily Stress Process. Almeida (2005) described a heuristic model for understanding the daily stress process. Two critical elements in this model are stressor exposure and reactivity. Exposure refers to likelihood that an individual will experience a negative event during a given period of time, and reactivity refers to the degree to which that individual reacts emotionally, physically and cognitively to experiencing the event. Before describing this research, it is important to examine how the daily stress process is studied and how exposure and reactivity are typically operationalized. Much of the research on daily stress has employed daily diary methods which require participants to answer questions about their experiences, activities and affective states during the previous day (e.g., Almeida 2005). This approach, which consists of paper and pen, electronic, or telephonic modes of assessment, has been widely used in aging research on daily stress. Individuals record whether or not they have experienced a stressful event and then answer questions about the event, including what type of stressor it was (e.g., an argument, a work overload, or other daily hassle) and how unpleasant or serious it was. Individuals also answer how they felt (e.g., happy, angry, tense, depressed) during the time proximal to this event. Emotional reactivity is operationalized as the amount by which negative affect increased on days when a stressor was reported relative to days when no stressor was reported, as in Figure 9.1. More recently *experience sampling* methods (ESM; Carstensen et al., 2011; Wrzus et al., 2012), which require individuals to stop and record their current experiences, thoughts, activities and feelings in real time, have also been used. The approach to measuring exposure and reactivity to daily stressors is similar in ESM and diary methods, however, frequency of assessments is a key advantage to the ESM approach to recording events and emotional reactions (Smyth & Stone, 2003). End-of-day reports

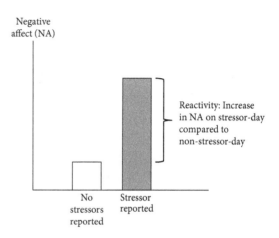

Figure 9.1. Diary operationalization of reactivity.

of event exposure may be biased by retrospective recall—outright forgetting as well as the outcome or resolution of an event determining whether it is reported at all. Similarly, when reporting emotions at the end of the day, it is often unclear whether the participant is drawing from the most intense (i.e., peak), most recent, global beliefs about him—or herself, or some aggregation of these heuristics. By asking individuals to recall events over a short period (e.g., few hours) and report their current emotional states (e.g., right now, last five minutes), ESM limit the influence of these biases.

Figure 9.2 presents ESM and diary assessments of exposure and reactivity on a sample day. In this example, five ESM surveys and one end-of-day diary were collected. In the diary report, the individual should report that 2 events occurred today, and as indicated by the difference between the grey and white rectangles, reports higher NA today than on other days when no stressors were reported. For ESM reports 2 and 4, the participant would respond affirmatively to the question, "Has a stressor occurred since your last survey?" For the rest of the ESM reports, the participant would report no stressor. Some recall may still be involved in ESM reports, as when ESM report 4 takes place some time after the second stressor, however, the recall window is much narrower than at the end of day report.

The fine grained temporal resolution afforded by ESM also provides the opportunity distinguish between immediate and enduring responses to events. We believe that the term "reactivity" should be used to describe the immediate response to an event, whereas the term "regulation" should be used

to refer to more enduring effects and responses to negative events. Regulation describes the "ways in which an individual manages their affective state" (Isaacowitz & Blanchard-Fields, 2012, p. 4). The extent that the emotional report quickly follows the experience of a stressor, this provides a good index of reactivity. Emotion reports which occur later in time, such a person's overall rating of today's mood provided by and end of day diary report, may better be described as the extent to which the individual has needed to regulate his or her emotions than as an index of their initial reaction.

This discussion raises two issues concerning the use of the term "reactivity" in daily stress research. First, it implies that the stressful event preceded and *caused* a change in NA. For example, if an individual reports an increase in NA for a day on which they also reported having an argument with their partner, we assume, but cannot demonstrate that the argument caused the increase in NA, and not the reverse (i.e., that the person got into an argument because they were grouchy). All that can be demonstrated in a daily diary study is that NA is higher on days when stressors occur relative to days on which there are no reported stressors.

A second issue with using the term "reactivity" is that it implies immediacy in the temporal sequencing between stressor and emotional state that may be beyond the temporal resolution afforded by assessments of daily stress (Sliwinski et al., 2009). Daily diary methods do not attain this level of temporal resolution in sequencing events and emotional states. Experience sampling methods provide a better, albeit imperfect, approach to distinguish immediate from enduring response to stressful

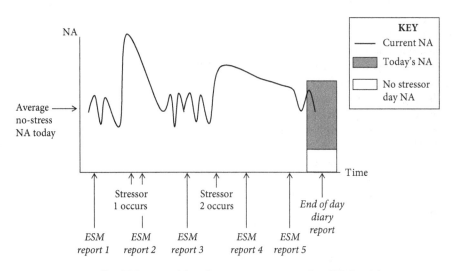

Figure 9.2. Exposure & negative affect (NA) measured for a day via experiencing sampling (ESM) and diary.

events. So even if the temporal sequencing between a daily stressor and report of NA is established (i.e., the argument preceded the bad mood), perhaps through the use of lagged analyses (e.g., Johnson et al., 2008; Ong, Bergeman, Bisconti, & Wallace, 2006; van Eck, Nicolson, & Berkhof, 1998), what is being described probably may have less to do with immediate reactivity and has more to do with an enduring response. This latter point implies that the use of the term "reactivity" in daily stress research is sometimes a misnomer. However, to be consistent with the literature, we will continue to use the term "reactivity" in the following section to describe findings on age differences in stress-related affect, even though this construct reflects something different than the immediate reactivity estimates derived in experimental stress studies.

Age differences in stress-related affect. Most research suggests that self-reports of exposure to daily stressors decline slightly with age (Almeida & Horn, 2004; Stawski et al., 2008). This finding is certainly consistent with theoretical perspectives that predict older adults more effectively select benign or positive social environments in order to avoid negative experiences (Carstensen, Fung, & Charles, 2003). The literature, however, is much less consistent with respect to the role of age in emotional responses to daily stressors. Using a daily diary method, Mroczek and Almeida (2004) reported one of the first studies to examine age differences in emotional responses to daily stressors. They found that negative emotional responses to everyday stressors, such as having an argument or having something unpleasant occur at work, were larger in older compared to younger adults. Other studies using similar methods have not always found amplified emotional responses to daily stressors. A 45-day diary study (Röcke et al., 2009) contrasting a small sample of younger (n=18) and older (n=19) found no age differences, whereas a 100 day study (Brose, Schmiedek, Lövdén, & Lindenberger, 2011) with a larger sample (101 and 103 younger and older adults, respectively) found evidence of *reduced* emotional reactivity for older adults. In an experiencing sampling study (Uchino, Berg, Smith, Pearce, & Skinner, 2006) that lasted only one day, but consisted of brief assessments every 45 minutes during a 9 hour period, older adults exhibited less emotional (but greater cardiovascular) reactivity to daily stress.

Whether or not age differences in emotional reactivity emerge depends upon the nature of the daily stress. With increasing age, adults tend to favor more passive strategies for dealing with potentially stressful situations (Birditt & Fingerman, 2005; Blanchard-Fields & Coats, 2008), such as avoiding potential arguments (Blanchard-Fields, Mienaltowski, & Seay, 2007). Charles et al. (2009) reanalyzed data from the NSDE, focusing on interpersonal daily stress. They found no age differences in negative emotional responses to arguments, but they observed decreased NA in response to *avoided* arguments in older adults. Charles concluded that proactively avoided negative situations may underlie age-related benefits in affective well-being when they are observed. Older adults may also have difficulty dealing with complex stressful situations that affect multiples aspects of their daily life compared to more circumscribed events. Wrzus et al. (2012) found no age difference in negative emotional responses to circumscribed stressors but observed that older adults responded more negatively than younger adults to complex daily stressors that affected multiple domains (e.g., home life and work).

Age differences in personal resources and psychosocial environments may also influence how people respond to daily stress. Day-to-day perceptions of control play an important role in emotional responses to daily stress (Hay & Diehl, 2010), and there is some evidence to suggest that older adults are less affected by short-term fluctuations in control than are younger adults (Neupert, Almeida, & Charles, 2007). Stawski et al. (2008)examined whether global perceived stress moderated reactivity to daily stress in a group of younger and older adults. Global perceived stress reflects the degree to which individuals perceive their lives to be unpredictable, uncontrollable, and overloaded (Cohen, Kamarck, & Mermelstein, 1983). Stawski and colleagues found that average negative emotion reactivity did not differ between young and older adults, but that older adults had higher reactivity than the younger adults after equating for age differences in global stress (which was significantly lower in the older group). Another study that used an experience sampling design revealed a similar pattern of results (Scott, Sliwinski, & Blanchard-Fields, under review). Scott et al. showed that older adults exhibited smaller negative emotional responses to momentary reports of disruptive events, but that this age advantage disappeared after controlling for individual differences in global perceived stress.

There is little longitudinal data addressing the question of how emotional responses to daily stress change as people age. Sliwinski et al. (2009) described longitudinal changes in two samples

(CHAP and NSDE) that were studied using a measurement burst design. Across the two samples, they found longitudinal increases in the association between daily NA and daily stress in adults between the ages of 35 to 90. The rate of increase did not depend upon age or neuroticism. The magnitude of emotional reactivity to daily stress did exhibit a within-person association with global perceived stress across 6 month assessment periods in the CHAP sample. That is, older adults were more reactive to daily stress during times when they are also dealing with chronic problems.

There are numerous reasons for these mixed findings. Obvious possibilities pertain to methodological differences between studies. Some studies allowed individuals to select the time of day for their assessment (e.g., Brose et al., 2011; Röcke et al., 2009), which could have afforded a benefit to older adults who have more flexible schedules than younger adults. There are also differences in how studies assess daily stress, which could influence the type, severity and frequency of reported events. For example in the Uchino et al. (2006) study, participants reported an average of 2.5 events when they were asked whether they were dealing with an "everyday hassle or problem." Other studies (e.g., Brose et al., 2011; Mroczek & Almeida, 2004) that have framed their daily stress assessment with respect to specific types of events (e.g., an argument, a stressful event that happened to a close friend) report events occurring on only between 20 percent and 40 percent of the days (e.g., a daily average of .2 or .4 events). These radically different reporting frequencies across studies suggest that they may be assessing different phenomena.

Another reason for apparently inconsistent findings regarding the role of age in the daily stress process is that most rely on cross-sectional comparisons among people of different ages. For example, comparing the effects of daily stressors in a group of mostly single young adults how are working or attending school full time may to a group of older adults who are mostly partnered and retired may reveal more about age-graded differences in social environment than maturational changes in how people cope with daily stressors. Cross-sectional comparisons may be particularly problematic given the dependency of daily reactivity on the broader temporal context in which daily stress occurs (e.g., chronic stress), which varies not only between people of very different ages (Stawski et al., 2008) but also within individuals across relatively short time periods (Sliwinski et al., 2009).

Despite the methodological challenges and inconsistencies across studies, there are conditions under which both positive and negative age differences in emotional responses to daily stress emerge. When operating under adverse conditions (e.g., high global stress) or dealing with a complex stressors (e.g., ones impacting multiple life domains), older adults appear to exhibit amplified negative emotional responses. However, when they are able to engage in their preferred emotion regulation strategies, such as avoiding an argument, older adults manifest less reactivity than younger adults. There is still a dearth of longitudinal data on how the daily stress process changes as people age, but the two available longitudinal studies to date suggest that individuals tend to become more reactive over time.

In the final section of this chapter, we discuss the implications of daily stress research for socioemotional theories of aging. We also explore promising future directions for research on daily stress that can integrate aging theory with theories of stress pathology.

Implications for Aging and Stress Theory

Maintaining a favorable balance of positive and negative emotions is important for both personal happiness and health. Although there is variability in research findings, converging evidence points to two regularities in the data on emotional aging. First, emotional well-being improves during much of adulthood, reaching a peak in the mid to late 60s. Second, average decreases in emotional well-being have been observed in several studies, beginning for people in their mid to late 60s. These regularities have several implications.

One implication is that the processes driving the reversal in emotional trajectories probably commence years before the peak in emotional well-being, as evidenced by the slowdown in emotional gains during the years prior to that peak. This notion is consistent with the insight advanced by Baltes (1995) that the process of adult aging reflects the interplay between maturational gains and involutional losses in functioning and capabilities. The average age at which losses offset gains is less important than evidence that such a reversal exists. Not only is there variability among studies in their estimates for age at which the peak in emotional well-being occurs, there is almost certainly considerable variability among individuals. The challenge for aging theory is to provide a principled account of the conditions under which gains compensate for losses, as well as conditions under which the reverse holds true.

We can acknowledge that the average 70 year old may be happier than the average 30 year old. However, we must also acknowledge that, on average, 70 year old people are more likely to exhibit a decline in emotional well-being over the next few years compared to people who are 30 years of age, who can expect an increase in well-being over the same period. A second implication from the literature on emotional aging is that decrements in emotional well-being may serve as a precursor or early sign of physical and mental health problems. There is some evidence (Kunzmann et al., 2000)that declines in emotional well-being are related to poor health in older adults. Subtle decrements in emotional well-being may therefore represent an early or preclinical sign of physical health problems (e.g., Gerstorf et al., 2010).

Theoretical Accounts of Aging and Daily Stress

The literature on the role of age in the daily stress process can help to elucidate the boundary conditions for age-related emotional enhancement. One of the most prominent theories, socioemotional selectivity theory (SST) has done exceptionally well not only in explaining age trends in emotional well-being through most of adulthood, but also in predicting results for age differences in daily stress. SST posits that as people age they perceive future time horizons to be shorter. These perceptions of limited time motivate older adults to invest more effort in meaningful relationships, and derive more satisfaction from these investments. A key prediction from SST is that people should report fewer negative experiences as they grow older, partly as a result of selecting into more favorable social environments (Carstensen et al., 2000). The evidence from daily diary studies have consistently confirmed this prediction by showing a negative association between age the frequency of reported daily stressors. That is, older adults report unpleasant experiences less frequently than younger adults. This is a particularly impressive result because the prediction was made prior tomuch of the research on the role of age in daily stress. However, SST offers no predictions about the intensity of negative emotions when they do occur (Carstensen et al. 2000), making it relatively agnostic on the issue of whether emotional responses to stressful experiences change with age. Nor does SST specify the boundary conditions that limit age-graded improvements in emotional well-being.

There are recent developments in aging theory that specify these boundary conditions. The Strength and Vulnerability Integration (SAVI) theory represents the most comprehensive of these developments (Charles, 2010). The key insight of SAVI is that age-graded changes in emotional well-being represent a balance of age-based strengths and vulnerabilities in dealing with unpleasant situations. SAVI acknowledges that with advancing age, people more frequently and effectively use attentional strategies (Charles, Mather, & Carstensen, 2003; Mather & Carstensen, 2005), reappraisals (Shiota & Levenson, 2009; Wrosch, Heckhausen, & Lachman, 2000), and behaviors (Coats & Blanchard-Fields, 2008) to de-escalate negative events or avoid them entirely. When circumstances permit effective utilization of these passive strategies for emotion regulation, older adults can exhibit enhanced emotional well-being compared to younger persons. However, these strengths in emotion regulation can be offset by age-related vulnerabilities in physiological flexibility (e.g., reduced heart rate variability resulting in sustained physiological arousal following stressors). This physiological inflexibility makes it more difficult for older adults to marshal resources to effectively cope with negative situations rapidly while they are occurring, or to regulate their emotions in the face of unrelenting demands (Charles, 2010).

The nature of these strengths and vulnerabilities imply two types of boundary conditions for age-related enhancements in emotional well-being. The first is temporal proximity to stressful experiences. Specifically, SAVI predicts that age benefits in emotional well-being will be reduced during times proximal to a stressor, and that age benefits will emerge as time passes, which enables older adults to use strategies of disengagement and reappraisal to regulate their emotions. Chronic stress represents a second boundary condition for age-related strengths in emotion regulation abilities. SAVI asserts that over time, chronic stress can wear away psychological andphysical reserves which can result in a decrease in emotion regulation capacity. Conditions of chronic and uncontrollable stress also make it difficult for older adults to disengage from or reappraise negative situations. When exposed to unavoidable stressors, SAVI predicts older adults to be as affected or even more affected than younger persons.

Consistent with this notion, older adults experience less event-related NA for avoided arguments than younger persons, but no age differences were found in NA responses to arguments which occurred (Charles et al., 2009). Older adults are also no less and perhaps more reactive than younger adults under comparable levels of global stress (Scott et al., under review; Stawski et al., 2008). If older adults are advantaged by selecting favorable psychosocial environments, then they may be disadvantaged relative to younger adults when required to operate in less benign environments characterized by chronic and uncontrollable sources of stress. Some of the inconsistency in the literature in regarding whether there are age-related increases, decreases or stability in negative emotional responses to daily stress could result from unmeasured age differences in chronic stress.

Dynamic integration theory (Labouvie-Vief, 2003) offers another possible boundary condition for age-related enhancements in emotion regulation. This theory suggests that older adults may be less effective at regulating their emotions than younger adults when situational demands exceed available cognitive resources. Work by Stawski and colleagues (2011; in press) emphasizes the importance of fluid cognitive ability in moderating emotional responses to daily stress. Specifically, they have found that emotional responses are more negative among people with lower levels of fluid cognitive ability compared to high ability people. To the extent that fluid ability declines with age (McArdle, Ferrer-Caja, Hamagami, & Woodcock, 2002; Verhaeghen & Salthouse, 1997), older adults may be at greater risk for elevated distress during times of excessive or overwhelming stress. Wrzus et al. (2012) proposed the *overpowering hypothesis*, which predicts that older adults will respond more strongly to unpleasant events than younger people when situational demands are complex (i.e., when events affect multiple life domains). Wrzus and colleagues found evidence for the overpowering hypothesis—older adults were more emotionally reactive to complex stressors compared to circumscribed daily stressors—and argued that variability in stressor complexity could account from some of the inconsistency in research on age differences in daily stress.

A common theme in theories of emotion regulation, particularly SAVI and the overpowering hypothesis, is that of context. Individuals may have fewer resources available to cope with daily stressors during times when, at a more global level, life's demands seem overwhelming and uncontrollable (Sliwinski et al., 2009). This may be particularly true for older adults who have fewer cognitive and physiological resources to deal with complex psychosocial demands (Charles, 2010; Wrzus et al., 2012). Further, there is some evidence to suggest that younger adults experience more perceived stress and that this difference can influence the magnitude

and direction of the relationship between age and the effects of daily events (Stawski et al., 2008). Consequently, studies that show an age equivalence or advantage in dealing with daily stressors may not reflect online processing (e.g., reactivity) but rather whether older adults benefit from living in more favorable, or less adverse, environments which may provide more resources to respond to disruptive events as they appear.

Implications for linking aging and stress theory. Earlier in the chapter we discussed how researchers label increases in NA that are coincident to daily stressor as "reactivity." We also discussed why this label might be a misnomer. One reason is that most studies of daily stress do not provide sufficient temporal resolution to determine the sequencing of when the stressor occurred in relation to shift in negative emotions. A second and related reason is that it is often not possible to determine whether elevated distress reflects an immediate reaction to or an enduring response to negative events. The issue of whether to call increases in NA in relation to daily stress "reactivity" is more than a technical or semantic detail. This is because recent developments in stress theory emphasize not heightened reactivity but the inability to "shut off" stress-related activation as the critical mechanism by which stress affects health.

Indeed, McEwen's (1998) concept of allostatic load, which has provided a major theoretical motivation for the study of stress in health and aging, does not entail increased stress reactivity as a critical pathogenic mechanism. Allostatic load, which refers to "wear and tear" on the body that results from chronic stress, arises from patterns of physiological responses to prolonged and repeated psychological stress. This notion has been further developed in the perseverative cognition hypothesis (Brosschot, Gerin, & Thayer, 2006), which posits that worry and rumination function as a "final psychological pathway by which stress exercises its deleterious effects on the body's systems"(Brosschot, Pieper, & Thayer, 2005, p. 1046). According to this hypothesis, the magnitude of stress reactivity is less important than whether the response is prolonged. That is, it's not how large the stress reaction is, but how long the response lasts that matters for health.

This notion is important for daily stress because changes in emotional states in relation to daily stress have almost always been termed "reactivity." In fact, such stress-related shifts affective states may primarily represent the enduring effects of daily stressors rather than initial reactions to them. When a person reports feeling mostly frustrated or anxious during the day very likely could be driven as much by their enduring states across the day, as by their emotional state in the minutes following a stressful event. This is both good and bad news for previous daily stress research. The good news is that the way in which response to stress has been operationalized likely reflects, at least to some degree, precisely the prolonged activation that makes stress pathogenic. The bad news is that by labeling it as reactivity researchers may not have been directing their attention at the most relevant underlying mechanisms. For example, the situational and person characteristics that cause a person to become very angry during an argument might not be the same factors that determine whether that individual is still angry 12 hours later. For these reasons, we advocate replacing the term "stress reactivity" with either "stress-related affect" or "stress responsivity" either of which de-emphasize the immediacy implied by the word "reactivity."

Identifying the reasons why some people, in some circumstances, remain activated, both emotionally and physiologically, long after cessation of the eliciting stimulus (i.e., the stressor) may be key to understanding how daily stressor can "pile up" to produce chronic stress and affect health (Grzywacz & Almeida, 2008). This issue becomes especially relevant in the context of SAVI's prediction that older adults need more time than younger adults to regulate effectively their emotions. It is a completely open question as to whether age-graded shifts in emotion regulation strategies represent a strength or vulnerability with respect the effects of daily stress on health. A promising line for future research on the role of aging in daily stress would be to determine whether the types of emotion regulation strategies favored by older adults lead to shortened or prolonged responses to daily stress.

Conclusions. Adults, on average, exhibit gains in emotional well-being through early adulthood and well into middle age. The literature, though not entirely consistent, suggests that these gains slow down and eventually reverse at some point in the mid to late 60s. This reversal in the positive trajectory of emotional well-being suggests there are limits or boundary conditions to positive socioemotional aging. These boundary conditions or limits may reflect physiological and cognitive changes that render people less able to deal with complex stressors. Understanding how people deal with everyday challenges and adversities holds considerable promise for elucidating mechanisms which determine limits or boundary conditions positive socioemotional aging and to further our understanding of how some people successfully navigate pitfalls that threaten healthy aging.

References

Almeida, D. M. (2005). Resilience and vulnerability to daily stressors assessed via diary methods. *Current Directions in Psychological Science, 14*(2), 64–68.

Almeida, D. M., & Horn, M. C. (2004). Is daily life more stressful during middle adulthood? In O. G. Brim, C. D. Ryff, & R. C. Kessler (Eds.), *How healthy are we? A national study of well-being at midlife* (pp. 425–451).

Baltes, M. M. (1995). Dependency in old age: Gains and losses. *Current Directions in Psychological Science, 4*(1), 14–19.

Birditt, K. S., & Fingerman, K. L. (2005). Do We Get Better at Picking Our Battles? Age Group Differences in Descriptions of Behavioral Reactions to Interpersonal Tensions. *The Journals of Gerontology Series B: Psychological Sciences and Social Sciences, 60*(3), P121–P128. doi:10.1093/geronb/60.3.P121

Blanchard-Fields, F., & Coats, A. H. (2008). The experience of anger and sadness in everyday problems impacts age differences in emotion regulation. *Developmental Psychology, 44*(6), 1547–1556. doi:10.1037/a0013915

Blanchard-Fields, F., Mienaltowski, A., & Seay, R. B. (2007). Age differences in everyday problem-solving effectiveness: older adults select more effective strategies for interpersonal problems. *The Journals of Gerontology Series B: Psychological Sciences and Social Sciences, 62*(1), P61–P64.

Bolger, N., & Schilling, E. A. (1991). Personality and the problems of everyday life: The role of Neuroticism in exposure and reactivity to daily stressors. *Journal of Personality, 59*(3), 355–386. doi:10.1111/j.1467-6494.1991.tb00253.x

Brose, A., Schmiedek, F., Lövdén, M., & Lindenberger, U. (2011). Normal aging dampens the link between intrusive thoughts and negative affect in reaction to daily stressors. *Psychology and Aging, 26*, 488–502. doi:10.1037/a0022287

Brosschot, J. F., Gerin, W., & Thayer, J. F. (2006). The perseverative cognition hypothesis: A review of worry, prolonged stress-related physiological activation, and health. *Journal of Psychosomatic Research, 60*(2), 113–124. doi:10.1016/j.jpsychores.2005.06.074

Brosschot, J. F., Pieper, S., & Thayer, J. F. (2005). Expanding stress theory: Prolonged activation and perseverative cognition. *Psychoneuroendocrinology, 30*(10), 1043–1049. doi:10.1016/j.psyneuen.2005.04.008

Cacioppo, J. T., Berntson, G. G., Malarkey, W. B., Kiecolt-Glaser, J. K., Sheridan, J. F., Poehlmann, K. M., Burleson, M. H., et al. (1998). Autonomic, neuroendocrine, and immune responses to psychological stress: the reactivity hypothesis. *Annals of the New York Academy of Sciences, 840*(1), 664–673. doi:10.1111/j.1749-6632.1998.tb09605.x

Carstensen, L. L., Fung, H. H., & Charles, S. T. (2003). Socioemotional Selectivity Theory and the regulation of emotion in the second half of life. Motivation and Emotion, *27*(2), 103–123. doi:10.1023/A:1024569803230

Carstensen, L. L., & Fredrickson, B. L. (1998). Influence of HIV status and age on cognitive representations of others. *Health Psychology, 17*(6), 494–503. doi:10.1037/0278-6133.17.6.494

Carstensen, L. L., Mikels, J. A., & Mather, M. (2006). Aging and the intersection of cognition, motivation, and emotion. In L. L. Carstensen, J. A. Mikels, & M. Mather (Eds.),

Handbook of the psychology of aging (6th ed., pp. 343–362). Amsterdam, Netherlands: Elsevier.

Carstensen, L. L., Turan, B., Scheibe, S., Ram, N., Ersner-Hershfield, H., Samanez-Larkin, G. R., Brooks, K. P., et al. (2011). Emotional experience improves with age: Evidence based on over 10 years of experience sampling. *Psychology and Aging, 26*(1), 21–33. doi:10.1037/a0021285

Charles, S. T. (2010). Strength and Vulnerability Integration: A model of emotional well-being across adulthood. *Psychological Bulletin, 136*(6), 1068–1091. doi:10.1037/a0021232

Charles, S. T., Mather, M., & Carstensen, L. L. (2003). Aging and emotional memory: The forgettable nature of negative images for older adults. *Journal of Experimental Psychology: General, 132*(2), 310–324. doi:10.1037/0096-3445.132.2.310

Charles, S. T., Piazza, J. R., Luong, G., & Almeida, D. M. (2009). Now you see it, now you don't: Age differences in affective reactivity to social tensions. *Psychology and Aging, 24*, 645–653. doi:10.1037/a0016673

Charles, S. T., Piazza, J. R., Mogle, J. M., Sliwinski, M. J., & Almeida, D. M. (in press). The wear-and-tear of daily stressors on mental health. *Psychological Science.*

Charles, S. T., Reynolds, C. A., & Gatz, M. (2001). Age-related differences and change in positive and negative affect over 23 years. *Journal of Personality and Social Psychology, 80*(1), 136–151. doi:10.1037/0022-3514.80.1.136

Coats, A. H., & Blanchard-Fields, F. (2008). Emotion regulation in interpersonal problems: The role of cognitive-emotional complexity, emotion regulation goals, and expressivity. *Psychology and Aging, 23*(1), 39–51. doi:10.1037/0882-7974.23.1.39

Cohen, S., Kamarck, T., & Mermelstein, R. (1983). A global measure of perceived stress. *Journal of Health and Social Behavior, 24*(4), 385–396.

DeLongis, A., Coyne, J. C., Dakof, G., Folkman, S., & Lazarus, R. S. (1982). Relationship of daily hassles, uplifts, and major life events to health status. *Health Psychology, 1*(2), 119–136. doi:10.1037/0278-6133.1.2.119

Elder, G. H. (1991). Family transitions, cycles, and social change. In P. A. Cowan & E. M. Hetherington (Eds.), Family Transitions (Vol. 2, pp. 32–58). Hillsdale, NJ: Lawrence Erlbaum Associates Inc.

Gerstorf, D., Ram, N., Mayraz, G., Hidajat, M., Lindenberger, U., Wagner, G. G., & Schupp, J. (2010). Late-life decline in well-being across adulthood in Germany, the United Kingdom, and the United States: Something is seriously wrong at the end of life. Psychology and Aging, 25(2), 477–485. doi:10.1037/a0017543

Griffin, P. W., Mroczek, D. K., & Spiro, A. (2006). Variability in affective change among aging men: Longitudinal findings from the VA Normative Aging Study. *Journal of Research in Personality, 40*(6), 942–965. doi:10.1016/j.jrp.2005.09.011

Grzywacz, J. G., & Almeida, D. M. (2008). Stress and binge drinking: A daily process examination of stressor pile-up and socioeconomic status in affect regulation. *International Journal of Stress Management, 15*(4), 364–380. doi:10.1037/a0013368

Hay, E. L., & Diehl, M. (2010). Reactivity to daily stressors in adulthood: The importance of stressor type in characterizing risk factors. *Psychology and Aging, 25*(1), 118–131. doi:10.1037/a0018747

Isaacowitz, D. M., & Blanchard-Fields, F. (2012). Linking process and outcome in the study of emotion and aging. *Perspectives on Psychological Science, 7*(1), 3–17. doi:10.1177/1745691611424750

Johnson, E. I., Husky, M., Grondin, O., Mazure, C. M., Doron, J., & Swendsen, J. (2008). Mood trajectories following daily life events. *Motivation and Emotion, 32*(4), 251–259. doi:10.1007/s11031-008-9106-0

Kamarck, T. W., Shiffman, S., Sutton-Tyrrell, K., Muldoon, M. F., & Tepper, P. (2012). Daily psychological demands are associated with 6-year progression of carotid artery atherosclerosis: the Pittsburgh Healthy Heart Project. *Psychosomatic Medicine, 74*(4), 432–439. doi:10.1097/PSY.0b013e3182572599

Kiecolt-Glaser, J. K., McGuire, L., Robles, T. F., & Glaser, R. (2002). Emotions, morbidity, and mortality: New perspectives from psychoneuroimmunology. *Annual Review of Psychology, 53*, 83–107. doi:10.1146/annurev.psych.53.100901.135217

Kunzmann, U., Little, T. D., & Smith, J. (2000). Is age-related stability of subjective well-being a paradox? Cross-sectional and longitudinal evidence from the Berlin Aging Study. *Psychology and Aging, 15*(3), 511–526. doi:10.1037/0882-7974.15.3.511

Labouvie-Vief, G. (2003). Dynamic integration: Affect, cognition, and the self in adulthood. *Current Directions in Psychological Science, 12*(6), 201–206. doi:http://dx.doi.org.ezaccess.libraries.psu.edu/10.1046/j.0963-7214.2003.01262.x

Mather, M., & Carstensen, L. L. (2005). Aging and motivated cognition: The positivity effect in attention and memory. *Trends in Cognitive Sciences, 9*(10), 496–502. doi:10.1016/j.tics.2005.08.005

McArdle, J. J., Ferrer-Caja, E., Hamagami, F., & Woodcock, R. W. (2002). Comparative longitudinal structural analyses of the growth and decline of multiple intellectual abilities over the life span. Developmental Psychology, 38(1), 115–142. doi:http://dx.doi.org.ezaccess.libraries.psu.edu/10.1037/0012-1649.38.1.115

McEwen, B. S. (1998). Stress, adaptation, and disease: Allostasis and allostatic load. *Annals of the New York Academy of Sciences, 840*, 33–44. doi:10.1111/j.1749-6632.1998.tb09546.x

Mroczek, D. K., & Almeida, D. M. (2004). The effect of daily stress, personality, and age on daily negative affect. *Journal of Personality, 72*(2), 355–378. doi:10.1111/j.0022-3506.2004.00265.x

Mroczek, D. K., & Kolarz, C. M. (1998). The effect of age on positive and negative affect: A developmental perspective on happiness. *Journal of Personality and Social Psychology, 75*(5), 1333–1349. doi:10.1037/0022-3514.75.5.1333

Neupert, S. D., Almeida, D. M., & Charles, S. T. (2007). Age differences in reactivity to daily stressors: The role of personal control. *The Journals of Gerontology Series B: Psychological Sciences and Social Sciences, 62*(4), P216–P225.

Ong, A. D., Bergeman, C. S., Bisconti, T. L., & Wallace, K. A. (2006). Psychological resilience, positive emotions, and successful adaptation to stress in later life. *Journal of Personality and Social Psychology, 91*(4), 730–749. doi:10.1037/0022-3514.91.4.730

Ostir, G. V., Markides, K. S., Peek, M. K., & Goodwin, J. S. (2001). The association between emotional well-being and the incidence of stroke in older adults. *Psychosomatic Medicine, 63*(2), 210–215.

Parrish, B. P., Cohen, L. H., & Laurenceau, J.-P. (2011). Prospective relationship between negative affective reactivity to daily stress and depressive symptoms. *Journal of Social and Clinical Psychology, 30*(3), 270–296. doi:10.1521/jscp.2011.30.3.270

Piazza, J. R., Charles, S. T., Sliwinski, M. J., Mogle, J. M., & Almeida, D. M. (in press). Affective reactivity to daily stressors and long-term risk of reporting a chronic health condition. *Annals of Behavioral Medicine.*

Pressman, S. D., & Cohen, S. (2005). Does positive affect influence health? *Psychological Bulletin, 131*(6), 925–971. doi:http://dx.doi.org/10.1037/0033-2909.131.6.925

Ready, R. E., Åkerstedt, A. M., & Mroczek, D. K. (2012). Emotional complexity and emotional well-being in older adults: Risks of high neuroticism. *Aging & Mental Health, 16*(1), 17–26. doi:10.1080/13607863.2011.602961

Robinson, M. D., & Clore, G. L. (2002). Belief and feeling: Evidence for an accessibility model of emotional self-report. *Psychological Bulletin, 128*(6), 934–960. doi:10.1037/0033-2909.128.6.934

Röcke, C., Li, S.-C., & Smith, J. (2009). Intraindividual variability in positive and negative affect over 45 days: Do older adults fluctuate less than young adults? *Psychology and Aging, 24*(4), 863–878. doi:10.1037/a0016276

Scheibe, S., & Carstensen, L. L. (2010). Emotional aging: recent findings and future trends. *The Journals of Gerontology Series B: Psychological Sciences and Social Sciences, 65B*(2), 135–144. doi:10.1093/geronb/gbp132

Scott, S. B., Sliwinski, M. J., & Blanchard-Fields, F. (in press). *Age differences in emotional responses to stress: It's more than just Psychology and Aging.*

Shiota, M. N., & Levenson, R. W. (2009). Effects of aging on experimentally instructed detached reappraisal, positive reappraisal, and emotional behavior suppression. *Psychology and Aging, 24*(4), 890–900. doi:10.1037/a0017896

Sliwinski, M. J., Almeida, D. M., Smyth, J., & Stawski, R. S. (2009). Intraindividual change and variability in daily stress processes: Findings from two measurement-burst diary studies. *Psychology and Aging, 24*(4), 828–840. doi:10.1037/a0017925

Sliwinski, M. J., Hoffman, L., & Hofer, S. M. (2010). Evaluating convergence of within-person change and between-person age differences in age-heterogeneous longitudinal studies. *Research in Human Development, 7*(1), 45–60. doi:10.1080/15427600903578169

Sliwinski, M. J., Smyth, J. M., Hofer, S. M., & Stawski, R. S. (2006). Intraindividual coupling of daily stress and cognition. *Psychology and Aging, 21*(3), 545–557. doi:10.1037/0882-7974.21.3.545

Smyth, J. M., & Stone, A. A. (2003). Ecological Momentary Assessment research in Behavioral Medicine. *Journal of Happiness Studies, 4*(1), 35–52. doi:10.1023/A:1023657221954

Stawski, R. S., Almeida, D. M., Lachman, M. E., Tun, P. A., Rosnick, C. B., & Seeman, T. (2011). Associations between cognitive function and naturally occurring daily cortisol during middle adulthood: Timing is everything. *The Journals of Gerontology Series B: Psychological Sciences and Social Sciences, 66B*(Supplement 1), i71–i81. doi:10.1093/geronb/gbq094

Stawski, R. S., Mogle, J. M., & Sliwinski, M. J. (in press). Associations among fluid and crystallized cognition and daily stress processes in older adults. *Psychology and Aging.*

Stawski, R. S., Sliwinski, M. J., Almeida, D. M., & Smyth, J. M. (2008). Reported exposure and emotional reactivity to daily stressors: The roles of adult age and global perceived stress. *Psychology and Aging, 23*(1), 52–61. doi:10.1037/0882-7974.23.1.52

Uchino, B. N., Berg, C. A., Smith, T. W., Pearce, G., & Skinner, M. (2006). Age-related differences in ambulatory blood pressure during daily stress: Evidence for greater blood pressure reactivity with age. *Psychology and Aging, 21*(2), 231–239. doi:10.1037/0882-7974.21.2.231

van Eck, M., Nicolson, N. A., & Berkhof, J. (1998). Effects of stressful daily events on mood states: Relationship to global perceived stress. *Journal of Personality and Social Psychology, 75*(6), 1572–1585. doi:10.1037/0022-3514.75.6.1572

Verhaeghen, P., & Salthouse, T. A. (1997). Meta-analyses of age-cognition relations in adulthood: estimates of linear and nonlinear age effects and structural models. *Psychological bulletin, 122*(3), 231–249.

Wells, K., Stewart, A., Hays, R. D., Burnam, M. A., Rogers, W., Daniels, M., Berry, S., et al. (1989). The functioning and well-being of depressed patients: Results from the medical outcomes study. *JAMA: The Journal of the American Medical Association, 262*(7), 914–919. doi:10.1001/jama.1989.03430070062031

Wichers, M., Geschwind, N., Jacobs, N., Kenis, G., Peeters, F., Derom, C., Thiery, E., et al. (2009). Transition from stress sensitivity to a depressive state: Longitudinal twin study. *The British Journal of Psychiatry, 195*(6), 498–503. doi:10.1192/bjp.bp.108.056853

Wrosch, C., Heckhausen, J., & Lachman, M. E. (2000). Primary and secondary control strategies for managing health and financial stress across adulthood. *Psychology and Aging, 15*(3), 387–399. doi:10.1037/0882-7974.15.3.387

Wrzus, C., Müller, V., Wagner, G. G., Lindenberger, U., & Riediger, M. (2012). Affective and cardiovascular responding to unpleasant events from adolescence to old age: Complexity of events matters. *Developmental Psychology,* Advance online publication. doi:10.1037/a0028325

Zautra, A. J. (2003). *Emotions, stress, and health.* New York: Oxford University Press.

Zautra, A. J., Affleck, G. G., Tennen, H., Reich, J. W., & Davis, M. C. (2005). Dynamic approaches to emotions and stress in everyday life: Bolger and Zuckerman reloaded with positive as well as negative affects. *Journal of Personality, 73*(6), 1511–1538. doi:10.1111/j.0022-3506.2005.00357.x

Tasks, Capacities, and Tactics: A Skill-Based Conceptualization of Emotion Regulation Across the Lifespan

Nathan S. Consedine *and* Iris Mauss

Abstract

Although widely asserted that emotion regulation improves with age, little empirical evidence is directly demonstrative of this claim. This essay examines the available work through the lens offered by developmental functionalism-a lifespan theory of emotion and emotion regulation. Following an outline of the theory and its emphasis on regulatory tasks, capacities, and tactics, the essay reviews experimental work testing age-related variation in emotion regulation. As predicted, depending on the specific skill, data indicate considerable variation in whether skills improve or decline with age. Although situational selection, positive reappraisal, use of social resource, and acceptance generally improve with age, regulatory skills relying on specific capacities (notably, executive processing) decline or remain unchanged. Patterns are interpreted in terms of age-related differences in regulatory tasks and capacities, as well as in the specific tactics used to accomplish particular regulatory ends. Directions for future empirical work are given.

Key Words: emotion, emotion regulation, lifespan development, later life, reappraisal, acceptance, suppression, developmental functionalism

Emotion and emotion regulation are centrally implicated in adaptive functioning across the lifespan. Predominantly studied among children and adolescents, regulatory capacities are nonetheless a cornerstone for adaptive success across the lifespan (Gross & Thompson, 2007; Troy, Shallcross, Wilhelm, & Mauss, 2010a) and appear among the most highly developed functions of adulthood (Muraven, Tice, & Baumeister, 1998). Less clear are questions regarding why emotions and emotion regulation change in the ways they do across the adult lifespan, which aspects of regulatory functioning improve and decline, whether people of different ages are regulating toward the same endpoints (targets), or how changes in basic capacities may be involved. This essay outlines the core assertions of developmental functionalism, a lifespan theory of emotion and its regulation. This view suggests that emotion regulatory processes are usefully conceptualized in terms of the conjoint influences of three phenomena—tasks, capacities, and tactics. From within this framework, it is argued that regulating the different components of emotions represent distinct regulatory tasks, particularly where the capacities necessary for varied forms of regulation are fluctuating developmentally; consequently, distinct patterns of regulatory tactics are used among adults from different ages. A systematic review of experimental work examining age-related variation in emotion regulation is presented and directions for future research based around the concepts of task, capacity, and tactic are outlined.

Developmental Functionalism: A Brief Overview

Developmental functionalism is a discrete emotions-based approach to the study of emotions (Consedine & Magai, 2003; Consedine, Magai, &

Bonanno, 2002; Consedine & Moskowitz, 2007), emotion regulation (Consedine, 2011a; 2011b; Magai, Consedine, Krivoshekova, McPherson, & Kudadjie-Gyamfi, 2006), and their links to adaptive outcomes that pays explicit attention to lifespan developmental contexts. In this view, discrete emotions are evolved adaptations that were selected because they historically helped promote adaptive responding to recurrent classes of adaptive challenge or opportunity (Nesse, 1990). They are evolutionarily adaptive and developmentally calibrated problem solvers.

Emotions: Tasks, Capacities, and Tactics

Developmental functionalism differs from other functionalist theories insofar as it attends to the fact that adaptive challenges (tasks) vary developmentally. Early challenges like ensuring parental attention (Bowlby, 1969), internalizing physical rules, and so on are supplanted across the lifespan by challenges such as mate choice and retention, alliance, and cheater detection (Tooby & Cosmides, 2008); knowledge transmission (Carstensen & Löckenhoff, 2003); and managing reductions in systemic resources (Baltes, 1997). Such variation implies that emotions' functions also vary developmentally. If (a) emotions were selected because they facilitated adaptive responding to challenges (Tooby & Cosmides, 2008) and (b) adaptive challenges vary developmentally, it logically follows that the functions of emotions also vary across the lifespan.

Second, developmental functionalism asserts that the ways in which emotions facilitate adaptive functioning are built on basic capacities that vary across the lifespan (Consedine, 2011b). Some capabilities are available early in life, some take time to develop, and some develop and then fade as the organism ages. The functional manifestations of emotions are seen in cognitive (Keltner, Ellsworth, & Edwards, 1993), physiological (Levenson, 1994), signal (Brown & Consedine, 2004), experiential (Izard, 1991), and behavioral channels (Consedine, Strongman, & Magai, 2003). Although components tend to co-occur, at least in early life and/or when emotions are intense, each may have distinct functional roles in adaptation (Averill, 1994; Consedine & Moskowitz, 2007). Importantly, whether the specific capabilities (e.g., locomotion, expressive control, representational ability) needed for particular functions have come online is critical; emotions can only manifest their functions through those aspects of the system that are available and

may thus constrain how functions manifest at different ages (Consedine, 2011b).

Because organisms of different ages are attempting to accomplish age-normatively varying tasks with capabilities that also fluctuate in an age-normative manner, developmental functionalism suggests that selective pressures create a *tactical* need to calibrate emotional functioning to the capabilities of the organism. Although emotions are predominantly selected for their utility in meeting early life demands (Baltes, 1997; Dennett, 1995; Schulz, Wrosch, & Heckhausen, 2002), there may be some exceptions in terms of deferred adaptations (Bjorklund & Pelligrini, 2002; Hernandez-Blasi & Bjorklund, 2003) or later life inclusive fitness (Carstensen & Löckenhoff, 2003). Traits may adjust dynamically through the interactions of inherited predispositions and current cues to fitness (Bjorklund & Bering, 2002; Ellis & Garber, 2000; Gottlieb, 2002a; 2002b). Logically, current cues may include evaluations of current capacity and, at least in theory, selective pressures on the postreproductive years can exist to the extent to which such characteristics enhance inclusive fitness (Carstensen & Löckenhoff, 2003; Gurven & Kaplan, 2009; Kachel, Premo, & Hublin, 2011). Emotions' functions are differentially manifest in the systems of infants, adolescents, and younger and older adults precisely *because* we have different physical, cognitive, experiential, behavioral, and social capacities at different developmental stages.

Emotion Regulation: Tasks, Capacities, and Tactics

In addition to providing a useful metaphor for conceptualizing the evolutionary processes underlying the design of emotions, developmental functionalism suggests that these same three concepts—task, capacity, and tactic—provide a useful framework for organizing observations regarding age-related variation in emotion regulation. Rather than assume (or infer) that the target of regulation is to maximize felt positive emotion (Charles, Mather, & Carstensen, 2003), developmental functionalism suggests vast differentiation in the targets of regulation—the tasks that individuals of different ages are attempting.

The highly differentiated emotional repertoire seen among humans exists because distinct emotions have generally proven adaptive in specific contexts (Consedine, 2011b). Some aspects of experiential regulatory motivations are thus likely to be constrained by the core functions of each discrete emotion's experience (e.g., shame is necessarily experienced as aversive) although other aspects (e.g., learning that shame experiences can be forestalled by skill acquisition, secrecy, or situational avoidance) are not. Although the question of age-related variation in regulatory goals remains poorly explored, research suggests that regulatory goals (in general) are well differentiated (Hackenbracht & Tamir, 2010; Rusk, Tamir, & Rothbaum, 2011; Tamir, 2011; Tamir & Ford, 2009).

Functionalist reasoning suggests that experiential versus expressive regulatory goals should be distinguished (Brown & Consedine, 2004) and that hedonic versus instrumental motivations are both evidenced in experiential regulatory processes (Tamir, Mitchell, & Gross, 2008). The ability of distinct emotional signals to influence the social environment (Brown & Consedine, 2004; Fridlund, 1994; Owren & Bachorowski, 2001) implies variation at the level of discrete emotions, and there is reason to expect further variation in whether regulatory targets concentrate on issues of experiential frequency, intensity, or duration. Consistent with other models (Gross, 1998; Westphal & Bonanno, 2004), developmental functionalism suggests that experiential and expressive regulatory targets are highly differentiated and (despite the current absence of data) that age-related variation in regulatory targets is a near certainty.

Furthermore, the view outlined here suggests that understanding age differences in emotion regulation requires an appreciation of (a) the resources necessary to accomplish regulatory goals and (b) age-normative variation in those capacities. Emotion regulation is a *skill* (Bonanno, Papa, Lalande, Westphal, & Coifman, 2004; Gross, 2001; Gross et al., 1997; Labouvie-Vief, Lumley, Jain, & Heinze, 2003; Magai et al., 2006; Troy et al., 2010a), and the capacity requirements underlying the deployment of regulatory skills remain unclear. The fact that emotion regulation emerges late in child development (Eisenberg, 2000) does, however, suggest that the these requirements are complex (Consedine, 2011a). Many emotion regulatory processes require aspects of self-awareness and cultural referencing (Saarni, 1989), executive functioning (Ochsner & Gross, 2005; Urry & Gross, 2010), linguistic capacities (Eisenberg, Sadovsky, & Spinrad, 2005), knowledge of others' beliefs, intentions, and desires (Charles & Piazza, 2009), and an understanding of the connections between emotions and internal processes (Thompson & Meyer, 2007). Developmental functionalism distinguishes between two broad classes of capacity—those reflecting basic biological capacities and those reflecting acquired characteristics (Consedine, 2011a)—suggesting that the former reflect basic competencies that fluctuate in line with general developmental processes while the latter denote acquired (learned) capacities and are, commensurately, more idiosyncratic.

The capacities needed for different forms of regulation have complex trajectories of improvement and decline across adulthood (see Figure 10.1). Relative to younger groups, older adults appear more reflective and conscious of emotions and themselves and have greater knowledge regarding emotions, the

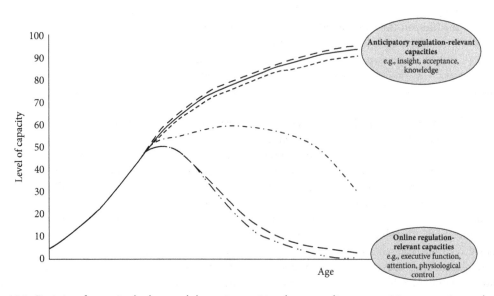

Figure 10.1. Depiction of normative developmental changes in capacities relevant to online versus anticipatory emotion regulation.

links between situations and emotions, and the effects of emotion on others (Charles & Piazza, 2009; Labouvie-Vief, Chiodo, Goguen, Diehl, & Orwoll, 1995; Labouvie-Vief, Hakin-Larson, DeVoe, & Schoeberlein, 1989). In developmental functionalism, these capacities are seen as being particularly important to anticipatory regulation. Conversely, however, older adults have fewer somatic resources, reduced energy (Panksepp & Miller, 1995), reduced physiological flexibility (De Meersman & Stein, 2006), as well as a reduced capacity for executive tasks such as planning, inhibition, task switching, abstraction, and selective attention (Gilhooly, Phillips, Wynn, Logie, & Della Sala, 1999; Kray & Lindenberger, 2000; Maylor & Lavie, 1998). In developmental functionalism, declines in these capacities may impair "online" or reactive-type regulation and creates a specific need for the use of alternate regulatory tactics.

As in the evolved design of the emotions themselves, developmental functionalism suggests that fluctuating capacity sets creates a need for alterations in the tactics individuals use to attain regulatory goals. Persons of different ages (and thus different regulatory tasks, goals, and capacities) operate in a manner that treats regulatory targets as problems to be solved. Because regulatory capacities change, different individuals *must* use distinct patterns of regulatory tactic. Over time, for example, some regulatory tasks may become automatized and require fewer resources (Mauss, Bunge, & Gross, 2007; Mauss, Evers, Wilhelm, & Gross, 2006); design-wise, automatization is a tactical solution to the trade-off between task and capacity. More broadly, developmental changes in capacity may make certain targets and tactics more and less viable and/or effective for individuals of different ages. Consistent with Baltes' model of selection, optimization, and compensation (Baltes, 1987; 1997), the view offered here suggests that changes in

regulatory capacities promote changes in both the targets of regulation as well as in the strategies used to attain them.

By definition, regulation requires effort and should deplete a finite regulatory reservoir (Baumeister, Bratslavsky, Muraven, & Tice, 1998). Where the resource pool is reduced, tactics may necessarily become more "efficient" in terms of desired outcomes. Consistent with this view, older adults appear to differentially favor regulatory tactics such as situational selection, conflict avoidance and minimization, and reduced interpersonal reactivity (Birditt, Fingerman, & Almeida, 2005), and exhibit greater flexibility in problem-solving (Blanchard-Fields, Chen, & Norris, 1997) and goal adjustment processes (Heckhausen, 1997). Emotional understanding acquired across a lifespan may permit later-life adults to more effectively seek and manage environments that further their emotional goals. It may be that the raw "amount" of some regulatory capacities declines in later life but that such reductions are offset by an increased ability to effectively *deploy* the resources that are available—a change in regulatory tactic. These relations are graphically depicted in Figure 10.2.

Empirical Findings: Age-Related Changes in Emotion Regulation Across the Lifespan

Although it has been widely suggested that emotion regulation improves with age (Blanchard-Fields, 2007; Carstensen, Fung, & Charles, 2003; Carstensen & Mikels, 2005; Urry & Gross, 2010), surprisingly little empirical evidence is directly demonstrative of this claim. One reason for this lack of unambiguous empirical evidence may be that we have often treated emotion regulation as a unitary construct, neglecting to consider that different regulatory tasks rely on different sets of age-related capacities (Opitz, Gross, & Urry, 2012; Shiota & Levenson, 2009; Urry & Gross, 2010). Because of

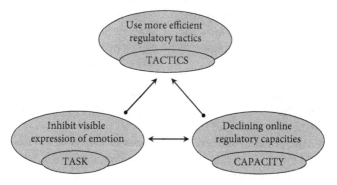

Figure 10.2. The task, capacity, and tactic framework as applied to changes in emotion regulation across the adult lifespan.

its focus on emotion regulation as a skill and the underlying capacity changes, developmental functionalism may help advance our thinking about the link between age and emotion regulation insofar as it leads to predictions about which specific *types* of emotion regulation may decline and which ones may improve with age.

As noted, advancing age typically sees executive cognitive functions such as planning, inhibition, task switching, abstraction, and selective attention decline (Gilhooly et al., 1999; Kray & Lindenberger, 2000; Maylor & Lavie, 1998; Nessler, Friedman, Johnson, & Bersick, 2007) whereas resources such as the capacity to generate positive emotional states, social skills, and emotional understanding appear to improve (Blanchard-Fields, 2007; Carstensen & Jacobs, 1993; Carstensen et al., 2011; Charles & Piazza, 2009; Nielsen, Knutson, & Carstensen, 2008; Scheibe & Blanchard-Fields, 2009). In developmental functionalism, this pattern of age-related changes in resources allows us to make predictions regarding the *types* of regulation that should decline and improve with age. Specifically, we would expect that greater age should bring declines in forms of regulation that rely primarily on executive functioning but improvements in types of regulation that are not so reliant and/or that reflect developmental changes in emotion-related motivations, social skills, or understanding/knowledge regarding emotions.

Here, we review the evidence on types of emotion regulation that either decline or improve with age. In this review, we focus on studies that have examined emotion regulation directly rather than its putative downstream effects, such as experienced emotion or emotional well-being. Where possible, we focus on studies that have evaluated successful (rather than attempted) regulation use because our predictions regard successful use of emotion regulation skills rather than attempted use (Troy, Shallcross, Wilhelm, & Mauss, 2010). Similarly, we concentrate on evidence from laboratory paradigms rather than surveys because laboratory data may be less biased by desirability, motivation, or the limits to introspection (Barrett, 1997; Robinson & Clore, 2002).

Types of Emotion Regulation That May Decline With Age

At least two comparatively well-studied types of emotion regulation rely primarily on executive capacities and should therefore decline with age: cognitive reappraisal used to decrease negative emotion and expressive suppression.

COGNITIVE REAPPRAISAL USED TO DECREASE NEGATIVE EMOTION

Reappraisal techniques, such as adopting a more detached perspective on an emotional event or making it less self-relevant, are among the most common strategies used to reduce negative experience (Gross, Richards, & John, 2006). Because such regulation is based on executive functions (Ochsner & Gross, 2005), age should be related to declines in the effectiveness of such strategies. Using a multimethod laboratory paradigm to index cognitive reappraisal success among adults aged 20–69, Shiota and Levenson (2009) found that age was related to declines in "detached reappraisal" (a type of reappraisal primarily aimed at decreasing negative emotion). Another work denotes a similar finding (Opitz, Rauch, Terry, & Urry, 2012). In this study, older relative to younger adults showed a lower ability to utilize cognitive reappraisal to decrease negative emotion. Thus, even though adults in their early 60s ("young old" people) report using cognitive reappraisal *more frequently* than do younger adults (John & Gross, 2004), older compared to younger adults appear to be less successful at using reappraisal to reduce negative experience.

EXPRESSIVE SUPPRESSION

Reducing the visible signals of an emotion—expressive suppression—appears to be similarly reliant on executive functions (Baumeister et al., 1998; Richards & Gross, 2000; Schmeichel, Volokhov, & Demaree, 2008). Consequently, aging should predict a reduced ability to suppress expressions of felt emotion. However, whereas self-report data suggest suppression is used less frequently with greater age (John & Gross, 2004), the question of "success" is unclear. Several recent studies testing whether age is related to suppression success (Emery & Hess, 2011; Kunzmann, Kupperbusch, & Levenson, 2005; Magai et al., 2006; Phillips, Henry, Hosie, & Milne, 2008; Shiota & Levenson, 2009) have failed to find age differences in expressive suppression. Although there has been some suggestion of age-related variation in the specific tactic used to attain successful suppression (Magai et al., 2006), it may also be that only the most severe declines in executive functioning lead to decrements in suppressive ability (Shiota & Levenson, 2009).

Types of Emotion Regulation That May Improve With Age

Four types of emotion regulation do not appear to rely primarily on executive functions or rely on the generation of positive emotional states, social skills, and understanding emotions. Such regulatory tasks should therefore show no declines or even reveal improvements with age.

POSITIVE REAPPRAISAL

Unlike reappraisal in the service of decreasing negative emotion, reappraisal in the service of increasing positive emotion ("positive reappraisal") may not require the types of executive function that decrease with age. This might be because the generation of positive emotion relies on different cognitive and neural mechanisms than the decrease of negative emotion (e.g., McRae, Ochsner, Mauss, Gabrieli, & Gross, 2008), including the strategic recall of positive memories and the "pull" (rather than effortful direction) of attention to positive aspects of a situation. Unlike executive functions, older adults appear more effective than younger adults at such approaches (Charles et al., 2003; Isaacowitz, Toner, & Neupert, 2009; Isaacowitz, Wadlinger, Goren, & Wilson, 2006; Mather & Carstensen, 2005). Relative to younger groups, older adults report greater reliance on positive reappraisal (Charles & Carstensen, 2008), and laboratory work shows that they are better at implementing a positive refocusing strategy (thinking of a positive memory while viewing a negative film clip) (Phillips et al., 2008). More recently, a multimethod study contrasting detached and positive forms of reappraisal found that older (vs. younger) adults showed improvements in positive but impairments in detached reappraisal (Shiota & Levenson, 2009). Taken as a whole, this evidence suggests that it is positive reappraisal in particular (vs. reappraisal to reduce negative emotion) that improves with age.

USING SOCIAL SUPPORT

Although the overall size of the social network tends to decrease over the lifespan (Morgan, 1988), older adults prioritize and may have a greater proportion of close relationships (Lang, 2001; Lang & Carstensen, 1994). Data suggest that older adults also experience fewer negative interactions and less anger in close relationships than do healthy younger adults (Akiyama, Antonucci, Takahashi, & Langfahl, 2003; Birditt & Fingerman, 2005; Birditt et al., 2005). Because their interactions are focused on close, relatively positive relationships from which they can draw support, older adults may have higher levels of social support than do younger adults (Opitz, Gross et al., 2012). Use of social support may represent a particularly effective means of regulating emotions in later life by

reducing negative emotion and increasing positive emotion (Cacioppo, Hughes, Waite, Hawkley, & Thisted, 2006; Steverink & Lindenberg, 2006). People who report experiencing more positive social relationships also score higher on measures of ability to strategically regulate emotions (Lopes et al., 2004; Lopes, Salovey, Cote, Beers, & Petty, 2005) perhaps implying that social support may facilitate other forms of emotion regulation. Together, this evidence supports the notion that, with age, adults become better at utilizing social resources to regulate emotion.

SITUATION SELECTION AND/OR MODIFICATION

Selecting or changing situations in such a way as to facilitate the avoidance/minimization of non-desired states and/or attainment of desired states is one emotion regulation strategy that may increase with age because it does not rely on executive functions and because it does rely on skills that appear to improve with age: knowledge about emotions, and, in particular, affective forecasting (Blanchard-Fields, Mienaltowski, & Seay, 2007; Scheibe, Mata, & Carstensen, 2011). Although available data provide only somewhat indirect evidence, studies suggest that older adults are more likely to effectively avoid (or avoid escalating) unpleasant social situations (Birditt et al., 2005; Blanchard-Fields, 2007; Blanchard-Fields et al., 1997; Charles & Carstensen, 2008; Charles & Piazza, 2009) and experience lower negative emotion in conflict situations (Charles, Piazza, Luong, & Almeida, 2009). This ability may be specific to social contexts because, in nonsocial problem situations, older adults are at least as likely as young adults to continue engaging in problem-focused (as compared to avoidant) coping (Blanchard-Fields, 2007; Blanchard-Fields et al., 2007). Perhaps as a result of increased ability to avoid unpleasant situations, exposure to daily stressors, particularly social ones, generally declines with age (Birditt et al., 2005; Stawski, Sliwinski, Almeida, & Smyth, 2008). Successful avoidance of situations that engender negative emotions and seeking out of situations that engender positive emotions in the service of emotion regulation might be due to increased understanding of what constitutes the most effective emotion-regulatory strategy in each particular context (Blanchard-Fields, 2007).

ACCEPTANCE

Given that it is not always possible to avoid negative emotional situations, acceptance is considered an effective strategy for managing the negative emotions that can result. Rather than simply giving up (as the term may at first glance suggest), acceptance is defined as the process of engaging with (vs. avoiding) negative experiences without judging them to be detrimental (Hayes, Luoma, Bond, Masuda, & Lillis, 2006). Acceptance is a promising candidate to consider as an emotion regulation strategy that may improve with age, for two reasons. First, acceptance does not appear to rely on cognitive functions that decline with age (Schloss & Haaga, 2011). Second, theoretical support of the idea that age is associated with increased acceptance comes from the literature on wisdom. *Wisdom* has been defined as a knowledge system that governs the conduct and understanding of life (Baltes & Smith, 2008). A key component of wisdom is acceptance of reality, including uncertainty, unpredictability, and impermanence and the negative emotions that often accompany these experiences (Ardelt, 2000). If we allow that wisdom generally increases with age (Clayton, 1982; Tentori, Osherson, Hasher, & May, 2001) and that acceptance is a key component of wisdom, it seems likely that acceptance may also increase with age.

A recent study found support for the hypothesis that acceptance increases with age (Shallcross, Ford, Floerke, & Mauss, 2013). A community sample of 340 adults, aged 21–73 years, completed measures of acceptance as well as multiple experiential and physiological indices of trait and state negative affect up to 6 months later. As expected, age was associated with greater acceptance, as well as with lower anger and anxiety (but not sadness) across measurement modalities. Moreover, acceptance mediated age-related decreases in anger and anxiety. These results suggest that, as hypothesized, acceptance increases with age and creates the possibility that acceptance may be an important mechanism in the link between aging and reductions in certain classes of negative emotion.

Discussion, Interpretations, and Future Directions

Although the number experimental works examining lifespan differences in emotion regulation has substantially increased across the past decade, the field remains in its infancy (Consedine, 2011a). Certainly, effective emotion regulation is a critical adaptive capacity in both younger (Bonanno et al., 2004; Westphal, Seivert, & Bonanno, 2010) and older (Carstensen et al., 2003; Charles & Carstensen, 2010; Consedine, 2011a) samples.

However, core descriptive questions regarding normative patterns of improvement or change are yet to be definitively answered, as are subsidiary questions regarding the typical targets of emotion regulation at different stages of development, the capacities needed for various forms of regulation, and the means by which individuals with fluctuating capacities attain regulatory ends. Similarly indistinct are questions regarding the links between emotion regulatory performance and the physical, social, and psychological health outcomes that are increasingly a focus in psychological research. In the preceding section, a developmental functionalist view of emotion regulation across adulthood was presented. In the next section, we revisit the available experimental work from this perspective before outlining preliminary conclusions, highlighting themes, and offering some directions for future empirical development.

Although other bodies of research (e.g., lifespan attachment and personality research) are relevant to the questions considered here, we elected to concentrate our review on studies employing *experimental* designs in which regulatory "success" was directly assessed (rather than inferred) and in which demand characteristics are likely lessened. To begin, it is worth noting that although there is an ongoing increase in the number of studies, the current corpus of data remains small; more work is quite clearly needed. Consistent with prior writers, however, the broadest conclusion we might draw from the current body of experimental work is that aging does not appear to bring a unilateral decline in emotion regulatory ability. Consistent with assertions from developmental functionalism, however, there are some early indications that different types of emotion regulatory task show distinct patterns of improvement and decline across age groups. Of particular note is the previous suggestion (Consedine, 2011a) that normative age reductions in executive-type tasks should mean that regulatory tasks relying on such capacities should be relatively impaired whereas those linked to positive emotion generation or social functioning might show preservation or improvement.

Findings were mixed regarding this broad prediction. Consistent with expectation, there appear to be improvements in types of emotion regulation linked to the generation of positive states (Charles et al., 2003; Isaacowitz et al., 2009; Isaacowitz et al., 2006; Mather & Carstensen, 2005; Phillips et al., 2008; Shiota & Levenson, 2009), in social contexts and/or through use of social supports as a regulatory resource (Akiyama et al., 2003; Birditt & Fingerman, 2005; Birditt et al., 2005; Lopes et al., 2004; 2005; Opitz, Gross et al., 2012), in situational selection/modification (Birditt et al., 2005; Blanchard-Fields, 2007; Blanchard-Fields et al., 1997; Blanchard-Fields et al., 2007; Charles & Carstensen, 2008; Charles & Piazza, 2009; Charles et al., 2009; Stawski et al., 2008), and, at least according to preliminary data, in acceptance (Shallcross et al., 2013).

Conversely, however, our review of empirical studies found that expressive suppression—which is thought to rely on executive functioning (Baumeister et al., 1998; Richards & Gross, 2000; Schmeichel et al., 2008)—found few differences across age groups (Emery & Hess, 2011; Kunzmann et al., 2005; Magai et al., 2006; Phillips et al., 2008; Shiota & Levenson, 2009). Although the absence of effects may reflect insufficient declines in executive functioning among the samples studied to date (Shiota & Levenson, 2009), the pattern might be taken as broadly inconsistent with developmental functionalism's assertions. Recall, however, that, in line with several other authors (Emery & Hess, 2011), developmental functionalism interprets data indicating differential effects of expressive regulation on experiential (Magai et al., 2006) or cognitive (Emery & Hess, 2011) systems as likely indicating that older and young adults achieve expressive control via different *tactics* (Consedine, 2011a). It may be that some forms of emotion regulation are, in fact, less (capacity) demanding for older groups (Scheibe & Blanchard-Fields, 2009), perhaps because the data are indexing age-related increases in the automatization of common forms of regulation with age (see below).

As expected, given the importance that developmental functionalism places on executive processes as a core capacity for real-time regulation (Ochsner & Gross, 2005), studies of reappraisal to decrease negative emotion showed a consistent reduction in this ability across age groups (Opitz, Rauch et al., 2012; Shiota & Levenson, 2009). These studies are significant for two reasons. First, the Opitz, et al. (2012) study provides among the first evidence of differential neural activation during emotion regulatory tasks across age groups, with lower activation in the left ventrolateral prefrontal cortex among older adults. Although differences in activation did not mediate age-related decrements in reappraisal ability, the study provides one of the few demonstrations that certain types of emotion regulatory task may be associated with age-related variation in activation in theoretically expected brain regions.

Second, because older samples report using cognitive reappraisal *more frequently* than do younger adults (John & Gross, 2004), these findings suggest that there may be clear capacity constraints to regulatory *success*.

More broadly, developmental functionalism offers a useful lens to consider the implications of the findings to date and to both consider what they are telling us as well as within which to consider the "next steps" in this important lifespan research agenda. In beginning to evaluate these findings, it is worth noting that age-related improvements were more consistently evident when *experience* was being regulated (positive reappraisal, use of social support/coping, situational selection/modification, and acceptance) but less reliable for regulatory tasks necessitating expressive control. Because different components of emotions have distinct functions (Averill, 1994), they likely represent distinct regulatory challenges (Consedine, 2011a). In particular, the regulation of signals (expressions) has capacity requirements that are distinct from those needed to regulate experience (Consedine et al., 2002). Developmentally then, this pattern may be telling us that the resource base necessary for effective experiential regulation is either maintained or enhanced with age whereas that needed for expressive regulation declines.

Although decrements in negative reappraisal must be borne in mind, one intriguing area for future work lies in automatic emotion regulation (AER). Although it is unclear whether all forms of AER are best characterized as skills, insofar as they are (a) not typically *volitionally* deployed (Mauss et al., 2007) and, in some instances such as repression, (b) may not be *capable* of being brought under voluntary control, AER minimizes resource demand and may thus become more common and useful with age. Although no research to date has directly examined age differences in AER (Consedine, 2011a), two considerations suggest that such studies may be of benefit. First, studies of personality factors closely linked to regulatory styles such as adult attachment consistently show greater dismissiveness in older cohorts (Consedine & Magai, 2003; Davila, Burge, & Hammen, 1997; Fiori, Consedine, & Magai, 2009; Kafetsios & Sideridis, 2006; Magai, Hunziker, Mesias, & Culver, 2000; Mickelson, Kessler, & Shaver, 1997; Webster, 1997; Zhang & Labouvie-Vief, 2004), implying that these adults will have more restrictive expressive and experiential goals (Consedine, Fiori, & Magai, 2012; Consedine & Magai, 2003). Assuming that these goals are fashioned in early life creates the possibility that current cohorts of older adults may habitually down-regulate the expression or experience of certain negative emotions and, thus, become differentially efficient at it.

Second, recent findings indicative of reduced effects of emotion regulation on other processes may imply that older adults are increasing their reliance on AER—in developmental functionalism, this is seen as a tactical adaptation to the problem posed by fewer resources available for online regulation (c.f., Baltes, 1997). In the Emery and Hess (2011) study, for example, suppression instructions led to reduced memory for emotional pictures in young adults but did not impair memory in older adults (Emery & Hess, 2011). Similarly, instructions to reduce negative feelings in response to a disgusting film clip impaired older adults' performance on a working memory task less than it did younger adults' performance (Scheibe & Blanchard-Fields, 2009). Reduced decrements in cognitive performance when regulating among older individuals are consistent with the possibility that older adults may make greater use of automatized forms of regulation. In theory, more habitual expressive suppression might lead to a situation in which fewer executive resources are consumed during suppression and, thus, more resources are available to concentrate on the emotional material. Alternately, such findings may also reflect greater compartmentalization of mental processes and/or the deployment of alternate tactics to accomplish the same regulatory goal (Magai et al., 2006). In contrast to the Emery and Hess (2011) study, the Magai et al. (2006) report showed that expressive suppression had a *greater* impact on both self-reported experience and language use among older adults, a finding that was interpreted as indicating suppression was being partially accomplished by controlling experience, such that a smaller amount of expressive regulation was required to begin with. Studies examining the possible moderational effects of trait regulatory tendencies on experimental regulatory performance are one approach to these questions.

However, although automatization appears a useful avenue within which to extend our understanding of age differences in emotion regulatory performance, an interpretation of improved experiential regulation as stemming from greater automatization would necessarily struggle to interpret findings indicating that older adults perform more poorly when asked to reappraise in a manner that decreases negative emotion (Opitz, Gross et al., 2012; Shiota & Levenson, 2009). If, (a) cohorts of older adults have more experiential goals aimed at minimizing negative emotional experience and (b) automatization occurs as a function of habitual deployment (i.e., repeated use across a lifespan), we might have expected greater ability in this area. That the available data point in the opposite direction may imply several possibilities worth examining. First, it may be that positive versus negative reappraisals rely on different mechanisms or capacities or that losses in executive capacity are insufficiently offset by any small gains acquired through automatization. Alternately, it may be a motivational or regulatory target issue, insofar as older adults are known to place a premium on positive emotional experience; it may be that they are more motivated regarding increasing positive (vs. decreasing negative) experience.

Conclusion

Recent years have seen somewhat of a groundswell in experimental studies examining aspects of emotion regulation across the adult lifespan. Despite ongoing insight, this literature remains in a fledgling state, and the review presented here suggests that three interrelated areas of study would provide fertile avenues for increasing our understanding of lifespan differences in emotion regulation.

1. What *tasks and goals* (emotional and otherwise) are typical at different stages of adulthood? How well differentiated are these goals, and can we move beyond hedonic characterizations to examine age-related differences in discrete emotions and/or the possibility that the regulatory goals of adults from different stages of development vary in terms of intensity, frequency, and duration?

2. What *capacities* are needed for effective emotion regulation, and how do they vary at different stages of adulthood? How should capacities be conceptualized, manipulated, and measured and in which research designs?

3. What are the age differences in the *tactics* used to achieve emotional and other goals? In particular, are there are differences in the ways adults from different stages of development (or with different capacity sets) accomplish reactive versus anticipatory regulatory goals?

References

Akiyama, H., Antonucci, T., Takahashi, K., & Langfahl, E. S. (2003). Negative interactions in close relationships across the life span. *Journals of Gerontology: Series B: Psychological Sciences and Social Sciences, 58B*(2), P70–P79.

Ardelt, M. (2000). Antecedents and effects of wisdom in old age: A longitudinal perspective on aging well. *Research on Aging, 22*(4), 360–394.

Averill, J. R. (1994). Emotions are many splendored things. In P. Ekman & R. J. Davidson (Eds.), *The nature of emotions: Fundamental questions* (pp. 99–102). New York: Oxford University Press.

Baltes, P. B. (1987). Theoretical propositions of life-span developmental psychology: On the dynamics between growth and decline. *Developmental Psychology, 23*(5), 611–626.

Baltes, P. B. (1997). On the incomplete architecture of human ontogeny: Selection, optimization and compensation as foundation of developmental theory. In U. M. Staudinger & U. Lindenberger (Eds.), *Understanding human development: Dialogues with lifespan psychology* (pp. 17–43). Dordrecht, Netherlands: Kluwer.

Baltes, P. B., & Smith, J. (2008). The fascination of wisdom: Its nature, ontogeny, and function. *Perspectives on Psychological Science, 3*(1), 56–64.

Barrett, L. F. (1997). The relationships among momentary emotion experiences, personality descriptions, and retrospective ratings of emotion. *Personality & Social Psychology Bulletin 23*(10) (Oct. 1997): 1100–1110, 23(10), 1100–1110.

Baumeister, R. F., Bratslavsky, E., Muraven, M., & Tice, D. M. (1998). Ego depletion: Is the active self a limited resource? *Journal of Personality and Social Psychology, 74*(5), 1252–1265.

Birditt, K. S., & Fingerman, K. L. (2005). Do we get better at picking our battles? Age group differences in descriptions of behavioral reactions to interpersonal tensions. *Journals of Gerontology: Series B: Psychological Sciences and Social Sciences, 60B*(3), P121–P128.

Birditt, K. S., Fingerman, K. L., & Almeida, D. M. (2005). Age differences in exposure and reactions to interpersonal tensions: A daily diary study. *Psychology & Aging, 20*(2), 330–340.

Bjorklund, D. F., & Bering, J. M. (2002). The evolved child: Applying evolutionary developmental psychology to modern schooling. *Learning & Individual Differences, 12*, 347–373.

Bjorklund, D. F., & Pellegrini, A. D. (2002). *The origins of human nature: Evolutionary developmental psychology*. Washington, DC: American Psychological Association.

Blanchard-Fields, F. (2007). Everyday problem solving and emotion: an adult developmental perspective. *Current Directions in Psychological Science, 16*(1), 26–31.

Blanchard-Fields, F., Chen, Y., & Norris, L. (1997). Everyday problem solving across the adult life span: Influence of domain specificity and cognitive appraisal. *Psychology and Aging, 12*, 684–693.

Blanchard-Fields, F., Mienaltowski, A., & Seay, R. B. (2007). Age differences in everyday problem-solving effectiveness: Older adults select more effective strategies for interpersonal problems. *Journals of Gerontology: Series B: Psychological Sciences and Social Sciences, 62B*(1), P61–P64.

Bonanno, G. A., Papa, A., Lalande, K., Westphal, M., & Coifman, K. (2004). The importance of being flexible: The ability to both enhance and suppress emotional expression predicts long term adjustment. *Psychological Science, 15*(7), 482–487.

Bowlby, J. (1969). *Attachment and loss: Vol. I. Attachment.* New York: Basic Books.

Brown, W. M., & Consedine, N. S. (2004). Just how happy is the happy puppet? an emotion signalling and kinship theory perspective on the behavioral phenotype of Angelman Syndrome children. *Medical Hypotheses, 63*(3), 377–385. doi: 10.1016/j.mehy.2004.05.010

Cacioppo, J. T., Hughes, M. E., Waite, L. J., Hawkley, L. C., & Thisted, R. A. (2006). Loneliness as a specific risk factor for depressive symptoms: Cross-sectional and longitudinal analyses. *Psychology and Aging, 21*(1), 140–151.

Carstensen, L. L., Fung, H. H., & Charles, S. T. (2003). Socioemotional selectivity theory and the regulation of emotion in the second half of life. *Motivation and Emotion, 27*(2), 103–123.

Carstensen, L. L., & Jacobs, J. E. (1993). Motivation for social contact across the life span: A theory of socioemotional selectivity. *Nebraska Symposium on Motivation, 1992: Developmental perspectives on motivation.* (pp. 209–254). Lincoln: University of Nebraska Press.

Carstensen, L. L., & Löckenhoff, C. E. (2003). Aging, emotion, and evolution: The bigger picture. *Proceedings of the National Academy of Sciences, 1000*, 152–179.

Carstensen, L. L., & Mikels, J. A. (2005). At the intersection of emotion and cognition. Aging and the positivity effect. *Current Directions in Psychological Science, 14*, 117–121.

Carstensen, L. L., Turan, B., Scheibe, S., Ram, N., Ersner-Hershfield, H., Samanez-Larkin, G. R., et al. (2011). Emotional experience improves with age: Evidence based on over 10 years of experience sampling. *Psychology and Aging, 26*(1), 21–33.

Charles, S. T., & Carstensen, L. L. (2008). Unpleasant situations elicit different emotional responses in younger and older adults. *Psychology and Aging, 23*(3), 495–504.

Charles, S. T., & Carstensen, L. L. (2010). Social and emotional aging. *Annual Review of Psychology, 61*, 383–409.

Charles, S. T., Mather, M., & Carstensen, L. L. (2003). Aging and emotional memory: The forgettable nature of negative images for older adults. *Journal of Experimental Psychology: General, 132*(2), 310–324.

Charles, S. T., & Piazza, J. R. (2009). Age differences in affective well-being: Context matters. *Social and Personality Psychology Compass, 3*(5), 711–724.

Charles, S. T., Piazza, J. R., Luong, G., & Almeida, D. M. (2009). Now you see it, now you don't: age differences in affective reactivity to social tensions. *Psychology and Aging, 24*(3), 645–653.

Clayton, V. (1982). Wisdom and intelligence: The nature and function of knowledge in the later years. *International Journal of Aging and Human Development, 15*(4), 315–321.

Consedine, N. S. (2011a). Capacities, targets, and tactics: Lifespan emotion regulation viewed from developmental functionalism. In I. Nyclicek, A. Vingerhoets, & M. Zeelenberg (Eds.), *Emotion regulation and wellbeing* (pp. 13–29). New York: Springer.

Consedine, N. S. (2011b). Emotion, regulation, and learning across the adult lifespan: Implications from developmental functionalism. In C. Hoare (Ed.), *Oxford handbook of reciprocal adult development and learning* (2nd ed., pp. 132–154). New York: Oxford University Press.

Consedine, N. S., Fiori, K. L., & Magai, C. (2012). Regulating emotion expression and regulating emotion experience: Divergent associations with dimensions of attachment among older women. *Attachment & Human Development, 14*(5), 477–500.

Consedine, N. S., & Magai, C. (2003). Attachment and emotion experience in later life: The view from emotions theory. *Attachment & Human Development, 5*, 165–187.

Consedine, N. S., Magai, C., & Bonanno, G. A. (2002). Moderators of the emotion inhibition-health relationship: A review and research agenda. *Review of General Psychology, 6*(2), 204–228. doi: 10.1037//1089-2680.6.2.204

Consedine, N. S., & Moskowitz, J. T. (2007). The role of discrete emotions in health outcomes: a critical review. *Journal of Applied and Preventive Psychology, 12*(2), 59–75. doi: 10.1016/j.appsy.2007.09.001

Consedine, N. S., Strongman, K. T., & Magai, C. (2003). Emotions and behavior: Data from a cross-cultural recognition study. *Cognition and Emotion, 17*(6), 881–902. doi: 10.1080/02699930302312

Davila, J., Burge, D., & Hammen, C. (1997). Why does attachment style change? *Journal of Personality & Social Psychology, 73*(4), 826–838.

De Meersman, R. E., & Stein, P. K. (2006). Vagal modulation and aging. *Biological Psychology, 74*(2), 165–176.

Dennett, D. C. (1995). *Darwins dangerous idea.* New York: Simon & Schuster.

Eisenberg, N. (2000). Emotion, regulation, and moral development. *Annual Review of Psychology, 51*, 665–697.

Eisenberg, N., Sadovsky, A., & Spinrad, T. L. (2005). Associations of emotion-related regulation with language skills, emotion knowledge and academic outcomes. *New Directions in Child and Adolescent Development, 109*, 109–118.

Ellis, B. J., & Garber, J. (2000). Psychosocial antecedents of variation in girls' pubertal timing: Maternal depression, stepfather presence, and marital and family stress. *Child Development, 71*(2), 485–501.

Emery, L., & Hess, T. M. (2011). Cognitive consequences of expressive regulation in older adults. *Psychology and Aging, 26*(2), 388–396. doi: 10.1037/a0020041

Fiori, K. L., Consedine, N. S., & Magai, C. (2009). Patterns of relating among men and women from seven ethnic groups. *Journal of Cross-Cultural Gerontology, 24*(2), 121–141.

Fridlund, A. J. (1994). *Human facial expression: An evolutionary view.* San Diego, CA: Academic Press.

Gilhooly, K. J., Phillips, L. H., Wynn, V., Logie, R. H., & Della Sala, S. (1999). Planning processes and age in the five-disc Tower of London task. *Thinking & Reasoning, 5*, 339–361.

Gottlieb, G. (2002a). Developmental-behavioral initiation of evolutionary change. *Psychological Review, 109*(2), 211–218.

Gottlieb, G. (2002b). On the epigenetic evolution of species specific perception: The developmental manifold concept. *Cognitive Development, 17*, 1287–1300.

Gross, J. J. (1998). The emerging field of emotion regulation: An integrative review. *Review of General Psychology, 2*, 271–299.

Gross, J. J. (2001). Emotion regulation in adulthood: Timing is everything. *Current Directions in Psychological Science, 10*(6), 214–219.

Gross, J. J., Carstensen, L. L., Pasupathi, M., Tsai, J., Goetestam-Skorpen, C. G., & Hsu, A. Y. C. (1997). Emotion and aging: Experience, expression, and control. *Psychology and Aging, 12*(4), 590–599.

Gross, J. J., Richards, J. M., & John, O. P. (2006). Emotion regulation in everyday life. In D. K. Snyder, J. Simpson, & J. N. Hughes (Eds.), *Emotion regulation in couples and families: Pathways to dysfunction and health* (pp. 13–35). Washington, DC: American Psychological Association.

Gross, J. J., & Thompson, R. A. (2007). Emotion regulation: conceptual foundations. In J. J. Gross (Ed.), *Handbook of emotion regulation* (pp. 3–24). New York: Guilford Press.

Gurven, M., & Kaplan, H. S. (2009). Beyond the grandmother hypothesis: evolutionary models of human longevity. In J. Sokolovsky (Ed.), *The cultural context of aging: worldwide perspectives* (3rd ed., pp. 53–66). Westport, CT: Praeger.

Hackenbracht, J., & Tamir, M. (2010). Preferences for sadness when eliciting help: Instrumental motives in sadness regulation. *Motivation and Emotion, 34*(3), 306–315.

Hayes, S. C., Luoma, J. B., Bond, F. W., Masuda, A., & Lillis, J. (2006). Acceptance and commitment therapy: Model, processes and outcomes. *Behaviour Research and Therapy, 44*(1), 1–25.

Heckhausen, J. (1997). Development regulation across adulthood: primary and secondary control of age-related challenges. *Developmental Psychology, 33*(1), 176–187.

Hernandez-Blasi, C., & Bjorklund, D. F. (2003). Evolutionary Developmental Psychology: A new tool for better understanding human ontogeny. *Human Development, 46*, 259–281.

Isaacowitz, D. M., Toner, K., & Neupert, S. D. (2009). Use of gaze for real-time mood regulation: Effects of age and attentional functioning. *Psychology and Aging, 24*(4), 989–994.

Isaacowitz, D. M., Wadlinger, H. A., Goren, D., & Wilson, H. R. (2006). Is there an age-related positivity effect in visual attention? A comparison of two methodologies. *Emotion, 6*(3), 511–516.

Izard, C. E. (1991). *The psychology of emotions.* New York: Plenum Press.

John, O. P., & Gross, J. J. (2004). Healthy and unhealthy emotion regulation: Personality processes, individual differences, and life span development. *Journal of Personality, 72*(6), 1301–1333.

Kachel, A. F., Premo, L. S., & Hublin, J.- J. (2011). Grandmothering and natural selection. *Proceedings of the Royal Society B, 278*, 384–391.

Kafetsios, K., & Sideridis, G. D. (2006). Attachment, social support and well-being in young and older adults. *Journal of Health Psychology, 11*(6), 863–875.

Keltner, D., Ellsworth, P. C. E., & Edwards, K. (1993). Beyond simple pessimism: Effects of sadness and anger on social perception. *Journal of Personality & Social Psychology, 64*, 740–752.

Kray, J., & Lindenberger, U. (2000). Adult age differences in task switching. *Psychology & Aging, 15*, 126–147.

Kunzmann, U., Kupperbusch, C. S., & Levenson, R. W. (2005). Behavioral inhibition and amplification during emotional arousal: a comparison of two age groups. *Psychology and Aging, 20*(1), 144–158.

Labouvie-Vief, G., Chiodo, L. M., Goguen, L. A., Diehl, M., & Orwoll, L. (1995). Representations of self across the life span. *Psychology and Aging, 10*(3), 404–415.

Labouvie-Vief, G., Hakin-Larson, J., DeVoe, M., & Schoeberlein, S. (1989). Emotions and self-regulation: A lifespan view. *Human Development, 32*, 279–299.

Labouvie-Vief, G., Lumley, M. A., Jain, E., & Heinze, H. (2003). Age and gender differences in cardiac reactivity and subjective emotion responses to emotional autobiographical memories. *Emotion, 3*(2), 115–126.

Lang, F. R. (2001). Regulation of social relationships in later adulthood. *Journals of Gerontology: Series B: Psychological Sciences and Social Sciences, 56B*(6), P321–P326.

Lang, F. R., & Carstensen, L. L. (1994). Close emotional relationships in late life: Further support for proactive aging in the social domain. *Psychology and Aging, 9*(2), 315–324.

Levenson, R. W. (1994). Human emotion: A functional view. In P. Ekman & R. J. Davidson (Eds.), *The nature* of emotion: Fundamental questions (pp. 123–126). New York: Oxford University Press.

Lopes, P. N., Brackett, M. A., Nezlek, J. B., Schutz, A., Sellin, I., & Salovey, P. (2004). Emotional intelligence and social interaction. Personality and Social Psychology Bulletin, 30(8), 1018–1034. doi: 10.1177/0146167204264762

Lopes, P. N., Salovey, P., Cote, S., Beers, M., & Petty, R. E. (2005). Emotion regulation abilities and the quality of social interaction. Emotion, 5(1), 113–118. doi: 10.1037/1528-3542.5.1.113

Magai, C., Consedine, N. S., Krivoshekova, Y. S., McPherson, R., & Kudadjie-Gyamfi, E. (2006). Emotion experience and expression across the adult lifespan: Insights from a multi-modal assessment study. Psychology & Aging, 21(1), 303–317.

Magai, C., Hunziker, Mesias, W., & Culver, L. C. (2000). Adult attachment styles and emotional biases. International Journal of Behavioral Development, 24, 301–309.

Mather, M., & Carstensen, L. L. (2005). Aging and motivated cognition: The positivity effect in attention and memory. Trends in Cognitive Sciences, 9(10), 496–502.

Mauss, I. B., Bunge, S. A., & Gross, J. J. (2007). Automatic emotion regulation. Social and Personality Psychology Compass, 1, 146–167. doi: 10.1111/j.1751-9004.2007.00005.x

Mauss, I. B., Evers, C., Wilhelm, F. H., & Gross, J. J. (2006). How to bite your tongue without blowing your top: Implicit evaluation of emotion regulation predicts affective responding to anger provocation Personality and Social Psychology Bulletin, 32(5), 589–602.

Maylor, E. A., & Lavie, N. (1998). The influence of perceptual load on age differences in selective attention. Psychology & Aging, 13, 563–573.

McRae, K., Ochsner, K. N., Mauss, I. B., Gabrieli, J. J. D., & Gross, J. J. (2008). Gender differences in emotion regulation: An fMRI study of cognitive reappraisal. Group Processes and Intergroup Relations, 11(2), 143–162.

Mickelson, K. D., Kessler, R. C., & Shaver, P. R. (1997). Adult attachment in a nationally representative sample. Journal of Personality & Social Psychology, 73, 1092–1106.

Morgan, D. L. (1988). Age differences in social network participation. Journals of Gerontology: Series B: Psychological and Social Sciences, 43(4), S129–S137.

Muraven, M., Tice, D. M., & Baumeister, R. F. (1998). Self-control as limited resource: Regulatory depletion patterns. Journal of Personality and Social Psychology, 74(3), 774–789.

Nesse, R. M. (1990). Evolutionary explanations of emotions. Human Nature, 1, 261–289.

Nessler, D., Friedman, D., Johnson, R., & Bersick, M. (2007). ERPs suggest that age affects cognitive control but not response conflict detection. Neurobiology of Aging, 28(11), 1769–1782. doi: 10.1016/j.neurobiolaging.2006.07.011

Nielsen, L., Knutson, B., & Carstensen, L. L. (2008). Affect dynamics, affective forecasting, and aging. Emotion, 8(3), 318–330.

Ochsner, K. N., & Gross, J. J. (2005). The cognitive control of emotion. Trends in Cognitive Sciences, 9(5), 242–249.

Opitz, P., Gross, J. J., & Urry, H. (2012). Selection, optimization, and compensation in the domain of emotion regulation: applications to adolescence, older age, and major depressive disorder. Social and Personality Psychology Compass, 6(2), 142–155.

Opitz, P., Rauch, L. C., Terry, D. P., & Urry, H. (2012). Prefrontal mediation of age differences in cognitive reappraisal. Neurobiology of Aging, 33(4), 645–655.

Owren, M. J., & Bachorowski, J.-A. (2001). The evolution of emotional experience: A "selfish-gene" account of smiling and laughter in early hominids and humans. In T. J. Mayne & G. A. Bonanno (Eds.), Emotions: Current issues and future directions (pp. 152–191). New York: Guilford.

Panksepp, J., & Miller, A. M. (1995). Emotions and the aging brain: Regrets and remedies. In C. Magai & S. H. McFadden (Eds.), Handbook of emotion, adult development and aging (pp. 3–26). San Diego, CA: Academic Press.

Phillips, L. H., Henry, J. D., Hosie, J. A., & Milne, A. B. (2008). Effective regulation of the experience and expression of negative affect in old age. Journals of Gerontology: Series B: Psychological Sciences and Social Sciences, 63B(3), P138–P145.

Richards, J. M., & Gross, J. J. (2000). Emotion regulation and memory: The cognitive costs of keeping one's cool. Journal of Personality and Social Psychology, 79(3), 410–424.

Robinson, M. D., & Clore, G. L. (2002). Belief and feeling: Evidence for an accessibility model of emotional self-report. Psychological Bulletin, 128(6), 934–960.

Rusk, N., Tamir, M., & Rothbaum, F. (2011). Performance and learning goals for emotion regulation. Motivation and Emotion, 1–17.

Saarni, C. (1989). Children's understanding of strategic control of emotional expression in social transaction. In C. Saarni & P. Harris (Eds.), Children's understanding of emotion (pp. 181–208). New York: Cambridge University Press.

Scheibe, S., & Blanchard-Fields, F. (2009). Effects of regulating emotions on cognitive performance: What is costly for young adults is not so costly for older adults. Psychology and Aging, 24(1), 217–223.

Scheibe, S., Mata, R., & Carstensen, L. L. (2011). Age differences in affective forecasting and experienced emotion surrounding the 2008 US presidential election. Cognition and Emotion, 25(6), 1029–1044.

Schloss, H. M., & Haaga, D. A. F. (2011). Interrelating behavioral measures of distress tolerance with self-reported experiential avoidance. Journal of Rational-Emotive & Cognitive Behavior Therapy, 29(1), 53–63. doi: 10.1007/s10942-011-0127-3

Schmeichel, B. J., Volokhov, R. N., & Demaree, H. A. (2008). Working memory capacity and the self-regulation of emotional expression and experience. Journal of Personality and Social Psychology, 95(6), 1526–1540.

Schulz, R., Wrosch, C., & Heckhausen, J. (2002). The lifespan theory of control: Issues and evidence. In S. H. Zarit, L. I. Pearlin, & K. W. Schaie (Eds.), Personal control in social and life course contexts (pp. 233–262). New York: Springer.

Shallcross, A. J., Ford, B. Q., Floerke, V. A., & Mauss, I. B. (2013). Getting better with age: the relationship between age, acceptance, and negative affect. Journal of Personality & Social Psychology, 104, 734–749.

Shiota, M. N., & Levenson, R. W. (2009). Effects of aging on experimentally instructed detached reappraisal, positive reappraisal, and emotional behavior suppression. Psychology and Aging, 24(4), 890–900.

Stawski, R. S., Sliwinski, M. J., Almeida, D. M., & Smyth, J. M. (2008). Reported exposure and emotional reactivity to daily stressors: The roles of adult age and global perceived stress. Psychology and Aging, 23(1), 52–61.

Steverink, N., & Lindenberg, S. (2006). Which social needs are important for subjective well-being? What happens to them with aging? Psychology and Aging, 21(2), 281–290.

Tamir, M. (2011). The maturing field of emotion regulation. *Emotion Review, 3*(1), 3–7.

Tamir, M., & Ford, B. Q. (2009). Choosing to be afraid: Preferences for fear as a function of goal pursuit. *Emotion, 9*(4),488–497.

Tamir, M., Mitchell, C., & Gross, J. J. (2008). Hedonic and instrumental motives in anger regulation. *Psychological Science, 19*(4), 324–328.

Tentori, K., Osherson, D., Hasher, L., & May, C. (2001). Wisdom and aging: Irrational preferences in college students but not older adults. *Cognition, 81*(3), B87–B96.

Thompson, R. A., & Meyer, S. (2007). Socialization of emotion regulation in the family. In J. J. Gross (Ed.), *Handbook of emotion regulation* (pp. 249–268). New York: Guilford.

Tooby, J., & Cosmides, L. (2008). The evolutionary psychology of the emotions and their relationship to internal regulatory variables. In M. Lewis, J. Haviland-Jones, & L. F. Barrett (Eds.), *Handbook of emotions* (3rd ed., pp. 114–137). New York: Guilford.

Troy, A. S., Shallcross, A. J., Wilhelm, F. H., & Mauss, I. B. (2010). Seeing the silver lining: Cognitive reappraisal ability moderates the relationship between stress and depression. *Emotion, 10*, 783–795.

Urry, H. L., & Gross, J. J. (2010). Emotion regulation in older age. *Current Directions in Psychological Science, 19*(6), 352–357.

Webster, J. D. (1997). Attachment style and well-being in elderly adults: A preliminary investigation. *Canadian Journal of Aging, 16*(1), 101–111.

Westphal, M., & Bonanno, G. A. (2004). Emotion self-regulation. In M. Beauregard (Ed.), *Consciousness, emotional self-regulation, and the brain* (pp. 1–34). Amsterdam: John Benjamins Publishing Company.

Westphal, M., Seivert, N. H., & Bonanno, G. A. (2010). Expressive flexibility. *Emotion, 10*(1), 92–100.

Zhang, F., & Labouvie-Vief, G. (2004). Stability and fluctuation in adult attachment style over a 6-year period. *Attachment & Human Development, 6*(4), 419–437.

Reconciling Cognitive Decline and Increased Well-Being With Age: The Role of Increased Emotion Regulation Efficiency

Erin Senesac Morgan *and* Susanne Scheibe

Abstract

Despite decreases in cognitive control with advancing age, older adults maintain high levels of well-being. On the surface, this is surprising, given that emotion regulation, which is often associated with well-being, has been shown to require cognitive control. This chapter discusses three possible explanations for these seemingly contradictory findings, with a particular focus on the recent hypothesis that older adults regulate emotions more efficiently than young adults, therefore requiring less cognitive control for successful regulation.

Key Words: emotion regulation, development, aging, cognitive control, well-being, affect, positivity effect, motivation, automatization

Western societies are "aging" with remarkable speed. In most developed countries, by 2050, there will be twice as many people over 60 as under 15 years of age (United Nations 2001). For many people, the idea of aging elicits negative expectations and fears (Hummert, Garstka, Shaner, & Strahm, 1994; Posthuma & Campion, 2009; Röcke & Lachman, 2008). And indeed, older adults normatively experience reduced physical fitness and health, cognitive slowing, and memory decline, as well as social losses. However, despite these negative aging correlates, research on emotional aging paints a surprisingly positive picture in which emotional balance is more likely to be achieved than at earlier life stages (e.g., Carstensen, Pasupathi, Mayr, & Nesselroade, 2000). Although no two people age the same way, research suggests that stable if not improved affective well-being and emotional stability are the norm rather than the exception at least into the 7th and 8th decades of life (e.g., Carstensen et al., 2000, 2011; Charles, Reynolds, & Gatz, 2001; Kessler & Staudinger, 2009). This finding has been termed the "well-being paradox of aging" (Kunzmann, Little, & Smith, 2000). One facet of this paradox is the seemingly contradictory relationship between older adults' affective well-being and cognitive decline. Older adults' high levels of well-being are often explained by motivational shifts, as well as by enhanced expertise in regulating emotions in older ages (Charles & Carstensen, 2010; Scheibe & Carstensen, 2010). Yet emotion regulation requires cognitive control (Ochsner & Gross, 2005), and one of the most predictable changes with age is cognitive decline. How can these divergent trajectories of well-being and cognition be reconciled? This chapter explores three possible explanations for how older adults maintain well-being in the face of cognitive declines. Specifically, we review (a) evidence for biological changes that may reduce emotional reactivity and therefore decrease the degree of cognitive resources needed to regulate emotions, (b) evidence for changes in motivation that may lead older adults to devote greater proportions of their cognitive resources to emotion regulation, and (c) evidence for changes in emotion-regulation strategy use that may lead to more efficient use of available cognitive resources.

Older Adults Maintain Emotional Well-being

Despite old age being a period of increasing losses in many domains of functioning, older adults appear to maintain a very positive profile of emotional experience, even in very old age (Charles & Carstensen, 2007; Chipperfield, Perry, & Weiner, 2003). Specifically, the frequency and intensity of positive and negative affect has been hypothesized to change, although results are somewhat mixed. Researchers have found small decreases in positive affect in some studies (Charles et al., 2001; Costa, McCrae, & Zonderman, 1987; Diener & Suh, 1997; Isaacowitz & Smith, 2003; Kunzmann et al., 2000; Stacey & Gatz, 1991), age-related stability in positive affect (Carstensen et al., 2000; Lawton, Kleban & Dean, 1993; Lawton, Kleban, Rajagopal, & Dean, 1992; Malatesta & Kalnok, 1984), and increases in positive affect with age in other studies (Diehl, Hay, & Berg, 2011; Kessler & Staudinger, 2009; Mroczek & Kolarz, 1998). It is possible that mixed results are a product of which emotions different studies use to measure positive affect, as low arousal positive affect appears to increase with age, but high arousal positive affect does not (Kessler & Staudinger, 2009; Ross & Mirowsky, 2008; Scheibe, English, Tsai & Carstensen, 2012). Further, other variables, like health, can impact the relationship of affect and age. For example, Kunzmann et al. (2000) found no differences in positive affect with age until health was accounted for. Then, a positive relationship with age was revealed, possibly because poor health with age increases opportunities for negative emotions. In addition to possible changes in the frequency or intensity of positive emotions, older adults appear to experience a higher ratio of positive-to-negative affect (Carstensen et al., 2011; Diehl et al., 2011). Furthermore, older adults may be more likely to have more stable positive affective states, with positive emotions lasting for longer periods of time for older age groups (Carstensen et al., 2000).

Changes in negative affect with age appear to be more consistent. Although a few studies find no change in negative affect with age (Diener & Suh, 1997; Kunzmann et al., 2000; Mroczek & Kolarz, 1998), the majority of studies do find that negative affect declines with age in both cross-sectional (Carstensen et al., 2000; Costa et al., 1987; Gross et al., 1997; Kessler & Staudinger, 2009; Lawton et al., 1992; Pethtel & Chen, 2010) and longitudinal studies (Charles et al., 2001, Stacey & Gatz, 1991; Windsor & Anstey, 2010). Furthermore, older adults' negative affect appears to be less long-lasting than young adults', with older adults' negative affect decreasing more quickly in experience sampling studies (Carstensen et al., 2000).

The previously discussed studies were largely conducted by asking participants to either rate their emotions many times across a period of time or by asking people to retrospect about how they usually feel. Other studies have measured changes in emotional reactions with age by exposing participants to emotional stimuli and examining their reactions. These types of studies also appear to support the idea that older adults experience a more positive emotion profile. Older adults report more positive and less negative emotions in response to hypothetical emotional scenarios (Löckenhoff, Costa, & Lane, 2008). Older adults also react with less anger when listening to audiotapes of people criticizing them (Charles & Carstensen, 2008). When describing social interactions with problematic partners, older adults are less likely than young adults to mention experiencing anger, they describe anger as less intense and of shorter duration, and they describe distress as less intense (Birditt & Fingerman, 2003). They are also more likely to forgive a hypothetical transgression by a friend (Allemand, 2008; Cheng & Yim, 2008). However, older adults may be more likely to experience sadness or loneliness in these situations (Birditt & Fingerman, 2003; Charles & Carstensen, 2008). In sum, findings relating to prevalence and intensity of positive and negative emotions across the adult lifespan suggest that older adults generally maintain emotional well-being and even improve in emotional well-being, although there is some variation in age trajectories depending on the emotions being studied. One prominent explanation for high levels of well-being in older ages is improvement or maintenance of the ability to regulate emotions.

Older Adults Appear to Be Masters of Emotion Regulation

The pattern of positive affect trajectories has been linked to age-related gains in emotion regulation (Scheibe & Carstensen, 2010; Urry & Gross, 2010). Not only do older adults report experiencing more positive and less negative emotions, they also report having greater control over their emotions. Older adults report greater ability to control their experience of emotions (Gross et al., 1997; Lawton et al., 1992). Further, feelings of control over emotions appear to be directly related to the magnitude of emotional experiences. For example, older adults' reports of better control of anger partly explains reduced negative affect and anxiety and improved quality of life relative to younger adults (Phillips, Henry, Hosie, & Milne, 2006). Also, the relationship between age and negative and positive affect is partly mediated by the perceived tendency to regulate affect during stressful events (Kessler & Staudinger, 2009).

Interestingly, improvement in emotion regulation may apply only to certain types of strategies. Gross's (1998) popular modal model of emotion regulation separates different types of emotion regulation strategies by the point in the emotion generation cycle at which each strategy occurs. Early in the cycle, people can influence emotions by selecting situations, modifying situations, deploying attention, or cognitively changing the meaning of stimuli (such as reappraisal); this is called *antecedent-focused emotion regulation*. Later in the cycle, once the emotion is already generated, the emotional response can still be altered or regulated (such as when facial expressions of emotions are suppressed); this is called *response-focused emotion regulation*.

Although older adults report being able to better control their experience of emotions (which could occur at any point during the emotion generation cycle), older adults do not consistently report themselves to be more capable of controlling the outward expression of emotion, which is a response-focused strategy (Gross et al., 1997). Indeed, older adults report using suppression less often than do young adults (John & Gross, 2004). Further, in experimental settings, older adults' ability to suppress their facial expressions when requested by an experimenter is no higher than that of young adults (Phillips, Henry, Hosie, & Milne, 2008; Shiota & Levenson, 2009).

Conversely, older adults appear to improve in their ability to use many (although not all) antecedent-focused strategies. Older adults engage effectively in situation selection, with studies demonstrating that older adults prefer familiar, close social partners who allow maximal emotional reward (Fredrickson & Carstensen, 1990; Lang & Carstensen, 1994). Especially in advanced old age, older adults increasingly prefer the routinization of daily activities, which offers increased control and predictability of daily life and likely helps to prevent negative experiences (Bouisson, 2002; Reich & Zautra, 1991). Older adults also engage effectively in situation modification, for example by avoiding arguments in the face of interpersonal conflicts (Birditt & Fingerman, 2005), thus resulting in lower negative affective reactivity to conflicts (Charles,

Piazza, Luong, & Almeida, 2009). Whether older adults improve in their ability to select and modify situations or are simply more motivated to select and modify situations to maximize emotional outcomes, as suggested by socioemotional selectivity theory (to be discussed later; Carstensen, 2006), is unclear.

Older adults further appear to effectively use attentional deployment to modulate emotional reactions and may even improve at this ability. For example, older adults who were asked to positively refocus (distract themselves by thinking about something positive but unrelated to the emotional stimulus) during a negative emotion induction were more effective at reducing negative emotional experience than were young adults (Phillips et al., 2008). Older adults may also be more likely to use attentional deployment to regulate emotions, such as orienting to and away from information in ways consistent with emotion regulation goals. For example, older adults evidence positivity biases (a tendency to attend to positive and ignore negative information; Charles, Mather, & Carstensen, 2003), and positivity effects are associated with more positive emotions (Isaacowitz, Toner, & Neupert, 2009, Kennedy, Mather, & Carstensen, 2004), although some researchers do caution against interpreting this correlation as evidence that positivity biases necessarily serve to regulate emotions (Isaacowitz & Blanchard-Fields, 2012). Young adults also can show positivity effects, although they seem to be less likely to display positivity biases when not instructed to do so (Kennedy et al., 2004).

Older adults also appear to improve at some forms of cognitive change (i.e., reappraisal), although this may depend on the type of reappraisal. Older adults who were asked to use positive reappraisal (think about the positive aspects of negative emotional films) were more effective than young adults in reducing negative reactions to emotional stimuli, as measured both by self-reported emotion and physiological measures (Shiota & Levenson, 2009). However, when asked to use detached reappraisal (to think about the negative films in an objective way), older adults were less successful than young adults (Shiota & Levenson, 2009). It is possible that this strategy is less often used in everyday life (and perhaps less effective at reducing negative emotion), and thus, less well practiced by older adults. It is also possible that detached reappraisal, which requires participants to totally eliminate emotional interpretation, is more difficult or resource demanding than positive reappraisal (Shiota & Levenson, 2009).

In conclusion, emotional outcomes appear to be spared in older adults. In daily life and in experiments, older adults report more positive and less negative emotions and greater emotional stability compared to younger adults. When asked to regulate their emotions, older adults are often capable of regulating emotions as successfully as or more successfully than young adults, leading to positive emotional outcomes. This improvement of outcomes appears to be related to improved feelings of control over emotions, suggesting that older adults have better emotional outcomes because they are better able to control their emotions compared to their younger counterparts. Interestingly, improved emotional outcomes and feelings of improved emotional control with age co-occur with declines in many aspects of cognitive functioning, including declines in executive functioning and cognitive control (Braver & West, 2008; Verhaeghen 2011). This appears to be especially paradoxical, given that emotion regulation has been shown to require cognitive control resources, as will be detailed in the following section.

Emotion Regulation Requires Cognitive Control

Interestingly, although older adults improve at emotion regulation and evidence more positive emotional outcomes than young adults, they decline in cognitive control (Braver & West, 2008; Salthouse, Atkinson, & Berish, 2003; Verhaeghen, 2011; Zacks, Hasher, & Li, 2000), which appears to be vital for emotion regulation. Evidence for the relationship of cognitive control and emotion regulation can be found in a variety of paradigms. Young adults who concurrently regulate emotions and perform a cognitive task often perform more poorly on the cognitive task than young adults who do not regulate emotions (Richards & Gross, 2000, 2006). Suppressing emotional expressions, exaggerating emotional expressions, and distracting oneself from an emotional situation all impair later memory for the emotional situation itself, as regulating in these ways draws on attentional resources that then cannot be used to process the emotional stimuli (Bonanno, Papa, Lalande, Westphal, & Coifman, 2004; Dillon, Ritchey, Johnson, & Labar, 2007; Richards & Gross, 2000, 2006). Other strategies, like reappraisal, do not impair later memory and may actually enhance it (Dillon et al., 2007). This does not mean that reappraisal does not require cognitive resources. Instead, reappraisal may orient attention toward the stimuli in order to alter

interpretations of it, and this deeper encoding may facilitate later memory. Costs of regulation have also been examined by looking at costs of regulation on a concurrent task. Scheibe and Blanchard-Fields (2009) found that young adults' performance on a difficult working memory task suffered when they concurrently downregulated negative emotions.

Working memory and cognitive control have also been related to emotion regulation success in correlational studies. Young adults higher in working memory capacity are better able to suppress expressions, regulate internal experience, and use reappraisal than are those low in working memory capacity (McRae, Jacobs, Ray, John, & Gross, 2012; Schmeichel, Volokhov, & Demaree, 2008). Other research finds a link between other executive functions and emotion regulation. The ability to detect errors, as measured by both brain and behavioral measures, predicts responses to daily stressors over the next 2 weeks, with higher cognitive control associated with lower negative affective reactivity to stressors (Compton et al., 2008, 2011). In addition, reappraisal ability is correlated with set-shifting costs (using the local global task, the cost in reaction time associated with having to alternate between two response rules; McRae et al., 2012) and verbal fluency (Gyurak et al., 2009). Importantly, the relationship between executive functioning and regulation appears to extend to older adults. Older adults with higher executive functioning are better able to resist mood declines by using positive gaze preferences during a frustrating task (Isaacowitz et al., 2009) and are more likely to exhibit positivity effects (Mather & Knight, 2005; Petrican, Moscovitch, & Schimmack, 2008), which are considered by some researchers to be a form of emotion regulation.

Further evidence that emotion regulation recruits cognitive control comes from studies in which emotional stimuli and cognitive trials are interleaved. When participants are asked to upregulate negative emotions and then perform a Stroop trial, interference effects are reduced (Moser, Most, & Simons, 2010). Similarly, when persons low in trait anger view hostile stimuli, they perform more successfully on a subsequent switching task (Wilkowski & Robinson, 2008). These researchers suggest that participants recruit cognitive control resources to deal with the emotional stimuli (to upregulate negative emotions or calm themselves in the presence of hostile stimuli) and that these resources are still available for the cognitive task trial that is presented immediately afterward, thereby aiding performance. In these studies, trials requiring emotion regulation and trials of cognitive tasks were closely interleaved (e.g., one hostile stimulus, one Stroop trial), but in studies with blocks of emotion regulation followed by blocks of cognitive tasks, emotion regulation does not appear to facilitate cognitive control, but instead may impair it.

Baumeister and his colleagues suggest that tasks that require self-control, like emotion regulation, draw on a limited self-control resource (Schmeichel, Vohs, & Baumeister, 2003). This self-control resource is temporarily depleted when it is used, which impairs performance on subsequently performed tasks that also rely on self-control. In a number of studies, suppressing internal and external signs of emotion has been demonstrated to cause deficits on later tasks requiring self-control (Dillon et al., 2007; Gailliot, Schmeichel, & Baumeister, 2006; Schmeichel et al., 2003; Shamosh & Gray, 2007). Importantly, self-control has been equated with cognitive control or executive functioning (Schmeichel et al., 2003; Shamosh & Gray, 2007), demonstrating once again that emotion regulation and cognitive control appear to rely on the same resources. More extended cognitive control efforts may deplete resources, temporarily impairing performance on other tasks that also rely on the same resources. However, at shorter intervals, such as one trial of emotion regulation followed by one trial of a cognitive task, depletion may not reach levels necessary to impair subsequent task performance. In studies such as those discussed in the prior paragraph, depletion may not play a role in cognitive task performance for this reason.

Finally, neuroscience research has suggested that emotion regulation and cognitive control appear to rely on the same brain areas, particularly areas of the prefrontal cortex (Ochsner & Gross, 2005). Neural models of emotion regulation assume that perceptual information about emotional stimuli pass through the thalamus to the amygdala and insula to elicit an initial emotional response (Green & Malhi, 2006; Zelazo & Cunningham, 2007). From there, activation reaches different regions of the lateral prefrontal cortex, which is involved in reflection, planning, and execution of emotion regulation strategies (Ochsner & Gross, 2004; Zelazo & Cunningham, 2007). The lateral prefrontal cortex, in turn, influences responding in the amygdala and other subcortical systems to modify emotional responding. Neuroimaging studies provide support for these assumptions by showing coupling between activation in prefrontal areas and reduced activation in the amygdala during exposure to emotional stimuli (Cunningham Raye, & Johnston, 2004; Green & Malhi, 2006; Kanske, Heissler, Schönfelder, Bonger, & Wessa, 2011; Ochsner, Bunge, Gross, & Gabrieli, 2002; Zelazo & Cunningham, 2007). Other areas of the prefrontal cortex, including the medial prefrontal cortex and the dorsal anterior cingulate cortex, are also implicated in emotion regulation, and appear to be involved in the ability to monitor internal responses and monitor inconsistencies between top-down reappraisal and bottom-up evaluations of (emotional) stimuli (Green & Malhi, 2006). The lateral and medial prefrontal cortex and the dorsal anterior cingulate cortex are also all implicated in cognitive control (Ochsner & Gross, 2005; Zelazo & Cunningham, 2007).

Reconciling Cognitive Declines With Maintenance of Emotional Well-Being

In light of known decreases in cognitive control with age and the requirement of cognitive control for emotion regulation, it is perplexing that older adults appear to have preserved or improved emotional outcomes and processes. We describe three potential explanations for this "paradox of aging," which will be detailed in the following sections (for an overview, see Figure 11.1). First, physical changes that occur with age may reduce emotional reactivity, lowering the difficulty of emotion regulation for older adults. Second, older adults may become more motivated to regulate their emotions and may therefore devote greater resources to regulating emotions. Finally, older adults may choose more efficient emotion regulation strategies or learn to use emotion regulation strategies more efficiently, which would allow them to effectively regulate emotions without devoting the same degree of resources to the emotion regulation task.

Physical Changes With Age Lower the Difficulty of Emotion Regulation for Older Adults

One possibility is that improved emotional functioning with age is a serendipitous by-product of biological decline in neural and autonomic emotion systems (Cacioppo, Berntson, Bechara, Tranel, & Hawkley, 2011; Cacioppo, Berntson, Klein, & Poehlmann, 1997; Mendes, 2010). For instance, structural and functional degradation of neural and autonomic emotion systems could diminish processing and physiological reactivity to negative stimuli, thereby reducing the impact of negative events. This would create less of an emotion-regulatory load in older adults and hence, reductions in executive

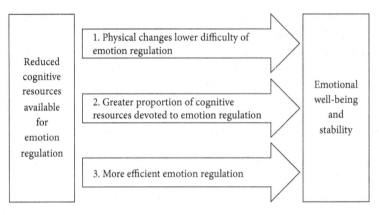

Figure 11.1. A schematic overview of the three proposed mechanisms underlying improved emotional well-being and stability despite reduced cognitive resources with age.

capacity with age would be irrelevant to affective well-being. Consistent with this hypothesis are a variety of findings in which older adults are less physiologically reactive to emotional stimuli than are young adults (Birditt, Fingerman, & Almeida, 2005; Charles & Almeida, 2007; Gavazzeni, Wiens, & Fischer, 2008; Levenson, Carstensen, Friesen, & Ekman, 1991; Levenson, Carstensen, & Gottman, 1994; Neupert, Almeida, & Charles, 2007; Tsai, Levenson, & Carstensen, 2000).

However, newly emerging evidence suggests that older adults sometimes show equivalent (Kunzmann & Richter, 2009; Stawski, Sliwinski, Almeida, & Smyth, 2008) or greater physiological reactivity to negative emotional events, especially in diary studies conducted outside of the laboratory (Charles, 2010; Mroczek & Almeida, 2004; Piazza, Charles, & Almeida, 2007; Uchino, Berg, Smith, Pearce, & Skinner, 2006; Uchino, Birmingham, & Berg, 2010; Uchino, Holt-Lunstad, Bloor, & Campo, 2005). Charles (2010) suggests in her model of strength and vulnerability integration (SAVI) that older adults are better able to prevent and down-regulate mild negative emotions, like those encountered in laboratory situations. However, once a strong emotional reaction has occurred and older adults' physiological systems have become aroused, older adults have difficulty downregulating arousal. This perspective would suggest that older adults should have particular difficulty in maintaining well-being in the presence of intense or enduring and unavoidable stressors in everyday life, such as caregiving or chronic health problems. In addition, reduced reactivity to negative emotional stimuli and increased activity in frontal regions associated with emotion regulation often co-occur, suggesting that reduced reactivity in older adults does not

necessarily result from physiological system degradation (Samanez-Larkin & Carstensen, 2011; Scheibe & Carstensen, 2010). Given increased emotional reactivity with age in some studies and the questionable nature of reduced brain reactivity, the hypothesis that the reduced physiological load of emotions leads to reduced need for cognitive resources in emotion regulation can at best be a partial explanation for maintenance of affective well-being with age. Moreover, it is possible that reduced physiological responding to mild or moderately intense emotional stimuli with age is the result of improved emotion regulation. This perspective is consistent with the following two explanations.

Older Adults Devote a Greater Proportion of Cognitive Resources to Regulating Emotions

Older adults may also compensate for cognitive resource declines by devoting greater resources to emotion regulation, especially as emotion regulation may become more valued in old age. Socioemotional selectivity theory (SST) suggests that, as people age, they become more aware of decreased time left in life and this awareness alters their motivations (Carstensen, 2006). Older adults shift away from prioritizing novel experiences and instead prioritize meaningful emotional experiences, which are often positive (Carstensen, 2006). Consequently, they begin to prioritize close, meaningful relationships, avoid unnecessary stressors, and seek out situations that encourage positive emotions (Carstensen, 1992, 2006).

One apparent outcome of this motivational shift is the age-related positivity effect, referred to earlier. Young adults typically process negative information more thoroughly than positive information, supposedly because it has a higher survival value (Baumeister, Bratslavsky, Finkenauer, and Vohs, 2001). Yet this general pattern is not consistently found in older adults. In fact, recent studies have suggested that older adults may preferentially process and remember positive information (Mather & Carstensen, 2005) or show a reduced negativity bias relative to young adults (Charles et al., 2003). Positivity effects or reduced negativity effects in older adults can be found in a variety of studies, including studies of attention (Mather & Carstensen, 2005; Isaacowitz, Wadlinger, Goren, & Wilson, 2006), working memory (Mikels, Larkin, Reuter-Lorenz, & Carstensen, 2005), autobiographical memory (Kennedy et al., 2004), memory for pictures and events (Langeslag & van Strien, 2009; Charles et al., 2003; Kryla-Lighthall & Mather, 2009), and decision-making (Mather & Johnson, 2000; Löckenhoff and Carstensen, 2007). Further, preferential processing of positive information and/or avoidance of negative information is associated with more positive emotional outcomes (Isaacowitz et al. 2009; Kennedy et al., 2004), suggesting that it serves an emotion regulation purpose. For example, young adults instructed to attend to positive faces and ignore negative faces exhibited less frustration than those who were given no attentional goals (Johnson, 2009). In addition, both older and younger adults who were instructed to concentrate on their emotions while recalling information about their past exhibited both a positivity effect in recall and more positive emotions (Kennedy et al., 2004).

The age-related positivity effect, as suggested by SST, appears to be based on changes in goals or motivation, evidenced in studies in which manipulations of attention to emotion in young adults produce positivity effects (e.g. Kennedy et al., 2004; Mather & Johnson, 2000) and in other studies in which shortened future time perspective is related to positivity effects (Pruzan & Isaacowitz, 2006). When younger adults are asked to concentrate on their current emotional states, for example, they display positivity biases in autobiographical memory instead of the typical negativity biases found when young adults are not oriented to their emotional state (Kennedy et al., 2004). People also tend to make choice-supportive memory errors when recalling the attributes of different options they chose from, which may reflect an attempt to maintain satisfaction with choices (Mather & Johnson, 2000). In studies measuring future time perspective, students with foreshortened time perspective (senior college students who were about to graduate) spent less time looking at negative faces than did their peers (Pruzan & Isaacowitz, 2006). Seniors may be more motivated to maintain positive emotions, given the impending ending of a chapter of their lives. Data from a study by Riediger, Schmiedek, Wagner, and Lindenberger (2009) further support the motivational argument in an experience-sampling study, in which older adults were more likely to report the desire to maintain positive and decrease negative emotions compared to middle-aged and younger adults (although they were less likely to report the desire to further increase positive emotions). Older adults may be more motivated to regulate emotions (via strategies like orienting away from negative and toward positive information), and this might explain why they appear to maintain or even increase in emotional well-being compared to younger people.

Importantly, motivation to regulate emotions may encourage older adults to devote a greater portion of their limited resources to regulation tasks. Riediger et al. (2011) report evidence that motivation to regulate emotions is associated with cognitive control costs. In an experience sampling study, these authors found that participants of various ages who were highly motivated to maintain positive emotions or decrease negative emotions showed small but significant decrements on a working memory task, relative to occasions with low motivation to regulate. The positivity effect also appears to require cognitive control. Mather and Knight (2005) found that older adults with higher cognitive control were more likely to display the positivity effect. Furthermore, under divided attention, older adults not only failed to display a positivity bias in later memory for the stimuli, but actually displayed a heightened negativity bias. The authors propose that two processes are involved in the positivity effect: the first is the search for the to-be-avoided negative information, which is relatively effortless, and the second is the process of orienting away from the negative information, which requires cognitive control. When older adults' resources are taxed by a dual-task paradigm, they no longer have sufficient resources to enact the second part of the process, and, consequently, they attend to the negative information. Similar results have also been found in studies of visual attention (Knight et al., 2007). When viewing negative and neutral face pairs in a full-attention condition, older adults oriented toward negative faces less often than did young adults. However, under divided attention conditions, older adults spent more time looking at negative faces than did young adults (Knight et al., 2007). These findings suggest that older adults' motivation to regulate emotions leads them to devote a greater portion of their limited resources to the task of emotion regulation when the task allows it. Consequently, older adults may be able to compensate for reduced cognitive resources and maintain well-being by altering the allotment of resources to emotion regulation tasks, relative to other tasks.

In summary, research investigating SST has often considered the positivity effect as a form of emotion regulation motivated by changes in future time perspective. This research has demonstrated that the positivity effect is related to motivations to regulate emotions (Kennedy et al., 2004; Mather & Johnson, 2000) and to future time perspective (Pruzan & Isaacowitz, 2006). The research has also demonstrated that those people who evidence positivity effects are often those who experience more positive emotions (Johnson, 2009; Kennedy et al., 2004) and that the positivity effect appears to draw on cognitive control resources (Mather & Knight, 2005). Together, these findings suggest that older adults may purposefully devote greater proportions of their limited cognitive control resources to maintaining positivity biases, which may serve to regulate their emotions.

However, recently, Isaacowitz and Blanchard-Fields (2012) have become concerned about the correlational rather than causal nature of the relationship between the positivity effect and emotional outcomes, and suggest that researchers be cautious in assuming that the positivity effect serves to regulate emotions until causal links can be established. They particularly point out that many studies that examine the positivity effect may actually be examining how people process valenced information that does not necessarily induce an emotion that requires regulation. If that is the case, positivity effects may not be related to emotion regulation. However, an implication of SST is that older adults value regulating emotions, even if positivity biases themselves do not turn out to be emotion regulatory in nature. Although devotion of resources when using emotion regulation strategies other than attentional deployment has not been examined, it seems consistent with SST to suppose that older adults would devote greater cognitive resources to enact *any* emotion regulation strategy when possible and necessary.

Although older adults may be willing to devote resources to emotion regulation, it may not always be necessary. Positivity effects may not always require the allotment of large amounts of resources, as older adults do sometimes show positivity/reduced negativity effects in dual-task paradigms.

When trying to perform a number parity task (judging whether two numbers are odd or even) in the presence of emotional distracter words, young adults' attention is negatively biased, but older adults attend equally to all word stimuli (Thomas & Hasher, 2006). Furthermore, in a study in which participants viewed images while listening to text and making a lexical decision, older adults fixated less on negative stimuli regardless of whether they were in full or divided attention conditions (Allard & Isaacowitz, 2008). Possibly, the manipulations in these two studies put less load on older adults' resources, which allowed them to maintain positivity effects despite limited resources. The findings suggest that, in some circumstances, older adults may be able to regulate emotions using positivity preferences without draining cognitive resources. In the next section, we discuss further evidence that older adults may be particularly efficient at using emotion regulation strategies.

Older Adults Regulate Emotions More Efficiently

A final way that older adults may overcome reduced cognitive resources to maintain well-being is to choose strategies that require fewer resources to successfully enact or to enact the same strategies with fewer resources. In other words, older adults may rely on more efficient types of emotion regulation that do not require cognitive resources to the same extent as the emotion regulation conducted by young adults. Consequently, reduced cognitive resources would not negatively influence the ability to maintain well-being. Below we consider three aspects of more efficient emotion regulation; namely, that older adults (1) use more effective emotion regulation strategies, (2) use less cognitively demanding strategies, and (3) as a result of practice and automatization, require less cognitive resources to enact the same strategies.

CHANGES IN STRATEGY USE

Much research suggests that older and younger adults differ in the types of emotion regulation strategies that they use in a given context. Older adults appear to improve in the selection of strategies used to regulate emotions in the face of everyday problems. Older adults, more than young adults, seem to cater their emotion regulation strategies to the particular situation (Blanchard-Fields, 2007). Specifically, older adults tend to include emotion regulation as part of their problem solving when problems are interpersonal and emotionally laden but use instrumental strategies (actions to solve the problem) in both interpersonal and instrumental problem situations. Young adults, on the other hand, tend to use instrumental strategies regardless of context (Blanchard-Fields, Chen, & Norris, 1997; Blanchard-Fields, Mienaltowski, & Seay, 2007; Watson & Blanchard-Fields, 1998). Further, experts rate older adults' strategy choices in these situations as more effective (Blanchard-Fields et al., 2007). This suggests that older adults are more effective at tailoring their strategies to the problem they are dealing with, including emotion regulation, as part of the problem-solving strategy when it is relevant.

Researchers have also examined the different types of emotion regulation strategies used in different contexts. Although use of passive emotion regulation strategies (such as denial, withdrawal, suppression) are often thought of as negative, passive strategies may be adaptive for older adults, since those strategies help them to avoid high levels of arousal (Blanchard-Fields, 2007). When reacting to interpersonal problems, older adults were more likely to use passive rather than proactive emotion regulation strategies (seeking out emotional support, directly confronting emotions; Coats & Blanchard-Fields, 2008). This may reflect, however, lower levels of anger experienced by older adult participants, as the higher intensity of anger may necessitate use of more proactive strategies (Blanchard-Fields, 2007). Older adults may be more likely to try to avoid anger using passive strategies, but when they do experience it, they report using proactive strategies (Blanchard-Fields, 2007; Coats & Blanchard-Fields, 2008). Again, this suggests a tailoring of strategy to situation, with older adults using appropriate strategies when they are needed. Further, the use of passive strategies in some situations may be more adaptive than proactive strategies—such as when a person needs to preserve a social relationship (Blanchard-Fields, 2007).

Passive strategies may have the additional benefit of being easier to use. Older adults with lower emotional complexity (lower understanding of how to use emotion to inform cognition) were more likely to use passive rather than proactive emotion regulation strategies (Coats & Blanchard-Fields, 2008). Older adults with low affective complexity may have more difficulty thinking about emotions in a complex way, and passive strategies may allow them to deal with emotions effectively without needing to process information in a complex way. This argument is consistent with Labouvie-Vief's dynamic integration theory (DIT; Labouvie-Vief, Grühn, & Mouras, 2009). These authors suggest that all adults are motivated to regulate emotions to some degree, but that older adults might have to regulate emotions in different ways due to their decreased cognitive resources. When emotion regulation load is low, such as when arousal is low, older adults should be able to use complex emotion schemas and emotion regulation strategies, such as those used by younger adults. However, when under cognitive load or under high emotion regulation load, older adults may compensate by switching to more heuristic, simpler emotion processing, allowing them to maintain well-being with reduced cognitive resources. In that case, older adults do not devote more resources to maintain well-being, but instead compensate for reduced resources by adopting simpler strategies. In summary, older adults faced with emotional interpersonal situations appear to use different strategies than do younger adults, and the strategies they use may be particularly adaptive and require less complex processing.

Research based on Gross' (1998) modal model of emotion regulation also supports age differences in strategy use. Older adults report greater and more effective use of specific strategies that are known to be effective and efficient regulation strategies. For example, older adults may be more likely to use distraction (Coats & Blanchard-Fields, 2008), which is a particularly effective way to downregulate high-intensity negative emotions (Sheppes & Gross, 2011; Sheppes & Meiran, 2007). Furthermore, older adults report greater use of reappraisal, a strategy in which people try to change their appraisal of a situation so that it has a different emotional meaning (John & Gross, 2004) and less use of the oftentimes problematic strategy, suppression of expression. Reappraisal is associated with effective change of emotional experience and greater well-being and psychological health, and is not associated with some of the negative physiological outcomes of suppression of expression. In addition, the ability of individuals to use cognitive reappraisal moderates the impact of high levels of stress on depressive symptoms (Troy, Wilhelm, Shallcross, & Mauss, 2010). Those individuals who were better able to regulate negative emotions in the laboratory setting experienced fewer depressive symptoms in response to cumulative stress outside of the laboratory. Suppression of expression, in contrast, is associated with increased physiological arousal, degraded memory for information that is concurrently presented, greater costs during social interaction, and reduced well-being (John & Gross, 2004).

In summary, in interpersonal problem solving, older adults are more likely to regulate emotions, and they appear to use strategies that are more effective and more likely to maintain social relationships. Older adults also appear to favor antecedent-focused emotion regulation and certain particularly effective strategies, like reappraisal and distraction. Using more effective strategies can preserve cognitive resources because negative emotions subside more quickly and cognitive resources can then be directed to other ongoing tasks.

DIFFERENT STRATEGIES, DIFFERENT COSTS

The fact that older adults use different strategies than young adults is also important, because different strategies appear to have different cognitive costs and may rely on cognitive resources to different degrees. Regulating emotions early in the unfolding emotion process (antecedent-focused regulation) may be less cognitively costly than regulating later in the process (response-focused regulation) because regulating early in the process prevents an emotional response and therefore curtails need for regulation later. Regulating emotion once it is under way, however, will require continual monitoring and regulation effort (Baumeister, Schmeichel and Vohs, 2007; Richards & Gross, 2000).

A variety of research supports varying cognitive costs for different emotion regulation strategies. One body of research examines the way that emotion regulation influences memory for items encountered during the regulation attempt, such as emotional pictures. It appears that using antecedent-focused strategies like reappraisal interferes with memory significantly less than using response-focused strategies like distraction or suppression of expression (Richards & Gross, 2000, 2006). Ostensibly, this occurs because distraction and suppression of expression draw attention away from the emotional stimuli and toward the regulation attempt, and therefore processing of the stimuli is impaired. The cause of memory decrements, however, does not necessarily imply that differential levels of cognitive resources are required for the different emotion regulation strategies. Instead, different strategies may simply direct resources in different directions. Whereas reappraisal encourages continued processing of the stimuli being reappraised, distraction and suppression may draw attention away from the stimuli (Richards & Gross, 2006). The magnitude of resources being put into reappraisal, suppression, or distraction cannot really be assessed in this memory paradigm.

However, other lines of research are consistent with different strategies actually requiring different levels of cognitive resources. For example, research examining the depletion of self-control suggests that suppression of expression requires self-control resources more so than reappraisal (Inzlicht & Gutsell, 2007; Vohs & Schmeichel, 2003), although the timing of the regulation effort may also matter (Sheppes, Catran, & Meiran, 2009; Sheppes & Meiran, 2008). Baumeister and colleagues propose that people have limited self-control resources that are temporarily depleted whenever they are used (Gailliot et al., 2006; Schmeichel et al., 2003). After performing a task that requires self-control (like regulating emotion), people temporarily have fewer resources with which to perform subsequent self-control tasks, causing their performance on those tasks to suffer (Schmeichel et al., 2003). Depleted self-control has been found when participants are asked to suppress, internally and externally, their emotional reactions (Dillon et al., 2007; Gailliot et al., 2006; Schmeichel et al., 2003; Shamosh & Gray, 2007). Also, participants asked to suppress expression demonstrate behavioral depletion effects, and the magnitude of these depletion effects is mediated by brain activity in areas associated with conflict monitoring, such that people who suppressed expression exhibited lower brain activity in these areas and lower performance on a subsequent self-control task (Inzlicht & Gutsell, 2007). Reappraisal, on the other hand, does not deplete self-control resources unless it is initiated late in the regulatory process (Sheppes & Meiran, 2008; Vohs & Schmeichel, 2003), and thus appears to be less effortful than suppression of emotional expression.

The suppression–reappraisal distinction in terms of cognitive costs, however, may be too simplistic. Other researchers have found that when reappraisal is initiated late in the emotion generation process, such as when it is instructed partway through a mood induction (in other words, when reappraisal is used to downregulate an already existing response rather than antecedently preventing a response), depletion costs do emerge (Sheppes & Meiran, 2008). This may occur because, once the emotion has been generated and the stimulus has been interpreted in an emotional way, it may be difficult to reappraise the meaning of the stimulus, so participants may have to put in more effort. Interestingly, late-enacted distraction is not associated with depletion costs, suggesting that distracting oneself from emotional situations can be effective and require few resources, whether it is engaged in early or late in an emotional situation (Sheppes & Meiran, 2008).

Research examining sympathetic activation during emotion regulation also provides evidence that different regulation strategies require different levels of effort. Sympathetic activation has been demonstrated to increase when people exert effort (Elliott, Bankart, and Light, 1970; Wegner & Gold, 1995), and therefore has been used in some research to examine effort during emotion regulation. The research dovetails nicely with the results just reported. When participants are instructed to suppress expression or reappraise before they encounter stimuli, suppression is associated with increased sympathetic activation when compared to reappraisal, but reappraisal is not different from a control condition (Gross, 1998, 2002; Gross & Levenson 1993, 1997). However, when instructed midway through an induction, reappraisal is also associated with increased sympathetic activation, but distraction is not (Sheppes et al., 2009). Taken together, these results suggest that suppression of expression requires effort and resources, reappraisal requires effort and resources only if enacted at a late time point but does not require resources if enacted early, and distraction does not appear to require effort or resources (although it interferes with memory processing).

As discussed earlier, older adults appear to use different strategies when regulating emotions than do young adults. Increased use of antecedent-focused strategies, like reappraisal or situation selection, could be especially adaptive in older adults, as they appear to require fewer cognitive resources to enact. In addition, increased use of distraction may be adaptive and help older adults maintain well-being without drawing on limited cognitive resources to the same extent as other strategies.

INCREASED EFFICIENCY OF
SPECIFIC STRATEGIES

Recently, researchers have begun to explore a new hypothesis: older adults may enact the same specific emotion regulation strategies more efficiently than do young adults (Scheibe & Blanchard-Fields, 2009). From research on attentional control, it is known that tasks that were once highly controlled and effortful can become more automatic and less effortful with practice, as indicated in task performance and brain activation (Chein & Schneider, 2005; Kaplan & Berman, 2010). Similarly, emotion researchers suggest that the same types of emotion regulation strategies that people can use intentionally can also become automatic over time (Mauss,

Bunge, & Gross, 2007). The relative automatization of emotion regulation is supported by theoretical arguments made by Bargh and Williams (2007), who argue that the goal of regulating emotions can become linked to contexts such that goals are automatically pursued when those contexts arise. Automatic pursuit can include unintentionality, effortlessness, and uncontrollability, and is enacted outside of awareness, although not all of these traits are always present. Hypothetically, if a person routinely, consistently, and successfully uses a particular strategy in a given situation, then that strategy should be activated and operated automatically in that situation over time. This should happen in adults of all ages. Further, research suggests that automatically pursued emotion regulation can be just as effective as intentional, controlled regulation (Williams, Bargh, Nocera, & Gray, 2009). In addition, some aspects of any particular emotion regulation strategy may be automatic while other aspects are controlled (Mather & Knight, 2005).

Theoretically, older adults could use certain strategies more efficiently than young adults if older adults' years of experience using specific emotion regulation strategies leads to relative automatization of these strategies, as described earlier. To the extent that older adults use emotion regulation strategies habitually in more situations (Blanchard-Fields, 2007); tailor strategies to specific situations, so that specific situations are associated with different regulation responses (Blanchard-Fields, 2007); and use a different set of regulation strategies more frequently (John & Gross, 2004), the emotion regulation strategies that become automated in specific situations for older adults may differ from those that are more automatic for young adults. For example, if older adults often use emotion regulation in conjunction with other problem-solving strategies, these emotion regulation strategies may deploy without intention, require less effort to engage in, and occur without conscious awareness. For young adults, who may have less experience in using emotion regulation with solving problems, using these same strategies may require both intention and effort. Several recent studies support the argument that older adults may expend fewer resources when regulating emotions, although it is not clear whether this is the product of strategy choice or degree of automatization.

OLDER ADULTS USE FEWER COGNITIVE
RESOURCES WHEN REGULATING EMOTIONS

Scheibe and Blanchard-Fields (2009) found that older adults could successfully regulate emotions while doing a concurrent task, with no cost to the concurrent task. Both young and older adults experienced a disgust emotion induction through a film clip and then were asked to perform a resource-demanding *N*-back task. Just before the *N*-back task, some people were given instructions to downregulate their negative emotions from the film clip while performing the *N*-back task. Although young adults who were asked to downregulate emotions showed deficits on the *N*-back task relative to young adults who were given no instructions, older adults performed the *N*-back task equivalently, regardless of the regulation instructions they received. This seems to suggest that older adults did not have to utilize more resources when regulating emotions than when not trying to regulate.

Scheibe and Blanchard-Fields gave participants general regulation instructions that asked them to downregulate their experience of emotion. But new evidence suggests that older adults' improved cognitive costs can also be associated with more specific regulation strategies. For example, Emery and Hess (2011) found that older adults who suppressed their expressions while viewing pictures did not show memory deficits compared to those simply viewing the stimuli, whereas young adults who suppressed expression had worse memory for the stimuli compared to young adults who only viewed the stimuli. The authors suggest that this pattern could emerge if older adults were using a different regulation strategy, such as reappraisal, that would increase attention to the stimuli. It could also occur if suppressing expression had become less effortful, allowing more attention to be paid to the stimuli and less to maintaining a stoic expression. Finally, Senesac and Blanchard-Fields (2012) recently found support for reduced cognitive costs associated with emotion regulation in a depletion paradigm. Whereas young adults who regulated disgust emotions during a film clip suffered from reduced performance on a subsequent Stroop task compared to young adults who maintained their disgust, older adults performed equivalently in all conditions. It appears that cognitive resources or executive control is required for performance in some emotion regulation tasks for older adults, yet older adults can other tasks.

Conclusion

Aging researchers are making headway in understanding how older adults can maintain well-being and emotion regulation capabilities despite decreases in cognitive functioning. The biological aging theory presented earlier suggests that older adults can maintain emotional well-being because their physical reactions are blunted, and this lower reactivity makes emotion regulation easier to accomplish. Socioemotional selectivity theory suggests that older adults have a reduced future time perspective and are therefore more motivated to regulate emotions. Consequently, they are willing to devote a greater proportion of their limited cognitive resources to regulating emotions. Finally, recently, researchers have suggested that not all emotion regulation requires the same amount of cognitive resources. Older adults may increasingly rely on the types of strategies that are efficient in terms of cognitive resources and may become more able to efficiently use specific strategies with practice.

Rather than simply thinking of old age as a time of improvement in emotion regulation for everyone, it is also important to examine individual differences in the trajectory of emotion regulation with age (e.g., Charles et al., 2001; Mroczek & Kolarz, 1998). Each of the explanations presented in this chapter provides new hypotheses that may help researchers to understand which older adults are at risk for emotional difficulties and which older adults may improve at emotion regulation. If biological aging makes older adults less reactive, then people with greater biological aging may be less reactive when encountering emotional stimuli. Such a perspective would suggest that those older adults who are biologically more aged may ironically have fewer difficulties maintaining well-being when emotionally challenged. Socioemotional selectivity theory, on the other hand, would suggest that older adults who have a more limited future time perspective should show stronger motivation to regulate emotions and may, therefore, be more likely to regulate emotions and maintain well-being. Finally, our third explanation suggests that older adults who have had more practice successfully regulating emotions should improve the most at emotion regulation. This explanation has found some support in studies indicating that some lifetime adversity improves resilience relative to no or very much adversity (Seery, 2011). However, the crucial determinant of whether someone improves at emotion regulation is not how often the need to regulate emotions arises, but how often the person successfully regulates emotions. Successful regulation in particular situations could lead to automatic coupling of the situation with the regulation strategy and use of the regulation strategy without effort.

This further suggests that each older adult should improve at specific types of emotion regulation and in specific contexts that have been successfully paired in the past.

Of course, within any individual person, each of these factors could play a role in emotion regulation success at a particular moment. One possible interface between the three hypotheses is provided in Figure 11.2. As can be seen from the flowchart, whether any particular instance of emotion regulation is successful could be determined by a number of different factors, including both person factors (biological aging, cognitive resources) and situational factors (familiar vs. novel situation, environmental constraints on resources). In this model, reactions to stimuli can be regulated either with or without a strong physiological reaction. The pathway that does not include a physiological reaction might be similar to an antecedent-focused regulation attempt, in which regulation is deployed before the emotion is generated, whereas the pathway that includes a physiological reaction is more like response-focused regulation. In this model, if a physiological reaction occurs that needs to be regulated, two pathways are available. If the emotion regulation task is familiar and emotion regulation can deploy automatically, then the person will be successful. On the other hand, if the emotion

regulation task is less familiar, then motivation and resources will play a role. If the person is motivated to regulate emotions (as when he or she has a limited future time perspective), then a regulation attempt will be made that may or may not be successful, depending on whether sufficient resources are available. If the person is less motivated to regulate emotions, then fewer resources may be allotted to the regulation attempt, and success will vary accordingly. The model in Figure 11.2 is an example, but future research should seek to determine how different factors interact to determine emotion regulation success.

Future Directions

Another concern for future research is the study of strategy selection. Many of the arguments made in this chapter are predicated on the assumption that older adults choose different types of strategies than young adults, but choice is rarely examined directly. Recently, Sheppes, Scheibe, Suri, and Gross (2011) introduced a new paradigm that allows researchers to test emotion regulation strategy choice in the face of varying contextual demands, which allows testing of this assumption more directly. In this set of studies, participants were initially trained to use reappraisal and distraction while viewing pictures or receiving electric shocks. During the test phase

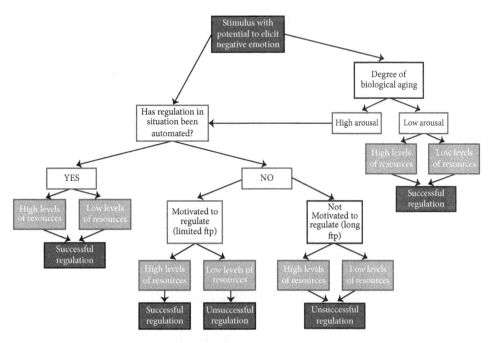

Figure 11.2. Flowchart illustrating one potential interface between the proposed mechanisms by which older adults maintain well-being in the face of cognitive declines. The chart demonstrates that there may be multiple paths to successful emotion regulation. ftp, future time perspective.

of the experiment, participants were allowed to choose between either strategy by pressing a button. A subset of trials, in which participants talked aloud about the strategy they were using, demonstrated that participants did indeed implement the strategy they chose.

Researchers should also consider how to reconcile the apparently conflicting theories about whether older adults must devote resources to regulate emotions. The suggestion that older adults may devote more resources to emotion regulation and the theory that emotion regulation may become more efficient with age could be integrated by suggesting that older adults, when faced with a situation in which emotion regulation has become relatively automatic, use minimal cognitive resources. However, when faced with an unfamiliar, novel, or unautomated emotion regulation context, older adults will devote cognitive resources to regulating, as consistent with their motivations. Understanding how the different explanations can complement each other and when each explanation will be useful is an important future aim.

Researchers should also take into consideration the ways that different components of executive function decline with age. Although overall cognitive functioning clearly declines with age, not all types of cognitive functioning follow the same age-related trajectories. In fact, some types of executive functioning may remain relatively intact with age, although which specific types remain intact and which decline is the subject of debate (Braver & West, 2008; Hasher, Lustig, & Zacks, 2007; Verhaeghen, 2011). Considering that some aspects of cognitive control remain intact, it is perhaps not surprising that emotion regulation ability is maintained in old age. However, more systematic study of the reliance of emotion regulation on executive functions and the relationship of specific domains of executive functioning to specific types of emotion regulation should be further explored.

References

Allard, E., & Isaacowitz, D. (2008). Are preferences in emotional processing affected by distraction? Examining the age-related positivity effect in visual fixation within a dual-task paradigm. *Neuropsychology, Development, and Cognition, Section B, Aging, Neuropsychology and Cognition, 15*, 725–743. doi: 10.1080/13825580802348562

Allemand, M. (2008). Age differences in forgivingness: The role of future time perspective. *Journal of Research in Personality, 42*, 1137–1147. doi: 10.1016/j.jrp.2008.02.009

Bargh, J. A., & Williams, L. E. (2007). On the automatic or nonconscious regulation of emotion. In J. Gross (Ed.), *Handbook of emotion regulation.* (pp. 1–39). New York: Guilford Press.

Baumeister, R. F., Bratslavsky, E., Finkenauer, C., & Vohs, K. D. (2001). Bad is stronger than good. *Review of General Psychology, 5*, 323–370. doi: 10.1037/1089-2680.5.4.323

Baumeister, R. F., Schmeichel, B. J., & Vohs, K. D. (2007). Self regulation and the executive function: The self as controlling agent. In A. W. Kruglanski & E. T. Higgins (Eds.), *Social psychology: Handbook of basic principles*, 2nd ed. (pp. 516–539). New York: Guilford Press.

Birditt, K. S., & Fingerman, K. L. (2003). Age and gender differences in adults' descriptions of emotional reactions to interpersonal problems. *The Journals of Gerontology, Series B: Psychological Sciences and Social Sciences, 58B*, 237–245. doi: 10.1093/geronb/58.4.P237

Birditt, K. S., & Fingerman, K. L. (2005). Do we get better at picking our battles? Age group differences in descriptions of behavioral reactions to interpersonal tensions. *The Journals of Gerontology, Series B: Psychological Sciences and Social Sciences, 60B*, (3) 121–128.

Birditt, K. S., Fingerman, K. L., & Almeida, D. M. (2005). Age differences in exposure and reactions to interpersonal tensions: A daily diary study. *Psychology and Aging, 20*, 330–340. doi: 10.1037/0882-7974.20.2.330

Blanchard-Fields, F. (2007). Everyday problem solving and emotion: An adult developmental perspective. *Current Directions in Psychological Science, 16*, 26–31. doi: 10.1111/j.1467-8721.2007.00469.x

Blanchard-Fields, F., Chen, Y., & Norris, L. (1997). Everyday problem solving across the adult life span: Influence of domain specificity and cognitive appraisal. *Psychology and Aging, 12*, 684–693. doi: 10.1037/0882-7974.12.4.684

Blanchard-Fields, F., Mienaltowski, A., & Seay, R. B. (2007). Age differences in everyday problem-solving effectiveness: Older adults select more effective strategies for interpersonal problems. *Journal of Gerontology, 62B*, 61–64.

Bouisson, J. (2002). Routinization preferences, anxiety, and depression in an elderly French sample. *Journal of Aging Studies, 16*, 295–302.

Bonanno, G. A., Papa, A., Lalande, K., Westphal, M., & Coifman, K. (2004). The importance of being flexible: The ability to enhance and suppress emotional expression as a predictor of long-term adjustment. *Psychological Science, 15*, 482–487. doi: 10.1111/j.0956-7976.2004.00705.x

Braver, T. S., & West, R. (2008). Working memory, executive control, and aging. In F. M. Craik & T. A. Salthouse (Eds.), *The handbook of aging and cognition*, 3rd ed. (pp. 311–372). New York: Psychology Press.

Cacioppo, J. T., Berntson, G. G., Bechara, A., Tranel, D., & Hawkley, L. C. (2011). Could an aging brain contribute to subjective well being?: The value added by a social neuroscience perspective. In S. T. F. A. Tadorov & D. Prentice (Eds.), *Social neuroscience: Toward understanding the underpinnings of the social mind* (pp. 249–262). New York: Oxford University Press.

Cacioppo, J. T., Berntson, G. G., Klein, D. J., & Poehlmann, K. M. (1997). The psychophysiology of emotion across the lifespan. *Annual Review of Gerontology and Geriatrics, 17*, 27–74.

Carstensen, L. L. (1992). Social and emotional patterns in adulthood: Support for socioemotional selectivity theory. *Psychology and Aging, 7*, 331–338. doi: 10.1037/0882-7974.7.3.331

Carstensen, L. L. (2006). The influence of a sense of time on human development. *Science, 312*, 1913–1915. doi: 10.1126/science.1127488

Carstensen, L. L., Pasupathi, M., Mayr, U., & Nesselroade, J. R. (2000). Emotional experience in everyday life across the adult life span. *Journal of Personality and Social Psychology, 79,* 644–655. doi: 10.1037//0022-3 514.79.4.644

Carstensen, L. L., Turan, B., Scheibe, S., Ram, N., Ersner-Hershfield, H., Samanez-Larkin, G. R., et al. (2011). Emotional experience improves with age: Evidence based on over 10 years of experience sampling. *Psychology and Aging, 26,* 21–33. doi: 10.1037/a0021285

Charles, S. (2010). Strength and vulnerability integration: A model of emotional well-being across adulthood. *Psychological Bulletin, 136,* 1068–1091. doi: 10.1037/a0021232

Charles, S., & Almeida, D. M. (2007). Genetic and environmental effects on daily life stressors: More evidence for greater variation in later life. *Psychology and Aging, 22,* 331–340. doi: 10.1037/0882-7974.22.2.331

Charles, S. T., & Carstensen, L. L. (2007). Emotion regulation and aging. In J. J. Gross (Ed.), *Handbook of emotion regulation* (pp. 307–327). New York: Guilford Press.

Charles, S. T., & Carstensen, L. L. (2008). Unpleasant situations elicit different emotional responses in younger and older adults. *Psychology and Aging, 23,* 495–504. doi: 10.1037/a0013284

Charles, S. T., & Carstensen, L. L. (2010). Social and emotional aging. *Annual Review of Psychology, 61,* 383–409.

Charles, S. T., Mather, M., & Carstensen, L. L. (2003). Aging and emotional memory: The forgettable nature of negative images for older adults. *Journal of Experimental Psychology: General, 132,* 310–324. doi: 10.1037/0096-3445.132.2.310

Charles, S. T., Piazza, J. R., Luong, G., & Almeida, D. M. (2009). Now you see it, now you don't: Age differences in affective reactivity to social tensions. *Psychology and Aging, 24,* 645–653. doi: 10.1037/a0016673

Charles, S., Reynolds, C. A., & Gatz, M. (2001). Age-related differences and change in positive and negative affect over 23 years. *Journal of Personality and Social Psychology, 80,* 136–151. doi: 10.1037//0022-3514.80.1.136

Chein, J. M., & Schneider, W. (2005). Neuroimaging studies of practice-related change: fMRI and meta-analytic evidence of a domain-general control network for learning. *Cognitive Brain Research, 25,* 607–623. doi: 10.1016/j.cogbrainres.2005.08.013

Cheng, S., & Yim, Y. (2008). Age differences in forgiveness: The role of future time perspective. *Psychology and Aging, 23,* 676–680. doi: 10.1037/0882-7974.23.3.676

Chipperfield, J. G., Perry, R. P., & Weiner, B. (2003). Discrete emotions in later life. *Journal of Gerontology, Psychological Sciences, 58B,* 23–34.

Coats, A., & Blanchard-Fields, F. (2008). Emotion regulation in interpersonal problems: The role of cognitive-emotional complexity, emotion regulation goals, and expressivity. *Psychology and Aging, 23,* 39–51. doi: 10.1037/0882-7974.23.1.39

Compton, R. J., Arnstein, D., Freedman, G., Dainer-Best, J., Liss, A., & Robinson, M. D. (2011). Neural and behavioral measures of error-related cognitive control predict daily coping with stress. *Emotion, 11,* 379–390. doi: 10.1037/a0021776

Compton, R. J., Robinson, M. D., Ode, S., Quandt, L. C., Fineman, S. L., & Carp, J. (2008). Error-monitoring ability predicts daily stress regulation. *Psychological Science, 19,* 702–708. doi: 10.1111/j.1467-9280.2008.02145.x

Costa, P. T., McCrae, R. R., & Zonderman, A. B. (1987). Environmental and dispositional influences on well-being: Longitudinal follow-up of an American national sample. *British Journal of Psychology, 78,* 299–306. doi: 10.1111/j.2044-8295.1987.tb02248.x

Cunningham, W. A., Raye, C. L., & Johnston, M. K. (2004). Implicit and explicit evaluation: fMRI correlates of valence, emotional intensity, and control in the processing of attitudes. *Journal of Cognitive Neuroscience, 16,* 1717–1729. doi: 10.1162/0898929042947919

Diehl, M., Hay, E. L., & Berg, K. M. (2011). The ratio between positive and negative affect and flourishing mental health across adulthood. *Aging and Mental Health, 15,* 882–893.

Diener, E., & Suh, E. (1997). Measuring quality of life: economic, social, and subjective indicators. *Social Indicators Research, 40,* 189–216. doi: 10.1023/A:1006859511756

Dillon, D. G., Ritchey, M., Johnson, B. D., & LaBar, K. S. (2007). Dissociable effects of conscious emotion regulation strategies on explicit and implicit memory. *Emotion, 7,* 354–365. doi: 10.1037/1528-3542.7.2.354

Elliott, R., Bankart, B., & Light, T. (1970). Differences in the motivational significance of heart rate and palmar conductance: Two tests of a hypothesis. *Journal of Personality and Social Psychology, 14,* 166–172. doi: 10.1037/h0028686

Emery, L., & Hess, T. M. (2011). Cognitive consequences of expressive regulation in older adults. *Psychology and Aging, 26,* 388–396. doi: 10.1037/a0020041

Fredrickson, B. L., & Carstensen, L. L. (1990). Choosing social partners: How old age and anticipated endings make us more selective. *Psychology and Aging, 5,* 335–347.

Gailliot, M. T., Schmeichel, B. J., & Baumeister, R. F. (2006). Self-regulatory processes defend against the threat of death: Effects of self-control depletion and trait self-control on thoughts and fears of dying. *Journal of Personality and Social Psychology, 91,* 49–62. doi: 10.1037/0022-3514.91.1.49

Gavazzeni, J., Wiens, S., & Fischer, H. (2008). Age effects to negative arousal differ for self-report and electrodermal activity. *Psychophysiology, 45,* 148–151. doi: 10.1111/j.1469-8986.2007.00596.x

Green, M., & Malhi, G. (2006). Neural mechanisms of the cognitive control of emotion. *Acta Neuropsychiatrica, 18,* 144–153. doi: 10.1111/j.1601-5215.2006.00149.x

Gross, J. J. (1998). Antecedent- and response-focused emotion regulation: Divergent consequences for experience, expression, and physiology. *Journal of Personality and Social Psychology, 74,* 224–237. doi: 10.1037/0022-3514.74.1.224

Gross, J. J. (2002). Emotion regulation: Affective, cognitive, and social consequences. *Psychophysiology, 39,* 281–291. doi: 10.1017.S0048577201393198

Gross, J. J., & Levenson, R. W. (1993). Emotional suppression: Physiology, self-report, and expressive behavior. *Journal of Personality and Social Psychology, 64,* 970–986. doi: 10.1037/0022-3514.64.6.970

Gross, J. J., & Levenson, R. W. (1997). Hiding feelings: The acute effects of inhibiting negative and positive emotion. *Journal of Abnormal Psychology, 106,* 95–103. doi: 10.1037/0021-843X.106.1.95

Gross, J. J., Carstensen, L. L., Pasupathi, M., Tsai, J., Skorpen, C., & Hsu, A. C. (1997). Emotion and aging: Experience, expression, and control. *Psychology and Aging, 12,* 590–599. doi: 10.1037/0882-7974.12.4.590

Gyurak, A., Goodkind, M. S., Madan, A., Kramer, J. H., Miller, B. L., & Levenson, R. W. (2009). Do tests of executive functioning predict ability to downregulate emotions spontaneously and when instructed to suppress? *Cognitive, Affective & Behavioral Neuroscience, 9*, 144–152. doi: 10.3758/CABN.9.2.144

Hasher, L., Lustig, C., & Zacks, R. T. (2007). Inhibitory mechanisms and the control of attention. In A. Conway, C. Jarrold, M. Kane, A. Miyake, A., & J. Towse (Eds.), *Variation in working memory* (pp. 227–249). New York: Oxford University Press.

Hummert, M. L., Garstka, T. A., Shaner, J. L., & Strahm, S. (1994). Stereotypes of the elderly held by young, middle-aged, and elderly adults. *Journals of Gerontology, Series B: Psychological Sciences, 49B*, 240–249.

Inzlicht, M., & Gutsell, J. N. (2007). Running on empty: Neural signals for self-control failure. *Psychological Science, 18*, 933–937. doi: 10.1111/j.1467-9280.2007.02004.x

Isaacowitz, D. M., & Blanchard-Fields, F. (2012). Linking process and outcome in the study of emotion and aging. *Perspectives on Psychological Science, 7 (1)*, 3–17.

Isaacowitz, D. M., & Smith, J. (2003). Positive and negative affect in very old age. *The Journals of Gerontology, Series B: Psychological Sciences and Social Sciences, 58B*, 143–152. doi: 10.1093/geronb/58.3.P143

Isaacowitz, D. M., Toner, K., & Neupert, S. D. (2009). Use of gaze for real-time mood regulation: Effects of age and attentional functioning. *Psychology and Aging, 24*, 989–994. doi: 10.1037/a0017706

Isaacowitz, D. M., Wadlinger, H. A., Goren, D., & Wilson, H. R. (2006). Is there an age-related positivity effect in visual attention? A comparison of two methodologies. *Emotion, 6*, 511–516. doi: 10.1037/1528-3542.6.3.511

John, O., & Gross, J. J. (2004). Healthy and unhealthy emotion regulation: Personality processes, individual differences, and life span development. *Journal of Personality, 72*, 1301–1333. doi: 10.1111/j.1467-6494.2004.00298.x

Johnson, D. R. (2009). Goal-directed attentional deployment to emotional faces and individual differences in emotional regulation. *Journal of Research in Personality, 43*, 8–13. doi: 10.1016/j.jrp.2008.09.006

Kanske, P., Heissler, J., Schönfelder, S., Bonger, A., & Wessa, M. (2011). How to regulate emotion? Neural networks for reappraisal and distraction. *Cerebral Cortex, 21*, 1379–1388.

Kaplan, S., & Berman, M. G. (2010). Directed attention as a common resource for executive functioning and self-regulation. *Perspectives on Psychological Science, 5*, 43–57. doi: 10.1177/1745691609356784

Kennedy, Q., Mather, M., & Carstensen, L. L. (2004). The role of motivation in the age-related positivity effect in autobiographical memory. *Psychological Science, 15*, 208–214. doi: 10.1111/j.0956-7976.2004.01503011.x

Kessler, E., & Staudinger, U. M. (2009). Affective experience in adulthood and old age: The role of affective arousal and perceived affect regulation. *Psychology and Aging, 24*, 349–362. doi: 10.1037/a0015352

Knight, M., Seymour, T. L., Gaunt, J. T., Baker, C., Nesmith, K., & Mather, M. (2007). Aging and goal-directed emotional attention: Distraction reverses emotional biases. *Emotion, 7*, 705–714. doi: 10.1037/1528-3542.7.4.705

Kryla-Lighthall, N., & Mather, M. (2009). The role of cognitive control in older adults' emotional well-being. In V. Bengston, D. Gans, N. Pulney, & M. Silverstein (Eds.), *Handbook of theories of aging*, 2nd ed. (pp. 323–344). New York: Springer Publishing.

Kunzmann U., Little. T., & Smith J. (2000). Is age-related stability of subjective well-being a paradox? Cross-sectional and longitudinal evidence from the Berlin Aging Study. *Psychology and Aging, 15*, 511–526. doi: 10.1037//0882-7974.15.3.511

Kunzmann, U., & Richter, D. (2009). Emotional reactivity across the adult life-span: The cognitive pragmatics make a difference. *Psychology and Aging, 24*, 879–889. doi: 10.1037/a0017347

Labouvie-Vief, G., Grühn, D., & Mouras, H. (2009). Dynamic emotion-cognition interactions in adult development: Arousal, stress, and the processing of affect. In H. B. Bosworth, C. Hertzog (Eds.), *Cognition in aging: Methodologies and applications*. Washington, DC: American Psychological Association.

Lang, F. R., & Carstensen, L. L. (1994). Close emotional relationships in late life: Further support for proactive aging in the social domain. *Psychology and Aging, 9*, 315–324. doi: 10.1037/0882-7974.9.2.315

Langeslag, S. E., & van Strien, J. W. (2009). Aging and emotional memory: The co-occurrence of neurophysiological and behavioral positivity effects. *Emotion, 9*, 369–377. doi: 10.1037/a0015356

Lawton, M., Kleban, M. H., & Dean, J. (1993). Affect and age: Cross-sectional comparisons of structure and prevalence. *Psychology and Aging, 8*, 165–175. doi:10.1037/0882-7974.8.2.165

Lawton, M., Kleban, M. H., Rajagopal, D., & Dean, J. (1992). Dimensions of affective experience in three age groups. *Psychology and Aging, 7*, 171–184. doi: 10.1037/ 0882-7974.7.2.171

Levenson, R. W., Carstensen, L. L., Friesen, W. V., & Ekman, P. (1991). Emotion, physiology, and expression in old age. *Psychology and Aging, 6*, 28–35. doi: 10.1037/ 0882-7974.6.1.28

Levenson, R. W., Carstensen, L. L., & Gottman, J. M. (1994). The influence of age and gender on affect, physiology, and their interrelations: A study of long-term marriage. *Journal of Personality and Social Psychology, 67*, 56–68. doi: 10.1037/0022-3514.67.1.56

Löckenhoff, C. E., & Carstensen, L. L. (2007). Aging, emotion, and health-related decision strategies: Motivational manipulations can reduce age differences. *Psychology and Aging, 22*, 134–146. doi: 10.1037/0882-7974.22.1.134

Löckenhoff, C. E., Costa, P. R., & Lane, R. D. (2008). Age differences in descriptions of emotional experiences in oneself and others. *The Journals of Gerontology, Series B: Psychological Sciences and Social Sciences, 63B*, 92–99.

Malatesta, C. Z., & Kalnok, M. (1984). Emotional experience in younger and older adults. *Journal of Gerontology, 39*, 301–308.

Mather, M., & Knight, M. (2005). Goal-directed memory: The role of cognitive control in older adults' emotional memory. *Psychology and Aging, 20*, 554–570. doi: 10.1037/0882-7974.20.4.554

Mather, M., & Carstensen, L. L. (2005). Aging and motivated cognition: The positivity effect in attention and memory. *Trends in Cognitive Sciences, 9*, 496–502. doi: 10.1016/j.tics.2005.08.005

Mather, M., & Johnson, M. K. (2000). Choice-supportive source monitoring: Do our decisions seem better to us as we age? *Psychology and Aging, 15*, 596–606. doi: 10.1037/0882-7974.15.4.596

Mauss, I. B., Bunge, S. A., & Gross, J. J. (2007). Automatic emotion regulation. *Social and Personality Psychology Compass, 1*, 146–167. doi: 10.1111/j.1751-9004.2007.00005.x

McRae, K., Jacobs, S. E., Ray, R. D., John, O. P., & Gross, J. J. (2012). Individual differences in reappraisal ability: Links to reappraisal frequency, well-being, and cognitive control. *Journal of Research in Personality, 46*, 2–7. doi: 10.1016/j.jrp.2011.10.003

Mendes, W. (2010). Weakened links between mind and body in older age: The case for maturational dualism in the experience of emotion. *Emotion Review., 2*, 240–244.

Mikels, J. A., Larkin, G. R., Reuter-Lorenz, P. A., & Cartensen, L. L. (2005). Divergent trajectories in the aging mind: Changes in working memory for affective versus visual information with age. *Psychology and Aging, 20*, 542–553. doi: 10.1037/0882-7974.20.4.542

Moser, J. S., Most, S. B., & Simons, R. F. (2010). Increasing negative emotions by reappraisal enhances subsequent cognitive control: A combined behavioral and electrophysiological study. *Cognitive, Affective & Behavioral Neuroscience, 10*, 195–207. doi: 10.3758/CABN.10.2.195

Mroczek, D. K., & Almeida, D. M. (2004). The effect of daily stress, personality, and age on daily negative affect. *Journal of Personality, 72*, 355–378. doi: 10.1111/j.0022-3506.2004.00265.x

Mroczek, D. K., & Kolarz, C. M. (1998). The effect of age on positive and negative affect: A developmental perspective on happiness. *Journal Of Personality and Social Psychology, 75*, 1333–1349. doi: 10.1037/0022-3514.75.5.1333

Neupert, S., Almeida, D. M., & Charles, S. T. (2007). Age differences in reactivity to daily stressors: The role of personal control. *Journals of Gerontology, Series B: Psychological and Behavioral Sciences, 62B*, 116–122.

Ochsner, K. N., Bunge, S. A., Gross, J. J., & Gabrieli, J. D. E. (2002). Rethinking feelings: An fMRI study of the cognitive regulation of emotion. *Journal of Cognitive Neuroscience, 14*, 1215–1299. doi: 10.1162/089892902760807212

Ochsner, K. N., & Gross, J. J. (2004). Thinking makes it so: A social cognitive neuroscience approach to emotion regulation. In R. B. K. Vohs (Ed.), *The handbook of self-regulation.* (pp. 221–225). New York, NY.: Guilford Press.

Ochsner, K. N., & Gross, J. J. (2005). The cognitive control of emotion. *Trends in Cognitive Sciences, 9*, 242–249. doi: 10.1016/j.tics.2005.03.010

Pethtel, O., & Chen, Y. (2010). Cross-cultural aging in cognitive and affective components of subjective well-being. *Psychology and Aging, 25*, 725–729. doi: 10.1037/a0018511

Petrican, R., Moscovitch, M., & Schimmack, U. (2008). Cognitive resources, valence, and memory retrieval of emotional events in older adults. *Psychology and Aging, 23*, 585–594. doi: 10.1037/a0013176

Phillips, L. H., Henry, J. D., Hosie, J. A., & Milne, A. B. (2006). Age, anger regulation and well-being. *Aging and Mental Health, 10*, 250–256. doi: 10.1080/13607860500310385

Phillips, L. H., Henry, J. D., Hosie, J. A., & Milne, A. B. (2008). Effective regulation of the experience and expression of negative affect in old age. *The Journals of Gerontology, Series B: Psychological Sciences and Social Sciences, 63B*, 138–145.

Piazza, J. R., Charles, S. T., & Almeida, D. M. (2007). Living with chronic health conditions: Age differences in affective well-being. *The Journals of Gerontology, Series B: Psychological Sciences and Social Sciences, 62B*, 313–321.

Posthuma, R. A., & Campion, M. A. (2009). Age stereotypes in the workplace: Common stereotypes in the workplace:, moderators, and future directions. *Journal of Management, 35*, 158–188. doi: 10.1177/0149206308318617

Pruzan, K., & Isaacowitz, D. M. (2006). An attentional application of socioemotional selectivity theory in college students. *Social Development, 15*, 326–338. doi: 10.1111/j.1467-9507.2006.00344.x

Richards, J. M., & Gross, J. J. (2000). Emotion regulation and memory: The cognitive costs of keeping one's cool. *Journal of Personality and Social Psychology, 79*, 410–424. doi: 10.1037/0022-3514.79.3.410

Richards, J. M., & Gross, J. J. (2006). Personality and emotional memory: How regulating emotion impairs memory for emotional events. *Journal of Research in Personality, 40*, 631–651. doi: 10.1016/j.jrp.2005.07.002

Reich, J. W., & Zautra, A. J. (1991). Analysing the trait of routinization in older adult. *International Journal of Aging and Human Development, 32(3)*, 161–180.

Riediger, M., Schmiedek, F., Wagner, G. G., & Lindenberger, U. (2009). Seeking pleasure and seeking pain: Differences in prohedonic and contra-hedonic Motivation from adolescence to old age. *Psychological Science, 20*, 1529–1535. doi: 10.1111/j.1467-9280.2009.02473.x

Riediger, M., Wrzus, C., Schmiedek, F., Wagner, G., G., & Lindenberger, U. (2011). Is seeking bad mood cognitively demanding? Contra-hedonic orientation and working memory capacity in everyday life. *Emotion, 11*, 656–665. doi: 10.1037/a0022756

Röcke, C., & Lachman, M. E. (2008). Perceived trajectories of life satisfaction across past, present, and future: Profiles and correlates of subjective change in young, middle-aged, and older adults. *Psychology and Aging, 23*, 833–847. doi: 10.1037/a0013680

Ross, C. E., & Mirowsky, J. (2008). Age and the balance of emotions. *Social Science and Medicine, 66*, 2391–2400. doi: 10.1016/j.socscimed.2008.01.048

Salthouse, T. A., Atkinson, T. M., & Berish, D. E. (2003). Executive functioning as a potential mediator of age-related cognitive decline in normal adults. *Journal of Experimental Psychology: General, 132*, 566–594. doi: 10.1037/0096-3445.132.4.566

Samanez-Larkin, G. R., & Carstensen, L. L. (2011). Socioemotional functioning and the aging brain. In J. Decety & J. T. Cacioppo (Eds.), *The Oxford handbook of social neuroscience* (pp. 507– 521). New York: Oxford University Press.

Scheibe, S., & Blanchard-Fields, F. (2009). Effects of regulating emotions on cognitive performance: What is costly for young adults is not so costly for older adults. *Psychology and Aging, 24*, 217–223. doi: 10.1037/a0013807

Scheibe, S., & Carstensen, L. L. (2010). Emotional aging: Recent findings and future trends. *The Journals of Gerontology, Series B: Psychological Sciences and Social Sciences, 65B*, 135–144.

Scheibe, S., English, T., Tsai, J. L., & Carstensen, L. L. (2012). Striving to feel good: Ideal affect, actual affect, and their correspondence across adulthood. *Psychology and Aging.* Advanced online publication. doi: 10.1037/a0030561

Schmeichel, B. J., Vohs, K. D., & Baumeister, R. F. (2003). Intellectual performance and ego depletion: Role of the self in logical reasoning and other information processing. *Journal of Personality and Social Psychology, 85*, 33–46. doi: 10.1037/0022-3514.85.1.33

Schmeichel, B. J., Volokhov, R. N., & Demaree, H. A. (2008). Working memory capacity and the self-regulation of emotional expression and experience. *Journal of Personality and Social Psychology, 95*, 1526–1540. doi: 10.1037/a0013345

Seery, M. D. (2001). Resilience: A silver lining to experiencing adverse life events?. *Current Directions in Psychological Science, 20*, 390–394.

Senesac, E., & Blanchard-Fields, F. (2012). Cognitive depletion in emotion regulation: Age differences depend on regulation strategy. Manuscript in preparation.

Shamosh, N. A., & Gray, J. R. (2007). The relation between fluid intelligence and self-regulatory depletion. *Cognition & Emotion, 21*, 1833–1843. doi: 10.1080/02699930701273658

Sheppes, G., Catran, E., & Meiran, N. (2009). Reappraisal (but not distraction) is going to make you sweat: Physiological evidence for self-control effort. *International Journal of Psychophysiology, 71*, 91–96. doi: 10.1016/j.ijpsycho.2008.06.006

Sheppes, G., & Gross, J. (2011). Is timing everything? Temporal considerations in emotion regulation. *Personality and Social Psychology Review, 15*, 319–331. doi: 10.1177/1088868310395778

Sheppes, G., & Meiran, N. (2007). Better late than never? On the dynamics of online regulation of sadness using distraction and cognitive reappraisal. *Personality and Social Psychology Bulletin, 33*, 1518–1532. doi: 10.1177/0146167207305537

Sheppes, G., & Meiran, N. (2008). Divergent cognitive costs for online forms of reappraisal and distraction. *Emotion, 8*, 870–874. doi: 10.1037/a0013711

Sheppes, G., Scheibe, S., Suri, G., & Gross, J. J. (2011). Emotion-Regulation Choice. *Psychological Science, 22*, 1391–1396. doi: 10.1177/0956797611418350

Shiota, M. N., & Levenson, R. W. (2009). Effects of aging on experimentally instructed detached reappraisal, positive reappraisal, and emotional behavior suppression. *Psychology and Aging, 24*, 890–900. doi: 10.1037/a0017896

Stacey, C. A., & Gatz, M. (1991). Cross-sectional age differences and longitudinal change on the Bradburn Affect Balance Scale. *Journal of Gerontology, 46*, 76–78.

Stawski, R. S., Sliwinski, M. J., Almeida, D. M., & Smyth, J. M. (2008). Reported exposure and emotional reactivity to daily stressors: The roles of adult age and global perceived stress. *Psychology and Aging, 23*, 52–61. doi: 10.1037/0882-7974.23.1.52

Thomas, R. C., & Hasher, L. (2006). The influence of emotional valence on age differences in early processing and memory. *Psychology and Aging, 21*, 821–825. doi: 10.1037/0882-7974.21.4.821

Troy, A. S., Wilhelm, F. H., Shallcross, A. J., & Mauss, I. B. (2010). Seeing the silver lining: Cognitive reappraisal ability moderated the relationship between stress and depressive symptoms. *Emotion, 10*, 783–795. doi: 10.1037/a0020262

Tsai, J. L., Levenson, R. W., & Carstensen, L. L. (2000). Autonomic, expressive and subjective responses to emotional films in younger and older adults of European American and Chinese descent. *Psychology and Aging, 15*, 684–693. doi: 10.1037//Q882-7974.15.4.684

Uchino, B. N., Berg, C. A., Smith, T. W., Pearce, G., & Skinner, M. (2006). Age-related differences in ambulatory blood pressure during daily stress: Evidence for greater blood pressure reactivity with age. *Psychology and Aging, 21*, 231–239. doi: 10.1037/0882-7974.21.2.231

Uchino, B. N., Birmingham, W., & Berg, C. A. (2010). Are older adults less or more physiologically reactive? A meta-analysis of age-related differences in cardiovascular reactivity to laboratory tasks. *The Journals of Gerontology, Series B: Psychological Sciences and Social Sciences, 65B*, 154–162.

Uchino, B. N., Holt-Lunstad, J., Bloor, L. E., & Campo, R. A. (2005). Aging and cardiovascular reactivity to stress: Longitudinal evidence for changes in stress reactivity. *Psychology and Aging, 20*, 134–143. doi: 10.1037/0882-7974.20.1.134

United Nations, Department of Economic and Social Affairs Population Division (2001). World population ageing: 1950–2050. Retrieved from http://www.un.org/esa/population/publications/worldageing19502050/pdf/preface_web.pdf

Urry, H. L., & Gross, J. J. (2010). Emotion regulation in older age. *Current Directions in Psychological Science, 19*, 352–357.

Verhaeghen, P. (2011). Aging and executive control: Reports of a demise greatly exaggerated. *Current Directions in Psychological Science 20*, 174–180. doi: 10.1177/0963721411408772

Vohs, K. D., & Schmeichel, B. J. (2003). Self-regulation and extended now: Controlling the self alters the subjective experience of time. *Journal of Personality and Social Psychology, 85*, 217–230. doi: 10.1037/0022-3514.85.2.217

Watson, T. L., & Blanchard-Fields, F. (1998). Thinking with your head and your heart: Age differences in everyday problem-solving strategy preferences. *Aging, Neuropsychology, and Cognition, 5*, 225–240. doi: 10.1076/anec.5.3.225.613

Wegner, D. M., & Gold, D. B. (1995). Fanning old flames: Emotional and cognitive effects of suppressing thoughts of a past relationship. *Journal of Personality and Social Psychology, 68*, 782–792. doi: 10.1037/0022-3514.68.5.782

Williams, L. E., Bargh, J. A., Nocera, C. C., & Gray, J. R. (2009). The unconscious regulation of emotion: Nonconscious reappraisal goals modulate emotional reactivity. *Emotion, 9*, 847–854. doi: 10.1037/a0017745

Wilkowski, B. M., & Robinson, M. D. (2008). Clear heads are cool heads: Emotional clarity and the down-regulation of antisocial affect. *Cognition & Emotion, 22*, 308–326. doi: 10.1080/02699930701394199

Windsor, T. D., & Anstey, K. J. (2010). Age differences in psychosocial predictors of positive and negative affect: A longitudinal investigation of young, midlife, and older adults. *Psychology and Aging, 25*, 641–652. doi: 10.1037/a0019431

Zacks, R. T., Hasher, L., & Li, K. Z.H. (2000). Human memory. In T. A. S. F. I. M. Craik (Ed.), *Handbook of aging and cognition*, 2nd ed. Mahwah, NJ: Lawrence Erlbaum.

Zelazo, P., & Cunningham, W. (2007). Executive function: Mechanisms underlying emotion regulation. In J. J. Gross (Ed.), *Handbook of emotion regulation* (pp. 135–158). New York: Guilford Press.

PART 3

Everyday Problem Solving

Contextual Variation in Adults' Emotion Regulation During Everyday Problem Solving

Michelle A. Skinner, Cynthia A. Berg, *and* Bert N. Uchino

Abstract

This chapter reviews research on the contextual variation that is seen in how older adults experience and regulate emotion evoked by interpersonal problem solving. It begins by exploring the general developmental shift toward the experience of more positive emotion and how this shift may be dependent on context and problem constraints by utilizing the concepts of Strengths and Vulnerability Integration. It examines four different everyday problem-solving contexts in middle-aged and older adult married couples and then considers the physiological processes that might be related to emotion regulation during adulthood.

Key Words: problem solving, emotion regulation, positive emotion, Strengths and Vulnerability Integration

Our understanding of how adults across the lifespan think about and act on emotions in everyday life owes a great deal of gratitude to Fredda Blanchard-Fields's creative insights. Her focus in this field on emotions was in stark contrast to the exclusive cognitive focus on everyday problem solving as an everyday manifestation of intellectual abilities (Willis & Schaie, 1986). From her dissertation published in the first year of the journal *Psychology and Aging* to her last work on daily everyday problem solving and biomarkers, she sought to understand how older adults' socio-emotional functioning is adaptive in spite of cognitive and physiological declines with age. Where other researchers saw older adults' everyday problem solving as limited by cognitive abilities, she saw their problem solving as enriched by their ability to regulate emotions and to integrate their emotional processing together with cognitive processing, exemplified well in the title of one of her articles "Thinking with Your Head and Your Heart" (Watson & Blanchard-Fields, 1998).

However, Blanchard-Fields's complex thinking allowed her quickly to see that older adults' ability to adaptively integrate emotion and cognition was not a universal seen across all types of everyday problems. Rather, her work provided empirical demonstrations for the contextual theoretical perspective that was so crucial for the initial investigations in the field of everyday problem solving (Baltes, Dittmann-Kohli, & Dixon, 1984; Sternberg, 1984). That is, the enhanced ability of older adults to integrate their experience of emotion together with their thinking was especially demonstrated when the content of everyday problems was interpersonal in nature (Blanchard-Fields, Mienaltowski, & Seay, 2007). Furthermore, older adults were also more likely to fit their strategies to different contexts (Blanchard-Fields, Chen, & Norris, 1997), with such strategy variability regarded as adaptive, given that a single type of everyday problem-solving strategy is not likely to be equally effective across different contexts.

In this chapter, we review our own research on the contextual variation that is seen in how married couples experience and regulate emotion evoked by interpersonal problem solving. We place our research in the context of the now active theoretical debate as to whether emotional experience and regulation skills are largely advantaged in late adulthood (Scheibe & Carstensen, 2010), as well as in theories that specify conditions under which such skills show an advantage or a disadvantage for older adults (Charles, 2010; Labouvie-Vief, Gruhn, & Studer, 2010). We first discuss the general developmental shift toward the experience of more positive emotion and how this shift may be dependent on context and problem constraints by utilizing the concepts of Strengths and Vulnerability Integration (SAVI; Charles, 2010). We next utilize our data that examine four different everyday problem-solving contexts in middle-aged and older adult married couples. These data illustrate variability in whether older adults experience greater positive and lower negative affect, which is moderated by the context of the problem or task.

We extend these findings by also considering the physiological (e.g., heart rate, blood pressure) processes that might be related to emotion regulation during adulthood. This is important because physiological responses will not always map onto subjective responses in a straightforward manner (Uchino, Birmingham, & Berg, 2010). Consistent with this possibility, many studies examining age differences in physiological reactivity do not find similar patterns between physiological and self-reported affective processes (Uchino et al., 2010). Physiological responses are thus thought to provide information about a different level of analysis that can provide an integrative perspective on adaptation, as well as on its implications for physical health (Cacioppo & Petty, 1986).

Age Differences in Emotion Regulation in Problem Solving

In the context of everyday problem solving, emotion regulation aids in how individuals approach, solve, and appraise everyday problems (Blanchard-Fields, 1996; Blanchard-Fields et al., 1997). Emotion regulation refers to how an individual consciously or unconsciously modulates emotional experience and expression through adapting to emotion-eliciting situations (Gross, 1999). An understanding of how the regulation of emotions unfolds temporally across the lifespan must take into account how emotion shifts with contexts and individual strengths and vulnerabilities at different developmental time points. Charles's (2010) recent theoretical model of

emotion regulation, SAVI, represents the potential for better emotion regulation in older adults based on strengths accumulated over a lifetime balanced by vulnerabilities that accumulate with advancing age. The acknowledgment of both strengths and vulnerabilities as being important for emotion regulation suggests that, in contexts in which older adults' strengths are maximized and vulnerabilities are minimized, they may have better emotion regulation. However, in contexts in which this does not occur, older adults may have poorer emotion regulation abilities compared to younger counterparts.

A wealth of information suggests that older adults focus more on emotional aspects of everyday problems than do younger adults. Most research makes a distinction among strategies that are aimed at resolving the problem (instrumental strategies such as planful problem solving and involving others), those aimed at dealing with one's emotions (e.g., emotional coping, seeking social support), and those that involve avoidance or distancing oneself from the problem (Berg, Meegan, & Deviney, 1998; Blanchard-Fields & Coats, 2008). Older adults utilize more emotion-focused strategies or strategies aimed at controlling the internal environment for managing everyday problems, but use less planful problem solving (Blanchard-Fields & Irion, 1988; Folkman, Lazarus, Pimley, & Novacek, 1987; Lazarus & Folkman, 1984; Levine & Bluck, 1997) and confrontive strategies than do young adults (Blanchard-Fields & Coats, 2008). For instance, Folkman et al. (1987) found that older adults were more likely to use strategies for coping that included distancing and positive reappraisal, whereas younger adults relied more on instrumental coping strategies for managing stressful experiences. Older adults are able to let go of negative feelings more rapidly than are younger adults and appear less distressed by negative emotion than their younger counterparts (Carstensen, Isaacowitz, & Charles, 1999). Similarly, Aldwin, Sutton, Chiara, and Spiro (1996) found that older adults denied having problems. These findings indicate that, as individuals age, they may be more likely to appraise everyday problems as less emotionally salient but also may be more effective at regulating negative affect generated by everyday problem situations through the use of cognitive control and reappraisal (Carstensen, 1991; Carstensen, Pasupathi, Mayr, & Nesselroade, 2000).

Increasing evidence exists to support a developmental shift in emotion regulation across the lifespan. Carstensen, and colleagues (2011) have shown that positive emotions increase over time in older adults who reported on their daily emotion over 10 years. The increase in positive emotion was also associated with survival over the 10-year period of the study. In general, older adults report equal or higher levels of emotional well-being (Charles & Carstensen, 2007; Consedine & Magai, 2006) and have increased motivation to regulate emotion compared to middle-aged and younger adults (Blanchard-Fields, 2009). Moreover, older adults are less likely than their younger counterparts to experience long periods of negative emotion and may strive to regulate these negative emotions; they often report less distress when these emotions occur (Carstensen et al., 2000).

Older adults' emotional modulation may be facilitated primarily by a shift of goals toward prioritizing emotional meaning over knowledge or information-seeking goals. In part, this shift may occur from older adults' increasing awareness of time limitations (Carstensen et al., 1999). Carstensen et al. suggest that older adults' goals shift toward maintaining and fostering interpersonal relationships that provide positive emotional experiences and that this shift promotes regulation of emotion, especially in interpersonal contexts. Antecedent-focused coping is defined as ways that individuals construct their environment and close relationship partners in their environment to alter the generation, experience, and expression of emotion (Gross, 1998a, 1998b). Thus, older adults may use selection of social partners and environments or contexts to regulate emotion (Gross, 1998a, 1998b; Urry & Gross, 2010).

Both selectivity and antecedent-focused coping may be two mechanisms that explain why older adults show specific strengths that limit negative emotional experience. When individuals can select situations that allow for more favorable emotional experiences or modify situations so that they fit better with their resources (Urry & Gross, 2010), older adults may report more favorable emotional experiences. For example, older adults report fewer problems and daily stressors in their lives compared with younger adults (Aldwin et al., 1996; Almeida & Horn, 2004; Folkman et al., 1987) and show enhanced regulation of emotion when they avoid problems (Charles, Piazza, Luong, & Almeida, 2009). However, when problems occur that are unavoidable, older adults are as reactive as younger counterparts (Charles et al., 2009). The suggestion is that older individuals are motivated to select environments that reduce negative emotion, and this

effect becomes more pronounced as older adults progress through life to much older age. For example, work has shown that 80-year-olds report fewer stressors than do 70-year-olds (Charles et al., 2011). One alternative explanation for these effects that cannot yet be ruled out is that older adults, by virtue of the reduction in their social roles (e.g., no longer parenting a child or being an employed worker), may encounter fewer stressors that require the regulation of negative emotions (Folkman et al., 1987; Sansone & Berg, 1993). However, older individuals do appear to draw on their situation selection strategies (e.g., strategies to avoid problems) to manage their emotional experience (Charles et al., 2009). When contextual demands, however, constrain the modification of the situation or make it more difficult through competing task demands that draw on resources, older adults may be less successful in maintaining positive emotional experience (Urry & Gross, 2010).

Consistent with the antecedent nature of emotion regulation, older adults employ selective attention strategies that facilitate focus away from negative information and toward positive information (Carstensen & Mikels, 2005; Isaacowitz, Toner, Goren, & Wilson, 2008). Such attentional shifts also promote emotion regulation but may not always be readily controlled by the individual. For example, in situations using fearful stimuli, older adults were not able to shift attention away (Mather & Knight, 2006). It is possible that not all contexts provide the personal control implied in antecedent-focused coping, especially when the situation has highly salient negative information. In general, use of selectivity may curb instances of frequent exposure to situations or stressors that produce negative emotional states and physiological reactivity (Gross, 1998a, 2002) and promote goals in older adulthood to focus on positive emotional experiences. Overall, the work on adult age differences in emotion regulation suggests that older adults are better able to use skills in emotion regulation that promote more positive emotional experience in daily life and skills that might serve a regulatory function in the face of stressful everyday problems.

However, older adults' greater ability to regulate emotion may not be applicable to all problem situations. If problems are uncontrollable or afford little flexibility in how they are approached, older adults may be unable to use selectivity to minimize negative emotional experience. Contextual variations of everyday life situations may not only affect selectivity but also affect other emotional processes, such as one's ability to modify the situation and cognitively reappraise the situation.

The Effect of Context on Emotion Regulation

Consideration of context is an important factor in how older adults may regulate emotion during everyday problem solving. For example, the use of a particular strategy and the effectiveness of that strategy will depend on contextual conditions such as interpersonal demands (Blanchard-Fields et al., 2007), problem definitions (Berg et al., 1998), and older adults' ability to employ strategies that are consistent with their emotional goals (Coats & Blanchard-Fields, 2008). Contextual variations in older adults' emotion regulation as they resolve daily everyday problems may be placed within the SAVI model (Charles, 2010). This theory posits that age-related changes in emotional regulation are a function of both greater awareness of limited time, which translates into shifts in motivation for positive well-being, and social expertise from life lived (Charles, 2010). Living longer can generate a wealth of experience and knowledge about everyday problems and how best to solve them, given the particular situation (Rothermund & Brandstadter, 2003). Thus, older adults may be better able to predict their own emotional responses and the responses of others that act as a cue to altering one's environments to mitigate negative emotional states (Magai, 2001).

Although work suggests that older individuals may have more strengths in approaching everyday problem solving, contexts in which older adults' age-related vulnerabilities are prominent may limit their better emotion regulation around problem-solving situations. For example, a significant vulnerability in aging comes with increasing chronic health conditions of the individual and those in his or her close social network (Hoffman, Rice, & Seung, 1996), which are detrimental for well-being (Piazza, Charles, & Almeida, 2007). Chronic health conditions are stressors in their own right and may affect cognitive and physical resources that can be drawn upon for emotion regulation. Furthermore, cognitive changes in older adulthood can make daily problems and decisions more difficult to resolve (Thornton & Dumke, 2005), with daily stressors also affecting cognitive performance (Sliwinski, Smyth, Hofer, & Stawski, 2006). SAVI highlights that when vulnerabilities begin to outweigh strengths, older adults may experience more negative emotions than do younger individuals. We now explore some contextual conditions of coping with everyday problems in which older adults experience strengths in regulation and when regulation may be hindered by vulnerabilities.

Interpersonal Context and Strengths in Emotion Regulation

Older adults' enhanced abilities to regulate emotions are especially salient when individuals manage interpersonal problems (Blanchard-Fields, 1997; Fredrickson & Carstensen, 1990; Sansone & Berg, 1993). For example, older adults have been found to be less reactive to interpersonal stressors than are middle-aged or younger adults (Neupert, Almeida, & Charles, 2007). Furthermore, older adults appear less reactive to arguments that have been avoided versus actual arguments (Charles et al., 2009), whereas younger adults experience similar emotional reactivity to avoided arguments and actual arguments (Charles et al., 2009).

Older adults' lessened emotional reactivity to interpersonal stressors may come about through multiple pathways. As suggested by *socioemotional selectivity theory* (SET), older adults' interpersonal goals may be less focused on resolving interpersonal problems, but instead be focused on creating interpersonal harmony and positive emotional regard in dealing with everyday interpersonal problems (Carstensen et al., 1999; Rook, Sorkin, & Zettel, 2004; Sorkin & Rook, 2006). In addition, older adults may experience activating emotions, such as anger, with reduced frequency that allows for a greater range of emotion regulation strategies (Blanchard-Fields & Coats, 2008). Older adults' abilities to regulate emotions more favorably in interpersonal situations may also be due to how others treat older adults (Fingerman & Charles, 2010). For instance, Fingerman, Miller, and Charles (2008) found that individuals of all ages report that they would use less confrontation and more avoidance in negative interactions with older adults than with younger adults. Thus, the motivations and emotional experience of older adults, as well as of those who interact with them, may contribute to older adults' greater emotional success in interpersonal situations.

Everyday problems vary in the extent to which they occur in a social context (Berg et al., 1998; Blanchard-Fields et al., 1997). Some everyday problems are oriented toward the solution of a problem that involves only the individual (Berg et al., 1998). However, adults report experiencing problems in their everyday lives in which other individuals are frequently the source of the problem, involved in the goals that individuals set, and are substantially involved in the solution of the problem (Berg et al., 1998; Meegan & Berg, 2002). For example, when asked to describe everyday problems, the family context and problems in managing health were most frequently mentioned by older adults, whereas middle-aged adults reported multiple contexts involving family and friends and work and leisure (Sansone & Berg, 1993). Older adults' problem domains are more characteristic of interpersonal contexts in which collaborators in problem solving are likely to be close relationship partners, such as a spouse (Strough, Patrick, Swenson, Chen, & Barnes, 2003).

When couples collaborate with close relationship partners, they may experience gains in emotion regulation by minimizing relevant vulnerabilities and maximizing appropriate strengths. For instance, older adults may be able to work with others by simultaneously relying on the skills of others and drawing out those skills to optimize performance, which could attenuate the effect of their own cognitive vulnerabilities. For example, Dixon and Gould (1998) found that older couples performed as well as younger couples on a text memory task in which typically substantial age differences are seen in individual performance. When examining the strategies for remembering text, they found that older couples used collaborative discussion of content to compensate for declines in each individual's retrieval of text content (Gould, Kurzman, & Dixon, 1994). Berg, Smith, Ko, Story, Beveridge, et al. (2007) also found that older women were especially able to fit their control over a collaborative task to their own cognitive capabilities, thereby enhancing performance on an errand-running task. Older adults' greater marital satisfaction and affiliation (Story, Berg, Smith, Beveridge, Henry, & Pearce, 2007) may also benefit collaborative performance. Berg, Johnson, Meegan, and Strough (2003) found that couples who were affiliative and warm performed better on an errand-running task and a vacation decision task that did those who were more separate and less warm. Collaborative contexts may facilitate positive interaction when the quality of the interaction is affiliative and warm, perhaps by mitigating the negative emotional arousal typically present in everyday stressors or problem contexts.

Although interpersonal contexts may provide a means by which older adults can use their expertise and reduce vulnerabilities, other contextual features may override the age-related strengths provided by interpersonal contexts. For example, tasks or problems that present cognitive challenge can pose a problem for older adults' emotion regulation if cognitive capacity is strained (Knight, Seymour, Gaunt, Baker, Nesmith & Mather, 2007; Mather & Knight, 2005). If a task or problem is unavoidable and selectivity or selective attention cannot be used, older adults may not be able to readily employ their expertise. Similarly, if cognitive decline restricts older adults' ability to actively use emotion regulation and problem-solving skills, there could be an incongruence between the features of the task in interaction with individual vulnerabilities and goals for experiencing more positive emotion (Labouvie-Vief et al., 2010).

Context and Physiological Vulnerability for Emotion Regulation

The importance of context is also salient when considering older adults' physiological responses to everyday stress as they endeavor to regulate emotion. Two different literatures have systematically investigated the links between age and physiological responses with divergent results. Researchers interested in physical health outcomes have modeled such links in an attempt to determine how aging might influence disease risk. These studies typically expose individuals of differing ages to standard psychological stressors (e.g., speech, math task) and examine cardiovascular reactions thought to underlie risk for disease. The most consistent finding from this literature is that age is related to greater blood pressure reactivity during stress (Garwood, Engel, & Capriotti, 1982; Steptoe, Moses, & Edwards, 1990; Uchino, Holt-Lunstad, Bloor, & Campo, 2005). However, studies from the age and emotion regulation literature have examined this question using more general autonomic nervous system assessments (e.g., pulse transit time, skin conductance) and other types of emotional tasks (e.g., exposure to affective film clips; Levenson, 2000). This literature generally reports that age is associated with lower physiological reactivity as indexed by heart rate and pulse transit time (Levenson, Carstensen, & Gottman, 1994; Tsai, Levenson, & Carstensen, 2000).

We recently conducted a meta-analysis of thirty-one studies across these literatures to determine the nature of the link between age and physiological reactivity during emotional tasks (Uchino et al., 2010). Across all studies, we found reliable evidence that older adults showed greater systolic blood pressure (SBP) reactions, but decreased heart rate reactivity, compared to younger adults. However, based on the larger literature on age-associated changes in relevant physiology, we argued that decreases in heart rate reactivity may be a more general age-related difference (not specific to emotion regulation) because it is found across other tasks such as exercise and sympathetic infusions (Esler et al., 1995; Turner, Mier, Spina, Schechtman, & Ehsani, 1999). Blood pressure, on the other hand, may provide a better index of age differences in self-regulation because it appears more specific to emotional tasks (Uchino et al., 2010).

These data highlight the importance of distinguishing between emotion (e.g., stress) and less emotional (e.g., exercise) contexts. Of course, even within emotional context there are a number of different elicitors and coping options (Birditt, Fingerman, & Almeida, 2005; Charles, et al., 2009; Coats & Blanchard-Fields, 2008; Hay & Diehl, 2010). Recent work suggests that such contextual processes are also relevant for understanding biological responses to emotion-based tasks. For instance, Kunzmann and Gruhn (2005) found that when videos with emotional themes relevant to the aging adult were utilized (e.g., loss of a loved one), there were no longer any age differences in biological reactivity as indexed by broad assessments of the autonomic nervous system (e.g., skin conductance, finger temperature). These results have been replicated and were not moderated by individual differences in cognitive functioning (Kunzmann & Richter, 2009).

As noted earlier, age differences in biological reactivity should be greatest under more highly arousing contexts. Such contextual variation in reactivity is consistent with dynamic integration theory and SAVI (Charles, 2010; Labouvie-Vief, 2008). According to dynamic integration theory, changing cognitive resources in older adults may result in some positive changes in emotion regulation (Labouvie-Vief, 2008). However, highly arousing situations may lead to the "breakdown" of systems that regulate cognitive-affective integration and can result in poorer emotion regulation, which would be predicted to increase physiological reactivity (Labouvie-Vief, 2008). The SAVI model also directly hypothesizes that biological systems become less flexible with age, and, hence, older adults may have difficulty in dealing with more intense or long-lasting stressors (Charles, 2010).

In our recent meta-analysis, we directly tested the possibility that high levels of arousal may

contribute to greater cardiovascular reactivity during stress in older adults (Uchino et al., 2010). This is a salient possibility because the work on age and reactivity in the health domain has typically used more evocative stressors (e.g., math task) compared to the prior work on age and emotion regulation (e.g., films). Importantly, we found that there were stronger links between age and SBP reactivity when the stressor was more intense or arousing (Uchino et al., 2010). Future work will need to examine different models (e.g., cognitive-affective complexity) that may predict such effects and highlight how different physiological and psychological mechanisms can compensate or override older adults' ability to regulate emotion in various contexts.

Age differences in emotion regulation typically seen in the literature may not consistently be applicable to physiological responses. We might expect that physiological responding and capacity become dysregulated, whereby older adults show a larger discrepancy between physiological response to stressors or everyday problems and self-reports of less negative affect or greater positive reappraisals. However, it remains unclear if there is a "tipping point" at which the demands of the task far outweigh the strengths of the individual and both self-reports and physiology become less discrepant. For instance, early work by Szafran (1963, 1966) suggests that correlations between cardiac measures and performance were more evident when older individuals were under higher cognitive load. More generally, an examination of physiology may provide a different glimpse of the regulation process and help to elucidate when older adults can no longer utilize strengths in emotion regulation (e.g., reappraisal, selectivity), which might then influence their health.

Contextual Variation in Emotional Experience

We now turn to an examination of the role of context in understanding aspects of emotion regulation in our own work with middle-aged and older couples. Marriage is the context for many important interpersonal exchanges surrounding daily life during adulthood. To understand how contextual variations may play a role in mitigating the emotional regulation and physiological reactivity of older adults in everyday problem contexts, we review data that examine how middle-aged and older adult couples are engaged in everyday stressors or problem-solving tasks in interpersonal contexts.

Our own data suggest that there is contextual variation in emotional experience across multiple everyday problem-solving tasks in long-term married couples. The data that we present comes from the Utah Health and Aging study, which involved 150 middle-aged (Wives, *M* = 43.9 years old, standard deviation [*SD*] = 3.8, range 32–54 years, Husbands, *M* = 45.8 years old, *SD* = 4.0, range 37–59 years) and 154 older married couples (Wives, *M* = 62.2 years old, *SD* = 4.5, range 50–71 years, Husbands, *M* = 64.7 years old, *SD* = 4.3, range 52–76 years). Couples engaged in four tasks that tapped into positive and negative affect while resolving problems representative of their daily lives: (1) recording daily stressful events and affect at random intervals across a single day while undergoing ambulatory blood pressure monitoring (Uchino, Berg, Smith, Pearce, & Skinner, 2006), (2) describing the most stressful event of the past week (Skinner, 2007), (3) reporting positive and negative affect while discussing an area of marital conflict in their lives (Smith et al., 2009*a*), and (4) performing a collaborative hypothetical errand-running task (Berg et al., 2007). In each of these tasks, assessments of individuals' positive and negative affect were collected. In the following section, we describe the results from published analyses, as well as reanalyses of these data that illustrate the variability that exists in whether age differences in emotional experience and physiological reactivity occur.

Reports of Daily Positive and Negative Affect

Participants completed a one-day diary (adapted from the Pittsburgh diary of ambulatory mood states; Kamarck, Peterman, & Raynor, 1998) on a nonwork day following ambulatory blood pressure assessment that took place at random intervals every 45 minutes. Individuals first completed general information relevant to blood pressure measurements (e.g., time, posture, activity level, location, consumption of caffeine). Next, participants rated their positive (e.g., active, interested, excited) and negative affective states (e.g., sad, stressed, frustrated, upset) on a 1 (not at all) to 4 (very much) point scale. Individuals were also asked to indicate whether they were dealing with an everyday hassle or stressor at that time.

Multilevel models revealed that after controlling for basic demographic variables (e.g., education), older adults reported lower overall ratings of negative affect and higher overall ratings of positive affect compared to middle-aged adults (Uchino et al.,

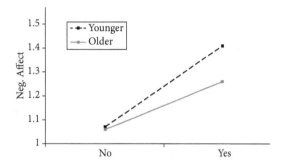

Figure 12.1. Predicted negative affect as a function of age (1 standard deviation [*SD*] above and below the mean) and daily stress (*no, yes*). Neg: negative.

2006). This main effect was qualified by an Age × Daily Stress interaction for negative affect only. As can be seen in Figure 12.1. older adults reported less of an increase in negative affect on occasions in which they reported a stressful event compared to middle-aged adults. No such interaction occurred for positive affect. These results for negative affect were in contrast to the ambulatory blood pressure data. Even when considering various important time-varying covariates (e.g., posture, caffeine), older adults' diastolic blood pressure increased on occasions in which they reported a stressful event, whereas middle-aged individuals showed little difference between occasions in which they reported a stressful event versus not. These analyses suggest that there was a greater uncoupling of self-reported negative affect and ambulatory blood pressure for older adults than for middle-aged adults. The uncoupling of self-reported affect and physiological responses might suggest a specific physiological vulnerability in older adults, whereas strength in reappraisal of emotion remains unaffected. However, it should be noted that the greater increase in diastolic blood pressure for older adults could be an indicator of older adults striving to remain controlled under stressful circumstances or use avoidant or passive coping strategies to mitigate emotional arousal (Heckhausen & Schulz, 1995; Sherwood, Dolan, & Light, 1990).

Positive and Negative Affect in Descriptions of Stressful Events

To further examine positive and negative affect in everyday stressors, narrative accounts of stressful events and coping strategies were elicited from participants as part of a structured interview. Participants were first oriented toward the week's events by asking them to recall something they did each day for the past 7 days.

Then they were asked to describe the most stressful event of the week (which could include a minor daily hassle or problem) in detail. Further, participants were asked to describe three coping strategies that they used to manage the stressor (i.e., things they did, thought, or felt). These narratives were audiotape recorded and transcribed verbatim. Next, the transcripts of these narratives were submitted to the Linguistic Inquiry and Word Count (LIWC) program developed by Pennebaker and Francis (1996, 1999). The LIWC provides textual analysis on a word-by-word basis and calculates the percentage of words (in proportion to the total number of words) in the text that match up to eighty-two language dimensions. Positive affect was indexed by words such as happy, excited, and calm. Negative affect was indexed by words such as sad, frustrated, and annoyed. In addition, participants were asked to make a rating of how the event made them feel on a 1 (not at all positive) to 7 (extremely positive) point scale.

A repeated measures analysis of variance (with spouse and valence as repeated measures and age as a between-subjects measure) indicated a main effect of age, $F(1,249) = 5.40$, $p <. 05$) such that middle-aged adults had a larger percentage of emotion words in their narratives than did older adults (2.17 vs. 1.95). However, the more important Age × Valence interaction was not significant, indicating no age differences in proportions of positive and negative affect words in the current sample. However, analyses of individuals' ratings of how positive the stressful event made them feel indicated a significant main effect of age ($F(1, 263) = 5.49$, $p <. 05$), such that older adults reported feeling more positive about the stressful event than did middle-aged adults (4.23 vs. 3.83). These analyses suggest that although there were few age differences in the proportion of adults' narratives that reflected positive and negative affect words, older adults appraised their stressful events as more positive overall than did middle-aged adults.

We then analyzed the domains of stressors (as coded qualitatively into interpersonal, work, finances, etc.) reported by husbands and wives to determine whether emotion was related differently to different stress contexts by age. We did not find any interactions between context and age for husbands. We found contextual effects for wives, such that older wives reported fewer negative emotion words than did middle-aged women when they discussed stressors involving household chores and time management, suggesting that, in the domains of household chores and time management, older

wives were able to describe events more positively. However, older wives mentioned *fewer* positive emotion words in stress narratives when stressors involved health problems than did middle-aged women. The same effect was found when they discussed health stressors of other individuals (i.e., typically relatives, friends). Similarly, in the work context, older wives reported *more* negative emotion words than did middle-aged wives. It is possible that stressors that are uncontrollable (e.g., heath stressors) evoke less positive feelings in older wives. This may also be seen in the work context if work provides fewer choices for selectivity of positive social interactions or unavoidable stressors. Although such contextual explanations are tentative because we do not have more specific information regarding the features of each context (e.g., did the work stressor involve people who were not preferred social partners), the results are suggestive that different contexts pull for different emotional content for wives. It is possible that this was not found for husbands because husbands tended to describe events using fewer emotional words overall.

Marital Conflict Discussion and Collaborative Problem-Solving Task

Finally, participants completed two tasks in a laboratory setting together with their spouse: a marital conflict discussion and a collaborative errand-running task. The marital conflict discussion occurred in a laboratory context in which couples discussed a topic that they jointly nominated as a source of frequent disagreement (e.g., household responsibilities, money). Individuals were told to select an issue for discussion that was a current issue that they could discuss for 15 minutes. Instructions indicated that couples were not expected to solve the particular issue but to view the discussion as an opportunity to make progress on the issue. A content analysis of couples' disagreement topics indicated that the most common conflicts involved their children, communication, money, and household responsibilities (Story et al. 2007). The collaborative problem-solving task involved a hypothetical errand-running task (Radziszewska & Rogoff, 1988) in which couples planned the shortest route involving the least amount of time to complete twelve everyday errands (e.g., going to the bank, shopping, dry cleaner, etc.). Couples had 15 minutes to complete the errands.

Before and after each of the tasks, individuals separately made ratings of how much they felt twelve different emotions focused on the interpersonal emotions of state anxiety and anger (e.g., calm, annoyed, tense, friendly, nervous, and angry). For the present analyses, we conducted factor analyses of these emotion words. The first two factors for each task and for females and males revealed two dimensions reflecting positive (i.e., calm, friendly, warm and kindhearted, relaxed) and negative emotions (i.e., annoyed, tense, nervous, angry, anxious, irritated, worried, and aggressive). A mixed ANOVA (with age group as a between-subjects factor and gender, task, and valence as within subjects factors) on change in emotions experienced revealed a significant Age × Valence by task interaction, $F(1, 278) = 6.58, p < .05$). Older adults experienced fewer decreases in positive emotion and fewer increases in negative emotion compared to middle-aged adults during the laboratory disagreement task. However, during the collaborative problem-solving task, older adults showed greater increases in negative emotion and decreases in positive emotion (see Figure 12.2). These analyses suggest that the typical positivity effect, in which older adults experience more positive and less negative affect, was found only for the marital disagreement task rather than for the collaborative task. These results should be interpreted with caution because the specific positive and negative emotion words used were selected to tap components of anger and anxiety rather than positive and negative affect more broadly. However, previous analyses of these same emotion words focusing on the distinction of anger and anxiety (Smith et al., 2009a) revealed similar results in that age differences varied depending on the context of the task, such that older adults did not show better emotion regulation in the collaborative errand-running task.

We also examined physiological responses in the conflict and collaboration tasks. Consistent with prior work, older couples had lower heart rate but higher SBP responses across tasks (Smith et al., 2009b). However, in the context of collaboration, older couples had similar heart rate reactions but higher SBP reactivity (especially men), higher diastolic blood pressure reactivity, and slower recovery (Smith et al., 2009b). These data may reflect that collaboration as a context holds greater demands for older rather than for middle-aged adults, perhaps due to the greater cognitive demands of this task and the use of collaboration as a compensatory coping strategy. Given that collaboration occurs more frequently in the lives of older married adults (Berg, Schindler, Smith, Skinner, & Beveridge, 2011), these data suggest the importance of the interpersonal context on the physiological mechanisms that may contribute to emotion regulation processes in older adults and subsequent health outcomes. To the extent that these data indicate that collaboration holds greater demands for the aging adult, it is consistent with the predictions of dynamic integration and SAVI theories' predictions of difficulty for older adults in these more demanding contexts. This interpretation is consistent with our meta-analytic finding of stronger links between age and blood pressure reactivity when the stressor was more intense or arousing (Uchino et al., 2010). Future work will need to examine the potential mechanisms responsible for such differences as predicted by these models (e.g., cognitive-affective complexity) and may highlight how different systems can compensate or override older adults' ability to regulate emotion in various contexts.

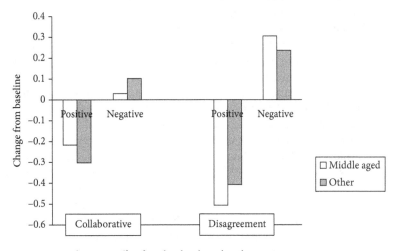

Figure 12.2. Change in positive and negative affect from baseline by task and age.

In sum, the results from the Health and Aging Study indicate that age differences in the experience of positive and negative emotions and the regulation of these emotions show contextual variability. In contexts in which older adults are afforded the most latitude to utilize their strengths in selectivity (e.g., selecting everyday experiences throughout the day), we find evidence that older adults report greater positive and less negative affect. Emotional experience in the context of naturally occurring stressful events demonstrates that older adults experience less negative affect in response to stressful events than do middle-aged adults. Examining narratives of stressful events, older adults' greater positivity is only seen in their appraisals of the positivity of the event but not in the count of the actual positive and negative affect words used to describe the events. This might suggest that older adults' strengths in emotion regulation may be based on reappraisal processes even when stressors cannot be avoided. Furthermore, positive and negative emotion words used to describe events may depend on the context of the stressor (e.g., domain of stressor) for older wives. These results might suggest that domains that individuals find most familiar and controllable are associated with older wives' more positive emotional descriptions. Finally, in a laboratory setting, older adults evince less reduction in positive affect and increases in negative affect only in a marital disagreement task. However, in a collaborative problem-solving task that drew on older adults' cognitive skills (Berg et al., 2007), older adults showed greater decreases in positive affect and increases in negative affect. We also examined physiological components of regulation in the disagreement and collaborative task. We found that, in the disagreement task, older adults had less physiological response, consistent with older adults' reports of fewer reductions in positive affect and fewer increases in negative affect. However, in the collaborative task, which appeared to be more challenging cognitively, physiological responding was heightened. We hypothesize that the age differences in regulation found in the Utah Health and Aging Project vary by task constraints, in particular, the freedom for older adults to use strengths in selection and problem avoidance while minimizing age-related vulnerabilities.

Future Directions

Future research is needed to understand the specific contextual features that may draw out older adults' strengths and vulnerabilities to understand emotion regulation in later adulthood. From our data, it appears that older adults' ability to regulate emotions is enhanced when contexts provide individuals the most freedom to selectively attend to features of the task, such as in the descriptions of everyday experiences. However, when tasks are more constrained and draw on older adults' vulnerabilities, older adults' ability to effectively regulate emotion may be reduced. For instance, in the collaborative problem-solving task, older adults were less able to regulate their emotion and also showed greater blood pressure reactivity than did middle-aged adults. The collaborative problem-solving task required that couples work together to approach a problem with specific constraints. This task required cognitive effort and simultaneous management of the interpersonal relationship. It is possible that competing task demands may prove to be especially challenging in terms of emotion regulation. It is interesting to note that we did not see similar emotional reactivity in older adults' ratings of emotions in response to everyday stressors or problems in the ambulatory diary portion of this study. In the daily context, better self-reported regulation was maintained even while physiological responses increased for older adults. Such inconsistencies hold potential for investigation into the type and number of task constraints that must be present for older adults' emotion regulation to be undermined. SAVI posits that emotion regulation is a function of the balance between older adults' strengths and vulnerabilities. Investigations into the links between specific physiological vulnerabilities associated with age and responses to emotionally salient everyday situations may provide nuanced information about when older adults' strengths are outweighed by vulnerabilities.

The examination of emotional regulation in various contexts is essential for understanding its development. Blanchard-Fields's work offered a model of how future inquiry could proceed to further understand contextual differences in adults' regulation of emotion and where in the process older adults may be able to better regulate emotions (Blanchard-Fields, 2009). Specifically, she suggested that older adults are motivated to reduce negative emotion much more so than younger counterparts. For example, older adults' avoidance of angry interpersonal stimuli occurs relatively early in the process of emotion regulation. Similarly, in response to disgust film clips, older adults were less cognitively impaired when they were told to down-regulate the emotional experience of disgust, thus suggesting that when older adults are free to regulate, they may use this ability to buffer against potential declines in memory performance. This result was present even though both older and younger adults had similar emotional reactions to the emotional film clip without specific directions to regulate emotional experience. When older adults were asked to suppress an already generated negative emotion, they had more impairment, thus suggesting that the cost of suppression is far greater than the cost of regulating negative emotion before full generation of negative emotion occurs. Through examination of several studies, she concluded that older adults' emotion regulation depends on their ability to flexibly select and apply strategies for emotion regulation. Thus, her work offers a road map for the type of detailed experimental work that might help to clarify remaining questions regarding contextual effects of emotion regulation.

In this chapter, we focused on different tasks within the interpersonal domain, and future work in this area would do well to focus on broader contexts outside of the interpersonal domain, as well as on measurement of people's reactions in various contexts. For example, manipulations of the cognitive challenge in a task may provide information about how difficult a task must be before older adults are unable to utilize their skills. Similarly, investigations in personal vulnerability (e.g., cognitive decline) or preferences for tasks (e.g., preferred contexts, enjoyable context) would be helpful. It is likely that there are individual difference characteristics that contribute to older adults' ability to regulate. For example, if the task is desirable, they may feel freer to regulate emotion, whereas if they would rather avoid the task, they may feel more constrained. An investigation of the contextual features that allow older adults to show their strengths or be affected by their vulnerabilities will need to take into account adults' appraisals of the meaning of the context (Berg et al., 1998). For example, work may be associated with greater goals for competence, which may be increasingly difficult to attain, thus contributing to less effective regulation in those contexts (Berg et al., 1998). Specific features may help clarify which contexts are detrimental to better regulation. These types of investigations with the addition of models of physiology can help support theories such as SAVI that seek to look at emotion regulation in older adults as a nuanced and carefully balanced set of processes.

One promising area of work that might help integrate these areas is the growing literature examining the brain mechanisms that might be associated with emotion-based differences between younger and older adults (MacPherson, Phillips, & Sala, 2002; Mather et al., 2004; Samanez-Larkin, Mikels, Robertson, Carstensen, & Gotlib, 2009; see St. Jacques, Bessette-Symons, & Cabeza, 2009, for a review). It is clear that self-report measures of psychological processes reflect complex information processing pathways that may rely on separable neural substrates (Eisenberger, Gable, & Lieberman, 2007; Lieberman, 2007). Some of these neural substrates are more closely linked to autonomic nervous system alterations than others (Gianaros & O'Connor, 2011). Although more work is needed, these studies generally show that older adults show greater recruitment of medial prefrontal structures and less amygdala activation in response to negative stimuli (St. Jacques et al., 2009).

Given that amygdala activation results in stronger peripheral biological responses (Gray, 1993), how would lower activation of the amygdala during negative stimuli in older adults explain the heightened blood pressure reactivity typically seen during everyday stress? It is important to note that these functional magnetic resonance imaging (fMRI) studies have examined low levels of emotional induction (e.g., pictures, words, faces) that might be related to comparable or better self-report and biological emotion regulation in older adults (Charles, 2010; Labouvie-Vief, 2008). It is thus possible that exposing older adults to more intense stressors might be related to less activation of medial prefrontal structures and greater activity in the amygdala, which should result in stronger peripheral biological responses although not necessarily changes in self-reported affect (as seen in our recent meta-analysis, Uchino et al., 2010). We propose a ventral medial prefrontal (vmPFC)/amygdala mechanism to be responsible for links between age and peripheral biological responses. That is, at low levels of stress, age differences in the vmPFC favors emotion regulation in older adults because this region has been linked to emotional and social goals (MacPherson et al., 2002). However, higher levels of stress have been shown to deactivate the vmPFC (Wager, Waugh, Lindquist, Noll, Fredrickson et al., 2009). In the case of older adults, higher levels of stress may have a stronger negative influence on vmPFC because it interferes with the pursuit of emotional and social goals as outlined by SET and SAVI. This might result in amygdala activation and greater subsequent peripheral biological responses during stress (Wager, Davidson, Hughes, Lindquist, & Ochsner, 2008) and more variable links to self-report processes. Future research will be needed to test the viability of this hypothesis using central and peripheral biological assessments, as well as self-reported emotions (see Wager et al., 2009*a*; Wager et al., 2009*b*).

Conclusion

The current chapter focused on discussion of the literature regarding the general developmental shift toward more positive emotion. We proposed that this shift may be dependent on context and problem constraints, as suggested by more recent theory, such as the SAVI model (Charles, 2010). This model integrates theory suggesting that older adults have better skills at regulation of emotion based on shift in motivation toward more positive emotional experiences in later life and that these skills are enhanced only under conditions in which strengths can be utilized and vulnerabilities minimized. We specifically utilized data that demonstrated contextual variability in the reports of positive affect based on different aspects of the task or conditions under which older adults were reporting everyday problems. We also discussed the physiological aspects of regulation and changes in older adulthood, in which different tasks are associated with either uncoupling of blood pressure reactivity and self-report affect (daily experiences of stressors or problems) or tasks in which blood pressure reactions may be more consistent with self-reported affect (e.g., collaborative problem solving). The results described in this chapter stand in contrast to much of the work in emotion regulation among older adults, which has stemmed from work in which the context is relatively unconstrained, such as reports of emotion in daily life, in which contexts may be largely dependent on older adults' skill at selectivity (Carstensen, 2011). Our work looking at individuals' responses across contexts that vary in constraints demonstrated that older adults' emotion regulation skills are more likely a function of strengths and vulnerabilities triggered by context, as suggested by the SAVI model (Charles, 2010). The physiological literature would suggest that emotional tasks or emotionally salient stressors can illicit dysregulation in physiological responses despite the evidence of better self-reported indices of emotion regulation. Together, both literatures suggest a complex picture in which contextual conditions, either as a function of task or real-life constraints (e.g., inability to use selectivity, unavoidable stressors) can tax older adults' ability to utilize their strengths. Older adults may experience overwhelming physiological arousal

or difficulty with managing cognitive challenges. In such conditions, older adults' better ability to regulate emotional experience may become threatened.

Acknowledgments

The study was supported by a grant from the National Institutes of Aging R01 AG 18903 awarded to Timothy Smith (PI) and Cynthia Berg (co-PI).

References

Aldwin, C. M., Sutton, K. J., Chiara, G., & Spiro, A. (1996). Age differences in stress, coping and appraisal: Findings from the normative aging study. *Journal of Gerontology, 51b*(4), 179–188.

Almeida, D. M., & Horn, M. C. (2004). Is daily life more stressful during middle adulthood? In O. G. Brim, C. D. Ryff, & R. C. Kessler (Eds.), *How healthy are we? A national study of well-being at midlife* (pp. 425–451). Chicago: University of Chicago Press.

Baltes, P. B., Dittmann-Kohli, F., & Dixon, R. A. (1984). New perspectives on the development of intelligence in adulthood: Toward a dual-process conception and a model of selective optimization with compensation. In P. B. Baltes & O. G. Brim, Jr. (Eds.), *Life-span development and behavior* (vol. 6, pp. 33–76). New York: Academic Press.

Berg, C. A., Johnson, M. M. S., Meegan, S. P., & Strough, J. (2003). Collaborative problem solving interaction in young and old married couples. *Discourse Processes, 35*, 33–58.

Berg, C. A., Meegan, S. P., & Deviney, F. P. (1998). A social-contextual model of coping with everyday problems across the life span. *International Journal of Behavioral. Development, 22*, 239–261.

Berg, C. A., Schindler, I., Smith, T. W., Skinner, M., & Beveridge, R. M. (2011). Perceptions of the cognitive compensation and interpersonal enjoyment functions of collaboration among middle-aged and older married couples. *Psychology and Aging, 26*, 167–173.

Berg, C. A., Smith, T. W., Ko, K., Story, N., Beveridge, R., Allen, N., Florsheim, P., Pearce, G., Uchino, B., Skinner, M., & Glazer, K. (2007). Task control and cognitive abilities of self and spouse in collaboration in middle-aged and older couples. *Psychology and Aging, 22*, 420–427.

Birditt, K. S., Fingerman, K. L., & Almeida, D. M. (2005). Age differences in exposure and reactions to interpersonal tensions: A daily diary study. *Psychology and Aging, 20*, 330–340.

Blanchard-Fields, F. (1996). Causal attributions across the adult life span: The influence of social schemas, life context, and domain specificity. *Applied Cognitive Psychology, 10*, 137–146.

Blanchard-Fields, F. (1997). The role of emotion is social cognition across the adult life span. In. K.W. Schaie & M.P. Lawton (Eds.), *Annual Review of Gerontology and Geriatrics* (Vol 17, pp. 238–265). New York: Springer.

Blanchard-Fields, F. (2009). Flexible and adaptive socioemotional problem solving in adult development. *Restorative Neurology and Neuroscience, 27*, 539–550.

Blanchard-Fields, F., Chen, Y., & Norris, L. (1997). Everyday problem solving across the life span: Influence of domain specificity and cognitive appraisal. *Psychology and Aging, 12*, 684–693.

Blanchard-Fields, F., & Coats, A. H. (2008). The experience of anger and sadness in everyday problems impacts age differences in emotion regulation. *Developmental Psychology, 44,* 1547–1556.

Blanchard-Fields, F., & Irion, J. (1988). The relation between locus of control and coping in two contexts: Age as a moderator variable. *Psychology & Aging, 3,* 197–203.

Blanchard-Fields, Mienaltowski, A., & Seay, R. B. (2007). Age differences in everyday problem-solving effectiveness: Older adults select more effective strategies for interpersonal problems. *Journal of Gerontology: Psychological Science, 62B,* P61-P64.

Cacioppo, J. T., & Petty, R. E. (1986). Social processes. In M. Coles, E. Donchin, & S. Porges (Eds.), *Psychophysiology: Systems, processes, and application* (pp. 646–679). New York: Guilford.

Carstensen, L. L. (1991). Selectivity theory: Social activity in life-span context. In K. W. Schaie (Ed.), *Annual review of gerontology and geriatrics* (vol. 11, pp. 195—217). New York: Springer.

Carstensen, L. L., Isaacowitz, D. M., & Charles, S. T. (1999). Taking time seriously: A theory of socioemotional selectivity. *American Psychologist, 54*(3), 165–181.

Carstensen, L. L., & Mikels, J. A. (2005). At the intersection of emotion and cognition. Aging and the positivity effect. *Current Directions in Psychological Science, 14*(3), 117?121.

Carstensen, L. L., Pasupathi, M., Mayr, U., & Nesselroade, J. R. (2000). Emotional experience in everyday life across the adult life span. *Journal of Personality and Social Psychology, 79,* 644–655.

Carstensen, L. L., Turan, B., Scheibe, S., Ram, N., Ersner-Hershfield, H., Samanez-Larkin, G. R., Brooks, K. P., & Nesselroade, J. R. (2011). Emotional experience improves with age: Evidence based on over 10 years of experience sampling. *Psychology and Aging, 26,* 21–33.

Charles, S. T. (2010). Strength and vulnerability integration: A model of emotional well-being across adulthood. *Psychological Bulletin, 136,* 1068–1091.

Charles, S. T., & Carstensen, L. L. (2007). Emotion regulation and aging. In J. J. Gross (Ed.), *Handbook of emotion regulation* (pp. 307–327). New York: Guilford Press.

Charles, S. T., Piazza, J., Luong, G., & Almeida, D. M. (2009). Now you see it, now you don't: Age differences in affective reactivity to social tensions. *Psychology & Aging, 24,* 645–653.

Coats, A. H., & Blanchard-Fields, F. (2008). Emotion regulation in interpersonal problems: The role of cognitive-emotional complexity, emotion regulation goals, and expressivity. *Psychology and Aging, 23*(1), 39–51.

Consedine, N. S., & Magai, C. (2006). Emotion development in adulthood: A developmental functionalist review and critique. In C. Hoare (Eds.), *The Oxford handbook of adult development and learning* (pp. 209–244). New York: Oxford University Press

Dixon, R. N., & Gould, O. N. (1998). Younger and older adults collaborating on retelling everyday stories. *Applied Developmental Science, 2,* 160–171.

Eisenberger, N. I., Gable, S. L., & Lieberman, M. D. (2007). fMRI responses relate to differences in real-world social experience. *Emotion, 7,* 745–754.

Esler, M. D., Thompson, J. M., Kaye, D. M., Turner, A. G., Jennings, L., Cox, H. S., Lambert, G. W., & Seals, D. R. (1995). Effects of aging on the responsiveness of the human cardiac sympathetic nerves to stressors. *Circulation 91,* 351–358.

Fingerman, K. L., & Charles, S. (2010). It takes two to tango: Why older people have the best relationships. *Current Directions in Psychological Science, 19,* 172–176.

Fingerman, K. L., Miller, L., & Charles, S. (2008). Saving the best for last: How adults treat social partners of different ages. *Psychology and Aging, 23,* 399–409.

Folkman, S., Lazarus, R. S., Pimley, S., & Novacek, J. (1987). Age differences in stress and coping processes. *Psychology and Aging, 2,* 171–184.

Fredrickson, B. F., & Carstensen, L. (1990). Choosing social partners: How old age and anticipated endings make people more selective. *Psychology and Aging, 5*(3), 335–347.

Garwood, M., Engel, B. T., & Capriotti, R. (1982). Autonomic nervous system function and aging: Response specificity. *Psychophysiology, 19,* 378–385.

Gianaros, P. J., & O'Connor, M. F. (2011). Neuroimaging methods in human stress science. In R. Contrada & A. Baum (Eds.), *Handbook of stress science* (pp. 543–563). New York: Springer.

Gould, O. N., Kurzman, D., & Dixon, R. A. (1994). Communication during prose recall by young and old dyads. *Discourse Process, 17,* 149–165.

Gray, T. S. (1993). Amygdaloid CRF pathways: Role in autonomic, neuroendocrine, and behavioral responses to stress. In Tache, Y. and Rivier, C. (Eds.), Corticotropin-releasing factor and cytokines: Role in the stress response. *Annals of the New York Academy of Sciences, 697,* 3–60.

Gross, J. J. (1998*a*). Antecedent—and response-focused emotion regulation: Divergent consequences for experience, expression, and physiology. *Journal of Personality and Social Psychology, 74,* 224–237.

Gross, J. J. (1998*b*). The emerging field of emotion regulation: An integrative review. [Special Issue: New directions in research on emotion.] *Review of General Psychology, 2*(3), 271–299.

Gross, J. J. (1999). Emotion Regulation: Past, present, and future. *Cognition & Emotion, 13* (5), 551–573.

Gross, J. J. (2002). Emotion regulation: Affective, cognitive, and social consequences. *Psychophysiology, 39,* 281–291.

Hay, E. L., & Diehl, M. (2010). Reactivity to daily stressors in adulthood: The importance of stressor type in characterizing risk and resilience factors. *Psychology and Aging, 25,* 118–131.

Heckhausen, J., & Schulz, R. (1995). A life-span theory of control. *Psychological Review, 102,* 284–304.

Hoffman, C., Rice, D., & Sung, H. Y. (1996). Persons with chronic conditions. Their prevalence and costs. *Journal of the American Medical Association, 276,* 1473–1479.

Isaacowitz, D. M.Toner, K., Goren, D., & Wilson, H. R. (2008). Looking while unhappy: Mood congruent gaze in young adults, positive gaze in older adults. *Psychological Science 19.* 843–853.

Kamarck, T. W., Peterman, A. H., & Raynor, D. A. (1998). The effects of the social environment on stress-related cardiovascular activation: Current findings, prospects, and implications. *Annals of Behavioral Medicine, 20*(4), 247–256.

Knight, M., Seyour, T. L., Gaunt, J. T., Baker, C., Nesmith, K., & Mather, M. (2007). Aging and goal-directed emotional attention: Distraction reverses emotional biases. *Emotion, 7,* 705–714.

Kunzmann, U., & Gruhn, D. (2005). Age differences in emotional reactivity: The sample case of sadness. *Psychology and Aging, 20*(1), 47–59.

Kunzmann, U., & Richter, D. (2009). Emotional reactivity across the adult life span: The cognitive pragmatics make a difference. *Psychology and Aging, 24*(4), 879–889.

Labouvie-Vief, G. (2008). Dynamic integration theory: Emotion, cognition, and equilibrium in later life. In V. Bengtson, M. Silverstein, N. Putney, & D. Gans (Eds.), *Handbook of theories of aging* (pp. 277–293). New York: Springer.

Labouvie-Vief, G., Gruhn, D., & Struder, J. (2010). Dynamic integration of emotional and cognition: Equilibrium regulation in development and aging. In M. Lamb, A. M. Freund, & R. M. Lerner (Eds.), *The handbook of life-span development, Vol. 2: Social and emotional development* (pp. 79–115). Hoboken, NJ: Wiley.

Lazarus, R. S., & Folkman, S. (1984). *Stress, appraisal, and coping*. New York: Springer.

Levine, L. J., & Bluck, S. (1997). Experienced and remembered emotional intensity in older adults. *Psychology & Aging, 12*(3), 514–423.

Levenson, R. W. (2000). Expressive, physiological, and subjective changes in emotion across adulthood. In S. H. Qualls & N. Abeles (Eds.), *Psychology and the aging revolution: How we adapt to longer life* (pp. 123–140). Washington, DC: American Psychological Association.

Levenson, R. W., Carstensen, L. L., & Gottman, J. M. (1994). Marital interaction in old and middle aged long-term marriages: Physiology, affect and their interrelations. *Journal of Personality and Social Psychology, 67*, 56–6

Lieberman, M. D. (2007). Social cognitive neuroscience: A review of core processes. *Annual Review of Psychology, 58*, 259–289.

MacPherson, S. E., Phillips, L. H., & Della Sala, S. (2002Age Executive function and social decision making: A dorsolateral prefrontal theory of cognitive aging. *Psychology and Aging, 17*, 598–609.

Magai, C. (2001). Emotions over the life span. In J. E. Birren & K. W. Schaie (Eds.), *Handbook of the psychology of aging* (pp. 165–183). San Diego, CA: Academic Press.

Mather, M., Canli, T., English, T., Whitfield, S., Wais, P., Ochsner, K., Gabrieli, J. D. E., & Carstensen, L. L. (2004). Amygdala responses to emotionally valenced stimuli in older and younger adults. *Psychological Science. 15*, 259–263.

Mather, M., & Knight, M. R. (2005). Goal-directed memory: The role of cognitive control in older adults' emotional memory. *Psychology and Aging, 20*, 554–570.

Mather, M., & Knight, M. R. (2006). Angry faces get noticed quickly: Threat detection is not impaired among older adults. *Journals of Gerontology Series B: Psychological Sciences and Social Sciences, 61*, P54–P57.

Meegan, S. P., & Berg, C. A. (2002). Contexts, functions, forms, and processes of collaborative everyday problem solving in older adulthood. *International Journal of Behavioral Development, 26*, 6–15.

Neupert, S. D., Almeida, D. M., & Charles, S. T. (2007). Age differences in reactivity to daily stressors: The role of personal control. *Journals of Gerontology. Series B, Psychological Sciences and Social Sciences, 62*, P216–P225.

Pennebaker, J. W., & Francis, M. E. (1996). Cognitive, emotional, and language processes in disclosure. *Cognition and Emotion, 10*, 601–626.

Pennebaker, J. W., & Francis, M. E. (1999). *Linguistic inquiry and word count: LIWC*. Mahwah, NJ: Erlbaum.

Piazza, J. R., Charles, S. T., & Almeida, D. M. (2007). Living with chronic health conditions: Age differences in affective well-being. *Journal of Gerontology: Psychological Sciences, 62B*(6), 313–321.

Radziszewska, B., & Rogoff, B. (1988). Influence of adult and peer collaborators on children's planning skills. *Developmental Psychology, 24*, 840–848.

Rook, K. S., Sorkin, D. H., & Zettel, L. A. (2004). Stress in social relationships: Coping and adaptation across the life span. In F. Lang & K. Fingerman (Eds.), *Growing together: Personal relationships across the lifespan*. New York: Cambridge University Press.

Rothermund, K., & Brandstadter, J. (2003). Coping with deficits and losses in later life: From compensatory action to accommodation. *Psychology and Aging, 18*(4) 896–905.

Samanez-Larkin, G. R., Robertson, E. R., Mikels, J. A., Carstensen, L. L., & Gotlib, I. H. (2009). Selective attention to emotion in the aging brain. *Psychology and Aging, 24*, 519–529.

Sansone, C., & Berg, C. A. (1993). Adapting to the environment across the life span: Different process or different inputs? *International Journal of Behavioral Development, 16*, 379–390.

Scheibe, S., & Carstensen, L. L. (2010). Emotional aging: Recent findings and future trends. *Journal of Gerontology: Psychological Science, 65B*, 135–144.

Sherwood, A., Dolan, C. A., & Light, K. C. (1990). Hemodynamics of blood pressure responses during active and passive coping. *Psychophysiology, 27*, 656–668.

Skinner, M. A. (2007). Relational and emotional language and spousal involvement in older and middle-aged couples' narratives of stressors and coping strategies (master's thesis), University of Utah.

Sliwinski, M. J., Smyth, J. M., Hofer, S., & Stawski, R. S. (2006). Intraindividual coupling of daily stressors and cognition. *Psychology and Aging, 21*, 545–557.

Smith, T. W., Berg, C. A., Florsheim, P., Uchino, B. N., Pearce, G., Hawkins, M., Henry, N. J. M., Beveridge, R., Skinner, M., & Olsen-Cerny, C. (2009a). Conflict and collaboration in middle-aged and older married couples: I: Effects on self-reported affect, spouse appraisals, and observed behavior. *Psychology and Aging, 24*, 259–273.

Smith, T. W., Uchino, B. N., Berg, C. A., Florsheim, P., Pearce, G., Hawkins, M., Henry, N. J. M., Beveridge, R., Skinner, Ko, K. J., & Olsen-Cerny, C. (2009b). Conflict and collaboration in middle-aged and older married couples: II; Age, sex, and task context moderate cardiovascular reactivity during marital interaction. *Psychology and Aging, 24*, 274–286.

Sorkin, D. H., & Rook, K. S. (2006). Dealing with negative social exchanges in later life: Coping responses, goals, and effectiveness. *Psychology and Aging, 21*, 715–725.

St. Jacques, P. L., Bessette-Symons, B., & Cabeza, R. (2009). Functional neuroimaging studies of aging and emotion: Fronto-amygdalar differences during emotional perception and episodic memory. *Journal of the International Neuropsychological Society, 9*, 792–810.

Steptoe, A., Moses, J., & Edwards, S. (1990). Age-differences in cardiovascular responses in mental stress tests in women. *Health Psychology, 9*, 18–34.

Sternberg, R. J. (1984). A contextual view of the nature of intelligence. In P. S. Fry (Ed.), *Changing conceptions of intelligence and intellectual functioning: Current theory and research* (pp. 7–34). Amsterdam: North-Holland.

Story, T. N., Berg, C. A., Smith, T., Beveridge, R., Henry, N. A., & Pearce, G. (2007). Positive sentiment bias in middle and older married couples. *Psychology and Aging, 22*, 719–727.

Strough, J., Patrick, J. H., Swenson, L. M., Cheng, S., & Barnes, K. A. (2003). Collaborative everyday problem solving: Interpersonal relationships and problem dimensions. *International Journal of Aging and Human Development, 56*, 43–66.

Szafran, J. (1963). Age differences in choice reaction time and cardio-vascular status among pilots. *Nature, 200*, 904–906.

Szafran, J. (1966). Age differences in the rate of gain of information, signal detection strategy and cardiovascular status among pilots. *Gerontologia, 12*, 6–17.

Thornton, W. J. L., & Dumke, H. A. (2005). Age differences in everyday problem-solving and decision-making effectiveness: A meta-analytic review. *Psychology and Aging, 20*, 85–99.

Tsai, J. L., Levenson, R. W., & Carstensen, L. L. (2000). Autonomic, subjective, and expressive responses to emotional films in older and younger Chinese Americans and European Americans. *Psychology and Aging, 15*, 684–693.

Turner, M. J., Mier, C. M., Spina, R. J., Schechtman, K. B., & Ehsani, A. A. (1999). Effects of age and gender on the cardiovascular responses to isoproterenol. *Journal of Gerontology: Biological Sciences, 54A*, B393–B400.

Wager, Davidson, Hughes, Lindquist, & Ochsner (2008). Prefrontal-sucortical pathways mediating successful emotion regulation. *Neuron, 59*(6), 1037–1050,

Wager, T. D., Waugh, C. E., Lindquist, M., Noll, D. C., Fredrickson, B. L., & Taylor, S. F. (2009 *a*). Brain mediators of cardiovascular responses to social threat, Part I: Reciprocal dorsal and ventral sub-regions of the medial prefrontal cortex and heart-rate reactivity. *NeuroImage, 47*, 821–835.

Wager, T. D., van Ast, V. A., Hughes, B. L., Davidson, M. L., Lindquist, M. A., & Ochsner, K. N. (2009*b*). Brain mediators of cardiovascular responses to social threat, Part II: Prefrontalsubcortical pathways and relationship with anxiety. *NeuroImage 47*, 836–851.

Watson, T. L., & Blanchard-Fields, F. (1998). Thinking with your head and your heart: Age differences in everyday problem-solving strategy preferences. *Aging, Neuropsychology, and Cognition, 5*, 225–240.

Willis, S. L., & Schaie, K. W. (1986). Practical intelligence in later adulthood. In R. J. Sternberg & R. K. Wagner (Eds.), *Practical intelligence: Nature and origins of competence in the everyday world* (pp. 236–268). New York: Cambridge University Press.

Uchino, B., Berg, C. A., Smith, T. S., Pearce, G., & Skinner, M. (2006). Age-related differences in ambulatory blood pressure during daily stress: Evidence for greater blood pressure reactions in older individuals. *Psychology and Aging, 21*, 231–239.

Uchino, B, N., Birmingham, W., & Berg, C. A. (2010). Are older adults less or more physiologically reactive? A meta-analysis of age-related differences in cardiovascular reactivity to laboratory tasks. *Journals of Gerontology: Series B Psychological Sciences and Social Science, 65B*(2), 154–162.

Uchino, B. N., Holt-Lunstad, J., Bloor, L. E., & Campo, R. A. (2005). Aging and cardiovascular reactivity to stress: Longitudinal evidence for changes in stress reactivity. *Psychology and Aging, 20*, 134–143.

Urry, H., & Gross, J. J. (2010). Emotion regulation in older age. *Current Directions in Psychological Science, 19*, 352–357.

Goals and Strategies for Solving Interpersonal Everyday Problems Across the Lifespan

JoNell Strough *and* Emily J. Keener

Abstract

In this chapter, we review research on interpersonal everyday problem solving from adolescence through old age. First, we provide a brief history of the emergence of research on interpersonal everyday problem solving as a distinct area of inquiry. We then outline a contextual and motivational model of interpersonal everyday problem solving across the lifespan. Drawing from this model, we discuss how dimensions of interpersonal relationships, in tandem with normative developmental tasks, give rise to age and gender differences in problem-solving goals and strategies. We review research that investigates links between goals and strategies, and evidence suggesting that goals may explain age and gender differences in problem-solving strategies. We also consider the extent to which a match between goals and strategies serves as an index of problem-solving effectiveness. We conclude by offering suggestions for future research.

Key Words: goals, strategies, everyday problem solving, gender, interpersonal relationships, adolescence, emerging adulthood, later adulthood, effective problem solving

Research on everyday problem solving seeks to understand people's ability to deal effectively with the challenges they face in their day-to-day lives. The navigation of daily life is not always smooth sailing. People often face obstacles or barriers that throw them off course. When it is not readily apparent how to overcome the obstacle, or the means of overcoming the obstacle are not immediately available, a problem exists (Chang, D'Zurilla, & Sanna, 2004). For example, an adolescent girl may have to choose between honoring plans to spend Saturday night with her best friend and accepting a boy's offer to go on a date. A middle-aged couple's financial planning for retirement may be derailed when their adult son returns home to live after college graduation. When writing his will, an aging man may struggle with how to divide his estate among his family. The problem-solving process unfolds as people attempt to overcome these obstacles and implement strategies to achieve their goals (Siegler & Alibali, 2005).

Chapter Overview

In this chapter, we review research on age and gender differences in interpersonal everyday problem solving across the lifespan, focusing primarily on the portion of the lifespan ranging from adolescence through old age. In our review, we consider how dimensions of interpersonal relationships may affect problem solving. More specifically, we apply a contextual and motivational model (see Figure 13.1) to consider how dimensions of interpersonal relationships (see Figure 13.2), in tandem with the normative developmental tasks operative for members of a given age group within contemporary Western culture, may affect goals and strategies for solving interpersonal everyday problems. Interpersonal everyday problems are a subset of the types of problems considered in

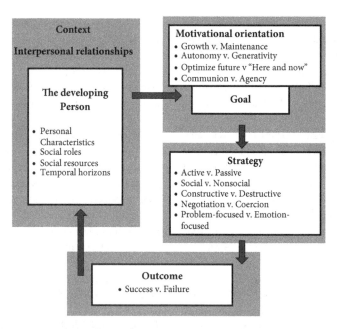

Figure 13.1. Contextual and motivational model of the problem-solving process.

the larger literature on everyday problem solving. To situate our focus on interpersonal everyday problem solving within this larger literature, we first provide a brief overview of the history of research on everyday problem solving (see, Coats, Hoppmann, & Scott, this volume, for a historical review of everyday problem-solving and coping research).

A Brief History of the Field of Everyday Problem Solving

One impetus behind the emergence of the field of everyday problem solving was to understand

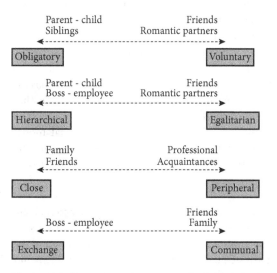

Figure 13.2. Dimensions of interpersonal relationships that may influence goals and strategies

intellectual development and problem solving in ecologically valid contexts. The emphasis on ecological validity reflected the growing recognition that intellectual development is embedded in sociohistorical and cultural contexts (see Berg, 2008, for a review). The traditional intelligence tests used to assess children and young adults who were immersed in academic environments, such as school, were suggested to be less relevant to adults because contexts become more variable with age across the lifespan (Baltes, Dittmann-Kohli, & Dixon, 1984). As such, understanding people's ability to solve problems occurring within the contexts of their everyday lives became a focal point of research (Berg & Sternberg, 1985; Blanchard-Fields & Chen, 1996; Denney, 1989).

Competency Perspective

Two broad perspectives toward understanding how people function in their day-to-day lives emerged (Berg & Klaczynski, 1996; Marsiske & Margrett, 2006). One perspective, labeled the "competency perspective" (Berg, 2008) builds on the psychometric tradition of intelligence testing. In the competency perspective, everyday problem-solving performance is theorized to reflect underlying primary mental abilities (Willis, 1996; Willis & Schaie, 1986). A central issue is to understand how age-related changes in primary mental abilities across the adult lifespan relate to performance when the abilities being tested are embedded in familiar stimuli, such as using information on a prescription medication label or modifying a recipe to address health concerns (e.g., Allaire & Marskise, 1999, 2002; Diehl, Willis, & Schaie, 1995; Thornton, Deria, Gelb, Shapiro, & Hill, 2007). Often, these problems are well-defined, such that there is one "best solution" or "correct answer." Research emanating from this perspective established that substantial overlap occurs between traditional measures of intelligence and performance on well-defined everyday problems (see Marsiske & Margrett, 2006; Thorton & Dumke, 2005 for reviews).

Despite this overlap between traditional measures of intelligence and performance on well-defined everyday problems, measures of everyday problem solving contribute to a more complete understanding of late-life functioning. Performance on well-defined everyday problem-solving tasks predicts mortality (Weatherbee & Allaire, 2008), daily functioning of patients with serious mental illness (Thornton, Kristinsson, DeFreitas, & Thornton, 2010), and individual differences in performance on Instrumental Activities of Daily Living (e.g., medication use, managing finances; Lawton & Brody, 1969), over and above the variance accounted for by traditional measures of intelligence (Allaire & Marsiske, 2002). Importantly, because many (but not all) cognitive abilities decline in late life, and because well-defined measures of everyday problem solving overlap with primary mental abilities, research guided by a competency perspective finds a trajectory of age-related decline in everyday problem-solving performance across adulthood (Thornton & Dumke, 2005).

Contextual Perspective

The other perspective toward understanding how people function in their day-to-day lives is the "contextual perspective" (Berg, 2008). When moving the study of problem solving from lab to life, the inherently social context within which people develop became part of the research terrain to be mapped. Early theoretical research emphasized that interpersonal skills were central for everyday problem solving (Berg, 1990; Ford, 1986; Meacham & Emont, 1989), and empirical research established that interpersonal features of problem contexts were salient to people across the lifespan when they described their own everyday problems (Berg, Strough, Calderone, Sansone, & Weir, 1998; Blanchard-Fields, Jahnke, & Camp, 1995; Strough, Berg, & Sansone, 1996). This research highlighted the necessity of considering individual differences in socioemotional skills

and abilities to understand how people function in their day-to-day lives—both to solve interpersonal conflicts and to work with others to overcome obstacles and complete specific tasks (i.e., collaborative problem solving; see Berg & Strough, 2011, for a review of collaborative problem solving across the lifespan).

In contrast to the age-related declines in everyday problem-solving performance found within the competency perspective, the trajectory of age differences that emerges in research guided by a contextual perspective is one of age-related maintenance and gains (Blanchard-Fields, 2007). This trajectory stands in marked contrast to the age-related declines that characterize many facets of aging, including the trajectory for well-defined everyday problem solving. The research on which this conclusion is based is reviewed in this chapter.

Conceptual Model of Everyday Problem-Solving Process

The problems used to assess performance from the contextual perspective are considered to be "ill-defined" (see Berg, Skinner, & Ko, 2009, for a review; Sinnott, 1989). Problems are ill-defined when the best strategy for solving the problem is debatable, a variety of different strategies may successfully resolve the problem, or the problem contains numerous elements such that the "core" or main problem is open to interpretation (Berg & Calderone, 1994). For instance, in the example of the middle-aged couple whose adult son moves back home, his mother might see the main problem as the son's failure to successfully navigate the transition to adulthood, but focus on her own feelings of guilt for not providing a successful foundation for his independence. Alternatively, his father could view the main problem in terms of financial strain on the family budget caused by the son's lack of ambition. Meanwhile, the son likely has his own interpretation. It may also be the case that none of the family members sees the situation as a problem. As detailed in our conceptual model here, we use problem solvers' goals to capture the essential elements of the problem from their own perspectives.

In regards to problem-solving strategies, in our model, each person's actions (or nonactions) are theorized to reflect his or her goals (see Figure 13.1). For instance, a goal of reducing guilt could be addressed by cognitively reframing the problem and blaming the economy instead of one's parenting skills. If the problem is defined as the son's lack of ambition, and the goal is to decrease the son's financial dependence, strategies might be directed toward regulating the son's behavior—for example, by finding him a job. Depending on the offspring's compliance with the attempt to regulate his behavior, the problem context will be transformed. If he resists the attempt to regulate his behavior, the situation may escalate into an interpersonal conflict.

As is apparent in this example, problem contexts are fluid and dynamic, constantly transforming over time. To understand the dynamic nature of interpersonal everyday problem solving across the lifespan, in our research, we adopt a contextual and motivational model that focuses on the problem solver's perspective of the essential features of the immediate problem-solving context (see Figure 13.1 and Berg & Strough, 2011). Recent research demonstrates that most of the variability in problem-solving strategies originates at the level of the problem situation or context (Hoppmann & Blanchard-Fields, 2011). Accordingly, it is essential to account for the problem context when investigating individual differences in problem-solving strategies. In our research, we account for problem context by considering what is salient about the context from the problem solver's perspective. To do so, we focus on goals—what the person wants to happen or accomplish. Goals are systematically related to strategies—the steps or actions a person takes to solve a problem (see Berg & Strough, 2011, for a review; Coats et al., this volume). Prior research demonstrates that goals account for additional variability in strategies, variability beyond that accounted for by problem context (Berg et al., 1998), thus demonstrating that goals may capture essential elements of the context from the person's perspective.

Motivational Orientations and Problem-Solving Goals

Our conceptualization of problem-solving goals acknowledges that goals range in their degree of specificity. That is, similar to the hierarchy posited within action-identification theory (Vallacher & Wegner, 1987), both higher and lower level goals exist. Higher level goals reflect the larger purpose that motivates a given strategy and may reflect broad motivational orientations corresponding to age, gender, developmental life tasks, or future time perspective. For instance, lifespan theorists emphasize that, in adolescence and early adulthood, people are oriented toward growth, whereas in midlife and later adulthood, their orientation shifts toward maintenance and preventing loss

(Baltes, 1987; Baltes, Lindenberger, & Staudinger, 2006). Socioemotional selectivity theory suggests that motivational orientations change systematically as a function of lifespan temporal horizons, from a focus on gaining knowledge for the future when time is perceived as unlimited, to optimizing meaningful interpersonal relationships in the "here and now," when temporal perspectives are restricted (Carstensen, 2006). Gender and cultural differences in agentic (focusing on independence and self-interest) and communal (focusing on interdependence and the self in relation to others) orientations (e.g., Bakan, 1966; Eagly, Wood, & Diekman, 2000; Markus & Kitayama, 1991) may be reflected in higher level goals. Higher level goals also may reflect normative transformations in interpersonal relationships, such as seeking autonomy from parents in adolescence (Collins & Steinberg, 2006) or increasing dependence on others in old age (Baltes & Silverberg, 1994). Developmental life tasks, such as establishing identity and intimate relationships in adolescence and early adulthood, maintaining relationships and caring for others in midlife, and maintaining integrity in the face of losses in late life (Erickson, 1968; McCormick, Kuo, & Masten, 2011) also may guide the goals that motivate interpersonal everyday problem solving across the lifespan. Within the everyday problem-solving literature, goals that pertain to developmental life tasks, such as autonomy (e.g., following own interests) and generativity (e.g., making a difference to others), have been investigated in relation to strategies for solving everyday problems with family members (Hoppmann & Blanchard-Fields, 2010), and goals that reflect communal and agentic orientations have been investigated in relation to interpersonal features of the problem-solving context (Strough et al., 1996).

Lower level goals are more concrete and correspond to the specific objectives people strive to accomplish when solving a specific problem. These goals serve as an action plan that is executed when a strategy is deployed. People often describe concrete goals (e.g., "prove that my way is best," "finish the project by 5:00 p.m.," "avoid upsetting my friend," "establish a trust fund for grandson"). These concrete goals reflect higher level goals (e.g., establishing independence or generativity), as well as the demands of the immediate problem-solving context (see Hoppmann, Coats, & Blanchard-Fields, 2008; Strough et al. 1996). Goals are systematically linked to strategies for solving everyday problems (Berg et al., 1998; Hoppmann et al., 2008).

Goals and Strategy Effectiveness

Concrete, specific goals may be particularly useful for evaluating the outcome or effectiveness (success or failure) of a person's problem-solving strategies. That is, goals serve as a reference point, both for the problem solver and for outside observers, to evaluate the extent to which a strategy moves the problem solver closer to or farther away from the desired end state (Carver & Scheier, 2002; Coats et al., this volume; Heath, Larrick, & Wu, 1999). Researchers have considered the match between goals and strategies—for example, the extent to which people use interpersonal strategies to pursue interpersonal goals (Berg et al., 1998) or use self-focused instrumental strategies to pursue autonomy goals (Hoppmann & Blanchard-Fields, 2010). However, it is important to emphasize that the presence of a match does not necessarily indicate effectiveness. In the earlier example of the son who moves back home, his mother may use a social strategy to regulate his behavior (e.g., drawing on her social connections to find him a job) that matches her social goal of facilitating her son's transition to adulthood. Yet, this goal–strategy match does not ensure that the strategy will have the intended outcome.

To use goal–strategy coherence to judge strategy effectiveness, the outcome of the strategy must be known. A focus on outcomes as an index of effectiveness has begun to emerge in work on emotion regulation (Blanchard-Fields, 2009) and stress and coping (Sorkin & Rook, 2006). More typically, however, other criteria (expert ratings, strategy fluency) have been used to judge the effectiveness of strategies (see Mienaltowski, 2011, for a review). Compared to younger adults, older adults' strategies for solving interpersonal problems are sometimes, but not always, found to be more closely aligned with experts' ratings (Artistico, Orom, Cervone, Krauss, & Houston, 2010; Blanchard-Fields, Mienaltowski, & Seay, 2007; Cornelius & Caspi, 1987; Crawford & Channon, 2002). Mixed findings may reflect variation across studies in the operational definition of a "problem-solving expert." Some studies use doctoral or master's level clinical psychologists' judgments of strategies (e.g., Artistico et al., 2010). In their seminal research, Cornelius and Caspi (1987) used laypersons, graduate students, and researchers as expert judges (see also Crawford & Channon, 2002). The expert judgments obtained by Cornelius and Caspi in the 1980s have been used in subsequent research (e.g., Blanchard-Fields et al., 2007; Galambos, MacDonald, Naphtali, Cohen, & de Frias, 2005; Marsiske & Willis, 1995). The

extent to which expert judgments of strategies obtained in the 1980s are valid for current cohorts is debatable (see McFall, 2010).

Strategy fluency (the number and diversity of strategies) is often used as an index of problem-solving effectiveness. Research indicates an inverse U-shaped function across adult age (e.g., Heidrich & Denney, 1994). There is some indication that these age differences may be attenuated by self-efficacy and problem familiarity (Artistico, Cervone, & Pezzuti, 2003). Others have questioned the use of this criterion because a single effective strategy may be sufficient, and older adults may disregard strategies they deem ineffective based on their experience (Berg, Meegan, & Klaczynski, 1999). One underlying assumption of using strategy fluency as an index of effectiveness is that participants pursue the goal set by the researcher, namely, to list as many strategies as possible.

Interpersonal Problem-Solving Contexts Across the Lifespan

Our model of everyday problem solving acknowledges that different social contexts are more or less prevalent depending on age. Peer relationships assume a more prominent position in adolescents' daily lives relative to childhood, while the prominence of family recedes (Collins & Steinberg, 2006). Romantic relationships become increasingly important across adolescence through early adulthood, often culminating in committed pair relationships, such as marriage or domestic partnerships (Roisman, Masten, Coatsworth, & Tellegen, 2004). In early adulthood and midlife, family and work relationships are prominent (Bornstein, Bradley, Lutfey, Mortimer, & Penmar, 2011). Relationships may "carry over" from earlier ages as social convoys move through life together (Antonucci, Birditt, & Ajrouch, 2011). New relationships may be formed and old relationships dissolved. For instance, in later adulthood, people winnow extraneous others from their social networks and selectively maintain and maximize relationships with a smaller, more select group (Carstensen, 2006), although there is some evidence to suggest that the specific relationships selected depend on culture (Fung, Stoeber, Yeung, & Lang, 2008). Our model also acknowledges that social contexts and specific interpersonal relationships are nested within more distal sociocultural and historical contexts. For example, relationships between parents and offspring during the developmental life stage of emerging adulthood—a period in the early 20s when offspring may remain financially and emotionally dependent on their parents—represents a relatively recent historical phenomenon within industrialized cultures (Arnett, 2000).

Dimensions of Interpersonal Relationships

In this chapter, we consider the extent to which individual characteristics such as age and gender, in tandem with dimensions of relationships such as those outlined in Figure 13.2, are related to the goals and strategies people select for solving interpersonal problems. Interpersonal relationships can be conceptualized as falling on a continuum across a number of dimensions (see Figure 13.2). On the dimension of closeness, interpersonal relationships with family and friends are distinct from more peripheral relationships with acquaintances or professionals (e.g., salesperson, dentist; Fingerman, Brown, & Blieszner, 2011; Levitt, & Cici-Gokaltun, 2011). Some close relationships, such as family, are obligatory, whereas others, such as friends, are voluntary (see Hartup & Stevens, 1997; Laursen, Finkelstein, & Townsend Betts, 2001). Communal norms operate in some relationships, partners respond to each other based on need without expecting equal benefits in return, whereas equity norms for "quid pro quo" operate in exchange relationships, in which people keep track of others' contributions (Clark, Mills, & Corcoran, 1989). Interpersonal relationships also differ in the extent to which they are hierarchical, where one person holds more power in the relationship (e.g., boss–employee) versus egalitarian, where partners expect to share power (e.g., friends). Over time, a relationships' placement on the continuum of a given dimension may change. For instance, parent–child relationships become more egalitarian as the child enters adolescence and adulthood. As parents age, they may become more dependent on their adult children. Moreover, socially proscribed roles and behaviors within relationships may differ according to age and gender. For instance, whereas parents are expected to support their children, stereotypical gender roles of homemaker mothers and breadwinner fathers assign emotional support to mothers and financial support to fathers (Eagly et al., 2000). In relationships with friends, girls' friendships are less overtly hierarchical and more egalitarian than those of boys (Maccoby, 1998). In our review, we thus consider socially proscribed roles as a factor that may increase the salience of particular goals when problems occur in interpersonal relationships.

Age Differences in Goals and Strategies for Solving Interpersonal Everyday Problems

A small number of studies include adolescents, young, middle-aged, and older adults within a single study and compare goals and strategies as a function of age group (Berg et al., 1998; Birditt & Fingerman, 2005; Blanchard-Fields, 1986; Hoppmann et al., 2008; Strough et al., 1996). Aside from these studies, much of the literature on interpersonal everyday problem solving uses between-group designs to compare younger and older adults. Thus, to map the developmental trajectory of interpersonal everyday problem solving from adolescence through old age, we draw from other literatures in addition to the everyday problem-solving literature, including peer conflict management, marital and romantic relationship conflict, and stress and coping (for reviews of these literatures, see Coats et al., this volume; Eldridge & Christensen, 2002; Laursen et al., 2001; Seiffge-Krenke, 2011). We use research from these literatures selectively to highlight how individual difference characteristics, such as age and gender, in tandem with dimensions of interpersonal relationships, may be associated with the pursuit of goals that give rise to specific problem-solving strategies.

Adolescence and Early Adulthood

Age-related differences in strategies for managing interpersonal conflicts with peers are well documented. Meta-analytic research (Laursen et al., 2001) indicates that children tend to use coercion (i.e., verbal or physical aggression, commands) more than negotiation (i.e., talking things out, compromising) or disengagement (i.e., withdrawing, passive-avoidance), whereas adolescents and young adults tend to manage interpersonal conflicts by using negotiation more than by using coercion or disengagement. Adolescents use coercion and disengagement equally, but young adults are less likely to use coercion than disengagement. This research suggests that interpersonally oriented strategies involving negotiation and involvement of both partners in conflict resolution increase from childhood to early adulthood, whereas coercion and disengagement decrease.

Age-related differences in strategies from childhood to adolescence may be due to goals that change in conjunction with developmental tasks (see Figure 13.1). For example, in adolescence, pubertal changes, advances in abstract thought, and increased social skills, spur the developmental task of identity development (see Diehl, Youngblade, Hay, & Chui,

2011; Erickson, 1968). Peers play an important role in this process—adolescents often affiliate with a specific "clique" or "crowd" of peers who provide them with a sense of identity and belongingness in the larger group (Brown, Mory, & Kinney, 1994). Friends serve as a key audience and source of support for identity development (Pasupathi & Hoyt, 2009). Age-related decreases in coercive strategy use and increases in the use of negotiation strategies from childhood to adolescence might reflect relationship maintenance goals. That is, if adolescents are motivated to maintain peer relationships because these relationships support identity development, they may use strategies that mitigate the escalation of conflict. Changes from adolescence to young adulthood may reflect experience. Young adults may become more socially adept as they make the transition to adulthood, reflecting experience with the success or failure of specific strategies.

Within the conflict management literature, researchers have begun to systematically investigate how strategies for managing interpersonal conflict vary across different interpersonal relationships (Seiffge-Krenke, 2011; Seiffge-Krenke, Aunola, & Nurmi, 2009). Adolescents are more likely to use negotiation strategies in conflicts with a romantic partner compared to a conflict with a friend, and are more likely to use negotiation strategies in conflicts with friends than acquaintances (Laursen et al., 2001). Laursen and colleagues (2001) reason that negotiation strategies might be least likely to be used with acquaintances because motivation to maintain relationships and preserve affiliative ties would be present in interactions with friends and romantic partners, but absent for acquaintances. When the interpersonal problem involves a sibling rather than a friend, the use of coercive strategies remains stable with age. This relationship difference could reflect the obligatory nature of sibling relationships in comparison to the voluntary nature of friendships (Laursen et al., 2001; see Figure 13.2). Because coercive strategies can damage a relationship, they are unlikely to be used when relationship maintenance goals are salient. Goals for maintaining a relationship may be less salient when the relationship is obligatory compared to when it is voluntary. Because obligatory relationships are more difficult to terminate, they may be less fragile and therefore able to withstand strategies that allow people to pursue goals that serve self-interests.

In a recent study, we compared young adult college students' strategies for managing conflict with friends of the same sex and romantic partners (Keener, Strough, & DiDonato, 2012). In conflicts with romantic partners, young adults were more likely to endorse strategies that involved discussing the problem. In contrast, when the conflict involved a friend, young adults were more likely to endorse strategies that reflected the pursuit of self-interests. These differences across relationships might reflect the developmental task of early adulthood of establishing a meaningful relationship with a romantic partner and the dimensions of romantic relationships. In early adulthood, friendships are likely to have a longer history compared to romantic relationships (Carver, Joyner, & Udry, 2003). Therefore friendships may be more durable and able to withstand one person's more selfish pursuit of self-interests. In contrast, not taking the partner's interests into account or using coercion could irreparably damage a newer, more fragile relationship. Younger adults may be more likely to endorse strategies that take both partners' needs into account as a way to protect newer and perhaps less durable romantic relationships. This would be consistent with a developmental task pertaining to the development of intimacy within romantic relationships.

Within the peer conflict management literature, research on gender often draws from classic work regarding stereotypical gender roles (Bem, 1974; Broverman, Broverman, Clarkson, Rosenkrantz, & Vogel, 1970; Gilligan, 1982). Classic work on stereotypical gender roles emphasizes that girls and women are relatively more likely than boys and men to approach interpersonal interactions with a communal or cooperative orientation that focuses on the needs of others in addition to one's own needs; whereas boys and men are relatively more likely than girls and women to approach interpersonal interactions with an agentic or competitive orientation that focuses more exclusively on the needs of the self. Contemporary research suggests that, after the second wave of the women's movement, women increasingly adopted stereotypical masculine personality traits (e.g., assertive) alongside feminine traits (e.g., compassionate), whereas men's traits stayed more stable across time and age (Strough, Leszczynski, Neely, Flinn, & Margrett, 2007; Twenge, 1997). In addition, there is substantial within-group variation in the extent to which individual men and women display behaviors associated with stereotypical gender roles (Costa, Terracciano, & McCrae, 2001; Hyde, 2005). Demands present within the immediate situation or context can increase and decrease gender-typed behavior (Leszczynski & Strough, 2008; Pickard & Strough,

2003a, 2003b). As such, it is important to take the social context into account when investigating gender differences and similarities in problem-solving goals and strategies.

There is some evidence that gender differences in strategies for managing peer conflict follow gender stereotypes. Stereotypical gender differences in aggression versus prosocial strategies become more pronounced from preadolescence to late adolescence (Lindeman, Harakka, & Keltikangas-Jarvinen, 1997). Other research shows that gender differences in strategies depend on the context of the interpersonal relationship. With same-sex friends, girls and women are more likely than boys and men to use or endorse negotiation, cooperation, or constructive strategies, such as expressing reassurance, discussing the conflict, or compromising (Black, 2000; de Wied, Branje, & Meeus, 2007; Keener, Strough, & DiDonato, 2012; Owens, Daly, & Slee, 2005). However, a different pattern of gender differences in strategies is found when the interpersonal context of the conflict shifts from friendships to romantic partners. When adolescents were asked how they generally manage conflict with a romantic partner, girls were more likely than boys to indicate they expressed anger or used strategies that escalated conflict (e.g., "get mad and yell" or "throw insults and digs"), and they also reported that they persisted in their efforts to resolve conflict (Cicognani, 2011; Feldman & Gowen, 1998; Simon & Furman, 2010). Our research on young adults (Keener et al., 2012) indicates that when the conflict involves a romantic relationship, women are relatively more likely than men to endorse strategies that involve standing their ground. These findings are in contrast to what would be predicted based on traditional gender stereotypes regarding girls' and women's concern with communion and interpersonal harmony (see also Suh, Moskowitz, Fournier, & Zuroff, 2004). However, they are consistent with research on marital conflict (e.g., Eldridge & Christensen, 2002). In marital conflicts, women often make demands whereas men are relatively more likely to withdraw or "stonewall" (Gottman, Coan, Carrere, & Swanson, 1998). Similarly, there is some evidence that adolescent boys also withdraw from conflict with romantic partners by using cognitive reframing strategies such as "tell myself it is not important" (Feldman & Gowen, 1998; see also Seiffge-Krenke, 2011).

Studies suggesting that gender differences in strategies depend on the interpersonal context have largely investigated same-sex friends and other-sex romantic partners. Thus, because the sex of the peer is confounded with the specific interpersonal relationship, the aspect of the context that may elicit gender differences is unclear. Some research suggests that goals and strategies vary depending on the sex of others with whom a person interacts. For example, when working on a collaborative problem-solving task, preadolescents' conversation strategies and goals vary systematically as a function of whether interacting peers are same-sex (i.e., boy-boy; girl-girl) versus other-sex (i.e., boy-girl; Strough & Berg, 2000). On a decision-making task, women received different responses to their suggestions depending on if they were discussing the decision with a male or female friend (Leaper, 1998). Adolescents' endorsements of gender-typed self-descriptors (e.g., communal traits) also vary systematically depending on the context of interactions with same- versus other-sex peers (Leszczynski & Strough, 2008). These findings suggest that part of the variation in adolescents' strategies for managing conflict in relationships with friends and romantic partners may reflect the same- versus other-sex nature of these relationships. Our ongoing research (Keener, 2010) is directed toward disentangling the same- versus other-sex composition of the relationship from the type of relationship by comparing adolescents' endorsement of strategies for managing conflict with same-sex friends, other-sex friends, and romantic partners. Initial results suggest that the type of relationship (romantic vs. platonic), rather than gender composition, is the key contextual factor.

Based on a literature review, Seiffge-Krenke (2011) suggested that girls are more concerned than boys with maintaining relationships and that this explains why they use different coping strategies than boys. Empirical research indicates that goals are linked to strategies (Rose & Asher, 1999), and that goals mediate gender differences in strategies (Strough & Berg, 2000). Specifically, when preadolescent boys and girls reported communal goals for working with a peer (mutual participation), their use of affiliative conversation strategies was similar. Research on young adults also indicates a link between goals and strategies. Keener and colleagues (2012) found that women were more likely than men to endorse discussion strategies for managing a hypothetical problem with a same-sex friend, but that endorsement of communal goals—goals to find a mutually beneficial solution to the problem—accounted for the association between gender and strategies.

Early and Later Adulthood

As just reviewed, the extent to which strategies depend on the features of the interpersonal context (e.g., siblings, friends, romantic relationships) is an emerging focus within the peer conflict management literature. Within the everyday problem-solving literature, the extent to which strategies (and age differences in strategies) depend on the problem context is an issue of long-standing interest. This long-standing interest reflects that the increasing variability of contexts of development with age (Baltes et al., 1984) was a key impetus for the emergence of the everyday problem-solving literature, as was noted earlier.

In their seminal research, Cornelius and Caspi (1987) examined problems occurring within six domains, including two explicitly interpersonal domains: friends and family. Cornelius and Caspi found age differences in people's reports of the extent to which they encountered specific hypothetical interpersonal problems. Young adults were more likely than middle-aged and older adults to report they encountered problems with friends; middle-aged adults were more likely than young and older adults to report they encountered problems with family. The differential prevalence of problems with friends and family in Cornelius and Caspi's study corresponds to research and theory regarding the differential importance of relationships across the lifespan outlined earlier in this chapter.

In comparison to Cornelius and Caspi's (1987) findings, a slightly different pattern of age differences is found when people respond to open-ended questions about problems they experience. From adolescence through old age, the proportion of reported tensions that involve family and friends is similar. Across age, a greater proportion of tensions involve family than friends (Birditt & Fingerman, 2005). When a variety of interpersonal relationships—both family and nonfamily (including acquaintances and strangers)—are considered, older adults report experiencing fewer interpersonal tensions (Birditt, Fingerman, & Almeida, 2005). Middle-aged adults are more likely than older and younger adults to report experiencing interpersonal problems (Strough et al., 1996). When older adults report tensions, they are more likely to mention spouses and are less likely to mention their children (Birditt et al., 2005). Gender differences are sometimes found, with women being more likely than men to describe interpersonal problems (Strough et al., 1996) and to report tensions with children (Birditt et al., 2005). Together, these findings

suggest that conclusions about the prevalence of problems within interpersonal relationships across age may depend on the method employed, the type of interpersonal relationship under investigation, and the roles (e.g., mother, father, child) of the persons involved.

Much research investigating age differences in everyday problem-solving strategies compares the strategies people generate or endorse when presented with hypothetical interpersonal problems (such as problems with friends) to hypothetical instrumental problems completing a task (e.g., dealing with a home cluttered with sentimental items; Artistico et al., 2010; Blanchard-Fields, Chen, & Norris 1997; Strough, McFall, Flinn, & Schuller, 2008). Time-sampling methods, daily diaries, interviews, and questionnaires have been employed to investigate age differences in strategies for solving problems and managing interpersonal tensions (Berg et al., 1998; Birditt & Fingerman, 2005; Birditt et al., 2005; Hoppmann & Blanchard-Fields, 2011). Other studies focus on age differences within a single interpersonal domain, such as family or friends (Blanchard-Fields, Stein, Watson, 2004; Coats & Blanchard-Fields, 2008; Crawford & Channon, 2002; Hoppmann & Blanchard-Fields, 2010).

When investigating strategies, everyday problem-solving researchers have used distinctions from the stress and coping literature between *problem-focused strategies* (e.g., independent actions, planning) and *emotion-focused strategies* (e.g., avoiding, denying, and depending on others; see Carver, Scheier, & Weintraub, 1989; Coats et al., this volume; Heckhausen & Schulz, 1995; Lazarus, 1996). The extent to which people of different ages use strategies that are active and constructive (e.g., discussing the problem), active and destructive (e.g., arguing), passive and constructive (e.g., doing nothing), or passive and destructive (e.g., avoiding, ignoring) also has been investigated (e.g., Birditt & Fingerman, 2005). Research investigating age differences in emotion-regulation strategies distinguishes strategies that are passive (e.g., suppressing feelings) from those that are proactive (e.g., venting; Coats & Blanchard-Fields, 2008), as well as strategies that are social versus those that involve only the self (Berg et al., 1998; Hoppmann & Blanchard-Fields, 2010).

To the extent that older adults are motivated to maintain meaningful interpersonal relationships and experience positive affect in the "here and now" (see Blanchard-Fields, 2007; Carstensen, 2006), they may use different strategies than do young adults to deal with interpersonal problems (see Figure 13.1). A large number of studies indicate systematic age differences in strategies depending on problem domain. When problems involve instrumental tasks devoid of interpersonal content, or when problem solvers pursue self-focused goals, both older and younger adults endorse problem-focused strategies (e.g., Berg et al., 1998; Blanchard-Fields et al., 1997, 2007). When problems are high in "emotional salience"—that is, when a problem is interpersonal (e.g., involves friends) or is emotionally charged—older adults are more likely than younger adults to endorse emotion-focused strategies such as avoidance-denial, to deliberate about the problem before taking action, and are less likely to argue (Birditt et al., 2005; Blanchard-Fields et al., 1997; Blanchard-Fields & Coats, 2008; Blanchard-Fields et al., 1995; Strough et al., 2008; Watson & Blanchard-Fields, 1998). These strategies deescalate interpersonal conflict and reduce arousal, which may facilitate emotion regulation and relationship maintenance. These strategies are in accord with developmental tasks focused on avoiding loss and maximizing one's experience of the "here and now" (see Carstensen, 2006). This pattern of age differences has been interpreted as indicating age-related improvements in the ability to manage emotions and deal with interpersonal everyday problems (Blanchard-Fields, 2007).

The studies reviewed here suggest that, in later adulthood, the strategies older adults use to deal with interpersonal problems are similar across relationships with family and friends. This similarity is somewhat surprising, given that these relationships differ on a number of the dimensions outlined in Figure 13.2 (e.g., voluntary, obligatory). One potential explanation is that researchers often specify problems that involve a "close friend" (e.g., Coats & Blanchard-Fields, 2008). Socioemotional selectivity theory (Carstensen, 2006) would predict that the friendships older adults have chosen to retain are emotionally close. The closeness of the relationship may constrain goals (see Strough et al., 1996). Age differences in goals and strategies across different interpersonal relationships may be more pronounced when the relationships differ on dimensions such as closeness.

Blanchard-Fields (2007) suggested that age differences in strategies for solving problems that are high in emotional salience reflect that older adults flexibly adjust their strategies to meet emotion-regulation goals. That is, older adults recognize that not all problems can be solved immediately and that managing one's own emotions is important. Older adults' focus on regulating emotions may reflect that the experience of negative emotions can be particularly toxic to older adults' well-being (Charles, 2010; Labouvie-Vief, 2009). As outlined by socioemotional selectivity theory (Carstensen, 2006), older adults' focus on regulating emotional reactions to interpersonal problems may reflect goals for maintaining important and emotionally meaningful relationships (rather than escalating conflict via attempts to regulate others). Indeed, Sorkin and Rook (2006) reported that older adults most frequently reported goals for maintaining interpersonal harmony in relationships when they experienced negative social exchanges.

In general, research suggests that people's strategies match their goals (Berg et al., 1998; Hoppmann & Blanchard-Fields, 2010; Hoppmann et al., 2008; Sorkin & Rook, 2006). Berg and colleagues (1998) found that, across the lifespan, when people describing their own everyday problems indicated pursuit of an interpersonal goal, they described using strategies that involved including or regulating others. Using hypothetical vignettes and a card sort task, Hoppmann and Blanchard-Fields (2010) found that autonomy goals were associated with self-focused strategies and generative goals were associated with other-focused strategies. Moreover, Hoppmann and Blanchard-Fields suggested that, compared to younger adults, older adults were better able to match strategies to goals. Others, however, reported a similar goal-strategy match across age (Berg et al. 1998). Thus, the literature is equivocal in regards to this issue.

Within the everyday problem-solving literature, attention to gender is sporadic, with only a few studies considering the intersection of age and gender. In published research, gender is not always included as a factor in the analyses (e.g., Berg et al., 1998; Blanchard-Fields, Mienaltowski, & Seay, 2007; Coats & Blanchard-Fields, 2008; Crawford & Channon, 2002; Hoppmann & Blanchard-Fields, 2010; Hoppmann et al., 2008). In these studies, it is not clear whether gender differences were not investigated, or whether gender differences were investigated, found to be nonsignificant, and thus not reported. The relative lack of attention to gender in the literature is somewhat surprising—given gender differences in longevity, aging is a gendered phenomenon (Kinsella & Wan, 2009).

When gender differences are reported, they are often consistent with stereotypical gender roles. For instance, men have been found to be more likely than women to select aggressive strategies (Diehl, Coyle, & Labouvie-Vief, 1996). In interpersonal conflicts with family members and when dealing with health problems, women are more likely to endorse strategies that involve seeking support from others (Strough et al., 2010; Watson & Blanchard-Fields, 1998). When dealing with problems with friends, women are more likely than men to endorse problem-focused and cognitive analysis strategies (Blanchard-Fields et al., 1997). However, gender similarities in strategies are found when participants generate their own strategies for solving problems with friends (Strough et al., 2008). Thus, when gender differences are reported, they appear to depend on problem domain or context, as well as the methods used.

A number of studies report gender differences in emotion-regulation strategies. Women use a greater number of strategies to regulate emotions compared to men (Blanchard-Fields, Stein, & Watson, 2004). Women are more likely than men to select emotion-regulation strategies that are either passive (suppressing feelings, avoidance) or proactive, such as venting (Birditt, Rott, & Fingerman, 2009; Blanchard-Fields & Coats, 2008; Blanchard-Fields et al., 2004; Diehl, Coyle, & Labouvie-Vief, 1996). Emotion-regulation strategies also differ as a function of age (e.g., Coats & Blanchard-Fields, 2008), raising the question of whether an age-by-gender interaction might exist. Detecting gender-by-age interactions often requires large samples to achieve the statistical power needed to detect small effects. Consistent with meta-analytic research on gender differences (Hyde, 2005), many of the reviewed gender differences are small to medium in magnitude; thus, most of these published studies likely lack sufficient power to detect significant interactions, if they do indeed exist.

Gender differences in reported use of emotion-regulation strategies may reflect that women report experiencing more sadness (Blanchard-Fields & Coats, 2008) and more intense emotions (Birditt & Fingerman, 2003) in response to interpersonal problems compared to men, and women report higher levels of neuroticism (Costa et al., 2001). If competence in interpersonal relationships is more central to women's socially proscribed gender role (e.g., Eagly et al., 2000), conflicts in interpersonal relationships may be more affectively arousing to women. Traditional gender stereotypes of women as the "emotional sex" (Plant, Hyde, Keltner, & Devine, 2000) may also facilitate greater willingness among women to disclose emotion. Stereotypical

gender roles and individual differences in the subjective experience of emotional states could combine to make goals for regulating emotion more salient for women than men.

In contrast to studies indicating gender differences in strategies, gender similarities characterize the results of other studies (Birditt et al., 2005, 2009; Blanchard-Fields et al., 1995). For instance, Birditt and colleagues (2009) found that mothers and fathers were equally likely to use both constructive and destructive strategies in conflicts with their adult children. Interestingly, the strategies examined in these studies often are similar to those examined in studies that indicate gender differences. As noted earlier, one issue that may contribute to the mixed results is statistical power. Contextual influences may also play a role. For instance, in the family domain, well-defined roles (e.g., parent), the closeness of the relationship, and its obligatory nature may override any gender differences in goals and strategies.

Within the extant literature, there is some support for the notion that gender similarities and differences in strategies depend on features of the context. For instance, in later adulthood, women are more likely than men to endorse interpersonal strategies for dealing with health problems, yet when problems have more severe consequences, men and women are equally likely to endorse interpersonal strategies (Strough et al., 2010). Similarly, both men and women endorse interpersonal strategies when they perceive limitations in their own problem-solving abilities, but perceived limitations correspond to gender-stereotyped domains of competence (Strough, Cheng, & Swenson, 2002). When older men and women work together to solve everyday problems, men are more influential than women, but only when the solution is ambiguous (Margrett & Marsiske, 2002). These findings demonstrate that gender similarities or differences may emerge depending on the context.

Recommendations for Future Research
Assessing Effectiveness
To advance research on interpersonal everyday problem solving across the lifespan, it is essential to continue to develop and refine methods for measuring problem-solving effectiveness. Recent work (Hoppmann & Blanchard Fields, 2010) has used coherence (the match between goals and strategies) as an indicator of effective problem solving. However, as noted by researchers who study judgment and decision making, this criterion is not without limitations (see Bruine de Bruin, 2012; Reyna

& Farley, 2006, for reviews). For instance, coherence could be present in links between goals (e.g., enacting revenge), strategies (e.g., physical or verbal aggression), and outcomes (e.g., harm is caused to another person), but this coherence may escalate long-term conflict and animosity, such that the strategy is ineffective. Thus, coherence is necessary, but not sufficient, for assessing competence. Focusing on outcomes, such as the extent to which a strategy maximizes positive outcomes and minimizes negative outcomes (D'Zurilla, Nezu, & Maydeu-Olivares, 2004), is another means of addressing effectiveness. However, due to the ill-defined nature of everyday problem solving, applying this definition presents challenges. Are immediate or long-term outcomes more important? In interpersonal conflicts, what is beneficial to one person may be detrimental to another. Moreover, good outcomes do not necessarily signal good processes because outcomes can occur by chance (Bruine de Bruin, 2012).

When evaluating everyday problem solving, both coherence and outcomes should be considered. Considering the coherence of the problem-solving process (links between goals and strategies), short-term outcomes of strategies such as physiological indexes of emotion (see Blanchard-Fields, 2009) and long-term outcomes of strategies such as relationship satisfaction (Hoppmann & Blanchard-Fields, 2011) would begin to address the debate within the everyday problem-solving literature regarding how to best measure strategy effectiveness. Resolving this debate is important because different conclusions about the trajectory of everyday problem-solving performance across the lifespan are reached depending on whether strategy fluency versus strategy quality (based on expert ratings or self-assessed effectiveness) are used as performance metrics (see Mienalotwski, 2011, for a review).

Goals and Strategies

Using diverse methods will increase our understanding of the extent that strategies reflect individual differences in goals. Within the adult development and aging literature, the majority of research investigating problem-solving goals has relied on retrospective self-reports (e.g., Berg et al., 1998; Hoppmann et al., 2008; Sorkin & Rook, 2006; Strough et al., 1996). These studies provide rich descriptive information about the goals that motivate everyday problem solving across the lifespan, but provide only limited information regarding causal relations. Hoppmann and Blanchard-Fields' (2010) research demonstrates

how incorporating an experimental manipulation can increase understanding of age differences in strategies. In their study, temporal horizons posited to correspond to age-related differences in motivational orientations (Carstensen, 2006) were manipulated. Older adults shifted their strategies to match the induced temporal horizons, but age differences in strategies corresponding to developmental tasks persisted. Methods developed by social psychologists to prime goals (Chartrand & Bargh, 1996) at either a conscious or unconscious level (Gollwitzer, Parks-Stamm, & Oettingen, 2009) may be useful in advancing understanding of the relation between goals and strategies across the lifespan.

Conclusion

Many gaps remain to be addressed, and numerous barriers must be overcome to develop an integrated understanding of interpersonal everyday problem solving across the lifespan. By using a conceptual model (see Figure 13.1) to integrate results across studies, and by ferreting out consistencies in the phenomena under investigation obscured by disparate terms (e.g., conflict management, problem solving), we have attempted to provide a foundation for future research. Researchers investigating adolescents have speculated that strategies are linked to goals. Empirical research within the adult development and aging literature demonstrates the utility of considering goals for understanding contextual influences on strategies. Conversely, the adolescent literature has begun to address how dimensions of relationships, such as those outlined in Figure 13.2, may influence strategies, whereas research on adult development and aging often compares interpersonal to instrumental problems. When different interpersonal relationships are compared, key dimensions of relationships, such as closeness, may be confounded. Most of the research we reviewed focuses on age differences rather than the intersection of age and other individual difference characteristics such as gender, race, and culture. Thus, questions regarding the generalizability of developmental trajectories remain open to investigation. In future research, we believe it is essential to use an array of methods to continue to disentangle the extent to which age differences in goals and strategies reflect age-related maturational changes or shifts in developmental contexts and tasks.

Acknowledgments
We thank Philip Lemaster for his assistance and Lisa DiDonato, Tara Karns, Nipat Pichayayothin,

and Philip Lemaster for comments on a previous draft of this chapter. Correspondence should be directed to JoNell Strough, Department of Psychology, West Virginia University, Morgantown, WV. Email: JoNell.Strough@mail.wvu.edu

References

Allaire J. C., & Marskise, M. (1999). Everyday cognition: Age and intellectual ability correlates. *Psychology and Aging, 14*(4), 627–644.

Allaire, J. C., & Marsiske, M. (2002). Well- and ill-defined measures of everyday cognition: Relationship to older adults' intellectual ability and functional status. *Psychology & Aging, 17*(1), 101–115.

Antonucci, T. C., Birditt, K. S., & Ajrouch, K. (2011). Convoys of social relations: Past, present, and future. In K. L. Fingerman, C. A. Berg, J. Smith., & T. C. Antonucci (Eds.), *Handbook of life-span development* (pp. 161–182). New York: Springer.

Arnett, J. J. (2000). Emerging adulthood: A theory of development from the late teens through the twenties. *American Psychologist, 55*(5), 469–480.

Artistico, D., Cervone, D., & Pezzuti, L. (2003). Perceived self-efficacy and everyday problem solving among young and older adults. *Psychology and Aging, 18*(1), 68–79.

Artistico, D., Orom, H., Cervone, D., Krauss, S., & Houston, E. (2010). Everyday challenges in context: The influence of contextual factors on everyday problem solving among young, middle-aged, and older adults. *Experimental Aging Research, 36*(2), 230–247.

Bakan, D. (1966). *The duality of human existence: An essay on psychology and religion*. Chicago: Rand McNally.

Baltes, P. B. (1987). Theoretical propositions of life-span developmental psychology: On the dynamics between growth and decline. *Developmental Psychology, 23*(5), 611–626.

Baltes, P. B., Dittmann-Kohli, F., & Dixon, R. A. (1984). New perspectives on the development of intelligence in adulthood: Toward a dual-process conception and a model of selective optimization with compensation. In P. B. Baltes & O. G. Brim, Jr. (Eds.), *Life-span development and behavior* (vol. 6, pp. 33–76). New York: Academic Press.

Baltes, P. B., Lindenberger, U., & Staudinger, U. M. (2006). Life span theory in developmental psychology. In R. M. Lerner & W. Damon (Eds.), *Handbook of child psychology*, 6th ed. (vol. 1, pp. 569–664). Hoboken, NJ: John Wiley and Sons.

Baltes, M. M., & Silverberg, S. B. (1994). The dynamics between dependency and autonomy: Illustrations across the life span. In D. L. Featherman, R. M. Lerner, & M. Perlmutter (Eds.), *Life-span development and behavior* (vol. 12, pp. 41–90). Hillsdale, NJ: Lawrence Erlbaum Associates.

Bem, S. L. (1974). The measurement of psychological androgyny. *Journal of Consulting and Clinical Psychology, 42*(2), 155–162.

Berg, C. A. (2008). Everyday problem solving in context. In S. Hofer & D. Alwin (Eds.), *Handbook of cognitive aging: Interdisciplinary perspectives* (pp. 207–223). Thousand Oaks, CA: Sage Publications.

Berg, C. A. (1990). What is intellectual efficacy over the life course? Using adults' conceptions to address the question. In J. Rodin, C. Schooler, & K. W. Schaie (Eds.), *Selfdirectedness: Cause and effects throughout the life course* (pp. 155–181). Hillsdale, NJ: Lawrence Erlbaum Associates.

Berg, C. A., & Calderone, K. S. (1994). The role of problem interpretations in understanding the development of everyday problem solving. In R. J. Sternberg & R. K. Wagner (Eds.), *Mind in context: Interactionist perspectives on human intelligence* (pp. 105–132). New York: Cambridge University Press.

Berg, C. A., & Klaczynski, P. (1996). Practical intelligence and problem solving: Searching for perspectives. In F. Blanchard-Fields & T. M. Hess (Eds.), *Perspectives on cognition in adulthood and aging* (pp. 323–357). New York: McGraw-Hill.

Berg, C. A., Meegan, S. P., & Klaczynski, P. (1999). Age and experiential differences in strategy generation and information requests for solving everyday problems. *International Journal of Behavioral Development, 23*, 615–639.

Berg, C. A., Skinner, M., & Ko, K. (2009). An integrative model of everyday problem solving across the adult life span. In M. C. Smith & N. DeFrates-Densch (Eds.), *Handbook of research on adult learning and development* (pp. 524–552). New York: Routledge.

Berg, C. A., & Sternberg, R. J. (1985). A triarchic theory of intellectual development during adulthood. *Developmental Review, 5*(4), 334–370.

Berg, C. A., & Strough, J. (2011). Problem solving across the life span. In K. L. Fingerman, C. A. Berg, J. Smith., & T. C. Antonucci (Eds.). *Handbook of life-span development* (pp. 239–267). New York: Springer.

Berg, C. A., Strough, J., Calderone, K. S., Sansone, C., & Weir, C. (1998). The role of problem definitions in understanding age and context effects on strategies for solving everyday problems. *Psychology and Aging, 13*(1), 29–44.

Birditt, K. S., & Fingerman, K. L. (2003). Age and gender differences in adults' descriptions of emotional reactions to interpersonal problems. *Journal of Gerontology: Psychological Sciences, 58B*(4), 237–245.

Birditt, K. S., & Fingerman, K. L. (2005). Do we get better at picking our battles? Age group differences in descriptions of behavioral reactions to interpersonal tensions. *Journal of Gerontology: Psychological Sciences, 60B*(3), 121–128.

Birditt, K. S., Fingerman, K. L., & Almeida, D. M. (2005). Age differences in exposure and reactions to interpersonal tensions: A daily diary study. *Psychology and Aging, 20*(2), 330–340.

Birditt, K. S., Rott, L. M., & Fingerman, K. L. (2009). "If you can't say something nice, don't say anything at all": Coping with interpersonal tensions in the parent-child relationship during adulthood. *Journal of Family Psychology, 23*(6), 769–778.

Black, K. (2000). Gender differences in adolescents' behavior during conflict resolution tasks with best friends. *Adolescence, 35*(139), 499–512.

Blanchard-Fields, F. (1986). Reasoning on social dilemmas varying in emotional saliency: An adult developmental perspective. *Psychology and Aging, 1*(4), 325–333.

Blanchard-Fields, F. (2007). Everyday problem solving and emotion: An adult development perspective. *Current Directions in Psychological Science, 16*(1), 26–31.

Blanchard-Fields, F. (2009). Flexible and adaptive socio-emotional problem solving in adult development and aging. *Restorative Neurology and Neuroscience, 27*(5), 539–550.

Blanchard-Fields, F., & Chen, Y. (1996). Adaptive cognition and aging. *American Behavioral Scientist, 39*(3), 231–248.

Blanchard-Fields, F., & Coats, A. H. (2008). The experience of anger and sadness in everyday problems impacts age differences in emotion regulation. *Developmental Psychology, 44*(6), 1547–1556.

Blanchard-Fields, F., Chen, Y., & Norris, L. (1997). Everyday problem solving across the adult life span: Influence of domain specificity and cognitive appraisal. *Psychology and Aging, 12*(4), 684–693.

Blanchard-Fields, F., Jahnke, H. C., & Camp, C. (1995). Age differences in problem-solving style: The role of emotional salience. *Psychology and Aging, 10*(2), 173–180.

Blanchard-Fields, F., Mienaltowski, A., & Seay, R. B. (2007). Age differences in everyday problem-solving effectiveness: Older adults select more effective strategies for interpersonal problems. *Journal of Gerontology: Psychological Sciences, 62B*(1), 61–64.

Blanchard-Fields, F., Stein, R., & Watson, T. L. (2004). Age differences in emotion-regulation strategies in handling everyday problems. *Journal of Gerontology: Psychological Sciences, 59B*(6), 261–269.

Bornstein, M. H., Bradley, R. H., Lutfey, K., Mortimer, J. T., & Penmar, A. (2011). Contexts and contents of socialization: A life-span perspective. In K. L. Fingerman, C. A. Berg, J. Smith., & T. C. Antonucci (Eds.), *Handbook of life-span development* (pp. 837–881). New York: Springer.

Broverman, I. K., Broverman, D. M., Clarkson, F. E., Rosenkrantz, P. S., & Vogel, S. R. (1970). Sex-role stereotypes and clinical judgments of mental health. *Journal of Consulting and Clinical Psychology, 34*(1), 1–7.

Brown, B. B., Mory, M. S., & Kinney, D. (1994). Casting adolescent crowds in a relational perspective: Caricature, channel, and context. In R. Montemayor, G. R. Adams, & T. P. Gullotta (Eds.), *Personal relationships during adolescence* (pp. 123–167). Thousand Oaks, CA: Sage Publications.

Bruine de Bruin, W. (2012). Judgment and decision making in adolescence. In M. K. Dhami, A. Schlottmann, & M. Waldmann (Eds.). *Judgment and decision making as a skill: Learning, development, and evolution.* (pp. 85–111). New York: Cambridge University Press.

Carstensen, L. (2006). The influence of a sense of time on human development. *Science, 312*(5782), 1913–1915.

Carver, K., Joyner, K., & Udry, J. R. (2003). National estimates of adolescent romantic relationships. In P. Florsheim (Ed.), *Adolescent romantic relations and sexual behavior* (pp. 23–56). Mahwah, NJ: Lawrence Erlbaum Associates.

Carver, C. S., & Scheier, M. F. (2002). Control processes and self-organization as complementary principles underlying behavior. *Personality and Social Psychology Review, 6*(4), 304–315.

Carver, C. S., Scheier, M. F., & Weintraub, J. K. (1989). Assessing coping strategies: A theoretically based approach. *Journal of Personality and Social Psychology, 56*(2), 267–283.

Chang, E. C., D'Zurilla, T. J., & Sanna, L. J. (2004). *Social problem solving.* Washington, DC: American Psychological Association.

Charles, S. T. (2010). Strength and vulnerability integration: A model of emotional well-being across adulthood. *Psychological Bulletin, 136*(6), 1068–1091.

Chartrand, T. L., & Bargh, J. A. (1996). Automatic activation of impression formation and memorization goals: Nonconscious goal priming reproduces effects of explicit task instructions. *Journal of Personality and Social Psychology, 71*(3), 464–478.

Cicognani, E. (2011). Coping strategies with minor stressors in adolescence: Relationships with social support, self-efficacy, and psychological well-being. *Journal of Applied Social Psychology, 41*(3), 559–578.

Clark, M., & Mills, J., & Corcoran, D. M. (1989). Keeping track of needs and inputs of friends and strangers. *Personality and Social Psychology Bulletin, 15*, 533–542.

Coats, A. H., & Blanchard-Fields, F. (2008). Emotion regulation in interpersonal problems: The role of cognitive-emotional complexity, emotion regulation goals, and expressivity. *Psychology and Aging, 23*(1), 39–51.

Coats, A. H., Hoppmann, C., & Scott, S. B. (this volume). Goals, strategies, and well-being across adulthood: Integrating perspectives from the coping and everyday problem-solving literatures. In P. Verhaeghen & C. Hertzog (Eds.), *Emotion, social cognition and everyday problem solving during adulthood.* New York: Oxford University Press.

Collins, W. A., & Steinberg, L. (2006). Adolescent development in interpersonal context. In N. Eisenberg, W. Damon, & R. M. Lerner (Eds.), *Handbook of child psychology*, 6th ed. (vol. 3, pp. 1003–1067). Hoboken, NJ: John Wiley and Sons.

Cornelius, S. W., & Caspi, A. (1987). Everyday problem solving in adulthood and old age. *Psychology and Aging, 2*(2), 144–153.

Costa, P. T., Terracciano, A., & McCrae, R. R. (2001). Gender differences in personality traits across cultures: Robust and surprising findings. *Journal of Personality and Social Psychology, 81*, 322–331.

Crawford, S., & Channon, S. (2002). Dissociation between performance on abstract tests of executive function and problem solving in real-life-type situations in normal aging. *Aging & Mental Health, 6*(1), 12–21.

Denney, N. W. (1989). Everyday problem solving: Methodological issues, research findings, and a model. In L. W. Poon, D. C. Rubin, & B. A. Wilson (Eds.), *Everyday cognition in adulthood and late life* (pp. 330–351). New York: Cambridge University Press.

de Wied, M., Branje, S. T., & Meeus, W. H. J. (2007). Empathy and conflict resolution in friendship relations among adolescents. *Aggressive Behavior, 33*(1), 48–55.

Diehl, M., Coyle, N., & Labouvie-Vief, G. (1996). Age and sex differences in strategies of coping and defense across the life span. *Psychology and Aging, 11*(1), 127–139.

Diehl, M., Willis, S., & Schaie, W. (1995). Everyday problem solving in older adults: Observational assessment and cognitive correlates. *Psychology and Aging, 10*(3), 478–491.

Diehl, M., Youngblade, L. M., Hay, E. L., & Chui, H. (2011). The development of self-representations across the lifespan. In K. L. Fingerman, C. A. Berg, J. Smith, & T. C. Antonucci (Eds.), *Handbook of life-span development* (pp. 611–646). New York: Springer.

D'Zurilla, T. J., Nezu, A. M., & Maydeu-Olivares, A. (2004). Social problem solving: Theory and assessment. In E. C. Chang, T. J. D'Zurilla, & L. J. Sanna (Eds.), *Social problem solving* (pp. 11–27). Washington, DC: American Psychological Association.

Eagly, A. H., Wood, W., & Diekman, A. B. (2000). Social role theory of sex differences and similarities: A current appraisal. In T. Eckes & H. M. Trautner (Eds.), *The developmental social psychology of gender.* Mahwah, NJ: Lawrence Earlbaum Associates.

Eldridge, K. A., & Christensen, A. (2002). Demand-withdraw communication during couple conflict: A review and analysis. In P. Noller & J. A. Feeney (Eds.), *Understanding marriage: Developments in the study of couple interaction* (pp. 289–322). New York: Cambridge University Press.

Erikson, E. H. (1968). *Identity: Youth and crisis.* New York: Norton.

Feldman, S. S., & Gowen, L. K. (1998). Conflict negotiation tactics in romantic relationships in high school students. *Journal of Youth and Adolescence, 27*(6), 691–717.

Ford, M. E. (1986). For all practical purposes: Criteria for defining and evaluating practical intelligence. In R. J. Sternberg & R. K. Wagner (Eds.), *Practical intelligence: Nature and origins of competence in the everyday world* (pp. 183–200). London: Cambridge University Press.

Fingerman, K. L., Brown, B., & Blieszner, R. (2011). Informal ties across the life span: Peers, consequential strangers, and people we encounter in daily life. In K. L. Fingerman, C. A. Berg, J. Smith., & T. C. Antonucci (Eds.), *Handbook of life-span development* (pp. 487–511). New York: Springer.

Fung, H. H., Stoeber, F. S., Yeung, D. Y., & Lang, F. R. (2008). Cultural specificity of socioemotional selectivity: Age differences in social network composition among Germans and Hong Kong Chinese. *Journal of Gerontology: Psychological Sciences, 63B*(3), 156–164.

Galambos, N. L., MacDonald, S. W. S., Naphtali, C., Cohen, A., & de Frias, C. M. (2005). Cognitive performance differentiates selected aspects of psychosocial maturity in adolescence. *Developmental Neuropsychology, 28*(1), 473–492.

Gilligan, C. (1982). *In a difference voice: Psychological theory and women's development.* Cambridge, MA: Harvard University Press.

Gottman, J. M., Coan, J., Carrere, S., & Swanson, C. (1998). Predicting marital happiness and stability from newlywed interactions. *Journal of Marriage and the Family, 60*(1), 5–22.

Hartup, W. W., & Stevens, N. (1997). Friendships and adaptation in the life course. *Psychological Bulletin, 121*(3), 355–370.

Heath, C., Larrick, R. P., & Wu, G. (1999). Goals as reference points. *Cognitive Psychology, 38*(1), 79–109.

Heckhausen J., & Schulz, R. (1995). A life-span theory of control. *Psychological Review, 102*(2), 284–304.

Heidrich, S. M., & Denney, N, W. (1994). Does social problem solving differ from other types of problem solving during the adult years? *Experimental Aging Research, 20*(2), 115–118.

Hoppmann, C. A., & Blanchard-Fields, F. (2010). Goals and everyday problem solving: Manipulating goal preferences in young and older adults. *Developmental Psychology, 46*(6), 1433–1443.

Hoppmann, C. A., & Blanchard-Fields, F. (2011). Problem solving variability on older spouses: How is it linked to situation-, person-, and couple-characteristics? *Psychology and Aging, 26*(3), 525–531.

Hoppmann, C. A., Coats, A. H., & Blanchard-Fields, F. (2008). Goals and everyday problem solving: Examining the link between age-related goals and problem-solving strategy use. *Aging, Neuropsychology, and Cognition, 15*(4), 401–423.

Hyde, J. S. (2005). The gender similarities hypothesis. *American Psychologist, 60*(6), 581–592.

Gollwitzer, P. M., Parks-Stamm, E. G., & Oettingen, G. (2009). Living on the edge: Shifting between nonconscious and conscious goal pursuit. In E. Morsella, J. A. Bargh, & P. M. Gollwitzer (Eds.), *Oxford handbook of human action* (pp. 603–623). New York: Oxford University Press.

Keener, E., Strough, J., & DiDonato, L. (2012). Gender differences and similarities in strategies for managing conflict with friends and romantic partners. *Sex Roles, 67*(1–2), 83–97.

Keener, E. (2010). Boys' and girls' strategies for managing peer conflict in adolescence. Unpublished doctoral dissertation. West Virginia University, Morgantown.

Kinsella, K. & Wan, H. (2009). *An aging world: 2008.* U. S. Census Bureau, International Population Reports, P95/09–1, U. S. Government Printing Office: Washington, DC.

Labouvie-Vief, G. (2009). Cognition and equilibrium regulation in development and aging. *Restorative Neurology and Neuroscience, 27*(5), 551–565.

Laursen B., Finkelstein, B. D., & Townsend Betts, N. (2001). A developmental meta-analysis of peer conflict resolution. *Developmental Review, 21*(4), 423–449.

Lawton, M. P., & Brody, E. M. (1969). Assessment of older people: Self-maintaining and instrumental activities of daily living. *The Gerontologist, 9*(3), 179–186.

Lazarus, R. S. (1996). The role of coping in the emotions and how coping changes over the life course. In C. Magai & S. H. McFadden (Eds.), *Handbook of emotion, adult development, and aging* (pp. 289–306). San Diego, CA: Academic Press.

Leaper, C. (1998). Decision making processes between friends: Speaker and partner gender effects. *Sex Roles, 39*(1–2), 125–133.

Leszczynski, J. P., & Strough, J. (2008). The contextual specificity of masculinity and femininity in early adolescence. *Social Development, 17*(3), 719–736.

Levitt, M. J., & Cici-Gokaltun, A. (2011). Close relationships across the life span. In K. L. Fingerman, C. A. Berg, J. Smith., & T. C. Antonucci (Eds.), *Handbook of life-span development* (pp. 457–486). New York: Springer.

Lindeman, M., Harakka, T., & Keltikanga-Järvinen, L. (1997). Age and gender differences in adolescents' reactions to conflict situations: Aggression, prosociality, and withdrawal. *Journal of Youth and Adolescence, 26*(3), 339–351.

Maccoby, E. E. (1998). *The two sexes: Growing up apart, coming together.* Cambridge, MA: Harvard University Press.

Markus, H. R., & Kitayama, S. (1991). Culture and the self: Implications for cognition, emotion, and motivation. *Psychological Review, 98*(2), 224-253.

Marsiske, M., & Margrett, J. A. (2006). Everyday problem solving and decision making. In J. E. Birren & K. W. Schaie (Eds.), *Handbook of the psychology of aging*, 6th ed. (pp. 315–342). New York: Academic Press.

Marsiske, M., & Willis, S. L. (1995). Dimensionality of everyday problem solving in older adults. *Psychology and Aging, 10*(2), 269–283.

Margrett, J. A., & Marsiske, M. (2002). Gender differences in older adults' everyday cognitive collaboration. *International Journal of Behavioral Development, 26*(1), 45–59.

McCormick, C. M., Kuo, S. I., & Masten, A. S. (2011). Developmental tasks across the lifespan. In K. L. Fingerman, C. Berg, T. C. Antonucci, & J. Smith (Eds.), *Handbook of life-span development* (pp. 117–140). New York: Springer.

McFall, J. P. (2010). *Effectiveness of strategies for solving everyday problems during early and later adulthood: A reexamination of the Everyday Problem Solving Inventory.* Unpublished doctoral dissertation, West Virginia University, Morgantown.

Meacham, J. A., & Emont, N. C. (1989). The interpersonal basis of everyday problem solving. In J. D. Sinnott (Ed.), *Everyday problem solving: Theory and applications* (pp. 7–23). New York: Praeger.

Mienaltowski, A. (2011). Everyday problem solving across the adult life span: Solution diversity and efficacy. *Annals of the New York Academy of Sciences, 1235,* 75–85.

Owens, L., Daly, A., & Slee, P. (2005). Sex and age differences in victimisation and conflict resolution among adolescents in a south Australian school. *Aggressive Behavior, 31*(1), 1–12.

Pasupathi, M., & Hoyt, T.(2009). The development of narrative identity in late adolescence and emergent adulthood: The continued importance of listeners. *Developmental Psychology 45*(2), 558–574.

Pickard, J., & Strough, J. (2003a). The effects of same-sex and other-sex contexts on masculinity and femininity. *Sex Roles, 48*, 421–432.

Pickard, J., & Strough, J. (2003b). Variability in goals as a function of same-sex and other-sex contexts. *Sex Roles, 49*(11-12), 643–652.

Plant, E. A., Hyde, J. S., Keltner, D., & Devine, P. G. (2000). The gender stereotyping of emotions. *Psychology of Women Quarterly, 24*(1), 81–92.

Reyna, V. F., & Farley, F. (2006). Risk and rationality in adolescent decision making: Implications for theory, practice, and public policy. *Psychological Science in the Public Interest, 7*(1), 1–44.

Roisman, G. I., Masten, S. D., Coatsworth, J. D., & Tellegen, A. (2004). Salient and emerging developmental tasks in the transition to adulthood. *Child Development, 75*(1), 123–133.

Rose, A. J., & Asher, S. R. (1999). Children's goals and strategies in response to conflicts within a friendship. *Developmental Psychology, 35*(1), 69–79.

Seiffge-Krenke, I. (2011). Coping with relationship stressors: A decade review. *Journal of Research on Adolescence, 21*(1), 196–210. doi:10.1111/j.1532-7795.2010.00723.x

Seiffge-Krenke, I., Aunola, K., & Nurmi, J. (2009). Changes in stress perception and coping during adolescence: The role of situational and personal factors. *Child Development, 80*(1), 259–279. doi:10.1111/j.1467-8624.2008.01258.x

Siegler, R. S., & Alibali, M. W. (2005). *Children's thinking* (4th ed.). Upper Saddle River, NJ: Prentice Hall.

Simon, V. A., & Furman, W. (2010). Interparental conflict and adolescents' romantic relationship conflict. *Journal of Research on Adolescence, 20*(1), 188–209.

Sinnott, J. D. (1989). A model for solution of ill-structured problems: Implications for everyday and abstract problem solving. In J. D. Sinnot (Ed.), *Everyday problem solving: Theory and applications* (pp. 72–99). New York: Praeger.

Sorkin, D. H., & Rook, K. S. (2006). Dealing with negative social exchanges in later life: Coping responses, goals, and effectiveness. *Psychology and Aging, 21*(4), 715–725.

Strough, J., & Berg, C. (2000). Goals as a mediator of gender differences in high-affiliation dyadic conversations. *Developmental Psychology, 36*(1), 117–125.

Strough, J., Berg, C. A., & Sansone, C. (1996). Goals for solving everyday problems across the life span: Age and gender differences in the salience of interpersonal concerns. *Developmental Psychology, 32*(6), 1106–1115.

Strough, J., Cheng, S., & Swenson, L. M. (2002). Preferences for collaborative and individual everyday problem solving in older adulthood. *International Journal of Behavior Development, 26*(1), 26–35.

Strough, J., Leszczynski, J. P., Neely, T. L., Flinn, J. A., & Margrett, J. (2007). From adolescence to later adulthood: Femininity, masculinity and androgyny in six age groups. *Sex Roles, 57*, 385–396.

Strough, J., McFall, J. P., Flinn, J. A., & Schuller, K. L. (2008). Collaborative everyday problem solving among same-gender friends in early and later adulthood. *Psychology and Aging, 23*(3), 517–530.

Strough, J., McFall, J. P., & Schuller, K. L. (2010). Endorsement of interpersonal strategies for dealing with hypothetical everyday arthritis problems as a function of marital status, gender, and problem severity. *The International Journal of Aging & Human Development, 70*(1), 39–59.

Suh, E. J., Moskowitz, D. S., Fournier, M. A., & Zuroff, D. C. (2004). Gender and relationships: Influences on agentic and communal behaviors. *Personal Relationships, 11*(1), 41–59.

Thornton, A. E., Kristinsson, H., DeFreitas, V. G., & Thornton, W. L. (2010). The ecological validity of everyday cognition in hospitalized patients with serious mental illness. *Journal of Clinical Neuropsychology, 32*(3), 299–308.

Thornton, W. L., Deria, S., Gelb, S., Shapiro, R. J., & Hill, A. (2007). Neuropsychological mediators of the links among age, chronic illness, and everyday problem solving. *Psychology and Aging, 22*(3), 470–481.

Thornton, W. J. L., & Dumke, H. A. (2005). Age differences in everyday problem-solving and decision-making effectiveness: A meta-analytic review. *Psychology and Aging, 20*(1), 85–99.

Twenge, J. M. (1997). Changes in masculine and feminine traits over time: A meta-analysis. *Sex Roles, 36*, 305–325.

Vallacher, R. R., & Wegner, D. M. (1987). What do people think they're doing? Action identification and human behavior. *Psychological Review, 94*(1), 3–15

Watson, T. L., & Blanchard-Fields, F. (1998). Thinking with your head and your heart: Age differences in everyday problem-solving strategy preferences. *Aging, Neuropsychology, and Cognition, 5*(3), 225–240.

Weatherbee, S. R., & Allaire, J. C. (2008). Everyday cognition and mortality: Performance differences and predictive utility of the Everyday Cognition Battery. *Psychology and Aging, 23*(1), 216–221.

Willis, S. L. (1996). Everyday cognitive competence in elderly persons: Conceptual issues and empirical findings. *The Gerontologist, 36*(5), 595–601.

Willis, S. L., & Schaie, K. W. (1986). Training the elderly on the ability factors of spatial orientation and inductive reasoning. *Psychology and Aging, 1*(3), 239–247.

Goals, Strategies, and Well-Being Across Adulthood: Integrating Perspectives From the Coping and Everyday Problem-Solving Literatures

Abby Heckman Coats, Christiane Hoppmann, *and* Stacey B. Scott

Abstract

How older adults cope with stress and handle everyday problems has been an important focus in adult developmental research. The extent to which individuals manage hassles in their lives predicts important outcomes that have implications for their independence and ability to age successfully. Traditionally, coping research has emerged from a clinical background, whereas everyday problem-solving research has emerged from a cognitive background. The aim of this chapter is to review research in coping and everyday problem solving with an eye toward integrating them. We review the history of coping and everyday problem-solving research, focusing on the importance of individuals' goals and the strategies individuals use to reach those goals. We discuss possible mechanisms underlying age differences in these strategies. We also address the challenge of determining what constitutes effective coping and everyday problem solving. The field would benefit from considering interdisciplinary perspectives as we consider ideas for future research.

Key Words: coping, everyday problem solving, aging, goals, strategies

How older adults cope with stress and handle everyday problems has been an important focus in adult developmental research (Blanchard-Fields, 2007; Lazarus, 1996). The extent to which individuals manage hassles in their lives predicts important outcomes that have implications for their independence and ability to age successfully (Berg & Strough, 2011; Marsiske & Margrett, 2006). Goals for managing life hassles are important because they guide strategy selection and reflect individuals' own ideas about what constitutes effective coping and everyday problem solving (Berg, Skinner, & Ko, 2009; Berg, Strough, Calderone, Sansone, & Weir, 1998). Traditionally, coping research has emerged from a clinical background, whereas everyday problem-solving research has emerged from a cognitive background. The focus in coping research is on responses to what can go wrong in one's life. The starting point of coping is with a stressor, such

as a medical diagnosis or a family conflict. This is in contrast to everyday problem-solving research, which examines changes in cognitive functioning. The focus in everyday problem-solving research is primarily on skills, resources, and effectiveness. Although the histories of these research areas differ, both offer important insights into effectively handling real-world challenges. The aim of this chapter is to review research in these areas with an eye toward identifying common and complementary themes. First, we review coping research, including its history and the importance of goals and strategies. Then, we review everyday problem-solving research, including its history and the importance of goals and strategies. Next, we consider the question of what constitutes effective coping and everyday problem solving. Then, mechanisms underlying age differences in coping and everyday problem solving are discussed. Finally, we close the chapter with some questions that may guide future research. The field would benefit from considering interdisciplinary perspectives as we consider ideas for helping older adults with their daily challenges.

Coping
History and Theory in Coping Research

Coping has been defined as "efforts to manage specific external and/or internal demands that are appraised as taxing or exceeding the resources of the person" (Lazarus & Folkman, 1984, p. 141). Interest in coping started with clinical and personality psychologists' observations of how clients and individuals handle stressful situations. Because of its history in clinical psychology, coping research often focuses on problematic life events, such as illnesses or dysfunctional family relationships. As coping research has progressed, it has moved beyond clinical psychology. In particular, transactional (state) and dispositional (trait) theories of coping have emerged as ways to describe how psychologically healthy individuals regulate stress.

TRANSACTIONAL VIEW OF COPING: COPING
AS A DYNAMIC PROCESS THAT UNFOLDS
OVER TIME

Lazarus's (1966; Lazarus & Folkman, 1984) transactional theory of stress and coping reoriented the field from its focus on pathology and unconscious processes rooted in ego psychology. Instead, Lazarus and colleagues highlighted the variety of cognitive and behavioral responses that people use in their everyday lives. In the transactional view of coping, coping is seen as a *dynamic process* rather than a *trait*. In this view, coping is a process in which individuals appraise, handle, and reappraise particular stressors in particular ways. Changing situational circumstances and demands are very important in this approach, and there is no one best strategy that is always effective, independent of the specific context.

Two components of this dynamic view of coping are key: the centrality of appraisal and the situational specificity of responses. First, coping is a response to an *appraisal* of stress. Reflecting the historical context of the time, Lazarus placed cognition at the center of the theory. This moved coping research beyond its origins in clinical observations. A stressful situation is one appraised as personally significant and as likely to strain or exceed the individual's resources. These are situations that produce negative affect and involve harm, loss, or threat to important goals. When encountering a situation, the individual weighs the demands of the situation with the resources she or he has available. Situations are appraised as irrelevant, benign-positive, or stressful (Lazarus & Folkman, 1984); those that are appraised as stressful are characterized by either harm or loss that has already been sustained, threat of harm or loss that may occur in the future, or a challenge that also requires a response but offers the opportunity for gain or growth.

Second, coping is viewed as situation-specific and dynamic (Folkman, Lazarus, Dunkel-Schetter, DeLongis, & Gruen, 1986). Appraisal is determined iteratively, via the unfolding balance between the stressor and the individual's response. The emphasis in this approach is on actual behaviors and thoughts elicited by a particular stressor, as well as on how these may change as the person engages with the stressor. The transactional approach describes coping as a dynamic feedback system that continues until the stressor is over. This is in contrast to a more dispositional perspective on coping (McCrae, 1989) in which individuals should show marked consistency in their coping behaviors across situations and time.

DISPOSITIONAL VIEW OF COPING:
COPING AS A *TRAIT*

In contrast to the transactional model's emphasis on the dynamic nature and situation-specificity of coping, some researchers have focused on dispositional preferences for certain coping styles. This view of coping as a *trait* posits that individuals bring dispositional tendencies to bear when experiencing stress. Indeed, McCrae and Costa (1986) found that controlling for personality (e.g., facets of neuroticism and extraversion) substantially reduced correlations between coping and well-being outcomes. When examined together, individuals' responses to global coping style measures have been found to be only weakly correlated with the strategies individuals report using in stressful situations (Carver & Scheier, 1994). One difficulty with most studies from the trait perspective is the reliance on retrospective self-reports. However, studies using time-sampling techniques also find weak correlations between trait and situational components of coping. For example, one study demonstrated that individuals often endorse relationship-focused coping strategies (such as compromise) when handling stressful marital conflicts. Individuals rarely use relationship-focused coping with misbehaving children (DeLongis & Holtzman, 2005). Global, trait-like coping style measures fail to capture these situation-specific responses (DeLongis & Holtzman, 2005). Further, dispositional features may affect both the strategies selected and their effectiveness. For example, adult attachment style, which is theoretically a dispositional characteristic drawn from early relationship experiences, was found to moderate the effect of daily pain catastrophizing and use of social coping in the context of chronic illnesses, such as osteoporosis and fibromyalgia (Kratz, Davis, & Zautra, 2012). Of course, the situational specificity issue is not limited to coping research.

DEVELOPMENTAL VIEW OF COPING: COPING ACROSS DIFFERENT LIFE PHASES

Despite the differing views of coping among transactional and dispositional approaches, by any of the definitions, coping is an important feature of adaptation to life's minor challenges and major events across the lifespan (Lupien, McEwen, Gunnar, & Heim, 2009; Ruth & Coleman, 1996). Given the diversity in responses that individuals display, a central question involves what produces these sets of responses. The possible contributions of personality were mentioned previously. However, much research has been devoted to understanding how coping resources develop throughout life. Interestingly, many of the classic coping theories were developed and tested in samples spanning the adult lifespan. Here, we overview theoretical accounts of the development of coping, as well as empirical findings of age differences and age-related change in coping across the lifespan.

The dispositional (e.g., McCrae and Costa) and transactional (e.g., Lazarus and Folkman) theories reviewed earlier are not explicitly developmental, but both imply predictions about changes or stability in coping (Labouvie-Vief, Hakim-Larson, & Hobart, 1987). That is, a dispositional approach proposes that personality emerges early in the lifespan and remains relatively stable across adulthood; therefore, age differences in coping are not expected after young adulthood. Cross-sectionally, McCrae found that middle-aged and older adults were less likely to use hostile reaction or escapist fantasy compared to younger adults (McCrae, 1982). However, later repeated measures and cross-sequential analyses of follow-up data did not replicate age differences in coping (McCrae, 1989). This lack of age differences or change is pointed to as evidence of modest stability in coping responses as enduring characteristics of individuals.

Conversely, from the transactional perspective, the primary determinants of a particular coping response are situational context and individual resources; age differences and developmental change are secondary and, by extension, may be apparent because of age differences in the types of contexts individuals engage in during different parts of the lifespan and the resources and skills they bring to the situation (Lazarus & DeLongis, 1983). In their study focused on coping in a middle-aged community sample, Lazarus and colleagues found no evidence of age differences in coping (Folkman & Lazarus, 1980). Instead, the authors argue against focusing solely on age differences in stress and coping because differential rates of biological aging will produce variability in the timing of any changes in activities and coping strategies (Lazarus & DeLongis, 1983). Further, they encourage examining individuals' patterns of commitment (i.e., goals, ideals) and beliefs about self and world (i.e., controllability) across the lifespan to understand the transactions between a developing person and different contextual stressors. Later, the transactional approach acknowledged the importance of developmental processes in coping. For example, younger adults reported more control over their stressful situations than did older adults, which led them to use problem-focused coping (Lazarus, 1996). Importantly, however, Lazarus argued that individual differences in life experiences and rates of aging overshadow general age trajectories in coping (Lazarus, 1996). Until recently, this argument was largely untested, leaving the field with little insight into predictors of age-related change in coping over time. A recent longitudinal study (Brennan, Holland, Schutte, & Moos, 2012) spanning 20 years found that, although there is a general age-related decline in the use of both approach and avoidance coping, individual differences in baseline (i.e., middle age) social and financial resources, as well as depressive symptoms, were related to the steepness of these declines.

Developmental psychologists such as Labouvie-Vief, Blanchard-Fields, and Aldwin took a different approach, applying a developmental perspective to coping research. Labouvie-Vief (1985) provided an explicitly developmental perspective on coping across the adult lifespan. She proposed that substantial conceptual reorganization occurs during adulthood, allowing a mature individual more cognitive complexity and flexibility in responding to challenges (Labouvie-Vief et al., 1987). Indeed, in cross-sectional work, maturity (e.g., a composite of age, ego level, and attributions about the nature of stressful experiences) was related to the use of particular coping strategies. Among individuals of the same chronological age, developmental maturity helped to explain individual differences in coping. Older adults used combinations of particular strategies that reflected more impulse control and positive reappraisal (Diehl, Coyle, & Labouvie-Vief, 1996), in comparison to adolescents and young adults.

Extending Labouvie-Vief's work, Blanchard-Fields studied the importance of controllability and context for the selection of coping strategies across the adult lifespan. Although older adults attributed the cause of stressors to be less controllable, no age differences were apparent in participants' appraisals of the controllability of the outcomes (Blanchard-Fields & Robinson, 1987). Age was found to moderate the relationship between locus of control and coping (Blanchard-Fields & Irion, 1988). Related to the core transactional idea of appraisal, age differences were found in the relationship between coping strategies and perceived effectiveness. In particular, older adults' use of planful problem solving and self-controlling were significantly related to appraised effectiveness (as compared to adolescents and young adults) (Irion & Blanchard-Fields, 1987).

Aldwin and colleagues (Aldwin & Stokols, 1988; Aldwin, Sutton, & Lachman, 1996), building off Lazarus and Folkman's transactional theory, also incorporated a developmental perspective on coping. Their deviation amplification model (Aldwin & Stokols, 1988) proposes that a person's coping response is primarily aimed at returning oneself to a preferred homeostasis. However, the way in which a person responds may also have long-term consequences beyond the encounter with the current stressor. These consequences can be positive (e.g., utilizing resources effectively may result in the development of additional resources for later use) or negative (e.g., already low levels of resources may be further depleted or exhausted when used) adaptive spirals. Aldwin and colleagues argued that this perspective is inconsistent with a dispositional coping styles approach. Instead, coping is viewed as "a process that extends across situations by resulting in general changes in coping resources…and, as such, can affect personality processes such as mastery and self-esteem" (Aldwin et al., 1996, p. 842). Across three samples (middle-aged and older men, men and women across the adult lifespan, and young adult to middle-aged college graduates), 80–90% of participants reported that they drew on prior experiences to help them cope with current problems. Furthermore, only for about 20% in each sample were these prior experiences similar stressors

to the present problem. Instead, many described confidence or perspective that they gained from their success in coping with previous stressors. The cross-sectional analyses of the lifespan sample suggest that almost all of those people who experienced low-point events in young adulthood reported finding advantages from the experience, but only 60% of those who experienced the low-point event in later life reported deriving advantages from the experience.

Overall, then, increasing maturity and accumulated experience seem to be related to more flexible and mature coping strategies. There are pronounced individual differences within each age group, however. Not all individuals learn from their life experiences or develop mature coping techniques. The importance of individual differences in coping is underscored by the wide variety of goals individuals bring to coping-related situations.

Goals and Coping

Goals are important factors related to individual differences in coping. In the context of coping, goals are hoped-for outcomes of stressful situations that are personally significant to the individual (Folkman & Moscowitz, 2004). They flag whenever there is a gap between current and desired end states (Lazarus, 1996). Researchers from the transactional view on coping (Lazarus & Folkman, 1984) argue that, to understand what constitutes a problem for a specific individual in a given situation, it is important to know (a) what this particular person was trying to achieve; (b) what is at stake in a given encounter, knowing that personal goals play a crucial role in this initial cognitive appraisal; and (c) the choice of strategies used to solve the problem (Lazarus, 1993, 1996; Lazarus & Folkman, 1984). Importantly, personal goals not only affect the initial appraisal of an encounter but also the evaluation of whether employed efforts have led to its successful solution (Lazarus, 1993, 1996; Lazarus & Folkman, 1984).

Individuals' coping goals are often complex and difficult to study. Most stressful situations elicit multiple goals, even from the same individuals. For example, one study demonstrated that more than 80% of adults reported having multiple goals in mind as they coped with interpersonal situations (Rook, Sorkin, & Zettel, 2004). In addition, goals often change as the stressful situation unfolds. For example, an initial goal might involve compromising with a relationship partner, but if efforts to compromise fail, the goal might change to reducing emotional distress (Rook et al., 2004). Goals also are influenced by available resources. For example, a widower may have a goal of remarriage, but this goal might change if no suitable partners are available (Rook et al., 2004). In addition, coping goals can be difficult to identify when stressors are chronic, such as ongoing illness, caregiving, and bereavement (Folkman & Moskowitz, 2004). In these situations, goals might be especially idiosyncratic, such as a goal to feel pain-free enough to attend a family event in the next week. The idiosyncratic nature of coping-related goals makes them difficult to study, but also makes them a rich source of insight into real-world coping processes.

Strategies and Coping

Although individuals develop different goals for coping with stressful situations, they also differ in the strategies they use to reach their goals. Strategies for coping encompass both thoughts and behaviors aimed at reducing negative emotions and/or resolving the threat. Lazarus and Folkman (1984) organized these responses broadly into problem- and emotion-focused coping. *Problem-focused coping* is aimed at problem-solving actions that involve acting to alter the stressor. *Emotion-focused coping* responses, conversely, are aimed at reducing or managing the emotional distress produced by the situation. As is clear from these descriptions, a given problem may involve both problem- and emotion-focused coping. The iterative feature of coping may become clear as the individual then appraises how successful his or her efforts were to manage emotions and resolve the threat. If the coping was successful, the stressor may now be perceived as benign and the threat passed. If the threat is still present, the individual may attempt other problem-focused techniques and return to emotion-focused coping to reduce the distress she or he is experiencing. Carver, Scheier, and Weintraub (1989), among others, further elaborated specific problem-focused (e.g., active coping, planning, suppression of other competing activities, restraint coping, seeking instrumental social support) and emotion-focused coping (seeking emotional social support, positive reinterpretation, acceptance, denial, and turning to religion) that individuals may use when encountering an event. In later years, Lazarus (1996) and others (Moos & Billings, 1982) recommended that researchers not use the problem- versus emotion-focused dichotomy as a classification system because it oversimplifies the way that coping responses actually function. The functions are not mutually exclusive;

rather, an emotion-focused response may help the individual focus enough to evaluate the resources needed to manage the problem directly. Similarly, a problem-focused, action-oriented strategy may help the person to bring his or her emotions in check.

In addition to the problem-focused and emotion-focused coping described by Folkman and Lazarus, recent research on the transactional model of coping has described relationship-focused coping. This is a type of coping focused on maintaining or managing relationships during stress (DeLongis & Holtzman, 2005; O'Brien & DeLongis, 1996). DeLongis's approach extends Folkman and Lazarus's transactional model of coping to the interactional context in which coping occurs. Examples of relationship-focused coping include empathy, giving support, and compromise. It is often used in stressful situations involving relationships with other people, especially a close family member or friend (O'Brien & DeLongis, 1996). Positive relationship-focused coping is associated with higher caregiver satisfaction (Kramer, 1993). Importantly, the effects of relationship-focused coping are often studied using time-sampling research and not just retrospective reports. This technique showed husbands' relationship-focused coping was associated with *higher* marital tension immediately after a stressful event, but *lower* marital tension the next day (DeLongis & Holtzman, 2005). This leads to unique insights with regards to the temporal ordering of coping-outcome associations. For example, coping strategies that are initially effective may be maladaptive in the long term.

Further study of relationship-focused coping, particularly how it is used in different social partnerships beyond married couples, is needed. This is important because sociological perspectives point out that most coping is in response to common and enduring strains from social roles (Pearlin & Schooler, 1978). Indeed, Pearlin and Schooler defined coping as "behavior that protects people from being psychologically harmed by problematic social experience" (1978, p. 2). Their work highlights normative coping responses to widely experienced life problems. Social evaluative threats, which are commonly experienced in interpersonal relationships, are potent biological stressors (Dickerson & Kemeny, 2004). Thus, research investigating coping responses to these stressors is especially important.

Finally, theories of coping must acknowledge the wide variety of coping behaviors. A research-based classification system for the numerous coping behaviors has yet to be established. Skinner, Edge,

Altman, and Sherwood (2003) reviewed 100 different coping measures, totaling 400 distinct ways of coping, and attempted to organize these responses. Rather than the typical distinctions (e.g., problem- vs. emotion-focused, approach vs. avoidance, cognitive vs. behavioral), they recommend that coping responses be organized by their action types (e.g., proximity seeking, mastery, accommodation) and how they are linked to adaptation to stress. Future research must incorporate all these complexities.

Everyday Problem Solving

Coping and everyday problem solving share many features, such as an emphasis on the importance of context (Skinner, Berg, & Uchino, this volume). Both processes involve using strategies to reach goals, and these strategies and goals differ greatly among individuals. The pattern of age differences in strategies is also similar for coping and everyday problem solving. One difference between coping and everyday problem solving is their different disciplinary backgrounds and approaches. In this section, we review the history and theory of everyday problem solving. We then turn our attention to the importance of goals. Finally, we review research on strategies used to solve everyday problems.

History and Theory in Everyday Problem-Solving Research

HISTORY OF EVERYDAY PROBLEM SOLVING

Interest in everyday problem solving originated from concerns about the generalizability of intelligence research. Intelligence tests were developed with the intention to predict academic performance in a school context (Woolfolk, 2011). Whether traditional intelligence tests predict nonacademic achievement, however, is controversial (Neisser et al., 1996). In particular, everyday problem-solving research arose from dissatisfaction with the predictive validity of intelligence measures for real-world behavior in adults, for whom school performance is no longer a meaningful criterion measure. Everyday problem solving aims to measure real-world knowledge and reasoning skills. These real-world tasks range from reading bus schedules to handling family conflicts. Hence, everyday problem solving is a strengths-based approach describing what works well in solving the problems people actually confront in their everyday lives.

Robert Sternberg suggested the importance of everyday problem solving with his idea of *practical intelligence* (Sternberg, 1985; Sternberg, Wagner,

Williams, & Horvath, 1995). He demonstrated that adults with accurate procedural knowledge in their job content were more successful in their careers. Sternberg's findings suggested that everyday success involved more than traditional intelligence. Similarly, Gisela Labouvie-Vief suggested that intelligence in adulthood is multidimensional (Labouvie-Vief, 1985). When faced with a problem, adults choose strategies based on practical and emotional factors, in addition to logical factors (Labouvie-Vief, 1992).

Another early researcher in the field was Nancy Denney. She and her colleagues presented hypothetical problems to young, middle-aged, and older participants (Denney & Pearce, 1989). They consistently found that middle-aged adults generated the largest number of safe and effective possible solutions (Denney, Pearce, & Palmer, 1982). Other researchers questioned whether mentioning more solutions was the same as effective problem solving. Experts rated older adults' proposed solutions as more effective than those of younger adults (Cornelius & Caspi, 1987).

More recently adopted contextual approaches to everyday problem solving take into account the problem-solvers' goals and the socioemotional context of the problem (Berg et al., 1998; Blanchard-Fields, Jahnke, & Camp, 1995). Recent approaches also include an evaluation of the usefulness of everyday problem solving for helping older adults remain independent (Marsiske & Willis, 1995).

Historically, researchers have distinguished well-structured from ill-structured problems (Berg, 2008; Strough & Keener, this volume; Wood, 1983). Well-structured problems generally have one correct answer. In contrast, ill-structured problems have several correct answers and often involve emotional and social aspects. Fredda Blanchard-Fields was a pioneer in the investigation of ill-structured problems. She brought attention to the importance of these problems in older adults' lives. Many everyday problems that adults spontaneously mention when reflecting on their lives are ill-structured (Blanchard-Fields & Coats, 2008). Recently, an attempt has been made to integrate these two approaches in everyday problem-solving research (Berg et al., 2009; Strough & Keener, this volume). This is important because an understanding of the full range of everyday problems could lead to improved well-being and independent functioning in older adults. For both types of everyday problem solving, individuals' goals for handling the situation are paramount.

Goals and Everyday Problem Solving

A growing number of studies show that age-related differences in the occurrence and management of everyday problems reflect not only differences in situational circumstances but also an individual's inner evaluations of these specific situations (Marsiske & Margrett, 2006; Sorkin & Rook, 2006). As a result, goal-based appraisals have attracted considerable interest in research on everyday problem solving in adulthood and aging (Berg et al., 1998; Blanchard-Fields, 1996; Strough, Berg, & Sansone, 1996).

Personal goals can be defined as cognitive representations of the self that guide behavior over time (Austin & Vancouver, 1996). Goals are defining features of everyday problem solving because they represent the standard for evaluating discrepancies between current and desired end states (Heath, Larrick, & Wu, 1999; Lazarus, 1996; Marsiske & Margrett, 2006). In turn, they influence the strategies that people use to minimize such discrepancies (Carver & Scheier, 2002; Marsiske & Margrett, 2006). Accordingly, Berg and colleagues (Berg et al., 1998) have called for an examination of everyday problem solving as filtered through an individual's subjective experiences, suggesting a focus on personal goals. This is similar to coping researchers' arguments that personal goals affect the appraisal of situation and also the evaluation of whether the situation has improved (Lazarus, 1993, 1996). Following this line of reasoning, it seems important to examine how individuals of different ages appraise an encounter based on their personal goals, which strategies they choose to overcome obstacles to their personal goals, and the extent to which employed strategies are effective in dealing with everyday problems in such a way as to enable continued goal pursuit.

Research conducted with individuals of different ages shows that goal content varies systematically across the lifespan and reflects developmental tasks and themes (Baltes, Lindenberger, & Staudinger, 1998; Cantor & Sanderson, 1999; Ebner, Freund, & Baltes, 2006; Erikson, 1966; Havighurst, 1952; Nurmi, 1992). For instance, in young adulthood, autonomy and independence play a central role, whereas in older adulthood, generative themes play an important role (McAdams, de St. Aubin, & Logan, 1993; Sheldon & Elliot, 1999). Beyond such common age-related themes, goals also become increasingly individualized over the adult lifespan and represent a domain of functioning in which growth and development are still possible well into old age (Hooker & McAdams, 2003; Hoppmann, Gerstorf, Smith, & Klumb, 2007; Hoppmann & Smith, 2007; Smith & Freund, 2002). Studying goals, therefore, offers important insight into individual differences in everyday problem solving because they reflect what an individual had been trying to achieve when confronted with a specific problem.

Strategies and Everyday Problem Solving

Another important facet of everyday problem-solving research is the strategies adults use to handle their problems. One way that the coping and everyday problem-solving literatures overlap is through categorizations of strategies for handling stressful or problematic situations. As described earlier, coping theorists distinguish between problem-focused strategies and emotion-focused strategies (Folkman, Lazarus, Pimley, & Novacek, 1987). Everyday problem-solving researchers have adapted these coping categories into their own work and demonstrated that emotion-focused strategies are more preferred by older adults than by young adults (Blanchard-Fields et al., 1995; Cornelius & Caspi, 1987). More recently, researchers have criticized the category of emotion-focused strategies for being too broad, arguing for distinctions to be made between different types of emotion-focused strategies, such as passive emotion regulation and proactive emotion regulation (Blanchard-Fields & Coats, 2008; Blanchard-Fields, Stein, & Watson, 2004; Coats & Blanchard-Fields, 2008; Martini & Busseri, 2010). Previous measures of emotion-focused strategies, broadly conceived, were actually dominated by passive strategies (such as avoidance) and neglected other types of emotion-focused strategies used in real, self-reported problems (Blanchard-Fields & Coats, 2008; Blanchard-Fields et al., 2004). Passive emotion regulation strategies involve withdrawing from the problem, distracting oneself away from the situation, or suppressing feelings. Proactive emotion regulation strategies involve approaching the emotion directly, through such actions as venting one's feelings toward the source of the problem, seeking advice, or analyzing emotions. Distinguishing between the two approaches to regulating emotions in everyday problems is important because emotional strategies can still be active, and passive and proactive strategies might be distinct subtypes of emotional strategies (Blanchard-Fields et al., 2004). Older adults report more passive and fewer proactive emotion regulation strategies than do young adults (Birditt & Fingerman, 2005; Blanchard-Fields & Coats, 2008).

Although there are age differences in strategy endorsements, individuals' strategy preferences depend on the type of problem they are experiencing. This is especially true for older adults, who often use combinations of several strategies to handle everyday problems. In particular, older adults endorse problem-focused strategies in combination with emotion-focused strategies more than young adults do (Watson & Blanchard-Fields, 1998). For example, following an argument with a family member over who should repair a broken refrigerator, older adults are likely to call a repair business (problem-focused strategy) while also accepting the family member's feelings (emotion-focused strategy). Conway, Magai, McPherson-Salandy, and Milano (2010) studied everyday problem-solving strategies in a large representative sample of four ethnic groups of older adults. A wide variety of strategies were mentioned, such as seeking social support and actively working to solve the problem. Similarly, the most mentioned strategies in a sample of German middle-aged adults were productive, problem-focused behaviors and nurturing interpersonal relationships (Jopp & Schmitt, 2010).

CONTEXT SPECIFICITY

Adults not only use multiple strategies, but they adapt their strategies to the context of the problem. Context specificity and flexibility in problem solving is important because different problem-solving strategies may be effective in some contexts, but not others (Blanchard-Fields, 2009; Bonanno, Papa, Lalande, Westphal, & Coifman, 2004). For example, a problem-focused strategy of going to court might be effective when one is the victim of a burglary. This same strategy might not be as effective in an emotionally charged custody fight between divorcing parents. Older adults, perhaps because of lifelong development and accumulated life experience, may understand when it is appropriate to step back from a conflict and when it is better to actively work to solve problems (Blanchard-Fields et al., 1995). In one example from an interview-based study, an older adult reported the following problem and her solution:

> An older woman's daughter-in-law just gave birth to her fifth grandchild. However, her daughter-in-law and son were quite insulting instructing her on how to hold the baby. In order not to escalate the conflict, the older woman gently gave the baby back to the mother and left the hospital room to vent her emotions alone. She did not want to cause a fight with her family at such a vulnerable time. Later,

when things calmed down, she would revisit the issue with her family. (Blanchard-Fields, 2009; Blanchard-Fields & Coats, 2008)

The woman in this situation felt that the context called for a passive emotion regulation strategy. Older adults, compared to young adults, often demonstrate context specificity by adapting their strategies, depending on various aspects of everyday problems. In particular, researchers have demonstrated context specificity based on problem domain, goals, and discrete emotions. Each of these aspects of context specificity is discussed below.

Problem Domain

Problem domains refer to different content areas, such as conflicts with friends and consumer problems. Blanchard-Fields has shown that in the interpersonal domain of conflict with friends, older adults endorsed more emotion-focused strategies than did young adults. In the instrumental domain of consumer problems, older adults tended to endorse problem-focused strategies. Thus, older adults adapted their strategies to fit the nature of the problem (Blanchard-Fields, Chen, & Norris, 1997). In another study, older adults were more problem-focused than were young adults in their approach to solving instrumental problems, whereas older adults endorsed more avoidant–denial strategies than did young adults when solving interpersonal problems (Blanchard-Fields, Mienaltowski, & Seay, 2007).

Goals

Older adults also adapt their strategies to match their goals for handling everyday problems. Previous studies on goals and everyday problem solving found that individuals of different ages interpret the same problem in systematically different ways based on their goals (Berg, Klaczynski, Calderone, & Strough, 1994; Sorkin & Rook, 2006). Furthermore, goals have been shown to be associated with the selection of problem-solving strategies (Berg et al., 1998). For example, adults who focus on more interpersonal goals when solving problems are more likely to use strategies that involve regulation and inclusion of others, whereas adults with competence goals report strategies that involve self-action (Berg et al., 1998).

In our own past work, we have demonstrated that developmentally relevant goals, such as generativity and autonomy, are closely linked with age-related differences in strategy use across a variety of problems. Using qualitative interviews from a lifespan sample, we showed, for instance, that in the domain of family and financial problems, autonomy goals were associated with instrumental self-focused problem solving, and generativity goals were related to the use of instrumental other-focused problem solving (Hoppmann, Coats, & Blanchard-Fields, 2008). Importantly, older adults showed a greater match between their goals and strategies than did young adults. In another study, we tested the mechanisms underlying previously observed goal and problem-solving links using hypothetical family problem vignettes and experimentally manipulated goals in young and older adults. In line with expectations, young adults expressed a preference for autonomy goals whereas older adults preferred generative goals. Autonomy goals were related to an elevated emphasis on self-focused instrumental problem solving and self-focused proactive emotion regulation strategies, whereas generative goals were associated with more other-focused instrumental problem-solving and other-focused proactive emotion regulation strategies. Importantly, participants who changed their goal preferences in response to the experimental manipulation (i.e., imagining an expanded future time perspective) also adjusted their problem-solving strategies (Hoppmann & Blanchard-Fields, 2010). These results suggest that goals do indeed represent an important mechanism behind age-related differences in strategy use.

Discrete Emotions

Finally, the last problem feature to illustrate context specificity in everyday problem solving is discrete emotions, such as anger and sadness. Older adults demonstrate context specificity as they adapt their problem-solving strategies to match the specific emotions elicited by different problems. In one study, adolescents and adults of all ages described the emotions they felt during problems encountered during their lives (Blanchard-Fields & Coats, 2008). Instead of reporting how they felt at one point during the problem, participants told interviewers how they felt and how they handled their feelings at each point during the sequence of events in the problem. Older adults reported fewer instances of anger than did adolescents, young adults, and middle-aged adults. Older adults also reported less use of proactive emotion regulation strategies, such as venting feelings and confronting the source of the problem. Importantly, the reduced experience of anger on the part of older adults partially accounted for why they did not use a high degree of proactive emotion regulation strategies. Older adults used proactive

emotion regulation strategies when they were angry and passive emotion regulation strategies when they were sad. Thus, they showed more context specificity than did younger individuals, whose strategies did not differ based on discrete emotions (Blanchard-Fields & Coats, 2008).

In another study focused on discrete emotions, young, middle-aged, and older adults read hypothetical problem situations that elicited anger or sadness (Coats & Blanchard-Fields, 2008). Participants rated the degree to which they would use several strategies to handle their feelings in each situation. As in past research, older adults endorsed proactive emotion regulation less than young adults did. However, important differences emerged based on discrete emotions. Older adults reported expressing less anger but more sadness than did young adults. Thus, older adults again show evidence of handling everyday problem situations differently, depending on the context. There also were individual differences within older adults in the degree to which they endorsed passive emotion regulation strategies. In this study, it was not the case that older adults uniformly preferred passive strategies more than young adults. Older individuals with lower levels of cognitive-emotional complexity, who may have had trouble tolerating strong angry feelings, were the ones who endorsed passive strategies more than did younger individuals (Coats & Blanchard-Fields, 2008).

Overall, there is some evidence that older adults adapt their problem-solving strategies to match the context of the situation. Not all older adults demonstrate context specificity, however, and individual difference variables play an important role in predicting adults' strategies. In particular, adults who prioritize emotion regulation goals, tend to be non-expressive, and are low in cognitive-emotional complexity are more likely to endorse passive emotion regulation strategies (Coats & Blanchard-Fields, 2008). Some researchers have suggested that adapting strategies to fit the context is a measure of problem-solving effectiveness (Blanchard-Fields, 2007). This issue is controversial, however, and other methods of effectiveness show different age-related patterns.

Assessing Effectiveness

What is effective coping and everyday problem solving? How do individuals know when to stop coping? When are everyday problems solved? Studies investigating age-related differences in everyday problem-solving effectiveness show that instrumental and interpersonal problem solving follow different trajectories across the lifespan (Baltes et al., 1998; Thornton & Dumke, 2005). Despite the fact that effectiveness is central to research on coping and everyday problem solving, there is no standard set of criteria to measure it. Researchers have suggested several indices for assessing effective coping and everyday problem solving. Each index has strengths and limitations.

Early research suggested that *the number of safe solutions* generated was a useful proxy for effectiveness (Denney & Pearce, 1989). The strength of this approach is that it avoids imposing value-laden criteria for judging effectiveness. For example, if an older adult is dealing with the problem of loneliness, participating in church activities and joining a bridge club are both valid solutions. Researchers are probably not in a position to say which is more effective, in general. Additionally, proponents of this approach point out that, in traditional problem-solving research, seeing multiple solutions to a problem is indicative of high problem-solving ability (Denney & Pearce, 1989). The limitation to this approach is that individuals who might not generate a lot of solutions for a given problem might have identified a few highly effective strategies. If one has identified a creative and useful solution to a problem, it is not necessary to try other strategies. In fact, throwing many strategies at a problem might be a sign of difficulty in generating an effective way to handle a problem (Berg, Meegan, & Klaczynski, 1999). When number of strategies is the index of effectiveness, older adults typically perform worse than young adults (Denney & Pearce, 1989).

To address the limitation of this index, other researchers recruited experts to objectively assess effectiveness. In this line of research, experts rated several possible strategies for handling hypothetical situations. Then, participants read the situations and chose which strategies they thought were best (Blanchard-Fields et al., 2007; Cornelius & Caspi, 1987). Participants' ratings were compared to *experts' ratings* to determine effectiveness. The strength of this approach is that it can be a direct method for assessing effectiveness. The limitation is that it depends on recruiting knowledgeable, unbiased experts. It can be difficult to validate expertise, particularly in everyday problem solving, in which experts do not have access to problem-solvers' motives and situational constraints. When the index of effectiveness is matched to an expert panel's ratings, older adults tend to perform better than younger individuals, especially for interpersonal problems (Blanchard-Fields et al., 2007; Cornelius & Caspi, 1987).

For well-structured problems (Strough & Keener, this volume), effective problem solving can be defined as using strategies that lead to *successful performance of instrumental tasks of daily living*, such as finance management, shopping, and transportation (Allaire & Marsiske, 2002). If individuals can independently take care of themselves, it suggests that they can handle well-structured, instrumental everyday problems well. When this index of effectiveness is used, older adults tend to perform worse than younger individuals (Allaire & Marsiske, 2002; Diehl, Willis, & Schaie, 1995), although this might be due to impairments in a subpopulation of older adults.

One difficulty with these effectiveness indices is their neglect of individuals' own ideas of what constitutes an effective solution to their problems. Research employing externally defined measures of problem-solving effectiveness, such as the accuracy of solutions as compared to absolute criteria or the number of safe and effective solutions, has limitations. As described earlier, these limitations include difficulty determining absolute criteria for "correct" or "effective" problem solving and difficulty choosing experts who are true experts. Another concern with respect to the externally defined measures of problem-solving effectiveness just enumerated is that this approach seems better suited to evaluate problem-solving effectiveness for problems, which usually have one right answer (e.g., understanding medication labels) as compared to evaluating problem-solving effectiveness with respect to complex social problems that typically have more than one possible solution. Hence, an alternative approach to examine age-related differences in problem-solving effectiveness may be to focus on goals because goals reveal what an individual would consider a good outcome given specific contextual circumstances.

Examining the match between goals and everyday problem solving offers a new perspective on conceptualizing problem-solving effectiveness. The match between goals and strategies can be used to compare problem-solving effectiveness across different age groups, while at the same time taking into account individual differences in problem interpretations. In that sense, a goal-based definition of problem-solving effectiveness instantiates a developmental contextualist perspective by suggesting that there is no universal standard for problem-solving effectiveness (Berg & Klaczynski, 1996). Imagine the following scenario:

A family is having difficulty finding a good weekend for their family reunion. The grandmother, who has the goal of engaging in a weekend full of emotionally meaningful interactions with her loved ones, might approach this problem by thinking through different alternative scenarios and spending a lot of time on the phone with family members to find out about their preferences. Her grandson, in contrast, who wants to become more autonomous and independent, might avoid getting too involved and suggest that they postpone by a year.

Hence, the same social problem can have very different implications for two members of the same family, depending on their goals. As a consequence, these two family members might use very different strategies that are both effective, depending on their individual goals. Initial evidence looking at age differences in goal–strategy matches suggests that older adults may be better at selecting strategies that match their problem-solving goals, thus rendering them more effective problem-solvers (Hoppmann & Blanchard-Fields, 2010). Hence, to better understand problem-solving effectiveness, it may be fruitful to incorporate goals into research on everyday problems across the lifespan and examine how these goals match the way everyday problems are appraised and approached (Blanchard-Fields, 2007; Hoppmann et al., 2008; Lazarus, 1991). An analysis of individuals' goals in context may help to explain why older adults manifest context specificity when solving everyday problems.

Mechanisms Underlying Age Differences in Coping and Everyday Problem-Solving Strategies

General trends suggest that older adults are more likely than young adults to use passive emotion regulation strategies (such as accepting everyday problems) and less likely to use proactive emotion regulation strategies (such as directly confronting the source of the problem). We have seen that older adults select a wider variety of strategies than do young adults. Recent research has examined possible mechanisms underlying these age differences in strategies. Candidate explanations include cognitive, motivational, and experience-based mechanisms.

Because everyday problem-solving research (in contrast to coping research) traces its roots to the *cognitive* perspective in psychology, some effort has been made to identify cognitive factors underlying strategy choices. Research on well-structured problem solving demonstrates that older adults with limited cognitive resources show poorer performance (Allaire & Marsiske, 1999). Older adults' reduced cognitive resources (Hess & Queen, this volume) may also lead to difficulty tolerating negative emotions and less complexity in everyday problem representations (Labouvie-Vief, 2003; Wurm, Labouvie-Vief, Aycock, Rebucal, & Koch, 2004). For example, older adults' thinking is disrupted by emotionally arousing stimuli (Wurm et al., 2004). Labouvie-Vief suggests that the inability of many older adults to handle intense negative emotions leads them to use passive emotion regulation strategies, such as acceptance of the problem and conflict avoidance (Labouvie-Vief, 2003; Labouvie-Vief, Gilet, & Mella, this volume). Another difference in cognition between young and older adults is that older adults are more likely to use a heuristic, experiential mode of thinking than are young adults (Klaczynski & Robinson, 2000). A recent study demonstrated that older adults relied more on experiential thought during everyday situations that called for counterfactual thinking (Horhota, Mienaltowski, & Blanchard-Fields, 2012). Thus, older adults may rely on mental shortcuts when choosing strategies for solving everyday problems.

Another explanation for age differences in strategies is *motivational*. Socioemotional selectivity theory posits that as individuals perceive a limited amount of time left in their lives, they prioritize emotional goals over information-gathering goals (Carstensen, Isaacowitz, & Charles, 1999). To maximize positive emotional outcomes, many older adults greatly value the preservation of close relationships. This affects the problem-solving strategies they use, especially in highly emotional situations (Blanchard-Fields et al., 1995; Coats & Blanchard-Fields, 2008). For example, expressing anger at a friend might not be the strategy of choice if one's goal is to maintain a harmonious friendship. If a young adult's goal is to influence the friend or to get one's own way, then expressing anger might be a useful strategy. In addition to age differences in interpersonal goals, some research suggests that older adults avoid focusing on negative stimuli (Isaacowitz, Toner, & Neupert, 2009; Mather & Carstensen, 2005). This positivity effect may be due to older adults' focus on emotion regulation, although this assumption is difficult to test directly (Isaacowitz & Blanchard-Fields, 2012). If older adults seek to avoid negativity, this could lead them to endorse passive emotion regulation strategies, such as accepting the situation and avoiding the problem.

Another possible mechanism underlying age differences in problem-solving strategies is older adults' accumulated *life experience* (Berg et al., 1999; Blanchard-Fields & Kalinauskas, 2009). Because older adults have spent many years handling everyday problems, some have gained expertise in choosing which strategies are most effective in different situations. Of course, accumulated experience does not necessarily lead to expertise, but the ability to learn from experience might be an important variable to examine when considering age differences in everyday problem solving. There also may be generational differences in strategy use. The cohort of older adults that grew up during the Great Depression was trained to "keep a stiff upper lip" and not express negative emotions, especially during interpersonal conflicts. Different age differences in strategies may emerge as the more expressive Baby Boomers age (Blanchard-Fields, 1996).

Future Directions: Integrating Coping and Everyday Problem-Solving Research

The underlying processes of coping (especially the transactional perspective of Folkman and Lazarus) and everyday problem solving (especially for ill-structured problems, as studied by Blanchard-Fields and Berg) are quite complex and share important features. Common characteristics of these approaches include the importance of appraisals, goals, context, and prior experience. Both involve appraisals of stressful or problematic situations. How individuals interpret a situation has a direct effect on how they cope with the stress or solve the problem. Goals are also central to both coping and everyday problem solving. Individuals have their own idiosyncratic ideas of what outcome they would like when confronted with stressful situations or everyday problems. When researchers acknowledge the importance of these idiosyncrasies, they move closer to discovering what matters to individuals in everyday life. Contextual factors are also important for coping and everyday problem solving. Effective coping and problem solving needs to take situational factors into account, such as the needs of other people, the emotions elicited, and the resources available. Finally, prior experience can be helpful or detrimental for coping and problem solving, as we see from the work of Aldwin (coping research; Aldwin & Stokols, 1988; Aldwin et al., 1996) and Berg (everyday

problem-solving research; Berg et al., 2009; Berg & Strough, 2011).

In both coping and everyday problem-solving research, there are several important open questions. To address concerns regarding the ecological validity of hypothetical problems and retrospective response biases associated with reports of previous stressful situations, we suggest complementing laboratory-based and questionnaire-based research with time-sampling studies. Such an approach examines coping and everyday problem solving as a dynamic process that unfolds over time. This would advance our thinking in several ways: First, it would allow investigations of the ecological validity of past laboratory-based research and its context specificity. For example, are older adults better at matching their daily strategies to their goals in social contexts than are young adults? Second, examining daily processes would help us to better understand if past research that is based on between-person differences transfers into within-person relationships. Specifically, are older adults better at adjusting their strategies to daily problems than are young adults, based on the goal that is elicited in a specific situation? Third, investigating daily processes opens new ways to study the effectiveness of goal–strategy matches in terms of time until solution and affective and physiological responses.

In addition to more time-sampling investigations, researchers should further examine the question of age differences in coping and everyday problem-solving effectiveness. Blanchard-Fields (2007) suggested that older adults are generally effective copers and problem solvers, at least in ill-structured, emotional situations. Other researchers, such as Denney (Denney & Pearce, 1989) and Labouvie-Vief (2003), suggested that coping and everyday problem-solving effectiveness peak in midlife. Discrepancies in age-related differences in effectiveness generally reflect different definitions of effectiveness, as described earlier. Developmental psychologists should strive to integrate these definitions, incorporating important factors such as emotions, well-being, functional independence, and relationship-based outcomes.

Interestingly, past research on coping and everyday problem solving mainly investigates samples of unrelated individuals (although this is starting to change; see Skinner, Berg, & Uchino, this volume). This is striking, given that, in many endeavors, social partners are involved to some extent. Based on an interactive minds perspective, we therefore call for an examination of how close others can influence each other's coping and problem solving, both positively and negatively (Baltes & Staudinger, 1996). Close others are important throughout the lifespan, but they may play different roles depending on age-related developmental themes and relationship types (Baltes & Silverberg, 1994). In old age, adults often share long histories with their relationship partners (such as spouses), selectively focus on close meaningful others, and have accumulated a lot of experience in handling social problems (Antonucci, Akiyama, & Merline, 2001; Baltes & Carstensen, 1998; Blanchard-Fields, 1996; Dixon, 1999; Lang, 2001). Hence, research on older adult couples, for example, may offer important insights into the maintenance of independence in older adults because long-term spouses may be able to achieve together what could not be done by each individual alone (Baltes & Carstensen, 1998; Hoppmann & Blanchard-Fields, 2011; Hoppmann & Gerstorf, 2009).

Researchers from the coping and everyday problem-solving traditions share an emphasis on strategies for handling stressful everyday situations. Perhaps theoretical and empirical integration in the challenge of strategy classifications can inspire further cross-discipline communication in the areas of appraisals, goals, context, and experience. This communication could lead to exciting developments, especially if dynamic interactions among social partners are examined on a moment-to-moment basis in real time. Fredda Blanchard-Fields emphasized the importance of context and interpersonal factors in her work. Her legacy continues when researchers are willing to tolerate complexity and incorporate a broad spectrum of developmental variables as they study coping and everyday problem solving. Research innovations and practical interventions in this area will lead to improved outcomes for older adults as they manage daily challenges.

References

Aldwin, C., & Stokols, D. (1988). The effects of environmental change on individuals and groups: Some neglected issues in stress research. *Journal of Environmental Psychology, 8*(1), 57–75.

Aldwin, C., Sutton, K. J., & Lachman, M. (1996). The development of coping resources in adulthood. *Journal of Personality, 64*(4), 837–871.

Allaire, J. C., & Marsiske, M. (1999). Everyday cognition: Age and intellectual ability correlates. *Psychology & Aging, 14,* 627–644.

Allaire, J. C., & Marsiske, M. (2002). Well- and ill-defined measures of everyday cognition: Relationship to older adults' intellectual ability and functional status. *Psychology & Aging, 17,* 101–115.

Antonucci, T. C., Akiyama, H., & Merline, A. (2001). Dynamics of social relationships in midlife. In M. E. Lachman (Ed.), *Handbook of midlife development* (pp. 571–598). New York: Wiley.

Austin, J. T., & Vancouver, J. B. (1996). Goal constructs in psychology: Structure, process, and content. *Psychological Bulletin, 120,* 338–375.

Baltes, M. M., & Carstensen, L. L. (1998). Social-psychological theories and their applications to aging: From individual to collective. In V. L. Bengtson & K. W. Schaie (Eds.), *Handbook of theories of aging* (pp. 209–226). New York: Springer.

Baltes, P. B., Lindenberger, U., & Staudinger, U. M. (1998). Life-span theory in developmental psychology. In R. M. Lerner (Ed.), *Handbook of child psychology* (vol. 1, pp. 1029–1143). New York: Wiley.

Baltes, M. M. & Silverberg, S. B. (1994). The dynamics between dependency and autonomy: Illustrations across the life span. In D. L. Featherman, R. M. Lerner, & M. Perlmutter (Eds.), *Life-span development and behavior* (pp. 41–90). Hillsdale, NJ: Lawrence Erlbaum.

Baltes, P. B., & Staudinger, U. M. (1996). *Interactive minds: Life-span perspectives on the social foundation of cognition.* New York: Cambridge University Press.

Berg, C. (2008). Everyday problem solving in context. In S. M. Hofer & D. F. Alwin (Eds.), *Handbook of cognitive aging: Interdisciplinary perspectives* (pp. 207–223). Los Angeles: Sage.

Berg, C. A., & Klaczynski, P. A. (1996). Practical intelligence and problem solving: Searching for perspectives. In F. Blanchard-Fields & T. M. Hess (Eds.), *Perspectives on cognitive change in adulthood and aging* (pp. 323–357). New York: McGraw-Hill.

Berg, C. A., Klaczynski, P., Calderone, K. S., & Strough, J. (1994). Adult age differences in cognitive strategies: Adaptive or deficient. In J. Sinnot (Ed.), *Interdisciplinary handbook of adult lifespan learning* (pp. 371–388). Westport, CT: Greenwood.

Berg, C. A., Meegan, S. P., & Klaczynski, P. (1999). Age and experiential differences in strategy generation and information requests for solving everyday problems. *International Journal of Behavioral Development, 23,* 615–639.

Berg, C. A., Skinner, M., & Ko, K. (2009). An integrative model of everyday problem solving across the adult life span. In M. Smith & N. DeFrates-Densch (Eds.), *Handbook of research on adult learning and development* (pp. 524–552). New York: Routledge.

Berg, C. A., & Strough, J. (2011). Problem solving across the life span. In K. Fingerman, C. A. Berg, T. Antonnuci, & J. Smith. (Eds.), *Handbook of life-span psychology* (pp. 239–267). New York: Springer.

Berg, C. A., Strough, J., Calderone, K. S., Sansone, C., & Weir, C. (1998). The role of problem definitions in understanding age and context effects on strategies for solving everyday problems. *Psychology & Aging, 13,* 29–44.

Birditt, K.S., & Fingerman, K. L. (2005). Do we get better at picking our battles? Age group differences in descriptions of behavioral reactions to interpersonal tensions. *Journal of Gerontology: Psychological Sciences, 60B,* 121–128.

Blanchard-Fields, F. (1996). Social cognitive development in adulthood and aging. In F. Blanchard-Fields & T. M. Hess (Eds.), *Perspectives on cognitive change in adulthood and aging* (pp. 454–487). New York: McGraw-Hill.

Blanchard-Fields, F. (2007). Everyday problem solving and emotion: An adult developmental perspective. *Current Directions in Psychological Science, 16,* 26–31.

Blanchard-Fields, F. (2009). Flexible and adaptive socio-emotional problem solving in adult development and aging. *Restorative Neurology and Neuroscience, 27*, 539–550.

Blanchard-Fields, F., Chen, Y., & Norris, L. (1997). Everyday problem solving across the adult life span: Influence of domain specificity and cognitive appraisal. *Psychology and Aging, 12*, 684–693.

Blanchard-Fields, F., & Coats, A. H. (2008). The experience of anger and sadness in everyday problems impacts age differences in emotion regulation. *Developmental Psychology, 44*, 1547–1556.

Blanchard-Fields, F., & Irion, J. C. (1988). The relation between locus of control and coping in two contexts: Age as a moderator variable. *Psychology and Aging, 3*(2), 197–203.

Blanchard-Fields, F., Jahnke, H. C., & Camp, C. (1995). Age differences in problem-solving style: The role of emotional salience. *Psychology and Aging, 10*, 173–180.

Blanchard-Fields, F., & Kalinauskas, A. S. (2009). Challenges for the current status of adult developmental theories: A new century of progress. In M. Cecil Smith & N. Densch-DeFrates (Eds.), *The handbook of research on adult learning and development* (pp. 3–33). New York: Routlege/Taylor & Francis Group.

Blanchard-Fields, F., Mienaltowski, A., & Seay, R. B. (2007). Age differences in everyday problem-solving effectiveness: Older adults select more effective strategies for interpersonal problems. *Journal of Gerontology: Psychological Sciences, 62B*, P61–P64.

Blanchard-Fields, F., & Robinson, S. L. (1987). Age differences in the relation between controllability and coping. *Journal of Gerontology, 42*(5), 497–501.

Blanchard-Fields, F., Stein, R., & Watson, T. L. (2004). Age differences in passive versus proactive emotion regulation strategies in handling everyday problems. *Journals of Gerontology: Psychological Sciences, 59*, 261–269.

Bonanno, G. A., Papa, A., Lalande, K., Westphal, M., & Coifman, K. (2004). The importance of being flexible: The ability to both enhance and suppress emotional expression predicts long-term adjustment. *Psychological Science, 15*, 482–487.

Brennan, P. L., Holland, J. M., Schutte, K. K., & Moos, R. H. (2012). Coping trajectories in later life: A 20 year predictive study. *Aging & Mental Health, 16*, 305–316.

Cantor, N., & Sanderson, C. A. (1999). Life task participation and well-being: The importance of taking part in daily life. In D. Kahneman & E. Diener (Eds.), *Well-being: The foundations of hedonic psychology* (pp. 230–243). New York: Russell Sage Foundation.

Carstensen, L. L., Isaacowitz, D. M., & Charles, S. T. (1999). Taking time seriously: A theory of socioemotional selectivity. *American Psychologist, 54*, 165–181.

Carver, C. S., & Scheier, M. F. (2002). Control processes and self-organization as complementary principles underlying behavior. *Personality & Social Psychology Review, 6*, 304–315.

Carver, C. S., & Scheier, M. F. (1994). Situational coping and coping dispositions in a stressful transaction. *Journal of Personality and Social Psychology, 66*(1), 184–195.

Carver, C. S., Scheier, M. F., & Weintraub, J. K. (1989). Assessing coping strategies: A theoretically based approach. *Journal of Personality and Social Psychology, 56*(2), 267–283.

Coats, A. H., & Blanchard-Fields, F. (2008). Emotion regulation in interpersonal problems: The role of cognitive-emotional complexity, emotion regulation goals, and expressivity. *Psychology and Aging, 23*, 39–51.

Conway, F., Magai, C., McPherson-Salandy, R., & Milano, K. (2010). Synergy between molecular and contextual views of coping among four ethnic groups of older adults. *International Journal of Aging and Human Development, 70*, 319–343.

Cornelius, S. W., & Caspi, A. (1987). Everyday problem solving in adulthood and old age. *Psychology and Aging, 2*, 144–153.

DeLongis, A., & Holtzman, S. (2005). Coping in context: The role of stress, social support, and personality in coping. *Journal of Personality, 73*, 1–24.

Denney, N. W., & Pearce, K. A. (1989). A developmental study of practical problem solving in adults. *Psychology and Aging, 4*, 438–442.

Denney, N. W., Pearce, K. A., & Palmer, A. M. (1982). A developmental study of adults' performance on traditional and practical problem solving tasks. *Experimental Aging Research, 5*, 115–118.

Dickerson S. S., & Kemeny, M.E. (2004). Acute stressors and cortisol responses: A theoretical integration and synthesis of laboratory research. *Psychological Bulletin, 130*, 355–391.

Diehl, M., Coyle, N., & Labouvie-Vief, G. (1996). Age and sex differences in strategies of coping and defense across the life span. *Psychology and Aging, 11*(1), 127–139.

Diehl, M., Willis, S. L., & Schaie, K. W. (1995). Everyday problem solving in older adults: Observational assessment and cognitive correlates. *Psychology and Aging, 10*, 478–491.

Dixon, R. A. (1999). Exploring cognition in interactive situations: The aging of N+1 minds. In T. M. Hess & F. Blanchard-Fields (Eds.), *Social cognition and aging* (pp. 267–290). San Diego: Academic Press.

Ebner, N. C., Freund, A. M., & Baltes, P. B. (2006). Developmental changes in personal goal orientation from young to late adulthood: From striving for gains to maintenance and prevention losses. *Psychology & Aging, 21*(4), 664–678.

Erikson, E. (1966). Eight ages of man. *International Journal of Psychiatry, 2*, 281–300.

Folkman, S., & Lazarus, R. S. (1980). An analysis of coping in a middle-aged community sample. *Journal of Health and Social Behavior, 21*(4), 219–239.

Folkman, S., & Moskowitz, J. T. (2004). Coping: Pitfalls and promise. *Annual Review of Psychology, 55*, 745–774.

Folkman, S., Lazarus, R. S., Dunkel-Schetter, C., DeLongis, A., & Gruen, R. J. (1986). Dynamics of a stressful encounter: Cognitive appraisal, coping, and encounter outcomes. *Journal of Personality and Social Psychology, 50*(5), 992–1003.

Folkman, S., Lazarus, R. S., Pimley, S., & Novacek, J. (1987). Age differences in stress and coping processes. *Psychology and Aging, 2*, 171–184.

Folkman, S., & Moskowitz, J. T. (2004). Coping: Pitfalls and promise. *Annual Review of Psychology, 55*, 745–774.

Havighurst, R. J. (1952). *Developmental tasks and education.* New York: David McKay Company.

Heath, C., Larrick, R. P., & Wu, G. (1999). Goals as reference points. *Cognitive Psychology, 38*, 79–109.

Hooker, K., & McAdams, D. P. (2003). Personality reconsidered: A new agenda for aging research. *Journal of Gerontology: Psychological Sciences, 58 B*, 296–304.

Hoppmann, C., & Blanchard-Fields, F. (2010). Goals and everyday problem solving: Manipulating goal preferences in young and older adults. *Developmental Psychology, 46*, 1433–1443.

Hoppmann, C., & Blanchard-Fields, F. (2011). Daily problem solving variability: How is it linked to situation-, person-, and couple-characteristics? *Psychology & Aging, 26*, 525–531.

Hoppmann, C., Coats, A. H., & Blanchard-Fields, F. (2008). Goals and everyday problem solving: Examining the link between age-related goals and problem-solving strategy use *Aging, Neuropsychology, and Cognition, 15,* 401–423.

Hoppmann, C., & Gerstorf, D. (2009). Spousal interrelations in old age- A mini review. *Gerontology, 55*(449), 459.

Hoppmann, C. A., Gerstorf, D., Smith, J., & Klumb, P. L. (2007). Linking possible selves and behavior: Do domain-specific hopes and fears translate into daily activities in very old age? *Journal of Gerontology: Psychological Sciences, 62B*(2), P104–P111.

Hoppmann, C. A., & Smith, J. (2007). Life-history related differences in possible selves in very old age. *International Journal of Aging and Human Development, 64*(2), 109–127.

Horhota, M., Mienaltowski, A., & Blanchard-Fields, F. (2012). If only I had taken my usual route...: Age-related differences in counter-factual thinking. *Aging, Neuropsychology, and Cognition, 19,* 339–361.

Irion, J. C., & Blanchard-Fields, F. (1987). A cross-sectional comparison of adaptive coping in adulthood. *Journal of Gerontology, 42*(5), 502–504.

Isaacowitz, D. M., & Blanchard-Fields, F. (2012). Linking process and outcome in the study of emotion and aging. *Perspectives on Psychological Science, 7,* 3–17.

Isaacowitz, D. M., Toner, K., & Neupert, S. D. (2009). Use of gaze for real-time mood regulation: Effects of age and attentional functioning. *Psychology and Aging, 24.* 989–994.

Jopp, D. S., & Schmitt, M. (2010). Dealing with negative life events: Differential effects of personal resources, coping strategies, and control beliefs. *European Journal of Ageing, 7,* 167–180.

Klaczynski, P. A., & Robinson, B. (2000). Personal theories, intellectual ability, and epistemological beliefs: Adult age differences in everyday reasoning biases. *Psychology and Aging, 15,* 400–416.

Kramer, B. J. (1993). Expanding the conceptualization of caregiver coping: The importance of relationship-focused coping strategies. *Family Relations, 42,* 383–391.

Kratz, A. L., Davis, M. C., & Zautra, A. J. (2012). Attachment predicts daily catastrophizing and social coping in women with pain. *Health Psychology, 31,* 278–285.

Labouvie-Vief, G. (1985). Intelligence and cognition. In J. E. Birren & K. W. Schaie (Eds.), *Handbook of the psychology of aging,* 2nd ed. (pp. 500–530). New York: Van Nostrand Reinhold.

Labouvie-Vief, G. (1992). A neo-Piagetian perspective on adult cognitive development. In R. J. Sternberg & C. A. Berg (Eds.), *Intellectual development* (pp.239–252). New York: Cambridge University Press.

Labouvie-Vief, G. (2003). Dynamic integration: Affect, cognition, and the self in adulthood. *Current Directions in Psychological Science, 12,* 201–206.

Labouvie-Vief, G., Hakim-Larson, J., & Hobart, C. J. (1987). Age, ego level, and the life-span development of coping and defense processes. *Psychology and Aging, 2*(3), 286–293.

Lang, F. R. (2001). Regulation of social relationships in later adulthood. *The Journals of Gerontology, 56B,* P321–P326.

Lazarus, R. S. (1966). *Psychological stress and the coping process.* New York: McGraw-Hill.

Lazarus, R. S. (1991). *Emotion and adaptation.* New York: Oxford University Press.

Lazarus, R. S. (1993). Why we should think of stress as a subset of emotion. In L. Goldberger & S. Breznitz (Eds.), *Handbook of stress: Theoretical and clinical aspects* (pp. 21–39). New York: The Free Press.

Lazarus, R. S. (1996). The role of coping and how coping changes over the life course. In C. Magai & S. H. McFadden (Eds.), *Handbook of emotion, adult development, and aging* (pp. 289–306). San Diego, CA: Academic Press.

Lazarus, R. S., & DeLongis, A. (1983). Psychological stress and coping in aging. *American Psychologist, 38*(3), 245–254.

Lazarus, R. S., & Folkman, S. (1984). *Stress, appraisal, and coping.* New York: Springer.

Lupien, S. J., McEwen, B. S., Gunnar, M. R., & Heim, C. (2009). Effects of stress throughout the lifespan on the brain, behaviour and cognition. *Nature Reviews Neuroscience, 10*(6), 434–445.

Marsiske, M., & Margrett, J. A. (2006). Everyday problem solving and decision making. In J. E. Birren & K. W. Schaie (Eds.), *Handbook of the psychology of aging* (pp. 315–342). New York: Academic Press.

Marsiske, M., & Willis, S. L. (1995). Dimensionality of everyday problem solving in older adults. *Psychology and Aging, 10,* 269–283.

Martini, T. S., & Busseri, M. A. (2010). Emotion regulation strategies and goals as predictors of older mothers' and adult daughters' helping-related subjective well-being. *Psychology and Aging, 25,* 48–59.

Mather, M., & Carstensen, L. (2005). Aging and motivated cognition: The positivity effect in attention and memory. *Trends in Cognitive Sciences, 9,* 496–502.

McAdams, D. P., de St. Aubin, E., & Logan, R. L. (1993). Generativity among young, midlife, and older adults. *Psychology & Aging, 8,* 221–230.

McCrae, R. R. (1982). Age differences in the use of coping mechanisms. *Journal of Gerontology, 37*(4), 454–460.

McCrae, R. R. (1989). Age differences and changes in the use of coping mechanisms. *Journal of Gerontology, 44*(6), P161–P169.

McCrae, R. R., & Costa Jr., P. T. (1986). Personality, coping, and coping effectiveness in an adult sample. *Journal of Personality, 54*(2), 385–404.

Moos, R. H., & Billings, A. G. (1982). Conceptualizing and measuring coping resources and coping processes. In L. Goldberger & S. Breznitz (Eds.), *Handbook of stress: Theoretical and clinical aspects* (pp. 212–230). New York: Free Press.

Neisser, U., Boodoo, G., Bouchard, A., Boykin, W., Brody, N., Ceci, S. J., et al. (1996). Intelligence: Knowns and unknowns. *American Psychologist, 51,* 77–101.

Nurmi, J.-E. (1992). Age differences in adult life goals, concerns, and their temporal extension: A life course approach to future-oriented motivation. *International Journal of Behavioral Development, 15,* 487–508.

O'Brien, T. B., & DeLongis, A. (1996). The interactional context of problem-, emotion-, and relationship-focused coping: The role of the Big Five personality factors. *Journal of Personality, 64,* 775–813.

Pearlin, L. I., & Schooler, C. (1978). The structure of coping. *Journal of Health and Social Behavior, 19*(1), 2–21.

Rook, K., Sorkin, D., & Zettel, L. (2004). Stress in social relationships: Coping and adaptation across the life span. In F. R. Lang & K. L. Fingerman (Eds.), *Growing together: Personal relationships across the life span* (pp. 210–239). Cambridge: Cambridge University Press.

Ruth, J.-E., & Coleman, P. (1996). Personality and aging: Coping and management of the self in later life. In J. E. Birren & K.

W. Schaie (Eds.), *Handbook of the psychology of aging* (4th ed., pp. 308–322). New York: Academic Press.

Sheldon, K. M., & Elliot, A. J. (1999). Goal striving, need satisfaction, and longitudinal well-being: The self-concordance model. *Journal of Personality & Social Psychology, 76,* 482–497.

Skinner, E. A., Edge, K., Altman, J., & Sherwood, H. (2003). Searching for the structure of coping: A review and critique of category systems for classifying ways of coping. *Psychological Bulletin, 129,* 216–269.

Smith, J., & Freund, A. (2002). The dynamics of possible selves in old age. *Journal of Gerontology: Psychological Sciences, 57B,* 492–500.

Sorkin, D. H., & Rook, K. S. (2006). Dealing with negative social exchanges in later life: Coping responses, goals and effectiveness. *Psychology and Aging, 21,* 715–725.

Sternberg, R. J. (1985). *Beyond IQ: A triarchic theory of human intelligence.* New York: Cambridge University Press.

Sternberg, R. J., Wagner, R. K., Williams, W. M., & Horvath, J. A. (1995). Testing common sense. *American Psychologist, 50,* 912–927.

Strough, J., Berg, C. A., & Sansone, C. (1996). Goals for solving everyday problems across life spans: Age and gender differences in the salience of interpersonal concerns. *Developmental Psychology, 32,* 1106–1115.

Thornton, W. J. L., & Dumke, H. (2005). Age differences in everyday problem-solving and decision-making effectiveness: A meta-analytic review. *Psychology & Aging, 20,* 85–99.

Watson, T. L., & Blanchard-Fields, F. (1998). Thinking with your head and your heart: Age differences in everyday problem-solving strategy preferences. *Aging, Neuropsychology, & Cognition, 5,* 225–240.

Wood, P. K. (1983). Inquiring systems and problem structure: Implications for cognitive development. *Human Development, 26,* 249–265.

Woolfolk, A. (2011). *Educational psychology* (11th ed.). Boston: Pearson.

Wurm, L. H., Labouvie-Vief, G., Aycock, J., Rebucal, K. A., & Koch, H. E. (2004). Performance in auditory and visual emotional Stroop tasks: A comparison of older and younger adults. *Psychology and Aging, 19,* 523–535.

PART 4

Social Cognition and Goals

My Heart Will Go On: Aging and Autonomic Nervous System Responding in Emotion

Michelle N. Shiota *and* Samantha L. Neufeld

Abstract

Visceral sensations mediated by activation of the autonomic nervous system are thought to play an important role in emotional experience. Autonomic physiology changes in important and complex ways with normal aging, with implications for several aspects of emotional responding. These changes are summarized, and current research on the relationship between emotion psychophysiology and emotional experience is reviewed in light of these structural alterations. Suggested directions for future research on aging and autonomic aspects of emotion are offered that take advantage of new methodological techniques and new knowledge about autonomic aging, as well as recent theoretical developments on emotion, aging, and their intersection.

Key Words: aging, emotion, affect, autonomic nervous system, psychophysiology

Human emotion is a complex, multifaceted phenomenon, commonly involving subjective feelings; facial, postural, and/or vocal expression; implications for cognitive processing; and motivated or goal-oriented behavior. In addition to these components, many theoretical definitions of emotion include peripheral physiological responses mediated by activation of the autonomic nervous system (ANS) (e.g., Damasio, 1999; Ekman, 1992; James, 1884; Levenson, 1999; Plutchik, 1980; Tooby & Cosmides, 2008). Psychology's first theory of emotion went so far as to propose physiological reactivity as a *defining* feature of emotion—that when we say we "feel" an emotion, we are primarily describing the body's instinctive response to some eliciting situation (James, 1884). Although this proposal has been and continues to be controversial, autonomic effects such as a pounding heart, perspiration, and muscle tension are certainly common and highly salient features of strong emotions.

Normal aging is accompanied by considerable change in the neural mechanisms supporting these effects (Kaye & Esler, 2008). Implications for emotional experience are potentially profound. Early research on these changes emphasized the reduction in sympathetic nervous system influence on the heart with increasing age, suggesting a general diminution of emotion-related physical arousal (e.g., Cacioppo, Berntson, Klein, & Poehlmann, 1997; Gross et al., 1997; Lawton, Kleban, Rajagopal, & Dean, 1992; Levenson, 2000). Research in the past decade suggests a more complex picture of autonomic aging, however (e.g., Kaye & Esler, 2008; Masi, Hawkley, Rickett, & Cacioppo, 2007; Monahan, 2007), with corresponding complexity in implications for emotion (e.g., Uchino, Birmingham, & Berg, 2010). Also, the implications of normal aging for emotional physiology and experience may differ across specific, "discrete" emotions (e.g., Kunzmann & Grühn, 2005; Seider, Shiota, Whalen, & Levenson, 2011; Tsai, Levenson, & Carstensen, 2000).

In this chapter, we offer an updated summary of autonomic aging, review recent literature on age-related changes and continuities in emotion psychophysiology, and discuss implications for the relationship between peripheral physiological responding and subjective emotional experience. We also discuss important limitations of and gaps in the presently available research and suggest a number of promising avenues for future work.

Normal Aging of the Autonomic Nervous System: A Complex Picture

The ANS, a branch of the peripheral nervous system, carries instructions from the hypothalamus and brainstem to visceral structures throughout the body. The ANS is subdivided into two major branches, commonly referred to as the "fight-flight" sympathetic branch and the "rest-digest" parasympathetic branch. Together, these two branches regulate the activity of dozens of organs across the cardiovascular, respiratory, digestive, endocrine, and reproductive systems, among others. As a general rule, increased sympathetic activation leads to increased "arousal," with features such as increased heart rate, rapid breathing, peripheral vasoconstriction, perspiration, piloerection, dryness of mouth, and gastric discomfort, whereas increased parasympathetic activation promotes opposing effects, including slowed heart rate and breathing, gastrointestinal mobility, and reproductive activity.

Lay people and research psychologists alike often refer to "arousal" as a unidimensional phenomenon, with the symptoms just listed all hanging together in a single factor. Indeed, the sympathetic branch of the ANS was long thought by physiologists to respond in an "all-or-none" fashion to physical or psychological challenge (e.g., Cannon, 1939). It is now clear, however, that the sympathetic and parasympathetic branches of the ANS each include multiple neural pathways that can be activated independently (e.g., Folkow, 2000; Jänig & Häbler, 2000). At a minimum, researchers often differentiate among sympathetic effects mediated by alpha-adrenergic receptors for norepinephrine/noradrenaline (e.g., increased heart rate), beta-adrenergic receptors for the same neurotransmitter (e.g., vasoconstriction), and cholinergic receptors for acetylcholine (e.g., perspiration and resulting increase in the skin's electrical conductivity), as well as among multiple "twigs" of the parasympathetic system.

Thus, the ANS has the potential to change developmentally and react to stimuli in far more complex ways than previously recognized—"arousal" is inherently multidimensional. This rich differentiation has strong implications for the relationship between physiological responding and emotional

experience (e.g., Kreibig, 2010; Levenson, 1988; Shiota, Neufeld, Yeung, Moser, & Perea, 2011; Stemmler, Aue, & Wacker, 2007)—a point we address in more detail later. Importantly, the various neural mechanisms and organ-level consequences of autonomic responding are also affected quite differently by normal aging.

At a broad level, some sympathetic neurotransmitter activity appears elevated in older adults. Specifically, "clearance," or removal of norepinephrine/noradrenaline from the synapse once it has been released, is reduced as we age, resulting in a potential for greater sympathetically mediated end-organ effects (Kaye & Esler, 2008; Moore, Mangoni, Lyons, & Jackson, 2003) and longer duration of such effects before returning to baseline. However, age-related reduction in norepinephrine clearance has different implications for different organs. Despite the increase in norepinephrine availability, maximum heart rate in response to physical exertion declines steadily throughout adulthood (e.g., Esler et al, 1995; Turner, Mier, Spina, Schechtman, & Ehsani, 1999). This effect is found in athletic as well as sedentary adults (Pugh & Wei, 2001) and is thought to reflect age-related decreases in cardiac beta-adrenergic receptor density and sensitivity, possibly in response to the increased levels of the neurotransmitter itself (e.g., Bertel, Buhler, Kiowski, & Lutold, 1980; Collins, Exton-Smith, James, & Oliver, 1980).

Like heart rate, skin conductance (caused by sweat gland activity, which is mediated by cholinergic rather than beta-adrenergic receptors) also decreases steadily with age, both in terms of baseline levels and in response to physical challenges such as standing and hyperventilation (Barontini, Lázzari, Levin, Armando, & Basso, 1997). As with heart rate, this likely reflects age-related changes in the target organs—in this case, the sweat glands themselves, which are less numerous in the skin of older adults (Catania, Thompson, Michalewski, & Bowman, 1980)—as well as changes in underlying neural processes.

Age-related changes in blood pressure show a quite different pattern. Activity of the sympathetic nerves communicating with muscles in the arterial wall increases linearly with age through the early 70s and shows a steeper slope in women than in men (Narkiewicz et al., 2005). This effect, combined with arterial stiffness due to progressive wear and tear, leads to higher blood pressures both at rest and in response to challenge (e.g., Ferrari, Radaelli, & Centolla, 2003; Palmer, Ziegler, & Lake, 1978; Steptoe, Moses, & Edwards, 1990).

Finally, aging is accompanied by decreased vagal parasympathetic control of the heart (e.g., DeMeersman, 1993; Masi et al., 2007). One important consequence is blunting of the baroreflex response, in which increases in blood pressure are sensed by baroreceptors in the arteries and trigger a compensating reduction in heart rate via vagal pathways (Monahan, 2007). Reduced flexibility in the arterial wall, combined with diminished vagal control of the heart, lead to a negative relationship between age and baroreflex intensity. As a result, older adults typically show reduced homeostatic buffering against transient increases in arterial pressure.

In sum, normal aging is characterized by a complex profile of changes in the ANS. Despite increased norepinephrine availability and reduced vagal influence on the heart (both of which should cause greater cardiac arousal), heart rate reactivity to challenge declines steadily throughout adulthood. Skin conductance reactivity also shows age-related decline. However, resting blood pressure and blood pressure reactivity both increase with age, and deterioration of mechanisms supporting the baroreflex reduce the body's ability to buffer against sudden increases in pressure. These changes may have correspondingly complex implications for physiological aspects of aging adults' emotional responding.

Aging and Intensity of Emotional Autonomic Responding

What are the implications of these structural changes for *emotion* psychophysiology? Subjectively, older adults report that they experience emotion as less physiologically arousing than do younger adults (e.g., Gross et al, 1997; Lawton et al., 1992), despite comparable or even more extreme ratings of the positive-negative valence of emotional experience (e.g., Burriss, Powell, & White, 2007; Labouvie-Vief, Lumley, Jain, & Heinze, 2003). Objective measures of autonomic responding have generally been consistent with these subjective reports. For example, an early study by Levenson and colleagues (1991) found that the magnitude of heart rate and skin conductance increases during relived emotion and directed facial action tasks was smaller in adults aged 71–83 years than had been observed in young adults. Levenson, Carstensen, and Gottman (1994) found that spouses in their 60s showed smaller increases in heart rate during a conversation about an area of marital conflict than did spouses in their 40s. Tsai and colleagues (2000) reported that adults aged 70–85 years showed

baseline-to-trial decreases in an arousal composite (derived from finger pulse amplitude, finger pulse transit time, ear pulse transit time, and finger temperature) while viewing amusing film clips, whereas those aged 20–34 years showed increases in arousal. Looking at a wider range of emotions and a sample with greater age variability (ages 15–88), Labouvie-Vief and colleagues (2003) observed a reduction across adulthood in intensity of cardiac reactivity during relived anger, fear, sadness, and happiness. Similarly, Burriss and colleagues (2007) found that heart rate reactivity to positive and negative emotion-eliciting photographs was significantly stronger in young adults (18–35 years) than in an older cohort (66–95 years).

A 1997 review by Cacioppo and colleagues concluded that normal aging is accompanied by reduction in cardiac reactivity in the context of emotional tasks. A new meta-analysis has reached the same conclusion (Uchino et al., 2010). However, recent studies have detected greater increases in blood pressure during emotional stress tasks among older adults than in their younger counterparts (Uchino et al., 2010). In addition to lab-based, cross-sectional studies, one study using ambulatory measures found that older adults showed greater increases in diastolic blood pressure during daily hassles (Uchino, Berg, Smith, Pearce, & Skinner, 2006), and another observed increases in 30- to 70-year-olds' systolic blood pressure during speech and mental arithmetic tasks in a short-term longitudinal design (intervals 7–16 months; Uchino, Holt-Lunstad, Bloor, & Campo, 2005). A 2010 meta-analysis of 31 studies concluded that normal aging is characterized by diminished emotional heart rate reactivity, but *augmented* increases in blood pressure, at least during stress tasks (Uchino et al., 2010).

The picture of emotion psychophysiology in normal aging is also complicated somewhat by distinguishing among specific emotions. Many studies, such as those using batteries of unpleasant photographs as stimuli, do not explicitly differentiate among fear, anger, disgust, and so forth. These studies, studies explicitly targeting fear or anger, and studies employing social stressors (such as the Trier serial subtraction and speech preparation tasks) have typically found the profile just described in older adults, with lower cardiac and electrodermal reactivity but increased blood pressure responding. However, multiple recent studies report overall physiological responses to sad stimuli that are as strong or stronger in aging adults than they are in young adults. Kunzmann and Grühn (2005) detected no difference between participants aged 20–30 versus 60–70 in cardiac interbeat interval (the inverse of heart rate), finger pulse transit time, or skin conductance reactivity while viewing loss-themed film clips. Participants aged 70–85 years showed, in a study by Tsai and colleagues (2000), greater cardiac arousal during a loss-themed film than did those aged 20–34, although the latter had been more aroused by an amusing film. Recently, Seider and colleagues (2011) found that participants in their 40s and 60s showed greater reactivity than those in their 20s on an 11-measure physiological composite while viewing loss-themed films, but not disgusting films. Not all studies have replicated this effect (see Labouvie-Vief et al., 2003, for a clear exception), so more research is needed to confirm it and investigate likely mechanisms. However, these findings highlight the possibility that physiological aspects of different emotions may be affected differentially by normal aging—a possibility that has rarely been explored.

Emotion Psychophysiology, Emotional Experience, and Regulation

As noted, many emotion theories hold that autonomic reactivity and the subjective experience of emotion are closely intertwined (Damasio, 1999; Ekman, 1992; James, 1884; Levenson, 1999; Plutchik, 1982; Tooby & Cosmides, 2008). If this is the case, then age-related changes in the autonomic system, as well as changes in the way this system responds to emotional stimuli, may have strong implications for how emotion is experienced by aging adults. On one hand, studies that do find age-related reduction in emotional arousal generally *fail* to detect a corresponding reduction in the intensity of subjective feeling (e.g., Labouvie-Vief, 2003; Tsai et al., 2000). Some studies even find greater intensity of reported felt emotion among older than younger adults in response to laboratory stimuli, despite weaker physiological reactivity (e.g., Burriss et al., 2007; Gavazzeni, Wiens, & Fischer, 2008).

On the other hand, programs of research on three issues—the relationship between arousal and the valence of felt affect, the extent to which different "discrete" emotions such as anger and fear are characterized by distinct autonomic patterns, and the relationship between effortful emotion regulation and autonomic reactivity—all address more subtle possible consequences of age-related changes in autonomic physiology. As we shall see, these studies each have important limitations, and we still have a great deal to learn about the effects

of autonomic aging on emotional experience. Next, we address each of these three topics in turn.

Relationship Between Arousal and Affect Valence

In research with young adults, arousal is commonly associated with both strong negative emotion and strong positive emotion. In a typical study of this phenomenon, undergraduate research participants are asked to view a large number of photographic images (often from the International Affective Picture System, or "IAPS" slides; Lang, Bradley, & Cuthbert, 2008) that range from extremely aversive (e.g., a mob dragging a mutilated corpse through the streets) through neutral (e.g., household objects), through highly positive (e.g., desserts), and rate each image on subjective pleasantness and subjective arousal. Studies using this approach consistently find a boomerang-shaped relationship between valence and arousal, such that arousal increases approximately linearly with greater extremes of affect valence (e.g., Bradley, Greenwald, Petry, & Lang, 1992; Greenwald, Cook, & Lang, 1989), although arousal is sometimes stronger on the negative end of the valence scale than the positive end (e.g., Ito, Cacioppo, & Lang, 1998). McManis and colleagues (2001) reported a similar subjective valence-arousal relationship in children aged 7–11 years and adolescents aged 12–14 years, as well as in college-aged adults.

There is a question as to whether this curvilinear relationship holds true for objectively measured physiological reactivity as well as for subjective arousal. Despite finding the curvilinear relationship between subjective ratings of valence and arousal just described, McManis and colleagues (2001) observed that skin conductance response magnitudes were consistently greater for unpleasant images than for neutral or pleasant images—a linear rather than curvilinear relationship. Burriss and colleagues (2007) also observed a clear linear relationship between subjective valence and skin conductance responses, with more aversive images eliciting greater magnitude responses in young (18–35) and middle-aged (36–65) adults. In a meta-analysis of studies comparing physiological responding in several emotions elicited via a range of techniques, Cacioppo and colleagues (2000) concluded that negative emotions are generally characterized by greater autonomic activity than are positive emotions.

However, a growing body of evidence supports the proposal that strong positive emotions can also be quite arousing, at least among young adults. In one early study, researchers found that skin conductance response magnitudes were greater for IAPS slides rated as either pleasant-arousing or unpleasant-arousing than they were for those rated as low-arousal regardless of valence (Bradley et al., 1992). Comparing several positive emotions in a single study, Shiota and colleagues (2011) found that visual images eliciting anticipatory enthusiasm, or the anticipation of reward, led to increased heart rate, increased number of skin conductance responses, increased respiration rate, and increased mean arterial pressure when compared with the effects of neutral images. Attachment and nurturant love were also associated with relative increases in heart rate in this study (Shiota et al., 2011). Other studies have documented clear increases in cardiac, vascular, and/or electrodermal activity with positive emotions such as amusement and joy (Christie & Friedman, 2004; Demaree, Schmeichel, Robinson, & Everhart, 2004; Giuliani, McRae, & Gross, 2008; Mauss, Levenson, McCarter, Wilhelm, & Gross, 2005; Neumann & Waldstein, 2001). In a recent review of the emotion psychophysiology literature, Kreibig (2010) concluded that a number of positive emotions may involve strong physiological reactivity. In sum, research with young adults suggests that physiological reactivity can be associated with intense emotional responding of either positive or negative valence, although it may be somewhat stronger in the latter case.

What happens to this relationship as people age? Although several recent studies have addressed this important question, different studies reach different conclusions. Some studies suggest that the relationship between arousal and subjective valence becomes more linear with increasing age (e.g., Backs, DaSilva, & Han, 2005; Grühn & Scheibe, 2008; Keil & Freund, 2009). In each case, the association of strong negative affect with greater arousal is preserved, but increasing positive affect is linked to *reduced* arousal. Backs and colleagues (2005) compared a sample of college students with a sample of older adults (mean age 66.26 years), examining their ratings of sets of IAPS images selected to be pleasant-arousing, pleasant-calm, unpleasant-arousing, and unpleasant but not arousing. They found that the younger cohort rated all pleasant images as more arousing than did the older cohort. Furthermore, they found that young adults rated pleasant-arousing category images as more pleasant than did older adults, whereas older adults offered more positive ratings than did young adults for images in the pleasant-calm group.

Rather than grouping images into categories, Grühn and Scheibe (2008) used several hundred IAPS slides representing the full spectrum of valence and arousal (each participant viewed a subset of images) and used a regression-based approach to examine valence-arousal relationships in each age group. They observed primarily linear relationships between the two variables, but the slope was significantly steeper in a cohort aged 63–77 years than in a younger cohort aged 18–31 years. Keil and Freund (2009) added a middle-aged cohort (aged 30–59 years, compared with 18–29 and 60–81 years) and observed a gradual trend in which the valence-arousal relationship became less quadratic and increasingly linear with advancing age. Keil and Freund (2009) also replicated the finding using a set of emotion verbs as target stimuli, in addition to a study with IAPS images.

There are good, theory-driven, and physiologically sound reasons to think that high-arousal positive affect may become less common as we age. For one, socioemotional selectivity theory (Carstensen, Isaacowitz, & Charles, 1999) suggests that positive emotion may become less appetitive (focused on acquiring new rewards) and more appreciative (enjoying rewards we already have) as we age, promoting a growing preference for low-arousal positive experiences and the corresponding emotions.

It is also possible that arousal itself becomes more aversive as we age. As noted earlier, structural changes in the ANS lead to reduced cardiac reactivity to emotional stimuli while increasing blood pressure reactivity and blunt the body's ability to homeostatically correct for sudden, transient increases in blood pressure. Taken as a whole, this may increase the probability that sympathetically mediated arousal will tend to cause a combination of increased heart rate and increased blood pressure. This profile has been associated with a subjective sense of psychological threat, as distinct from increased heart rate in the absence of high blood pressure—a profile associated with more positive, empowered psychological "challenge" (Tomaka, Blascovich, Kibler, & Ernst, 1997). If distinct physiological responses are the basis of subjective emotional feelings, as suggested by William James (1884), these age-related changes in autonomic physiology may induce a profile of arousal that feels more like threat. To our knowledge, attempts to generate subjective feelings of threat versus challenge by experimentally manipulating physiological profiles (e.g., by having research participants exercise or engage in a warm vs. cold pressor task in conjunction with a stressful mental arithmetic task) have failed to detect statistically significant effects (e.g., Tomaka et al., 1997). However, sample sizes in these studies were small (approximately n - 20 per condition), and the effect size associated with the warm- vs. cold-pressor manipulation was nontrivial, $F(1, 42) = 2.58$, $p >. 12$. Thus, the possibility remains that structural bias toward a "threat" profile of cardiovascular arousal might also bias older adults toward experiencing any arousal as threat.

However, these studies of aging and the relationship between valence and arousal have important limitations as well as strengths. Foremost, all three relied on self-reports of arousal rather than actually measuring physiological reactivity to emotional stimuli. Prior research has often documented strong correlations between subjective arousal and objective skin conductance response magnitudes across large stimulus sets (e.g., Bradley et al., 1992; Burriss et al., 2007). However, other studies suggest that these effects are inconsistent, may not generalize to physiological measures beyond skin conductance, and vary from individual to individual (e.g., Hubert & de Jong-Meyer, 1990; Sze, Gyurak, Yuan, & Levenson, 2010).

Also, these studies rely heavily, and in most cases exclusively, on the IAPS set to provide emotional stimuli. Although the IAPS images are diverse, intense, and richly validated, the content of the pleasurable images may not map well to the full domain of positive emotion stimuli. Pleasant photos in this set consist mostly of erotic images, extreme sports, desserts, and peaceful nature scenes. It's possible that aging adults find sky diving and impersonal nudity somewhat less appealing than do young adults, yet still experience high-arousal positive emotion in response to kinds of stimuli that are not included in this particular stimulus set.

Some studies do offer hints that this may be the case. Burriss and colleagues (2007), using a different subset of IAPS images, observed the same quadratic relationship between subjective valence and self-reported arousal in their young, middle-aged, and older cohorts. This study also relied on subjective rather than objective measures of arousal. However, we recently turned to archival data from a study of aging and emotion regulation, which did include a composite measure of autonomic reactivity, to ask whether we could find evidence of high-arousal positive affect in older adults (Neufeld, Shiota, & Levenson, 2007). In this study 222 adults in their 20s, 40s, or 60s watched brief film clips, one showing a character responding to the death of a loved one and the other showing a character eating animal viscera (either cow intestine or horse rectum; see Shiota & Levenson, 2009, for additional details regarding the sample, procedures, and measures). Although these clips were geared toward evoking sadness and disgust, respectively, they were also affectively complex, eliciting positive as well as negative emotional feelings (Shiota & Levenson, 2012). Specifically, the sad clips elicited strong reports of compassion and interest, whereas the disgusting clips elicited strong reports of amusement and considerable laughter.

During each film clip (and a 60-second baseline preceding each clip) eight measures of autonomically mediated physiological reactivity were assessed: cardiac interbeat interval, skin conductance level, finger pulse amplitude, finger pulse transit time, finger temperature, ear pulse transit time, respiration depth, and mean arterial pressure. Epoch-level averages were calculated for the baseline and trial periods for each of these variables, z-scored, reversed when appropriate (based on preliminary principal components analyses), and averaged to create an overall physiological reactivity index. After each film clip, in addition to rating other aspects of their subjective experience, participants also rated the valence of their affect while watching the clip, on a scale in which 0 = very negative, 4 = neutral, and 8 = very positive.

Within each age cohort, and for each film type (sad vs. disgusting), we calculated the linear product-moment correlation between subjective affect valence and the physiological reactivity index. We then computed the quadratic relationship between subjective valence and physiological reactivity by centering and squaring participants' valence scores and entering this quadratic term as the second block in a stepwise regression (with the nontransformed valence scores as the first step) predicting the physiological reactivity index. This approach tests the significance of the curvilinear relationship after controlling for the linear relationship. Scatterplots depicting the results are presented in Figures 15.1 and 15.2.

Data from the sad film clips were consistent with the pattern observed in previous studies using IAPS slides and self-report measures of arousal, as discussed earlier. The linear correlation between valence and physiological reactivity was positive but not significant in the 20s cohort, $r =. 12$, $p =. 31$, as well as in the 40s cohort, $r =. 10$, $p =. 41$. Among the 60s cohort, a significant negative relationship was observed, $r = -.30$, $p =. 01$. A Fisher's z test for

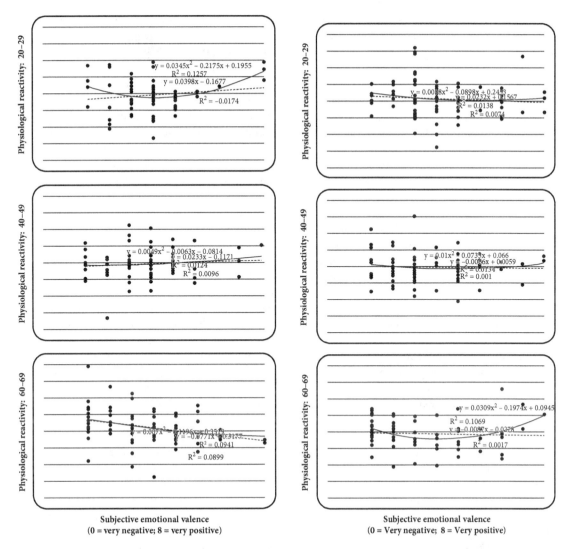

Figure 15.1. Scatterplots of subjective emotional valence and objective physiological reactivity for participants aged 20–29, 40–49, and 60–69 while viewing sad films. Dashed lines indicate linear line of best fit, unbroken lines quadratic line of best fit.

Figure 15.2. Scatterplots of subjective emotional valence and objective physiological arousal for participants aged 20–29, 40–49, and 60–69 while viewing disgusting films. Dashed lines indicate linear line of best fit, unbroken lines quadratic line of best fit.

each pair of cohorts revealed that these correlations did not significantly differ between the 20s and 40s ($z = 0.12$, $p = 0.90$); however, the 60s cohort differed significantly from both the 20s cohort ($z = -.26$, $p = 0.01$) and the 40s cohort ($z = -2.42$, $p = 0.02$). Thus, the relationship between emotion valence and physiological arousal was well characterized by a linear slope for older adults, and this trend significantly distinguished the older cohort from the younger and middle-aged cohorts. For the 20s cohort, the quadratic valence term explained a significant amount of variance in physiological reactivity over and above the linear term, $\Delta R^2 = .128$, $p = .002$. Specifically, young adults who reported extremes of either positive or negative subjective

valence showed greater physiological reactivity than did those who reported more neutral valence. This was not the case for either the 40s cohort, $\Delta R^2 = .003$, *n.s.*, or the 60s cohort, $\Delta R^2 = .004$, *n.s.*

The picture looked quite different, however, with the disgusting film clips. Within each cohort, the linear correlation between valence and physiological reactivity was negative but nonsignificant: for 20s, $r = -.08$, *n.s.*; for 40s, $r = -.03$, *n.s.*; for 60s, $r = -.04$, *n.s.* For our 20s cohort, the effect of the quadratic valence term was not significant, $\Delta R^2 = .006$, *n.s.*; nor was it significant for our 40s cohort, $\Delta R^2 = .012$, *n.s.* Yet the quadratic valence term did significantly predict physiological reactivity, after controlling for the linear valence term, among participants in their 60s, ΔR^2 =. 104, p =. 006. Thus, older adults who reported extremes of *either* positive or negative subjective valence showed greater physiological reactivity than did those who reported more neutral valence.

These results point to the possibility that older adults can experience high-arousal, subjectively positive emotion, given the right stimulus—in this case, a funny one. Of course, this approach has its own important limitations with respect to age differences in the relationship between valence and arousal. Our stimuli were two film clips. Each of these clips primarily targeted a specific negative emotion, although positive-valence feelings were both plausible and observed in the sample. More importantly, the small number of stimuli necessitated a between-subjects approach to examining the valence-arousal relationship. However, relationships between different aspects of emotional responding (such as subjective feeling and arousal) are best studied by way of intraindividual correlations across a larger number of stimuli (Mauss et al., 2005). The ideal study of adult development in the relationship between subjective valence and physiological reactivity is yet to be conducted. Such a study would use objective measures of physiological responding, as we did, but with a large number of complex stimuli covering a comprehensive range of emotion elicitors and the sophisticated, within-subjects analyses used by previous researchers, thereby marrying the best elements of these separate lines of research.

Autonomic Differentiation Among "Discrete" Emotions

Much of the research just discussed presumes that subjective valence and physiological arousal are the key defining features of affective state, consistent with theoretical perspectives such as the *circumplex model* of core affect (e.g., Russell, 1980, 2003). Beyond defining affective experience in terms of valence, arousal, and their interrelationship lies the possibility, first proposed by William James (1884), that different "shades of emotion" might correspond to qualitatively distinct profiles of physiological responding. This proposal, known as the *autonomic specificity hypothesis* and linked closely to discrete emotions theoretical perspectives, has been investigated extensively in young adults. Although the findings of individual studies are not always consistent, and the autonomic implications of a given type of emotion may be moderated by the method used to elicit that emotion in the lab, certain points of difference among sadness, fear, anger, and disgust have

been supported by major reviews and meta-analyses of the available research (e.g., Cacioppo et al., 2000; Friedman, 2010; Kreibig, 2010; Levenson, 1992; Rozin, Haidt, & McCauley, 2000.

Few studies have explicitly addressed the question of possible age differences in the extent of autonomic specificity across emotions. In one study of adults aged 71–83 years, Levenson and colleagues (1991) compared physiological profiles associated with anger, fear, sadness, disgust, happiness, and surprise as elicited by relived personal experiences and directed, muscle-by-muscle facial expression posing. Although the magnitude of physiological responses was small in these participants (compared with young adults in a previous study using the same methods), certain key distinctions among emotions nonetheless were observed. Specifically, heart rate increases were greater for anger, fear, and sadness than for disgust, and drop in finger temperature (indicating peripheral vasoconstriction) was larger in fear than in anger.

Other studies including both young and older adult cohorts have typically compared physiological responses in anger versus fear, the negative emotions most clearly differentiated in prior research with young adults (see Cacioppo et al., 1997, for a review). Older adults' heart rate, respiration rate, and skin conductance best differentiated anger and fear, whereas diastolic blood pressure, facial temperature, finger temperature, and stroke volume most effectively differentiated these emotions among young adults. Thus, older and younger adults each showed evidence of autonomic specificity, but in somewhat different peripheral measures. Although this possibility was clearly raised by the review, it has not to our knowledge been followed up by studies explicitly targeting it as a hypothesis.

Physiological Aspects of Emotion Regulation

In the past decade and change, a strong literature has developed regarding the implications of normal aging for emotion regulation processes (Urry & Gross, 2010). Older adults report having greater control over their emotions (e.g., Gross et al., 1997; Lawton et al., 1992) and show signs of being better at emotion regulation overall, as well as more skilled at selecting specific regulation strategies to fit a given stressor (Blanchard-Fields, 2007; Scheibe & Carstensen, 2010). With respect to specific strategies, aging adults are increasingly likely to rely on situation selection, avoiding unpleasant social situations in particular (e.g., Birditt

& Fingerman, 2005; Blanchard-Fields, 2007; Coats & Blanchard-Fields, 2008; Hess & Pullen, 1994), and as likely as young adults to use problem-solving coping approaches to practical problems (e.g., Blanchard-Fields, 2007; Blanchard-Fields, Chen, & Norris, 1997). Attentional and memory biases appear to move away from negative and toward positive stimuli as we age, leading to an emotional positivity bias (e.g., Isaacowitz, Wadlinger, Goren, & Wilson, 2006; Mather & Carstensen, 2003, 2005). Although older adults may not be fully aware of this bias, it is reduced when they are distracted, suggesting that it is implemented in a regulatory manner requiring cognitive control (e.g., Knight et al., 2007).

Most of this research has relied on self-report measures of emotion regulation, but a growing number of studies examine the implications of aging for emotional experience, expression, and physiology in response to emotion regulation instruction in the lab (e.g., Kunzmann, Kupperbusch, & Levenson, 2005; Shiota & Levenson, 2009). On the whole, these studies suggest considerable continuity in emotion regulation ability and in implications for physiological responding in emotion. Kunzmann and colleagues (2005) instructed adults aged 18–28 and 60–85 to watch brief films of surgical procedures without trying to change their expression, while attempting to suppress any emotional expressions, and while trying to amplify such expressions on three different trials; physiological effects of the suppression and amplification instructions were not moderated by age. Similarly, Shiota and Levenson (2009) found that participants in their 20s, 40s, and 60s all showed similar subjective, expressive, and physiological responses to instruction to suppress expression. Shiota and Levenson (2009) did find that the physiological benefit (in terms of reduced baseline-to-trial physiological reactivity during the film clip) derived from detached reappraisal instruction diminished with age, whereas the benefit from instructed positive reappraisal increased with age. However, this effect was paralleled by comparable effects in self-reported emotional experience, consistent with adult development in the ability to implement these particular regulation strategies rather than distinctive age effects on emotion physiology per se.

Physiological measures of emotion regulation success are and will continue to be a useful tool for assessing age differences in implementing various emotion regulation strategies. Beyond this application, age-related changes in the ANS may have implications for emotion regulation that have not

yet, to our knowledge, been explored. We noted earlier that vagal influence on the heart is diminished with increasing age. Several studies have linked vagal parasympathetic activity (and its marker, cardiac respiratory sinus arrhythmia) to self-regulatory effort and/or ability in emotional as well as non-emotional contexts (e.g., Butler, Wilhelm, & Gross, 2006; Pu, Schmeichel, & Demaree, 2010; Di Simplicio et al., 2012). Although the psychological meaning of vagal activation is controversial, and causal direction (if any) in the vagal influence–self-regulation relationship is not at all clear, theorists have proposed that vagal influence on the heart is one important mechanism by which mammals down-regulate stress responses (e.g., Porges, 2011). If this is correct, aging adults may actually face a physiology-based challenge in managing distress in the face of stressors that cannot be avoided or fixed. This would be consistent with the profile of emotion regulation strategies that aging adults appear to use selectively, which lean toward averting stressors. Future research is needed to explore this possibility and, if it is supported, to seek out "workarounds" that allow aging adults to remain engaged with potentially stressful situations (when needed) while still managing emotions effectively.

Implications, Limitations, and Future Directions: A "To-Do" List

The ANS, which plays an important role in emotional responding, changes structurally in a number of ways with normal aging. Although early research suggested that autonomic reactivity simply diminished across the board with age, studies from the last decade indicate a more complex profile, with some pathways becoming less reactive and others more so. These changes may have correspondingly complex implications for subjective emotional experience, not just reducing intensity (and, in fact, evidence contradicts this proposal) but rather altering profiles of felt emotion and the ways in which we manage our emotions.

The literature on aging and autonomic aspects of emotion is growing in important ways, but still has significant limitations and gaps. As a result, there is great need for new research addressing these topics. First and foremost, studies of "arousal" and emotion rely far too often on subjective feelings of arousal in the absence of objective measures of autonomic reactivity. Those that do include objective physiological measures tend to focus on skin conductance, which reflects only one mechanism of sympathetic nervous system influence. Given the diversity of age effects on alpha-adrenergic, beta-adrenergic, cholinergic sympathetic, and vagal parasympathetic mechanisms discussed earlier (not to mention other mechanisms not addressed in this review), there is need for studies using markers of all of these mechanisms to index "arousal." We may find that the subjective experience of arousal is actually linked to different underlying physiological processes as we age. At a minimum, the mechanisms' differential relationship to aging itself suggests a need to measure them directly and independently whenever possible. New, efficient techniques for teasing apart neural mechanisms of autonomic influence are now readily available (e.g., impedance cardiography, spectral analysis-based approaches to measuring vagal influence on the heart) and feasible for a greater number of researchers.

Research is also needed that considers differences among possible discrete emotions with respect to aging. The "discrete versus dimensional" debate in emotion science continues to be heated and shows no signs of going away (e.g., Barrett, 2006; Panksepp & Watt, 2011). However, the evidence supporting at least some degree of emotion-specific autonomic patterning (e.g., Cacioppo et al., 2000; Kreibig, 2010; Levenson, 1992; Shiota et al., 2011; Stephens, Christie, & Friedman, 2010), as well as evidence that there may be something special about sadness for aging adults, suggest it would be wise to ask explicitly whether different emotions "age" in different ways, rather than assuming that valence and overall arousal capture any important variability. Choice of emotion constructs should be theory-driven and should aim to cover a reasonable span of emotional experience, rather than focusing on one or two constructs (and associated elicitors) and assuming that the resulting findings can be generalized to other states. Restriction of the scope of emotion in this research is especially notable in the area of positive emotion. Although the IAPS set is a tremendous resource for emotion scientists, most images targeting positive emotion states fall into a few, fairly narrow categories (e.g., desserts, erotic images, extreme sports, peaceful nature scenes). If this content does not reflect the key elicitors of positive emotion for aging adults, we may miss important processes in the adult development of positive emotion.

More studies examining autonomic aspects of emotion across the adult lifespan are also needed. Many studies discussed earlier include a young adult sample and an aging sample, but omit a midlife cohort (e.g., Kunzmann & Grühn, 2005;

Kunzmann et al., 2005; Tsai et al., 2000). Others do have greater variability and treat age as a continuous variable, but use statistical analyses that only allow for linear relationships with other variables (e.g., Uchino et al., 2005). Other aspects of emotional responding, such as the subjective experience of positive and negative emotions and emotional complexity (the co-occurrence of positive and negative emotions) have been found to show nonlinear trajectories across adulthood (e.g., Carstensen, Pasupathi, Mayr, & Nesselroade, 2000; Mroczek, 2001), suggesting that we should be open to quadratic relationships in other aspects of emotional responding as well. Studies explicitly examining possible culture × age interactions in emotion physiology are also needed (e.g., Tsai et al., 2000), even if the result is to confirm that age effects on autonomic aspects of emotion generalize across cultures and ethnicities.

One subtle limitation of some work in this area is a tendency to confound physiological arousal, emotional reactivity, and emotion regulation. For example, if older adults show milder cardiac responses to a stress task, is that because their hearts are not as responsive to sympathetic nervous system input as they used to be, because they do not find the task as psychologically stressful as young adults, or because they manage that stress more effectively? Some analyses have sought to tease these issues apart. For example, studies often find that some aspect of emotion physiology changes with age, but the subjective experience of emotion does not (e.g., Tsai et al., 2000). Other studies have demonstrated that age differences in physiological reactivity hold up even after controlling for age differences in subjective experience (e.g., Levenson et al., 1994; Uchino et al., 2005). This is an area in which research is already improving, and we expect it will continue to do so.

Finally, research is needed that addresses the implications of age-related changes in emotion psychophysiology for other emotional processes. For example, autonomic aspects of emotion are thought to mediate the emotional facilitation of memory (e.g., Bradley et al., 1992; Cahill, Prins, Weber, & McGaugh, 1994), as well as play a role in aspects of judgment and decision making (e.g., Damasio, 1999). If emotion physiology is itself changing with age, these emotion-cognition relationships may be changing as well.

The existing literature offers a strong foundation for understanding the implications of normal aging for autonomic aspects of emotion. However, the past decade has brought new methodological techniques; rich theoretical developments in emotion, aging, and their intersections; and new information about the physiological aging of the ANS. Together, these advances set the stage for a new push forward in understanding the complex interplay of aging, biology, and emotion.

References

Backs, R. W., Da Silva, S. P., & Han, K. (2005). A comparison of younger and older adults' Self-Assessment Manikin ratings of affective pictures. *Experimental Aging Research, 31*, 421–440.

Barontini, M., Lázzari, J. O., Levin, G., Armando, I., & Basso, S. J. (1997). Age-related changes in sympathetic activity: Biochemical measurements and target organ responses. *Archives of Gerontology and Geriatrics, 25*, 175–186.

Barrett, L. F. (2006). Are emotions natural kinds? *Perspectives on Psychological Science, 1*(1), 28–58.

Bertel, O., Buhler, F. R., Kiowski, W., & Lutold, B. E. (1980). Decreased beta adrenoreceptor responsiveness as related to age, blood pressure, and plasma catecholamines in patients with essential hypertension. *Hypertension, 2*, 130–138.

Birditt, K. S., & Fingerman, K. L. (2005). Do we get better at picking our battles?: Age group differences in descriptions of behavioral reactions to interpersonal tensions. *Journals of Gerontology Series B: Psychological Sciences and Social Sciences. 60*, 121–128.

Blanchard-Fields, F. (2007). Everyday problem solving and emotion: An adult developmental perspective. *Current Directions in Psychological Science, 16*(1), 26–31.

Blanchard-Fields, F., Chen, Y., & Norris, L. (1997). Everyday problem solving across the adult lifespan: Influence of domain specificity and cognitive appraisal. *Psychology and Aging, 12*, 684–693.

Bradley, M. M., Greenwald, M. K., Petry, M. C., & Lang, P. J. (1992). Remembering pictures: Pleasure and arousal in memory. *Journal of Experimental Psychology: Learning, Memory, and Cognition, 18*(2), 379–390.

Burriss, L., Powell, D. A., & White, J. (2007). Psychophysiological and subjective indices of emotion as a function of age and gender. *Cognition and Emotion, 21*(1), 182–210.

Butler, E. A., Wilhelm, F. H., & Gross, J. J. (2006). Respiratory sinus arrhythmia, emotion, and emotion regulation during social interaction. *Psychophysiology, 43*(6), 612–622.

Cacioppo, J. T., Berntson, G. G., Klein, D. J., & Poehlmann, K. M. (1997). The psychophysiology of emotion across the lifespan. *Annual Review of Gerontology and Geriatrics, 17*, 27–74.

Cacioppo, J. T., Berntson, G. G., Larsen, J. T., Poehlmann, K. M., & Ito, T. A. (2000). The psychophysiology of emotion. In R. Lewis & J. M. Haviland-Jones (Eds.), *The handbook of emotion* (2nd edition, pp. 173–191). New York: Guilford Press.

Cahill, L., Prins, B., Weber, M., & McGaugh, J. L. (1994). β-Adrenergic activation and memory for emotional events. *Nature, 371*, 702–704.

Cannon, W. B. (1939). *The wisdom of the body* (2nd edition). Oxford, England: Norton & Co.

Carstensen, L. L., Isaacowitz, D. M., & Charles, S. T. (1999). Taking time seriously: A theory of socioemotional selectivity theory. *American Psychologist, 54*, 165–181.

Carstensen, L. L., Pasupathi, M., Mayr, U., & Nesselroade, J. R. (2000). Emotional experience in everyday life across the adult life span. *Journal of Personality and Social Psychology, 79*(4), 644–655.

Catania, J. J., Thompson, L. W., Michalewski, H. A., & Bowman, T. E. (1980). Comparisons of sweat gland counts, electrodermal activity, and habituation behavior in young and old groups of subjects. *Psychophysiology, 17*(2), 146–152.

Christie, I. C., & Friedman, B. H. (2004). Autonomic specificity of discrete emotion and dimensions of affective space: A multivariate approach. *International Journal of Psychophysiology, 51*, 143–153.

Coats, A. H., & Blanchard-Fields, F. (2008). Emotion regulation in interpersonal problems: The role of cognitive-emotional complexity, emotion regulation goals, and expressivity. *Psychology and Aging, 23*(1), 39–51.

Collins, K. J., Exton-Smith, A. N., James, M. H., & Oliver, D. J. (1980). Functional changes in autonomic nervous responses with ageing. *Age and Ageing, 9*(1), 17–24.

Damasio, A. (1999). *The feeling of what happens: Body and emotion in the making of consciousness.* Fort Worth, TX: Harcourt College.

Demaree, H. A., Schmeichel, B. J., Robinson, J. L., & Everhart, D. E. (2004). Behavioral, affective, and physiological effects of negative and positive emotional exaggeration. *Cognition and Emotion, 18*(8), 1079–1097.

DeMeersman, R. (1993). Aging as a modulator of respiratory sinus arrhythmia. *Journal of Gerontology: Biological Sciences, 48*, B74–B78.

Di Simplicio, M., Costoloni, G., Western, D., Hanson, B., Taggart, P., & Harmer, C. J. (2012). Decreased heart rate variability during emotion regulation in subjects at risk for psychopathology. *Psychological Medicine, 42*(8), 1775–1783.

Ekman, P. (1992). An argument for basic emotions. *Cognition and Emotion, 6*, 169–200.

Esler, M. D., Thompson, J. M., Kaye, M. D., Turner, A. G., Jennings, G. L., Cox, H. S., Lambert, G. W., & Seals, D. R. (1995). Effects of aging on the responsiveness of the human cardiac sympathetic nerves to stressors. *Circulation, 91*, 351–358.

Ferrari, A. U., Radaelli, A., & Centola, M. (2003). Aging and the cardio- vascular system. *Journal of Applied Physiology, 95*, 2591–2597.

Folkow, B. (2000). Perspectives on the integrative functions of the "sympatho-adrenomedullary system." *Autonomic Neuroscience: Basic and Clinical, 83*, 101–115.

Friedman, B. H. (2010). Feelings and the body: The Jamesian perspective on autonomic specificity of emotion. *Biological Psychology, 84*(3), 383–393.

Gavazzeni, J., Wiens, S., & Fischer, H. (2008). Age effects to negative arousal differ for self-report and electrodermal activity. *Psychophysiology, 45*(1), 148–151.

Giuliani, N., McRae, K., & Gross, J. J. (2008). The up- and down- regulation of amusement: Experiential, behavioral, and autonomic consequences. *Emotion, 8*, 714–719.

Greenwald, M. L., Cook, E. W., & Lang, P. J. (1989). Affective judgment and psychophysiological response: Dimensional covariation in the evaluation of pictorial stimuli. *Journal of Psychophysiology, 3*(1), 51–64.

Gross, J. J., Carstensen, L. L., Pasupathi, M., Tsai, J., Skorpen, C. G., & Hsu, A. Y. C. (1997). Emotion and aging: Experience, expression, and control. *Psychology and Aging, 12*(4), 590–599.

Grühn, D., & Scheibe, S. (2008). Age-related differences in valence and arousal ratings of pictures from the International

Affective Picture System (IAPS): Do ratings become more extreme with age? *Behavior Research Methods, 40,* 512–521.

Hess, T. M., & Pullen, S. M. (1994). Adult age difference in informational biases during impression formation. *Psychology and Aging, 9,* 237–250.

Hubert, W., & de Jong-Meyer, R. (1990). Psychophysiological response patterns to positive and negative film stimuli. *Biological Psychology, 31,* 73–93.

Isaacowitz, D. M., Wadlinger, H. A., Goren, D., & Wilson, H. R. (2006). Is there an age-related positivity effect in visual attention? A comparison of two methodologies. *Emotion 6*(3), 511–516.

Ito, T. A., Cacioppo, J. T., & Lang, P. J. (1998). Eliciting affect using the IAPS: trajectories through evaluative space. *Personality and Social Psychology Bulletin, 24*(8), 855–879.

James, W. (1884). What is an emotion? *Mind, 9,* 188–205.

Jänig, W., & Häbler, H.-J. (2000). Specificity in the organization of the nervous system: A basis for precise neuroregulation of homeostatic and protective body functions. *Progress in Brain Research, 122,* 351–367.

Kaye, D. M., & Esler, M. D. (2008). Autonomic control of the aging heart. *Neuromolecular Medicine, 10,* 179–186.

Keil, A., & Freund, A. M. (2009). Changes in the sensitivity to appetitive and aversive arousal across adulthood. *Psychology and Aging, 24,* 668–680.

Knight, M., Seymour, T. L., Gaunt, J. T., Baker, C., Nesmith, K., & Mather, M. (2007). Aging and goal-directed emotional attention: Distraction reverses emotional biases. *Emotion, 7,* 705–714.

Kreibig, S. D. (2010). Autonomic nervous system activity in emotion: A review. *Biological Psychology, 84,* 394–421.

Kunzmann, U., & Grühn, D. (2005). Age differences in emotional reactivity: The simple case of sadness. *Psychology and Aging, 20*(1), 47–59.

Kunzmann, U., Kupperbusch, C. S., & Levenson, R. W. (2005). Behavioral inhibition and amplification during emotional arousal: A comparison of two age groups. *Psychology and Aging, 20*(1), 144–158.

Labouvie-Vief, G., Lumley, M. A., Jain, E., & Heinze, H. (2003). Age and gender differences in cardiac reactivity and subjective emotion responses to emotional autobiographical memories. *Emotion, 3*(2), 115–126.

Lang, P. J., Bradley, M. M., & Cuthbert, B. N. (2008). *International affective picture system (IAPS):* Affective ratings of pictures and instruction manual. Technical Report A-8. University of Florida, Gainesville, FL.

Lawton, M. P., Kleban, M. H., Rajagopal, D., & Dean, J. (1992). The dimensions of affective experience in three age groups. *Psychology and Aging, 7,* 171–184.

Levenson, R. W. (1988). Emotion and the autonomic nervous system: A prospectus for research on autonomic specificity. In H. L. Wagner (Ed.), *Social psychophysiology and emotion: Theory and clinical applications* (pp. 17–42). Oxford: Wiley & Sons.

Levenson, R. W. (1992). Autonomic nervous system differences among emotions. *Psychological Science, 3,* 23–27.

Levenson, R. W. (1999). The intrapersonal functions of emotion. *Cognition & Emotion, 13,* 481–504.

Levenson, R. W. (2000). Expressive, physiological, and subjective changes in emotion across adulthood. In S. H. Qualls & N. Abeles (Eds.), *Psychology and the aging revolution: How we adapt to longer life* (pp. 123–140). Washington DC: American Psychological Association.

Levenson, R. W., Carstensen, L. L., Friesen, W. V., & Ekman, P. (1991). Emotion, physiology, and expression in old age. *Psychology and Aging, 6*(1), 28–35.

Levenson, R. W., Carstensen, L. L., & Gottman, J. M. (1994). The influence of age and gender on affect, physiology, and their interrelations: A study of long-term marriages. *Journal of Personality and Social Psychology, 67,* 56–68.

Masi, C. M., Hawkley, L. C., Rickett, E. M., & Cacioppo, J. T. (2007). Respiratory sinus arrhythmia and disease of aging: Obesity, diabetes mellitus and hypertension. *Biological Psychology, 74,* 212–223.

Mather, M., & Carstensen, L. L. (2003). Aging and attentional biases for emotional faces. *Psychological Science, 14,* 409–415.

Mather, M., & Carstensen, L. L. (2005). Aging and motivated cognition: The positivity effect in attention and memory. *Trends in Cognitive Sciences, 9,* 496–502.

Mauss, I. B., Levenson, R. W., McCarter, L., Wilhelm, F. H., & Gross, J. J. (2005). The tie that binds? Coherence among emotion experience, behavior, and physiology. *Emotion, 5*(2), 175–190.

McManis, M. H., Bradley, M. M., Berg, W. K., Cuthbert, B. N., & Lang, P. J. (2001). Emotional reactions in children: Verbal, physiological, and behavioral responses to affective pictures. *Psychophysiology, 38,* 222–231.

Monahan, K. (2007). Effect of aging on baroreflex function in humans. *American Journal of Physiology, 293,* R3–R12.

Moore, A., Mangioni, A. A., Lyons, D., & Jackson, S. H. D. (2003). The cardiovascular system in the ageing patient. *British Journal of Clinical Pharmacology, 56,* 254–260.

Mroczek, D. K. (2001). Age and emotion in adulthood. *Current Directions in Psychological Science, 10*(3), 87–90.

Narkiewicz, K., Phillips B. G., Kato, M., Hering, D., Bieniaszewski, L., & Somers, V. K. (2005). Gender-selecting interaction between aging, blood pressure, and sympathetic nerve activity. *Hypertension, 45,* 522–525.

Neufeld, S. L., Shiota, M. N., & Levenson, R. W. (2007, October). *Age differences in the relationship between emotional valence and cardiovascular reactivity.* Poster presented at the annual meeting of the Society for Psychophysiological Research, Savannah, GA.

Neumann, S. A., & Waldstein, S. R. (2001). Similar patterns of cardiovascular response during emotional activation as a function of affective valence and arousal and gender. *Journal of Psychosomatic Research, 50,* 245–253.

Palmer, g. J., Ziegler, M. G., & Lake, C. R. (1978). Response of norepinephrine and blood pressure to stress increases with age. *Journal of Gerontology, 33,* 482–487.

Panksepp, J., & Watt, D. (2011). What is basic about basic emotions? Lasting lessons from affective neuroscience. *Emotion Review, 3*(4), 387–396.

Plutchik, R. (1980). *Emotion: A psychoevolutionary synthesis.* New York: Harper & Row.

Porges, S. W. (2011). *The polyvagal theory: Neurophysiological foundations of emotions, attachment, communication, and self-regulation.* New York: Norton.

Pu, J., Schmeichel, B. J., & Demaree, H. A. (2010). Cardiac vagal control predicts spontaneous regulation of negative emotional expression and subsequent cognitive performance. *Biological Psychology, 84*(3), 531–540.

Pugh, K. g., & Wei, J. Y. (2001). Clinical implications of physiological changes in the aging heart. *Drugs & Aging, 18,* 263–276.

Rozin, P., Haidt, J., & McCauley, C. R. (2000). Disgust. In M. Lewis & J. M. Haviland (Eds.), *Handbook of emotions* (2nd edition, pp. 637–653). New York: Guilford Press.

Russell, J. A. (1980). A circumplex model of affect. *Journal of Personality and Social Psychology*, *39*(6), 1161–1178.

Russell, J. A. (2003). Core affect and the psychological construction of emotion. *Psychological Review*, *110*, 145–172.

Scheibe, S., & Carstensen, L. L. (2010). Emotional aging: Recent findings and future trends. *Journals of Gerontology: Series B: Psychological Sciences and Social Sciences*, *65B*, 135–144.

Seider, B. H., Shiota, M. N., Whalen, P., & Levenson, R. W. (2011). Greater sadness reactivity in late life. *Social, Cognitive, and Affective Neuroscience*, *6*(2), 186–194.

Shiota, M. N., & Levenson, R. W. (2009). Effects of aging on experimentally instructed detached reappraisal, positive reappraisal, and emotional behavioral suppression. *Psychology and Aging*, *24*(4), 890–900.

Shiota, M. N., & Levenson, R. W. (2012). Turn down the volume, or change the channel?: Emotional effects of detached versus positive reappraisal. *Journal of Personality and Social Psychology*, *103*(3), 416–429.

Shiota, M. N., Neufeld, S. L., Yeung, W. H., Moser, S. E., & Perea, E. F. (2011). Feeling good: Autonomic nervous system responding in five positive emotions. *Emotion*, *11*(6), 1368–1378.

Stemmler, G., Aue, T., & Wacker, J. (2007). Anger and fear: Separable effects of emotion and motivational direction on somatovisceral responses. *International Journal of Psychophysiology*, *66*(2), 141–153.

Stephens, C. L., Christie, I. C., & Friedman, B. H. (2010). Autonomic specificity of basic emotions: Evidence from patterns classifications and cluster analysis. *Biological Psychology*, *84*(3), 463–473.

Steptoe, A., Moses, J., & Edwards, S. (1990). Age-related differences in cardiovascular reactions to mental stress tests in women. *Health Psychology*, *9*, 18–34.

Sze, J. A., Gyurak, A., Yuan, J. W., & Levenson, R. W. (2010). Coherence between emotional experience and physiology: Does bodily awareness training have an impact? *Emotion*, *10*(6), 803–814.

Tomaka, J., Blascovich, J., Kibler, J., & Ernst, J. M. (1997). Cognitive and physiological antecedents of threat and challenge appraisal. *Journal of Personality and Social Psychology*, *73*(1), 63–72.

Tooby, J., & Cosmides, L. (2008). The evolutionary psychology of the emotions and their relationship to internal regulatory variables. In M. Lewis, J. M. Haviland-Jones & L. F. Barrett (Eds.), *Handbook of emotions* (3rd ed., pp. 114–137). New York: Guilford Press.

Tsai, J. L., Levenson, R. W., & Carstensen, L. L. (2000). Autonomic, subjective, and expressive responses to emotional films in older and younger Chinese Americans and European Americans. *Psychology and Aging*, *15*(4), 684–693.

Turner, M. J., Mier, C. M., Spina, R. J., Schechtman, K. B., & Ehsani, A. A. (1999). Effects of age and gender on the cardiovascular responses to isoproterenol. *Journal of Gerontology: Biological Sciences*, *54A*, B393–B400.

Uchino, B. N., Berg, C. A., Smith, T. W., Pearce, G., & Skinner, M. (2006). Age-related differences in ambulatory blood pressure reactivity during stress: Evidence for greater blood pressure reactivity with age. *Psychology and Aging*, *21*, 231–239.

Uchino, B. N., Birmingham, W., & Berg, C. A. (2010). Are older adults less or more physiologically reactive? A meta-analysis of age-related differences in cardiovascular reactivity to laboratory tasks. *Journal of Gerontology: Psychological Sciences*, *65B*(2), 154–162.

Uchino, B. N., Holt-Lunstad, J., Bloor, L. E., & Campo, R. A. (2005). Aging and cardiovascular reactivity to stress: Longitudinal evidence for changes in stress reactivity. *Psychology and Aging*, *20*, 134–143.

Urry, H. L., & Gross, J. J. (2010). Emotion regulation in older age. *Current Directions in Psychological Science*, *19*(6), 352–357.

Aging Influences on Judgment and Decision Processes: Interactions Between Ability and Experience

Thomas M. Hess *and* Tara L. Queen

Abstract

Research on age differences in judgment and decision making (JDM) processes are explored from a social-cognitive/contextual perspective, with a focus on the impact of declining cognitive resources, increased experience, and adaptive/compensatory processes. This review of JDM processes illustrates the complex interplay between multiple factors in determining age differences in performance. It further suggests that a simplistic perspective (e.g., one focusing solely on the impact of reduced cognitive resources) on understanding the impact of aging provides an incomplete understanding of the positive impact of experience and compensatory processes on promoting continued levels of adaptive functioning in everyday life.

Key Words: aging, decision making, social cognition, judgments

The publication of the volume on *Social Cognition and Aging* (Hess & Blanchard-Fields, 1999) recognized the emergence of interest in the study of social cognitive processes during adulthood. Perhaps more importantly, however, was the associated advocacy for taking a social-cognitive perspective in examining adaptive cognitive functioning in later life. That is, such an approach was viewed as not just helpful for understanding social functioning, but also as useful in understanding, more broadly, cognition in context. In this chapter, we explore the utility of such an approach in characterizing adult age differences in judgment and decision making (JDM) processes. We also explore what such processes reveal about adaptive functioning in adulthood. Our focus is primarily on work conducted in our lab, but we also explore connections with relevant research from other sources.

Blanchard-Fields and Hess (1999) identified two basic aspects of a social-cognitive perspective with particular utility for the study of adult development. The first involves understanding the

cognitive underpinnings of basic social psychological phenomena. For example, an important focus in the field of social cognition has been on how individual and situational constraints on processing (e.g., working memory) influence the ability to form accurate impressions of others or judge the causal factors underlying the behavior of others in social situations (e.g., Srull & Wyer, 1989). Of further interest is how automatic processes might compensate for such constraints or, alternatively, introduce biases when cognitive control is compromised. This focus on basic mechanisms and the impact of constraints on their operation provides a useful perspective for understanding the impact of aging-related cognitive limitations on social functioning. Importantly, however, the social-cognitive perspective goes beyond just the examination of basic cognitive mechanisms—or *cold cognition*—and extends to the examination of factors that energize and direct their operation. This focus on *hot cognition* emphasizes the important role played by affect, motivation, and goals in energizing and directing the cognitive system (e.g., Metcalfe & Mischel, 1999). For example, how do specific inter-action goals and the degree of personal investment in them influence the extent to which individuals engage in elaborative processing of social informa-tion (e.g., Fiske & Neuberg, 1990)? An additional layer of complexity is added to the study of these "hot" factors when applied to understanding adult development, where consideration must also be given to the possibility that age is associated with changes in fundamental aspects of their nature. For example, research has demonstrated that age is associated with increased efficiency of some emotion-regulation processes, but decreased effi-ciency of others (e.g., Shiota & Levenson, 2009). In addition, goals and motivation are also sensitive to the changing context associated with the aging pro-cess (e.g., Carstensen, Isaacowitz, & Charles, 1999; Hess, Emery, & Neupert, 2012). Consideration of such factors and their interaction with the situation permits a more complete understanding of adult age differences in social functioning and broadens the potential constellation of determinants of observed age differences in cognitive performance.

The second aspect of a social-cognitive per-spective identified by Blanchard-Fields and Hess (1999) concerned a focus on social competencies. Conceptualized as a form of social intelligence (e.g., Cantor & Kihlstrom, 1989), social competencies are adaptations based on the availability and use of knowledge specific to contexts in which the indi-vidual functions. Thus, such competencies will vary as a function of life context and experience, both of which may differ for people of different ages. In addition, competency is not only reflected in knowledge, but in its appropriate application in a given context. Although the social-cognitive per-spective focuses on social competency, we argue that this general focus on the benefits of knowledge can be used to help understand adaptive cognitive functioning in everyday contexts, as well as in social behavior. For example, research on wisdom (e.g., Baltes & Staudinger, 2000) and social expertise (e.g., Hess & Auman, 2001) have much in com-mon with the study of expertise in other domains, such as chess (e.g., Charness, 1981), in that both emphasize the importance of accumulated knowl-edge in defining the problem situation and focusing attention on the most important information.

In this chapter, we explore the process and com-petency factors highlighted by the Blanchard-Fields and Hess (1999) social-cognitive perspective within the context of adult developmental research on JDM. Until recently, judgment and—especially—decision-making processes have not been con-sidered from a developmental perspective and have mostly been studied in young adult samples. Studying aging within a JDM framework, however, provides an excellent context for examining every-day cognitive functioning in older adulthood. The process of forming judgments and making decisions is multidimensional in nature, allowing for exami-nation of the aforementioned cognitive, affective, and experienced-based influences. These underly-ing mechanisms are also quite relevant to the study of aging. In thinking about the influence of aging on decision making, one prediction may be that declines in cognitive functioning will limit older adults' ability to form accurate judgments or make optimal decisions. Age-related declines in delibera-tive processes may also result in greater reliance on affective processing, experience, and accrued knowl-edge (Peters, Hess, Västfjäll, & Auman, 2007). Such a shift could result in poorer performance in certain situations, but could also serve to counteract cog-nitive losses. Increased reliance on experiential pro-cesses could also lead to improved decision making in older adulthood in situations where, for example, affective information is beneficial to making good decisions.

In the next three sections, we review work from our lab and elsewhere on JDM processes in social and nonsocial contexts. We begin by examining how age differences in ability and basic cognitive mechanisms may impact the efficiency of JDM pro-cesses and the types of information that are used in constructing responses. Of specific interest in the latter case is a focus on dual-process JDM perspec-tives and the possibility that age-related decline in deliberative processes may lead to an overreliance on affective processes (e.g., processing of evalua-tive content). We then focus on the competency factor, with specific interest in the relationship between experience and the availability and use of knowledge in making judgments and decisions in social and nonsocial contexts. Finally, we consider interactions between mechanisms and competen-cies as individuals adapt to changes that occur in later adulthood. Of particular interest here is older adults' selective engagement of resources and the development of processing shortcuts (e.g., heuris-tics) that take advantage of experience and mini-mize the demands on cognitive resources.

To foreshadow, we argue that cognitive limita-tions associated with age may negatively impact JDM processes primarily when (a) successful performance depends on efficient deliberative processes, (b) individuals possess little experience within the domain being examined, and (c) self-relevance of the task is low. In contrast, when successful judgments or decisions can be informed by affective processing or when individuals have extensive experience within the task domain, age differences in performance will be attenuated and may even favor middle-aged and older adults. Finally, JDM performance also reveals adaptive aspects of functioning in late adulthood as individuals use their knowledge to compensate for declining deliberative skills, conserve mental energy by selectively engaging cognitive resources, and adjust the nature of processing to take into account chronic goals and personal experience.

The Impact of Affective Versus Deliberative Processes on JDM

Age-related declines in basic cognitive processes such as processing speed (Salthouse, 1996), working memory (West, 1996), inhibitory functions (Hasher & Zacks, 1988), and executive skills (Braver & West, 2008) are well documented in the cognitive aging literature. To the extent that effective JDM processes depend on the ability to, for example, process information within a limited time period, handle large amounts of information, and control the impact of irrelevant information, it seems reasonable to expect that performance will be negatively impacted with increasing age.

SOCIAL INFERENCES

Several early studies in our lab focused on how age-related declines in cognitive abilities might impact negatively on social inferences and representations. Of particular interest was how hypothesized declines in basic processing resources (e.g., working memory) might result in less specific social representations in later life. Hess and Tate (1991) examined whether young and older adults differed in the extent to which inconsistent information was integrated in cognitive representations of other people. Participants read descriptions of a target person that consisted mostly of behaviors that were evaluatively consistent with each other (i.e., reflected similarly valenced affective content) but that also contained a minority that were evaluatively inconsistent. They were instructed to form impressions of the target based on this information and then were given an unexpected memory test. Younger adults exhibited an inconsistency effect in recall, whereby they recalled a greater proportion of the inconsistent than of the consistent behaviors; no such effect was

observed for older adults. The recall advantage for inconsistencies is thought to reflect the more extensive processing accorded to such information due to its unexpected nature (e.g., Hastie, 1984), with one possible explanation for the age difference observed by Hess and Tate being that reduced processing resources in later life negatively affected the ability to engage in such processing.

Other research we have conducted suggests that aging may be associated with less specific processing, which in turn could also reflect reduced processing resources. For example, Hess and Follett (1994) presented young and old adults [1] with lists of traits attributed to different target people, with some people being characterized by more positive than negative traits and others being characterized by the opposite pattern. When asked to make inferences about whether the targets would perform specific behaviors, all participants were influenced by the difference in the number of positive versus negative behaviors and made inferences consistent with the direction of this difference. Younger adults, however, were more likely to make inferences based on the specific nature of the traits that they had previously viewed. Similar effects were obtained by Hess, Follett, an1d McGee (1998) using a reverse procedure in which participants were exposed to behaviors and then made trait inferences. All participants were biased toward making trait attributions that were consistent with the majority valence of the presented behaviors. Younger adults were more likely than older adults, however, to discriminate between traits with and without behavioral referents. Together, the findings suggest that age has minimal impact on the processing of evaluative information but that the encoding of more specific information suffers in later life.

A subsequent study (Hess, Pullen, & McGee, 1996) focused on age differences in learning about the characteristics that define social groups, with results that were consistent with this conclusion regarding age differences in the processing of evaluative versus content-specific information. Specifically, we exposed young and older adults to descriptions of individuals who were members or nonmembers of a fictitious social group and examined their ability to abstract group membership information. In one condition, this information was based on a series of attributes with no evaluative consistency (i.e., a mix of an equal number of positive, neutral, and negative traits), thereby requiring a focus on encoding of specific attribute—as opposed to general evaluative—content in order to determine group membership criteria. Younger adults were much more successful than older adults at abstracting this information. In contrast, when group membership was based on a series of evaluatively consistent attributes, older adults performed similarly to younger adults and even exhibited a slight learning advantage. (This may, in part, have reflected younger adults engaging in more deliberative processing when in fact performance would have benefitted by a more holistic and passive approach.) Thus, once again, age differences were minimal in situations in which performance depended on processing of evaluative information, but older adults exhibited a disadvantage when the processing of more specific information was required.

There is also evidence that aging effects on executive control might have a negative impact on the ability to control the impact of irrelevant information when making social inferences. For example, Hess, McGee, Woodburn, and Bolstad (1998) presented young and older adults with an ambiguous description of a person and then asked them to describe this person. This was preceded by priming with positive or negative trait information. When unaware that the priming had occurred, all participants produced descriptors that were consistent with the prime. When aware of the prime, older adults still produced evaluatively consistent descriptors, whereas younger adults were less likely to do so. This suggests that the younger adults were able to exert cognitive control over the impact of the primes on their judgments, whereas older adults were not.

Another realm of social information processing that appears to be negatively influenced by age-related declines in cognitive ability has to do with attribution processes. The research in this area has focused primarily on examining the extent to which the causes of another's behavior are attributed to the person, the circumstances surrounding the behavior, or some combination of the two. Of particular interest is the extent to which age differences exist in what has been termed the *correspondence bias* (Jones & Davis, 1965). This reflects the tendency of observers—at least in Western societies—to infer that observed behaviors are due to (i.e., *correspond* to) stable traits possessed by the actor. An overreliance on such inferences has been termed the *fundamental attribution error* (FAE; Ross, 1977) when dispositional attributions are made in spite of the fact that sufficiently strong facilitative forces are present in the environment. One of the most famous examples of this was in a study by Jones

and Harris (1967), who found that college students were likely to attribute the viewpoint expressed in a class assignment to the writer even though clear information was provided that the instructor had given the writer the task of supporting that viewpoint. Research on the circumstances governing the FAE suggests that it is influenced by the observer's goals (e.g., Tetlock, 1985), as well as by available cognitive resources (e.g., Gilbert & Krull, 1988).

From an aging perspective, it might be expected that declines in cognitive resources would result in a higher probability of correspondence biases in later life. Relatedly, age-related declines in cognitive complexity (e.g., Labouvie-Vief, Chiodo, Goguen, Diehl, & Orwoll, 1995) might result in a similar shift, as older adults focus on fewer pieces of information in constructing social inferences. Several studies have found that older adults are more likely to exhibit correspondent biases than middle-aged adults and, in some cases, younger adults (Blanchard-Fields, 1994; Blanchard-Fields, Chen, Schocke, & Hertzog, 1998; Blanchard-Fields & Norris, 1994; Follett & Hess, 2002). There is also evidence that this increase in the correspondence bias may reflect, in part, task demands. Chen and Blanchard-Fields (1997) found that when participants were asked to make immediate attribution ratings, older adults were more likely to make dispositional attributions than were younger adults. This may reflect older adults' greater dependence on relatively automatic processing when time constraints for response are high. However, when given more time to reflect, older adults' attributions became less dispositional and age differences disappeared. This appears to reflect a correction process on the part of older adults (Gilbert, Pelham, & Krull, 1988), suggesting engagement in more deliberative processing when task constraints are low. Thus, the age differences in dispositional ratings may be most evident when making spontaneous inferences due to reductions in cognitive resources in later life (see also Chen & Blanchard-Fields, 2000). Other research has found little evidence that the age differences in the correspondence bias are mediated by complexity associated with social reasoning (Follett & Hess, 2002). Complexity has been shown to moderate age effects, however, with age differences in attribution strongest for those who are low in complexity (Horhota & Blanchard-Fields, 2006).

Although the age effects observed in much of the foregoing research are consistent with a reduced cognitive resource explanation, it must also be acknowledged that there have been few successful attempts made to identify the specific resources mediating these effects. For example, several studies have found that working memory is inconsistent in accounting for age or individual differences in social judgments (e.g., Blanchard-Fields, Hertzog, & Horhota, 2012; Chen & Blanchard-Fields, 2000). These findings do not necessarily downplay the importance of processing resources in accounting for age effects, given that working memory may be just one aspect of such resources. They do, however, argue for more precision in identifying the nature of these resources and their specific role in determining social information processing and age differences therein.

DECISION MAKING

The preceding discussion of social inferences introduced the idea that age differences in JDM processes may depend on the interplay between deliberative and more automatic processing modes. This notion of dual modes of information processing has also provided a framework for characterizing the underlying mechanisms involved in decision making (for review, see Payne & Bettman, 2004). This model has been particularly useful in understanding the influences of age on decision making because deliberative and automatic modes of processing seem to be differentially affected by age (Peters et al., 2007). In contrast to affective information processing, which is relatively automatic in nature and requires minimal cognitive effort (for review, see Bargh, 1994), successful deliberative information processing depends on efficient use of controlled attentional and cognitive resources. When confronted with a complex decision, individuals may be required to search through many pieces of information, suppress less relevant information, and weigh the pros and cons of several possible choices. Active deliberation therefore requires the coordination of multiple cognitive processes, including working memory and executive functioning. Given normative age-related declines in cognitive resources, older adults may be less able to engage in sustained active deliberation when faced with these types of decisions. Affective processing, on the other hand, seems to be less susceptible to the effects of age, with older adults maintaining or possibly improving the efficiency of such processing. Thus, age differences in decision making may be most evident in situations demanding the use of deliberative processing, as opposed to those that allow for global evaluations.

Several studies have identified situations in which older adults appear to display less efficient decision making. In a series of early studies on aging and decision making, older adults were often observed to use less complex information search strategies and to consider fewer pieces of information than younger adults in making decisions (Hershey, Walsh, Read, & Chulef, 1990; Johnson, 1990, 1993; Johnson & Drungle, 2000; Riggle & Johnson, 1996; Streufert, Pogash, Piasecki, & Post, 1990). In addition, some studies have found that older adults use less systematic strategies (e.g., Riggle & Johnson, 1996). These researchers hypothesized that the greater use of information-minimizing search strategies with increasing age may have reflected changes in cognitive ability.

Related results have been reported in more recent studies of age differences in decision strategy selection. In a task examining strategy adaptation in simple and complex decision environments, age differences in strategy selection could be accounted for by cognitive ability (Mata, Schooler, & Rieskamp, 2007). That is, poorer memory, reasoning, and speed of processing were associated with selection of less cognitively demanding decision strategies. Similarly, Henninger, Madden, and Huetel (2010) reported that ability, specifically processing speed and memory, were negatively associated with decision quality on tasks of risky decision making. These results suggest that the effects of cognitive decline may be most pronounced under conditions of increased task complexity. In an attempt to measure decision competence, Finucane, Mertz, Slovic, and Schmidt (2005) found that increasing age was associated with more comprehension errors and greater inconsistency in responses across decision tasks. Although they did not find an interaction between age and task complexity, a substantial amount of the age-related variance in task performance could be accounted for by fluid cognitive ability and health. In spite of some inconsistency in complexity effects—perhaps reflecting differences in the operationalization of this construct across studies—these investigations all highlight the importance of basic cognitive processes in determining observed age effects in decision making.

Successful decision making, however, does necessarily require preserved deliberative abilities. Indeed, several of the aforementioned studies that found age differences in search behaviors obtained no evidence of age differences in decision outcomes (e.g., Hershey et al., 1990; Johnson, 1993; Riggle & Johnson, 1996). Such findings may reflect the increasing reliance on experiential processing—including use of past experience and a focus on affective information—as deliberative processes decline in later adulthood (e.g., Peters et al., 2007), which in turn may support effective decision making in many situations.

We have observed such differences in decision-making performance in our own work concerning the role of active deliberation in decision making. In one study (Queen & Hess, 2010), young and older adults were presented with a consumer decision (e.g., choosing a bank) involving two types information arrays. In the first, the optimal decision could be derived through global evaluations of each of the choice options; that is, the best choice was that defined by the most positive attributes. For the second set of information, the optimal choice was defined by only a subset of the choice information, requiring participants to inhibit nonessential decision information in order to arrive at the best decision. Following presentation of the choices in each task, participants engaged in tasks designed to encourage either conscious or unconscious processing for 3 minutes (see Dijksterhuis & Nordgren, 2006). In the former condition, they were asked to actively think about and compare the four choices. In the unconscious conditions, such active deliberation was prevented by having the participants complete an anagrams task for the same period of time. Participants were then asked to select the best option.

We first examined participants' ratings of each of the choice attributes and determined that young adults more accurately represented the decision information than did older adults in both information contexts. Decision making for those who were accurate in their representations was best when there was congruence between the manner in which the information was presented and the way in which it was processed. That is, participants performed better under unconscious processing conditions when choice optimality was based on the number of positive descriptors. Similarly, when choice effectiveness relied on deliberative abilities, participants performed better when engaging in conscious thought. Age differences were minimal when choice information could be processed on an evaluative level, but when deliberative processing was required, older adults' performance suffered. These results suggest that, although the ability to process information at a deliberative level may decline in older adulthood, affective processing remains quite effective.

These results were mirrored in a follow-up study (Hess, Queen, & Patterson, 2012) that examined the influence of online processing. The added deliberation associated with conscious thought was not beneficial to decision quality when task materials could be evaluated through online processing, but was helpful when task materials required more focused attention. Age differences were most apparent when the task required active deliberation, with older adults possessing fewer years of education and poorer cognitive abilities performing worse under these conditions.

Consistent with a dual-process characterization of age effects, there is also evidence that age differences are attenuated in tasks in which performance may rely on affective processing. For example, young and older adults are often observed to perform similarly on the Iowa Gambling Task (IGT; Bechara, Damasio, Damasio, & Anderson, 1994), which is highly dependent on cortical structures associated with processing of affect (e.g., Kovalchik, Camerer, Grether, Plott, & Allam, 2005; MacPherson, Phillips, & Della Sala, 2002; Wood, Busemeyer, Koling, Cox, & Davis, 2005; but see Denburg et al., 2009; Denburg, Tranel, & Bechara, 2005). When Wood et al. (2005) examined performance more closely on this task, they found that younger adults relied more on representations of cumulative outcomes, suggesting that younger adults were utilizing both deliberative and affective processes in guiding their choices between the disadvantageous (i.e., high gain, higher loss) and the advantageous (i.e., low gain, lower loss) card decks. In contrast, older adults were more influenced by recent gains and losses, suggesting greater reliance on affective information. In the IGT, however, this latter approach can prove quite beneficial in guiding performance, given that the value of losses becomes stronger than that of gains over time in the disadvantageous decks, whereas the opposite is true in the advantageous decks. This supports the view that preserved affective functions in later life may compensate for losses in deliberative functions in some situations.

Taken together, this review of social and nonsocial JDM processes suggests that older adults might engage in less deliberative processing than observed in younger adults, particularly under complex task conditions. This will often result in older adults displaying less complex inferences in social situations, simpler information search strategies, and less than optimal decisions. In addition, some of the observed age effects have been tied to reductions in cognitive ability. Note, however, that inefficient deliberative processing does not always constrain older adults' performance, even on tasks that might be considered quite complex (e.g., the IGT). The research reviewed in this section suggests that attenuation of age differences in some of these tasks may reflect the extent to which effective performance relies on preserved affective processing. As discussed in the next section, however, this may not be the only avenue supporting preserved decision-making competence in later life.

Age-Related Experience and JDM Competence

In contrast to the potentially negative influence of age-related normative declines in cognitive ability, accumulated experience in adulthood may result in enhanced competencies in making judgments and decisions and—in some case—counteract biases that are observed in younger adults. This experience can serve to focus attention (e.g., discriminate between relevant and irrelevant information), as well as aid in the development of heuristic devices that facilitate one's ability to make effective decisions while putting minimal demands on cognitive resources (Gigerenzer, 2008). In this section, we examine research that is consistent with this perspective, focusing first on social inferences and then on decision-making processes.

SOCIAL COMPETENCE

The foregoing discussion suggested that age-related deficits in cognitive resources negatively affect the effectiveness of social information processing. An alternative view is that progression through adulthood is associated with the accumulation of both (a) social knowledge that results in a better understanding of the bases of behaviors and (b) actual experiences that guide or bias social inferences. This might result in middle-aged and older adults being more likely than younger adults to (a) consider multiple sources of information in making social attributions, acknowledging the complex determinants of behavior; (b) identify and focus on the most relevant aspects of situations in making judgments; or (c) make effective decisions based on their specific life experiences.

Although work on attribution processes has suggested that older adults make less complex inferences due to changing cognitive resources, other research has suggested that the bases for the observed age trends is more complicated. For example, whereas older adults are more likely than younger and middle-aged adults to make dispositional attributions, there is also evidence that these same older adults are more likely to make interactive

attributions, in which dual dispositional and situational factors are judged to be determinants of behavior (Blanchard-Fields, 1994; Blanchard-Fields & Norris, 1994). Age differences in the FAE are also reduced when a plausible motivation is provided that increases the individual's attention to extenuating circumstances surrounding a target's behavior (Blanchard-Fields & Horhota, 2005).

Important for an experiential perspective, there is also evidence that the age-related increase in correspondence bias might be tied to beliefs and social schemas related to experience and goals. For example, Stanley and Blanchard-Fields (2011) observed that older adults had a stronger belief that people are unlikely to act in a manner that was inconsistent with their attitudes. This, in turn, partly accounted for age differences in the strength of dispositional attributions. Blanchard-Fields and colleagues (Blanchard-Fields et al., 1998; Blanchard-Fields et al., 2012; Chen & Blanchard-Fields, 1997; Horhota & Blanchard-Fields, 2006) have also demonstrated that age differences exist in experience-based schemas regarding social relationships and that the higher levels of dispositional attributions in later life may reflect beliefs based in such schemas. Indeed, Horhota and Blanchard-Fields (2006) found that the attitude–attribution linkage was stronger in later life than in young adulthood.

In sum, work from a traditional attribution framework demonstrates that older adults are more likely to exhibit correspondence bias than are other age groups, but this does not appear to simply reflect age-related declines in underlying cognitive mechanisms. Although low levels of cognitive resources and attributional complexity may result in higher levels of dispositional responses in older adults, these factors may only be influential under specific circumstances (e.g., minimal time to make judgments). Instead, it appears that a substantial portion of age-related variations in causal attributions regarding the behavior of others may be based in age-related changes in beliefs and social experience. One view is that older adults are more reliant on heuristic devices in making social inferences, rather than starting from scratch each time. To the extent that these heuristics are based in positive previous social experience regarding likely outcomes, the shifts in attribution may be adaptive.

In work from our lab, we have approached the examination of social inferences from a somewhat different but complementary perspective. Specifically, we have examined how different-aged individuals make inferences about personality traits underlying an individual's behavior and then use this information to make both general and context-specific evaluative judgments. Of particular interest in this work is the extent to which individuals selectively attend to and process different types of information and how this selectivity is related to (a) culturally shared beliefs about personality, (b) social experience, and (c) situational and chronic goals.

Much research has demonstrated that judgments about self and others tend to be organized along two underlying dimensions (e.g., Abele & Wojciszke, 2007; Fiske, Cuddy, & Glick, 2007; Judd, James-Hawkins, Yzerbyt, & Kashima, 2005). Although different names have been used to characterize these dimensions, there is relative consistency in the definition of the constructs associated with these dimensions. For present purposes, we will borrow from work by Abele and Wojciszke (2007) and refer to these dimensions as *agency* and *communion*. The agency dimension is related to traits that are typically beneficial or detrimental to the individual possessing them (e.g., ambition, intelligence) and are thus deemed *self-profitable* (Peeters & Czapinski, 1990). In contrast, the communion dimension is more reflective of traits that have primary benefit or harm implications for others (e.g., helpfulness, honesty) and thus are characterized as *other-profitable*. Although specific traits are often associated with these dimensions, the focus of the behavior— as implied by the labels of self- versus other-focus—is more important in determining whether the behavior is viewed as more relevant to one dimension versus the other. For example, Wojciszke (1997; Abel & Wojciszke, 2007) has argued that behaviors typically associated with agentic traits may also be viewed more in communal terms, to the extent that the observable behavior benefits others.

Of particular interest for our research is the fact that behavioral information associated with each dimension is selectively processed according the valence of the behavior. When behaviors relate to agency, people focus more on positive behaviors than on negative ones to characterize people, whereas the opposite is true for behaviors associated with communion (e.g., Hess & Auman, 2001; Skowronski & Carlston, 1987; Wojciszke, Brycz, & Borkenau, 1993). This differential weighting of positive and negative behaviors across trait domains represents variations in culture-specific beliefs regarding the *diagnosticity* of behaviors (i.e., the information value of a behavior in inferring possession of a specific trait; Skowronski & Carlston, 1989). Positive behaviors involving self are typically thought more reflective of agentic traits than are negative behaviors because there are fewer alternative explanations for the former. For example, if someone receives an "A" on a calculus test, we are likely to infer that she has strong math skills because there are few other explanations for this outcome. Alternatively, failing a calculus test might reflect low ability, but it could also be due to the individual not studying, being sick, poor test construction, and so forth, making it more difficult to establish with certainty where the individual falls on the ability dimension. The opposite is true for the communal dimension. For example, only dishonest people perform dishonest deeds, but even dishonest people will engage in some honest behaviors, thus making these behaviors less diagnostic of where individuals fall on the communal dimension.

Selectivity in social information processing is further evident when individuals form global evaluations of others (e.g., likability judgments, social partner selection) based on these trait inferences. Attributions regarding communion are generally given more weight than are attributions about agency in such evaluations, given the inherent relevance of other-profitable traits for social relationships (e.g., Abele & Wojciszke, 2007). These weightings may shift, however, with changes in social goals and interdependence between self and other (i.e., the extent to which personal outcomes are dependent on others). For example, in some relationships, the self-profitable behavior of one person may also have positive benefits for a close social partner (e.g., someone with good carpentry skills assisting in a home improvement project), resulting in more communal interpretation—and increased weighting—of typically agentic traits (Abele & Wojciszke, 2007; Wojciszke & Abele, 2008).

We have interpreted this selectivity as a form of social expertise, reflecting the individual's knowledge of adaptive social knowledge, as well as of the appropriate application of such knowledge. Consistent with this interpretation, such selectivity should be associated with increased social experience in adulthood as individuals not only gain social knowledge but also use such knowledge in response to appropriate situational cues.

Our initial work in this area examined how individuals adjusted their trait inferences about others following exposure to new behavioral information (Hess, Bolstad, Woodburn, & Auman, 1999; Hess & Pullen, 1994). Young, middle-aged, and older adults formed impressions of target individuals based on descriptions that focused on positive or negative agentic information (e.g., behaviors relating to intelligence) or communal information (e.g., behaviors relating to honesty). They were then presented with new information that was inconsistent with the initial impression (e.g., negative information about a person initially portrayed in a positive manner) and told to adjust their impressions. Of interest was the impact of the diagnosticity versus valence of this new information on the degree to which initial impressions were altered. Consistent with expectations, impressions underwent greater change when the original descriptions were based on nondiagnostic information (e.g., positive communal behaviors) and new diagnostic information (e.g., negative communal behaviors) was presented. Less change was evident when the original descriptions contained diagnostic information and new nondiagnostic information was presented. In addition, the impact of diagnosticity was stronger for middle-aged and older adults than for younger adults, who focused more on the valence of the behaviors. Interestingly, perceptions of the diagnostic value of individual behaviors did not vary across age groups, suggesting that the differences in social inferences were not based in such knowledge.

Based on these results, we hypothesized that the age differences in focus on the diagnostic value of behavioral information might be reflective of a form of social expertise based on the accumulation of social experience over adulthood. Specifically, we argued that an understanding of the diagnostic value of specific behaviors might be seen as a form of declarative knowledge reflecting shared cultural beliefs regarding the determinants of behavior. Further, the use of this knowledge in guiding our perceptions of others can be viewed as a form of procedural knowledge, reflecting the application of declarative knowledge. This might be evident in more automatic activation of trait schemas in response to specific behaviors, which in turn might be indexed by differential allocation of attentional resources to diagnostic versus nondiagnostic information. The results of our initial work suggested that there were few age differences in declarative knowledge (e.g., subjective judgments of the diagnostic value of specific pieces of information) but that procedural knowledge—as reflected in the impact of this information on attention allocation and trait inferences—benefited from the additional social experience of middle-aged and older adults. Consistent with perspectives on the development of expertise (e.g., Anderson, 1983), these trends suggest that declarative knowledge in this domain develops before procedural knowledge. Furthermore, work with children suggests that relevant declarative knowledge may develop from late childhood to adolescence. For example, Aloise (1993) found that third- and fifth-grade children required more information than did college students to make trait attributions, suggesting that the association between trait schemas and specific behaviors (i.e., declarative knowledge) was weaker in children. In line with our findings, although college students were more willing to infer traits from less information, the strength of their inferences in response to positive and negative behaviors did not vary based on the trait dimension represented by the behavior (i.e., agency vs. communion).

Other research has provided further support for the social expertise perspective. Several studies (e.g., Hess & Auman, 2001; Hess, Osowski, & Leclerc, 2005; Leclerc & Hess, 2007) have examined the impact of diagnostic behavioral information on impressions using descriptions of people that have equal numbers of positive and negative behaviors relating to either agentic or communal traits. In the former case, attention and impressions were biased toward positive information, whereas the opposite was true for communal traits. In addition, consistent with the social expertise notion, the emphasis on the diagnostic value of behaviors as opposed to evaluative content (i.e., valence) was greater in middle-aged and older adults than in younger adults. Hess et al. (2005) also found that age-related expertise was not just confined to descriptive implications of behaviors (i.e., the specific traits typified, such as honesty), but also to the degree to which behaviors would be considered self- or other-profitable. As noted previously, if behaviors have primary implications for others, people tend to interpret them in terms of communal traits and to weight negative behaviors more strongly than positive ones in making trait attributions. In contrast, if behaviors have implications primarily for self, then they are interpreted primarily in terms of agentic traits, and the focus is on positive information in making social inferences. We found both patterns of behavior to be true, but, once again, the differential focus on positive versus negative behavior as a function of self- versus other-profitability increased with age. Thus, for example, when participants were presented both positive and negative behaviors relating to honesty—typically a communal trait—but that also had implications for self (e.g., cheated playing solitaire; enrolled in literacy program after admitting to self he could not read), people not only made negative trait attributions relating to honesty, but also positive attributions associated with agency (e.g., competence). In addition, this trend was positively associated with age. In other words, increasing age in adulthood was associated with more complex social inferences relating to the processing of multiple types of diagnostic information. This complexity of reasoning was further evident in the factors that predicted individuals' global evaluations (e.g., likability) of people. In situations in which descriptive content (e.g., honesty) and focus (e.g., on self) were inconsistent with typical occurrences, older adults' evaluations were grounded in both communal and agentic trait attributions, whereas younger adults' evaluation were more simplistic, being based primarily on attributions of communal traits.

This research provides an interesting contrast to work on the positivity effect (see Mather & Carstensen, 2005), which suggests that—relative to young adults—older adults exhibit a bias toward positive or away from negative information. Framed within socioemotional selectivity theory (SST; Carstensen et al., 1999), this bias is thought to be reflective of regulatory functions designed to promote positive affective functioning in later life. On the surface, older adults' differential focus on positive versus negative information across trait domains in making trait inferences appears to be inconsistent with SST, or at least with recent extrapolations of the theory that focus on positivity. As we discuss later, however, promotion of positive affective goals in social situations may depend on attention to important negative information, particularly if it is diagnostic of potentially negative social outcomes. Consistent with an expertise framework, we have hypothesized that the age differences observed in the impact of diagnosticity on attention and trait inferences are due to the greater breadth and accessibility of relevant knowledge with increasing social experience in adulthood (Leclerc & Hess, 2007). One implication of this hypothesis is that relevant situational cues may need to be made more salient in order to activate knowledge associated with determining the diagnosticity of behavioral information in those with insufficient expertise. This is consistent with the notion that young adults may have appropriate declarative knowledge (e.g., understanding that a specific behavior is more diagnostic than another one) but may not have well-developed procedural knowledge (e.g., automatically activated links between this knowledge and specific instantiations of such behaviors). Supporting this idea, Betz,

Gannon, and Skowronski (1992) and Skowronski and Carlston (1992) found that younger adults were more likely to make trait inferences based on diagnosticity when the behavioral cues were extreme exemplars of trait-relevant behaviors. In addition, Leclerc and Hess (2007) found that age differences in trait inferences were attenuated when the diagnosticity of behavioral information was made more salient by increasing either the amount or extremity of this information. These findings suggest that the proposed age differences in procedural knowledge are, in part, reflections of the greater ease with which relevant declarative knowledge is activated by cues in the social environment. That the development of such procedural knowledge is related to social experience is further supported by findings that self-reported social activity moderates age differences in the use of diagnostic information in making social inferences (Hess et al., 2005). Thus, younger adults with high levels of social activity are more likely to attend to diagnostic information than are those who do not and are more likely to perform like middle-aged and older adults.

DECISION-MAKING COMPETENCE

Just as age-related experience appears to be adaptive in promoting social information processing, similar effects are apparent when examining decision making. As noted previously, research involving information search has suggested that older adults engage in less complex information search. In spite of such differences in strategy use, however, age differences in decision quality are often absent (Hershey et al., 1990; Mata & Nunes, 2010; Riggle & Johnson, 1996). In a manner similar to that associated with social expertise, experience and knowledge may guide search and make it more efficient. For example, studies examining decisions about over-the-counter (OTC) medications (Johnson & Drungle, 2000; Stephens & Johnson, 2000) found that older adults were likely to focus on factors of personal relevance (e.g., active ingredients, interactions with other drugs) and to be more systematic in their information searches than were younger adults, presumably reflecting their greater experience with using these drugs. Consistent with this view, Fisk and Rogers' (2000) review of existing research provided evidence that decisions in well-learned environments are preserved with age, and Meyer, Talbot, and Ranalli (2007) found the cognitive resources were primarily predictive of cancer treatment decisions for older adults only when treatment knowledge was low.

Other studies have suggested that experience may account for observations of less biased decisions for older compared to younger adults. Using a consumer decision task, Tentori, Osherson, Hasher, and May (2001) found that older adults were less susceptible to *preference reversals*, the tendency to adjust a preference for one product over another when a third product is introduced. Young adults, however, tended to reverse their preferences between the two initial choices even though the third product provided no new information regarding these choices. A subsequent study demonstrated that this age effect was not associated with domain knowledge, but it was attenuated in domains with which younger adults had more interest (Kim & Hasher, 2005). Thus, similar to our work on social expertise, this suggests that age differences in decision making in familiar domains may be based more in procedural knowledge (e.g., general skilled decision making) as opposed to declarative knowledge.

The framing effect involves another situation in which decision consistency may be affected by the manner in which information is framed. The classic study involves having participants choose between risky and nonrisky choices. When the choices are presented (i.e., framed) in terms of losses, people tend to be risk adverse and choose the nonrisky option. The opposite is true when the choices are presented as gains (Tversky & Kahneman, 1981). Age differences tend to be minimal in this task (e.g., Rönnlund, Karlsson, Laggnäs, Larsson, & Lindström, 2005; Mayhorn, Fiske, & Whittle, 2002), but there is evidence that perhaps young and older adults arrive at their decision differently. Woodhead, Lynch, and Edelstein (2011) found that age differences in susceptibility to framing could be accounted for by strategy (Woodhead et al., 2011). A qualitative analysis revealed that older adults' resistance to framing effects was at least in part due to their reliance on examples of personal experience, compared to young adults' data-driven strategy. This experiential focus made them less susceptible to the frames in which the information was presented. This suggests that this particular decision-making bias may be less tied to age and changes in ability than it is with specific experiences that individuals have. To the extent that older adults have relevant experience—which is more likely in everyday than in hypothetical domains—they may not be susceptible to framing effects and may, in some cases, exhibit less susceptibility than younger adults.

A similar pattern of results can be found in studies examining the *sunk-cost fallacy*, which involves the tendency to continue investing resources into a situation in which costs cannot be recovered (e.g., sit though a bad movie because they had paid to see it). These investments are considered irrational because the individuals would be unlikely to invest resources without the prior commitment. Research has demonstrated that the susceptibility to sunk costs decreases with age in adulthood (e.g., Bruine de Bruin, Parker, & Fischoff, 2007; Strough, Mehta, McFall, & Schuller, 2008; Strough, Schlosnagle, & DiDonato, 2011), and this appears—in part—to reflect older adults' reduced focus on loss-related information; in other words, the loss of the initial investment is not seen as being as important for older as it is for younger adults.

In sum, our review of social and decision-making competence suggests that older adults may benefit from experience and practice accumulated during adulthood. This may serve to selectively focus attention on the most important aspects of the environment—and away from irrelevant details—or allow them access to relevant experience-based schemas that can be used to draw conclusions about, for example, the determinants of social behavior. This experience may allow them to overcome deficits that might occur if they had to rely solely on deliberative functions to make judgments and arrive at decisions (see below). Thus, the development of social expertise and decision-making competence can be viewed as an adaptive developmental process, as well as a means for compensating for negative changes in basic cognitive skills. Although experience may promote adaptive functioning in relevant contexts, it should also be acknowledged that such experience may be maladaptive to the extent that such knowledge is rigidly or inappropriately applied. Such maladaptive behavior might be more prevalent in later life if, for example, normative changes in executive skills limit older adults' ability to counteract such automatically activated knowledge (e.g., Pachur, Mata, & Schooler, 2009).

Age-Related Adaptive and Compensatory Processes

In the previous section, we focused on competencies that were correlated with age in adulthood and can be thought to reflect adaptations to individual's life contexts. From some perspectives, however, these competencies might not necessarily be viewed as developmental in the strict sense since age—other than being correlated with the passage of time and accumulation of experience—is not necessarily an integral component of these competencies.

However, developmental processes reflecting adaptive functioning can be seen in JDM mechanisms in a number of ways. For example, they may reflect age-related adjustments in chronic goals due to normative changes in life contexts or compensatory processes in response to normative changes in basic cognitive abilities. In this final section, we discuss research relevant to these adaptive functions.

Responses to Reductions in Cognitive Resources

The previously discussed literature has addressed the influences of age-related cognitive decline on JDM processes. Although declines in cognitive ability may very well have a negative influence on the efficiency of older adults' deliberative processing, the use of simpler, but effective, strategies (e.g., heuristics) may be an adaptive mechanism in helping reduce cognitive load. Similarly, older adults might come to rely more on knowledge informed by experience to direct processing and reduce the demands on resources. For example, expertise in both cognitive (e.g., Hess & Kotter-Grühn, 2011) and noncognitive (e.g., Charness, 1981) domains may serve to direct attention, organize information, and focus memory search in domain-relevant situations. In addition, research in the decision-making realm often finds that decision quality is unrelated to age (e.g., Mata & Nunes, 2010), suggesting that these various compensatory mechanisms act as buffer for losses in ability experienced in older adulthood.

When seeking information to support the construction of effective judgments or decisions, one may imagine an information maximizing strategy as being superior to an information minimizing heuristic. Some researchers, however, argue the contrary (for example, Gigerenzer, 2008), suggesting that heuristic devices with reduced resource demands are often just as—if not more—effective as more complex strategies. This is an interesting concept to consider within the context of aging because older adults may be more inclined to use simpler strategies to reduce cognitive load. Although, at first glance, this shift in strategy preference may be seen as being a negative effect of cognitive decline, it may actually be an effective compensatory mechanism for older adults. The efficiency of simpler search strategies may depend on the decision environment, making it necessary for older adults to be cognizant of the demands of the task. Research on age differences in strategy selection, however, has found some support for older adults being adaptive in their strategy selection. For example, Mata, Schooler, and

Rieskamp (2007) presented young and older adults with two different decision-making contexts: one that required the use of a cognitively demanding strategy and the other that could be navigated with a simpler heuristic. Although, overall, older adults viewed less information, spent more time on the task, and tended to select an information minimizing strategy, they were also able to adapt their strategy depending on the decision context. Similar to young adults, they engaged in a more information maximizing strategy when the context was more cognitively demanding and switched to heuristics when performance on the task allowed for a simpler strategy. A meta-analysis examining age differences in predecision information search (Mata & Nunes, 2010) found that, when compared to young adults, older adults displayed only a small decline in amount of information searched. Furthermore, this decline did not seem to affect decision quality, suggesting that older adults can adaptively apply information minimizing strategies without negatively influencing the quality of their decisions.

We have found similar patterns of adaptive behavior in our own research, specifically in a study investigating the interactions between age and task complexity (Queen, Hess, Ennis, Dowd, & Grühn, 2012). Using process tracing software, we presented young, middle-aged, and older adults with simple and complex decision matrices. We found no age differences in the use of simple versus complex decision strategies. Instead, adults of all age groups were adaptive in their use of both strategies, adjusting their search to the demands of the task. These results echo those of Mata and colleagues', suggesting that older adults are adaptive in their ability to monitor situations in which different strategies are necessary.

Reliance on experience may also act as a compensatory mechanism by guiding search and highlighting important pieces of information. This idea is nicely illustrated in the results of a study investigating age differences in a battery of decision-making tasks. Across seven different tasks, Bruine de Bruin, Parker, and Fischoff (2007) found that age was positively associated with performance on three subtests and negatively associated on two subtests. Older adults displayed better performance on subtests related to everyday decisions and experience, suggesting that knowledge may act as a compensatory mechanism when performance benefits from the incorporation of such information.

This idea is also adressed in a study investigating age differences in decisions surrounding cancer treatment. Meyer et al. (2007) presented young and older adults with information on the treatment of two different cancers. Participants were able to make an immediate decision or were given the option of delaying the decision until a later time. The researchers found that increased relevance of or interest in the topic of cancer treatment was related to older adults with higher cognitive ability delaying decisions. The researchers suggest that the motivation for delaying a decision would be to spend more time seeking additional information. Increased interest or knowledge about medical treatments seems to have been a motivation to make a more informed choice.

Selective Engagement

Another way in which older adults appear to deal with changes in cognitive resources is by becoming more selective in engaging these resources (Hess, 2006, 2013; Hess & Emery 2012). The costs associated with cognitive activity appear to increase in later life, both in terms of the amount of resources required to achieve a specific cognitive outcome (e.g., Cabeza, 2002; Craik & Anderson, 1999; Gold, 2005) and the consequences of that effort (e.g., Gold, 2005; Neupert, Soederberg, & Lachman, 2006; Seeman & Robbins, 1994). For example, Hess and Ennis (2012; Ennis, Hess, & Smith, 2013) examined changes in systolic blood pressure—which has been found to be a reliable index of mental effort (e.g., Gendolla & Wright, 2005)—in response to sustained cognitive activity. They found that, relative to younger adults, older adults (a) had to exert more effort to support performance, (b) exerted disproportionately more effort as task difficulty increased, and (c) exhibited stronger fatigue-related effects associated with effort on a later task. We have argued that the greater costs associated with cognitive activity in later life result in older adults being less likely to engage resources in tasks that have minimal implications for self (e.g., personal relevance). In other words, older adults conserve resources by being more selective regarding the situations in which they will invest cognitive effort. This conservation behavior results in the self-implications of the task having a stronger impact on performance in later adulthood, with age differences in performance being attenuated in situations viewed as personally meaningful.

Support for this perspective has been found in several studies from our lab. Relative to younger adults, increasing self-relevance or social accountability resulted in disproportionate enhancement of older adults' performance, as reflected in the accuracy of social inferences and memory (Hess, Rosenberg, & Waters, 2001), the ability to filter out irrelevant affective content when making evaluative judgments (Hess, Germain, Rosenberg, Leclerc, & Hodges, 2005), and the use of important but cognitively demanding information in making both social and consumer judgments (Hess, Leclerc, Swaim, & Weatherbee, 2009; see also Chen, 2004). Two additional projects obtained further evidence for selective engagement at the process level. Using Jacoby's (1998) process-dissociation procedure with a person-memory task, Hess, Germain, Swaim, and Osowski (2009) found that accountability disproportionately increased estimates of controlled recollection processes on performance for older adults; neither age nor accountability had a significant impact on estimates of automatic processing. Germain and Hess (2007) examined how personal relevance moderated age differences in inhibitory functions. Young (17–26 years) and older (58–86 years) adults read prose passages interspersed with distracting text. Relevance was manipulated by varying the age-based content of the passages. Across three studies, increased relevance facilitated reading speed and comprehension and decreased memory for distracting text, with the effects being generally stronger for older adults.

Goal-Based Processes

Adaptive processes associated with adult development are also seen in normative changes in the chronic goals tied to specific behavior domains and contexts. These goals may bias information processing by influencing either attention to specific types of information or the direction of processing, which might result in qualitative changes in the nature of processing across age groups. In theory, such goal congruent shifts in the nature of processing should facilitate adaption by producing judgments and decisions that are consistent with these goals. Occasions may arise, however, when the bias introduced by chronic goals might be detrimental to effective decisions when, for example, attention is not focused on information essential for achieving a situational goal.

A few studies have investigated the impact of shifting social goals proposed by socioemotional selectivity theory. This theory posits that decreases in future time perspective associated with aging motivate older adults to focus on emotion-based goals, whereas a more expansive future time perspective orients younger adults to focus more knowledge-based goals (Carstensen et al., 1999). These shifts in chronic goals are thought to result in older adults focusing more on emotional content than do younger adults, with a particular bias toward processing positive information. Interest has been focused on whether such a bias emerges in decision making and whether task characteristics interact with age-related biases in determining the effectiveness of the decision-making process.

In one study, Löckenhoff and Carstensen (2007) presented young and older adults with a decision matrix containing information about healthcare plans. Each plan was rated on several different attributes, with the matrix describing whether the plan rated very good to very poor on each specific attribute. When asked to recall the information they viewed, older adults recalled more positive information about the choice options. When participants were encouraged to focus on the details of the task materials as opposed to their emotional reactions, age differences in memory for the choices were attenuated. The researchers suggest that older adults naturally attend to the affective information of the choices, which may ultimately guide their decisions.

Similarly, Mikels and colleagues (2010) examined how a focus on meeting emotion-based goals impacts decision quality. Before being presented with a healthcare decision, young and older adults were asked to focus on the specific details of the choices or their emotional responses to the choices. After assessing the choice options, participants were asked to make a decision. These researchers found that older adults' decision quality was best when they were asked to assess the choices based on their emotional reactions, whereas young adults made optimal decisions when they focused on the details of the options. Taken together with the previous study, these findings suggest chronic goals may influence the nature of the decision-making process, with effectiveness in both young and older adults in part based on the congruence between task structure and chronic goals.

In a recent set of studies on examining social inferences from our lab (Hess & Kotter-Grühn, 2011), we investigated whether chronic goals might interfere with the use of expert knowledge in characterizing people. For example, if aging is associated with a focus on positive information, it may be that older adults will be less likely to focus on important negative information (e.g., diagnostic behaviors related to communal traits) in situations in which interaction goals are emphasized and, presumably, chronic social goals would be more salient. Instead, we found that older adults focused on the diagnostic value of social information—whether it was positive or negative—when making trait inferences based on a target person's behaviors, regardless of situational goals. We did find, however, that the manner in which this information was used in making evaluative judgments did vary as a function of age and situational goals. For example, young, middle-aged, and older adults all focused more on communal trait inferences in making judgments as to whether the target person would be a good social partner, but more on agentic traits in making judgments about the person as a work partner. In addition, in all cases, older adults tended to weight communal traits more strongly than did young and middle-aged adults. Given that such traits relate to how well individuals treat others, this appears to be consistent with the hypothesized increase in the focus on affective outcomes of social interactions in later life. Thus, even though these results appear to be inconsistent with the recent focus on positivity effects based in SST (e.g., Mather & Carstensen, 2005), the general focus on communal traits can be viewed as relevant to older adults' focus on maximizing positive affect in social interactions. Somewhat counterintuitively from a positivity perspective, the differential focus on negative communal traits can also be seen as supportive of such efforts. To the extent that these traits are particularly predictive of characteristics that may be associated with negative social outcomes, it would be adaptive for older adults to attend to such characteristics and avoid individuals possessing them, thereby increasing the chances for positive affective experiences by reducing potentially negative interactions. Taken together, the research findings discussed in this section demonstrate adaptive and compensatory aspects of JDM processes in later life. Extensive experience within a specific domain can be used to guide top-down processing to compensate for declines in deliberative functions that may impede more elaborative bottom-up processing. In addition, older adults appear to adapt to the increased costs of cognitive engagement in later life by becoming more selective in their use of, and thereby conserving, cognitive resources. Importantly, the research reported here also suggests that age differences in performance are significantly attenuated in situations that older adults find personally relevant, which is associated with resource engagement. Finally, studies have also demonstrated that adults of all ages appear to adjust JDM processes in an adaptive manner that facilitates achievement of both situational and age-related chronic and social goals.

Conclusion

In this chapter, we have reviewed research on judgments and decision making, building on the social-cognitive perspective advocated by Blanchard-Fields and Hess (1999). A review of this literature provides details of the complex interplay between multiple forces in determining age differences in performance, illustrating both the negative impact of declining cognitive abilities in later life and the positive impact of experience and compensatory processes. Three general trends are evident. First, changes in basic cognitive skills, such as processing speed, working memory, and executive functions, appear to have a negative impact on the complexity of JDM processes. This is particularly evident in situations involving complex information and of low personal relevance. Second, the accumulation of age-correlated experience can benefit performance and result in enhanced judgments and decisions in later life by (a) providing knowledge with which to organize processing and focus attention and (b) providing practice in application of such knowledge. Finally, evidence of adaptive and compensatory processes can also be seen by examining JDM processes in adulthood. Adults of all ages appear to adaptively adjust their processing to be consistent with chronic and situational goals. Older adults also compensate for negative changes in cognitive resources in later life through (a) utilization of knowledge built up over a lifetime of experience and (b) selective application of cognitive resources to those situations that are most relevant to their lives.

These findings emphasize the importance of taking a contextual perspective in understanding cognitive functioning in adulthood by considering the interplay between situational factors (e.g., self-relevance, task demands), ability (e.g., cognitive resources), experience (e.g., social expertise), goals, and affective-motivational processes. This perspective is particularly important in understanding how aging affects everyday functions, where the impact of motivation and experience are most likely to be observed. In our advocacy of the contextual approach, we acknowledge that our review has been selective, with a heavy focus on work from our lab. The contextual perspective can be expanded, for example, to include adaptive and compensatory processes that include the social context in which the individual functions (e.g., collaborative decision making involving spouses or family). Our review has also focused primarily on research involving older adults with minimal identified cognitive impairment. It is likely that cognitive constraints will be more influential and disruptive to JDM processes in older adults experiencing, for example, mild cognitive impairments.

Acknowledgments

Writing of this chapter was supported by NIA grants R01 AG005552, R01 AG020153.

Note

1. In the studies reviewed, young adults typically range in age from 19 – 40 years, middles-aged adults from 40 – 65, and older adults from 65 years and older.

References

Abele, A. E., & Wojciszke, B. (2007). Agency and communion from the perspective of self vs. others. *Journal of Personality and Social Psychology, 93*, 751–776.

Aloise, P. A. (1993). Trait confirmation and disconfirmation: The development of attribution biases. *Journal of Experimental Child Psychology, 55*, 177–193.

Anderson, J. R. (1983). *The architecture of cognition*. Cambridge, MA: Harvard University Press.

Baltes, P. B., & Staudinger, U. M. (2000). Wisdom: A meta-heuristic (pragmatic) to orchestrate mind and virtue toward excellence. *American Psychologist, 55*, 122–136.

Bargh, J. A. (1994). The four horsemen of automaticity: Awareness, intention, efficiency, and control in social cognition. In R. S. Wyer, Jr., & T. K. Srull (Eds.), *Handbook of social cognition* (vol. 1; pp. 1–40). Hillsdale, NJ: Lawrence Erlbaum Associates.

Betz, A. L., Gannon, K. M., & Skowronski, J. J. (1992). The moment of tenure and the moment of truth: When it pays to be aware of recency effects in social judgments. *Social Cognition, 10*, 397–413.

Blanchard-Fields, F. (1994). Age differences in causal attributions from an adult developmental perspective. *Journal of Gerontology: Psychological Sciences, 49*, P43–P51.

Blanchard-Fields, F., Chen, Y., Schocke, M., & Hertzog, C. (1998). Evidence for content-specificity of causal attributions across the adult life span. *Aging, Neuropsychology, and Cognition, 5*, 241–263.

Blanchard-Fields, F., Hertzog, C., & Horhota, M. (2012). Violate my beliefs? Then you're to blame! Belief content as an explanation for causal attribution biases. *Psychology and Aging, 27*, 324–337.

Blanchard-Fields, F., & Hess, T. M. (1999). The social cognitive perspective and the study of aging. In Thomas M. Hess & Fredda Blanchard-Fields (Eds.), *Social cognition and aging* (2–15). San Diego, CA: Academic Press.

Blanchard-Fields, F., & Horhota, M. (2005). Age differences in the correspondence bias: When plausible explanation matters. *Journals of Gerontology: Psychological Sciences, 60B*, 259–267.

Blanchard-Fields, F., & Norris, L. (1994). Causal attributions from adolescence through adulthood: Age differences, ego level, and generalized response style. *Cognition and Aging, 1*, 67–86.

Braver, T. S., & West, R. (2008). Working memory, executive control, and aging. In F. I. M. Craik & T. A. Salthouse (Eds.),

The handbook of aging and cognition (3rd ed., pp. 311–372). New York: Psychology Press.

Bruine de Bruin, W., Parker, A. M., & Fischhoff, B. (2007). Individual differences in adult decision-making competence. *Journal of Personality and Social Psychology, 92*, 938–956.

Cabeza, R. (2002). Hemispheric asymmetry reduction in older adults: The HAROLD model. *Psychology and Aging, 17*, 85–100.

Cantor, N., & Kihlstrom, J. F. (1989). Social intelligence and cognitive assessments of personality. In R. S. Wyer, Jr & …K. Srull (Eds.), *Advances in social cognition* (vol. 2, pp. 1–59). Hillsdale, NJ: Lawrence Erlbaum Associates.

Carstensen, L. L., Isaacowitz, D. M., & Charles, S. T. (1999). Taking time seriously: A theory of socioemotional selectivity. *American Psychologist, 54*, 165–181.

Charness, N. (1981). Search in chess: Age and skill differences. *Journal of Experimental Psychology: Human Perception and Performance, 7*, 467–476.

Chen, Y. (2004). Age differences in correction of context-induced biases: Source monitoring and timing of accountability. *Aging, Neuropsychology and Cognition, 11*, 58–67.

Chen, Y., & Blanchard-Fields, F. (1997). Age differences in stages of attributional processing. *Psychology and Aging, 12*, 694–703.

Chen, Y., & Blanchard-Fields, F. (2000). Unwanted thought: Age differences in the correction of social judgments. *Psychology and Aging, 15*, 475–482.

Craik, F. I. M., & Anderson, N. D. (1999). Applying cognitive research to problems of aging. In D. Gopher, & A Koriat (eds.), *Attention and performance: Vol. XVII.Cognitive regulation of performance: Interaction of theory and application* (pp. 583–615). Cambridge, MA: MIT Press.

Bechara, A., Damasio, A. R., Damasio, H., & Anderson, S. W. (1994). Insensitivity to future consequences following damage to human prefrontal cortex. *Cognition, 50*, 7–15.

Denburg, N. L., Tranel, D., & Bechara, A. (2005). The ability to decide advantageously declines prematurely in some older persons. *Neuropsychologica, 43*, 1099–1106.

Denburg, N. L., Weller, K. L., Yamada, T. H., Shivapour, D. M., Kaup, A. R., LaLoggia, A., et al. (2009). Poor decision making among older adults is related to elevated levels of neuroticism. *Annals of Behavioral Medicine, 37*, 164–172.

Dijksterhuis, A., & Nordgren, L. F. (2006). A theory of unconscious thought. *Perspectives on Psychological Science, 1*, 95–109.

Ennis, G.E., Hess, T.M., & Smith, B.T. (2013). The Impact of age and motivation on cognitive effort: Implications for cognitive engagement in older adulthood. *Psychology and Aging, 28*, 495–504.

Finucane, M. L., Mertz, C. K., Slovic, P., & Schmidt, E. S. (2005). Task complexity and older adults" decision making competence. *Psychology and Aging, 20*, 71–84.

Fisk, A. D., & Rogers, W. A. (2000). Influence of training and experience on skill acquisition and maintenance in older adults. *Journal of Aging and Physical Activity, 8*, 373–378.

Fiske, S. T., & Neuberg, S. L. (1990). A continuum of impression formation, from category-based to individuating processes: Influences of information and motivation on attention and interpretation. In M. P. Zanna (Ed.), *Advances in experimental social psychology* (vol. 23, pp. 1–74). San Diego, CA: Academic.

Fiske, S. T., Cuddy, A. J. C., & Glick, P. S. (2007). Universal dimensions of social cognition: Warmth and competence. *Trends in Cognitive Sciences, 11*, 77–83.

Follett, K. J., & Hess, T. M. (2002). Aging, cognitive complexity, and the fundamental attribution error. *Journal of Gerontology: Psychological Sciences, 57B*, P312–P323.

Gendolla, G. H. E., & Wright, R. A. (2005). Motivation in social settings: Studies of effort-related cardiovascular arousal. In J. P. Forgas, K. Williams, & B. von Hippel (Eds.), Social motivation: Conscious and nonconscious processes. Cambridge University Press.

Germain, C. M., & Hess, T. M. (2007). Motivational influences on controlled processing: Moderating distractibility in older adults. *Aging, Neuropsychology, and Cognition, 14*, 462–486.

Gigerenzer, G. (2008). Why heuristics work. *Perspectives on Psychological Science, 3*, 20–29.

Gilbert, D., & Krull, D. S. (1988). Seeing less and knowing more: The benefits of perceptual ignorance. *Journal of Personality and Social Psychology, 54*, 193–202.

Gilbert, D., Pelham, B., & Krull, D. (1988). On cognitive busyness: When person perceivers meet persons perceived. *Journal of Personality and Social Psychology, 54*, 733–740.

Gold, P.E. (2005). Glucose and age-related changes in memory. *Neurobiology of Aging, 26S*, S60 – S64.

Hasher, L., & Zacks, R. T. (1988). Working memory, comprehension, and aging: A review and a new view. In G. H. Bower (Ed.), *The psychology of learning and motivation* (vol. 22, pp. 193–225). New York: Academic Press.

Hastie, R. (1984). Causes and effects of causal attribution. *Journal of Personality and Social Psychology, 46*, 44–56.

Henninger, D., Madden, D., & Huetel, S. (2010). Processing speed and memory mediate age-related differences in decision making. *Psychology and Aging, 25*, 262–270.

Hershey, D. A., Walsh, D. A., Read, S. J., & Chulef, A. S. (1990). The effects of expertise on financial problem solving: Evidence for goal-directed, problem-solving scripts. *Organizational Behavior and Human Decision Processes, 46*, 77–101.

Hess, T. M. (2006). Adaptive aspects of social cognitive functioning in adulthood: Age-related goal and knowledge influences. *Social Cognition, 24*, 279–309.

Hess, T.M. (2013). *Selective engagement of cognitive resources: adaptive processes in older adults' cognitive functioning.* Manuscript under review.

Hess, T. M., & Auman, C. (2001). Aging and social expertise: The impact of trait-diagnostic information on impressions of others. *Psychology and Aging, 16*, 497–510.

Hess, T. M., & Blanchard-Fields, F. (1999). *Social cognition and aging.* San Diego, CA: Academic Press.

Hess, T. M., Bolstad, C. A., Woodburn, S. M., & Auman, C. (1999). Trait diagnosticity versus behavioral consistency as determinants of impression change in adulthood. *Psychology and Aging, 14*, 77–89.

Hess, T. M., & Emery, L. (2012). Memory in context: The impact of age-related goals on performance. In M. Naveh-Benjamin & N. Ohta (Eds.), *Perspectives on memory and aging.* New York: Psychology Press.

Hess, T. M., Emery, L., & Neupert, S. (2012). Longitudinal relationships between resources, motivation, and functioning. *Journals of Gerontology, Series B: Psychological Sciences and Social Sciences, 67*, 299–308.

Hess, T.M., & Ennis, G. E. (2012). Age differences in the effort and cost associated with cognitive activity. *Journals of Gerontology, Series B: Psychological Sciences and Social Sciences, 67B*, 447–455.

Hess, T. M.,& Follett, K. J. (1994). Adult age differences in the use of schematic and episodic information in making social judgments. *Aging and Cognition, 1*, 54–66.

Hess, T. M., Follett, K. J., & McGee, K. A. (1998). Aging and impression formation: The impact of age-related differences in processing skills and goals. *Journal of Gerontology: Psychological Sciences, 53B,* P175–P187.

Hess, T. M., Germain, C. M., Rosenberg, D. C., Leclerc, C. M., & Hodges, E. A. (2005). Aging-related selectivity and susceptibility to irrelevant affective information in the construction of attitudes. *Aging, Neuropsychology, and Cognition, 12,* 149–174.

Hess, T. M., Germain, C. M., Swaim, E. L., & Osowski, N. L. (2009). Aging and selective engagement: The moderating impact of motivation on older adults' resource utilization. *Journals of Gerontology, Series B: Psychological Sciences and Social Sciences, 64B,* 447–456.

Hess, T. M., & Kotter-Grühn, D. (2011). Social knowledge and goal-based influences on social information processing in adulthood. *Psychology and Aging, 26,* 792–802.

Hess, T. M., Leclerc, C. M., Swaim, E., & Weatherbee, S. R. (2009). Aging and everyday judgments: The impact of motivational and processing resource factors. *Psychology and Aging, 24,* 735–740.

Hess, T. M., McGee, K. A., Woodburn, S. M., & Bolstad, C. A. (1998). Age-related priming effects in social judgments. *Psychology and Aging, 13,* 127–137.

Hess, T. M., Osowski, N. L., & Leclerc, C. M. (2005). Age differences in sensitivity to diagnostic cues and the flexibility of social judgments. *Psychology and Aging, 20,* 447–459.

Hess, T. M., & Pullen, S. M. (1994). Adult age differences in impression change processes. *Psychology and Aging, 9,* 237–250.

Hess, T. M., Pullen, S. M., & McGee, K. A. (1996). The acquisition of prototype-based information about social groups in adulthood. *Psychology and Aging, 11,* 179–190.

Hess, T. M., Queen, T. L., & Patterson, T. (2012). To deliberate or not to deliberate: Interactions between age, task characteristics, and cognitive activity on decision making. *Journal of Behavioral Decision Making, 25,* 29–40.

Hess, T. M., Rosenberg, D. C., & Waters, S. J. (2001). Motivation and representational processes in adulthood: The effects of social accountability and information relevance. *Psychology and Aging, 16,* 629–642.

Hess, T. M., & Tate, C. S. (1991). Adult age differences in explanations and memory for behavioral information. *Psychology and Aging, 6,* 86–92.

Horhota, M., & Blanchard-Fields, F. (2006). Do beliefs and attributional complexity influence age differences in the correspondence bias? *Social Cognition, 24,* 310–337.

Jacoby, L. L. (1998). Invariance in automatic influences of memory: Toward a user's guide for the process-dissociation procedure. *Journal of Experimental Psychology: Learning, Memory, & Cognition, 24,* 3–26.

Johnson, M. M. (1990). Age differences in decision making: A process methodology for examining strategic information processing. *Journals of Gerontology, 45,* 75–78.

Johnson, M. M. (1993). Thinking about strategies during, before, and after making a decision. *Psychology and Aging, 8,* 231–241.

Johnson, M. M. S., & Drungle, S. C. (2000). Purchasing over the counter medication: The influence of age and familiarity. *Experimental Aging Research, 26,* 245–261.

Jones, E. E., & Davis, K. E. (1965). From acts to dispositions: The attribution process in person perception. In L. Berkowitz (Ed.), *Advances in experimental social psychology* (vol. 2, pp. 220–266). New York: Academic Press.

Jones, E., & Harris, V. (1967). The attribution of attitudes. *Journal of Experimental Social Psychology, 3,* 1–24.

Judd, C. A., James-Hawkins, L., Yzerbyt, V., & Kashima, Y. (2005). Fundamental dimensions of social judgment: Understanding the relations between judgments of competence and warmth. *Journal of Personality and Social Psychology, 89,* 899–913.

Kim, S., & Hasher, L. (2005). The attraction effect in decision making: Superior performance by older adults. *Quarterly Journal of Experimental Psychology A: Human Experimental Psychology, 58A,* 120–133.

Kovalchik, S., Camerer, C. F., Grether, D. M., Plott, C. R., & Allman, J. M. (2005). Aging and decision making: A comparison between neurologically healthy elderly and young individuals. *Journal of Economic Behavior and Organization, 58,* 79–94.

Labouvie-Vief, G., Chiodo, L., Goguen, L., Diehl, M., & Orwoll, L. (1995). Representations of self across the life span. *Psychology and Aging, 10,* 404–415.

Leclerc, C. M., & Hess, T. M. (2007). Age differences in the bases for social judgments: Tests of a social expertise perspective. *Experimental Aging Research, 33,* 95–120.

Löckenhoff, C. E., & Carstensen, L. L. (2008). Decision strategies in health care choices for self and others: Older but not younger adults make adjustments for the age of the decision target. *Journals of Gerontology, Series B: Psychological Sciences and Social Sciences, 63B,* P106–P109.

MacPherson, S. E., Phillips, L. H., & Della Sala, S. (2002). Age, executive functioning, and social decision making: A dorsolateral prefrontal theory of cognitive aging. *Psychology and Aging, 17,* 598–609.

Mata, R., & Nunes, L. (2010). When less is enough: Cognitive aging, information search, and decision quality in consumer choice. *Psychology and Aging, 25,* 289–298.

Mata, R., Schooler, L., & Rieskamp, J. (2007). The aging decision maker: Cognitive aging and the adaptive selection of decision strategies. *Psychology and Aging, 22,* 796–810.

Mather, M., & Carstensen, L. L. (2005). Aging and motivated cognition: The positivity effect in attention and memory. *Trends in Cognitive Sciences, 9,* 496–502.

Mayhorn, C. B, Fisk, A. D., Whittle, J.D. (2002). Decisions, decisions: Analysis of age, cohort, and time of testing on framing risky decision options. *Human Factors, 44,* 515–521.

Metcalfe, J., & Mischel, W. (1999). A hot/cool-system analysis of delay of gratification: Dynamics of will power. *Psychological Review, 106,* 3–19.

Meyer, B. J. F., Talbot, A. P., & Ranalli, C. (2007). Why older adults make more immediate treatment decisions about cancer than younger adults. *Psychology and Aging, 22,* 505–524.

Mikels, J., Löckenhoff, C. E., Maglio, S., Carstensen, L. L., Goldstein, M., & Garber, A. (2010). Following your heart or your head: Focusing on emotions versus information differentially influences the decision of younger and older adults. *Journal of Experimental Psychology: Applied, 16,* 87–95.

Neupert, S. D., Soederberg, L. M., & Lachman, M. E. (2006). Physiological reactivity to cognitive stressors: Variations by age and socioeconomic status. *International Journal of Aging and Human Development, 62,* 221–235.

Pachur, T., Mata, R., & Schooler, L. J. (2009). Cognitive aging and the adaptive use of the recognition in decision making. *Psychology and Aging, 24,* 901–915.

Payne, J. W., & Bettman, J. R. (2004). Walking with the scarecrow: The information processing approach to decision research. In N. Harvey and D. Koehler (Eds.), *Blackwell handbook of judgment and decision making* (pp. 110–132). Oxford, UK: Blackwell.

Peeters, G., & Czapinski, J. (1990). Positive-negative asymmetry in evaluations: The distinction between affective and informational negativity effects. In M. Hewstone & W. Stroebe (Eds.), *European review of social psychology* (vol. *1*, pp. 33–60). Chichester, UK: Wiley.

Peters, E., Hess, T. M., Västfjäll, D., & Auman, C. (2007). Adult age differences in dual information processes and their influence on judgments and decisions: A review. *Perspectives on Psychological Science, 2*, 1–23.

Queen, T. L., & Hess, T. M. (2010). Age differences in the effects of conscious and unconscious thought in decision-making. *Psychology and Aging, 25*, 251–261.

Queen, T. L., Hess, T. M., Ennis, G. E., Dowd, K., & Grühn, D. (2012). Search characteristics in a decision-making task: Age, complexity, and strategy. *Psychology and Aging. 27*, 817–824.

Riggle, E. D. B., & Johnson, M. M. S. (1996). Age differences in political decision making: Strategies for evaluating political candidates. *Political Behavior, 18*, 33–43.

Rönnlund, M., Karlsson, E., Laggnäs, E., Larsson, L., & Lindström, T. (2005). Risky decision making across three arenas of choice: Are young and older adults differentially susceptible to framing effects? *Journal of General Psychology, 132*, 81–92.

Ross, L. (1977). The intuitive psychologist and his shortcomings: Distortions in the attribution process. In L. Berkowitz (Ed.), *Advances in experimental social psychology* (vol. *10*, pp. 174–221). New York: Academic Press.

Salthouse, T. A. (1996). The processing speed theory of adult age differences in cognition. *Psychological Review, 103*, 403–428.

Seeman, T. E., & Robbins, R. J. (1994). Aging and hypothalamic-pituitary-adrenal response to challenge in humans. Endocrinology Review, 15, 233–260.

Shiota, M. N., & Levenson, R. W. (2009). Effects of aging on experimentally instructed detached reappraisal, positive reappraisal, and emotional behavior suppression. *Psychology and Aging, 24*, 890–900.

Skowronski, J. J., & Carlston, D. E. (1987). Social judgment and social memory: the role of cue diagnosticity in negativity, positivity, and extremity biases. *Journal of Personality and Social Psychology, 52*, 689–99.

Skowronski, J. J., & Carlston, D. E. (1989). Negativity and extremity biases in impression formation: A review of explanations. *Psychological Bulletin, 105*, 131–142

Srull, T. K., & Wyer, R. S. (1989). Person memory and judgment. *Psychological Review, 96*, 58–83.

Stanley, J. T., & Blanchard-Fields, F. (2011). Beliefs about behavior account for age differences in the correspondence bias. *Journals of Gerontology: Psychological Sciences, 66B*, 169–176.

Stephens, E. C., & Johnson, M. M. S. (2000). Dr. Mom and other influences on younger and older adults" OTC medication purchases. *Journal of Applied Gerontology, 19*, 441–459.

Strough, J., Mehta, C. M., McFall, J. P., & Schuller, K. L. (2008). Are older adults less subject to the sunk-costs fallacy than younger adults? *Psychological Science, 19*, 650–652.

Strough, J., Schlosnagle, L., & DiDonato, L. (2011). Understanding decisions about sunk costs from older and younger adults' perspectives. *Journals of Gerontology, Series B: Psychological Sciences and Social Sciences, 66B*, P681–P686.

Streufert, S., Pogash, R., Piasecki, M., & Post, G. M. (1990). Age and management team performance. *Psychology and Aging, 5*, 551–559.

Tentori, K., Osherson, D., Hasher, L., & May, C. (2001). Wisdom and aging: Irrational preferences in college students but not older adults. *Cognition, 81*, 87–86.

Tetlock, P. E. (1985). Accountability: A social check on the fundamental attribution error. *Social Psychology Quarterly, 48*, 227–236.

Tversky, A., & Kahneman, D. (1981). The framing of decisions and the psychology of choice. *Science, 211*, 453–458.

West, R. L. (1996). An application of prefrontal cortex function theory to cognitive aging. *Psychological Bulletin, 120*, 272–292.

Wojciszke, B. (1997). Parallels between competence—versus morality-related traits and individualistic versus collectivistic values. *European Journal of Social Psychology, 27*, 245–256.

Wojciszke, B., & Abele, A. E. (2008). The primacy of communion over agency and its reversals in evaluations. *European Journal of Social Psychology, 38*, 1139–1147.

Wojciszke, B., Brycz, H., & Borkenau, P. (1993). Effects of information content and evaluative extremity on positivity and negativity biases. *Journal of Personality and Social Psychology, 64*, 327–335

Wood, S., Busemeyer, J., Koling, A., Cox, C. R., & Davis, H. (2005). Older adults as adaptive decision makers: Evidence from the Iowa Gambling Task. *Psychology and Aging, 20*, 220–225.

Woodhead, E. L., Lynch, E. B., & Edelstein, B. (2011). Decisional strategy determines whether frame influences treatment preferences for medical decisions. *Psychology and Aging, 26*, 285–294.

Wisdom and Emotions

Monika Ardelt *and* Michel Ferrari

Abstract

This chapter explores the paradoxical relationship between wisdom and emotions. Whereas a wise philosopher is considered knowledgeable but dispassionate, an Eastern sage cares deeply about others and exudes positive emotions. However, since emotions are vital signals to ourselves and others, both types of wisdom necessarily involve emotion. Specific emotions depend on specific cognitive scenarios and how they implicate us in our own personal projects, whether they are emotional reactions that urge immediate change or long-term emotional sentiments that sustain our positive and negative commitments to others. Emotions make experience memorable and also invite reflection on the commitments they imply. The chapter's findings agree with Blanchard-Fields and Norris who, in 1995, pointed out that wisdom necessitates the integration of emotion and cognition to develop toward self-awareness, self-transcendence, and wholeness—leading wise people to promote a good life for themselves and their communities.

Key Words: wisdom, emotions, cognition, reflection, mindfulness, compassion, emotion regulation, narrative, self-transcendence, personal identity

Voici mon secret. Il est très simple: on ne voit bien qu'avec le coeur.
L'essentiel est invisible pour les yeux.
[Here is my secret. It is very simple: one sees well only with the heart. The essential is invisible to the eyes.]
— Antoine de Saint Exupéry (*Le Petit Prince*, 1943, chapter 21)

Wisdom appears to have a paradoxical relationship with emotion, producing two conflicting images of a wise person. The first is the image of a wise philosopher or scholar who knows about the deeper meaning of life, dispenses wise advice to those who seek it, and knows what to do in any conceivable situation. In fact, one of the most prominent conceptualizations of wisdom, the *Berlin Wisdom Paradigm*, treats wisdom as expert knowledge or expertise in the fundamental pragmatics of life related to life meaning and conduct, including life management, life planning, and life review (Baltes & Smith, 2008; Baltes,

Smith, Staudinger, & Sowarka, 1990; Baltes & Staudinger, 2000; Smith, Dixon, & Baltes, 1989). This image of a wise person is dominated by rational and analytic cognition and the absence of emotions that might bias thought or decision-making processes (Curnow, 1999; Keltner & Gross, 1999). Yet the second image that might come to mind is that of a wise sage who not only knows as much as the wise philosopher/scholar does but also cares deeply about others and exudes positive emotions, such as love, sympathy, compassion, and goodwill. This image of a wise person is also close to the conceptualization of wisdom in the East, where the emphasis is not only on knowledge but also on self-insight, intuition, and compassion (Birren & Svensson, 2005; Jeste & Vahia, 2008; Ñanamoli, 2001; Takahashi & Overton, 2005). In fact, according to the Eastern wisdom tradition, wisdom-related knowledge cannot be gained by the intellect alone but requires the development of intuition and compassion (Clayton & Birren, 1980).

If researchers ask lay persons for their implicit definitions of wisdom, a similar split occurs. In the West, some people define wisdom in predominantly cognitive terms, as a combination of knowledge, understanding, and life experiences, whereas others perceive wisdom as an integration of cognitive, reflective, and affective features that also includes acceptance of others, empathy, orientation toward goodness, and love for humanity (Clayton & Birren, 1980; Glück & Bluck, 2011). In the East, people tend to adopt the integrative view of wisdom, comprising knowledge, benevolence, compassion, openness, profundity, modesty, and unobtrusiveness (Takahashi & Bordia, 2000; Yang, 2001).

How can we solve this paradox? Might there be different types of wisdom or different types of emotions? Both wisdom researchers and lay people tend to agree that wisdom contains cognitive and reflective dimensions. There is less consensus, however, whether an affective dimension is an integral part of wisdom (Ardelt, 2004). This chapter will try to solve the paradox by showing that the development of the cognitive wisdom dimension necessitates the transcendence of basic emotional reactions through the reflective dimension of wisdom. Yet, through the transcendence of the self, a selfless compassionate concern for others arises that is not a fleeting emotion but represents a long-term emotional sentiment, expressed through one's conduct in life.

Emotion (or *affect*, we will use these terms synonymously) can be understood in several ways, which might explain part of the paradox. For the purposes of this chapter, we will use Oatley's (2004, 2012) definition of emotions as vital signals to ourselves and others about what matters most to us; they urge us to act. More specifically, emotions signal relations between personal plans and events in the world. To use an image from Oatley (2012, p. 36), emotions are "compass-readings of our lives"—they invite the question, "to what direction is this emotion pointing?" In this sense, emotions not only make experience memorable, they also invite reflection on that experience.

According to Wierzbicka (1999), six main cognitive scenarios are implicated in emotions: (1) "something good happened" (e.g., joy), (2) "something bad happened" (e.g., sadness or grief), (3) "something bad can/will happen" (e.g., fear or anxiety), (4) "I don't want things like this to happen" (e.g., anger), (5) "thinking about other people" (e.g., compassion or envy), and (6) "thinking about ourselves" (e.g., shame or remorse). Moreover, emotions have different time horizons. Some emotions (what some call "basic emotions") are immediate reactions—for example, the psychological and physical experience of anger, sadness, or joy. Other emotions (what Oatley [2004] calls sentiments) signal long-term emotional stances that orient and sustain our commitments to others, either as positive commitments, like the love of one's child or family, or as negative commitments, like an enduring disappointment or the hostility one feels toward someone.

In 1995, Fredda Blanchard-Fields and Lisa Norris (p. 105) warned us not to equate wisdom with knowledge because "wisdom is not simply one aspect of knowledge, but knowledge is only one aspect of wisdom." They emphasized that wisdom and maturity require the integration of emotion and cognition to grow in consciousness and awareness and, ultimately, reach a stage of self-transcendence and wholeness (Blanchard-Fields & Norris, 1995). We attempt to outline the steps of this journey in this chapter.

Cognitive Wisdom Dimension

Both lay persons and wisdom experts consider knowledge an essential element of wisdom. For example, the Berlin Wisdom Paradigm defines wisdom as expert knowledge in the meaning and conduct of life (Baltes & Smith, 2008; Baltes & Staudinger, 2000), which includes rich factual knowledge about life matters and the human condition, rich procedural knowledge about dealing with problems of life meaning and conduct, knowledge about the contexts of life and how these change over time, knowledge of value relativism, which considers the relativism of values and life goals, and knowledge about the management of uncertainty in life (Baltes & Smith, 2008; Baltes & Staudinger, 2000; Staudinger & Baltes, 1996). Recently, Staudinger (Mickler & Staudinger, 2008; Staudinger, Dörner, & Mickler, 2005) has distinguished general from personal wisdom-related knowledge, in which personal wisdom is experienced in the first person and general wisdom from the third-person point of view. Similarly, the cognitive dimension of Ardelt's (1997,

2003) three-dimensional wisdom model (3D-WM) refers to a desire to know the truth and gain deeper knowledge about the intrapersonal and interpersonal aspects of life (Ardelt, 2000*b*; Blanchard-Fields & Norris, 1995; Kekes, 1983; Osbeck & Robinson, 2005). This includes knowledge and acceptance of the positive and negative aspects of human nature (including one's own being), of the inherent limits of knowledge, and of life's unpredictability and uncertainties. Sternberg's (1998, p. 347) balance theory of wisdom defines wisdom as the application of tacit (i.e., enacted, not necessarily conceptualized) knowledge that balances intrapersonal, interpersonal, and extrapersonal interests to adapt to or shape existing environments or to select new environments. Lay people have also described wisdom consisting of knowledge, life knowledge, self-knowledge, exceptional understanding, understanding of others, judgment, and insight (Bluck & Glück, 2005; Brown, 2004; Clayton & Birren, 1980; Holliday & Chandler, 1986; Montgomery, Barber, & McKee, 2002; Sternberg, 1990). To gain this kind of knowledge and deep insight into human affairs and to make judgments and decisions based on this knowledge, wise people first need to overcome self-serving and egocentric emotions.

The Attainment of Wisdom-Related Knowledge

Because wisdom-related knowledge concerns either one's own person or one's relations with other people or the world in general, it is inherently personal, applied, and involved rather than theoretical, abstract, and detached (Ardelt, 2000*b*; Clayton, 1982; Dittmann-Kohli & Baltes, 1990; Holliday & Chandler, 1986; Kramer, 1990; Strijbos, 1995; Taranto, 1989). It is knowledge related to the ultimate questions in life, such as "What is the meaning and purpose of life?" and "How should I best live my life?" (Blanchard-Fields & Norris, 1995; Clayton & Birren, 1980; Csikszentmihalyi & Rathunde, 1990; Kupperman, 2005). Therefore, pure intellectual or theoretical knowledge is not sufficient for wisdom (Ardelt, 2000*b*, 2004). In fact, Kekes (1983) argued that wise individuals do not necessarily know more facts than other people but that they understand the significance and deeper meaning of generally known facts, such as "humans are mortal" or proverbs such as the Golden Rule. Hence, wisdom requires experiential or tacit knowledge that can only be gained through a willingness to learn from experiences and be transformed in the process (Ardelt, 2005; Moody, 1986; Sternberg, 1998). As such, wisdom-related

knowledge cannot be devoid of emotions, as scientific, intellectual, and theoretical knowledge might be. Without emotion, knowledge is abstract and not personally vital. Yet, as has been argued by Greek philosophers as well as Christian and Eastern mystics (Curnow, 1999), certain emotions, such as greed, pride, fear, anxiety, anger, resentment, jealousy, or depression, bias cognitive appraisal and will not allow a person to "see through illusion" (McKee & Barber, 1999) to perceive reality clearly (Keltner & Gross, 1999; Pascual-Leone, 2000). Based on our earlier discussion of emotions, it seems clear that what is at stake is the kind of cognitive scenario one implicitly or explicitly engages when interpreting a situation that determines whether that emotion is to be mastered or simply provides a compass direction to orient toward good actions that promote better quality of life.

In general, humans have the tendency to blame others or external circumstances for their own or their in-group's failures and attribute successes to their own skills and abilities (Bradley, 1978; Hewstone, 1990; Sherwood, 1981). Failures result in cognitive scenarios that might generate feelings of resentment, bitterness, anger, jealousy, or depression, whereas successes might evoke feelings of pride, superiority, greed, and elation. Subjective scenarios and projections prevent people from seeing the truth about the relationship among themselves, others, and the world around them (Kramer, 1990; Levenson & Aldwin, 2014). According to Weinsheimer (1985, pp. 165–166), "Understanding always involves projecting oneself. What we understand therefore is ourselves, and thus how we understand ourselves has an effect on everything else we understand." Hence, an important step in the development of wisdom is to become aware of unconscious subjective scenarios and projections and the related emotions that are triggered by them, which bias perceptions and our interpretation of phenomena and events (Blanchard-Fields & Norris, 1995; Kramer, 1990). Through the cultivation of awareness, it becomes possible to understand the deeper causes of those emotions, facilitating their regulation and ultimately their transcendence so that a more objective reality can be perceived (Hart, 1987). To achieve this awareness, regulation, and transcendence of self-centered emotions necessitates the reflective dimension of wisdom.

Wise Judgment and Decision Making

All judgments and decisions that are deemed wise contain elements of uncertainty. Whereas much intellectual and scientific knowledge involves decisions in which all the parameters are known, wisdom-related knowledge is required for judgments and decisions under conditions of uncertainty (Ardelt, 2000*b*; Baltes & Smith, 2008; Baltes & Staudinger, 2000; Staudinger & Baltes, 1996). In fact, Brugman (2000) defines wisdom as expertise in handling the cognitive, emotional, and behavioral aspects of uncertainty. Wise persons realize the limits of their knowledge and the fact that the more they know, the more they are aware of the uncharted territory that is as yet unknown (Ardelt, Achenbaum, & Oh, 2014; Arlin, 1990). Yet wise individuals are not paralyzed by anxiety or doubt when they have to make important life decisions that involve uncertainty, such as with whom to share their life, which career path to pursue, and how best to balance intrapersonal, interpersonal, and extrapersonal interests to maximize the good for all (Kramer, 1990; Sternberg, 1998). Because wise persons see reality more clearly, they can discern the right course of action without being derailed by emotional reactions, such as anxieties, fears, impulses, passions, and desires (Curnow, 1999; Kunzmann, 2004). For example, lustful passions might interfere when selecting a mate, or greed for money, power, fame, or prestige might impede the pursuit of the common good when choosing a career or deciding the fate of others in one's profession. Even the fear of death has no power over wise individuals, as the examples of many martyrs show who continued to do what they perceived to be right and just rather than back down in the face of danger. Wise people know what to do because they are able to stay calm and present in the flow of the moment (Csikszentmihalyi, Abuhamdeh, & Nakamura, 2005; Csikszentmihalyi & Nakamura, 2010), what Tolle (2004) has called *The Power of NOW*. For example, in a qualitative study that asked college students to describe the characteristics of persons they considered wise rather than knowledgeable or intelligent (Ardelt, 2008*a*, p. 86), one student explained that

> I also associate a certain degree of calmness with wisdom. The wise person can weather the storm without losing his head. My father has always exemplified this trait, amazing me with his ability to think rationally even under the most unnerving circumstances.

The development of this mindful presence is accomplished through the reflective wisdom dimension.

Reflective Wisdom Dimension

Ardelt's (1997, 2003) 3D-WM defines the reflective dimension of wisdom as perceiving phenomena and events from multiple perspectives without a self-serving bias that might ignore unpleasant truths. Reflective thinking enables wise individuals to uncover the deeper causes of phenomena and events and comprehend the complex and sometimes contradictory nature of human behavior (Clayton, 1982; Csikszentmihalyi & Rathunde, 1990; Labouvie-Vief, 1990; Staudinger et al., 2005). This includes emotional intelligence (Goleman, 1995; Zacher, McKenna, & Rooney, in press), consisting of empathy or interpersonal intelligence, which is the ability to recognize other people's emotions and respond appropriately, but also intrapersonal intelligence, that is, the ability to look at oneself from an outside perspective through self-reflection and self-examination (Gardner, 1983), which results in self-insight, self-knowledge, and a reduction in self-centeredness (Csikszentmihalyi & Nakamura, 2005). Through the practice of mindful self-reflection and self-examination, wise individuals become aware, understand, and regulate their immediate emotional reactions and, ultimately, transcend their subjectivities and projections to see through the illusion of isolated selfhood (Gowans, 2003; Kekes, 1995; Kramer, 2000; Levitt, 1999; McKee & Barber, 1999; Sternberg, 1998). Because wise individuals do not view phenomena and events from a self-centered perspective and are able to accept reality "as it is" (Maslow, 1970), they are more likely to be grateful than embittered when they look back at their life (Glück, 2011).

Emotion Regulation

Wisdom researchers generally agree that wise individuals have learned to regulate their emotional reactions (Blanchard-Fields & Norris, 1995; Kunzmann & Baltes, 2003*a*; Labouvie-Vief & Medler, 2002; Webster, 2003, 2007). They have developed the skill to recognize and down-regulate their emotional reactions so that these emotions do not harm themselves or others (Csikszentmihalyi & Nakamura, 2005; Kunzmann, 2004). Consequently, they are more likely to sustain an affective stance that is peaceful, calm, and contented than exuberant, angry, or depressed (Hart, 1987; Kunzmann & Baltes, 2005). For example, wisdom-related knowledge was inversely related to the experience of both negative emotional reactions, such as being angry, afraid, hostile, sad, or disappointed, and also positive emotional reactions, such a being exuberant, happy, proud, amused, and cheerful (Kunzmann & Baltes, 2003b). Similarly, one student described his wise grandfather as follows (Ardelt, 2008a, p. 85):

> [One] reason I consider my grandfather to be wise is his composure. He is always very even keeled and I have never honestly seen him get worked up about anything. Even at times of absolute joy all one sees is a very satisfied smile. I believe that this is an important mark of wisdom as he understands that there is always going to be good and bad events in one's life and that fussing about it changes nothing. Furthermore, he is able to live by this in addition to understanding it. The balance he lives his life by is ultimately the reason I consider him to be wise.

Seeing events from multiple perspectives and taking the views of others into account tend to result in long-term emotional sentiments of tolerance and patience, which function as an antidote to negative emotional reactions of anger and hatred, leading to a calm and peaceful state of mind (Dalai Lama & Cutler, 1998; Levenson, Aldwin, & Cupertino, 2001). However, this does not mean that the wise will ignore or suppress negative emotional reactions if they arise. On the contrary, through self-awareness and self-observation, wise individuals are able to acknowledge their emotional reactions without further reacting to them (Hart, 1987). In particular, the practice of mindfulness and mindfulness meditation seems be one mechanism that enables individuals to observe and ultimately transcend emotional reactions of anger, hatred, anxiety, and depression (Barbieri, 1997; Farb et al., 2010; Grabovac, Lau, & Willett, 2011; Kabat-Zinn, 2003; Speca, Carlson, Goodey, & Angen, 2000). In fact, one empirical study found that wisdom, assessed by Ardelt's (2003) Three-Dimensional Wisdom Scale 3D-WS, consisting of cognitive, reflective, and compassionate (affective) wisdom dimensions, was positively related to mindfulness (Beaumont, 2011).

According to the teachings of the Buddha, emotional reactions are difficult to observe mindfully, but it is possible to learn how to observe their underlying bodily sensations with awareness and equanimity (Hart, 1987). By not reacting to these sensations with desire or aversion, the sensations gradually lose their strength and the accompanying emotions will pass. Reacting to emotions and sensations, by contrast, intensifies the emotions and increases suffering. As the Buddha explained, freedom from emotional suffering is directly related to seeing reality more clearly—or, to put it another way, to creating cognitive scenarios that are more

relational and accepting of impermanence. For example, people tend to react with anger and even hatred if they imagine a scenario in which their plans (considered in isolation of others and circumstances) have been frustrated, or they have been treated unfairly. With this anger, their body temperature and blood pressure rise, which might cause them to shout, scream, or even fight, thus intensifying their anger. Anger and hatred, in turn, cloud people's judgments and prevent them from making the right decisions. As the Dalai Lama (Dalai Lama & Cutler, 1998, p. 250) remarked:

> When such intense anger and hatred arises, it obliterates the best part of your brain, which is the ability to judge between right and wrong, and the long-term and short-term consequences of your actions. Your power of judgment becomes totally inoperable; it can no longer function. It is almost like you have become insane. So, this anger and hatred tends to throw you into a state of confusion, which just serves to make your problems and difficulties much worse.

The emotional appraisal implied here is egocentric—the focus is on the self and not on the relationship between self and other. If, however, people manage to observe their bodily agitation with detachment and equanimity when they feel anger arising, they are less likely to succumb to their anger, blood pressure will return to normal, the body will relax, and they can perceive the whole situation more objectively and thus devise a course of action that is beneficial for all of the parties involved.

For example, in a qualitative study on how wise people cope with crises and obstacles in their lives (Ardelt, 2005, p. 12), a wise older man explained how emotion regulation enables him to stay in control:

> I've had as much bad things to happen as good things, but I've never allowed any outside force to take possession of my being.... Every time something happens, I say where does that feeling come from? If it comes from within you, then you need to handle it. You can handle it. I can't make you angry. You get angry. I can't make you embarrassed. You get embarrassed. (laughing)...I mean, it's silly, but you think of it, if it is a feeling that comes from within, I am responsible to control it.

In this way, emotion regulation is inherently related to implicit cognitive scenarios of reality. When emotions take over, cognitive scenarios become biased, causing individuals to react blindly rather than wisely. Of course, wise persons who habitually engage in reflective thinking might become aware of their biased cognitive scenarios earlier and make a conscious effort to attune them more to reality, which allows them to be less affected by negative emotions because they can understand the other party's point of view (Zacher et al., in press) or perceive the larger picture. Because wise people are aware of the uncertainties in life, they do not dwell on negative events, but try to make the best of every situation (Ardelt, 2005). Self-reflection and self-honesty also tend to reduce fears and anxieties that others might expose one's weaknesses (Dalai Lama & Cutler, 1998). It appears that wise individuals have learned to master the inner world through the development of a more stable affective stance of equanimity, irrespective of external circumstances (Assmann, 1994; Hanna & Ottens, 1995).

Transcendence of Subjectivity and Projections Through Emotional Suffering

One way to transcend biased subjective scenarios and projections is through mindful awareness and self-reflection, but another pathway is through enduring crises and hardships in life (Kramer, 1990; Pascual-Leone, 2000; Randall & Kenyon, 2001). In fact, the First Noble Truth of the Buddha's teaching is that life is suffering:

> Now this, *bhikkhus*, is the noble truth of suffering: birth is suffering, aging is suffering, illness is suffering, death is suffering; union with what is displeasing is suffering; separation from what is pleasing is suffering; not to get what one wants is suffering; in brief, the five aggregates subject to clinging are suffering. (Samyutta Nikāya 56.11, cited in Gowans, 2003, p. 31)

Indeed, one of the insights that wisdom brings is the awareness that life is complex, uncertain, and fragile and often consists of suffering (Csikszentmihalyi & Nakamura, 2005; Staudinger & Kunzmann, 2005). The Buddha's Second Noble Truth is that desires and aversions are the underlying reasons for emotional suffering. A person who sees through the illusion of subjectivity and projections recognizes that we suffer because we often cannot get what we desire or because things happen to us that we do not want. Even if we get what we desire, it will not stay with us forever due to the ever-changing nature and impermanence of life (Gowans, 2003; Hart, 1987; Rosch, 2014). Yet the Buddha also contended (as his Third Noble Truth) that the realization that life is suffering can act as

a motivating force to search for the path of liberation from all suffering and greater wisdom.[1] A similar insight seems to inform Pascual-Leone's (2000, p. 247) claim that ultimate limit situations can promote the development of wisdom.

> [*U*]*ltimate limit situations* that cannot be undone and are nonetheless faced with consciousness and resolve—situations like death, illness, aging, irremediable oppression or loss, extreme poverty, rightful resistance or rebellion, guilt, absolute failure, danger, uncontrollable fear, etc., lead to the natural emergence of a transcendental self, if they do not destroy the person first. (emphasis in the original)

For most people, ultimate limit situations (and the realization that life necessarily involves suffering) will evoke feelings of distress, anguish, anger, or depression. However, they also provide an opportunity for the transcendence of subjectivity and projections and, hence, growth in wisdom. Suffering might prompt individuals to examine their life thoroughly and to construct cognitive scenarios from an outside perspective, helping them to see reality and their own situation more clearly, which might result in a change in life priorities, a reduction of selfcenteredness, stress-related growth, and, ultimately, increased wisdom and a more meaningful life (Bianchi, 1994; Kramer, 1990; Linley, 2003; Martin & Kleiber, 2005; Park, Cohen, & Murch, 1996)).

For example, chronic pain patients recounted how, through reflection and self-reflection, they came to accept their situation, learned to cope with it, and experienced a transformation of their personality by growing in humility, gratitude, (self-) compassion, spirituality, and wisdom (Plews-Ogan, Owens, & May, 2012). More specifically, chronic pain patients learned to accept and observe their pain without reacting to it, which decreased their emotional suffering and helped them to become more compassionate and less self-centered. As one pain patient recalled,

> There have been certain times in my life when I've experience pain, and you want to go "No, no, no" to the pain. That just increases the pain. But the more you can accept it, first mentally, and then start using different techniques, the more you find the pain subsiding. So you have to surrender to it if you want to get through it.... The more you fight it, the worse it becomes, because not only are you having a physical experience, now you're having a mental and emotional experience, which seems to increase the negative physical experience. So if you're able to

surrender, it's as if you're telling yourself, *Yes. I am most definitely in pain right now, but mentally and emotionally I'm fine.* (pp. 51–52, emphasis in original)

Similarly, older wisdom nominees of low and moderate financial means reported that they had learned valuable life lessons through crises and hardships in their lives, such as how to maintain a positive attitude in adversity through acceptance, perseverance, forgiveness, patience, and gratitude (Choi & Landeros, 2011). Older adults who were rated and scored relatively high on wisdom characteristics also told that coping with past adversity had helped them to learn how to use mental distancing to reflect on a stressful situation and stay calm, to engage in active coping to mentally reframe and/ or take physical control of the situation, and to apply the lessons gained from previous life experiences, such as the awareness and acceptance of life's unpredictability and uncertainty, to new crises and hardships in life (Ardelt, 2005). Moreover, studies of middle-aged and young-old adults found that the encounter with a life-threatening event, such as a serious illness, accident, or medical intervention, often led to renewed appreciation of life, a deeper sense of meaning and spirituality, and greater love, caring, and compassion for others (Ardelt, Ai, & Eichenberger, 2008; Kinnier, Tribbensee, Rose, & Vaughan, 2001). In fact, wise individuals are able to find meaning in suffering rather than submitting to despair. Instead of resigning themselves to their fate and "giving up," they have learned to "give in" and "go with the flow" (Randall & Kenyon, 2001, p. 30), to open themselves to life's lessons.

Facing death, in particular, either one's own or that of a loved one, can trigger emotional reactions of fear, dread, anguish, anger, sadness, isolation, alienation, loneliness, grief, hopelessness, helplessness, frustration, guilt, and/or depression (Attig, 1995). Yet people might also develop long-term emotional sentiments that help them to understand the deeper meaning of the finitude of life and how to live one's life accordingly. According to Kekes (1983, p. 280),

The significance of death is not merely that it puts an end to one's projects, but also that one's projects should be selected and pursued in the light of the knowledge that this will happen.... What a wise man knows... is how to construct a pattern that, given the human situation, is likely to lead to a good life.

Erikson (1964, p. 133) remarked that wisdom is "detached concern with life itself in the face of death itself." Paradoxically, by accepting the finality of life,

wise individuals live life more meaningfully (Ardelt et al., 2008; Kekes, 1983). For example, in a study of older community residents, hospice patients, and nursing home residents (Ardelt, 2007), wisdom was positively related to purpose in life and negatively to death anxiety and death avoidance. Yet wisdom was also inversely correlated with cognitive scenarios in which death is considered an escape from a dreadful existence. Wise older persons continue to cherish life even as they are unafraid of death. As the terminally ill Morrie Schwartz told Mitch Albom (Albom, 1997, p. 118) in *Tuesdays with Morrie:*

It's very simple. As you grow, you learn more. If you stayed at twenty-two, you'd always be as ignorant as you were at twenty-two. Aging is not just decay, you know. It's growth. It's more than the negative that you're going to die, it's also the positive that you *understand* you're going to die, and that you live a better life because of it.

The experience of crises and hardships does not lead to emotional sentiments of bitterness and despair in the lives of wise individuals but to compassion and gratitude. For example, a participant in one study characterized a wise woman as follows (Glück, 2011, p. 70):

Her wisdom is in the way she sees life. She knows that bad things can happen, and some have hit her hard, but there is no bitterness when she looks back, just a slightly detached perspective, an observer's perspective—an empathetic observer.

In another study, an older wise woman exclaimed (Ardelt, 2005, p. 18), "I just feel so blessed all the time. That's why I don't have time for feeling bad or thinking bad [when negative events happen]. I'm not going to waste my time doing that."

Yet, life crises and hardships do not automatically result in the transcendence of subjectivity and projections and greater wisdom (Glück & Bluck, 2014; Holliday & Chandler, 1986). Depending on individuals' personal, social, and economic resources, crises and hardships might lead to the emotional sentiments of anguish, depression, and despair rather than stress-related growth and wisdom (Aldwin, Levenson, & Kelly, 2009; Park, 1998; Park & Fenster, 2004; Pascual-Leone, 2000). For example, among middle-aged adults who suffered from economic deprivation during the Great Depression, those who were rated as relatively wise 40 years later increased in psychological health in the years after the Great Depression, whereas those who were rated low on wisdom characteristics in old age declined in psychological health after the Great Depression years (Ardelt, 1998). Similarly, among World War II veterans with heavy combat exposure, those who reached Erikson's (1980) psychosocial stage of generativity in midlife scored higher on wisdom characteristics, physical and psychological health, and subjective well-being at midlife and in old age than did those who failed to achieve generativity at midlife (Ardelt, Landes, & Vaillant, 2010).

It appears that cognitive scenarios that transcend subjectivity and projections allow growth in wisdom through an openness to all kinds of experiences, including the awareness and acknowledgment of one's own subjectivity and projections. As Kramer (1990, p. 296) has stated, "Paradoxically, it is the awareness of one's subjectivity—or one's projections—that allows one to begin the task of overcoming that subjectivity." Through openness, awareness, self-reflection, and a willingness to learn the lessons that life teaches, individuals grow wiser through the experience of adversity, reduce their self-centeredness, and are transformed in the process (Kramer, 1990; Pascual-Leone, 2000; Plews-Ogan et al., 2012; Randall & Kenyon, 2001; Staudinger & Kunzmann, 2005; Taranto, 1989).

Self-Transcendence

The realization that emotional reactions are not easy to control but that mindful self-reflection and attention to the underlying sensations calms and dissolves the accompanying emotions leads to cognitive scenarios in which the self is not as solid as one might have previously thought but is more process than substance (Gowans, 2003; Grabovac et al., 2011). For example, an individual's self-concept of a proud, angry, jealous, or depressed person cannot be sustained after realizing that those emotions are not permanent and unchanging features of one's being. In fact, wise individuals are generally believed to have transcended the attachment to a substantial or essentialist view of self (Ardelt, 2008b; Curnow, 1999; Levenson & Aldwin, 2014; Levenson et al., 2001; Takahashi, 2000).

It appears that a dialectical relationship exists between self-transcendence and self-knowledge (Curnow, 1999; Levenson & Crumpler, 1996; Levitt, 1999). As mentioned earlier, the quest for wisdom includes a desire to know the truth not only about the external world but also about the internal world of one's own being. Therefore, one of the truths that persons on the path to wisdom will discover is that the self is not a solid entity, but a social construction and socially performed narrative that incorporates attachments and aversions related to cognitive, emotional, and behavioral tendencies, habits, and preferences derived from culture, socialization, and inherited genes (Gowans, 2003; Levenson et al., 2001; Mead & Morris, 1934; Metzinger, 2003). Through mindful self-reflection and self-examination, those attachments and aversions grow weaker, and the person becomes less constrained by past conditioning and more open to experience reality "as it is," including the reality of a self that is more fluid than stable (Levenson & Aldwin, 2014). This insight loosens the attachment to the isolated self but also makes it possible to accept the totality of one's being by reducing the need to suppress or deny any negative emotional reactions or tendencies that do not fit into one's positive self-conception. By not suppressing undesirable emotions, true self-knowledge becomes possible. People who understand that everything is impermanent can accept their positive as well as negative emotions without holding on to them. That is, emotional reactions, such as anger, fear, depression, or elation, are acknowledged but do not become essential to (or threaten) one's self-concept. In this way, self-centeredness and self-importance are reduced, leading to self-transcendence. This process is consistent with the core features of most of the world's wisdom traditions, described by Curnow (1999) as self-knowledge, detachment, self-integration, and self-transcendence.

Wise people understand that being attached to a self that is necessarily ever-changing inevitably results in suffering (Rosch, 2014) because aging and death cannot be avoided, despite massive research efforts in anti-aging medicine (Morabia & Costanza, 2012) and a multimillion dollar anti-aging industry (Perls, 2004; Smirnova, 2012). Because wise individuals are more likely to live in the moment, they are less likely to dread the aging process and the accompanying changes of the body. As an 85-year-old wise woman explained (Ardelt, 2005, p. 13),

Ah, there's a lot of people,...they're so negative, all they say is "I'm so old." And I tell them, "Look, I don't know what it's like on the other side, but I know what it is here, and I like it [being old]." (laughing).... You know, as the years go by,...you don't even think about some of these things. I never just think, well, I'm going to be so, this age or that age. It happened, and I was 40, I was 50, I was 60, and I just, like everything else in my life, I took it in my stride. I'm not ashamed of how old I am. I'd be ashamed if I was like some people that I know [who] are so negative, don't realize what they have, you know. Ah, there's so much that you can do. There's people, there's children, there's people that need help.

Through self-awareness and self-knowledge, wise people recognize that the correct way to view the self is not as substance but as a process, which decreases the attachment to that self and increases tolerance and empathy toward others who still struggle with ego-centered self-understanding. This, in turn, leads to selftranscendence as demonstrated by thoughts, feelings, and actions that promote the good of all people rather than the individual (Kupperman, 2005; Levenson & Aldwin, 2014; Levitt, 1999; Rosch, 2014).

Affective Wisdom Dimension

Although we have been considering emotion all along in relation to cognition and reflection, let us now examine this dimension in its own right, as it specifically relates to wisdom. The affective or emotional dimension of wisdom is defined as sympathetic and compassionate love for others and the motivation to foster the well-being of all in Ardelt's 3D-WM (Ardelt, 1997, 2003; Bergsma & Ardelt, 2012). These emotions emerge with the gradual transcendence of the egocentric self and therefore can be described as involving long-term emotional sentiments, in contrast to the self-centered emotional reactions that distort the perception of reality (Curnow, 1999). The transcendence of self-centeredness, in turn, is intrinsically rewarding and liberating and brings forth joy, contentment, and a general sense of eudaimonic well-being that is quite distinct from the hedonic happiness and well-being that depends on the fulfillment of self-centered desires (Ardelt et al., 2014; Csikszentmihalyi & Nakamura, 2005; Dambrun & Ricard, 2011; Gowans, 2003; Ryan & Deci, 2001).

Wisdom and Eudaimonic Well-Being

Past studies have shown that wisdom, assessed as an integration of cognitive, reflective, and compassionate personality qualities, was positively related to life satisfaction and subjective well-being in samples of children, adolescents, and younger, middle-aged, and older adults (Ardelt, 2003; Ardelt & Vaillant, 2007; Brugman, 2000; Ferrari, Kahn, Benayon, & Nero, 2011; Le, 2011), even after controlling for objective circumstances such as physical health, socioeconomic status, financial situation, physical environment, and social involvement (Ardelt, 1997, 2000a). A positive correlation between wisdom, measured as an integration of an analytic (knowledge database and abstract reasoning) and synthetic (reflective understanding, emotional empathy, and emotional regulation) mode, and life satisfaction was also found in samples of middle-aged and older American and Japanese adults (Takahashi & Overton, 2002). Finally, self-transcendent wisdom was positively related to happiness among college students (Beaumont, 2009) and negatively to neuroticism and alienation in an age-diverse sample (Levenson, Jennings, Aldwin, & Shiraishi, 2005).

Yet when wisdom was operationalized and assessed without the compassionate component, the association between wisdom and well-being often turned out to be insignificant. For example, in a sample of middle-aged adults, practical wisdom (assessed by cognitive, reflective, and mature self-descriptive adjectives from the Adjective Check List) and transcendent wisdom (ratings of respondents' examples of their own wisdom) were unrelated to life satisfaction (Wink & Helson, 1997). Similarly, wisdom, defined as expertise in uncertainty and measured by the Epistemic Cognition Questionnaire (ECQ15), was neither related to life satisfaction in a sample of Dutch older adults nor to depressive symptoms in a sample of middleaged and older Dutch adults, although the ECQ15 was positively correlated with life satisfaction in the latter sample (Brugman, 2000). In a German sample of younger and older adults, general wisdom-related knowledge was weakly correlated with greater life satisfaction but not with personal wisdom, measured as a combination of self-knowledge, growth and self-regulation, interrelating the self, self-relativism, and tolerance of ambiguity (Mickler & Staudinger, 2008). These findings suggest that seeing reality more clearly without developing the self-transcendent emotions of self-acceptance, (self-)compassion, and sympathetic love might not result in greater well-being, but rather in worries, self-criticism, and the realization that the path to complete wisdom is indeed very long (Mickler & Staudinger, 2008; Staudinger et al., 2005; Staudinger & Glück, 2011; Zacher et al., in press).

The relation between this affectively integrated wisdom and well-being might be explained by multiple pathways. One pathway is through *emotional intelligence*. In two samples of college students and online workers, the positive association between Ardelt's (2003) 3D-WS and subjective well-being (life satisfaction and positive affect) was fully mediated by Wong and Law's (2002) emotional intelligence scale, measured by the appraisal of one's own and others' emotions, use of emotions, and emotion regulation (Zacher et al., in press). Primarily through the reflective component of wisdom, it appears that wise people can recognize and accept their own and other people's emotions and that they are able to regulate harmful emotional reactions before they adversely affect their subjective well-being (Csikszentmihalyi & Nakamura, 2005; Kunzmann, 2004). Of course, this emotional intelligence must be set within a cognitive scenario of concern for others, or emotional intelligence can be just as easily turned against others, as anyone who has been duped by a master salesman into buying something they did not want or need can well appreciate.

A second pathway is through improved coping strategies, resilience, mastery, and the reduction of stress. The relation between the 3D-WS and subjective well-being in samples of older adults was mediated by problem-focused coping, growth-oriented coping, life engagement, and perceived control in one study (Etezadi & Pushkar, 2013) and greater resilience, mastery, and less perceived stress in another study (Ardelt & Jeste, 2012). Because wisdom often develops through successful coping with adversity and hardship in life, as outlined earlier, it is likely that wise individuals have learned valuable skills to deal with future crises and that they have grown resilient in the process (Linley, 2003). According to Masten (2011, p. 494), "resilience can be defined most broadly as: The capacity of a dynamic system to withstand or recover from significant challenges that threaten its stability, viability, or development." Hence, resilience reduces the probability of experiencing stress under duress and makes it more likely that subjective well-being is maintained despite the presence of adversity and stressful life events.

A third pathway is probably through increases in psychological well-being, which, according to Ryff (1989), consists of self-acceptance, positive relations with others, a sense of autonomy, environmental mastery, purpose in life, and an orientation toward continued personal growth. Ryff argued that psychological well-being assesses eudaimonic well-being or the realization of human potential, in line with theories of human development and growth, such as Erikson's (1980) model of psychosocial stages, Jung's (1933) idea of individuation, and Maslow's (1968) conception of self-actualization. As such, psychological well-being is different from hedonic well-being that seeks to increase self-centered happiness or pleasure but should be related to wisdom.

Indeed, wisdom, assessed by the 3D-WS and also by Webster's (2003, 2007) Self-Assessed Wisdom Scale (SAWS, consisting of a combination of critical life experiences, reminiscence/life reflection, openness to experiences, emotional regulation, and humor), was positively related to all of the indicators of psychological well-being (Ardelt, 2003, 2011). Indicators of psychological well-being, in turn, tend to be positively related to indicators of subjective well-being, such as happiness, life satisfaction, and the absence of depressive symptoms (Ryff, 1989; Ryff & Keyes, 1995). This suggests that it might be easy to distinguish between subjective (hedonic) well-being and psychological (eudaimonic) well-being conceptually but difficult to determine empirically whether the happiness, joy, and life satisfaction a person feels stem from ego-centric pursuits or rather from growth-centered and other-focused endeavors.

A fourth pathway might be through greater self-forgiveness and self-compassion. Self-forgiveness was positively correlated with both the 3D-WS and the SAWS (Ardelt, 2011). Another study found that the reflective and compassionate dimensions of the 3D-WS were positively related to self-compassion, and all three variables were associated with greater happiness (Neff, Rude, & Kirkpatrick, 2007). Baseline self-compassion also predicted reductions or smaller increases in depressive symptoms over five months (Raes, 2011). According to Neff (2003), self-compassion entails an accepting and warm attitude toward the totality of one's life and one's being that includes (a) self-kindness, acceptance, and the absence of critical self-judgment in instances of perceived inadequacy and emotional suffering, (b) the recognition that suffering and failure are an inherent aspect of our shared humanity, and (c) the ability to acknowledge painful emotions and thoughts mindfully and with equanimity without overidentifying with them. It should be noted that self-compassion is not compassion for an isolated unchanging essential self. Rather, it arises from insight that the self is an ever-changing process and, as such, is more similar to other process selves than a distinct, ego-centric self ever could be. It is the realization that we are more alike than distinct at our basic level of being that fosters self-compassion and compassion for others (Levenson & Aldwin, 2014). According to the Buddha, true happiness becomes possible if we give up the illusion of a permanent, unchanging self. As Gowans (2003, p. 199) explained,

> Liberated from the thought of ownership, there will no longer be a deep sense of identification with "my

desires" as things that must be fulfilled for "me" to be happy. Liberated from the thought of being distinct from other beings, there will be compassion and loving-kindness for all creatures. Liberated from the thought of having [a fixed] identity, there will no longer be a preoccupation with regrets about the past and anxieties for the future. The result will be tranquility, happiness, freedom from the unsatisfying scenario of constantly striving to find some stable good to attach myself to in a relentlessly frail and fragile world.

Because wise individuals are likely to understand their life narrative as a changing process rather than as the activities of an immutable self that is permanent and unchanging, they have less need to suppress the negative aspects of their life experience, which allows them to accept the totality of their being and forgive their imperfections. Paradoxically, personality growth and the development of wisdom require that individuals can accept their failures and faults and let go of the idea of perfection. The compassionate love for others that results from a reduction in self-centeredness is extended to one's own being, which frees wise persons to enjoy the present moment even under conditions of external and internal imperfections.

Compassionate Concern for the Good of All

Although wise people tend to perceive reality with equanimity and detachment (Grabovac et al., 2011; Hart, 1987; Levenson et al., 2001; Maslow, 1970), they are not indifferent to the fates of others (Csikszentmihalyi & Nakamura, 2005). Research by Helson and Srivastava (2002) found that wise women were more likely than creative women to be rated as warm, compassionate, benevolent, caring, and accessible. Similarly, wisdom-related knowledge was positively related to the importance of other-enhancing values, such as the well-being of friends, societal engagement, and the protection of the environment, and inversely to the importance of living a pleasurable, hedonistic life (Kunzmann & Baltes, 2003b). Having transcended their ego-centered selves, wise individuals have a lesser need to focus on their own personal well-being but are instead emotionally committed to fostering the well-being of others (Clayton, 1982; Kunzmann, 2004; Kupperman, 2005; Sternberg, 1998). For example, two students described their wise grandfather as follows (Ardelt, 2008a, p. 100):

[My wise] grandfather shows a lot of sympathy and compassion for people. He never holds grudges

and always knows what is best for everyone. He never seems concerned about his own welfare, but more concerned about the welfare of the people around him.

Amongst the many lessons my [wise] great grandfather taught me, the most valuable was the one that I learned watching him live his daily life. In every situation, my great grandfather looked for the good in people. He always put himself on the line for others and truly knew the value of charity. He was extremely self-less and caring.

There is general consensus that wise individuals know how to live a life that benefits themselves, others, and society in general (Baltes & Staudinger, 2000; Csikszentmihalyi & Nakamura, 2005; Kekes, 1995; Kramer, 2000; Kupperman, 2005; Sternberg, 1998). Because wise individuals have transcended egocentric concerns, they are more emotionally committed toward the realization of the common good (Kunzmann & Baltes, 2003a; Yang, 2008) but without worrying about the outcome. As the Dalai Lama (Dalai Lama & Cutler, 1998, p. 272) pointed out, the purity of the motivation behind one's actions is more important than the outcome itself:

If you develop a pure and sincere motivation, if you are motivated by a wish to help on the basis of kindness, compassion, and respect, then you can carry on any kind of work, in any field, and function more effectively with less fear or worry, not being afraid of what others think or whether you ultimately will be successful in reaching your goal. Even if you fail to achieve your goal, you can feel good about having made the effort.

Yet it is important to emphasize that a wise person's motivation to make the world a better place is based on a cognitive scenario that evokes compassion and benevolent concern for the good of all rather than on anger or outrage about ego-centered injustice or maltreatment. Distinguishing between immediate emotional reaction and long-term emotional commitments leads us to understand why efforts must be made to master an immediate reaction of anger. For example, the Dalai Lama replied to an interviewer who suggested that anger might function as a motivator for action, "I know what you mean, but with anger, your wish to help doesn't last. With compassion, you never give up" (as quoted in Courtin, 2012, p. 5). The Dalai Lama (Dalai Lama & Cutler, 1998, p. 249) cautioned that even though positive anger that arises out of compassion or a sense of responsibility might act as a motivator and bring extra energy,

> All too often, however, . . . that energy is also blind, so it is uncertain whether it will become constructive or destructive in the end. So, even though under rare circumstances some kinds of anger can be positive, generally speaking, anger leads to ill feeling and hatred. And, as far as hatred is concerned, it is never positive. It has no benefit at all. It is always totally negative.

Similarly, the Buddhist monk and teacher Thich Nhat Hanh (as quoted in Lozoff, 2000, p. 207) remarked,

> If we use anger at injustice as the source of our energy, we may do something harmful, something that we will later regret. . . . Compassion is the only source of energy that is useful and safe. With compassion, your energy is born from insight; it is not blind energy.

The implication behind this worry about even righteous anger is that it implies opposition, not cooperation, and so it reinforces the wrong kinds of mental habits. Even if wise individuals use a forceful action to get a particular point across, as Jesus of Nazareth did when he forcefully evicted the money exchangers from the temple, they do so within a narrative of interpersonal care that evokes emotions of love and compassion rather than self-righteous anger and hatred (Hart, 1987; Lozoff, 2000). As the Dalai Lama (Dalai Lama & Cutler, 1998, p. 258) explained,

> [Y]ou can take a strong stand and even take strong countermeasures out of a feeling of compassion, or a sense of concern for the other, rather than out of anger. One of the reasons why there is a need to adopt a very strong countermeasure against someone is that if you let it pass—whatever the harm or the crime that is being perpetrated against you—then there is a danger of that person's habituation in a very negative way, which, in reality, will cause that individual's own downfall and is very destructive in the long run for the individual himself or herself. Therefore a strong countermeasure is necessary, but with this thought in mind, you can do it out of compassion and concern for that individual.

A wise person's display of "anger" is not an egocentric reaction to a personal affront but an attempt to get the attention of people who cannot be reached by subtler means. Wise individuals know that those who participate in injustice or maltreatment of others ultimately hurt themselves by increasing negative emotions, such as greed, hatred, jealousy, arrogance, or feelings of superiority that strengthen rather than weaken the self-centered ego and ultimately result in misery. Hence, wise persons are more likely to respond to others' transgressions with forgiveness and compassion rather than with anger and hatred, even if it is expressed as "tough love" (Ardelt, 2008b).

The compassion that emanates from wise people is likely to improve interpersonal relationships (Ardelt, 2011) and might have a profound positive impact on others (Achenbaum & Orwoll, 1991; Ardelt, 2000a, 2008a; Kunzmann & Baltes, 2003b). Hence, wise individuals can serve as role models that might help others to live a more ethical and moral life (Kupperman, 2005) and to overcome their negative emotions. In this way, wise people might gradually change the world for the better.

Conclusion

We began this chapter by describing a paradoxical relationship between wisdom and emotion. On the one hand, we have the image of a wise philosopher or scholar who is considered knowledgeable, but dispassionate: someone who is not swayed by emotion. On the other hand, we also have the image of the wise person as a sage who cares deeply about others and exudes positive emotions, such as love, sympathy, compassion, and good will. But, as we have seen in this chapter, both of these images of wisdom emphasize different aspects of emotion. Following Oatley (2004, 2012), we have argued that emotions are vital signals to ourselves and others about what matters most to us. More specifically, emotions signal relations between personal plans and events in the world captured in narratives or cognitive scenarios about ourselves and what matters most to us. Specific emotions depend on specific cognitive scenarios and how they implicate us in our own important personal projects, whether through an emotional reaction that urges us to initiate immediate change or long-term emotional sentiments or stances that orient and sustain our positive and negative commitments to others.

As Metzinger (2003, 2009) pointed out, our emotional experiences are situated within an "ego tunnel" that creates a projected model of both self and the external world. Therefore, what we understand is ourselves, and how we do so affects everything else we understand (Weinsheimer, 1985). Beyond immediate experience, however, we also create narratives about our lives and what our experiences mean, based on historical and literary examples that are provided by our culture (Ricœur, 1992)—a skill that only becomes fully developed in adolescence (Ferrari & Vuletic, 2010; Habermas & Bluck, 2000).

It takes careful examination of experience to lessen the tendency to see things from an egocentric point of view. In this sense, emotions not only make experience memorable, they also invite reflection on that experience and the commitments our emotions imply. Our emotional experiences of joy and suffering provide a window into the fundamental nature of self and human experience. With right mindfulness, one discovers that this extended narrative about our own core experiences is not a substantial entity, but a dynamic social construction that persists through attachments and aversions derived from historical and literary culture, socialization, and genetic inheritance (Gowans, 2003; Levenson et al., 2001; Mead & Morris, 1934; Metzinger, 2003).

On the basis of these distinctions, wisdom necessarily involves emotion because wisdom itself involves knowledge and action of vital emotional importance to us. What matters is the kind of cognitive scenario one implicitly or explicitly engages in a situation. In some cases, wisdom allows us to determine that an immediate emotional reaction, like anger, is to be mastered through self-reflection and emotion regulation to avoid causing suffering. In other cases, a long-term emotional stance like compassionate love provides an emotional compass direction orienting us toward actions that promote better quality of life for ourselves and others. More specifically, as related to wisdom, we have argued that scenarios that generate positive emotional sentiments will necessarily show a deeper understanding of the relationship between self and others, or self and circumstances—one that is dialectic and self-transcendent, leading wise people to promote a good life for themselves and their communities.

Note

1. The Fourth Noble Truth is that the way out of suffering involves following an eightfold path, often condensed to three main aspects: right ethical behavior (right speech, right action, and right livelihood), right concentration (right effort, right mindfulness, and right concentration), and right wisdom (right view and right intention) (Gowans, 2003; Ñanamoli, 2001).

References

Achenbaum, A. W., & Orwoll, L. (1991). Becoming wise: A psycho-gerontological interpretation of the Book of Job *International Journal of Aging and Human Development, 32*(1): 21–39.

Albom, M. (1997). *Tuesdays with Morrie. An old man, a young man, and life's great lesson.* New York: Broadway Books.

Aldwin, C. M., Levenson, M. R., & Kelly, L. (2009). Life span developmental perspectives on stress-related growth. In C. L. Park, S. C. Lechner, M. H. Antoni & A. L. Stanton (Eds.), *Medical illness and positive life change: Can crisis lead to personal transformation?* (pp. 87–104). Washington, DC: American Psychological Association.

Ardelt, M. (1997). Wisdom and life satisfaction in old age. *Journal of Gerontology: Psychological Sciences, 52B* (1), P15–P27.

Ardelt, M. (1998). Social crisis and individual growth: The long-term effects of the Great Depression *Journal of Aging Studies, 12*(3): 291–314.

Ardelt, M. (2000a). Antecedents and effects of wisdom in old age: A longitudinal perspective on aging well. *Research on Aging, 22*(4), 360–394.

Ardelt, M. (2000b). Intellectual versus wisdom-related knowledge: The case for a different kind of learning in the later years of life. *Educational Gerontology: An International Journal of Research and Practice, 26*(8), 771–789.

Ardelt, M. (2003). Empirical assessment of a three-dimensional wisdom scale *Research on Aging, 25*(3): 275–324.

Ardelt, M. (2004). Wisdom as expert knowledge system: A critical review of a contemporary operationalization of an ancient concept *Human Development, 47*(5): 257–285.

Ardelt, M. (2005). How wise people cope with crises and obstacles in life *ReVision: A Journal of Consciousness and Transformation, 28*(1): 7–19.

Ardelt, M. (2007). Wisdom, religiosity, purpose in life, and death attitudes of aging adults. In A. Tomer, G. T. Eliason, & P. T. P. Wong (Eds.), *Existential and spiritual issues in death attitudes* (pp. 139–158). Hillsdale, NY: Lawrence Erlbaum.

Ardelt, M. (2008a). Being wise at any age. In S. J. Lopez (Ed.), *Positive Psychology: Exploring the Best in People* (Vol. 1: Discovering Human Strengths, pp. 81–108). Westport, CT: Praeger.

Ardelt, M. (2008b). Self-development through selflessness: The paradoxical process of growing wiser. In H. A. Wayment & J. J. Bauer (Eds.), *Transcending self-interest: Psychological explorations of the quiet ego* (pp. 221–233). Washington, DC: American Psychological Association.

Ardelt, M. (2011). The measurement of wisdom: A commentary on Taylor, Bates, and Webster's comparison of the SAWS and 3D-WS *Experimental Aging Research, 37*(2): 241–255. doi: 1 0.1080/0361073X.2011.554509.

Ardelt, M., Achenbaum, A. W., & Oh, H. (2014). The paradoxical nature of personal wisdom and its relation to human development in the reflective, cognitive, and affective domains. In M. Ferrari & N. M. Weststrate (Eds.), *The scientific study of personal wisdom: From contemplative traditions to neuroscience* (pp. 265–295). New York: Springer.

Ardelt, M., Ai, A. L., & Eichenberger, S. E. (2008). In search for meaning: The differential role of religion for middle-aged and older persons diagnosed with a life-threatening illness *Journal of Religion, Spirituality and Aging, 20*(4): 288–312.

Ardelt, M., & Jeste, D. (2012). *Explaining the pathway between wisdom and well-being: Mediating effects of resilience and mastery.* Paper presented at the Gerontological Society of America Annual Meetings, San Diego, CA.

Ardelt, M., Landes, S. D., & Vaillant, G. E. (2010). The long-term effects of World War II combat exposure on later life well-being moderated by generativity *Research in Human*

Development, 7(3): 202–220. doi: 10.1080/15427609.2010.504505

Ardelt, M., & Vaillant, G. E. (2007). *Wisdom as a cognitive, reflective, and affective three-dimensional personality characteristic.* Paper presented at the Gerontological Society of America Annual Meetings, San Francisco, CA.

Arlin, P. K. (1990). Wisdom: The art of problem finding. In R. J. Sternberg (Ed.), *Wisdom: Its nature, origins, and development* (pp. 230–243). New York: Cambridge University Press.

Assmann, A. (1994). Wholesome knowledge: Concepts of wisdom in a historical and cross-cultural perspective. In D. L. Featherman, R. M. Lerner & M. Perlmutter (Eds.), *Life-span development and behavior* (vol. 12, pp. 187–224). Hillsdale, NJ: Lawrence Erlbaum.

Attig, T. (1995). Coping with mortality: An essay on self-mourning. In L. A. DeSpelder & A. L. Strickland (Eds.), *The path ahead. Readings in death and dying* (pp. 337–341). Mountain View, CA: Mayfield.

Baltes, P. B., & Smith, J. (2008). The fascination of wisdom: Its nature, ontogeny, and function *Perspectives on Psychological Science, 3*(1): 56–64.

Baltes, P. B., Smith, J., Staudinger, U. M., & Sowarka, D. (1990). Wisdom: One facet of successful aging? In M. Perlmutter (Ed.), *Late-life potential* (pp. 63–81). Washington, DC: Gerontological Society of America.

Baltes, P. B., & Staudinger, U. M. (2000). Wisdom: A meta-heuristic (pragmatic) to orchestrate mind and virtue toward excellence *American Psychologist, 55*(1): 122–136.

Barbieri, P. (1997). Habitual desires: The destructive nature of expressing your anger *International Journal of Reality Therapy, 17*(1): 17–23.

Beaumont, S. L. (2009). Identity processing and personal wisdom: An information-oriented identity style predicts self-actualization and self-transcendence *Identity: An International Journal of Theory and Research, 9*(2): 95–115. doi: 10.1080/15283480802669101

Beaumont, S. L. (2011). Identity styles and wisdom during emerging adulthood: Relationships with mindfulness and savoring *Identity: An International Journal of Theory and Research, 11*(2): 155–180. doi: 10.1080/15283488.2011.557298

Bergsma, A., & Ardelt, M. (2012). Self-reported wisdom and happiness: An empirical investigation *Journal of Happiness Studies, 13*(3): 481–499. doi: 10.1007/s10902-011-9275-5

Bianchi, E. C. (1994). *Elder wisdom. Crafting your own elderhood.* New York: Crossroad.

Birren, J. E., & Svensson, C. M. (2005). Wisdom in history. In R. J. Sternberg & J. Jordan (Eds.), *A handbook of wisdom. Psychological perspectives* (pp. 3–31). New York: Cambridge University Press.

Blanchard-Fields, F., & Norris, L. (1995). The development of wisdom. In M. A. Kimble, S. H. McFadden, J. W. Ellor, & J. J. Seeber (Eds.), *Aging, spirituality, and religion. A handbook* (pp. 102–118). Minneapolis, MN: Fortress Press.

Bluck, S., & Glück, J. (2005). From the inside out: People's implicit theories of wisdom. In R. J. Sternberg & J. Jordan (Eds.), *A handbook of wisdom. Psychological perspectives* (pp. 84–109). New York: Cambridge University Press.

Bradley, G. W. (1978). Self-serving biases in the attribution process: A reexamination of the fact or fiction question *Journal of Personality and Social Psychology, 36*(1): 56–71.

Brown, S. C. (2004). Learning across the campus: How college facilitates the development of wisdom *Journal of College Student Development, 45*(2): 134–148.

Brugman, G. M. (2000). *Wisdom: Source of narrative coherence and eudaimonia.* Delft, The Netherlands: Eburon.

Choi, N. G., & Landeros, C. (2011). Wisdom from life's challenges: Qualitative interviews with low—and moderate-income older adults who were nominated as being wise *Journal of Gerontological Social Work, 54*(6): 592–614. doi: 10.1080/01634372.2011.585438

Clayton, V. P. (1982). Wisdom and intelligence: The nature and function of knowledge in the later years *International Journal of Aging and Development, 15*(4): 315–323.

Clayton, V. P., & Birren, J. E. (1980). The development of wisdom across the life-span: A reexamination of an ancient topic. In P. B. Baltes & O. G. Brim, Jr. (Eds.), *Life-span development and behavior* (vol. 3, pp. 103–135). New York: Academic Press.

Courtin, R. (2012). Transforming anger: A Buddhist perspective. *A Little Good News, Spring* 2012, 5–6.

Csikszentmihalyi, M., Abuhamdeh, S., & Nakamura, J. (2005). Flow. In A. J. E. C. S. Dweck (Ed.), *Handbook of competence and motivation* (pp. 598–608). New York: Guilford.

Csikszentmihalyi, M., & Nakamura, J. (2005). The role of emotions in the development of wisdom. In R. J. Sternberg & J. Jordan (Eds.), *A handbook of wisdom. Psychological perspectives* (pp. 220–242). New York: Cambridge University Press.

Csikszentmihalyi, M., & Nakamura, J. (2010). Effortless attention in everyday life: A systematic phenomenology *Effortless attention: A new perspective in the cognitive science of attention and action* (pp. 179–189). Cambridge, MA: MIT Press.

Csikszentmihalyi, M., & Rathunde, K. (1990). The psychology of wisdom: An evolutionary interpretation. In R. J. Sternberg (Ed.), *Wisdom: Its nature, origins, and development* (pp. 25–51). New York: Cambridge University Press.

Curnow, T. (1999). *Wisdom, intuition, and ethics.* Brookfield, VT: Ashgate.

Dalai Lama, & Cutler, H. C. (1998). *The art of happiness: A handbook for living.* New York: Riverhead Books.

Dambrun, M., & Ricard, M. (2011). Self-centeredness and selflessness: A theory of self-based psychological functioning and its consequences for happiness *Review of General Psychology, 15*(2): 138–157. doi: 10.1037/a0023059

de Saint-Exupéry, A. (1943). *Le petit prince.* New York: Reynal & Hitchcock.

Dittmann-Kohli, F., & Baltes, P. B. (1990). Toward a neofunctionalist conception of adult intellectual development: Wisdom as a prototypical case of intellectual growth. In C. N. Alexander & E. J. Langer (Eds.), *Higher stages of human development. Perspectives on adult growth* (pp. 54–78). New York: Oxford University Press.

Erikson, E. H. (1964). *Insight and responsibility. Lectures on the ethical implications of psychoanalytic insight.* New York: Norton.

Erikson, E. H. (1980). *Identity and the life cycle.* New York: Norton.

Etezadi, S., & Pushkar, D. (2013). Why are wise people happier? An explanatory model of wisdom and emotional well-being in older adults *Journal of Happiness Studies, 14*(3): 929–950. doi: 10.1007/s10902-012-9362-2

Farb, N. A. S., Anderson, A. K., Mayberg, H., Bean, J., McKeon, D., & Segal, Z. V. (2010). Minding one's emotions: Mindfulness training alters the neural expression of sadness *Emotion, 10*(1): 25–33. doi: 10.1037/a0017151

Ferrari, M., Kahn, A., Benayon, M., & Nero, J. (2011). Phronesis, sophia, and hochma: Developing wisdom in Islam and Judaism *Research in Human Development, 8*(2): 128–148. doi: 10.1080/15427609.2011.568869

Ferrari, M., & Vuletic, L. (2010). The intentional personal development of mind and brain through education. In M. Ferrari & L. Vuletic (Eds.), *The developmental relations among mind, brain, and education: Essays in honor of Robbie Case* (pp. 293–323). Amsterdam: Springer.

Gardner, H. (1983). *Frames of mind: The theory of multiple intelligences.* New York: Basic Books.

Glück, J. (2011). "She looks back without bitterness:" Wisdom as a developmental opposite of embitterment? In M. Linden & A. Maercker (Eds.), *Embitterment: Societal, psychological, and clinical perspectives* (pp. 70–82). Vienna/New York: Springer.

Glück, J., & Bluck, S. (2011). Laypeople's conceptions of wisdom and its development: Cognitive and integrative views. *Journals of Gerontology: Series B: Psychological Sciences and Social Sciences, 66B* (3), 321–324. doi: 10.1093/geronb/gbr011

Glück, J., & Bluck, S. (2014). The MORE life experience model: A theory of the development of wisdom. In M. Ferrari & N. Weststrate (Eds.), *Personal wisdom* (pp. 75–97). New York: Springer.

Goleman, D. (1995). *Emotional intelligence.* New York: Bantam Books Inc.

Gowans, C. W. (2003). *Philosophy of the Buddha.* London/New York: Routledge.

Grabovac, A. D., Lau, M. A., & Willett, B. R. (2011). Mechanisms of mindfulness: A Buddhist psychological model *Mindfulness, 2*(3): 154–166. doi: 10.1007/s12671-011-0054-5

Habermas, T., & Bluck, S. (2000). Getting a life: The emergence of the life story in adolescence *Psychological Bulletin, 126*(5): 748–769. doi: 10.1037/0033-2909.126.5.748

Hanna, F. J., & Ottens, A. J. (1995). The role of wisdom in psychotherapy *Journal of Psychotherapy Integration, 5*(3): 195–219.

Hart, W. (1987). *The art of living. Vipassana meditation as taught by S. N. Goenka.* San Francisco: Harper.

Helson, R., & Srivastava, S. (2002). Creative and wise people: Similarities, differences and how they develop *Personality and Social Psychology Bulletin, 28*(10): 1430–1440.

Hewstone, M. (1990). The "ultimate attribution error?" A review of the literature on intergroup causal attribution *European Journal of Social Psychology, 20*(4): 311–335.

Holliday, S. G., & Chandler, M. J. (1986). *Wisdom: Explorations in adult competence.* Basel/New York: Karger.

Jeste, D. V., & Vahia, I. (2008). Comparison of the conceptualization of wisdom in ancient Indian literature with modern views: Focus on the Bhagavad Gita *Psychiatry: Interpersonal and Biological Processes, 71*(3): 197–209.

Jung, C. G. (1933). *Modern man in search of a soul.* New York: Harcourt Brace.

Kabat-Zinn, J. (2003). Mindfulness-based interventions in context: Past, present, and future *Clinical Psychology: Science and Practice, 10*(2): 144–156. doi: 10.1093/clipsy/bpg016

Kekes, J. (1983). Wisdom *American Philosophical Quarterly, 20*(3): 277–286.

Kekes, J. (1995). *Moral wisdom and good lives.* Ithaca, NY: Cornell University Press.

Keltner, D., & Gross, J. J. (1999). Functional accounts of emotions *Cognition and Emotion, 13*(5): 467–480.

Kinnier, R. T., Tribbensee, N. E., Rose, C. A., & Vaughan, S. M. (2001). In the final analysis: More wisdom from people who have faced death *Journal of Counseling & Development, 79*(2): 171–177.

Kramer, D. A. (1990). Conceptualizing wisdom: The primacy of affect-cognition relations. In R. J. Sternberg (Ed.), *Wisdom: Its nature, origins, and development* (pp. 279–313). New York: Cambridge University Press.

Kramer, D. A. (2000). Wisdom as a classical source of human strength: Conceptualization and empirical inquiry *Journal of Social and Clinical Psychology, 19*(1): 83–101.

Kunzmann, U. (2004). Approaches to a good life: The emotional-motivational side to wisdom. In P. A. Linley & S. Joseph (Eds.), *Positive psychology in practice* (pp. 504–517). Hoboken, NJ: John Wiley & Sons.

Kunzmann, U., & Baltes, P. B. (2003a). Beyond the traditional scope of intelligence: Wisdom in action. In R. J. Sternberg, J. Lautrey & e. al. (Eds.), *Models of intelligence: International perspectives* (pp. 329–343). Washington, DC: American Psychological Association.

Kunzmann, U., & Baltes, P. B. (2003b). Wisdom-related knowledge: Affective, motivational, and interpersonal correlates. *Personality and Social Psychology Bulletin, 29*(9), 1104–1119.

Kunzmann, U., & Baltes, P. B. (2005). The psychology of wisdom: Theoretical and empirical challenges. In R. J. Sternberg & J. Jordan (Eds.), *A handbook of wisdom. Psychological perspectives* (pp. 110–135). New York: Cambridge University Press.

Kupperman, J. J. (2005). Morality, ethics, and wisdom. In R. J. Sternberg & J. Jordan (Eds.), *A handbook of wisdom. Psychological perspectives* (pp. 245–271). New York: Cambridge University Press.

Labouvie-Vief, G. (1990). Wisdom as integrated thought: Historical and developmental perspectives. In R. J. Sternberg (Ed.), *Wisdom: Its nature, origins, and development* (pp. 52–83). New York: Cambridge University Press.

Labouvie-Vief, G., & Medler, M. (2002). Affect optimization and affect complexity: Modes and styles of regulation in adulthood *Psychology and Aging, 17*(4): 571–587.

Le, T. N. (2011). Life satisfaction, openness value, self-transcendence, and wisdom *Journal of Happiness Studies, 12*(2): 171–182. doi: DOI 10.1007/s10902-010-9182-1

Levenson, M. R., & Aldwin, C. (2014). The transpersonal in personal wisdom. In M. Ferrari & N. M. Weststrate (Eds.), *The scientific study of personal wisdom: From contemplative traditions to neuroscience* (pp. 213–228). New York: Springer.

Levenson, M. R., Aldwin, C. M., & Cupertino, A. P. (2001). Transcending the self: Towards a liberative model of adult development. In A. L. Neri (Ed.), *Maturidade & Velhice: Um enfoque multidisciplinar* (pp. 99–116). Sao Paulo, BR: Papirus.

Levenson, M. R., & Crumpler, C. A. (1996). Three models of adult development *Human Development, 39*(3): 135–149.

Levenson, M. R., Jennings, P. A., Aldwin, C. M., & Shiraishi, R. W. (2005). Self-transcendence: Conceptualization and measurement *International Journal of Aging & Human Development, 60*(2): 127–143.

Levitt, H. M. (1999). The development of wisdom: An analysis of Tibetan Buddhist experience *Journal of Humanistic Psychology, 39*(2): 86–105.

Linley, P. A. (2003). Positive adaptation to trauma: Wisdom as both process and outcome *Journal of Traumatic Stress, 16*(6): 601–610.

Lozoff, B. (2000). *It's a meaningful life. It just takes practice.* New York: Viking.

Martin, L. L., & Kleiber, D. A. (2005). Letting go of the negative: Psychological growth from a close brush with death *Traumatology, 11*(4): 221–232.

Maslow, A. H. (1968). *Toward a psychology of being* (2nd ed.). Oxford: Van Nostrand.

Maslow, A. H. (1970). *Motivation and personality* (2nd ed.). New York: Harper & Row.

Masten, A. S. (2011). Resilience in children threatened by extreme adversity: Frameworks for research, practice, and translational synergy *Development and Psychopathology, 23*(2): 493–506. doi: 10.1017/s0954579411000198

McKee, P., & Barber, C. (1999). On defining wisdom *International Journal of Aging and Human Development, 49*(2): 149–164.

Mead, G. H., & Morris, C. W. (1934). *Mind, self and society: From the standpoint of a social behaviorist.* Oxford: University of Chicago Press.

Metzinger, T. (2003). *Being no one: The self-model theory of subjectivity.* Cambridge, MA: MIT Press.

Metzinger, T. (2009). *The ego tunnel: The science of the mind and the myth of the self.* New York: Basic Books.

Mickler, C., & Staudinger, U. M. (2008). Personal wisdom: Validation and age-related differences of a performance measure *Psychology and Aging, 23*(4): 787–799. doi: 10.1037/a0013928

Montgomery, A., Barber, C., & McKee, P. (2002). A phenomenological study of wisdom in later life *International Journal of Aging and Human Development, 54*(2): 139–157.

Moody, H. R. (1986). Late life learning in the information society. In D. A. Peterson, J. E. Thornton, & J. E. Birren (Eds.), *Education and aging* (pp. 122–148). Englewood Cliffs, NJ: Prentice-Hall.

Morabia, A., & Costanza, M. C. (2012). Aging medicine: Not evidence-based medicine yet. *Preventive Medicine: An International Journal Devoted to Practice and Theory, 54* (Suppl), S1–S3. doi: 10.1016/j.ypmed.2012.04.005

Ñanamoli, B. (2001). *The life of the Buddha. According to the Pali Canon.* Seattle: BPS Pariyatti Editions.

Neff, K. D. (2003). Self-compassion: An alternative conceptualization of a healthy attitude toward oneself. *Self and Identity, 2,* 85–102.

Neff, K. D., Rude, S. S., & Kirkpatrick, K. L. (2007). An examination of self-compassion in relation to positive psychological functioning and personality traits *Journal of Research in Personality, 41*(4): 908–916. doi: 10.1016/j.jrp.2006.08.002

Oatley, K. (2004). *Emotions: A brief history.* Malden, VT: Blackwell.

Oatley, K. (2012). *The passionate muse: Exploring emotion in stories.* New York: Oxford University Press.

Osbeck, L. M., & Robinson, D. N. (2005). Philosophical theories of wisdom. In R. J. Sternberg & J. Jordan (Eds.), *A handbook of wisdom. Psychological perspectives* (pp. 61–83). New York: Cambridge University Press.

Park, C. L. (1998). Stress-related growth and thriving through coping: The roles of personality and cognitive processes *Journal of Social Issues, 54*(2): 267–277.

Park, C. L., Cohen, L. H., & Murch, R. L. (1996). Assessment and prediction of stress-related growth *Journal of Personality, 64*(1): 71–105.

Park, C. L., & Fenster, J. R. (2004). Stress-related growth: Predictors of occurrence and correlates with psychological adjustment *Journal of Social and Clinical Psychology, 23*(2): 195–215.

Pascual-Leone, J. (2000). Mental attention, consciousness, and the progressive emergence of wisdom *Journal of Adult Development, 7*(4): 241–254.

Perls, T. T. (2004). Anti-aging quackery: Human growth hormone and tricks of the trade—more dangerous than ever. *Journals of Gerontology: Series A: Biological Sciences and Medical Sciences, 59A* (7), 682–691. doi: 10.1093/gerona/59.7.B682

Plews-Ogan, M., Owens, J.E., & May, N. (2012). *Choosing wisdom: Strategies and inspiration for growing through life-changing difficulties.* West Conshohocken, PA: Templeton Press.

Raes, F. 2011. The effect of self-compassion on the development of depression symptoms in a non-clinical sample *Mindfulness, 2*(1): 33–36. doi: 10.1007/s12671-011-0040-y

Randall, W. L., & Kenyon, G. M. (2001). *Ordinary wisdom: Biographical aging and the journey of life.* Westport, CT: Praeger.

Ricœur, P. (1992). *Oneself as another.* Chicago: University of Chicago Press.

Rosch, E. (2014). The Grinch who stole wisdom. In M. Ferrari & N. M. Weststrate (Eds.), *The scientific study of personal wisdom: From contemplative traditions to neuroscience* (pp. 229–249). New York: Springer.

Ryan, R. M., & Deci, E. L. (2001). On happiness and human potentials: A review of research on hedonic and eudaimonic well-being. *Annual Review of Psychology, 52,* 141–166. doi: 10.1146/annurev.psych.52.1.141

Ryff, C. D. (1989). Happiness is everything, or is it? Explorations on the meaning of psychological well-being *Journal of Personality and Social Psychology, 57*(6): 1069–1081.

Ryff, C. D., & Keyes, C. L. M. (1995). The structure of psychological well-being revisited *Journal of Personality and Social Psychology, 69*(4): 719–727.

Sherwood, G. G. (1981). Self-serving biases in person perception: A reexamination of projection as a mechanism of defense *Psychological Bulletin, 90*(3): 445–459.

Smirnova, M. H. (2012). A will to youth: The woman's anti-aging elixir *Social Science & Medicine, 75*(7): 1236– 1243. doi: 10.1016/j.socscimed.2012.02.061

Smith, J., Dixon, R. A., & Baltes, P. B. (1989). Expertise in life planning: A new research approach to investigating aspects of wisdom. In M. L. Commons, J. D. Sinnott, F. A. Richards, & C. Armon (Eds.), *Adult development, Vol. 1: Comparisons and applications of developmental models.* (pp. 307–331). New York: Praeger.

Speca, M., Carlson, L. E., Goodey, E., & Angen, M. (2000). A randomized, wait-list controlled clinical trial: The effect of a mindfulness meditation-based stress reduction program on mood and symptoms of stress in cancer outpatients *Psychosomatic Medicine, 62*(5): 613–622.

Staudinger, U. M., & Baltes, P. B. (1996). Interactive minds: A facilitative setting for wisdom-related performance *Journal of Personality and Social Psychology, 71*(4): 746–762.

Staudinger, U. M., Dörner, J., & Mickler, C. (2005). Wisdom and personality. In R. J. Sternberg & J. Jordan (Eds.), *A handbook of wisdom. Psychological perspectives* (pp. 191–219). New York: Cambridge University Press.

Staudinger, U. M., & Glück, J. (2011). Psychological wisdom research: Commonalities and differences in a growing field *Annual Review of Psychology, 62*(1): 215–241. doi: doi:10.1146/annurev.psych.121208.131659

Staudinger, U. M., & Kunzmann, U. (2005). Positive adult personality development: Adjustment and/or growth? *European Psychologist, 10*(4), 320–329.

Sternberg, R. J. (1990). Wisdom and its relations to intelligence and creativity. In R. J. Sternberg (Ed.), *Wisdom: Its nature, origins, and development* (pp. 142–159). New York: Cambridge University Press.

Sternberg, R. J. (1998). A balance theory of wisdom *Review of General Psychology, 2*(4): 347–365.

Strijbos, S. (1995). How can systems thinking help us in bridging the gap between science and wisdom *Systems Practice, 8*(4): 361–376.

Takahashi, M. (2000). Toward a culturally inclusive understanding of wisdom: Historical roots in the East and West *International Journal of Aging and Human Development, 51*(3): 217–230.

Takahashi, M., & Bordia, P. (2000). The concept of wisdom: A cross-cultural comparison *International Journal of Psychology, 35*(1): 1–9.

Takahashi, M., & Overton, W. F. (2002). Wisdom: A culturally inclusive developmental perspective *International Journal of Behavioral Development, 26*(3): 269–277.

Takahashi, M., & Overton, W. F. (2005). Cultural foundations of wisdom: An integrated developmental approach. In R. J. Sternberg & J. Jordan (Eds.), *A handbook of wisdom. Psychological perspectives* (pp. 32–60). New York: Cambridge University Press.

Taranto, M. A. (1989). Facets of wisdom: A theoretical synthesis *International Journal of Aging and Human Development, 29*(1): 1–21.

Tolle, E. (2004). *The power of NOW: A guide to spiritual enlightenment* (Rev. ed.). Novato, CA: New World Library.

Webster, J. D. (2003). An exploratory analysis of a self-assessed wisdom scale *Journal of Adult Development, 10*(1): 13–22.

Webster, J. D. (2007). Measuring the character strength of wisdom *International Journal of Aging & Human Development, 65*(2): 163–183.

Weinsheimer, J. C. (1985). *Gadamer's Hermeneutics: A reading of truth and method.* New Haven, CT: Yale University Press.

Wierzbicka, A. (1999). *Emotions across languages and cultures: Diversity and universals.* New York: Cambridge University Press.

Wink, P., & Helson, R. (1997). Practical and transcendent wisdom: Their nature and some longitudinal findings *Journal of Adult Development, 4*(1): 1–15.

Wong, C.-S., & Law, K. S. (2002). The effects of leader and follower emotional intelligence on performance and attitude: An exploratory study *Leadership Quarterly, 13*(3): 243–274. doi: 10.1016/s1048-9843(02)00099-1

Yang, S.-Y. (2001). Conceptions of wisdom among Taiwanese Chinese *Journal of Cross-Cultural Psychology, 32*(6): 662–680.

Yang, S.-Y. (2008). Real-life contextual manifestations of wisdom *International Journal of Aging & Human Development, 67*(4): 273–303.

Zacher, H., McKenna, B., & Rooney, D. (in press). Effects of self-reported wisdom on happiness: Not much more than emotional intelligence? *Journal of Happiness Studies.* doi: 10.1007/s10902-012-9404-9

Values Across Adulthood: A Neglected Developmental Construct Guiding Thought and Action Over Time

Johannes O. Ritter *and* Alexandra M. Freund

Abstract

This chapter discusses the role of personal values in adult development. Personal values can be seen as higher order goals that an individual personally endorses and as a more general attitude about what people ought to do or what is generally important in life. Research has repeatedly demonstrated a gap between expressed values and actual behavior; nevertheless, we maintain that values can serve as an overarching cognitive compass to evaluate one's future as well as past behaviors and goals. On the basis of empirical research on goals we posit that personal values and their function change over the lifespan. We argue that personal values might be especially relevant for life planning in adolescence and early adulthood and for life review in later adulthood.

Key Words: adult development, personal values, behavior, behavior change, adulthood

One of the central questions of research on lifespan development is which constructs are suited to describe and explain the processes and direction of development. In this chapter, we explore the potential of a construct that has been largely neglected in research on the development of social cognition across adulthood, namely, that of values. Although pioneers of lifespan development such as Erikson (1959) and Havighurst (1956) called attention to the importance of values, little research investigates how values change across adulthood and how they affect adults' thoughts and actions at different points in their development. We shared an interest in the role of values for adult development and aging with the late Fredda Blanchard-Fields, explored it in many discussions with her, and had planned a joint research program on the topic. Sadly, our time with Fredda was cut short, so these discussions and research plans with her did not come to fruition. In this chapter, we lay out some of our mainly theoretical ideas about the social-cognitive function of values in adult development.

Starting with general definitions and theories of values, we will turn to the question of whether personal values change across adulthood. Several authors suggest that such a change occurs and that this change represents an adaptive process of developmental regulation that helps us to cope with developmental demands and challenges. We will review these accounts and related empirical findings and extend these findings using cross-sectional data from the World Values Survey (WVS). On this basis, we will discuss the influence of values on behavior in general and on developmental regulation in particular. Based on findings from social psychology, we argue that temporal distance might be a key variable moderating the value-behavior relationship. We hypothesize that there is a developmental trend toward value-behavior congruency and that values have specific functions related to developmental regulation.

What Are Values? A Definition Spanning Individual Values and Social Norms

Values are "principles, or criteria, for selecting what is good (or better, or best) among objects, actions, ways of life, and social and political institutions and structures. Values operate at the level of individuals, of institutions, and of entire societies" (Schwartz, 1990, p. 8). Institutions and societies embody values by providing conditions or opportunity structures that either increase or decrease the likelihood of individuals to act and express themselves in a certain way. Such structures, or *social norms*, can take the form of laws securing a basic set of values (such as not taking another person's material possessions or life) or institutional rules (such as affirmative action policies). In lifespan developmental psychology, socially shared values have a function similar to that of social norms or expectations. They provide information about opportunity structures that provide resources for the pursuit of certain goals (e.g., Freund, 2007; Heckhausen, 1999). For instance, the societal value of education is expressed in many societies by offering or even requiring children and adolescents to attend school. Individual and social norms are highly interdependent. Cultural and societal values are transmitted to individuals by institutions (e.g., schools), family, and cultural artifacts (e.g., books, TV programs). Individual values, in turn, can also have an impact on social norms (such as the values expressed by the "flower power" generation of the 1960s). For the most part, this research focuses on basic cultural differences between Western and Eastern cultures in how people perceive the world and themselves (Nisbett, 2003). To a large degree, the literature on values is concerned with the description of values over historical time and across nations (e.g., Inglehart, 1990). An example of this kind of research is the investigation of the change of values held by adolescents over historical time (e.g., Deutsche Shell, 2002) or differed between West and the former East Germany (e.g., Reitzle & Silbereisen, 2000). To a lesser degree, research on values investigates the reasons *why* individuals or groups hold certain values over others and how they develop over the course of the lifespan.

Sacred Values and Moral Mandates

More recently, the concept of *sacred values* was introduced (e.g., Baron & Spranca, 1997; Hanselmann & Tanner, 2008; Tetlock, 2003). People endorsing a sacred value are not willing to alter or even compare this value with other values. This is because they assign a basic, unquestionable, or even transcendental importance to it (Tetlock, Kristel, Elson, Green, & Lerner, 2000). Sacred values are normally shared by a community that endorses a common morality and concern issues such as human rights, environment, justice, and health. An example of a sacred value that many share is that there is simply no amount of money that can buy a human life. Violations of a sacred value elicit strong emotional reactions, moral outrage, distress, and disturbance (Tetlock, 2003). Moreover, sacred values are strong motivators of behavior (Tanner & Medin, 2004). People endorsing sacred values experience a moral obligation to protect the value. Such an endorsement of a sacred value implies at least a partial neglect of the consequences of an action. For instance, imagine that someone endorses the value of nature and environment as a sacred value. This person might object to genetically engineered plants without considering the potential beneficial effects on nutrition. It seems highly likely that sacred values are involved to some extent in the actions of political activist groups, as well as in activities related to civic responsibility (Skitka & Baumann, 2008; Skitka, Bauman, & Sargis, 2005). It may be that those who hold strong sacred values are more likely to take part in extreme political actions or justify using violence when they are threatened (e.g., anti-abortionists who attack or even murder physicians who perform abortions). To our knowledge, no research has been conducted on the development of sacred values across the lifespan.

Values as Dispositions

Early research on values focused primarily on values as an entity that lies within a person, like a personality trait or a disposition to prefer certain basic attitudes over others. This research, similar to other dispositional approaches, mainly describes individuals as having stable individual differences in their values, such as political conservatism or liberalism (e.g., Major & Deaux, 1982). Empirical research discovered that values—possibly with the exception of extremely strongly held values or sacred values—are generally poor predictors of behavior over time and across situations. People do not always—or even very often—act on their beliefs, attitudes, and values (e.g., Eagly & Chaiken, 1993; Wicker, 1969). An interesting question, then, is the function of values for individual thought and behavior. Only fairly recently has this question rekindled the interest mainly of social psychologists and, although to a much lesser extent, developmental psychologists. In general, research on values has put relatively little emphasis on the development of values and how values might influence social-cognitive processes across adulthood. We will address this question in the next section.

Value Theories: From the Search of Universals to the Study of Culture

Universal Value Theories

Instrumental and Terminal Values

One of the most influential psychological theories of universal values was developed by Rokeach (1973). Rokeach distinguished between a set of 18 instrumental values and 18 terminal values. *Terminal values* refer to end states of human existence or ultimate or ideal modes of living, whereas *instrumental values* pertain to modes of conduct and refer to socially desirable behavior. Table 18.1 presents some examples of terminal and instrumental values.

Relating Values to Human Needs

Some universal theories relate values to fundamental human needs. For instance, Ryan and Deci (2000) propose that goals and activities that are related to materialistic values or endeavors for fame, power, or physical attractiveness have detrimental effects on personal growth and well-being. In contrast, if personal goals and daily activities serve the three proposed universal human needs of autonomy, social relatedness, and competence, well-being is likely to be enhanced. They criticize the cultural values expressed in the "American dream" as conflicting with fundamental and universal human needs.

Similarly, S. Schwartz (1992) proposed that values represent the universal requirements of human existence. According to his theory, there are three basic universal requirements of human existence: (1) biological needs (e.g., hedonism), (2) coordinated social interactions (e.g., power), and (3) survival and welfare needs of a group (e.g., tradition). This does not imply that these values are prescriptive, in the sense that everyone endorses them to the same extent. In contrast to such an extreme position on the universality of values, Schwartz assumes that people differ with respect to the extent to which they endorse values related to these three basic requirements of human existence. Consequently, in his questionnaire, Schwartz asks respondents to report how important they feel the 57 target values are as "guiding principles of [their] life." He derived a total of 10 distinct values from studies in more than 60 countries with 60,000 individuals (see Table 18.2).

Beyond Universalism: What Are the Main Cultural Differences in Values?

Most universal theories of values do not deny the existence of interindividual and cultural differences but acknowledge that individuals and cultures differ

Table 18.1. Examples of terminal and instrumental values (Rokeach, 1973)

Type	Value	Explanation
Terminal	Equality	Brotherhood and equal opportunity for all
	Family Security	Taking care of loved ones
	Inner Harmony	Freedom from inner conflict
	Freedom	Independence and free choice
	Health	Physical and mental well-being
	Wisdom	A mature understanding of life
Instrumental	Imaginative	Daring and creative
	Capable	Competent, effective
	Courageous	Standing up for your beliefs
	Helpful	Working for the welfare of others
	Loyal	Faithful to friends or the group
	Obedient	Dutiful, respectful

Table 18.2. Ten distinct (universal) values (S. Schwartz, 1992)

Power	Social status, prestige, control, and dominance over people/resources
Achievement	Personal success and admiration
Hedonism	Pleasure and self-gratification
Stimulation	Exciting life
Self-direction	Independence, creativity, freedom
Universalism	Social justice and tolerance
Benevolence	Promoting the welfare of others
Tradition	Respect for traditions and customs
Conformity	Obedience
Security	Safety, harmony, and welfare of society and of oneself

with respect to the importance placed on certain values over others. The universality claim is mostly related to the basic value dimensions and their inter-relationships across cultures. Focusing on the differences between cultures (instead of individual values), Shweder presents three moral or value domains that he believes encompass all cultural systems: autonomy (based on rights violations), community (based on communal values and hierarchy violations), and divinity (based on concepts such as sanctity and purity) (Shweder, Much, Mahapatra, & Park, 1997).

Hofstede's (1980) highly influential distinction between collectivistic versus individualistic cultures can be viewed as conceptualizing two of these domains (autonomy and community) as opposite poles of a single continuous dimension. Drawing on Hofstede, but in contrast to the one-dimensional approach, Triandis (1995) proposed that individualism and collectivism could be viewed as two separate and multidimensional value constructs. Individualism entails a focus on self-reliance, self-enhancement, and the attainment of personal needs, with the related values of power, achievement, hedonism, stimulation, and self-direction. In contrast, collectivism denotes an orientation toward others (particularly other members of one's own group) and a focus on relationships with others, with the related values of benevolence, tradition, and security. Although there is a large overlap with the values proposed by S. Schwartz, he explicitly cautions against equating certain values with individualism or collectivism. According to Schwartz' view, individualism and collectivism refer to cultural values; although values such as power can serve individual interests, on the group level, they might actually be given higher priority in collectivist cultures.

Note that theories stressing cultural differences in values do not assume that there is no interindividual or intraindividual variability in values in a given culture. Obviously, not all Chinese, for instance, are collectivists, nor are all Westerners individualists. Moreover, although these theories do not imply a static view of value orientations across the lifespan, they are, to our knowledge, mute regarding intraindividual changes over time. However, these approaches do assume that the differences between cultural groups are larger than the individual differences within these groups.

A Materialistic Versus Post-Materialistic Value Orientation

Inglehart (1997), a political scientist, proposed that, with increasing wealth, societies move away from a materialistic to a more post-materialistic value orientation. Materialistic values are reflected in concerns about law and order, as well as economic stability or growth. In contrast, post-materialistic values are related to egalitarian concerns such as the right to express oneself and to enhance one's lifestyle. Inglehart argues that a "silent revolution" takes place in that, with increasing wealth, Western societies become increasingly oriented toward post-materialistic values such as self-expression, aesthetics, and social belonging and increasingly less oriented toward materialistic values related to economic and security concerns.

Questions about the role of values in personal development can be split into two separate categories: (1) Do personal values change across the lifespan? And (2) does the influence of values on thought and behavior change across the lifespan? We will discuss both questions separately in the remainder of this chapter.

Change of Values Across Adulthood

Very little theoretical and empirical research has investigated how values change across adulthood. One of the exceptions is Erikson (1959, 1968, 1982), who suggested age-related differences in generativity. Generativity is defined as a caring for future generations by passing knowledge down to younger cohorts (e.g., by rearing children or more formal kinds of education) or more generally by trying to improve the living conditions for the next generation (e.g., sustaining the environment). In fact, generativity tends to increase across adulthood, with middle-aged adults demonstrating greater self-reported and behavioral generativity than young adults (McAdams, de St. Aubin, & Logan, 1993; but see Whitbourne, Zuschlag, Elliot, & Waterman, 1992). McAdams and colleagues have shown that generative concerns remain stable from middle into late adulthood, whereas generative behaviors seem to actually decrease. One of the reasons for the difference between generative concerns and behaviors might be that older adults encounter fewer opportunities for generative behavior as a function of children leaving home, retirement, and other age-related life events (e.g., health-related constraints that prevent active engagement in education or environmental causes).

Recently, Brandstädter and colleagues (Brandstädter, Rothermund, Kranz, & Kühn, 2010) presented a series of studies investigating a shift from extrinsic/instrumental to intrinsic/value-rational goals with advancing age. *Extrinsic/*

instrumental goals prioritize personal future benefits and are guided by the question, "What is my future gain from this action?" In contrast, intrinsic/value-rational goals transcend the personal benefit and are guided by the question, "What value does my action follow?" The fundamental distinction between these two types of goals is that instrumental goals derive their value from future events and are therefore time bound, whereas value-rational goals carry an inherent value regardless of their potential personal benefit. Brandtstädter and colleagues assume that a shift toward a greater emphasis on intrinsic/value-rational goals with a decreasing future time perspective (i.e., when nearing death) might serve important regulatory functions. More specifically, as the attainment of future benefits becomes more and more unlikely with a diminishing future time perspective, older adults might derive greater satisfaction by concentrating on values that they consider to be important in and of themselves and hence carry immediate positive meaning. Adopting intrinsic/value-rational goals is proposed to benefit older adults more than adopting extrinsic/instrumental goals. Empirical evidence on self-reported values from young, middle-aged, and older adults supports the proposed shift in value orientation from early to late adulthood. Strengthening this descriptive evidence, experimentally inducing an awareness of life's finitude was found to result in a decrease in instrumental orientation but left the value-rational orientation unaffected (Brandtstädter et al., 2010).

The Influence of Values on Thought and Action Across Adulthood

In line with Brandtstädter and colleagues, Hoppmann and Blanchard-Fields (2010) showed that, whereas young adults preferred autonomy goals, older adults preferred generative goals. However, after they manipulated (lengthened) future time perspective, older adults' preferences for autonomy goals were on a level comparable to that of younger adults. Goal preferences affected cognitive processes, such that autonomy goals were related to self-focused instrumental problem solving and generative goals were related to other-focused problem solving. In addition, there is some indication that the effectiveness of the match between goal type and problem-solving strategy also follows a developmental trend across these goal domains (Hoppmann, Coats, & Blanchard-Fields, 2008). Younger adults seemed to be more effective in matching problem-solving strategies to autonomy

goals, and older adults were more effective in matching problem-solving strategies to generative goals.

In Blanchard-Fields' research program on everyday problem solving across adulthood (e.g., Blanchard-Fields, 2007; Blanchard-Fields, Jahnke, & Camp, 1995; Blanchard-Fields, Mienaltowski, & Seay, 2007), she established that there seem to be no systematic age-related differences in either the use of instrumental problem-solving strategies or finding effective solutions (Blanchard-Fields et al., 1995). However, when she took different kinds of problems into account (instrumental vs. interpersonal/emotionally salient problems), she found that older adults engaged in emotion-regulatory strategies when dealing with interpersonal problems more than did younger adults. More specifically, in a number of studies (e.g., Blanchard-Fields et al., 1995; Blanchard-Fields et al., 2007), she demonstrated that older adults approached emotionally salient problem situations with more passive-dependent (i.e., wanting somebody else to take care of the problem) and avoidant-denial strategies (i.e., denying that there is a problem) than did younger adults. Moreover, Blanchard-Fields' research showed that older adults exhibited a more flexible and effective choice of strategy than did younger adults when problems were emotionally salient (Blanchard-Fields et al., 2007). This "expertise" in the domain of emotional and interpersonal problems can be seen as a heightened concern with the emotional consequences of everyday problems. Older adults, then, might place higher value on emotion regulation than on finding an instrumental solution. This explanation is consistent with predictions from socioemotional selectivity theory (Carstensen, Isaacowitz, Charles, 1999).

Socioemotional selectivity theory (SST) sets out to explain why people of different age groups pursue different kinds of goals in their actions and decisions and how this selection of goals helps maintain or even increase subjective well-being over the lifespan (Carstensen et al., 2011). Socioemotional selectivity theory posits a shift from a focus on instrumental and informational values of goals to social and emotional values of goals as people age. According to SST, younger people select their goals with respect to what they can learn from a certain action or what future benefits it entails. Older people, in contrast, focus on the affective consequences, for example, the contribution to personal well-being and the social aspects of an action (i.e., how it affects one's relationships to other people). Similar to Brandtstädter and colleagues (2010), they see the driving force behind this developmental shift in the length of the personal future horizon (Lang & Carstensen, 2002). Whereas a young person's future seems rather expansive, older people face an increasingly apparent limit to their future.

A major line of research within the theoretical framework of SST focuses on what Carstensen and colleagues have subsumed under the term *positivity effect* (e.g., Charles, Mather, & Carstensen, 2003; Fung & Carstensen, 2003; Mather & Carstensen, 2003), which refers to age-related differences in attention, processing, and memory of positively valenced stimuli over negatively valenced stimuli. In one set of studies (Charles et al., 2003), younger (18–29 years), middle-aged (41–53 years), and older adults (65–85 years) were presented with positive, negative, and neutral pictures. A subsequent memory test revealed that the ratio of positive to negative recalled pictures increased with age. These findings were corroborated in further studies that additionally employed event-related functional magnetic resonance imaging (Mather et al., 2004). Here, older participants showed higher activation in the amygdala when presented with positive as compared to negative pictures. Other studies focused on attention to valenced stimuli (Mather & Carstensen, 2003) or on autobiographical memory (Kennedy, Mather, & Carstensen, 2004). In sum, proponents of SST were able to provide evidence for the positivity effect in various cognitive paradigms (but see Murphy & Isaacowitz, 2008, for a meta-analysis that does not provide evidence supporting the positivity effect in attentional paradigms). From the theoretical perspective of SST, the positivity effect is due to an age-related increase in the motivation to maximize positive emotional experiences in the here and now when future time perspective is decreasing. In line with Brandtstädter's account of value-related changes across adulthood, one might argue that, according to SST, older adults, because of their limited future, become more hedonistic, focusing on experiencing positive emotions right now rather than investing in the acquisition of knowledge that might only pay off at some point in the future. Rather than focusing on the development of specific values (knowledge vs. emotional well-being), we adopt a more comprehensive perspective and explore age-related changes in a large set of values.

Age Differences in Values in the World Values Survey

We used data from the WVS to explore age-related differences in values. The WVS is a worldwide network of social scientists conducting representative national surveys in more than 80 societies. The survey focuses on central values and beliefs in the context of societal and technological change. Originating from the theoretical work of Inglehardt (1997), the primary aim was to test the hypothesis that values change from materialistic to post-materialistic as a function of economic development (as discussed earlier). Cohort analyses of the post-materialistic–materialistic dimension also revealed age-related trends associated with economic indicators. To date, the WVS comprises five waves that started in 1981. The fifth wave (2005–2007) included an assessment of the 10 universal values identified by S. Schwartz (1992, 1994; see Table 18.2). Whereas Inglehart's conceptualization has a rather narrow focus on the economic aspects of values, Schwartz's set of values is assumed to include all major motivationally distinct values.

The American subsample in the WVS (5th wave) comprises a total of $N = 1,249$ respondents with an age range from 18 to 91 years (M = 48 years; 50 percent female). In order to compare the importance of values for different adult age groups, we divided the sample into young (18–30 years, $n = 235$), middle-aged (40–50 years, $n = 264$), and older adults (65–91 years, $n = 230$).[1] The value questionnaire was a short version of the Schwartz Value Inventory (SVI) with one item for each value. (e.g., *"It is important to this person to have a good time; to "spoil" himself/herself"* to assess hedonism; participants rated their similarity to the described person on a 6-point rating scale).

First, we found that age groups differ significantly in the importance ratings of the values, regardless of the content of the respective value (F (2, 680) = 5.45; $p < .01$; *partial η^2 = .02*). This effect might be due to different scale use between age groups. To prevent such a methodological artifact and following Schwartz's recommendations, we centered value importance for each value content at the individual mean across value contents.[2] Results of an analysis of variance (with age group as the between-participant factor and value as the within-participant factor) showed that the importance of different values varies systematically by age group (F (14, 4809) = 8.34; $p < .001$; *partial η^2 = .02*). Figure 18.1 depicts means of value importance for the different value contents and age groups with their 95 percent confidence intervals.

In a next step, we tested for age trends in all 10 Schwartz values separately. We subjected the importance ratings for each value to a contrast analysis

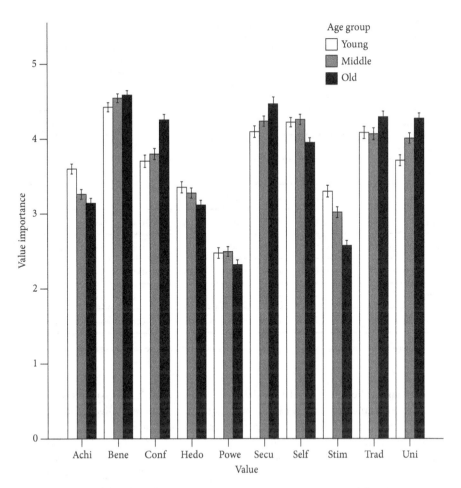

Figure 18.1. Importance ratings for the 10 Schwartz values by age group. Error bars represent 95 percent confidence intervals of the means. Achi = Achievement, Bene = Benevolence, Conf = Conformity, Hedo = Hedonism, Powe = Power, Secu = Security, Self = Self-direction, Stim = Stimulation, Trad = Tradition, Uni = Universalism.

testing a linear and a quadratic trend across the age groups. The demographic variables gender, education, social class, and income were controlled for in these analyses. However, tests without these covariates led to a comparable pattern of results. Table 18.3 presents the coefficients and statistics of these analyses.

Half of the values included in this study declined across age: self-determination, power, hedonism, achievement, and stimulation. These values are primarily self-related and are geared toward maximizing subjective well-being, self-fulfillment, and one's social position. In contrast to predictions from SST, then, hedonism declines with age. The other half of the values increases with age: security, benevolence, conformity, universalism, and tradition. With the exception of security, all of these values reflect a social orientation. There was hardly any indication of quadratic age trends, with the exception of conformity. The effect sizes of the linear trends

were of small to medium size. The largest effect sizes emerged for the age-related decline in the importance of achievement and stimulation and the age-related increase in the importance of conformity and universalism. This pattern of results maps nicely onto Schwartz theoretical model of two independent bipolar dimensions. On the first dimension, hedonism, achievement, and power form the pole "self-enhancement," and universalism and benevolence form the opposite pole "self-transcendence." On the second dimension, stimulation and self-direction mark the pole "openness to change" and opposes the pole "conservation," which is comprised of security, conformity, and tradition. On the basis of Schwartz's structure, one could summarize the age-related differences in importance of values by stating that, unlike younger adults, older adults value self-transcendence over self-enhancement and conservation over openness to change. An increase in self-transcendence with age is in line

Table 18.3. Age trends for the 10 Schwartz values

	Linear contrast				Quadratic contrast			
	Contrast	SE	p	$r_{effect size}$	Contrast	SE	P	$r_{effect size}$
Achievement	−0.37	0.07	<.001	.20	0.07	0.07	.29	.04
Benevolence	0.16	0.06	.01	.10	−0.03	0.06	.60	.02
Conformity	0.40	0.08	<.001	.18	0.16	0.08	<.05	.08
Hedonism	−0.19	0.07	.01	.10	−0.05	0.07	.50	.03
Power	−0.18	0.07	.01	.10	−0.07	0.07	.28	.04
Security	0.30	0.08	<.001	.15	<0.01	0.08	.98	<.01
Self-Determination	−0.19	0.07	.01	.10	−0.10	0.07	.15	.06
Stimulation	−0.53	0.08	<.001	.26	−0.04	0.08	.62	.02
Tradition	0.20	0.08	.02	.09	0.08	0.08	.32	.04
Universalism	0.42	0.08	<.001	.21	−0.01	0.07	.86	.01

Contrast analyses with demographic variables as covariates (gender, education, social class, income)

with Brandstädter and colleagues' (2010) model. An increase in the importance of conservation over openness to change would fit with results from personality development that show that openness to new experiences declines with age (e.g., Donnellan & Lucas, 2008).

To further explore this result, we averaged the importance ratings of the respective values that are, according to Schwartz's theory, indicative of self-enhancement, self-transcendence, openness to change, and conservation. Results of the analysis of variance with age group as a between-participants factor and value pole as a within-participants factor showed the expected interaction ($F(5,1773) = 16.45$; $p < .001$; *partial η^2* = .04). [3,4]

As depicted in Figure 18.2 older adults do, in fact, consider self-enhancement values to be less important than do younger adults. At the same time, they place more value on self-transcendence than do younger adults. Regarding the dimension of conservation versus openness to change, older adults value conservation more than younger adults but place less emphasis on openness to change. As is true for all cross-sectional designs, we cannot disentangle age from cohort effects (e.g., Schaie, 1965). However, the present findings nicely dovetail the theoretical accounts and empirical evidence of Brandtstädter and colleagues' (2010) work. Moreover, they extend Brandstädter's findings by using a comprehensive set of values and a large sample spanning

the entire adult lifespan. However, one important question remains: Given the weak (or nonexisting) association between values and actual behavior (Kristiansen & Hotte, 1996; Rohan, 2000), why should we care about the kinds of values different age groups endorse? In the remainder of this chapter, we argue that, under certain conditions, values should matter for developmental regulation.

When Do Values Matter?

In this section, we address the question of when values exert an influence on thought and behavior and whether the degree of this influence remains constant across adulthood. We argue that values play a role in life planning and life review and that this function might change as a function of life stage. Whereas adolescents and young adults rely relatively often on values as guiding principles for selecting life goals, middle-aged adults generally use more pragmatic standards for behavioral and attitudinal decisions. It is only in older age that values resurface in their function to guide action. Note that this proposed U-shaped developmental trend parallels the common folk psychological observation that, when moving from adolescence to adulthood, people have to give up their idealistic perspective to a certain degree and adopt a more pragmatic one in order to cope with the "developmental rush hour" in early/middle adulthood and its affordances (e.g., personal career, economic welfare, rearing children,

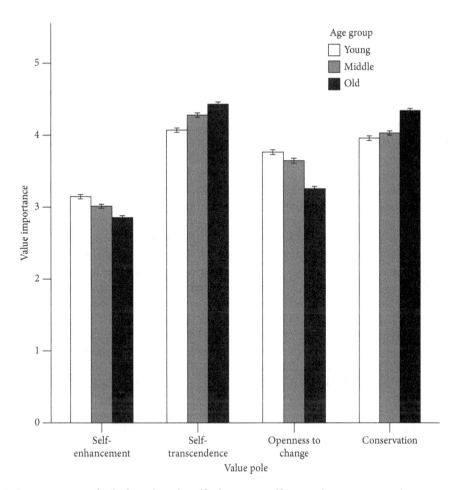

Figure 18.2. Importance ratings for the four value poles, self-enhancement, self-transcendence, openness to change, conservation, as a function of age group. Error bars represent 95 percent confidence intervals of the means.

etc.). Only in late adulthood, when people face fewer external constraints and demands, might there be sufficient freedom to adopt an idealistic perspective again.

Whereas this observation builds on age-graded affordances and constraints for explaining this trend, we adopt a more psychological rationale. Let us revisit the definition of values and their assigned role for thought and action. Values are abstract beliefs about what is generally desirable in life (Kluckhohn, 1951). Given their abstract nature, values are not directly related to concrete actions in specific situations. More proximate factors might exert a stronger influence on behavior, such as situational constraints, feasibility considerations, competing proximal goals, or expectations from other people. Thus, it is not surprising that the empirical link between values and behavior is generally rather weak and indirect (Kristiansen & Hotte, 1996; Rohan, 2000; but see Bardi & Schwartz, 2003).

However, values can also be seen as providing clear and simple rules that enable people to shortcut decisional or evaluative processes. In this perspective, values can be seen as a kind of heuristic (e.g., Sunstein, 2005). Once a situation is perceived as concerning a strongly held value, the appraisal of the situation and behavioral reactions might be straightforward (Tetlock, 2003). For example, consider a person for whom the protection of the environment is an important and strongly held value. If he or she conceives of the deforestation of the rainforest as a threat to the environment, he or she will condemn it without qualifications regarding the potential economic and social consequences. Without such a strong value, the evaluation might be derived from a more complex decision process that weighs costs and benefits. In this sense, then, strong values can serve as simplifying guidelines to evaluate the appropriate lines of action in a given situation. The respective value results in a simple rule of do's and don'ts: do what upholds the value and refrain from actions that disregard it (see also the research on "sacred values," Tanner & Medin,

2004; Tetlock, 2003). Nevertheless, apart from these rather pronounced cases, the general notion in the literature is that values exert their influence indirectly by acting as criteria or standards to select and evaluate goals (e.g., Schwartz, 1996).

Extensive theorizing and empirical research has attempted to close the value-behavior gap by identifying moderating and mediating variables (e.g., Maio & Olson, 1995; Maio, Olson, Allen, & Bernard, 2001; Kristiansen & Hotte, 1996). For example, Kristiansen and Hotte (1996) showed that the level of moral reasoning can have an impact on the value-behavior relationship. People with a higher level of moral reasoning also exhibit higher congruence between values and behavior. Verplanken and Holland (2002) suggested the centrality of a value within the self-concept as a moderator, with more central values exhibiting a stronger influence on behavior. Finally, Vallacher and Wegner (1987) proposed that the mental representation of a situation is a determining factor in the value-behavior relationship. According to their action identification theory, situations that are conceptualized in value-related terms are likely to elicit the corresponding behavior.

Time Perspective and the Influence of Values

Building on the action identification theory, Trope and colleagues (Trope & Liberman, 2003, 2010) developed a theoretical framework linking the subjective conceptualization, or *construal*, of a situation to time perspective. More specifically, the construal level theory (CLT) posits that increasing temporal distance to an event is associated with a more abstract cognitive representation of the event. The closer an event or an object, the more detailed information is available. For close events, mental construals can comprise a vast amount of concrete details, whereas construals of distant events are based on overarching core features and generally lack detailed information.

The concept of temporal distance has been extended to various kinds of "psychological distances," for example, social distance, hypothetical distance, spatial distance, and the like that are assumed to be equally related to construal abstractness (Liberman & Trope, 2008).

In an extensive research program, Trope and colleagues were able to provide evidence for the link between psychological distance and abstractness of mental construals in various domains ranging from gambling over negotiations to consumer behavior (e.g., Henderson, Trope, & Carnevale,

2006; Liberman & Trope, 1998; Liberman, Trope, & Wakslak, 2007; Sagristano, Liberman, & Trope, 2002).

More recently, Eyal and colleagues (Eyal, Liberman, & Trope, 2008; Eyal, Sagristano, Trope, Liberman, & Chaiken, 2009) applied CLT to values. Given the abstract nature of values, they predicted that the greater the psychological distance to an event, the more values should matter for behavior and thought. This should be the case because construing one's actions in abstract terms refers to the reason and meaning of the action (Liberman & Trope, 1998; Vallacher & Wegner, 1989) and is therefore more likely to invoke one's values. Confirming the higher link between values and actions, Eyal et al. (2008) found that people rate the likelihood of engaging in certain behaviors in the distant future more on the basis of their values than when the behaviors are temporally close.

In a similar vein, Kivetz and Tyler (2007) showed that a distal time perspective makes more idealistic versus pragmatic conceptions of the self accessible. Kivetz and Tyler suggested that, when people think of themselves in a time remote from the present, they tend to focus more on the core features of themselves and the values and principles that they adhere to rather than on pragmatic considerations. The focus on one's central values entails value-congruent behavior (Verplanken & Holland, 2002). In their studies, participants showed the proposed focus on personal values for distal decisions for which they made value-congruent choices. For proximal decisions, however, pragmatic concerns dominated the decisions. Agerström and Björklund (2009) investigated the effect of temporal distance on altruistic versus selfish behavioral intentions in the context of moral dilemmas. They found that people showed more moral and altruistic concern for distant events than for proximal events. This effect, however, was moderated by value importance. The time perspective changed the thinking only for people who endorsed the relevant moral values. In an additional mediation analysis, the authors found evidence for the assumption that the effect is mediated by value salience. The authors' conclusion is that a distal temporal perspective is able to activate personal values that subsequently guide behavior.

In sum, recent research suggests that time perspective might act as a central variable determining the value-behavior congruence: adopting a distal time perspective seems to enhance value-behavior congruence whereas adopting a proximal time perspective blurs it. The theoretical side of this moderation—that is, the mechanism of how time perspective interacts with values on the one side and behavior and thought on the other—is still not clear. Some authors seem to suggest that time perspective changes the representation of a situation in such a way that it is more likely to invoke values or value-related descriptions (Eyal et al., 2009). Other authors focus more on the representation of the self, claiming that a distal time perspective activates values within the self-concept (Kivetz & Tyler, 2007). Finally, it might also depend on the match between the representations of the situation and the self. More research is needed to distinguish among these three accounts. For our purposes, however, it is sufficient to state that there is reason to assume that a more distant time perspective makes it more likely to invoke values than a more proximal time perspective. Taking a developmental perspective, the link between time perspective and the relevance of personal values for thought and action implies that the function of values to provide direction for future actions and to serve as a standard of comparison to evaluate one's actions increases when people engage in temporally distal construals of themselves and their actions. We propose that there are two primary developmental activities that are likely to invoke a distal perspective on oneself and one's actions: life planning and life reviewing.

LIFE PLANNING: SETTING PERSONAL GOALS FOR THE FUTURE

One of the tenets of lifespan psychology is that people proactively shape their development by setting and pursuing goals (Brandtstädter, 1998; Freund & Baltes, 2000). During adolescence and early adulthood, people start to form ideas of the kind of person they want to become (Nurmi, 1991). Researchers have used different concepts to describe these long-term construals of oneself and one's life, such as personal strivings (Emmons, 1985), current concerns (Klinger, 1977), personal projects (Little, 1983), possible selves (Markus & Nurius, 1986), or identity goals (Gollwitzer, 1986), but they all share the idea that such future projections of the self become an important motivational source that provides structure and meaning for the individual life. In general, these future projections are closely linked to age-graded developmental tasks (Freund, 2007; Heckhausen, 1999; Nurmi, 1992) and thus reflect expectations about life events that are age-graded, such as when to finish education, when to start a family, or at what age to retire.

Reviewing the research on the content of goals, Freund and Riediger (2006) found that for younger adults these goals or concerns are often related to education, career, and family. Middle-aged adults focus more on their children's lives and their property. And for older adults, these goals concern health, retirement, future generations, and the state of the world in general. This change in the content of goals and its dependence on cultural scripts and opportunity structures is well established. Far less research exists on the temporal extension of planning one's life through setting personal goals. One of the few exceptions is a study by Nurmi (1992), who reports a decrease in the temporal extension of goals with age. Comparing goals of the same life domain, he found that younger people extend their planning further into the future than do older people. These findings corroborate data from Lens and Gally (1980), who also found a decrease in the temporal extension of life planning in a cross-sectional study based on a representative sample. A simple explanation for this finding is that, due to the decrease in future time perspective, developmental tasks and age-related life events are less extended into the future as people age. Thus, when life planning might be most important, namely, in adolescence and early adulthood, people adopt a distal time perspective that also invokes distal construals of oneself and one's actions. Building on the social-cognitive literature on construal level theory cited earlier, this implies that life planning likely invokes the activation of values that match this level of cognitive representation of oneself and one's life in the future. In this way, then, values are likely to guide life planning and, thereby, goal selection. As elaborated by Freund (2007), goals not only guide specific behavior in a specific situation, but guide actions across situations and time. Goals thereby serve an important function of developmental regulation. Indirectly, then, values have an impact on development because they are likely to be involved in future life planning that forms the overarching frame for the selection of goals.

LIFE REVIEW: LOOKING BACK ON THE PAST

Life review refers to the process of remembering and analyzing personal life events or life in general (Staudinger, 2001). Many lifespan theories posit that life review is an important component of development regulation. For example, Erikson (1959, 1982) stated that by reviewing their lives, people are able to resolve the eighth and last main psychosocial crisis of the life circle and to integrate their lives.

McAdams (1999) highlighted the importance of life review for one's sense of identity by reasoning and evaluating one's memories. Neugarten (1968) saw the primary function of life review in the reassessment and restructuring of one's life.

In general, life review is seen as bearing at least a twofold function (e.g., Bluck, Alea, Habermas, & Rubin, 2005; Staudinger, 2001): first, life review serves to build a coherent life story and to make sense of one's past. This function of life review is often referred to in the therapeutical context (e.g., Serrano, Latorre, Gatz, & Montanes, 2004). In this context, values can take center stage as a standard of comparison to evaluate one's past actions. The second function of life review is to guide and direct present and future thought and behavior. By reflecting on past experiences, people can gain insight into their motives and values and use this knowledge to plan their future. Staudinger (2001) pointed out that there are several social-cognitive processes underlying life review. For the explanation and evaluation component of life review, categorization and abstraction are among the key processes. Even when the content of life review consists of specific episodes, people categorize them in more general and more abstract themes, such as friendship, partnership, achievements. Through this abstraction process, it becomes more likely that the contents of life review appeal directly—or at least more directly—to personal values, which are then used as evaluative criteria.

Although people may engage in life review at any life stage beyond childhood (Staudinger, 2001), many developmental theorists posit a developmental trend, with older people showing more or more frequent engagement in life review than do younger people (e.g., Erikson, 1959; Neugarten, 1968). According to this perspective, then, values should regain importance in later adulthood when one looks back at life and more distal events to review one's life. The engagement in life review in later adulthood then stands as one factor—among others;, for example, personal resources (Brandtstädter et al., 2010)—that might lead to a greater relevance of personal values in this life phase.

Taken together, we posit that values play an important role in guiding development during adolescence and early adulthood, when life planning involves a long-term future perspective. Values regain importance as a standard of evaluating one's own life in later adulthood, when life review entails a longer past. Values, then, guide future actions in adolescence and early adulthood and thoughts about the past in later adulthood.

Conclusion

In this chapter, we set out to explore the role of values for personal development. Although values have been a topic of extensive investigation in psychology and related disciplines, they have rarely been considered a developmental construct. As an attempt to fill this gap, we posed two questions concerning values across the lifespan: (1) Does the content of values change across adulthood? (2) Does the impact of values on thought and action change across adulthood?

With regard to the first question, we reviewed developmental theories that posit the existence of age-related changes in value contents. This change in values is commonly assumed to affect behavior by shifting goal preferences (e.g., SST posits a shift from knowledge-related/informational to socio-emotional goals). Several authors see the future time perspective as a central determinant of this change. Future time perspective in this context is seen as a resource that makes future goals attainable. Aging is closely associated with the shrinking of the future, which, according to SST, stresses the importance of more immediate satisfaction of goals. Because emotional goals can be satisfied in any given situation, SST posits that they outweigh other goals such as gaining more knowledge (which might only pay off in the distant future). The accounts of Brandstädter and colleagues and of Carstensen and colleagues converge in the assumption that people master this challenge—at least in part—by a change in values. More precisely, both agree that people experience a shift toward a focus on immediate, emotionally gratifying experiences and close social relations. For Brandstädter, this list also includes time-transcending values, such as moral or ethical orientations. Extending this literature, we used the comprehensive measure of values by Schwartz (1994) included in the WVS to detect cross-sectional age differences in values. We obtained partly converging results: age was associated with a shift from self-enhancement to self-transcendence and with a shift from openness to change to conservation. Taken together, there is mounting evidence for a value change across the adult lifespan. Although the field needs further and more detailed research that is also able to disentangle cohort- and age-related trends, this value change might be relevant in many social-cognitive and developmental contexts.

The second question concerned the relative impact of values on thought and action across adulthood. We discussed theoretical reasons why— with the exception of very strongly held or sacred values—the impact of values on behavior is generally weak to nonexisting. Building on findings in social psychology, we identified time perspective as a central determinant of the value-behavior relationship. Time perspective is closely related to the cognitive representation of the self and events. Distal as opposed to proximal time perspective is associated with more abstract construals of events, individuals, and actions that match the level of abstractness typically associated with values. When levels of representation are matched, this should also lead to a higher likelihood of values guiding actions. Applying this reasoning to the developmental context, we hypothesized that personal values will gain directive influence whenever people are likely to construe themselves or their actions in a more distal perspective.

There are two main developmental activities that invoke such distal construals: life planning and life review. We assume that the influence of value on personal development takes place via these two activities. Because people are more likely to engage in life planning involving the distal future during adolescence and early adulthood, values are assumed to serve a guiding function for the selection of personal goals during these life stages. Values might take central stage again in later adulthood when people engage in life review involving the distant past. In this context, values serve as comparison standards for one's past actions. At present, these hypotheses await empirical testing—an endeavor we had planned to undertake with Fredda Blanchard-Fields, to whom we are greatly indebted for the many thought-provoking and stimulating discussions on this topic.

Notes

1. Analyses using age as a continuous variable rather than age groups yielded the same results. Because graphing the findings is easier when distinct age groups are used, we also present the analyses using age as a categorical variable.
2. Analyses were also conducted with raw scores that yielded comparable results.
3. The interaction qualified main effects of value pole (F $(3,1773) = 304.52$; $p < .001$; $partial\ \eta^2 = .30$)[4] and age group (F $(2,707) = 3.34$; $p = .04$; $partial\ \eta^2 = .01$). A planned contrast for the interaction, pitting the opposing value poles against each other, was also significant and yielded a larger effect (F $(2,707) = 29.47$; $p < .001$; $partial\ \eta^2 = .08$).
4. The degrees of freedom were adjusted using the Huynh-Feldt correction because the sphericity assumption was violated.

References

Agerström, J., & Björklund, F. (2009). Moral concerns are greater for temporally distant events and are moderated by value strength. *Social Cognition, 27*, 261–282.

Bardi, A., & Schwartz, S. H. (2003). Values and behavior: Strength and structure of relations. *Personality & Social Psychology Bulletin, 29*, 1207–1220.

Baron, J., & Spranca, M. (1997). Protected values. *Organizational Behavior and Human Decision Processes. 70*, 1–16.

Blanchard-Fields, F. (2007). Everyday problem solving and emotion: An adult developmental perspective. *Current Directions in Psychological Science, 16*, 26–31.

Blanchard-Fields, F., Jahnke, H. C., & Camp, C. (1995). Age differences in problem solving style: The role of emotional salience. *Psychology and Aging, 10*, 173–180.

Blanchard-Fields, F., Mienaltowski, A., & Seay, R. B. (2007). Age differences in everyday problem-solving effectiveness: Older adults select more effective strategies for interpersonal problems. *Journals of Gerontology: Psychological Science, 62*, 61–64.

Bluck, S., Alea, N., Habermas, T., & Rubin, D. C. (2005). A tale of three functions: The self-reported uses of autobiographical memory. *Social Cognition, 23*, 91–117.

Brandtstädter, J. (1998). Action perspectives on human development. In R. M. Lerner & W. Damon (Eds.), *Handbook of child psychology: Vol. 1. Theoretical models of human development* (5th ed., pp. 807–863). New York: Wiley.

Brandtstädter, J., Rothermund, K., Kranz, D., & Kühn, W. (2010). Final decentrations: Personal goals, rationality perspectives, and the awareness of life's finitude. *European Psychologist, 15*, 152–163.

Carstensen, L. L., Isaacowitz, D. M., Charles, S. T. (1999). Taking time seriously: A theory of socioemotional selectivity. *American Psychologist, 54*, 165–181.

Carstensen, L. L., Turan, B., Scheibe, S., Ram, N., Ersner-Hershfield, H., Samanez-Larkin, G. R., Brooks, K. P., & Nesselroade, J. R. (2011). Emotional experience improves with age: Evidence based on over 10 years of experience sampling. *Psychology and Aging, 26*, 21–33.

Charles, S., Mather, M., & Carstensen, L. L. (2003). Aging and emotional memory: The forgettable nature of negative images for older adults. *Journal of Experimental Psychology: General, 132*, 310–324.

Deutsche Shell. (2002). *Jugend 2002: 14. Shell Jugendstudie* [Adolescence 2002: 14th Shell adolescence study]. Frankfurt am Main, Germany: Fischer.

Donnellan, M. B., & Lucas, R. E. (2008). Age differences in the Big Five across the life span: Evidence from two national samples. *Psychology and Aging, 23*, 558–566.

Eagly, A. H., & Chaiken, S. (1993). *The psychology of attitudes.* Fort Worth, TX: Harcourt Brace Jovanovich.

Emmons, R. A. (1985). Personal strivings: An approach to personality and subjective well-being. *Journal of Personality and Social Psychology, 51*, 1058–1068.

Erikson, E. H. (1959). *Identity and the life cycle.* New York: International Universities.

Erikson, E. H. (1968). *Identity, youth, and crisis.* New York: Norton.

Erikson, E. H. (1982). *The life cycle completed.* New York: Norton.

Eyal, T., Liberman, N., & Trope, Y. (2008). Judging near and distant virtue and vice. *Journal of Experimental Social Psychology, 44*, 1204–1209.

Eyal, T., Sagristano, M. D., Trope, Y., Liberman, N., & Chaiken, S. (2009). When values matter: Expressing values in behavioral intentions for the near vs. distant future. *Journal of Experimental Social Psychology, 45*, 35–43.

Freund, A. M. (2007). Differentiating and integrating levels of goal representation: A life-span perspective. In B. R. Little,

K. Salmela-Aro, J. E. Nurmi, & S. D. Phillips (Eds.), *Personal project pursuit: Goals, action and human flourishing* (pp. 247–270). Mahwah, NJ: Erlbaum.

Freund, A. M., & Baltes, P. (2000). The orchestration of selection, optimization, and compensation: An action-theoretical conceptualization of a theory of developmental regulation. In W. J. Perrig & A. Grob (Eds.), *Control of human behavior, mental processes, and consciousness* (pp. 35–58). Mahwah, NJ: Erlbaum.

Freund, A. M., & Riediger, M. (2006). Goals as building blocks of personality and development in adulthood. In D. K. Mroczek & T. D. Little (Eds.), *Handbook of personality development* (pp. 353–372). Mahwah, NJ: Erlbaum.

Fung, H., & Carstensen, L. L. (2003). Sending memorable messages to the old: Age differences in preferences and memory for advertisements. *Journal of Personality and Social Psychology, 85*, 163–178.

Gollwitzer, P. M. (1986). Striving for specific identities: The social reality of self-symbolizing. In R. Baumeister (Ed.), *Public self and private self* (pp. 143–159). New York: Springer-Verlag.

Hanselmann, M., & Tanner, C. (2008). Taboos and conflicts in decision making: Sacred values, decision difficulty and emotions. *Judgment and Decision Making, 3*, 51–63.

Havighurst, R. J. (1956). Research on the developmental task concept. *School Review: A Journal of Secondary Education, 64*, 215–223.

Henderson, M. D., Trope, Y., & Carnevale, P. (2006). Negotiation from a near and distant time perspective. *Journal of Personality and Social Psychology, 91*, 712–729.

Heckhausen, J. (1999). *Developmental regulation in adulthood: Age-normative and sociostructural constraints as adaptive challenges.* New York: Cambridge University Press.

Hofstede, G. (1980). *Culture's consequences: International differences in work-related values.* Newbury Park, CA: Sage.

Hoppmann, C., & Blanchard-Fields, F. (2010). Goals and everyday problem solving: Manipulating goal preferences in young and older adults. *Developmental Psychology, 46*, 1433–1443.

Hoppmann, C. A., Coats, A., & Blanchard-Fields, F. (2008). Goals and everyday problem solving: Examining the link between age-related goals and problem-solving strategy use. Aging, *Neuropsychology, and Cognition, 15*, 401–423.

Inglehart, R. (1990). *Culture shift in advanced industrial society.* Princeton, NJ: Princeton University Press.

Inglehart, R. (1997). *Modernization and postmodernization.* Princeton, NJ: Princeton University Press.

Kennedy, Q., Mather, M., & Carstensen, L. L. (2004). The role of motivation in the age-related positivity effect in autobiographical memory. *Psychological Science, 15*, 208–214.

Kivetz, Y., & Tyler, T. R. (2007). Tomorrow I'll be me: The effect of time perspective on the activation of idealistic versus pragmatic selves. *Organizational Behavior and Human Decision Processes, 102*, 193–211.

Klinger, E. (1977). *Meaning and void: Inner experience and the incentives in people's lives.* Minneapolis: University of Minnesota Press.

Kluckhohn, C. (1951). Values and value-orientations in the theory of action. In E. Shils (Ed.), *Toward a general theory of action* (pp. 388–433). Cambridge, MA: Harvard University Press.

Kristiansen, C. M., & Hotte, A. (1996). Morality and the self: Implications for the when and how of value-attitude-behavior relations. In C. Seligman, J. M. Olson, & M. P. Zanna (Eds.), *The psychology of values: The Ontario symposium.* Hillsdale, NJ: Lawrence Erlbaum Associates.

Lang, F. R., & Carstensen, L. L. (2002). Time counts: Future time perspective, goals, and social relationships. *Psychology and Aging, 17*, 125–139.

Lens, W., & Gailly, A. (1980). Extension of future time perspective in motivational goals of different age groups. *International Journal of Behavioral Development, 3*, 1–17.

Liberman, N., & Trope, Y. (1998). The role of feasibility and desirability considerations in near and distant future decisions: A test of temporal construal theory. *Journal of Personality and Social Psychology, 75*, 5–18.

Liberman, N., & Trope, Y. (2008). The psychology of transcending the here and now. *Science, 322*, 1201–1205.

Liberman, N., Trope, Y., & Wakslak, C. (2007). Construal level theory and consumer behavior. *Journal of Consumer Psychology, 17*, 113–117.

Little, B. R. (1983). Personal projects. A rationale and method for investigation. *Environment and Behavior, 15*, 273–309.

Maio, G. R., & Olson, J. M. (1995). Relations between values, attitudes, and behavioral intentions: The moderating role of attitude function. *Journal of Experimental Social Psychology, 31*, 266–285.

Maio, G. R., Olson, J. M., Allen, L., & Bernard, M. M. (2001). Addressing discrepancies between values and behavior: The motivating effect of reasons. *Journal of Experimental Social Psychology, 37*, 104–117.

Markus, H., & Nurius, P. (1986). Possible selves. *American Psychologist, 41*, 954–969.

Major, B., & Deaux, K. (1982). Individual differences injustice behavior. In J. Greenberg & R. L. Cohen (Eds.), *Equity and justice in social behavior.* San Diego, CA: Academic Press.

Mather, M., & Carstensen, L. L. (2003). Aging and attentional biases for emotional faces. *Psychological Science, 14*, 409–415.

Mather, M., Canli, T., English, T., Whitfield, S., Wais, P., Ochsner, K., Gabrieli, J. D. E., & Carstensen, L. L. (2004). Amygdala responses to emotionally valenced stimuli in older and younger adults. *Psychological Science, 15*, 259–263.

McAdams, D. P. (1999). Personal narratives and the life story. In L. Pervin & O. John (Eds.), *Handbook of personality: Theory and research* (2nd edition, pp. 478–500). New York: Guilford Press.

McAdams, D. P., de St. Aubin, E., & Logan, R. L. (1993). Generativity among young, midlife, and older adults. *Psychology and Aging, 8*, 221–230.

Murphy, N. A., & Isaacowitz, D. M. (2008). Preferences for emotional information in older and younger adults: A meta-analysis of memory and attention tasks. *Psychology and Aging, 23*, 263–286.

Neugarten, B. L. (1968). *Adult personality: Toward a psychology of the life cycle.* Chicago, IL: University of Chicago Press.

Nisbett, R. E. (2003). *The geography of thought: Why we think the way we do.* New York: Free Press.

Nurmi, J.-E. (1991). How do adolescents see their future? A review of the development of future orientation and planning. *Developmental Review, 11*, 1–59.

Nurmi, J.-E. (1992). Age differences in adult life goals, concerns, and their temporal extension: A life course approach to future-oriented motivation. *International Journal of Behavioral Development, 15*, 487–508.

Reitzle, M., & Silbereisen, R. K. (2000). Adapting to social change: Adolescents' values in Eastern and Western Germany. In J. Bynner & R. K. Silbereisen (Eds.), *Adversity and challenge in life in the New Germany and in England* (pp. 123–152). London: Macmillan.

Rohan, M. J. (2000). A rose by any name? The values construct. *Personality & Social Psychology Review, 4*, 255–277.

Rokeach, M. (1973). *Understanding human values*. New York: Free Press.

Ryan, R. M., & Deci, E. L. (2000). Self-determination theory and the facilitation of intrinsic motivation, social development, and well-being. *American Psychologist, 55*, 68–78.

Sagristano, M. D., Trope, Y., & Liberman, N. (2002). Time-dependent gambling: Odds now, money later. *Journal of Experimental Psychology: General, 131*, 364–376.

Schaie, K. W. (1965). A general model for the study of developmental problems. *Psychological Bulletin, 64*, 92–107.

Schwartz, B. (1990). The creation and destruction of value. *American Psychologist, 45*, 7–15.

Schwartz, S. H. (1992). Universals in the content and structure of values: Theoretical advances and empirical tests in 20 countries. In M. Zanna (Ed.) *Advances in experimental social psychology* (Vol. 25, pp. 1–65). Orlando, FL: Academic Press.

Schwartz, S. H. (1994). Are there universal aspects in the content and structure of values? *Journal of Social Issues, 50*, 19–45.

Schwartz, S. H. (1996). Value priorities and behavior: Applying a theory of integrated value systems. In C. Seligman, J. M. Olson, & M. P. Zanna (Eds.), *The psychology of values: The Ontario Symposium* (Vol. 8, pp. 1–24). Hillsdale, NJ: Erlbaum.

Serrano, J. P., Latorre, J. M., Gatz, M., & Montanes, J. (2004). Life review therapy using autobiographical retrieval practice for older adults with depressive symptomatology. *Psychology and Aging, 19*, 272–277. doi: 10.1037/08827974.19.2.272

Shweder, R. A, Much, N. C., Mahapatra, M., & Park, L. (1997). The "big three" of morality (autonomy, community, divinity) and the "big three" explanations of suffering. In A. M. Brandt & P. Rozin (Eds.), *Morality and health* (pp. 119–169). New York: Routledge.

Skitka, L. J., & Bauman, C. W. (2008). Moral conviction and political engagement. *Political Psychology, 29*, 29–54.

Skitka, L. J., Bauman, C. W., & Sargis, E. G. (2005). Moral conviction: Another contributor to attitude strength or something more? *Journal of Personality and Social Psychology, 88*, 895–917.

Staudinger, U. (2001). Life reflection: A social-cognitive analysis of life review. *Review of General Psychology, 5*, 148–160.

Sunstein, C. R. (2005). Moral heuristics. *Behavioral and Brain Sciences, 28*, 531–542.

Tanner, C., & Medin, D. L. (2004). Protected values: No omission bias and no framing effects. *Psychonomic Bulletin & Review, 11*, 185–191.

Tetlock, P. E. (2003). Thinking the unthinkable: Sacred values and taboo cognitions. *Trends in Cognitive Sciences, 7*, 320–324.

Tetlock, P. E., Kristel, O.Elson, B.Green, M., & Lerner, J. S. (2000). The psychology of the unthinkable: Taboo trade-offs, forbidden base rates, and heretical counterfactuals. *Journal of Personality and Social Psychology, 78*, 853–870.

Triandis, H. C. (1995). *Individualism and collectivism*. Boulder, CO: Westview.

Trope, Y., & Liberman, N. (2003). Temporal construal. *Psychological Review, 110*, 403–421.

Trope, Y., & Liberman, N. (2010). Construal level theory of psychological distance. *Psychological Review, 117*, 440–463.

Vallacher, R. R., & Wegner, D. M. (1987). What do people think they're doing? Action identification and human behavior. *Psychological Review, 94*, 3–15.

Vallacher, R. R., & Wegner, D. M. (1989). Levels of personal agency: Individual variation in action identification. *Journal of Personality and Social Psychology, 57*, 660–671.

Verplanken, B., & Holland, R. W. (2002). Motivated decision making effects on activation and self-centrality of values on choices and behavior. *Journal of Personality and Social Psychology, 82*, 434–447.

Whitbourne, S. K., Zuschlag, M. K., Elliot, L. B., & Waterman, A. S. (1992). Psychosocial development in adulthood: A 22-year sequential study. *Journal of Personality and Social Psychology, 63*, 260–271.

Wicker, A. W. (1969). Attitudes versus actions: The relationship of verbal and overt behavior response to attitude objects. *Journal of Social Issues, 25*, 41–78.

World Values Survey Association (2009). *World values survey 2005 official data v.20090901* [Data file]. Retrieved from http://www.wvsevsdb.com/wvs/WVSData.jsp

Causal Attributions Across the Adult Lifespan

Michelle Horhota, Andrew Mienaltowski, *and* Yiwei Chen

Abstract

This chapter reviews the literature on causal attributions in adulthood. The authors first provide a brief history of the research on causal attributions from the social psychological literature and illustrate how a lifespan developmental approach extends our understanding of causal attributions. The authors then outline the age differences in attributions that emerge in performance and social contexts and discuss the two mechanisms that have been proposed to account for these age differences: cognitive resource limitations and social knowledge differences. Finally, the authors conclude with suggestions for future directions in the field.

Key Words: causal attributions, aging, cognitive resources, social beliefs, emotion and motivation, social cognition, social judgments

Why did that happen? From the moment an event occurs, individuals are motivated to generate an explanation for what caused the event. Sometimes events are easy to understand (e.g., being pulled over by a police officer because you were driving 15 miles over the speed limit), whereas other events may be much more difficult to explain (e.g., why a couple's marriage dissolves). The need for explanation occurs at the individual level in our daily lives and at a cultural level, as evidenced by the fact that we are surrounded by media providing round-the-clock analysis of the events of the day. It appears that humans are inherently interested in making causal attributions about events and human behavior.

Understanding the underlying causes of events is an adaptive part of our everyday reasoning (Weiner, 1985). If one can determine the cause of events, it is possible to avoid them in the future or to maximize the chance that a positive event will reoccur. Attributions help individuals to understand what to do next and how to adjust to the situations that they

encounter. Over the course of one's lifetime, individuals gather information about causes and effects, antecedents and outcomes, and they ultimately develop a knowledge base of general patterns of behavior that can then be applied to specific events that are encountered in daily life.

Social psychologists have long been interested in understanding the types of attributions and the variables that influence them. Young adults make relatively consistent patterns of attributions for their own behavior in performance contexts (e.g., minimizing fault following poor performance on a memory task; Blank & Levesque, 1993) and for the behavior of others in social scenarios (e.g., the actor-observer effect; Jones & Nisbett, 1971; Watson, 1982). However, causal attributions can be influenced by the cognitive abilities of the perceiver (Gilbert & Malone, 1995); individual difference variables, such as attributional complexity (Blumberg & Silvera, 1998); and the cultural norms in which the perceiver is immersed (Choi & Nisbett, 1998).

A major aim of lifespan developmental psychologists is to understand (1) the domains in which older adults show different levels of functioning compared to young adults and (2) whether these differences reflect aging-related limitations or are functional adaptations. Researchers turned to studying causal attributions as an area in which older adults may show gains in reasoning ability, reflecting a lifetime of experiences in social contexts and making social judgments (see Hess & Queen, this volume). The attributions that older adults make are influenced by age-related declines in relevant cognitive processes, such as working memory, as well as by motivations, personal beliefs, and the increasing importance of emotional experiences. When age differences in attributions emerge, these differences do not simply reflect changing cognitive abilities; rather, the judgments of older adults may reflect age differences in sensitivity to context and social knowledge (Blanchard-Fields, 1999; Hess, 2006). Thus, age differences in causal attributions may be functionally adaptive with respect to an individual's developmental stage in life.

The goal of this chapter is to provide an overview of the causal attribution literature with respect to aging. The chapter is divided into several sections. First, we provide a brief review of the social psychological literature on attributional processes, focusing on those areas of the literature that have informed the lifespan developmental approach to attributions. Second, we describe how adopting a lifespan developmental approach has expanded the understanding of attributional processing in the areas of performance attributions, as well as of social judgments. Next, we discuss several factors, ranging from cognitive change to social cognitive mechanisms, that determine when age-related differences emerge and when they will not. Finally, we discuss what we envision as future directions for the field.

A Brief History of Causal Attribution Research in Young Adults

Causal explanations and attributions have been of interest to social psychologists for the better part of the past century. The publication of Heider's (1958) seminal book, *The Psychology of Interpersonal Relations*, encouraged psychologists to examine biases and errors in causal reasoning as manifested in daily interactions with others. Heider's approach assumed two primary dimensions on which individuals make attributions: internal and external. Internal, or dispositional, attributions are those that attribute the cause of an event as being due to some personal characteristic, such as motivations, desires, personality, and beliefs. For example, if I do well on a test, it is because I am smart. External, or situational, attributions refer to the cause of an event being due to something situational or outside of an individual. For example, if I do poorly on a test, it is because the test was unfair. Heider presumed that these underlying causes were mutually exclusive, in that a cause could be classified as one or the other but not both (Heider, 1958). This dichotomy is still referenced today and forms the basis of many of the causal attribution paradigms that have been adopted in the literature on aging and social judgments (e.g., Blanchard-Fields & Horhota, 2005).

Early work that followed tested and then extended Heider's model to account for variance in attributions that individuals make for human performance. Weiner et al. (1971) crossed the internal-external dimension with a stable-unstable dimension to produce four categories—ability, effort, task characteristics, and luck. Ability reflected a stable internal trait, suggesting that ability was a resource that would be available to a person across a variety of tasks. Effort reflected an unstable internal trait, in that it could differ from task to task. The task characteristics category refers to elements of the task that are consistent; thus, it is a stable external trait, and the category of luck refers to elements that fluctuate each time the person engages in the task and is therefore an unstable external trait. Weiner (1979) later added another property called *controllability* to differentiate between unstable factors that were within or outside of a person's control. These categories remain in use today, primarily in the literature examining attributions for individuals' cognitive performance, including memory performance (Banziger & Drevenstedt, 1982; Blatt-Eisengart & Lachman, 2004).

Social psychologists have investigated the differing types of attributions made under a variety of different circumstances and the subsequent influences of those attributions on affect and behavior (Kelley & Michela, 1980), and they have clarified conceptual components of the theory (Blank, 1987). A number of general inferences are warranted from this voluminous literature. Attributions made about the self tend to be self-enhancing; for example, if a person does well on a test, it is much more likely that she will report internal reasons for success, such as ability and effort, rather than external factors, such as that the test was easy (Weiner, 1985). When judging others, individuals are prone to making automatic dispositional attributions despite the availability of situational factors, a phenomenon known as the *fundamental attribution error* (Ross, 1977). That is, the observer is highly likely to assume that an actor's actions are based on some aspect of the actor's personal character (e.g., due to a personality trait) rather than due to characteristics of the situation (Watson, 1982). Even when observers do take into account situational pressures, they often fail to adjust their dispositional attributions to a great extent (Gilbert, Pelham, & Krull, 1988).

This is not to say that it is impossible to find individuals who adjust their attributions for situational pressures. Researchers find a decrease in dispositional tendencies when a perceiver's goals are manipulated so that he or she focuses on situational context. For instance, when a perceiver is asked to form judgments relative to a series of dispositional and situational casual explanations that are evenly balanced, dispositional attributions become less dominant (Trope & Gaunt, 2000). Furthermore, there are cultural differences in attributional preferences such that individuals in Eastern cultures (e.g., Korea and China) are more likely to emphasize situational attributions compared to participants from Western cultures (Blanchard-Fields, Chen, Horhota, & Wang, 2007; Choi & Nisbett, 1998).

Extending the Research Into an Adult Developmental Context

Until the 1980s, the bulk of attributional research had been conducted with college-aged young adult samples, with some extensions to clinical subpopulations (e.g., Blank, 1987). In the mid-1980s, some researchers began to argue for the use of lifespan developmental perspectives to inform attributional research (Banzinger, 1987; Blanchard-Fields, 1986; Blank, 1987). These researchers outlined a wide variety of reasons why young adults' attributional behavior might not generalize across the adult lifespan (Sears, 1987). Undergraduate populations reflect a highly selective sample of individuals with high cognitive abilities, a limited age range, and higher levels of education than the general population. Furthermore, college-aged students may differ from individuals of other ages, as well as from nonstudents, in terms of personality characteristics and goals. In fact, a primary concern from a lifespan perspective (e.g., Baltes, 1987) was that individuals' priorities and concerns shift over the course of a lifespan, with attention to candidate explanations shifting toward whatever life concern is most salient to an individual (Blank & Levesque, 1993). Thus, the processes underlying attributions may differ

across different age groups. For example, young adults focus on academic achievement goals due to their current student status, whereas older individuals report more other-focused goals, reflecting generativity concerns (Strough, Berg, & Sansone, 1996). Consistent with Erikson's psychosocial developmental theory, Sheldon and Kasser (2001) also found that older adults listed more personal strivings concerning generativity and ego integrity (e.g., helping younger generations to leave a legacy and reflecting on one's place in the larger scheme of life) and fewer strivings related to identity and intimacy (e.g., searching for one's true character and forming meaningful relationships with others) than did young adults. These differences in goals and motivations can produce age differences in attributions, particularly when the judgments are interpersonal in nature. Furthermore, it was argued that attributions may be domain specific, with age differences emerging in some domains, such as interpersonal contexts, but not others, such as achievement contexts (Blanchard-Fields, Chen, & Norris, 1997). From this point forward, researchers no longer assumed that young adults' performance was a universal standard that reflected the attributional processes across the lifespan.

Causal Attributions in Performance Contexts

When individuals of different ages fail on a memory task, what are the causes of the failure? Some of the earliest attribution researchers to take a developmental approach were those who studied causal attributions in performance contexts (Banziger & Drevenstedt, 1982; Dweck, 1986). It is important to understand individuals' attributions for memory performance because they relate to how these individuals will approach memory tasks in the future. Individuals who attribute performance to internal controllable factors may be more likely to use strategies and put forth effort to perform well on future tasks, whereas those who attribute performance to task characteristics or luck may not try as hard (Blatt-Eisengart & Lachman, 2004).

Recent research suggests that there are few age differences in perceptions of one's personal control over current and future memory performance (e.g., Horhota, Lineweaver, Ositelu, Summers & Hertzog, 2011); however, both young and older adults expect a pattern of declining memory performance over time (Lineweaver & Hertzog, 1998). Both young and older adults attribute older adults' memory failures to internal, stable factors, such as lack of ability or other factors that are unlikely to change in later performance contexts (Banziger & Drevenstedt, 1982; Lachman & McArthur, 1986). Alternatively, similar failures by young adult targets are attributed to internal unstable causes (e.g., lack of effort; Erber, Szuchman, & Rothberg, 1990). When older adults experience successful performance, it is typically attributed to luck or task-specific effort rather than to an underlying stable trait (Lachman & McArthur, 1986).

The internal, stable patterns of attributions for older adults' memory failures suggest that individuals apply an *entity theory* to judgments of older adults' memory performance. Entity theory suggests that an individual's ability is fixed. This is in contrast to *incremental skill theory*, which suggests that an individual's ability can improve over time (Dweck, 1986; Elliott & Dweck, 1988). Skill theory is viewed as the more adaptive of the two patterns because it allows for improvement of an ability over time. An entity view can be maladaptive because a person with this view is more likely to avoid challenges and fail to persist when a task is difficult (Dweck, 1986; Elliott & Lachman, 1989). In combination with the belief that memory declines with age, holding an entity orientation may result in poor memory performance because a lack of motivation undercuts the investment of effort into memory tasks (Elliott & Lachman, 1989).

Although several studies find an entity theory is applied to the attributions of older adults' memory failures, there is also evidence that not all older individuals adopt this approach.

Studies examining self-ratings have found that older adults make adaptive patterns of attributions for imagined failures, for example, internalizing successes but minimizing blame for failure, much like young adults do to preserve their self-image (Blank & Levesque, 1993; Lachman & Jelalian, 1984; Lachman & McArthur, 1986). Older adults also manifest stable attributions for success and nonstable attributions for failure, again suggesting an adaptive strategy to protect self-image (Blank & Levesque, 1993). The previous examples involve forming attributions about imagined scenarios and fictional targets, but attributions for personal performance on recently completed tasks show similar results. Participants who perform well on a memory task make more internal attributions (e.g., due to effort), and older adults who make internal attributions for good performance have been shown to perform equally as well as young adults (Devolder & Pressley, 1992). Furthermore, Blatt-Eisengart

and Lachman (2004) found that older adults made more adaptive patterns of attributions compared to young adults; older adults made stronger internal uncontrollable attributions for good performance as opposed to poor performance. Collectively, these findings suggest that individuals who hold more adaptive views of learning contexts (i.e., hold a skill orientation) have better cognitive performance overall.

There is also evidence that individuals adjust their attributions depending on the context of the memory failure. For example, older adults are more likely than young adults to report that the task was difficult if an older target's failure occurred in long-term memory for highly familiar information (Erber, Szuchman, & Rothberg, 1990) and are less likely than young adults to report that long-term memory failures, such as forgetting the name of a long-time acquaintance, are serious (Erber, 1989). It is also the case that the attribution that is made depends on one's knowledge of the target person. When an older target is described as having an "old" lifestyle, perceivers react less negatively to the target's memory failure than when the older target is described as having a youthful lifestyle (Erber, Szuchman, & Prager, 1997). Thus, when the expectation of the older person is consistent with the behavior, the attributions are more positive. However, when the expectations for the older adult are high, and the older adult fails, that target is judged more harshly (Erber et al., 1997).

In sum, the literature is quite consistent in terms of the attributions that individuals make about older adults in memory and performance contexts. When thinking about others, the failures of older adults are perceived to reflect the age of the target person, a stable internal trait; however, when thinking about oneself, attributions of success and failure reflect more adaptive modes of self-preservation. For individuals who adopt this adaptive pattern of attribution for memory, it is much more likely that their performance will improve, whether due to persistence, motivation, or use of more effective strategies (Elliott & Lachman, 1989). From a developmental perspective, it is also important to ask how attributions about cognition affect older adults in their daily lives. For example, do everyday cognitive failures translate into concerns about cognitive loss? Furthermore, it is important to ask whether attributions differ across different domains. Research finds that older adults are more likely than young adults to spontaneously report success and failures in social scenarios rather than achievement scenarios (Blank, 1986; Blank & Levesque, 1993; Lachman, 1990). This finding reflects the notion that the stage in life matters; college-aged students focus on memory-demanding achievement contexts, given that schooling is their top priority, whereas older adults focus more on social relationships and interactions, reflecting their current goals and priorities in life.

Attributions of Others in Social Judgment Contexts

The majority of everyday experiences involve interacting with other people. From ordering a coffee in the morning on the way to work to interacting with colleagues, friends, and family members, individuals engage in interactive experiences throughout the day. If one of these interactions results in a negative outcome, people seek to understand what went wrong and how to proceed. Within the attributional literature, research has focused on the tendency of individuals to use internal, dispositional attributions to account for other people's behavior while minimizing or discounting external situational attributions. This is known in the literature as the correspondence bias (Gilbert & Malone, 1995; Jones & Harris, 1967) or the fundamental attribution error (Ross, 1977).

The correspondence bias is well documented in the social psychology literature using young adult participants (Gilbert & Malone, 1995); a developmental perspective can add to our understanding of this phenomenon because priorities shift across the lifespan, and older adults value social relationships more strongly (Carstensen, 2006; Carstensen, Issacowitz, & Charles, 1999). According to Labouvie-Vief (1980, 2008), adults gain in cognitive-affective complexity, the ability to coordinate diverse emotions into a complex, organized structure that promotes greater awareness of one's own and others' perspectives and motivations. Because cognitive-affective complexity involves accepting contradicting emotions (e.g., positive and negative emotions), it can help adults think more maturely about real-world dilemmas (Labouvie-Vief, 2003; see also Labouvie-Vief, this volume). In fact, when presented with real-life emotional problem scenarios, older adults were more likely than young adults to use relativistic and dialectical thought and to consider the complex emotional experience of the actors involved in the hypothetical situations (Blanchard-Fields, 1986). Furthermore, older adults have been shown to take situational cues into account in their everyday

problem solving (Blanchard-Fields & Norris, 1994). Therefore, it was thought that, in social attributional contexts, older individuals would recognize the role of situational factors in event outcomes and, in turn, may show more situational and interactive attributions in comparison to young individuals (Blanchard-Fields, 1996).

Work in this area makes use of research paradigms that present participants with vignettes depicting interpersonal and achievement situations that result in a negative outcome. Participants then rate what was responsible for the outcome: a character in the vignette (dispositional attribution), some aspect of the situation (situational attribution), or some combination of these factors (interactive attribution). Consistent with predictions of the post-formal literature, older adults were found to report more interactive attributions when compared to young adults (Blanchard-Fields, 1994). However, contrary to predictions, older adults were also more likely to make internal dispositional judgments relative to adolescents and young adults. Furthermore, older adults reported higher levels of dispositional attributions than interactive attributions overall (Blanchard-Fields, 1994). Although some older adults acknowledged that situational factors may interact with dispositional factors to affect an outcome, the majority of older adults preferred to make dispositional judgments that blamed one of the primary characters. The dispositional tendency shown by older adults has been replicated several times in the literature using vignette-based paradigms (Blanchard-Fields, 1996; Blanchard-Fields & Beatty, 2005; Chen & Blanchard-Fields, 1997), as well as more traditional correspondence bias paradigms (Blanchard-Fields & Horhota, 2005; Horhota & Blanchard-Fields, 2006).

Why might this be? What underlying mechanisms could account for these age-related differences in attributional processing? Research points toward two candidate explanations: cognitive resources and social cognitive factors such as beliefs, motivation, and emotional content.

Cognitive Resources

Well-documented age differences in cognition, including working memory, inductive reasoning, speed of processing, and episodic memory (Salthouse, 1996, Zacks, Hasher, & Li, 2000), have been hypothesized as candidate explanations for the differences found in young and older adults' attributions. Within the basic causal attribution framework, participants read vignettes or make judgments of individuals after being provided with information. If older adults are unable to remember all of the details associated with an actor's behaviors, or if they are unable to maintain details in working memory when forming a judgment, then older adults' attributions will be based on less evidence than attributions made by young adults who, on average, have a larger working memory capacity.

In general, the attributional process is thought to involve three stages: categorization, characterization, and correction. The categorization stage involves perceiving an event, the characterization stage involves characterizing the event in terms of forming an internal attribution of the actor, and, in the final correction stage, the perceiver adjusts the initial characterization for situational pressures on the event (Gilbert & Malone, 1995). The first two stages, categorization and characterization, are relatively automatic and result in dispositional attributions, whereas correcting for situational pressures is more cognitively effortful (Gilbert et al., 1988). Most attributions are dispositional because the correction phase will not occur if an individual (a) lacks awareness of the situational constraints or (b) does not have the resources to fully adjust the initial attribution (Gilbert & Malone, 1995; Gilbert et al., 1988).

Several studies suggest that cognitive abilities play a role in older adults' social judgment biases. When given additional time before making their judgments, age-related differences in dispositional attributions are eliminated; older adults benefit from having additional time to further consider situational pressures and correct their initial dispositional judgments (Chen & Blanchard-Fields, 1997). Furthermore, when asked to complete a more complex task that involved disregarding false information, older adults made inaccurate dispositional judgments and behaved much like young adults performing the task under divided-attention conditions (Chen & Blanchard-Fields, 2000). This finding suggests that older adults in the full-attention condition have fewer cognitive resources to invest into correction than do young adults. Minimizing the cognitive effort needed to make a judgment by providing older adults with more environmental support (e.g., providing clear instructions of the difference between target and situational context) has also been shown to reduce their judgmental biases, again suggesting that cognitive abilities play a role in older adults' judgments (Wang & Chen, 2004).

These findings implicate the role of cognitive abilities in social judgments; however, they do not imply that cognitive abilities are the only explanation for the age-related attributional differences observed in the literature. In fact, there is research that shows that cognitive abilities are unrelated to social judgments in some contexts (Sullivan & Ruffman, 2004), and other research suggests that cognitive abilities do not completely account for age differences in social judgments (Blanchard-Fields, Hertzog, & Horhota, 2012; Chen & Blanchard-Fields, 1997). Instead, a growing body of evidence suggests that cognitive abilities work in concert with one's motivations, beliefs, and social knowledge base to impact social judgments. Thus, the tendency for older adults to selectively allocate their resources to specific contextual features of the social landscape when forming social judgments may actually reflect an adaptive way of processing social information (Hess, 2006; see Hess and Queen, this volume). Similar motivational explanations for heuristic processing and for strategic resource allocation have also been proposed in the judgment and decision-making literature (Hanoch, Wood, & Rice, 2007; Mata, 2007; Mata & Nunes, 2010; Mikels, Reed, & Simon, 2009).

In fact, many studies show that, through a lifetime of experiences, older adults rely on their wealth of knowledge, heuristics, and preferred social information processing strategies when making social judgments (Hess, Osowski, & Leclerc, 2005; Hess & Queen, this volume; Leclerc & Hess, 2007). Through their accumulated experience, older adults have a more elaborated underlying theory of relations between behaviors and traits that can result in differential accessibility of that information and subsequent interpretations about the cause of behaviors (Leclerc & Hess, 2007). Furthermore, older adults appear to search for the most relevant information in order to focus their resources on the information that is most relevant to the judgment (Hess & Auman, 2001; Hess et al., 2005). Despite potentially having a wide range of information when judging the behavior of others, there is value in limiting one's judgment to the most relevant predictor of the trait on which the target is being evaluated. Thus, age differences in social judgments may not reflect cognitive impairment; rather, older adults' judgments may reflect a form of social expertise (Hess, 2006; Hess & Queen, this volume).

Social Cognitive Factors

A growing body of literature suggests that the social beliefs of a perceiver color the social judgment context in which the perceiver forms an attribution, and this impacts the interpretation of a scenario, as well as the motivation of the perceiver to engage in the effort required to adjust one's social judgments.

PERSONAL BELIEFS AND SOCIAL KNOWLEDGE

Prior knowledge and the information that is available in the situation interact to inform the causal attribution process (Hilton, 2007). In particular, social schemas (i.e., knowledge structures that reflect an individual's understanding of social situations) are easily accessible heuristics that individuals use to make social judgments (Baldwin, 1992). Some research finds that the connection between social schema beliefs and social judgments is stronger in older adults than in young adults (Blanchard-Fields, 1996; Hess & Follett, 1994), and older adults who hold strong views may access those beliefs more quickly and use them to inform their social judgments without engaging in elaborative processing (Blanchard-Fields, 1996).

A beliefs approach suggests that age differences will emerge when there are differences in the beliefs that individuals hold (Blanchard-Fields & Hertzog, 2000). Thus, cohort differences in social norms held by young and older adults may account for some of the age differences in attributional judgments (Blanchard-Fields, 1996; Blanchard-Fields, Chen, Schocke, & Hertzog, 1998). Blanchard-Fields (1996) found both age differences and context specificity in the schematic beliefs that were generated for different social and achievement vignettes. For instance, older adults were more likely than young adults to report schemas related to social rules regarding marriage, such as "marriage is more important than a career," reflecting either cohort differences in socialization norms or differences in current life goals and values (Blanchard-Fields, 1996). In addition, the age relevance of a target character in combination with the age relevance of the problem makes an impact on the judgments that emerge (Blanchard-Fields, Baldi, & Stein, 1999). Older adults blamed middle-aged and older targets more strongly than young targets in work contexts in which an individual failed to achieve a self-defined goal (Blanchard-Fields et al., 1999). Moreover, individuals blamed characters who violated a social rule that they identified with and absolved characters of responsibility when they identified with the character (Blanchard-Fields & Beatty, 2005). In a more recent study, individuals who held traditional beliefs were more likely to blame nontraditional characters (and vice versa), and, although these beliefs related to identification

with the characters, identification alone was not sufficient to explain the age differences in attributions. Instead, social beliefs were more predictive of age differences in attributions and even fully mediated the relationship between working memory and attributions (Blanchard-Fields et al., 2012).

Although cohort differences in beliefs exist for many issues, there are also individual differences in beliefs within age groups. Furthermore, some social judgment scenarios will reflect beliefs that a participant feels very strongly about, but other social judgment scenarios will tap into beliefs that are less controversial or strongly held, regardless of an individual's age. Thus, individuals of all ages could show the same biases if their beliefs are similar. Studies examining this hypothesis have generally provided support for this idea. Individuals who provided strong dispositional attributions were more likely to report more evaluative rule statements that related to the main character in a vignette (i.e., providing information about how the main character violated a social rule). When these rules were examined, researchers found that age differences in the reported schemas accounted for some of the age differences in attributional judgments (Chen & Blanchard-Fields, 1997). In another study, participants' justifications for their attributions were analyzed using cluster analysis to determine whether certain attributions were provided by certain types of responders. The clusters that emerged were weakly related to age; instead, cluster membership was more strongly associated with individuals' beliefs (Blanchard-Fields et al., 1998).

One possibility is that when a strongly held belief is activated and violated by a target character, the dispositional attribution evoked is tagged with an emotional valence (Peters, Hess, Vastfjall, & Auman, 2007). It would be expected that when a character's behavior results in a strongly negative reaction from the participant that a negative attribution of the offending character will occur, even if situational information is available. Past research has found that negative mood states lead to differential outcomes for young and older adults' decision-making and social judgment performance (Mienaltowski & Blanchard-Fields, 2005; Phillips, Smith, & Gilhooly, 2002). After being induced to experience a negative mood, young adults are less likely to display the correspondence bias (Forgas, 1998). However, after experiencing a negative mood, older adults are more likely to display this bias (Mienaltowski & Blanchard-Fields, 2005).

Other evidence for the role of beliefs comes from the cross-cultural literature. Social psychologists have shown that individuals who belong to individualistic Western cultures are more likely to make dispositional attributions compared to individuals who belong to Eastern cultures, which tend to be more collectivistic (Choi & Nisbett, 1998). Adding a developmental component, Blanchard-Fields, Chen, Horhota, and Wang (2007) replicated these cultural differences in a sample that included older adults; Chinese individuals showed less dispositional bias compared to American individuals. But, contrary to the findings in US samples, this study did not find age differences in attributions within the Chinese sample. Furthermore, members of the Chinese sample were more likely to acknowledge the role of situational factors in qualitative responses describing their reasoning. These findings suggest that cultural beliefs can have a strong impact on the ways in which social information is acquired and how it is implemented when forming a social judgment.

MOTIVATION

Do the beliefs that an individual holds impact one's motivation for engaging in the additional effort that is required to adjust one's dispositional attributions for situational pressures? This hypothesis was tested in a series of studies using a traditional correspondence bias paradigm, in which participants read an essay and determined whether the essay's content reflected the true belief of the writer. The key manipulation in this correspondence bias paradigm is that, in one condition, participants are told that the writer chose to write on the topic of the essay, and, in the other condition, participants are told that the writer did not have a choice about the essay topic. Using this method, older adults showed greater dispositional attributional tendencies than young adults unless they were provided with a plausible explanation for why the target would behave counter to their own beliefs (Blanchard-Fields & Horhota, 2005). This finding suggested that older adults believed in a strong behavior-attitude correspondence. A follow-up study further confirmed this interpretation; older adults hold a stronger behavior-attitude consistency belief than do young adults, and this tendency accounted for age differences in dispositional attributions (Stanley & Blanchard-Fields, 2011).

Motivations can also be impacted by underlying personality traits of the perceiver. Researchers have investigated a wide range of personality traits

to examine the connection between traits and attributional judgments, including need for structure (Hess, 2001), need for closure (Blanchard-Fields et al., 2012), and attributional complexity (Follett & Hess, 2002; Horhota & Blanchard-Fields, 2006). Need for structure and need for closure are highly related and reflect an aversion to ambiguity and the need for simple, well-defined structures when understanding and organizing the world. Older adults have been shown to have higher need for structure scores (Hess, 2001); however, the evidence is mixed in terms of the impact of this trait on attributions. Need for closure has been found to relate to traditional patterns of beliefs (Blanchard-Fields, Hertzog, Stein, & Pak, 2001); however, it does not consistently emerge as a predictor of attributional judgments when taking other factors, such as beliefs and values, into account (Blanchard-Fields et al., 2012; Hess, 2006). The findings for attributional complexity, the degree to which an individual considers complex rather than simple explanations, are more consistent. Few to no age differences emerge in attributions among individuals with high levels of attributional complexity, but, among individuals with low attributional complexity, older adults show more dispositional attributions than do young adults (Follett & Hess, 2002; Horhota & Blanchard-Fields, 2006).

Participant motivation can also be manipulated through task instructions. Chen (2004) found that participants who were told they would be accountable for their judgments invested additional effort in making a more accurate social judgment. Using a different paradigm, Hess, Rosenberg, and Waters (2001) found that older adults were less likely to invest cognitive resources into a judgment task when they knew that they would not be held accountable for their judgments, even if they had available resources. Motivation has also been manipulated by altering the personal relevance of the judgment task to increase participant's involvement in the task. When the task is meaningful to participants, older adults engage their cognitive resources, and this results in a reduction of age differences in trait judgments (Hess, Follett, & McGee, 1998) and increased memory performance in a social judgment task (Hess, Germain, Swaim, & Osowski, 2009). When the task is less meaningful, older adults invest less effort in the task (Hess, Leclerc, Swaim, & Weatherbee, 2009).

In sum, age differences in social judgments of others appear to reflect changes in social beliefs, motivations, and goals that alter the amount of cognitive effort that an individual invests in the social judgment task. These differences in processing may not be maladaptive; rather, they may reflect a form of social expertise on the part of older adults. Drawing from their wealth of knowledge, older adults are guided by their schema and their tacit knowledge of the way that social relationships operate. This knowledge helps them to minimize the cognitive resources necessary to form the judgment by narrowing down the information to the most critical points that they selectively process when forming a judgment. When age differences in beliefs are accounted for, age differences in social judgments and the role of cognitive abilities appear to be minimized.

Future Directions

Much progress has been made in the area of causal attributions and aging; however, many questions remain. Here, we suggest key areas that are in need of clarification, elaboration, and study.

Improving the Measurement of Attributions

One important issue that future research needs to address is the measurement of attributions. As reviewed earlier, different attribution paradigms have used different measurements of attribution. Some focused on types of attributions (e.g., Kelley & Michela, 1980), and others focused on the process of attributions (e.g., Gilbert et al., 1988). Some used dispositional attribution ratings as the index of the correspondence bias (e.g., Chen & Blanchard-Fields, 1997), and others used extreme scores deviating from a neutral point (e.g., Blanchard-Fields et al., 2007). Although there have been variations in the style of measurement, researchers have consistently used artificial situations in which participants read a vignette and judged target characters. Yet, in everyday life, people make attributions in dynamic interactive contexts. The literature would benefit from studies of real-time attributions in everyday contexts. For example, there are a range of attributions that may be correct or adaptive in everyday contexts. The literature suggests that interactive attributions are most often correct because they reflect deliberation over both dispositional and situational causal explanations; however, it may be the case that, in some situations, a dispositional attribution may be equally or more correct.

Furthermore, the research thus far has been cross-sectional in nature, examining young and

older adults at a single instance in time. The literature would benefit from longitudinal designs that investigate age-related changes in causal attributions over time. For example, is it the case that older individuals become more dispositionally biased with age? Or, is it possible that some individuals are more dispositionally biased throughout their lifetime? Is the developmental trajectory of attributions similar across individuals, or are there individual differences in patterns over time? Longitudinal studies would also help to clarify the underlying mechanisms for any age-related changes that are observed. For example, longitudinal studies could answer the question of whether within-subject changes in cognitive functioning or beliefs are correlated with changes in dispositional attributions.

Further Investigation of Cognitive and Belief Mechanisms

What cognitive resources matter for predicting age-related changes in dispositional attributions? Studies have found that global measures of working memory do not predict dispositional attributions (Blanchard-Fields et al., 2012; Chen & Blanchard-Fields, 2000). However, it may be the case that more precise cognitive measures are necessary. Chen and Blanchard-Fields (2000) found that source memory errors, but not working memory, predicted failure to discount false information in order to correct dispositional attributions. This finding suggests that we need a more precise process model for the cognitions underlying social judgments, one that takes into account the manner with which information is usually organized, stored, and later accessed when forming judgments.

It is also the case that the literature would benefit from more sensitive measures of beliefs. Thus far, beliefs have been measured by asking participants to agree or disagree with schema statements or by coding qualitative responses from participants. However, these explicit measures may be susceptible to socially desirable responding and therefore may not capture the true strength of a person's beliefs. Implicit measures of beliefs may be better measures of belief strength and may result in increased predictive ability (Blanchard-Fields et al., 1998). Another component of beliefs is the emotional valence that beliefs may impart to a dispositional attribution. For example, when a target violates one's beliefs, it may be the case that the dispositional judgment is also associated with a strong negative valence (Blanchard-Fields et al., 2012). Measurement of underlying emotional and physiological reactivity to the belief statements themselves or to the characters that violate one's beliefs may provide a more sensitive measure of belief strength and be more predictive of resulting attributions.

With more precise measurement of cognitive processes and belief structures, researchers will be better able to determine the conditions under which cognitive processes will drive attributions and when social beliefs will be the more important factor. In particular, it will be important to determine how cognitive processes and beliefs relate to motivation. Past work has shown that beliefs relate to motivation in attributional contexts (Blanchard-Fields & Horhota, 2005; Stanley & Blanchard-Fields, 2011), but these studies did not emphasize the relationship between cognition and motivation. Recent work suggests that physical and cognitive decline negatively affect motivation for cognitive and social activities (Hess, Emery, & Neupert, 2012) but has yet to connect these variables to attributions. An approach that integrates measurement of beliefs, cognition, and motivation with attributional processing will provide a clearer model of attributional reasoning processes across the lifespan.

Connections to Social Neuroscience

Our understanding of age differences will also benefit from work in the emerging area of social neuroscience. Experimental psychologists have used many models to describe various holistic approaches to information processing that include automatic and deliberate forms of thought (Bargh, 1984; Kahneman, 2003; Peters et al., 2007; Shiffrin & Schneider, 1977; Simon, 1990; Sloman, 1996). Recently, an integrative model that builds on these past approaches and ties in the role of various brain systems has emerged. With respect to attributions, individuals rely on a reflexive, automatic system (aka, the X-system) to help the observer quickly identify behaviors that are relevant to a social judgment, as well as a reflective, deliberate system (aka, the C-system) to engage in more controlled processing. The C-system tempers the output of the X-system by correcting for biases, errors, or extenuating environmental information (Lieberman, Gaunt, Gilbert, & Trope, 2002; Satpute & Lieberman, 2006). These systems reflect the role of both accumulated experience (which shapes the X-system) and the availability of cognitive resources (which drive the C-system).

These two different systems are linked to different areas of the brain. In general, the X-system contributes to attributions via (a) subcortical activity in the amygdala and basal ganglia linked to threat and probabilistic reward (Satpute & Lieberman, 2006), (b) lateral temporal cortex activation associated with recognizing cues that signal social engagement (Spunt, Falk, & Lieberman, 2010), and (c) ventral medial prefrontal and orbitofrontal activation associated with the internal representation of social norms as they relate to the observer's own intentions (Kreuger, Barbey, & Grafman, 2009; Van Overwalle, 2009). Conversely, the C-system contributes to attributions via (a) anterior cingulate cortex (ACC) activation associated with error monitoring and identifying the intention of the target (Guroglu, van den Bos, van Dijk, Rombouts, & Crone, 2011; Satpute & Lieberman, 2006), (b) activation of the lateral prefrontal cortex (PFC) associated with behavioral inhibition and emotion regulation (Satpute & Lieberman, 2006), and (c) dorsal medial PFC activation associated with goal setting and theory of mind (Kreuger et al., 2009). Given age-related degradation that emerges in those frontal regions of the cortex that drive controlled processing (cf. Mather, 2010), one is left to wonder what role individual differences in brain biology play in the social judgment process of older adults (e.g., Krendl, Heatherton, & Kensinger, 2009). Other regions (e.g., ventromedial PFC) are often spared with age (Fjell et al., 2009). Consequently, judgments that rely more on the maintained cortical regions than on the degraded ones are not likely to change with age (e.g., Ritchey, Bessette-Symons, Hayes, & Cabeza, 2011). Thus, the application of models like that of Lieberman and colleagues to the field of social cognition and aging could help to clarify the extent to which age differences in the social judgment process are tied to biological determinants (e.g., resource decline) or to social determinants (e.g., individual differences in beliefs or lifespan shifts in motives).

Social Consequences of Attributions

Future attributional research should not only focus on the underlying mechanisms of attributional processing. The literature would also benefit from research into the social consequences of the attributions that we make when judging others. When we think of older people in our community, both positive (e.g., wise, friendly, generous) and negative (e.g., forgetful, smelly, hard-of-hearing) attributes come to mind (Hummert, 2011). These stereotypes can impact the type of interaction that we have with older people. For example, the older a person is, the more likely the person will be negatively stereotyped as less competent. These attributions of lack of competence may translate to overaccomodative styles of speech, including slowing and simplifying speech, particularly when the context supports the negative stereotype, such as in hospital settings (Hummert, Garstka, Ryan, & Bonnesen, 2004; Hummert, Shaner, Garstka, & Henry, 1998). It is important to note that old age does not always lead to negative attributions. Young and older observers are both more likely to attribute a social transgression, such as walking out of a store without paying for an item, to forgetfulness for an older target than for a young target (Erber, Szuchman, & Prager, 2001). Additionally, in response to transgressions by an older target, young and older observers are less likely to pursue aggressive or confrontational strategies for righting the wrong (Miller, Charles, & Fingerman, 2009). Instead, older transgressors are given the benefit of the doubt; observers offer more forgiveness and less blame, and they are more likely to avoid making the situation worse. Ultimately, these findings suggest that aging is also associated with more leniency and kind-heartedness from others. Such leniency may have positive consequences for the quality of life of older adults (Fingerman, Miller, & Charles, 2008). More research is needed to characterize the conditions under which older adults are treated more harshly as well as more kindly than young adults by observers.

Conclusion

In sum, the causal attribution process is an important part of daily life. In the domain of performance attributions, the types of attributions that are made can lead to adaptive or maladaptive outcomes. Attributing failures to internal stable factors may lead to decreased effort on subsequent tasks, whereas attributing failure to a lack of effort may lead one to invest more resources in the task in the future. In the social domain, it is clear that attributions are shaped by cognitive resources, as well as by social cognitive factors that work together to drive social information processing (Blanchard-Fields, 1999; Hess, 2006). Although older adults show cognitive resource declines relative to young adults, older adults are also more strategic when identifying how best to weigh multiple pieces of information available about a target when forming a social judgment (Hess & Auman, 2001). Moreover, both younger and older adults rely on their respective collective and individual social knowledge bases, using heuristics like schema and beliefs to shape social judgments (Blanchard-Fields & Beatty, 2005; Blanchard-Fields et al., 1998, 2012). Thus, this literature represents an area in which older adults may not always show declines relative to young adults. Rather, in certain contexts, the resulting attributions may be equivalent across the lifespan.

Many questions remain in the area, and we urge researchers to further refine their measurements of cognitive resources, social beliefs, and causal attributions. In addition, the literature would benefit from longitudinal studies that could further tease apart the role of cognitive mechanisms and social beliefs from attributions. Several factors remain relatively unexplored, such as the role of emotional reactivity and age-related changes in brain structures on attributional processes. It also remains unclear whether attributional processing will differ if measured in more interactive and realistic contexts.

References

Baldwin, M. W. (1992). Relational schemas and the processing of social information. *Psychological Bulletin, 112*, 461–484.

Baltes, P. B. (1987). Theoretical propositions of life-span developmental psychology: On the dynamics between growth and decline. *Developmental Psychology, 23*, 611–626.

Banzinger, G. (1987). Contemporary social psychology and aging: Issues of attribution in a life-span perspective. In R. P. Abeles (Ed.), *Life-span perspectives and social psychology* (pp.85–102). Hillsdale, NJ: Lawrence Erlbaum Associates.

Banzinger, G., & Drevenstedt, J. (1982). Achievement attributions by young and old judges as a function of perceived age of stimulus person. *Journal of Gerontology, 37*, 468–474.

Bargh, J. A. (1984). Automatic and conscious processing of social information. In R. S. Wyer, Jr., & T. K. Srull (Eds.), *Handbook of social cognition* (Vol. 3, pp. 1–43). Hillsdale, NJ: Erlbaum.

Blanchard-Fields, F. (1986). Reasoning on social dilemmas varying in emotional saliency: An adult developmental perspective. *Psychology and Aging, 1*, 325–333.

Blanchard-Fields, F. (1994). Age differences in causal attributions from an adult developmental perspective. *Journals of Gerontology, 49*, 43–51.

Blanchard-Fields, F. (1996). Causal attributions across the adult life span: The influence of social schemas, life context, and domain specificity. *Applied Cognitive Psychology, 10*, 137–146.

Blanchard-Fields, F. (1999). Social schematicity and causal attributions. In T. Hess & F. Blanchard-Fields (Eds.), *Social cognition and aging* (pp. 219–236). San Diego, CA: Academic Press.

Blanchard-Fields, F., Baldi, R., & Stein, R. (1999). Age relevance and context effects on attributions across the adult lifespan. *International Journal of Behavioral Development, 23*, 665–683.

Blanchard-Fields, F., & Beatty, C. (2005). Age differences in blame attributions: The role of relationship outcome ambiguity and personal identification. *Journals of Gerontology: Psychological Sciences & Social Sciences, 60B*, P19–P26.

Blanchard-Fields, F., Chen, Y., & Norris, L. (1997). Everyday problem-solving across the adult life span: Influence of domain specificity and cognitive appraisal. *Psychology and Aging, 12,* 684–693.

Blanchard-Fields, F., Chen, Y., Schocke, M, & Hertzog. (1998). Evidence for content-specificity of causal attributions across the adult life span. *Aging, Neuropsychology, & Cognition, 5,* 241–263.

Blanchard-Fields, F., Chen, Y., Horhota, M., & Wang, M. (2007). Cross cultural and age differences in the correspondence bias. *Journals of Gerontology: Psychological Sciences, 62B,* P362–P365.

Blanchard-Fields, F., & Hertzog, C. (2000). Age differences in schematicity. In U. von Hecker, S. Dutke, & G. Sedek (Eds.), *Processes of generative mental representation and psychological adaptation* (pp. 175–198). Dordrecht, The Netherlands: Kluwer.

Blanchard-Fields, F., Hertzog, C., & Horhota, M. (2012). Violate my beliefs?—Then you're to blame! Belief content as an explanation for causal attribution biases. *Psychology and Aging, 27,* 324–337. doi: 10.1037/a0024423.

Blanchard-Fields, F., Hertzog, C., Stein, R., & Pak, R. (2001). Beyond a stereotyped view of older adults' traditional family values. *Psychology and Aging, 16,* 483–496. Doi: 10.1037//0 882-7974.16.3.483.

Blanchard-Fields, F., & Horhota, M. (2005). Age differences in the correspondence bias: When a plausible explanation matters. *Journals of Gerontology: Psychological Sciences, 60B,* P259–P267.

Blanchard-Fields, F., & Norris, L. (1994). Causal attributions from adolescence through adulthood: Age differences, ego level and generalized response style. *Aging and Cognition, 1,* 67–86.

Blank, T. O. (1986). Meaning and motivation in adult perceptions of causality. *Basic and Applied Social Psychology, 6,* 111–120.

Blank, T. O. (1987). Attributions as dynamic elements in a lifespan social psychology. In R. P. Abeles (Ed.), *Life-span perspectives and social psychology* (pp. 61–84). Hillsdale, NJ: Lawrence Erlbaum Associates.

Blank, T. O., & Levesque, M. J. (1993). Constructing success and failure: Age differences in perceptions and explanations of success and failure. *International Journal of Aging & Human Development, 37,* 105–118.

Blatt-Eisengart, I., & Lachman, M. E. (2004). Attributions for memory performance in adulthood: Age differences and mediation effects. *Aging, Neuropsychology, and Cognition, 11,* 68–79.

Blumberg, S. J., & Silvera, D. H. (1998). Attributional complexity and cognitive development: A look at the motivational and cognitive requirements for attribution. *Social Cognition, 16,* 253–266.

Carstensen, L. L. (2006). The influence of a sense of time on human development. *Science, 312,* 1913–1915.

Carstensen, L. L., Isaacowitz, D. M., & Charles, S. T. (1999). Taking time seriously: A theory of socioemotional motivation. *American Psychologist, 54,* 165–181.

Chen, Y. (2004). Age differences in correction of context-induced biases: Source monitoring and timing of accountability. *Aging, Neuropsychology, & Cognition, 11,* 58–67.

Chen, Y., & Blanchard-Fields, F. (1997). Age differences in stages of attributional processing. *Psychology & Aging, 12,* 694–703.

Chen, Y., & Blanchard-Fields, F. (2000). Unwanted thought: Age differences in the correction of social judgments. *Psychology & Aging, 15,* 475–482.

Choi, I., & Nisbett, R. E. (1998). Situational salience and cultural differences in the correspondence bias and actor-observer bias. *Personality and Social Psychology Bulletin, 24,* 949–960.

Devolder, P. A., & Pressley, M. (1992). Causal attributions and strategy use in relation to memory performance differences in younger and older adults. *Applied Cognitive Psychology, 6,* 629–642.

Dweck, C. S. (1986). Motivational processes affecting learning. *American Psychologist, 41,* 1040–1048.

Elliott, E. S., & Dweck, C. S. (1988). Goals: An approach to motivation and achievement. *Journal of Personality and Social Psychology, 54,* 5–12.

Elliott, E. S., & Lachman, M. E. (1989). Enhancing memory by modifying control beliefs, attributions and performance goals in the elderly. In P. S. Fry (Ed.), *Psychological perspectives of helplessness and control in the elderly* (pp. 339–367). Oxford, England: North Holland.

Erber, J. T. (1989). Young and older adults' appraisal of memory failures in young and older adult target persons. *Journal of Gerontology: Psychological Sciences, 44,* 170–175

Erber, J. T., Szuchman, L. T., & Prager, I. G. (1997). Forgetful but forgiven: How age and lifestyle affect perceptions of memory failure. *Journals of Gerontology Series B: Psychological Sciences and Social Sciences, 52B,* 303–307.

Erber, J. T., Szuchman, L. T., & Prager, I. G. (2001). Ain't misbehavin': The effects of age and intentionality on judgments about misconduct. *Psychology and Aging, 16,* 85–95.

Erber, J. T., Szuchman, L. T., & Rothberg, S. T. (1990). Age, gender and individual differences in memory failure appraisal. *Psychology and Aging, 5,* 236–241.

Fingerman, K. L., Miller, L., & Charles, S. (2008). Saving the best for last: How adults treat social partners of different ages. *Psychology and Aging, 23,* 399–409.

Fjell, A. M., Westlye, L. T., Amlien, I., Espeseth, T., Reinvang, I., Raz, N., Agartz, I., Salat, D. H., Greve, D. N., Fischl, B., Dale, A. M., & Walhovd, K. B. (2009). High consistency of regional cortical thinning across multiple samples. *Cerebral Cortex, 19,* 2001–2012.

Follett, K., & Hess, T. M. (2002). Aging, cognitive complexity, and the fundamental attribution error. *Journals of Gerontology: Psychological Sciences & Social Sciences, 57B,* P312–P323.

Forgas, J. P. (1998). On being happy and mistaken: Mood effects on the fundamental attribution error. *Journal of Personality and Social Psychology, 75,* 318–331.

Gilbert, D. T., & Malone, P. S. (1995). The correspondence bias. *Psychological Bulletin, 117,* 21–38.

Gilbert, D. T., Pelham, B. W., & Krull, D. S. (1988). On cognitive busyness: When person perceivers meet persons perceived. *Journal of Personality and Social Psychology, 54,* 733–740.

Guroglu, B., van den Bos, W., van Dijk, E., Rombouts, S. A. R. B., & Crone, E. A. (2011). Dissociable brain networks involved in development of fairness considerations: Understanding intentionality behind unfairness. *NeuroImage, 57,* 634–641.

Hanoch, Y., Wood, S., & Rice, T. (2007). Bounded rationality, emotions and older adult decision making: Not so fast and yet so frugal. *Human Development, 50,* 333–358. doi: 10.1159/000109835

Heider, F. (1958). *The psychology of interpersonal relations.* Hoboken, NJ: John Wiley & Sons

Hess, T. M. (2001). Ageing-related influences on personal need for structure. *International Journal of Behavioral Development, 25,* 482–490.

Hess, T. M. (2006). Adaptive aspects of social cognitive functioning in adulthood: Age-related goal and knowledge influences. *Social Cognition, 24,* 279–309.

Hess, T. M., & Auman, C. (2001). Aging and social expertise: The impact of trait-diagnostic information on impressions of others. *Psychology & Aging, 16*, 497–510.

Hess, T. M., Emery, L., & Neupert, S. D. (2012). Longitudinal relationships between resources, motivation, and functioning (2012). *Journals of Gerontology, Series B: Psychological Sciences and Social Sciences, 67*, 299–308. doi: 10.1093/geronb/gbr100.

Hess, T. M., & Follett, K. J. (1994). Adult age differences in the use of schematic and episodic information in making social judgments. *Aging, Neuropsychology, & Cognition, 1*, 54–66.

Hess, T. M., Follett, K. J., & McGee, K. A. (1998). Aging and impression formation: The impact of processing skills and goals. *Journal of Gerontology: Psychological Sciences, 53B*, 175–187.

Hess, T. M., Germain, C. M., Swaim, E. L., & Osowski, N. L. (2009). Aging and selective engagement: The moderating impact of motivation on older adults' response utilization. *Journals of Gerontology: Series B: Psychological Sciences and Social Sciences, 64B*, 447–456.

Hess, T. M., Leclerc, C. M., Swaim, E., & Weatherbee, S. R. (2009). Aging and everyday judgements: The impact of motivational and processing resource factors. *Psychology and Aging, 24*, 735–740. doi: 10.1037/10096340

Hess, T. M., Osowski, N. L., & Leclerc, C. M. (2005). Age and experience influences on the complexity of social inferences. *Psychology and Aging, 20*, 447–459.

Hess, T. M., Rosenberg, D., C., & Waters, S. J. (2001). Motivation and representational processes in adulthood: The effects of social accountability and information relevance. *Psychology & Aging, 16*, 629–642.

Hilton, D. (2007). Causal explanation: From social perception to knowledge-based causal attribution. In A. W. Kruglanski & E. Higgins (Eds.), *Social psychology: Handbook of basic principles* (2 ed., pp. 232–253). New York: Guilford Press.

Horhota, M., & Blanchard-Fields, F. (2006). Do beliefs and attributional complexity influence age differences in the correspondence bias? *Social Cognition, 24*, 310–337.

Horhota, M., Lineweaver, T., Ositelu, M., Summers, K., & Hertzog, C. (2011). Young and older adults' beliefs about effective ways to mitigate age-related memory decline. *Psychology and Aging, 27*, 293–304.

Hummert, M. (2011). Age stereotypes and aging. In K. W. Schaie & S. L. Willis (Eds.), *Social psychology: Handbook of the Psychology of Aging* (7th ed., pp. 249–262). San Diego, CA: Academic Press.

Hummert, M. L., Garstka, T. A., Ryan, E. B., & Bonnesen, J. L. (2004). The role of age stereotypes in interpersonal communication. In J. F. Nussbaum & J. Coupland (Eds.), *Handbook of communication and aging research* (2nd ed., pp. 91–114). Mahwah, NJ: Lawrence Erlbaum Associates.

Hummert, M. L., Shaner, J. L., Garstka, T. A., & Henry, C. (1998). Communication with older adults: The influence of age stereotypes, context, and communicator age. *Human Communication Research, 25*, 124–142.

Jones, E. E., & Harris, V. A. (1967). The attributions of attitudes. *Journal of Experimental Social Psychology, 3*, 1–24.

Jones, E. E., & Nisbett, R. E. (1971). *The actor and the observer: Divergent perceptions of the causes of behavior.* New York: General Learning Press.

Kahneman, D. (2003). A perspective on judgment and choice: Mapping bounded rationality. *American Psychologist, 58*, 697–720. doi: 10.1037/0003-066X.58.9.697

Kelley, H. H., & Michela, J. L. (1980). Attribution theory and research. *Annual Review of Psychology, 31*, 457–501.

Krendl, A. C., Heatherton, T. F., & Kensinger, E. A. (2009). Aging minds and twisting attitudes: An fMRI investigation of age differences in inhibiting prejudice. *Psychology and Aging, 24*, 530–541.

Kreuger, F., Barbey, A. K., & Grafman, J. (2009). The medial prefrontal cortex mediates social event knowledge. *Trends in Cognitive Sciences, 13*, 103–109.

Labouvie-Vief, G. (1980). Beyond formal operations: Uses and limits of pure logic in life-span development. *Human Development, 23*, 141–160.

Labouvie-Vief, G. (2003). Dynamic integration: Affect, cognition, and the self in adulthood. *Current Directions in Psychological Science, 12*, 201–206.

Labouvie-Vief, G. (2008). When differentiation and negative affect lead to integration and growth. *American Psychologist, 63*, 564–565.

Lachman, M. E. (1990). When bad things happen to older people: Age differences in attributional style. *Psychology and Aging, 5*, 607–609.

Lachman, M. E., & Jelalian, E. (1984). Self-efficacy and attributions for intellectual performance in young and elderly adults. *Journal of Gerontology, 39*, 577–582.

Lachman, M. E., & McArthur, L. Z. (1986). Adulthood age differences in causal attributions for cognitive, physical and social performance. *Psychology and Aging, 1*, 127–132.

Leclerc, C. M., & Hess, T. M. (2007). Age differences in the bases for social judgments: Tests of a social expertise perspective. *Experimental Aging Research, 33*, 95–120. doi: 10.1080/03610730601006446

Lieberman, M. D., Gaunt, R., Gilbert, D. T., & Trope, Y. (2002). Reflexion and reflection: A social cognitive neuroscience approach to attributional inference. *Advances in Experimental Social Psychology, 34*, 199–249.

Lineweaver, T. T., & Hertzog, C. (1998). Adults' efficacy and control beliefs regarding memory and aging: Separating general from personal beliefs. *Aging, Neuropsychology, & Cognition, 5*, 264–296.

Mata, R. (2007). Understanding the aging decision maker. *Human Development, 50*, 359–366. doi: 10.1159/000109836

Mata, R., & Nunes, L. (2010). When less is enough: Cognitive aging, information search, and decision quality in consumer choice. *Psychology and Aging, 25*, 289–298. doi: 10.1037/a0017927

Mather, M. (2010). Aging and cognition. *Wiley Interdisciplinary Reviews: Cognitive Science, 1*, 346–362.

Mienaltowski, A., & Blanchard-Fields, F. (2005). The differential effects of mood on age differences in the correspondence bias. *Psychology and Aging, 20*, 589–600.

Mikels, J. A., Reed, A. E., & Simon, K. I. (2009). Older adults place lower value on choice relative to young adults. *Journal of Gerontology: Psychological Sciences, 64B*, 443–446. doi: 10.1093/geronb/gbp021

Miller, L. M., Charles, S. T., & Fingerman, K. L. (2009). Perceptions of social transgressions in adulthood. *Journals of Gerontology: Psychological Sciences, 64B*, P551–P559.

Peters, E., Hess, T. M., Vastfjall, D., & Auman, C. (2007). Adult age differences in dual information processes: Implications for the role of affective and deliberative processes in older adults' decision making. *Perspectives on Psychological Science, 2*, 1–23. doi: 10.1111/j.1745-6916.2007.00025.x

Phillips, L. H., Smith, L., & Gilhooly, K. J. (2002). The effects of adult aging and induced positive and negative mood on planning. *Emotion, 2,* 263–272.

Ritchey, M., Bessette-Symons, B., Hayes, S. M., & Cabeza, R. (2011). Emotion processing in the aging brain is modulated by semantic elaboration. *Neuropsychologia, 49,* 640–650.

Ross, L. (1977). The intuitive psychologist and his shortcomings: Distortions in the attribution process. In L. Berkowitz (Ed.), *Advances in experimental social psychology* (vol. 10, pp. 174–214). New York: Academic Press.

Salthouse, T. A. (1996). The processing-speed theory of adult age differences in cognition. *Psychological Review, 103(3),* 403–428.

Satpute, A. B., & Lieberman, M. D. (2006). Integrating automatic and controlled processes into neurocognitive models of social cognition. *Brain Research, 1079,* 86–97.

Sears, D. O. (1987). Implications of the lifespan approach for research on attitudes and social cognition. In R. P. Abeles (Ed.), *Lifespan perspectives and social psychology* (pp. 17–60). Hillsdale, NJ: Lawrence Erlbaum Associates.

Sheldon, K. M., & Kasser, T. (2001). Getting older, getting better? Personal strivings and psychological maturity across the life span. *Developmental Psychology, 37,* 491–501.

Shiffrin, R. M., & Schneider, W. (1977). Controlled and automatic human information processing: II. Perceptual learning, automatic attending and a general theory. *Psychological Review, 84,* 127–190. doi: 10.1037/0033-295X.84.2.127

Simon, H. A. (1990). Invariants of human behavior. *Annual Review of Psychology, 41,* 1–19. doi: 10.1146/annurev.ps.41.020190.000245

Sloman, S. A. (1996). The empirical case for two systems of reasoning. *Psychological Bulletin, 119,* 3–22. doi: 10.1037/0033-2909.119.1.3

Spunt, R. P., Falk, E. B., & Lieberman, M. D. (2010). Dissociable neural systems support retrieval of how and why action knowledge. *Psychological Science, 21,* 1593–1598.

Stanley, J. T., & Blanchard-Fields, F. (2011). Beliefs about behavior account for age differences in the correspondence bias. *Journals of Gerontology: Series B: Psychological Sciences and Social Sciences, 66B,* 169–176.

Strough, J., Berg, C. A., & Sansone, C. (1996). Goals for solving everyday problems across the lifespan: Age and gender differences in the salience of interpersonal concerns. *Developmental Psychology, 32,* 1106–1115.

Sullivan, S., & Ruffman, T. (2004). Social understanding: How does it fare with advancing years? *British Journal of Psychology, 95,* 1–18.

Trope, Y., & Gaunt, R. (2000). Processing alternative explanations of behavior: Correction or integration? *Journal of Personality and Social Psychology, 79,* 344–354.

Van Overwalle, F. (2009). Social cognition and the brain: A meta-analysis. *Human Brain Mapping, 30,* 829–858.

Wang, M., & Chen, Y. (2004). Age differences in the correction processes of context-induced biases: When correction succeeds. *Psychology & Aging, 19,* 536–540.

Watson, D. (1982). The actor and the observer: How are their perceptions of causality divergent? *Psychological Bulletin, 92,* 682–700.

Weiner, B. (1985). "Spontaneous" causal thinking. *Psychological Bulletin, 97,* 74–84

Weiner, B. (1979). A theory of motivation for some classroom experiences. *Journal of Educational Psychology, 71,* 3–25.

Weiner, B., Frieze, I. H., Kukla, A., Reed, L., Rest, S., & … Rosenbaum, R. M. (1971). *Perceiving the causes of success and failure.* Morristown, NJ: General Learning Press.

Zacks, R. T., Hasher, L., & Li, K. Z. H. (2000). Human memory. In F. I. M. Craik & T. A. Salthouse (Eds.), *The handbook of aging and cognition* (2nd ed., pp. 293–357). Mahwah, NJ: Lawrence Erlbaum Associates.

Stereotype Threat in Older Adults: When and Why Does It Occur and Who Is Most Affected?

Sarah J. Barber *and* Mara Mather

Abstract

Stereotype threat occurs when people fear that poor performance on their part will confirm a negative, self-relevant stereotype. In response to this threat, people tend to underperform compared to their potential, thereby conforming to the stereotype. For example, older adults are stereotyped as having poorer memory abilities than younger adults; when this stereotype becomes salient to older adults, their memory performance decreases, thereby conforming to the stereotype. The current chapter provides an overview of when, how, and why stereotype threat impacts memory performance in older adults. In particular, we identify situations that lead to stereotype threat in the context of aging and memory. We also discuss the potential mechanisms underlying this effect within older adults and outline how individual differences can make older adults more, or less, susceptible to this form of stereotype threat. We conclude by discussing the potential implications, including those on health, of this form of stereotype threat and delineate future research avenues that remain unexplored.

Key Words: stereotype threat, aging, memory

Stereotypes about aging are prevalent and almost unconditionally accepted in the United States (e.g., Kite & Johnson, 1988; for reviews, see Hummert, 1999; Kite, Stockdale, Whitley, & Johnson, 2005), as well as in other industrialized countries—even in Asian countries (Cuddy et al., 2009). Like stereotypes about other minority groups, stereotypes about aging are multifaceted in nature (e.g., Brewer, Dull, & Lui, 1981), with both positive and negative components (e.g., Cuddy, Fiske, & Glick, 2008; Hummert, Garstka, Shaner, & Strahm, 1994). For example, older adults are generally perceived as being high in warmth but low in competence (Cuddy, Norton, & Fiske, 2005), a combination that is the signature of pitying stereotypes (Cuddy et al., 2008). In addition, although positive stereotypes about older adults exist, negative stereotypes about older adults are more prevalent (Crockett & Hummert, 1987). For example, older

adults are often perceived as being forgetful, slow, timid, weak, and set in their ways (for a review, see Nelson, 2004).

These negative stereotypes about aging are present across the lifespan; even preschool-aged children endorse negative stereotypes about older adults (e.g., Isaacs & Bearison, 1986). For example, in one study, children were shown a picture of an 80-year-old man and asked to imagine how they will feel at that age. The majority of children gave responses that were coded negatively (e.g., "I'll be sick and tired and ready to be buried," p. 509). This was especially true among the youngest groups of children, who were in preschool through fourth grade (Seefeldt, Jantz, Galper, & Serock, 1977). Furthermore, being older does not ameliorate negative attitudes about aging. An online study with more than 60,000 respondents found that people have strong implicit associations between "bad" and

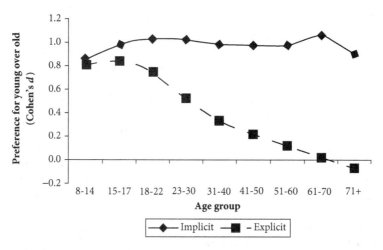

Figure 20.1. Implicit and explicit negative views of aging as a function of respondent age (from Nosek et al., 2002).

"older" (Nosek, Banaji, & Greenwald, 2002; see Figure 20.1). On average, these implicit negative attitudes about aging were stronger than any other implicit attitudes tested, including race. Even more striking is that the implicit negative attitudes were strongly negative no matter the respondents' age, even though explicit preferences for young over old diminished as the respondents' age increased.

A common negative stereotype about aging is the belief that cognitive abilities decline with age. People generally associate aging with forgetfulness, incompetence, and more senile thinking (Hummert et al., 1994; see also Kite & Johnson, 1988). For example, both younger and older adults believe that memory abilities begin to decline in middle adulthood and continue to decline throughout the lifespan (e.g., Lineweaver & Hertzog, 1998; Ryan, 1992; Ryan & See, 1993). These negative views about age-related cognitive decline can have a variety of effects on behavior (for a review, see Hummert, 2011). For example, they can affect how younger adults perceive older adults. Younger adults asked to judge the cause of a target person's memory failure are more likely to attribute it to poor memory abilities when the target person is an older, rather than younger, adult (e.g., Bieman-Copland, & Ryan, 1998; Erber, Szuchman, & Rothberg, 1990; Parr & Siegert, 1993). They are also more sympathetic when older, rather than younger, adults experience memory failures (Erber, Szuchman, & Prager, 1997).

Negative stereotypes about age-related cognitive decline can also affect cognitive performance in older adults. The current review focuses on this type of stereotype threat. In the following sections, we first define stereotype threat and review when it occurs for older adults. We then discuss the potential mechanisms underlying this effect in older adults and identify which older adults are most susceptible to it. Finally, we discuss applications of these findings in real-world settings.

What Is Stereotype Threat and When Does It Occur?

Stereotype threat occurs when members of a stigmatized group feel that if they perform poorly on a task they will confirm, or be judged by, a negative self-relevant stereotype. Ironically, their reactions to this threat may inadvertently cause them to conform to the negative stereotype by impairing their performance. Stereotype threat was first reported by Steele and Aronson in 1995 to explain why African-American students tend to underperform on standardized tests. Steele and Aronson reasoned that African-American students are aware of cultural stereotypes depicting them as intellectually inferior to their Caucasian peers, and fear of confirming these stereotypes causes them to underperform on standardized tests compared to their potential. Results supported these predictions. African-American students performed worse than Caucasian students when a test was described as being diagnostic of intellectual abilities, but not when it was described as being diagnostic of problem-solving abilities.

Hundreds of studies have now documented stereotype threat effects for a wide variety of situations and populations. For instance, women are often stereotyped as being less competent at math than are men. When this stereotype becomes salient to women, their performance on math-based tasks actually decreases, thereby conforming to the stereotype (e.g., Spencer, Steele, & Quinn, 1999). Similarly, stereotype threat impairs negotiation and driving abilities in women (e.g., Kray, Galinsky, & Thompson, 2002; Yeung & von Hippel, 2008), and academic performance in students from low socioeconomic backgrounds (e.g., Croizet & Claire, 1998).

Stereotype threat can also be induced in groups that are not typically thought to be subject to negative stereotypes and that are not chronically the victims of stigmatization. For example, when Caucasian men think they are being compared to Asian men, their math performance decreases (Aronson, Lustina, Good, Keough, Steele, & Brown, 1998). When they think they are being compared to African-American men, their athletic performance decreases (Stone, Lynch, Sjomeling, & Darley, 1999). So, stereotype threat can theoretically be experienced by *anyone* encountering negative self-relevant stereotypes about his or her performance.

In the current review, we focus primarily on how stereotype threat affects memory performance in older adults. This effect was well-demonstrated in a study by Hess, Auman, Colcombe, and Rahhal (2003). Here, younger and older adults read fictional news articles describing research about how aging affects memory. For participants in the control (no-threat) condition, these articles were relatively positive and described the maintenance of memory abilities across the lifespan. In contrast, for participants in the stereotype threat condition, these articles were relatively negative and described age-related declines in memory. For example, they were told that "older adults may have to increasingly depend upon the help of memory tools as well as friends and family" to cope with age-related memory declines. A short time after reading these articles, all participants were given a memory test that involved learning and recalling a list of words. Results revealed age differences in memory performance, but only within the stereotype threat condition. Younger and older adults did *not* differ in recall after reading articles that described maintenance of memory abilities across the lifespan. In contrast, younger adults had significantly higher recall than older adults after reading articles that described age-related memory declines. This result is consistent with stereotype threat theory. When negative stereotypes about age-related memory decline were made salient to older adults, their memory performance actually declined, thereby conforming to the stereotype.

How Is Stereotype Threat Induced in Older Adults?

Stereotype threat about age-related cognitive decline can be evoked in a number of different ways. In some studies, such as the one by Hess and colleagues (2003) just described, participants are exposed to fictitious news stories or conference proceedings confirming that cognitive abilities decline with age (e.g., Coudin & Alexopoulos, 2010; Hess & Hinson, 2006). In other cases, researchers have simply stated that the purpose of the experiment is to examine age-related declines or differences in memory (e.g., Abrams, Eller, & Bryant, 2006; Hess, Emery, & Queen, 2009; Hess, Hinson, & Hodges, 2009). However, stereotype threat can also be induced using more subtle manipulations. For example, Kang and Chasteen (2009) induced threat in older adults by having them explicitly report their age before completing the experiment alongside a younger adult confederate. These subtle indications that the researchers were examining age-related differences in memory were enough to induce stereotype threat and reduce memory performance relative to older adults in a control condition.

As another example of how subtle situational cues can induce stereotype threat, age-related stereotype threat can occur when researchers simply state that the purpose of the experiment is to examine memory performance (e.g., Desrichard & Kopetz, 2005; Rahhal, Hasher, & Colcombe, 2001). This is likely because older adults' negative stereotypes about age-related cognitive decline are activated when they know that their memory is being examined. Because of this, older adults tend to have higher performance on a test if it is *not* described as assessing memory, compared to when it *is* described as assessing memory.

Similar results have been obtained in other lines of research that were not necessarily designed to examine stereotype threat, but rather to examine how memory is affected by the intentionality of processing performed at encoding and/or retrieval. Looking first at encoding, several studies have reported a reduction of, or even an elimination of, age differences in memory performance when participants complete the encoding task without awareness that there will be an upcoming memory test. That is, age differences in memory performance are sometimes attenuated when *incidental* encoding instructions rather than *intentional* encoding instructions are used (for reviews, see Perlmutter & Mitchell, 1982; Yonelinas, 2002). Although some subsequent research has failed to replicate this effect (e.g., Kausler, Lichty, & Freund, 1985; Verhaeghen, Marcoen, & Goossens, 1992), when there are increased age differences for intentional rather than incidental encoding instructions, this may in part be due to stereotype threat. This is because stereotypes about age-related memory decline are more likely to come to mind when older adults are explicitly told their memory will be assessed.

Similar results have also been found from studies that manipulated the intentionality of processing at retrieval rather than at encoding (for reviews, see Fleischman & Gabrieli, 1998; Light, Prull, La Voie, & Healy, 2000). Age differences are typically observed on explicit memory tests, which involve the intentional and conscious retrieval of past events. In contrast, age differences are sometimes reduced, or even eliminated, on implicit memory tests. Here, memory is assessed as changes in behavior that are a result of prior experience, but that are (importantly) unaccompanied by intentional or conscious recall of previous learning (e.g., Mitchell & Bruss, 2003). Although performance on these implicit tests is highly variable and likely dependent on a myriad of additional factors, there do tend to be larger age differences in memory performance when participants are consciously aware that their memory is being tested. Again, this may in part be due to stereotype threat. When participants are aware that memory is being assessed, the threat is "in the air" (Steele, 1997).

A Distinction Between Implicit and Explicit Stereotype Activation

So far, we have only discussed how explicitly inducing stereotype threat can affect performance in older adults. However, some of the first research examining the influence of age-related stereotype activation on performance used implicit priming. Here, performance is examined after subliminally exposing participants to age-related primes. In the typical paradigm, negative age-related words (e.g., *feeble, forgot, incompetent, senile*) or positive age-related words (e.g., *accomplished, knowledgeable, successful, wise*) are briefly flashed on the screen at a faster speed than can be consciously perceived (e.g., Hess, Hinson, & Statham, 2004). Participants then complete a subsequent task. The expectation is that participants will show a different pattern of performance when primed with the negative, versus positive, age-related words. Results generally support this prediction. Older adults walk slower (Hausdorff, Levy, & Wei, 1999), have poorer handwriting (Levy, 2000), have poorer physical balance (Levy & Leifheit-Limson, 2009), have increased physiological responses to stress (Levy, Hausdorff, Hencke, & Wei, 2000), and are more likely to refuse health interventions to artificially prolong life (Levy,

Ashman, & Dror, 1999–2000) when exposed to negative, rather than positive, age-related primes.

Implicit priming can also affect memory performance. In general, older adults perform worse on a memory test following negative, rather than positive, age-related primes (Hess et al., 2004; Levy, 1996; Levy & Leifheit-Limson, 2009; Stein, Blanchard-Fields, & Hertzog, 2002). Although this has been inconsistently observed across memory measures, the general pattern suggests that unconsciously activated stereotypes about aging can negatively affect memory.

How do these implicit priming effects differ from the explicit stereotype threat effects discussed earlier? Some research has suggested that the two effects differ in magnitude (Hess et al., 2004). However, in contrast to this proposition, a recent meta-analysis found no difference in effect magnitude as a function of whether participants were aware of the stereotype or not (Meisner, 2012). Rather, the primary difference between implicit priming and explicit stereotype threat appears to be in whether the effects are limited to people personally stigmatized by the stereotype (for a review, see Wheeler & Petty, 2001). This can be illustrated by examining how younger adults are affected by stereotype threat (about age-related cognitive decline) versus by implicit stereotype activation (about age-related stereotypes). Results show that younger adults do not exhibit changes in memory performance as a function of explicit stereotype threat (e.g., Chasteen, Bhattacharyya, Horhota, Tam, & Hasher, 2005; Desrichard & Kopetz, 2005; Hess et al., 2003; Rahhal et al., 2001). For example, memory performance for younger adults does not vary as a function of whether the experiment is described as examining age-related declines in memory performance or not. In contrast, younger adults sometimes exhibit implicit stereotype activation effects similar to those exhibited by older adults. Priming age-related stereotypes in younger adults can result in assimilation to these stereotypes: they walk slower (Bargh, Chen, & Burrows, 1996), respond more slowly (Dijksterhuis, Spears, & Lépinasse, 2001), drive more cautiously (Gray & Branaghan, 2009), and sometimes remember less (Dijksterhuis, Aarts, Bargh, & van Knippenberg, 2000; but see Hess et al., 2004, for conflicting results and discussion of this issue).

Thus, younger adults are differentially affected by stereotype threat (about age-related cognitive decline) versus implicit stereotype activation (about age-related stereotypes). These differences are likely because the two effects emerge for different reasons (e.g., Marx & Stapel, 2006). Reviewed in more depth below, stereotype threat is typically thought to occur when people fear that poor performance on their part may confirm a negative, self-relevant, stereotype. That is, stereotype threat requires conscious awareness both of the stereotype and of its applicability to one's own performance. Furthermore, its effects seem to rely on these conscious mediation processes. In contrast, building upon James's (1890) idea of ideomotor action, implicit stereotype threat activation can affect behavior because action can proceed directly from perception. When stereotypes are unconsciously activated, people tend to behave in line with them (e.g., Bargh et al., 1996; Dijksterhuis, 2001). Interestingly, when stereotypes are self-relevant, they may therefore induce both stereotype threat as well as ideomotor effects (Dijksterhuis, 2001; Dijksterhuis & Bargh, 2001). In summary, although implicit priming and explicit stereotype threat both reflect how stereotypes can affect performance (and are therefore sometimes grouped together even within meta-analyses, see Horton, Baker, Pearce, & Deakin, 2008), they are due to different mechanisms.

Why Does Stereotype Threat Occur?

Although a large body of research has clearly demonstrated that stereotype threat effects occur, across studies, it is less clear *why*. Below, we briefly outline four potential mechanisms: negative affective responses, lowered performance expectations, executive control interference, and changes in motivational orientation. We also review how well each of these mechanisms can account for older adults' stereotype threat effects.

The Role of Negative Affective Responses

Negative affective responses were one of the first mechanisms proposed to underlie stereotype threat effects (e.g., Steele & Aronson, 1995). In particular, stereotype threat is assumed to be associated with increased negative affective states (such as test anxiety), which in turn are associated with negative thoughts or increased levels of anxiety, which in turn lead to performance decrements (Steele, 1997; Steele, Spencer, & Aronson, 2002).

Results in support of this mechanism have been mixed. Within the broader stereotype threat literature using younger adult participants, some studies have found that self-reported anxiety partially mediates stereotype threat effects (e.g., Osborne, 2001), others have found no mediation (e.g., Spencer et al.,

1999), and still others have found that mediation occurs only for people with a high personal investment in the domain being threatened (Delgado & Prieto, 2008). Mixed results have also been obtained when examining how stereotype threat affects memory performance in older adults. One study reported that older adults under threat experienced greater test anxiety, and that this increased anxiety mediated the extent of subsequent memory performance decrements (Abrams et al., 2006). However, a large number of additional studies have failed to demonstrate a mediating relationship between stereotype threat manipulations and either anxiety (e.g., Chasteen et al., 2005; Hess et al., 2003; Hess & Hinson, 2006), or negative mood states (e.g., Hess et al., 2009; Kang & Chasteen, 2009) in older adults. This is true even when examining skin conductance responses, an index of autonomic nervous system functioning (Hess et al., 2009) rather than self-reports of anxiety or arousal. In particular, although skin conductance increased for older adults in the stereotype threat condition relative to the control condition, this did not mediate the subsequent memory performance decrements (Hess et al., 2009).

In summary, stereotype threat has traditionally been explained as arising from hot motivational factors such as anxiety or arousal (see Wheeler & Petty, 2001). Although older adults sometimes display these negative affective responses in response to threat, this does *not* appear to be a key cause of stereotype threat–related memory impairments.

The Role of Lowered Performance Expectations

In contrast to the conflicting findings about the role of negative affective responses, results have consistently implicated performance expectations in modulating stereotype threat effects. The idea here is that when people expect to do poorly on a task then they will underperform compared to their potential (e.g., Kray, Thompson, & Galinsky, 2001). This appears to play a role in explaining stereotype threat effects. For example, younger adult women under threat about their spatial abilities expect to perform worse on a subsequent spatial abilities test than do younger adult women not under threat (Stangor, Carr, & Kiang, 1998). These decreased performance expectations partially mediate subsequent stereotype threat effects (Cadinu, Maass, Frigerio, Impagliazzo, & Latinotti, 2003). Similar results have also been reported for older adults. Older adults under threat about their memory abilities expect to do worse on a subsequent memory tasks, and these lowered expectations mediate stereotype threat performance decrements (Desrichard & Kopetz, 2005, see also Hess et al., 2009). Although this factor has not yet received a great deal of investigation in older adults, extant results suggest it may be a key factor contributing to their stereotype threat–related memory impairments.

The Role of Executive Control Interference

As noted, in this review, we focus only on a few potential mechanisms underlying stereotype threat effects. However, across studies, a variety of affective, motivational, physiological, and cognitive factors have all been shown to mediate stereotype threat effects. To reconcile these disparate results, a recent model proposes that executive control interference is the common distal mediator linking these aforementioned factors (Schmader, Johns, & Forbes, 2008). Here, we outline this integrated model before reviewing whether evidence from older adults supports it.

In brief, this integrated model (Schmader et al., 2008) proposes that stereotype threat is caused by three interrelated mechanisms that selectively impair performance on tasks that require executive control resources (i.e., the set of interrelated abilities involved in controlling and directing attention). First, stereotype threat is thought to induce physiological stress. When people encounter stereotype threat, they sometimes show increases in stress-based arousal (e.g., Ben-Zeev, Fein, & Inzlicht, 2005) and this, in turn, can negatively affect task performance (e.g., Eysenck & Calvo, 1992). This is particularly true for tasks that rely on executive control and prefrontal cortex functioning, since prefrontal function and performance on executive control–based tasks are known to be especially sensitive to stress-based arousal (e.g., Arnsten, 2009; Schoofs, Wolf, & Smeets, 2009). Second, stereotype threat can increase performance monitoring and concerns about task performance (e.g., Beilock, Rydell, & McConnell, 2007). Because performance concerns and stereotype threat concerns compete for executive control resources, they together induce a divided attention state in the participant. This, in turn, can impair performance. Finally, stereotype threat may also induce negative moods and thoughts that people then attempt to regulate (e.g., Steele, 1997; Steele et al., 2002). Suppression of negative moods and thoughts is cognitively costly, requiring executive control resources to complete

(e.g., Muraven & Baumeister, 2000). Thus, emotion regulation processes also compete for executive control resources, leaving even fewer resources available to perform the task at hand. In summary, this integrated model proposes that stereotype threat leads to increased stress, increased performance monitoring, and an increased need to regulate negative affective states. This, in turn, leads to lowered availability of executive control resources and hence lower performance on tasks that require the use of executive control resources.

Although research supports this model in younger adults (e.g., Beilock, Jellison, Rydell, McConnell, & Carr, 2006; Régner, Smeding, Gimmig, Thinus-Blanc, Monteil, & Hugert, 2010; Schmader & Johns, 2003), empirical evidence has been mixed when examining older adults. Looking first at evidence in favor of the model, research has shown that stereotype threat preferentially decreases older adults' ability to use controlled, rather than automatic, memory processes (Mazerolle, Régner, Morisset, Rigalleau, & Huguet, 2012). Similarly, older adults under threat tend to respond more on the basis of familiarity and less on the basis of recollection when completing a memory test under time pressure (Hess et al., 2009). Given that controlled memory processes and recollection-based judgments rely more heavily on executive control resources than on automatic memory processes and familiarity-based judgments, these findings support the notion that stereotype threat temporarily reduces the amount of executive control resources available and hence preferentially affects tasks that require executive control.

However, there has also been evidence suggesting that executive control interference is not a key factor underlying stereotype threat effects in older adults. For example, stereotype threat does not impair older adults' ability to selectively prioritize learning high- versus low-value information (Barber & Mather, 2012), even though this ability depends on executive control (Castel, Balota, & McCabe, 2009). Furthermore, although performance on a working memory measure is impaired following stereotype threat for younger adults (Johns, Inzlicht, & Schmader, 2008), it is not for older adults (Hess et al., 2009) unless it is described as being a test of memory abilities (Mazerolle et al., 2012; see also Abrams et al., 2006; Desrichard & Kopetz, 2005; experiment 2). The finding that working memory is not necessarily impaired for older adults following stereotype threat is problematic for an executive resource account of stereotype threat. A possibility that seems more consistent with these findings using working memory tasks is that stereotype threat reduces older adults' performance on all tasks clearly identified as memory tasks by lowering performance expectations.

In summary, although executive control interference appears to be a key cause of stereotype threat in younger adults, based on the extant literature, it is unclear what role it plays for older adults. One possibility is that executive control interference mediates stereotype threat more strongly in younger, compared to older, adults due to age-related changes in emotion regulation abilities. As noted earlier, arousal increases as a function of stereotype threat in older adults, but this does not mediate subsequent performance decrements (Hess et al., 2009). This may be because regulating negative emotions is less cognitively costly for older, compared with younger, adults. For example, research has shown that conducting emotion regulation while performing a cognitive task leads to performance decrements for younger, but not older, adults (Scheibe & Blanchard-Fields, 2009). So, although stereotype threat may induce negative affective states that people try to regulate, this may be more cognitively costly for younger than for older adults.

Motivational Orientations: The Role of Regulatory Fit

The final mechanism that we review here is a motivation-based explanation of stereotype threat that hinges on the role of *regulatory fit* (Seibt & Förster, 2004). This explanation is drawn from regulatory focus theory (Higgins, 1997, 1999), which proposes that people differ in how they pursue goals. People with a *promotion focus* concentrate on goal-related rewards and aspirations, and are sensitive to the presence or absence of rewards. Furthermore, people with a promotion focus tend to use approach strategies when completing tasks (e.g., try to gain hits and minimize misses during a recognition memory test). In contrast to this, people with a *prevention focus* concentrate on goal-related losses and responsibilities, and are sensitive to the presence or absence of losses. Furthermore, people with a prevention focus tend to use avoidance strategies when completing tasks (e.g., try to avoid false alarms and ensure correct rejections).

Although regulatory focus can directly affect performance, its precise role depends on the nature of the task. People tend to have higher task performance when their regulatory focus matches the reward structure of the task; that is, when there is

a *regulatory fit* (e.g., Shah, Higgins, & Friedman, 1998). People with a promotion focus typically do better when the task emphasizes gaining rewards rather than avoiding losses. The reverse is true for prevention focus.

Plenty of research suggests that people differ in their dispositional promotion and prevention focus tendencies (e.g., Higgins, Shah, & Friedman, 1997). However, a variety of factors can also affect an individual's temporary situational regulatory focus (e.g., Förster, Higgins, & Idson, 1998; Freitas, Liberman, & Higgins, 2002; Friedman & Förster, 2001). One such variable may be stereotype threat. In particular, stereotype threat may invoke a prevention focus, in which people are concerned with minimizing losses and avoiding risks (Seibt & Förster, 2004; see also Smith, 2004). Interestingly, an extension of this proposition is that stereotype threat impairments reported in previous research may be due to the fact that studies have almost exclusively used reward-based tasks (e.g., how many hits were gained?). This is problematic because these situations represent a regulatory mismatch for people with a prevention focus (Grimm, Markman, Maddox, & Baldwin, 2009). In other words, although stereotype threat is usually thought of as impairing performance, this may only occur when the task emphasizes rewards. In contrast, performance under stereotype threat may *increase* when the task emphasizes losses (i.e., when there is regulatory fit).

Results have tended to support this theory. Looking first at younger adults, stereotype threat is associated with an increased focus on prevention-, rather than promotion-related concepts (Seibt & Förster, 2004, see also Oyserman, Uskul, Yoder, Nesse, & Williams, 2007). Furthermore, younger adults under stereotype threat respond more slowly during a task (Seibt & Förster, 2004) and are more risk-averse in their decision making (Carr & Steele, 2010), as would be expected by a more cautious prevention focus. Also as predicted, stereotype threat effects disappear, and sometimes even reverse, when the task has a losses-based structure rather than a gains-based structure (Grimm, et al., 2009; Seibt & Förster, 2004). For example, one study examined whether women's performance on a math task depended on both stereotype threat and the task's reward structure. Results showed that women under threat underperformed when the math task had a reward-based structure (i.e., more points awarded for correct than incorrect answers), but showed no impairment when the task had a losses-based structure (i.e., more points lost for incorrect than correct answers; Grimm et al., 2009).

Support for this theory has also been found when examining older, rather than younger, adults. Consistent with the idea that stereotype threat induces a prevention focus, older adults under stereotype threat are more risk-averse in their decision making than are older adults not under stereotype threat (Coudin & Alexopoulos, 2010). Furthermore, more direct evidence for this theory can be seen in results from our own laboratory (Barber & Mather, 2012). In two experiments, older adults (either under stereotype threat or not) were asked to learn a series of words paired with point values. Some words led to point gains if remembered, whereas others led to point losses if forgotten. Memory was then tested using both a free recall test (Experiments 1 and 2), as well as a subsequent recognition test (Experiment 2). Supporting the prediction that stereotype threat induces a prevention focus, in both experiments, there was a significant interaction between stereotype threat condition and point value. Older adults under stereotype threat recalled fewer of the gain-related items, but *more* of the loss-related items than did older adults in the nonthreat condition. Furthermore, on the subsequent recognition test, older adults under stereotype threat had more conservative response biases than did older adults in the nonthreat condition. Together, these results are consistent with a prevention focus, which is associated with an increased concern with losses, minimizing errors, and avoiding risk. This mechanism predicts that stereotype threat will not always impair memory performance in older adults. Rather, stereotype threat could even *improve* memory when the task is framed as relating to losses rather than gains.

Interactions Between the Different Explanations of Stereotype Threat

In the previous section, we outlined four potential reasons why stereotype threat might occur. However, it is important to note that this is not an exhaustive list. For example, stereotype threat may also impact behavior by reducing the effort people exert toward the task (e.g., Schimel, Arndt, Banko, & Cook, 2004; Stone, 2002), by depleting their ability to engage in self-control and effortful processing (e.g., Inzlicht, McKay, & Aronson, 2006), by increasing attention or effort toward procedural tasks that are best performed automatically (e.g., Beilock et al., 2006), or by causing participants to use an inefficient task strategy (e.g., Hess et al., 2003). In the present review, we have focused only on the subset of mechanisms that have been widely cited as accounting for stereotype threat effects or that have received a large amount of experimental support when examining memory performance in older adults.

It is also important to note that although we have outlined these four potential mechanisms as independent causes of stereotype threat, in actuality, they likely interact with one another. For example, the regulatory fit model of stereotype threat is not incongruent with the executive interference hypothesis. For example, within the integrated executive control interference model proposed by Schmader, Johns, and Forbes (2008), regulatory focus is included as one of the reasons that stereotype threat induces task-monitoring behavior (e.g., by increasing vigilance toward avoiding errors). This, in turn, is thought to reduce the number of executive control resources available for completing the task at hand.

As a second example of the interaction between these mechanisms, it is possible that performance expectations are related to regulatory focus. People with a prevention focus tend to have performance avoidance goals, whereas people with a promotion focus tend to have performance approach goals (Smith, 2004, 2006). One way that these differences in task strategy may manifest themselves is through performance expectations. Avoidance goals may lead people to be concerned with failure to meet minimal expectations (i.e., vigilant not to be the worst) rather than with the ability to meet maximal performance (i.e., eager to be the best). This could, in turn, cause people in a prevention focus to set low performance expectations. So, the mediating role of performance expectations may actually be due to the fact that stereotype threat induces a prevention focus.

To summarize, although stereotype threat effects are robust and occur across a wide variety of situations for a wide variety of populations, the precise mechanisms underlying these effects are still unclear. However, research examining older adults has tended to support two mechanisms. First, stereotype threat appears to reduce performance expectations and this, in turn, mediates the amount of stereotype threat–induced memory impairments observed in older adults (e.g., Desrichard & Kopetz, 2005). Second, regulatory fit appears to be a key factor modulating stereotype threat effects in older adults. According to this model (Seibt & Förster, 2004), stereotype threat induces a prevention focus in which people focus on loss-, rather than gain-related information, and are concerned with minimizing mistakes and risks. Although some recent research in our own lab supports this proposition (Barber & Mather, 2012), future research is needed to more fully examine the role of regulatory fit in underlying stereotype threat effects in older adults. Furthermore, future research is also needed to clarify the conflicting findings about executive control interference's role in underlying stereotype threat effects in older, compared to younger, adults.

Who Is Most Affected by Stereotype Threat?

In the previous section, we examined four potential mechanisms underlying the occurrence of stereotype threat in older adults. We now turn to an examination of individual differences in older adults' susceptibility to stereotype threat. In particular, we examine how domain and group identification, intergenerational interactions, and perceptions of societal and cultural views of aging may modulate the extent to which older adults experience stereotype threat.

Identification With the Threatened Domain

Stereotype threat effects have long been thought to be moderated by how much people value achievement within the threatened domain (e.g., Aronson et al., 1998; Steele, 1997). People are only expected to feel threatened about how their performance will be perceived if they personally care about, or care about the societal implications of, whether they have the ability being tested (e.g., Brunstein & Gollwitzer, 1996; Steele, 1997). Results have generally been consistent with this (e.g., Stone et al., 1999). For example, when younger adult Caucasian men think that their math performance is being compared to younger adult Asian men, their performance generally decreases. However, this is only true for Caucasian men who strongly care about their math abilities (Aronson et al., 1999).

Similar results have also been found when examining how older adults respond to stereotype threat about their memory abilities. In fact, some research has suggested a strong relationship between these factors. When under stereotype threat (but not within a control condition), the amount by which older adults value their memory has a large negative association with the amount of information they recall, $r = -.70$ (Hess et al., 2003). Although subsequent research has failed to replicate this effect (Hess & Hinson, 2006), it suggests that stereotype threat may have the greatest negative impact on older adults who value their memory abilities. This may explain why stereotype threat impairments on memory are strongest for older adults with high levels of education (Barber & Mather, 2012; Hess et al., 2009; but see Andreoletti & Lachman, 2004). High levels of education may be associated with increased identification with the ability to perform well on memory tests (as this is a common occurrence in higher education).

It is interesting to note that although stereotype threat effects may be moderated by domain identification, it is also true that stereotype threat affects domain identification. In particular, stereotype threat may lead people to disidentify with the domain being threatened to preserve their self-esteem (e.g., Osborne, 1997; Steele, 1997; Steele & Aronson, 1995). This logic can explain why there are so few women who study math and engineering. Stereotypes about women's incompetence in math may cause women to disidentify with domains related to math and therefore decide not pursue this type of career. To our knowledge, this has not yet been studied with aging stereotypes. However, it would suggest that exposure to negative age-related stereotypes leads older adults to devalue memory performance.

Identification With the Threatened Group

Domain identification is not the only factor that can modulate stereotype threat. Group identification may also play a role. For example, younger adult women generally underperform on math tests when the link between their performance and gender is salient. However, this is moderated by group identification; only women whose gender is central to their self-identity are susceptible to these effects (Schmader, 2002). Although support for this has also been found when looking at age-related stereotypes in late middle-aged adults (O'Brien & Hummert, 2006), little research has directly examined older adults. Results of one study suggest that the more that people self-identify as older adults, the lower their memory performance. However, this did not moderate the observed threat effects (Kang & Chasteen, 2009). Future research is needed to explore the relationship between age-group identification and stereotype threat effects within older adults.

As was the case with domain identification, it is worth noting that although stereotype threat effects may be moderated by group identification, it is also true that stereotype threat affects group identification. Although identification with the older adult age group can actually help older adults cope with perceived age discrimination (Garstka, Schmitt, Branscombe, & Hummert, 2004), research suggests that stereotype threat *decreases* identification with the older adult age group. For example, correlational research suggests that older adults who perceive there to be greater age-related stigma also report less identification with the older adult age group (Hess & Dikken, 2010). A similar result has also been found experimentally. When older adults are presented with negative stereotypes about aging, they subsequently direct their gaze away from pictures of older adults and toward pictures of middle-aged adults. They also perceive themselves as being more similar to middle-aged, compared to older, adults (Weiss & Freund, 2012). This distancing may be accomplished via social comparisons (e.g., considering oneself as being better off than other members of one's age group; see Heckhausen & Krueger, 1993). It may also explain why older adults report subjectively feeling younger than their chronological age (e.g., Kleinspehn-Ammerlahn, Kotter-Grühn, & Smith, 2008; Montepare & Lachman, 1989; Rubin & Berntsen, 2006).

Intergenerational Interaction

The previous two factors, domain and group identification, both serve to make older adults *more* susceptible to stereotype threat effects. However, there are also protective factors that make older adults *less* susceptible to stereotype threat effects. One such factor appears to be positive intergenerational interactions.

A large body of literature has shown that, under the appropriate conditions, intergroup contact is one of the most effective ways of reducing prejudice and stereotypes (Allport, 1954; for a review or a meta-analysis of these effects see Pettigrew, 1998, and Pettigrew & Tropp, 2000, respectively). For example, younger adults who experience positive interactions with older adults hold fewer stereotypes about older adults (e.g., Hale, 1998; Schwartz & Simmons, 2001). Of greater interest to the current review, such interactions can also reduce stereotype threat for the outgroup members. This is because older adults who have had positive interactions with younger adults may be less anxious about being compared to younger adults and may be less likely to bring to mind negative age-related stereotypes (Crisp & Abrams, 2002). Results have been in line with this; intergenerational contact moderates

stereotype threat–related memory performance in older adults such that stereotype threat–related memory impairments are less likely to occur as older adults report increases in positive intergenerational contact within their daily lives (Abrams et al., 2006). Interestingly, these benefits can also occur for older adults who simply *imagine* positive interactions with younger adults (in this case, on a test of math abilities; Abrams, Crisp, Marques, Fagg, Bedford, & Provias, 2008).

The benefits of intergenerational contact on reducing stereotype threat in older adults likely arose for two reasons. First, older adults who reported having positive intergenerational contact also felt less anxious in response to stereotype threat. Furthermore, after accounting for these differences in anxiety, there was no remaining benefit of intergenerational contact in reducing stereotype threat effects (Abrams et al., 2006). Second, older adults who reported having positive intergenerational contact were also less likely to self-identify as an older adult (Abrams et al., 2006). This may serve as a protective factor, since identification with the threatened group tends to amplify stereotype threat effects (e.g., O'Brien & Hummert, 2006). Thus, intergenerational contact reduces stereotype threat by making older adults feel less anxious about the possibility of being compared to younger adults, and also by decreasing their identification with the older adult age group.

In summary, although intergenerational interaction is relatively uncommon (e.g., Hagestad & Uhlenberg, 2005), it can have positive consequences both for younger and older adults. This appears to be true even when the contact does not actually occur and is simply imagined. Given the relative ease of imagining a positive intergenerational interaction, this may be an effective means of reducing stereotype threat in real-world settings (for a review, see Crisp & Abrams, 2002; but for criticisms see Bigler & Hughes, 2010). Future research is needed to examine the use of this as an intervention, particularly among older adults most susceptible to stereotype threat effects (such as those who highly value their memory abilities).

Perception of Age-Related Stereotypes

Finally, cultural and personal perceptions about age-related cognitive decline may also affect the amount of stereotype threat impairments observed. Looking first at the role of culture, some of the first work examining stereotype threat suggested that older adults from cultures presumed to hold positive perceptions about aging (i.e., Chinese and the American Deaf) showed fewer age-related memory impairments than did older adults from cultures presumed to hold more negative perceptions of aging (i.e., Americans). Also, the relationship between culture and memory was mediated by the extent to which older adults held positive views about aging (Levy & Langer, 1994). This result could be explained as being caused by stereotype threat. That is, older adults from cultures that hold more positive views of aging are less likely to experience stereotype threat when their memory is being tested, and so show less age-related declines in memory performance when compared to older adults from cultures that hold more negative views of aging.

Although these results are compelling, a subsequent failure to completely replicate this effect has made the relationship between cultural views of aging and age-related memory decline less clear. In a study by Yoon and colleagues (2000), there was a reduction in age-related memory impairments for people from a culture that presumably has positive views on aging (i.e., Chinese immigrants who had recently moved to Canada) compared to people from a culture that has negative views on aging (i.e., Anglophone Canadians). However, in contrast to the results reported by Levy and Langer (1994), this was not mediated by the extent to which older adults held positive views about aging. In fact, there was no significant correlation between beliefs about aging and memory performance (Yoon, Hasher, Feinberg, Rahhal, & Winocur, 2000; see also Kahn, Zarit, Hilbert, & Niederehe, 1975; Scogin, Storandt, & Lott, 1985).

Thus, although studies suggest that age-related memory impairments are reduced for people from cultures with more positive views about aging, it is unclear whether this is in fact due to cultural views about aging. One alternative is that these results may have been due to cultural differences in the amount of positive intergenerational interactions among the older adults. For example, Yoon and colleagues (2000) note that a unique feature of their Chinese, compared to Anglophone, Canadians was that they tended to live in multigenerational households. So, it is possible that cultural differences in the extent to which older adults engage in intergenerational interactions, a factor known to reduce stereotype threat–related memory impairments (e.g., Abrams et al., 2006), is the driving force behind the reduction in age-related memory differences. It is also worth noting that recent evidence suggests that

Eastern and Western cultures have mostly similar ageist stereotypes (Boduroglu, Yoon, Luo, & Park, 2006). For example, recent evidence shows that Asian cultures, like Western cultures, have multifaceted stereotypes about older adults in which they are perceived as high in warmth but low in competence (Cuddy et al., 2009).

In contrast to the conflicting literature on the role of cultural perceptions of aging, there is more consistent evidence implicating personal perceptions of age-related stereotypes in modulating stereotype threat. Research in this area has examined the role of perceived stereotype threat. This is defined as the extent to which people expect and perceive others to be stereotyping them. It can occur both as general stigma consciousness (Pinel, 1999), in which people tend to expect or perceive negative stereotypes in their daily lives. It can also occur as a situational perception of threat within a specific context (Kang & Chasteen, 2009). Research has shown that perceptions of stereotype threat can moderate stereotype threat–related memory impairments in older adults. Older adults who tend to perceive a high degree of threat in their environment are more susceptible to stereotype threat, as evidenced by poorer memory performance when under threat (Kang & Chasteen, 2009; see also Chasteen et al., 2005).

What Are the Implications of Stereotype Threat?

So far, we have examined what stereotype threat is, why it occurs for older adults, and which older adults are most affected by it. We now turn our attention to examining how stereotype threat might impact older adults in real-world settings. Although some have argued that stereotype threat exerts little effect outside of the laboratory (e.g., Cullen, Hardison, & Sackett, 2004; Stricker & Ward, 2004), recent research has called this conclusion into question. For example, Danaher and Crandall (2008) reanalyzed data from Stricker and Ward (200) and found that when students were asked to indicate their gender after (rather than before) an AP Calculus test, there was a 33% reduction in the gender gap between male and female performance. Building on the notion that stereotype threat likely has many important ecological implications (e.g., Burgess, Warren, Phelan, Dovidio, & van Ryn, 2010), here we briefly outline ways that stereotype threat may influence older adults outside of the laboratory.

First, it is likely that stereotype threat negatively impacts memory performance in many everyday settings. This could be evidenced as forgetting appointments or the name of an acquaintance when placed in situations where age-related stereotypes are prevalent. If these everyday memory failures occur frequently, they may lead older adults to seek neuropsychological testing to determine whether their memory failures are indicative of dementia. Here, stereotype threat–related memory impairments can have serious clinical implications. In a recent study, 70% of older adults met diagnostic criteria for dementia when assessed under stereotype threat, compared to only 14% when not assessed under threat (Haslam, Morton, Haslam, Varnes, Graham, & Gamaz, 2012). This increase in false-positive diagnoses could lead to a myriad of negative outcomes for older adults. Not only would these older adults face the anxiety and stigma of receiving the dementia label, but they could also face monetary costs associated with follow-up testing, or could needlessly be prescribed antidementive drugs. Given that one out of every five Americans is expected to be older than 65 by 2030 (US Census, 2011), and given that there is increased advocation that older adults receive routine dementia screenings (e.g., Ashford et al., 2007), in the future, it will be increasingly important for clinicians to be aware of how stereotype threat may influence older adults' neuropsychological test performance (see also Burgess et al., 2010).

Stereotype threat may also exacerbate the degree to which older adults are dependent on younger adults. Previous research has shown that younger adults tend to perceive older adults as being less cognitively capable, and so tend to intervene and provide older adults with task assistance. For example, in nursing home settings, caregivers overwhelmingly reward residents for being dependent on them (e.g., by praising residents for accepting help or by discouraging them from executing tasks without help), and this is true even when the residents themselves are exhibiting independent behavior (e.g., Barton, Baltes, & Orzech, 1980). This pattern also occurs in community, rather than institutional, settings (Baltes & Wahl, 1992). Problematically, this assistance may lead to subsequent performance decrements for the older adults being assisted. For example, in one study, older adults were either provided with assistance in completing a puzzle or were simply given verbal encouragement while completing a puzzle. Interestingly, the older adults provided with assistance showed *decreased* performance over time, whereas the older adults provided with verbal encouragement showed *increased* performance over

time (Avorn & Langer, 1982). One possibility is that this was due to stereotype threat, such that providing older adults with cognitive assistance made salient for them stereotypes about age-related cognitive declines, which in turn lowered their cognitive performance and made them more dependent on younger adults. In line with this, research has shown that older adults under stereotype threat request assistance from younger adults more frequently than do older adults not under threat (Coudin & Alexopoulos, 2010). This increased dependency on younger adults is particularly problematic because dependency is associated with a number of negative outcomes. For example, dependent older adults frequently show a loss of motivation, depression, and other health problems (e.g., Solomon, 1990). Furthermore, unnecessary reliance on caregivers for activities of daily living, such as getting dressed, may needlessly accelerate the aging process through disuse of muscles or motor skills. In contrast, increasing feelings of independence in older adults in nursing homes is associated with increases in happiness and activity levels (e.g., Langer & Rodin, 1976; for a review, see Rowe & Kahn, 1987).

Finally, views about aging can also exert a direct impact on health. In general, having positive views about aging is associated with better physical recovery from heart attacks among older adults (Levy, Slade, May, & Caracciolo, 2006). In contrast, having negative views about aging is associated with greater hearing loss over time (Levy, Slade, & Gill, 2006) and decreased longevity (Levy, 2002). Not only can views about aging affect health, but stereotype threat can also play a role. Older adults under stereotype threat rate their own health as being subjectively worse than do older adults not under threat. They also rate themselves as lonelier than older adults not under threat (Coudin & Alexopoulos, 2010). This is problematic because lonely people show greater age-related increases in blood pressure and poorer sleep quality than do people who do not perceive themselves as being lonely (Cacioppo et al., 2002). They also have higher rates of mortality, even after accounting for a variety of health-related behaviors (Berkman & Syme, 1979). Although the current review focuses on how stereotype threat impacts cognitive performance, it is important to keep in mind that it also exerts other effects, some that have negative health implications.

Conclusion

Negative stereotypes about age-related cognitive decline are prevalent in the United States (e.g., Kite

& Johnson, 1988). As in many stereotypes, there is some truth to these generalizations—the normal aging process is associated with some degree of memory decline. However, of interest to the current review, negative stereotypes about age-related cognitive decline can also exacerbate these deficits via stereotype threat. When older adults encounter negative stereotypes about age-related cognitive decline, their memory performance decreases (e.g., Hess et al., 2003). This has important implication in assessing how age impacts memory abilities. For example, older adults recruited to participate in a study about "aging and memory" will likely underperform compared to their potential. This will, in turn, exacerbate, or possibly even create, age differences in memory performance, rendering it difficult to draw strong conclusions about how aging (in and of itself) affects memory processing.

Although it is now clear that stereotype threat occurs, it is less clear why. Within the older adult age group, two mechanisms appear to play a critical role. First, stereotype threat influences performance expectations. When faced with stereotype threat, older adults do not expect to perform well on the subsequent memory test and so underperform compared to their potential (Desrichard & Kopetz, 2005). Second, regulatory focus also appears to play a role (Barber & Mather, 2012). Stereotype threat induces older adults to focus more on goal-relevant losses and to adopt a conservative, risk-averse approach to performing tasks. Although this may lead to performance benefits in some situations, it will generally lead to performance decrements when the task emphasizes gains (e.g., learning as many words as possible). However, future research is needed to more fully examine both of these potential mechanisms, as well as to examine how they might be interrelated.

Finally, the individual differences factors identified in this chapter also have important implications in designing prevention or intervention strategies. Based on the extant literature, it appears that older adults who place a great importance on memory abilities (Hess et al., 2003), or who tend to perceive stereotype threat in everyday situations (Kang & Chasteen, 2009) are the most susceptible to stereotype threat effects. In contrast, intergenerational contact (Abrams et al., 2006), even when it is imagined (Abrams et al., 2008), appears to be a protective influence against stereotype threat. Given that it is likely difficult to change domain identification, this suggests that interventions may be more effective if they aim to either reduce the perception of

stereotype threat in ambiguous situations or if they aim to increase positive contact between younger and older adults. Because stereotype threat exerts negative influences across a wide variety of domains for older adults (e.g., memory performance, group identification, dependency, subjective health), designing effective stereotype threat interventions could improve the quality of life for older adults in a variety of different domains.

Future Directions

A large number of areas remain open for future research. Here, we outline what we consider to be some of the most important.

First, there needs to be a targeted examination of whether stereotype threat's effects on older adults' memory depend on the type of memory being tested or on the type of stimuli being examined. For example, no research has yet examined whether stereotype threat affects all forms of memory equally. Is semantic memory as affected by stereotype threat as episodic memory? Is prospective memory as affected as retrospective memory? Is associative memory as affected as item memory? Given that age-related memory impairments vary in magnitude across different forms of memory, it is possible that stereotype threat effects may also vary in magnitude as well. For instance, if older adults' stereotype threat effects are due to executive control interference, then stereotype threat should exert larger effects on memory tasks requiring executive control—which are also often the tasks most impaired in normal aging (e.g., Mather, 2010). As a related issue, it is not yet known whether stereotype threat's effects on memory depend on the type of stimuli being examined. Given that older adults tend to have better memory for socially meaningful (e.g., Cassidy & Gutchess, 2012) or emotional (e.g., Mather, 2004) information, it is possible that older adults will be less affected by stereotype threat on these types of materials. This is an important issue when one considers whether stereotype threat will exert equivalent effects in ecological settings as it does in the laboratory. In everyday life, people are often trying to remember personally relevant or emotional information (rather than lists of words). Thus, determining whether stereotype threat effects are affected by the type of stimuli has implications in determining how stereotype threat will affect the every-day memories of older adults.

A second important but unexplored area of inquiry is to determine how individuals who have cognitive impairments, such as Alzheimer disease

(AD), are affected by stereotype threat (for a discussion of this issue, see Scholl & Sabat, 2008). One possibility is that individuals with AD may be more susceptible to stereotype threat–related memory impairment than are healthy older adults. This likely occurs for several reasons. First, these individuals are subject to both stereotypes about age-related memory decline and also to stereotypes about AD-related memory failures. Second, people with AD do experience frequent memory problems, which likely increases the salience of memory decline–related stereotypes. Finally, these individuals interact with caregivers who likely expect them to perform poorly on memory tasks. Together, these factors may increase stereotype threat for these individuals and, in turn, increase their memory failures. This is particularly problematic as it will exacerbate their existing memory problems.

Finally, given that the development of effective stereotype threat interventions relies on an accurate understanding of its underlying mechanisms, one area of particular importance is to clarify why stereotype threat occurs for older adults. Three key areas of inquiry are needed to answer this question. First, although research has tended to support the role of reduced performance expectations (Desrichard & Kopetz, 2005) and regulatory fit (Barber & Mather, 2012) in underlying stereotype threat in older adults, these mechanisms have only been directly examined in a small number of studies. To have confidence that they are the key causes of stereotype threat in older adults, they need to be replicated in future research. Second, there have been contradictory findings about executive control interference's role in underlying stereotype threat effects in older adults. To clarify this, we suggest that future studies include measures of executive control abilities following stereotype threat, but importantly, not describe these tests as assessing memory abilities. This will elucidate whether stereotype threat reduces performance on memory tests or reduces executive control resources in older adults. Finally, there is a need for targeted research examining whether the mechanisms underlying stereotype threat change with age. This is important in determining whether the results from stereotype threat experiments with younger adults will hold when examining how stereotype threat affects older adults.

In summary, we conclude by noting that stereotype threat adversely affects a wide range of domains and populations beyond those covered in the current review. Because of this, future research that increases our understanding of why stereotype threat occurs and under what conditions stereotype threat–related performance impairments are eliminated has the potential to increase both health and educational outcomes for variety of vulnerable populations.

Acknowledgments

Writing of this chapter was supported by a grant from the National Institute on Aging (T32-AG00037).

References

Abrams, D., Crisp, R. J., Marques, S., Fagg, E., Bedford, L., & Provias, D. (2008). Threat inoculation: Experienced and imagined intergenerational contact prevents stereotype threat effects on older people's math performance. *Psychology and Aging, 23,* 934–939.

Abrams, D., Eller, A., & Bryant, J. (2006). An age apart: The effects of intergenerational contact and stereotype threat on performance and intergroup bias. *Psychology and Aging, 21,* 691–702.

Allport, G. W. (1954). *The nature of prejudice.* Reading, MA: Addison-Wesley.

Andreoletti, C., & Lachman, M. E. (2004). Susceptibility and resilience to memory aging stereotypes: Education matters more than age. *Experimental Aging Research, 30,* 129–148.

Arnsten, A. F. T. (2009). Stress signaling pathways that impair prefrontal cortex structure and function. *Nature Reviews Neuroscience, 10,* 410–422.

Aronson, J., Lustina, M. J., Good, C., Keough, K., Steele, C. M., & Brown, J. (1999). When White men can't do math: Necessary and sufficient factors in stereotype threat. *Journal of Experimental Social Psychology, 35,* 29–46.

Ashford, J. W., Borson, S., O'Hara, R., Dash, P., Frank, L., Robert, P., et al. (2007). Should older adults be screened for dementia? It is important to screen for evidence of dementia! *Alzheimer's and Dementia, 3,* 75–80.

Avorn, J., & Langer, E. J. (1982). Induced disability in nursing home patients: A controlled trial. *Journal of the American Geriatric Society, 30,* 397–400.

Baltes, M. M., & Wahl, H.-W. (1992). The dependency-support script in institutions: Generalization to community settings. *Psychology and Aging, 7,* 409–418.

Barber, S. J., & Mather, M. (2012). Stereotype threat in older adults: The key role of regulatory fit. *Manuscript under review.*

Bargh, J. A., Chen, M., & Burrows, L. (1996). Automaticity of social behavior: Direct effects of trait construct and stereotype activation on action. *Journal of Personality and Social Psychology, 71,* 230–244.

Barton, E. M., Baltes, M. M., & Orzech, M. J. (1980). Etiology of dependence in older nursing home residents during morning care: The role of staff behavior. *Journal of Personality and Social Psychology, 38,* 423–431.

Beilock, S. L., Jellison, W. A., Rydell, R. J., McConnell, A. R., & Carr, R. H. (2006). On the causal mechanisms of stereotype threat: Can skills that don't rely heavily on working memory still be threatened? *Personality and Social Psychology Bulletin, 32,* 1059–1071.

Beilock, S. L., Rydell, R. J., & McConnell, A. R. (2007). Stereotype threat and working memory: Mechanisms, alleviation, and spillover. *Journal of Experimental Psychology: General, 136,* 256–276.

Ben-Zeev, T., Fein, S., & Inzlicht, M. (2005). Arousal and stereotype threat. *Journal of Experimental Social Psychology, 41,* 174–181.

Berkman, L. F., & Syme, S. L. (1979). Social networks, host resistance, and mortality: A nine year follow-up of Alameda County residents. In A. Steptoe & J. Wardle (Eds.), *Psychosocial processes and health: A reader* (pp. 43–67). New York: Cambridge University Press.

Bieman-Copland, S., & Ryan, E. B. (1998). Age-based interpretation of memory successes and failures in adulthood. *The Journals of Gerontology: Series B: Psychological Sciences and Social Sciences, 53,* 105–111.

Bigler, R. S., & Hughes, J. M. (2010). Reasons for skepticism about the efficacy of simulated social contact interventions. *American Psychologist, 65,* 132–133.

Boduroglu, A., Yoon, C., Luo, T., & Park, D. C. (2006). Age-related stereotypes: A comparison of American and Chinese cultures. *Gerontology, 52,* 324–333.

Brewer, M. B., Dull, V., & Lui, L (1981). Perceptions of the elderly: Stereotypes as prototypes. *Journal of Personality and Social Psychology, 41,* 656–670.

Brunstein, J., & Gollwitzer, P. M. (1996). Effects of failure on subsequent performance: The importance of self-defining goals. *Journal of Personality and Social Psychology, 70,* 395–407.

Burgess, D. J., Warren, J., Phelan, S., Dovidio, J., & van Ryn, M. (2010). Stereotype threat and health disparities: What medical educators and future physicians need to know. *Journal of General Internal Medicine, 25,* 169–177.

Cacioppo, J. T., Hawkley, L. C., Crawford, E., Ernst, J. M., Burleson, M. H., Kowalewski, R. B., et al. (2002). Loneliness and health: Potential mechanisms. *Psychosomatic Medicine, 64,* 407–417.

Cadinu, M., Maass, A., Frigerio, S., Impagliazzo, L., & Latinotti, S. (2003). Stereotype threat: The effect of expectancy on performance. *European Journal of Social Psychology, 33,* 267–285.

Carr, P. B., & Steele, C. M. (2010). Stereotype threat affects financial decision making. *Psychological Science, 21,* 1411–1416.

Cassidy, B. S., & Gutchess, A. H. (2012). Social relevance enhances memory for impressions in older adults. *Memory, 20,* 332–345.

Castel, A. D., Balota, D. A., & McCabe, D. P. (2009). Memory efficiency and the strategic control of attention at encoding: Impairments of value-directed remembering in Alzheimer's disease. *Neuropsychology, 23,* 297–306.

Chasteen, A. L., Bhattacharyya, S., Horhota, M., Tam, R., & Hasher, L. (2005). How feelings of stereotype threat influence older adults' memory performance. *Experimental Aging Research, 31,* 235–260.

Coudin, G., & Alexopoulos, T. (2010). "Help me! I'm old!" How negative aging stereotypes create dependency among older adults. *Aging & Mental Health, 14,* 516–523.

Crisp, R., & Abrams, D. (2002). Improving intergroup attitudes and reducing stereotype threat: An integrated contact model. *European Review of Social Psychology, 19,* 242–284.

Crockett, W. H., & Hummert, M. L. (1987). Perceptions of aging and the elderly. In K. W. Schaie (Ed.), *The annual review of gerontology and geriatrics* (vol. 7, pp. 217–241). New York: Springer.

Croizet, J.–C., & Claire, T. (1998). Extending the concept of stereotype and threat to social class: The intellectual

underperformance of students from low socioeconomic backgrounds. *Personality and Social Psychology Bulletin, 24,* 588–594.

Cullen, M. J., Hardison, C. M., & Sackett, P. R. (2004). Using SAT-grade and ability-job performance relationships to test predictions derived from stereotype threat theory. *Journal of Applied Psychology, 89,* 220–230.

Cuddy, A. J. C., Fiske, S. T., & Glick, P. (2008). Warmth and competence as universal dimensions of social perception: The Stereotype Content Model and the BIAS Map. In M. P. Zanna (Ed.), *Advances in experimental social psychology* (vol. 40, pp. 61–149). New York: Academic Press.

Cuddy, A. J. C., Fiske, S. T., Kwan, V. S. Y., Glick, P., Demoulin, S., Leyens, J. –P., et al. (2009). Stereotype content model across cultures: Toward universal similarities and some differences. *British Journal of Social Psychology, 48,* 1–33.

Cuddy, A. J. C., Norton, M. I., & Fiske, S. T. (2005). This old stereotype: The pervasiveness and persistence of the elderly stereotype. *Journal of Social Issues, 61,* 265–283.

Danaher, K., & Crandall, C. S. (2008). Stereotype threat in applied settings re-examined. *Journal of Applied Social Psychology, 38,* 1639–1655.

Delgado, A. R., & Prieto, G. (2008). Stereotype threat as validity threat: The anxiety-sex-threat interaction. *Intelligence, 36,* 635–640.

Desrichard, O., & Kopetz, C. (2005). A threat in the elder: The impact of task instructions, self-efficacy and performance expectations on memory performance in the elderly. *European Journal of Social Psychology, 35,* 537–552.

Dijksterhuis, A. (2001). Automatic social influence: The perception-behavior link as an explanatory mechanism for behavior matching. In J. Forgas & K. D. Williams (Eds.), *Social Influence* (pp. 95–108). Philadelphia: Psychology Press.

Dijksterhuis, A., Aarts, H., Bargh, J. A., & van Knippenberg, A. (2000). On the relation between associative strength and automatic behavior. *Journal of Experimental Social Psychology, 36,* 531–544.

Dijksterhuis, A., & Bargh, J. A. (2001). The perception-behavior expressway: Automatic effects of social perception on social behavior. In M. P. Zanna (Ed.), *Advances in experimental social psychology* (vol. 33, pp. 1–40). San Diego, CA: Academic Press.

Dijksterhuis, A., Spears, R., & Lépinasse, V. (2001). Reflecting and deflecting stereotypes: Assimilation and contrast in impression formation and automatic behavior. *Journal of Experimental Social Psychology, 37,* 286–299.

Erber, J. T., Szuchman, L. T., & Prager, I. G. (1997). Forgetful but forgiven: How age and life style affect perceptions of memory failure. *The Journals of Gerontology: Series B: Psychological Sciences and Social Sciences, 52,* 303–307.

Erber, J. T., Szuchman, L. T., & Rothberg, S. T. (1990). Age, gender, and individual differences in memory failure appraisal. *Psychology and Aging, 5,* 600–603.

Eysenck, M. W., & Calvo, M. G. (1992). Anxiety and performance: The processing efficiency theory. *Cognition and Emotion, 6,* 409–434.

Fleischman, D. A., & Gabrieli, J. D. E. (1998). Repetition priming in normal aging and Alzheimer's disease: A review of findings and theories. *Psychology and Aging, 13,* 88–119.

Förster, J., Higgins, E. T., & Idson, L. C. (1998). Approach and avoidance strength during goal attainment: Regulatory focus and the "goal looms larger" effect. *Journal of Personality and Social Psychology, 75,* 1115–1131.

Freitas, A. L., Liberman, N., & Higgins, E. T. (2002). Regulatory fit and resisting temptation during goal pursuit. *Journal of Experimental Social Psychology, 38,* 291–298.

Friedman, R. S., & Förster, J. (2001). The effects of promotion and prevention cues on creativity. *Journal of Personality and Social Psychology, 81,* 1001–1013.

Garstka, T. A., Schmitt, M. T., Branscombe, N. R., & Hummert, M. L. (2004). How young and older adults differ in their responses to perceived age discrimination. *Psychology and Aging, 19,* 326–335.

Gray, R., & Branaghan, R. (2009). Changing driving behavior through unconscious stereotype activation. *Proceedings of the 5th International Driving Symposium on Human Factors in Driving Assessment and Design,* 104–109.

Grimm, L. R., Markman, A. B., Maddox, W. T., & Baldwin, G. C. (2009). Stereotype threat reinterpreted as a regulatory mismatch. *Journal of Personality and Social Psychology, 96,* 288–304.

Hagestad, G. O., & Uhlenberg, P. (2005). The social separation of old and young: A root of ageism. *Journal of Social Issues, 61,* 343–360.

Hale, N. (1998). Effects of age and interpersonal contact on stereotyping of the elderly. *Current Psychology: Developmental, Learning, Personality, Social, 17,* 28–47.

Haslam, C., Morton, T. A., Haslam, S. A., Varnes, L., Graham, R., & Gamaz, L. (2012). "When the age is in, the wit is out": Age-related self-categorization and deficit expectations reduce performance on clinical tests used in dementia assessment. *Psychology and Aging, 27,* 778–784.

Hausdorff, J. M., Levy, B. R., & Wei, J. Y. (1999). The power of ageism on physical function of older persons: Reversibility of age-related gait changes. *Journal of the American Geriatrics Society, 47,* 1346–1349.

Heckhausen, J., & Krueger, J. (1993). Developmental expectations for the self and most other people: Age grading in three functions of social comparison. *Developmental Psychology, 29,* 539–548.

Hess, M., & Dikken, J. (2010). The association between ageism and subjective age of older people in Europe. *International Journal of Social Sciences and Humanity Studies, 2,* 99–109.

Hess, T. M., Auman, C., Colcombe, S. J., & Rahhal, T. A. (2003). The impact of stereotype threat on age differences in memory performance. *The Journals of Gerontology: Series B: Psychological Sciences and Social Sciences, 58,* 3–11.

Hess, T. M., Emery, L., & Queen, T. L. (2009). Task demands moderate stereotype threat effects on memory performance. *The Journals of Gerontology: Series B: Psychological Sciences and Social Sciences, 64,* 482–486.

Hess, T. M., & Hinson, J. T. (2006). Age-related variation in the influences of aging stereotypes on memory in adulthood. *Psychology and Aging, 21,* 621–625.

Hess, T. M., Hinson, J. T., & Hodges, E. A. (2009). Moderators of and mechanisms underlying stereotype threat effects on older adults' memory performance. *Experimental Aging Research, 35,* 153–177.

Hess, T. M., Hinson, J. T., & Statham, J. A. (2004). Explicit and implicit stereotype activation on memory: Do age and awareness moderate the impact of priming? *Psychology and Aging, 19,* 495–505.

Higgins, E. T. (1997). Beyond pleasure and pain. *American Psychologist, 52,* 1280–1300.

Higgins, E. T. (1999). Promotion and prevention as a motivational duality: Implications for evaluative processes. In S. Chaiken & Y. Trope (Eds.), *Dual-process theories in social psychology* (pp. 503–525). New York: Guilford Press.

Higgins, E. T., Shah, J., & Friedman, R. (1997). Emotional responses to goal attainment: Strength of regulatory focus as moderator. *Journal of Personality and Social Psychology, 72,* 515–525.

Horton, S., Baker, J., Pearce, G. W., & Deakin, J. M. (2008). On the malleability of performance: Implications for seniors. *Journal of Applied Gerontology, 27,* 446–465.

Hummert, M. L. (1999). A social cognitive perspective on age stereotypes. In T. M. Hess & F. Blanchard-Fields (Eds.), *Social cognition and aging* (pp. 175–195). New York: Academic Press.

Hummert, M. L. (2011). Age stereotypes and aging. In K. W. Schaie & S. L. Willis (Eds.), *Handbook of the psychology of aging,* 7th ed. (pp. 249–262). San Diego, CA: Elsevier Academic Press.

Hummert, M. L., Garstka, T. A., Shaner, J. L., & Strahm, S. (1994). Stereotypes of the elderly held by young, middle-aged, and elderly adults. *Journals of Gerontology, 49,* 240–249.

Inzlicht, M., McKay, L., & Aronson, J. (2006). Stigma as ego depletion: How being the target of prejudice affects self-control. *Psychological Science, 17,* 262–269.

Isaacs, L. W., & Bearison, D. J. (1986). The development of children's prejudice against the aged. *The International Journal of Aging & Human Development, 23,* 175–194.

James, W. (1890). *Principles of psychology* (vol. 2). New York: Holt, Dover edition.

Johns, M., Inzlicht, M., & Schmader, T. (2008). Stereotype threat and executive resource depletion: Examining the influence of emotion regulation. *Journal of Experimental Psychology: General, 137,* 691–705.

Kahn, R. L., Zarit, A. H., Hilbert, N. M., & Niederehe, G. (1975). Memory complaint and impairment in the aged: The effect of depression and altered brain function. *Archives of General Psychiatry, 32,* 1569–1573.

Kang, S. K., & Chasteen, A. L. (2009). The moderating role of age-group identification and perceived threat on stereotype threat among older adults. *The International Journal of Aging & Human Development, 69,* 201–220.

Kausler, D. H., Lichty, W., & Freund, J. S. (1985). Adult age differences in recognition memory and frequency judgments for planned versus performed activities. *Developmental Psychology, 21,* 647–654.

Kite, M. E., & Johnson, B. T. (1988). Attitudes toward older and younger adults: A meta-analysis. *Psychology and Aging, 3,* 233–244.

Kite, M. E., Stockdale, G. D., Whitley, B. E., & Johnson, B. T. (2005). Attitudes toward younger and older adults: An updated meta-analytic review. *Journal of Social Issues, 61,* 241–266.

Kleinspehn-Ammerlahn, A., Kotter-Grühn, D., & Smith, J. (2008). Self-perceptions of aging: Do subjective age and satisfaction with aging change during old age? *The Journals of Gerontology: Series B: Psychological Sciences and Social Sciences, 63,* 377–385.

Kray, L. J., Galinsky, A. D., & Thompson, L. (2002). Reversing the gender gap in negotiations: An exploration of stereotype regeneration. *Organizational Behavior and Human Decision Processes, 87,* 386–409.

Kray, L. J., Thompson, L., & Galinsky, A. (2001). Battle of the sexes: Gender stereotype confirmation and reactance in negotiations. *Journal of Personality and Social Psychology, 80,* 942–958.

Langer, E., & Rodin, J. (1976). The effects of choice and enhanced personal responsibility for the aged: A field experiment in an institutional setting. *Journal of Personality and Social Psychology, 134,* 191–198.

Levy, B. (1996). Improving memory in old age through implicit self-stereotyping. *Journal of Personality and Social Psychology, 71,* 1092–1107.

Levy, B. (2000). Handwriting as a reflection of aging self-stereotypes. *Journal of Geriatric Psychiatry, 33,* 81–94.

Levy, B. R. (2002). Implicit ageism. In T. D. Nelson (Ed.), *Ageism: Stereotyping and prejudice against older persons* (pp. 49–75). Cambridge, MA: The MIT Press.

Levy, B., Ashman, O., & Dror, I. (1999–2000). To be or not to be: The effects of aging stereotypes on the will to live. *Journal of Death and Dying, 40,* 409–420.

Levy, B. R., Hausdorff, J. M., Hencke, R., & Wei, J. Y. (2000). Reducing cardiovascular stress with positive self-stereotypes of aging. *The Journals of Gerontology: Series B: Psychological Sciences and Social Sciences, 55,* 205–213.

Levy, B., & Langer, E. (1994). Aging free from negative stereotypes: Successful memory in China among the American deaf. *Journal of Personality and Social Psychology, 66,* 989–997.

Levy B. R., & Leifheit-Limson, E. (2009). The stereotype-matching effect: Greater influence on functioning when age stereotypes correspond to outcomes. *Psychology and Aging, 24,* 230–233.

Levy, B. R., Slade, M. D., & Gill, T. M. (2006). Hearing decline predicted by elders' stereotypes. *The Journals of Gerontology: Series B: Psychological Sciences and Social Sciences, 61,* 82–87.

Levy, B. R., Slade, M. D., May, J., & Caracciolo, E. A. (2006). Physical recovery after acute myocardial infarction: Positive age self-stereotypes as a resource. *The International Journal of Aging & Human Development, 62,* 285–301.

Light, L. L., Prull, M. W., La Voie, D. J., & Healy, M. (2000). Dual process theories of memory in old age. In T. J. Perfect & E. A. Maylor (Eds.), *Models of cognitive aging* (pp. 239–300). Oxford: Oxford University Press.

Lineweaver, T. T., & Hertzog, C. (1998). Adults' efficacy and control beliefs regarding memory and aging: Separating general from personal beliefs. *Aging, Neuropsychology, and Cognition, 5,* 264–296.

Marx, D. M., & Stapel, D. A. (2006). Distinguishing stereotype threat from priming effects: On the role of the social self and threat-based concerns. *Journal of Personality and Social Psychology, 91,* 243–254.

Mather, M. (2004). Aging and emotional memory. In D. Reisberg & P. Hertel (Eds.), *Memory and emotion* (pp. 272–307). New York: Oxford University Press.

Mather, M. (2010). Aging and cognition. *Wiley Interdisciplinary Reviews: Cognitive Science, 1,* 346–362.

Mazerolle, M., Régner, I., Morisset, P., Rigalleau, F., & Huguet, P. (2012). Stereotype threat strengthens automatic recall and undermines controlled processes in older adults. *Psychological Science, 23,* 723–727.

Meisner, B. A. (2012). A meta-analysis of positive and negative age stereotype priming effects on behavior among older adults. *The Journals of Gerontology: Series B: Psychological Sciences and Social Sciences, 67B,* 13–17.

Mitchell, D. B., & Bruss, P. J. (2003). Age differences in implicit memory: conceptual, perceptual, or methodological? *Psychology and Aging, 18,* 807–822.

Montepare, J. M., & Lachman, M. E. (1989). "You're only as old as you feel": Self-perceptions of age, fears of aging, and life satisfaction from adolescence to old age. *Psychology and Aging, 4,* 73–78.

Muraven, M., & Baumeister, R. F. (2000). Self-regulation and depletion of limited resources: Does self-control resemble a muscle? *Psychological Bulletin, 126,* 247–259.

Nelson, T. D. (2004). *Ageism: Stereotyping and prejudice against older persons.* Cambridge, MA: MIT Press.

Nosek, B. A. A., Banaji, M., & Greenwald, A. G. (2002). Harvesting implicit group attitudes and beliefs from a demonstration web site. *Group Dynamics: Theory, Research, and Practice, 6,* 101–115.

O'Brien, L. T., & Hummert, M. L. (2006). Memory performance in late middle-aged adults: Contrasting self-stereotyping and stereotype threat accounts of assimilation to age stereotypes. *Social Cognition, 24,* 338–358.

Osborne, J. W. (1997). Race and academic disidentification. *Journal of Educational Psychology, 89,* 728–735.

Osborne, J. W. (2001). Testing stereotype threat: Does anxiety explain race and sex differences in achievement? *Contemporary Educational Psychology, 26,* 291–310.

Oyserman, D., Uskul, A. K., Yoder, N., Nesse, R. M., & Williams, D. R. (2007). Unfair treatment and self-regulatory focus. *Journal of Experimental Social Psychology, 43,* 505–512.

Parr, W. V., & Siegert, R. (1993). Adults' conceptions of everyday memory failure in others: Factors that mediate the effects of target age. *Psychology and Aging, 8,* 599–605.

Perlmutter, M., & Mitchell, D. B. (1982). The appearance and disappearance of age differences in adult memory. In F. I. M. Craik & S. Trehub (Eds.), *Aging and cognitive processes* (pp. 127–144). New York: Plenum.

Pettigrew, T. F. (1998). Intergroup contact theory. *Annual Review of Psychology, 49,* 65–85.

Pettigrew, T. F., & Tropp, L. R. (2000). Does intergroup contact reduce prejudice: Recent meta-analytic findings. In S. Oskamp (Ed.), *Reducing prejudice and discrimination* (pp. 93–114). Mahwah, NJ: Lawrence Erlbaum Associates Publishers.

Pinel, E. C. (1999). Stigma consciousness: The psychological legacy of social stereotypes. *Journal of Personality and Social Psychology, 76,* 114–128.

Rahhal, T. A., Hasher, L., & Colcombe, S. J. (2001). Instructional manipulations and age differences in memory: Now you see them, now you don't. *Psychology and Aging, 16,* 697–706.

Régner, I., Smeding, A., Gimmig, D., Thinus-Blanc, C., Monteil, J.-M., & Huguet, P. (2010). Individual differences in working memory moderate stereotype-threat effects. *Psychological Science, 21,* 1646–1648.

Rowe, J. W., & Kahn, R. L. (1987). Human aging: Usual and successful. *Science, 237,* 143–149.

Ryan, E. B. (1992). Beliefs about memory changes across the adult life span. *Journals of Gerontology, 47,* 41–46.

Ryan, E. B., & See, S. K. (1993). Age-based beliefs about memory changes for self and others across adulthood. *Journals of Gerontology, 48,* 199–201.

Rubin, D. C., & Berntsen, D. (2006). People over forty feel 20% younger than their age: Subjective age across the lifespan. *Psychonomic Bulletin & Review, 13,* 776–780.

Scheibe, S., & Blanchard-Fields, F. (2009). Effects of regulating emotions on cognitive performance: What is costly for young adults is not so costly for older adults. *Psychology and Aging, 24,* 217–223.

Schimel, J., Arndt, J., Banko, K. M., & Cook, A. (2004). Not all self-affirmations were created equal: The cognitive and social benefit of affirming the intrinsic (vs extrinsic) self. *Social Cognition, 22,* 75–99.

Schmader, T. (2002). Gender identification moderates stereotype threat effects on women's math performance. *Journal of Experimental Social Psychology, 38,* 194–201.

Schmader, T., & Johns, M. (2003). Converging evidence that stereotype threat reduces working memory capacity. *Journal of Personality and Social Psychology, 85,* 440–452.

Schmader, T., Johns, M., & Forbes, C. (2008). An integrated process model of stereotype threat effects on performance. *Psychological Review, 115,* 336–356.

Scholl, J. M., & Sabat, S. R. (2008). Stereotypes, stereotype threat and ageing: implications for the understanding and treatment of people with Alzheimer's disease. *Ageing & Society, 28,* 103–130.

Schoofs, D., Wolf, O. T., & Smeets, T. (2009). Cole pressor stress impairs performance on working memory tasks requiring executive functions in healthy young men. *Behavioral Neuroscience, 123,* 1066–1075.

Schwartz, L. K., & Simmons, J. P. (2001). Contact quality and attitudes toward the elderly. *Educational Gerontology, 27,* 127–137.

Scogin, F., Storandt, M., & Lott, L. (1985). Memory-skills training, memory complaints, and depression in older adults. *Journal of Gerontology, 40,* 562–568.

Seefeldt, C., Jantz, R. K., Galper, A., & Serock, K. (1977). Using pictures to explore children's attitudes toward the elderly. *The Gerontologist, 17,* 506–512.

Seibt, B., & Förster, J. (2004). Stereotype threat and performance: How self-stereotypes influence processing by inducing regulatory foci. *Journal of Personality and Social Psychology, 87,* 38–56.

Shah, J., Higgins, T., & Friedman, R. S. (1998). Performance incentives and means: How regulatory focus influences goal attainment. *Journal of Personality and Social Psychology, 74,* 285–293.

Smith, J. (2004). Understanding the process of stereotype threat: A review of meditational variables and new performance goal directions. *Educational Psychology Review, 16,* 177–206.

Smith, J. (2006). The interplay among stereotypes, performance-avoidance goals, and women's math performance expectation. *Sex Roles, 54,* 287–296.

Solomon, K. (1990). Learned helplessness in the elderly: Theoretical and clinical considerations. *Occupational Therapy in Mental Health, 10,* 31–51.

Spencer, S. J., Steele, C. M., & Quinn, D. M. (1999). Stereotype threat and women's math performance. *Journal of Experimental Social Psychology, 35,* 4–28.

Stangor, C., Carr, C., & Kiang, L. (1998). Activating stereotypes undermines task performance expectations. *Journal of Personality and Social Psychology, 75,* 1191–1197.

Steele, C. M. (1997). A threat in the air: How stereotypes shape intellectual identity and performance. *American Psychologist, 52,* 613–629.

Steele, C. M., & Aronson, J. (1995). Stereotype threat and the intellectual test performance of African Americans. *Journal of Personality and Social Psychology, 69,* 797–811.

Steele, C. M., Spencer, S. J., & Aronson, J. (2002). Contending with group image: The psychology of stereotype and social identity threat. *Advances in experimental social psychology, 34,* 379–440.

Stein, R., Blanchard-Fields, F., & Hertzog, C. (2002). The effects of age-stereotypes priming on the memory performance of older adults. *Experimental Aging Research, 28,* 169–181.

Stone, J. (2002). Battling doubt by avoiding practice: The effects of stereotype threat on self-handicapping in white athletes. *Personality and Social Psychology Bulletin, 28,* 1667–1678.

Stone, J., Lynch, C. I., Sjomeling, M., & Darley, J. M. (1999). Stereotype threat effects on Black and White athletic performance. *Journal of Personality and Social Psychology, 77,* 1213–1227.

Stricker, L. J., & Ward, W. C. (2004). Stereotype threat, inquiring about test takers' ethnicity and gender, and standardized test performance. *Journal of Applied Social Psychology, 34,* 665–693.

Verhaeghen, P., Marcoen, A., & Goossens, L. (1992). Facts and fiction about memory aging: A quantitative integration of research findings. *Journal of Gerontology: Psychological Sciences, 48,* 157–171.

Weiss, D., & Freund, A. M. (2012). Still young at heart: Negative age-related information motivates distancing from same-aged people. *Psychology and Aging, 27,* 173–180.

Wheeler, S. C., & Petty, R. E. (2001). The effects of stereotype activation on behavior: A review of possible mechanisms. *Psychological Bulletin, 127,* 797–826.

Yeung, N. C. J., & von Hippel, C. (2008). Stereotype threat increases the likelihood that female drivers in a simulator run over jaywalkers. *Accident Analysis and Prevention, 40,* 667–674.

Yonelinas, A. P. (2002). The nature of recollection and familiarity: A review of 30 years of research. *Journal of Memory and Language, 46,* 441–517.

Yoon, C., Hasher, L., Feinberg, F., Rahhal, T. A., & Winocur, G. (2000). Cross-cultural differences in memory: The role of culture-based stereotypes about aging. *Psychology and Aging, 15,* 694–704.

INDEX

ability, 289
acceptance, negative emotional situations, 147–148
achievement
    age trends, 280t
    importance ratings by age, 279f
adaptive processes
    age-related, 248–252
    goal-based processes, 250–252
    responding to reductions in cognitive resources, 249–250
    selective engagement, 250
Adjective Check List, 264
adolescence
    life review, 284
    problem solving in, 195–197
adulthood
    causal attribution research in young adults, 289–290
    change of values across, 276–277
    influence of values on thought and action across, 277–278
    life review, 283–284
    problem solving in adolescence and early, 195–197
    problem solving in early and later, 198–200
    social cognitive perspective in, 238–239
adults. See older adults
affect, emotion, 257
affect balance, 64t, 65
affect complexity, 34
affective complexity
    affect co-occurrence, 74–75, 75t
    affect differentiation, 74, 75t, 75–76
    age differences, 72
    heterogeneity of research, 73–74
affective experiences
    affect co-occurrence, 74–75, 75t
    affect differentiation, 74, 75t, 75–76
    age differences, 63–67
    age differences in complexity of, 72–76
    ambulatory assessment for studying age differences, 62–63

central findings of age difference studies, 64t
    positive vs. negative affects, 65
    reactivity effects, 63
    subfacets of everyday, 64t, 65
affective neuroscience perspective
    benefits, 40–41
    linking affective and self-relevant, 41
    positivity effect, 40
    self-referential processing, 40–41
affective reactivity, unpleasant experiences in daily life, 70–72
affective stability
    age differences in, 63–67
    central findings of age difference studies, 64t
affective well-being
    age differences in, 63–67
    age differences in affect-regulation orientations, 69–70, 73t
    association vs. causal relation, 67
    central findings of age difference studies, 64t
    conceptions of, 61–62
    contra-hedonic orientations, 69–70
    daily hassles and motivational conflicts, 67–69, 73t
    potential contributors to age trajectories in, 67–72, 73t
    pro-hedonic orientations, 69–70
    reactivity to unpleasant experiences in daily life, 70–72
affect optimization, 34
affect-regulation, age differences in orientations, 69–70, 73t
affect valence, relationship of arousal to, 228–232
age-convergence approach, age trends, 131–132
age differences
    affect co-occurrence, 74–75
    affective reactivity to unpleasant experiences in daily life, 70–72
    affect-regulation orientations, 69–70

association with emotional well-being, 129–132
causal attributions, 289–290
change of values across adulthood, 276–277
combining emotional and eye gaze cues, 17–18
coping and everyday problem solving, 217–218
daily hassles and motivational conflicts, 67–69
decoding genuine and posed smiles, 12–13
detecting and following eye gaze, 15–16
detecting deception, 16–17
emotional body movements, 13
emotional reactivity, 136–137
emotional well-being, 115–119
emotion perception measures, 14–15
emotion recognition, 105
emotion regulation and vulnerability, 179–180
emotion regulation in problem solving, 176–178
future directions for social perception research, 21–23
goals and strategies for interpersonal everyday problem solving, 195–200
joint attention, 16
life experience, 21
motivational factors, 21
perceiving basic facial expressions, 10–12
personal beliefs and social knowledge, 294–295
positivity biases, 20–21
social cue, 15–18
social expertise, 246–247
social inferences, 240–242
social neuroscience, 297
social perception, 18–20
stress undoing, 122
understanding beyond basic emotions, 12
values in World Values Survey (WVS), 278–280

expressive suppression, 146

future directions, 111, 118–119, 148–150, 167–168

individual differences, 100t, 104–105

interpersonal context and strengths in, 178–179

motivation, 100t, 102–103

older adults, 93–94, 156–158, 160–162

optimizing emotional experience in later life, 117–118

perceiver context, 99, 100t, 102–105

physiological aspects of, 232–233

positive reappraisal, 147

requiring cognitive control, 158–159

situation selection and/or modification, 147

stimulus and task form, 101t, 107–108

stimulus context, 101t, 105–108

strength and vulnerability integration (SAVI) model, 118

stress, 4

tension and equilibrium expansion in early development, 89–90

types declining with age, 146

types improving with age, 146–148

using social support, 147

vulnerability of later life regulation capacities, 91–94

wisdom, 259–261

emotions

antecedent and consequents of age-related differences, 3–4

auditory expressions, 13–14

autonomic differentiation, 232

cognitive scenarios, 257

facial morphology, 3

health and positive, 119–123

lifespan aging effects on perceiving, 11t

multimodal presentation of, 14

normal aging and autonomic aspects of, 234–235

older adults and, 3

perception tasks by age group, 11f

physiological reactivity, 225

relationship between wisdom and, 4, 256–257, 267–268

role in cognition, 2

wisdom and eudaimonic well-being, 264–267

emotion science, discrete vs. dimensional debate, 234

encoding, memory, 29–30

entity theory, performance, 291

Epistemic Cognition Questionnaire (ECQ15), 264

equilibrium

biological, 85–86

cognitive-emotional development, 88f

complexity and tension in adulthood and later life, 90–91

complexity and tension in development, 88–89

emotional development, 85–91

mechanisms of tension and, in early development, 89–90

psychological and biological factors in regulation, 87–88

psychological construct, 86–87

eudaimonic well-being, wisdom and, 264–267

evaluative well-being, global self-reports, 131

event-related potentials (ERPs)

emotional regulation, 89–90

emotion recognition, 103–104, 110

everyday problem solving. *See also* coping

age differences in emotion regulation, 176–178

age differences in goals and strategies for interpersonal, 195–200

assessing effectiveness, 194–195, 200–201, 214–216

competency perspective, 191–192

conceptual model of process, 192–195

context specificity, 213–214

contextual perspective, 192

coping and, 211–214

coping research, 206–207

dimensions of interpersonal relationships, 195

discrete emotions, 214

emotion regulation, 4

future directions in research, 217–218

goals and, 194, 201, 212, 213–214

history and theory in, 211

history of field of, 191–192

interpersonal, across lifespan, 190–191, 194–195

marital conflict and collaborative problem-solving, 182–184

mechanisms underlying age differences, 216–217

motivational orientations and problem-solving goals, 193

research, 190

strategies and, 212–214

strategy effectiveness, 194, 201

executive control

aging effects, 241

performance and stereotype threat concerns, 307–308, 309, 310, 315

executive functioning, expressive suppression, 149

experience sampling, ambulatory assessment, 62–63, 76

experience sampling methods (ESM), daily stressors, 133–134

experimental designs, emotion regulation, 148

explicit stereotype threat, implicit vs., 305–306

exploitation, detecting, 17

expressive suppression

emotion regulation, 146, 149

older adults and emotion regulation, 163–164

extrinsic/instrumental goals, 276–277

eye gaze

combining emotional and, 17–18

detecting and following, 15–16

face identity perception task, emotion, 19

faces, lifespan aging effects on perceiving emotions, 11t

FACES Lifespan Database of Facial Expressions, 50

Facial Action Coding System, 103

facial aging

individual differences, 51

intergenerational interaction, 53–55

morphology, 49–50

morphology of, and emotional expression, 50–51

stereotyping process, 51–53

facial anomaly, 55

facial expressions

age differences in perceiving basic, 10–12

cues in person perception, 48–49

decoding genuine and posed smiles, 12–13

future research, 56

facial identity, own-age biases, 12

facial maturity, implications for theory, 55–56

facial morphology

age changes, 3, 47, 49–50, 57

directions for future research, 56–57

emotional expression, 50–51

facial maturity and emotional expression, 48, 55–56

race/ethnicity, 57

facial structure

age changes, 49

cues in person perception, 48–49

directions for future research, 56

ecological theory, 48–49

fear

age differences in decoding, 10–12

age differences in emotion recognition, 109

combining emotional and eye gaze cues, 17

facial maturity and emotional expression, 48

point-light display, 13

"fight-flight," sympathetic branch, 226

First Noble Truth, Buddha, 261

flashbulb memory, 27

fluidization, crystallized processes, 90

fluid processes, aging and loss of, 90, 91–94

Fourth Noble Truth, Buddha, 268n.1

framing effect, decision making, 248

fraud, detecting, 17

functional imaging, activation of medial prefrontal cortex (MPFC), 103–104

functional magnetic resonance imaging (fMRI), 38, 39

emotional processing, 89

emotional regulation in older adults, 185